Ancillary Relief Handbook

Sixth Edition

Ancillary Relief Handbook

Sixth Edition

Roger Bird LLB, Solicitor
Former District Judge

JORDANS

Published by
Jordan Publishing Limited
21 St Thomas Street
Bristol BS1 6JS

British Library Cataloguing-in-Publication Data

A catalogue record for this book is available from the British Library.

ISBN 978 1 84661 073 8

Typeset by Letterpart Ltd, Reigate, Surrey

Printed in Great Britain by Antony Rowe Limited, Chippenham, Wilts

CONTENTS

FOREWORD TO FIRST EDITION

Within the wider field of family law the comparative importance of ancillary relief is not always recognised. I am in no doubt that there is a ready market for a practitioners' handbook and who better to write one than Roger Bird. There can be few, if any, district judges who have greater experience of the work in court. Furthermore, he has been an invaluable member of the Lord Chancellor's Ancillary Relief Advisory Group almost since its inception. He is, thus, extremely well informed on policy issues and the perceived weaknesses in the existing law and practice. His concluding chapter, 'A Summing Up' well illustrates Roger's virtues. It is so succinct that it challenges the reader to detect some deficiency. But he will search in vain. It is refreshingly practical and it is the product of original and reflective writing.

I am confident that significant changes in law and practice are imminent. So it is easy to predict that the ancillary relief handbook will be for Roger a demanding creation.

The Rt Hon Lord Justice Thorpe
October 1998

PREFACE

The sixth edition of this book has been made necessary by a plethora of new decisions and by rule changes, notably with reference to costs. It had been hoped to publish earlier in the year, but, in view of the pending decision of the Court of Appeal in *Charman v Charman*, it was thought wise to wait to see whether the court gave any significant guidance as to how the two recent landmark decisions of the House of Lords should be interpreted. In the event, the decision to wait seems to have been justified.

However, this illustrates the invidious position in which the profession now finds itself. It cannot be said that the law is clear on many significant major issues. Every decision of the higher courts seems to add a new stratum of comment through which to strive to discern the proper approach to a particular case. Practitioners constantly ask themselves whether the current 'big money' case is going to be the one which provides the answer to the unresolved issues. In fact, it is becoming clear that the discretion based system which has served us well for over thirty years is in need of overhaul and repair.

That overhaul can now only be carried out by Parliament which, for understandable reasons, has shown little interest in the subject. It would be necessary to take important decisions as to policy and politicians, who try to discern the will of the public, might well find themselves in some difficulty. It has to be said that another problem is that the system works quite well and predictably in the great majority of cases; whether politicians would want to devote precious parliamentary time to debating the merits of a new scheme for the very rich is debatable.

At one time, of course, the government of the day would have instructed the Law Commission to examine the issues and report to Parliament, and such a report would at least have formed the basis for legislative action. Whether that rational and civilised way of framing new legislation will be adopted remains to be seen.

The law stated in this book is believed to be correct as at today's date.

Roger Bird
9 June 2007

TABLE OF CASES

References are to paragraph numbers.

TABLE OF STATUTES

References are to paragraph numbers.

TABLE OF STATUTORY INSTRUMENTS

References are to paragraph numbers.

TABLE OF CONVENTIONS

References are to paragraph numbers.

TABLE OF ABBREVIATIONS

CCA 1984	County Courts Act 1984
CCR	County Court Rules 1981
CETV	cash equivalent transfer value
CJJA 1982/1991	Civil Jurisdiction and Judgments Act 1982/1991
the Convention	European Convention for the Protection of Human Rights and Fundamental Freedoms 1950
CPR	Civil Procedure Rules 1998
CSA 1991	Child Support Act 1991
CS(MASC) Regs 1992	Child Support (Maintenance Assessments and Special Cases) Regulations 1992
CSPSSA 2000	Child Support, Pensions and Social Security Act 2000
DPMCA 1978	Domestic Proceedings and Magistrates' Courts Act 1978
ECHR	European Court of Human Rights
FA	first appointment
FDR	financial dispute resolution
FLA 1996	Family Law Act 1996
FPR 1991	Family Proceedings Rules 1991
HRA 1998	Human Rights Act 1998
I(PFD)A 1975	Inheritance (Provision for Family and Dependants) Act 1975
Information Regulations 2000	Pensions on Divorce etc (Provision of Information) Regulations 2000
LPA 1925	Law of Property Act 1925
MCA 1973	Matrimonial Causes Act 1973
MFPA 1984	Matrimonial and Family Proceedings Act 1984
Pensions Regulations 2000	Divorce etc (Pensions) Regulations 2000, SI 2000/1123
PPF	Pension Protection Fund
RSC	Rules of the Supreme Court 1965, SI 1965/1776
SCA 1981	Supreme Court Act 1981
SERPS	State Earnings Related Pensions Scheme
the 1999 Rules	Family Proceedings Rules 1991, SI 1991/1247, as amended by Family Proceedings (Amendment No 2) Rules 1999, SI 1999/3491
TLATA 1996	Trusts of Land and Appointment of Trustees Act 1996
WRPA 1999	Welfare Reform and Pensions Act 1999

Chapter 1

INTRODUCTION TO ANCILLARY RELIEF

SCOPE OF THIS CHAPTER

1.1 Ancillary relief comprises those orders of a financial nature which the court may make in proceedings for divorce, judicial separation or nullity of marriage. In this chapter, the range of possible orders is set out and the general principles on which orders are made are considered. In later chapters, each type of order (eg periodical payments orders) is examined in detail; in this chapter, certain matters common to all such orders are considered, although where any individual factor merits more detailed examination it is the subject of a chapter in its own right.

This book also deals with one type of ancillary relief which does not depend on the issue of proceedings for divorce etc, namely, applications for neglect to maintain under s 27 of the Matrimonial Causes Act 1973 (MCA 1973). The principles applicable to such applications are considered in Chapter 14.

1.2 It would be unusual for the court to consider making one type of order only. That might in fact be the result of a particular case, but the court must have regard to the overall position, and the result of most applications is that a combination of orders is made. The court must take an overview of the whole case.

DEFINITIONS

1.3 'Ancillary relief' is defined by the Family Proceedings Rules 1991 (FPR 1991)[1] as:

'(a) an avoidance of disposition order,
(b) a financial provision order,
(c) an order for maintenance pending suit,
(d) a property adjustment order,
(e) a variation order, or
(f) a pension sharing order.'

---

[1]   Rule 1.2.

The FPR 1991[2] define an avoidance of disposition order as an order under s 37(2)(b) or (c) of MCA 1973 and a variation order as an order under s 31 of MCA 1973. Further definitions of the remaining types of orders are contained in Part II of MCA 1973.

1.4   A financial provision order is:

(a)   an order that a party must make in favour of another person such periodical payments, for such term, as may be specified in the order (a 'periodical payments order');

(b)   an order that a party must, to the satisfaction of the court, secure in favour of another person such periodical payments, for such term, as may be specified (a 'secured periodical payments order');

(c)   an order that a party must make a payment in favour of another person of such lump sum or sums as may be specified (an 'order for the payment of a lump sum').[3]

1.5   A property adjustment order is:

(a)   an order that a party must transfer such of his or her property as may be specified in favour of the other party or a child of the family;

(b)   an order that a settlement of such property of a party as may be specified must be made, to the satisfaction of the court, for the benefit of the other party and of the children of the family, or either or any of them;

(c)   an order varying, for the benefit of the parties and of the children of the family, or either of them, any marriage settlement;

(d)   an order extinguishing or reducing the interest of either of the parties under any marriage settlement.[4]

In addition to the orders set out above, it should be noted that the court may make an order for sale of property (see Chapter 7).[5]

THE PRINCIPLES GOVERNING THE EXERCISE OF THE COURT'S DISCRETION

1.6   Section 25 of MCA 1973 contains the matters to which the court is to have regard in deciding how to exercise its powers under ss 23, 24 and 24A. It

---

[2]   Rule 1.2.
[3]   MCA 1973, s 21(2).
[4]   Ibid, s 21(2).
[5]   Ibid, s 24A.

has frequently been said[6] that the statutory 'guidelines' must be the principal determining factors for the court; decided cases showing how the court's discretion has been exercised on other occasions are of limited relevance although, clearly, guidance from appellate courts as to occasions on which courts have misdirected themselves are valuable.

In a leading case,[7] Butler–Sloss LJ, as she then was, stated the position as follows:

> 'There is a danger that practitioners in the field of family law attempt to apply too rigidly the decisions of this court and of the Family Division, without sufficiently recognising that each case involving a family has to be decided upon broad principles adapted to the facts of the individual case. Ancillary relief applications are governed by the statutory framework set out in the Matrimonial Causes Act 1973 as amended in 1984. Sections 25 and 25A provide the guidelines and require the court to have regard to all the circumstances of the individual case and to exercise the discretion of the court to do justice between the parties.'

Although *White v White*, from which these words are taken, was subsequently the subject of appeal to the House of Lords (and will be frequently mentioned in the following pages), the guidance given in this extract remains compelling law. Indeed, as will be seen, the House of Lords reinforced the principle that the provisions of the statute are pre-eminent.

Each case will turn on its own facts, and reference to the statutory criteria is therefore always essential. The primacy of the statute was underlined in another case[8] where there was a dispute between the parties as to the true ownership of the home. The court at first instance, and on appeal, allowed a purported claim by the wife under the Trusts of Land and Appointment of Trustees Act 1996 (TLATA 1996) to be consolidated with the ancillary relief application and to be tried at great length and cost as a preliminary issue. On further appeal, Thorpe LJ described this as 'about as appalling a litigation history as it would be possible to discover for an ancillary relief dispute'. Where property is jointly owned by the husband and wife and there are no real, as opposed to spurious, third party claims or interests, the only pertinent statutory provisions are those found in MCA 1973, s 25 which, once invoked, override the general and statutory provisions of real property and trust law.[9]

There now follows a summary of the 's 25 guidelines' followed by a discussion of the importance of 'equality' and 'fairness'. It is the practice of the courts to consider such of the guidelines as are relevant in the following order, and Form E[10] is designed to set out the evidence of the parties in this order.

---

6   Notably, first in *Sharpe v Sharpe* (1981) Fam Law 121, (1981) *The Times*, February 7.
7   *White v White* [1998] 2 FLR 310, CA.
8   *Tee v Tee and Hillman* [1999] 2 FLR 613, CA.
9   For the procedure where there is a genuine third party claim, see *TL v ML and Others* [2005] EWHC 2680 (Fam), [2006] 1 FLR 1263.
10   See Chapter 16 at para **16.11**.

ALL THE CIRCUMSTANCES OF THE CASE

1.7   In deciding whether to exercise its powers under ss 23 to 24A, and, if so, in what manner, it is the duty of the court to 'have regard to all the circumstances of the case'.[11] The section goes on to set out particular factors, but the term 'all the circumstances' must be taken to mean what it says. It is in wide terms, and it has been held that the court must not confine itself to the specified factors.[12] It is necessary to consider all other circumstances, whether past, present or future. For example, the remarriage of one of the parties is not specifically referred to as one of the statutory factors, but it has been held that it is one of the circumstances into which the court may properly enquire.[13] Another circumstance which is not specifically set out in the statute but which is none the less important is the existence of an agreement between the parties. This is considered in more detail at para **1.44**.

In *A v T (Ancillary Relief: Cultural Factors)*,[14] a case where the cultural values of both parties were not those of this country, it was held that in such a case and where the parties had only a secondary attachment to the English jurisdiction, the court should give due weight to the primary cultural factors and not ignore the differential between what one party might anticipate from determination here as opposed to another jurisdiction.[15]

As will be seen when the decisions of the House of Lords in *White v White*[16] and succeeding cases are considered below, two further extra-statutory principles, 'the yardstick of equality' and 'fairness', must now be borne in mind at all times (see para **1.51**).

FIRST CONSIDERATION THE WELFARE OF CHILDREN

1.8   It is provided that 'the first consideration' of the court must be given to:

> 'the welfare while a minor of any child of the family who has not attained the age of eighteen.'[17]

This requirement is therefore limited to children of the family, 'child of the family' being defined as any child who has been treated by both of the parties

---

[11]   MCA 1973, s 25(1).
[12]   See e g *Kokosinski v Kokosinski* [1980] Fam 72 at 183; *Trippas v Trippas* [1973] Fam 134 at 144.
[13]   *H v H* [1975] Fam 9; *Jackson v Jackson* [1973] Fam 99 at 104. However, prospects of remarriage are not a 'guessing game' and findings must be supported by some reasonable evidence: *Wachtel v Wachtel* [1973] Fam 72 at 86. A spouse is under a duty to be frank and give complete disclosure.
[14]   [2004] 1 FLR 977.
[15]   For another example see *G v G (Matrimonial Property: Rights of Extended Family)* [2005] EWHC 1560 (Admin), [2006] 1 FLR 62.
[16]   [2000] 2 FLR 981, HL.
[17]   MCA 1973, s 25(1).

to the marriage as a child of their family.[18] It includes stepchildren and, where the parties have lived together with a child, it is difficult to imagine circumstances in which a stepchild would not be a child of the family.[19]

The child must be under 18 years of age, and the scope of the court's duty under this provision is limited to the period ending with the child's eighteenth birthday. This is not to say that the court may or should not have regard to dependent children who are over 18,[20] but such consideration would arise from one of the other factors such as the financial obligations or responsibilities of the parties, or as one of the circumstances of the case, and would not be the first consideration of the court.

1.9 As to the meaning of 'the first consideration', it has been held that this is not the same as the paramount consideration.[21] The welfare of a child is not to be regarded as taking precedence over all other matters but is the first matter to which the court should direct itself (see para **1.10**).

NO ONE FACTOR MORE IMPORTANT THAN OTHERS

1.10 The statute sets out a list of matters to be considered, first when making orders as between the parties to the marriage and secondly when making orders in relation to children. The court is directed to have regard to all the matters contained in the subsection, and there is nothing in the Act to indicate that any one factor shall be more important than any other. Clearly, in some cases, consideration of one factor (eg discrepancies in age, or the length of the marriage) will occupy more of the time of the court than the others, and it may be that, in the circumstances of a particular case, one factor will prove to be more important than the others. In principle, however, there is no intrinsic reason why one factor should outweigh the importance of the others.[22]

In another case,[23] Thorpe LJ, after considering the historical evolution of s 25, and the deletion in 1984 of the statutory duty to attempt to place the parties in the financial position in which they would have been had the marriage not broken down, observed that even prior to that amendment the Court of

---

[18]   MCA 1973, s 52(1).
[19]   See eg *Teeling v Teeling* [1984] FLR 808, CA.
[20]   *Lilford (Lord) v Glyn* [1979] 1 WLR 78.
[21]   *Suter v Suter and Jones* [1987] Fam 111, CA. In that case, it was held that the judge had been wrong to elevate the children's interests so as to control the outcome of the case. However, see also *R v R* [1988] 1 FLR 89, CA, where it was said that, broadly speaking, a person having an obligation to maintain his children has an obligation to order his financial affairs with due regard to his responsibility to pay reasonable maintenance for them and to meet his reasonable financial obligations.
[22]   It used to be argued, for example, that if significant conduct were proved, this might be the major determining factor in the case. This is not, and never has been, so. See also *Piglowska v Piglowski* [1999] 2 FLR 763, HL.
[23]   *White v White* [1998] 2 FLR 310, CA.

Appeal[24] had defined the judge's ultimate aim as being to do that which is fair, just and reasonable between the parties, and that had continued to be the judicial interpretation of the objective of the section. Parliament had not chosen to lay any emphasis on any one of the eight specific factors above any other.[25] He continued:

> 'Although there is no ranking of the criteria to be found in the statute, there is as it were a magnetism that draws the individual case to attach to one, two, or several factors as having a decisive influence on its determination. . . . That said there is, if not a priority, certainly a particular importance attaching to s 25(2)(a).'

The reasons for that priority will be considered further at para **1.11**. Thorpe LJ concluded this part of his judgment as follows:

> 'It has often been said, and cannot be too often repeated, that each case depends on its own unique facts and those facts must determine which of the eight factors is to be given particular prominence in determination.'

In *Charman v Charman*[26] the Court of Appeal gave guidance on a further difficult question, namely how to resolve any irreconcilable conflict between the result suggested by one principle and that suggested by another. At para [73] of the judgment of the court, Sir Mark Potter P said:

> 'Often conflict can be reconciled by recourse to an order for periodical payments: as for example in *McFarlane*, per Baroness Hale at [154]. Ultimately, however, in cases in which it is irreconcilable, the criterion of fairness must supply the answer. It is clear that, when the result suggested by the needs principle is an award of property greater than the result suggested by the sharing principle, the former result should in principle prevail: per Baroness Hale in *Miller* at [142] and [144]. At least in applying the needs principle the court will have focussed upon the needs of both parties; analogous focus on the respondent is not present in the compensation principle and we leave for another occasion the proper treatment of irreconcilable conflict between that principle and one of the others. It is also clear that, when the result suggested by the needs principle is an award of property less than the result suggested by the sharing principle, the latter result should in principle prevail.'

FINANCIAL RESOURCES

1.11   The financial resources of the parties are crucial to any application for ancillary relief. It is only when the court has all the evidence as to the resources of the parties that it can decide whether, and if so, how, to redistribute them.

---

[24]   In *Page v Page* (1981) FLR 198, CA, at 206.
[25]   See also *Smith v Smith* [1991] 2 FLR 432, CA, per Butler-Sloss LJ.
[26]   [2007] EWCA Civ 503, [2007] All ER (D) 425 (May).

As Coleridge J put it in *Charman v Charman* at first instance,[27] 'the obvious starting point for all these applications is the financial position of the parties now'.

The court must have regard to:

> 'the income, earning capacity, property and other financial resources which each of the parties to the marriage has or is likely to have in the foreseeable future, including in the case of earning capacity any increase in that capacity which it would in the opinion of the court be reasonable to expect a party to the marriage to take steps to acquire.'[28]

In *White v White*, referred to in para **1.10**, Thorpe LJ underlined the importance of this factor by saying that, in almost every case, it is logically necessary to determine what is available before considering how it should be allocated, and repeated his opinion, first expressed in *H v H (Financial Provision: Capital Allowance)*,[29] that the discretionary powers of the court to adjust capital shares between spouses should not be exercised unless there was a manifest need for intervention upon the application of the s 25 criteria.

It has to be said that the second part of that statement cannot survive unscathed the decisions of the House of Lords in *White v White* and of the Court of Appeal in *Lambert v Lambert*. It is certainly still the case that the court has to fulfil a fact-finding role but even then some caution must be exercised. In *Parra v Parra*[30] Thorpe LJ was concerned that the judge had examined the financial position of the parties at very great length and in extraordinary detail and gave the following guidance:

> 'The outcome of ancillary relief cases depends upon the exercise of a singularly broad judgment that obviates the need for the investigation of minute detail and equally the need to make findings on minor issues in dispute.'

The task of the judge in ancillary relief litigation was different from that of the judge in the civil justice system; on the one hand, his quasi-inquisitorial role gave him a certain independence from the arguments of the parties but, on the other, he had an obligation to eschew over-elaboration and to

> 'endeavour to paint the canvas of his judgment with a broad brush rather than with a fine sable. Judgments in this field need to be simple in structure and simply explained.'

The duty of full disclosure

1.12 The exercise by the court of its statutory powers will be frustrated if one or other party is less than frank. The parties are therefore under an obligation

---

27 Approved by the CA at para [59] of its judgment.
28 MCA 1973, s 25(2)(a).
29 [1993] 2 FLR 335 at 347.
30 [2003] 1 FLR 942, CA.

to make full and frank disclosure of all relevant circumstances.[31] It is not appropriate to give partial disclosure, nor to wait for the other party to demand certain information. The information must be given voluntarily and completely. Failure to give full disclosure may result in the court exercising its powers to make interlocutory orders, for example for disclosure and production of documents,[32] will probably lead to the offender being condemned in costs, and, in extreme cases, may be regarded as conduct of a financial nature which it would be inequitable to disregard.[33] Readers are referred to the Protocol which is discussed at para **16.36**.

A related issue is the extent to which disclosure of potentially incriminating documents or evidence is privileged. In *S v S (Inland Revenue: Tax Evasion)*[34] Wilson J dismissed an application by the Revenue to keep a transcript which had irregularly come into its possession and to inspect affidavits and documents, on the ground that the public interest in encouraging full and frank disclosure in ancillary relief proceedings outweighed the interest in countering tax evasion. However, in *R v R (Disclosure to Revenue)*,[35] he permitted the Revenue to retain a transcript because it contained explicit findings as to evasion which had already resulted in action by the Revenue.

In *A v A; B v B*,[36] Charles J went further. A party to ancillary relief proceedings should be aware that if he or she does not claim protection against self-incrimination, the court may make or authorise disclosure in the overall public interest to a prosecuting or other public authority. The risk of serious harm being done to the administration of justice does not outweigh the public interest in the payment of all sums lawfully due to the Revenue. Where a court is satisfied that there has been illegal or unlawful conduct it should generally report the relevant material to the relevant authority. Advisers and courts should be alert to warning parties of their privilege against self-incrimination, but the fact that such a party may have assumptions made against him or her that result in a high award is not something that founds a public interest that disclosure should not be made.

Since those decisions the position has become yet more difficult for practitioners with the coming into force of the Proceeds of Crime Act 2002 (as to which, see Chapter 21).

---

[31] *Livesey (Formerly Jenkins) v Jenkins* [1985] AC 424, HL.
[32] See FPR 1991, rr 2.62(7) and 2.63. For more detail, see Chapter 16, para **16.31**.
[33] *P v P (Financial Relief: Non-disclosure)* [1994] 2 FLR 381; *B v B (Real Property: Assessment of Interests)* [1988] 2 FLR 490. See also *Minwalla v Minwalla* [2004] EWHC 2823 (Fam), [2005] 1 FLR 771; where the court finds that a party has set out to conceal resources and to obstruct proper investigation it may draw adverse inferences and reflect such conduct in costs. See also para **1.37**.
[34] [1997] 2 FLR 774.
[35] [1998] 1 FLR 922.
[36] [2000] 1 FLR 701.

Income and earning capacity

1.13 Further consideration will be given to this matter in the section on periodical payments at para **2.9**. Here it may be noted that the court will make an order on the basis of what the parties may reasonably be expected to receive if their opportunities are fully exploited. A party who chooses not to work when he or she could do so, or who chooses not to take advantage of opportunities to earn or to receive funds which are available to him or her, will find that the court draws adverse inferences from such unwillingness.[37] This is referred to as earning capacity, as opposed to earning potential which is dealt with at para **1.14**.

The income to be taken into account does not normally include welfare benefits, so that it would be unusual, to say the least, to make a periodical payments order against a person whose only income was income support.[38] Nevertheless, the availability of welfare benefits to one party may be a source of comfort to a court which feels unable to make an order in favour of that party.

Earning potential

1.14 Slightly different considerations arise when the court considers any increase in earning capacity which it might be reasonable to expect a party to take steps to acquire, and the subsection recognises this by making it a separate matter. This wording was added to the statute by the Matrimonial and Family Proceedings Act 1984 (MFPA 1984), and must be read together with s 25A which is considered below at para **2.21** et seq.

Property

1.15 Property includes all real and personal property owned by a party or in which he or she has an interest. It therefore includes land, beneficial interests under trusts,[39] shares in public or private companies, partnership assets, business stock, choses in action, money, jewellery, chattels, and so on. Nothing of value which is within the control of the party concerned should be excluded.[40]

---

[37] See e g *Hardy v Hardy* [1981] 1 FLR 321. But, for a contrary decision in a 'big money' case, see *A v A (Financial Provision)* [1998] 2 FLR 180.

[38] *Barnes v Barnes* [1972] 3 All ER 872; *Stockford v Stockford* (1982) FLR 58, CA; *Fletcher v Fletcher* [1985] Fam 92 at 100.

[39] For the position as to a discretionary trust, see e g *Charman v Charman* (above); the husband had appealed against the decision of Coleridge J to the effect that the assets which were in a Bermudan discretionary trust (a very sizeable proportion of the total) were to be regarded as assets over which he had control. The CA rejected the appeal.

[40] See *Donaldson v Donaldson* [1958] 2 All ER 660 (husband derived his living, food and accommodation from running a farm, and his only other source of income was a pension. He was ordered to pay an equivalent sum to the whole of the pension to his wife and children). However, where a spouse receives income under a discretionary trust over which he or she genuinely has no control, the court should only take account of the actual income received (this would not apply where the spouse had de facto control): *Howard v Howard* [1945] P 1; see also *B v B (Financial Provision)* (1982) FLR 298, CA.

In *White v White*,[41] the husband and wife had traded in a farming partnership for many years. This was a genuine, working partnership and not a mere tax vehicle. The assets were between £4.4m and £4.8m, and the judge found that the wife should, prima facie, have £1.5m. Nevertheless, he awarded her a lump sum of £800,000 on *Duxbury* principles.[42] The Court of Appeal allowed the wife's appeal and increased the lump sum to £1.5m. Thorpe LJ said that the first fundamental issue was what was the financial worth of each of the parties as if on the immediate dissolution of the farm partnership. Although, as will be seen at para **1.48**, the reasoning of the Court of Appeal was subsequently criticised by the House of Lords, the need to establish the means (and contributions) of the parties remains an integral part of the court's duty.

The position as to property acquired after the separation remains in doubt. In *Charman v Charman* the Court of Appeal[43] considered that a bonus generated by work done 14 months after separation was clearly an asset of the husband, but that the way the court should treat such an asset (eg by applying different percentages for 'sharing') was a 'grey area which this court may need to survey upon a suitable appeal'.

An entitlement under a pension scheme is frequently a valuable asset and, were it not for s 25B, would have to be considered in detail here. However, that section makes separate provision for pensions, and so pensions will be considered in detail in Chapter 10.

Expectations

1.16   The court must have regard to income, property, etc which a party has or is likely to have in the foreseeable future. This does not include pensions, which are dealt with separately.

The most common example of a financial expectation is where one party is, or is likely to be, a beneficiary under a will or an intestacy. However, here the court must recognise that wills may be changed and that testators may outlive beneficiaries. The court also has problems of evidence, since it cannot compel a potential benefactor to disclose his or her intentions nor can it always accurately estimate the size of the potential inheritance.

What is the foreseeable future may also be debatable. In one case, it was held that the prospects of a 64-year-old woman inheriting from her mother who was in poor health should be disregarded.[44] In another, where the husband was indefeasibly entitled under German law to a substantial inheritance from his father, and the parties had always made their financial arrangements on that basis, the wife's application was adjourned until the death of the father.[45]

---

[41]   [1998] 2 FLR 310.
[42]   See Chapter 4, para **4.17**.
[43]   [2007] EWCA Civ 503, [2007] All ER (D) 425 (May) at [104].
[44]   *Michael v Michael* [1986] 2 FLR 389.
[45]   *MT v MT (Financial Provision: Lump Sum)* [1992] 1 FLR 362.

When *Miller v Miller* was decided by the Court of Appeal,[46] it was held that when she married a rich man the wife had a 'legitimate expectation' to be maintained thereafter as the wife of a rich man. As will be seen (see para **1.53** et seq), the House of Lords rejected this finding (while re-emphasising) the importance of s 25(2)(c) (standard of living – see para **1.22**).

1.17 Before the coming into force of s 25B of MCA 1973 in 1996, there were authorities to the effect that the entitlement of a serviceman to a lump sum on retirement cannot be taken into account because of the provisions of the Army Act 1955 and similar statutes. It was also held that expectations which were more than a few years away were to be disregarded.[47]

These decisions have been reversed by s 25B, which is considered in Chapter 10.

1.18 Another common example of a financial expectation is a claim for personal injuries.[48] For this to be relevant, the court would have to be satisfied as to the likelihood of success, and the amount likely to be recovered. It should also be said that since, in serious cases, the award of damages would be intended to compensate a party for past and future loss, the damages would fall into a different category than, say, investments acquired during the marriage or a windfall inheritance.

In *D v D (Lump Sum Order: Adjournment of Application)*,[49] it was held that a court which decides to adjourn a lump sum application is doing no more than exercising the discretion vested in it, albeit that this step should be taken only rarely, where justice to the parties could not otherwise be done. One such circumstance was the real possibility of capital from a specific source becoming available in the near future.

In another somewhat unusual case[50] after a short marriage which ended 21 years ago a claim for a lump sum had been adjourned generally to allow the wife to apply again when the husband received an inheritance and the judge made the order for lump sum many years later. The needs of the children were said to be the most important factor.

Financial needs, obligations and responsibilities

1.19 The court is directed to have regard to:

---

[46] [2005] EWCA Civ 984, [2006] 1 FLR 151.
[47] *Roberts v Roberts* [1986] 2 FLR 152; see also *Priest v Priest* (1980) FLR 189 and *Happe v Happe* [1991] 4 All ER 527.
[48] *Daubney v Daubney* [1976] Fam 267; *Roche v Roche* (1981) Fam Law 243, CA; *Wagstaff v Wagstaff* [1992] 1 All ER 275, CA; *C v C (Financial Provision: Personal Damages)* [1995] 2 FLR 171, FD.
[49] [2001] 1 FLR 633, Connell J.
[50] *Re G (Financial Provision: Liberty to Restore Application for Lump Sum)* [2004] EWHC 88 (Fam), [2004] 1 FLR 997, Wilson J.

'the financial needs, obligations and responsibilities which each of the parties to the marriage has or is likely to have in the foreseeable future.'[51]

In most cases, the task of the court will be to calculate the reasonable needs of the parties, in particular the needs of a parent who is caring for the children of the family, and to make a decision as to whether there should be a transfer between the parties of assets or income to meet those needs. In such a case, it is also necessary to ensure that the 'paying party' is left with sufficient to meet his or her reasonable needs.[52]

In average income cases, the subsistence level indicated by benefit rates, together with the cost of housing is frequently regarded as a minimum figure for needs.[53]

1.20 What constitute obligations and responsibilities may be more debatable. Legal obligations assumed by one party from which it would be impossible to withdraw will normally be accepted.[54] The cost of maintaining a second family is clearly frequently contentious, particularly where the result is that that party is rendered unable to afford to maintain the first family. However, the court must be realistic, and must recognise that a second family which is being maintained by a person of average income will not have access to State benefits, whereas the first family would. There is nothing which the court can do to stop someone from establishing a second union and assuming the responsibility for children.

Where assets are surplus to needs it may be that a different approach will be adopted.[55]

Where there are children, the liability of either party under the Child Support Act 1991 (CSA 1991) is an obligation to be taken into account.

It has been held that the court should make a distinction between 'hard debts' such as debts to banks, and 'soft debts' such as money borrowed from relatives.[56]

---

[51] MCA 1973, s 25(2)(b).

[52] *Allen v Allen* [1986] 2 FLR 265, CA.

[53] Ibid; but see *Freeman v Swatridge* [1984] FLR 762.

[54] See eg *Stockford v Stockford* (1981) FLR 58, CA, where a husband had left his wife and first family in the former matrimonial home and bought a new house for his own occupation with the aid of a large mortgage. The court decided not to make an order against him since to do so would mean that he could not service the mortgage. Contrast *Slater v Slater and Another* (1982) FLR 364 where the court thought that the husband had been extravagant in deciding to live in a country house with heavy expenses, and took no account of the unreasonable expenses. See also *Campbell v Campbell* [1998] 1 FLR 828, CA.

[55] For two different approaches in relatively big money cases see *Norris v Norris* [2002] EWHC 2996 (Fam), [2003] 1 FLR 1142 (new children ignored) and *H-J v H-J (Financial Provision: Equality)* [2002] 1 FLR 415 (account taken of new responsibilities).

[56] *M v B (Ancillary Proceedings: Lump Sum)* [1998] 1 FLR 53, CA, at 56 and 60.

1.21 It was once the case that different considerations applied to 'big money cases' where the parties enjoy considerable affluence. This is the subject of a separate section in Chapter 4 at para **4.14**, where it will be seen that, until the recent decision of the House of Lords in *White v White*, the concept of 'reasonable requirements' was used in place of that of needs. It has now been established that reasonable requirements were an unwarranted judicial gloss on the words of the statute and that consideration of the needs of the parties is all that the statute permits (although an award will not necessarily be limited to a party's needs).

STANDARD OF LIVING DURING MARRIAGE

1.22 Before the changes introduced by the 1984 Act, the court was directed to put the parties in the position in which they would have been if the marriage had not broken down. That was frequently impossible, and is no longer one of the concerns of the court. However, the court is still directed to have regard to 'the standard of living enjoyed by the family before the breakdown of the marriage'.[57] This was upheld by the House of Lords in the conjoined appeals of *Miller v Miller* and *McFarlane v McFarlane*[58] (see para **1.53**).

It is perhaps important to note that the subsection refers to 'the family' and not to the parties; taken with the 'first consideration', this might entitle the court to take steps to ensure that the children of the family suffered as little as possible, even at the expense of one of the parents.

In most cases, the concern of the court will be to ensure that the standard of life of one party does not deteriorate to a greater extent than that of the other.[59]

1.23 Separate considerations may arise in cases of a short marriage and in big money cases. These are considered in more detail at para **1.25** and Chapter 4, para **4.14**, respectively. However, it may be helpful to note here that it has been held that, where there has been a high degree of affluence in the marriage, it is not necessary to ensure that the same high degree of affluence is maintained for both parties.[60]

Ages of parties and duration of marriage age

1.24 The next factor in the s 25 checklist is 'the age of each party to the marriage and the duration of the marriage'.[61] The age of the parties is normally relevant in relation to their earning capacity. Subject to the needs of young

---

[57] MCA 1973, s 25(2)(c).
[58] [2006] 1 FLR 1186, HL.
[59] See generally *M v M (Financial Provision)* [1987] 2 FLR 1; *Leadbeater v Leadbeater* [1985] FLR 789; *P v P (Financial Relief: Non-disclosure)* [1994] 2 FLR 381.
[60] See eg *F v F (Ancillary Relief: Substantial Assets)* [1995] 2 FLR 45.
[61] MCA 1973, s 25(2)(d).

children, a young wife will normally be taken to have an earning potential, and the provisions of s 25A will apply (see Chapter 2).

Very different considerations apply to a woman aged over 50 who has not worked for many years. The court will take the age of such a person into account when deciding whether she has an earning potential.[62]

Duration of marriage: short marriage

1.25 When a marriage has subsisted for more than the average number of years, the significance of its duration is not normally an important factor; the usual guidelines apply and there is no separate point to be made about the length of the marriage. Duration is really only significant in the case of a short marriage, which is a topic which must now be considered.

The duration of a short marriage is not, of course, an isolated factor; associated with a short marriage are normally such other important factors as contributions (or lack of contributions), children, and earning potential. For example, when all the capital contributions have come from one party, and the marriage ends after a short period, in the absence of other factors the non-contributing party could not expect a substantial redistribution of assets.

The proper approach to a short marriage has now been considered by the House of Lords in the conjoined appeals of *Miller v Miller* and *McFarlane v McFarlane*.[63] It may be helpful first to summarise the leading pre-*Miller/ McFarlane* cases and then to contrast these with the House of Lords guidance.

Pre-Miller/McFarlane cases

1.26 In *Attar v Attar (No 2)*,[64] the marriage had lasted for only 6 months and the actual cohabitation only 7 weeks. It was held that because of those facts it was impossible to have regard to all the usual s 25 factors; the only proper approach was to have regard to the effect on the parties of the marriage and its dissolution. There were no children, the husband was very wealthy, and the order was for a limited term of periodical payments to enable the wife to readjust.

In *C v C (Financial Relief: Short Marriage)*,[65] the facts of the case were described as 'highly unusual' with features that made it 'unique'. There was, however, a child of the marriage. The judge had ordered periodical payments with no term, and this was upheld by the Court of Appeal. Ward LJ said that the appropriateness of a term order depended on all the s 25 checklist criteria,

---

[62] See the cases cited in Chapter 2 on Periodical Payments, in particular 'The Clean Break' at para **2.21** et seq.

[63] [2006] 1 FLR 1186, HL.

[64] [1985] FLR 653.

[65] [1997] 2 FLR 26, CA; for a longer discussion of this case, see Chapter 2 at para **2.23**.

including the welfare of any child; it was not appropriate simply to presume the imposition of a term whenever there was a short-term marriage.

In *Hedges v Hedges*,[66] the marriage had lasted 4½ years; there were no children, and the wife had continued to work. She was awarded half the husband's liquid assets to help deal with her housing needs, and periodical payments for 18 months to help her to readjust. This was upheld by the Court of Appeal.

In *Hobhouse v Hobhouse*,[67] the parties divorced after 4 years of marriage; there were no children. The wife had inherited £0.5m and expected to inherit a further £1.5m on her mother's death. The husband's wealth was indicated by the fact that he pleaded the 'millionaire's defence'.[68] The wife was likely to return to Australia and her family home there within 3 to 5 years. The judge awarded her a lump sum of £175,000. The wife's appeal was dismissed. The marriage was childless and brief; the wife had not sacrificed any financial advantage; she had been allowed 3 to 5 years to rebuild her life. There was no obvious bracket, and the award was well within the judge's discretion.

In *G v G (Financial Provision: Separation Agreement)*,[69] the marriage lasted 4½ years. The wife brought into the marriage her two children from a previous marriage and they enjoyed a luxurious lifestyle. It was held that the short duration of the marriage was only one factor; both parties had made significant contributions to the welfare of the family and were likely to continue to do so. The husband's total wealth exceeded £4.5m; the wife earned £11,500 per annum and had a house (purchased for her by the husband) worth £250,000. She was awarded a lump sum of £240,000.

For an example of a more recent decision involving substantial assets see *K v K (Ancillary Relief: Prenuptial Agreement)* which is discussed at greater length at para **1.43**. The most interesting point to emerge from that case in this context is that, after dealing with the capital claims of the wife, the judge dealt with the needs of the child of the family almost as a discrete issue and as if it were an application under Sch 1 to the Children Act 1989. The husband was ordered to provide a home and furnishings for the child at a cost of £1.2m, to revert to him eventually.[70]

In *Foster v Foster*[71] the Court of Appeal allowed an appeal from a circuit judge and restored the order of a district judge awarding a wife 61% of the assets after a very short marriage where she had introduced the bulk of the capital. The district judge had sought to give the parties back what they had brought

---

66 [1991] 1 FLR 196, CA.
67 [1999] 1 FLR 961, CA.
68 See Chapter 4, para **4.12**.
69 [2000] 2 FLR 18, Connell J.
70 For an even more generous order in favour of a child made under Sch 1 see *Re P (Child: Financial Provision)* [2003] EWCA Civ 837, [2003] 2 FLR 865 and para **11.29**.
71 [2003] 2 FLR 299.

into the marriage at the value it held at that date, and that was not unfair. That was the only possible reason to depart from equality in this case. As will be seen below, this case is probably the most important of the pre-2006 cases.

In *B v B (Mesher Order)*[72] the marriage had lasted 10 months and there was one child. The district judge found the wife needed £220,000 to rehouse herself and awarded her a lump sum of £175,000 and periodical payments. The husband appealed and argued, inter alia, that there should have been a *Mesher* order. This was rejected on the ground that, given the wife's continuing contributions to bringing up the child, her prospects of being able to generate capital were small whereas the husband's were good. A *Mesher* order would therefore produce inequality of outcome. It was also held that a term order for periodical payments for the wife was not appropriate in view of the uncertainty and that the proper approach was to impose no term and to leave it to the payee to seek variation.

1.27 Perhaps the best way to summarise these decisions would be to reaffirm the importance of considering all the s 25 factors without preconceptions, while recognising that many of those factors will have little relevance in many cases of a short marriage. It was important to consider what had been the effect of the marriage on the parties, and, perhaps, to ask what they had lost in financial terms.

Where there is a child, it cannot be denied that this will have a significant effect on the parent caring for the child, and this would seem to make it prima facie inappropriate to impose a term on periodical payments.[73]

Miller/McFarlane guidance

1.28 The House held that, if it were not clear before *Foster v Foster*, it must now be clear that the old law relating to short marriages was swept away by *White v White*. The old principle of trying to restore one party, normally the wife, to her position before the marriage, was no longer applicable.

The principles of *White*, particularly the yardstick of equality and the concept of sharing, apply as much to short as to long marriages. *Foster v Foster* had made clear that all the s 25 guidelines must be applied in such a case. Having said that, in his speech Lord Nicholls also made clear that the application of these principles will not necessarily result in equal division. When he said that the length of the marriage 'will affect the quantum of the financial fruits of the

---

72   [2003] 2 FLR 285, [2003] Fam Law 462.
73   See also *Re G (Financial Provision: Liberty to Restore Application for Lump Sum)* [2004] EWHC 88 (Fam), [2004] 1 FLR 997, where after a short marriage a claim for a lump sum was adjourned generally with liberty to restore to enable the wife to apply in the event of the husband's inheritance; it was said that the interests of the children changed the perception of fairness.

partnership' he can only mean that the court must look at what the partnership produced during the term of the relationship, and that will be one of the factors to be considered.

Unsurprisingly, Baroness Hale agreed with the approval of her judgment in *Foster*. Referring to Foster, she said that:

> '[a]lthough one party had earned more and thus contributed more in purely financial terms to the acquisition of those assets, both contributed what they could, and the fair result was to divide the product of their joint endeavours equally.'

1.29 An issue associated with the length of the marriage may be the significance which the court should give to cohabitation outside marriage. As to pre-marital cohabitation, the law is reasonably clear; the court may have regard only to the period between the marriage and the breakdown when considering the length of the marriage.[74] The same applies to post-marital cohabitation.[75]

Perhaps a more contemporary approach can be derived from *GW v RW (Financial Provision: Departure from Equality)*[76] where it was held that where a marriage moved seamlessly from cohabitation to marriage it was unrealistic and artificial to treat the periods differently. However, it was equally unrealistic to treat the period of estrangement conducted under the umbrella of a divorce petition as part of the duration of the marriage.

Cohabitation of the party who applies for financial relief after divorce will be considered in more detail in Chapter 2 at para **2.10**.

---

[74] *Foley v Foley* [1981] Fam 160; *Campbell v Campbell* [1976] Fam 347.

[75] *Hill v Hill* [1997] 1 FLR 730, an unusual case which turned on other issues, eg whether an order made in 1969 could be set aside on the ground of 25 years' cohabitation after dissolution. 'Under English law, a relationship of cohabitation no matter how long nor how great the dependence does not give the wife any right to claim nor power in the court to order either maintenance or discretionary capital provision', per Holman J. See also *Hewitson v Hewitson* [1995] 1 FLR 241, CA. See also *CO v CO* [2004] EWHC 287 (Fam), [2004] 1 FLR 1095, where Coleridge J held that committed settled relationships which endure for years outside marriage must be regarded as every bit as valid as marriage; where such an arrangement existed and seamlessly preceded the marriage it is as capable of being as important a non-financial circumstance as any other.

[76] *GW v RW (Financial Provision: Departure from Equality)* [2003] EWHC 611 (Fam), [2003] 2 FLR 108, Nicholas Mostyn QC. See also *S v S (Financial Provision) (Post-Divorce Cohabitation)* [1994] 2 FLR 228; another unusual case, involving cohabitation of 6 years before, 8 years during and 15 years after marriage. Douglas Brown J held that it was necessary to have regard to all the circumstances and awarded the wife a lump sum of £185,000 out of the husband's free capital of £400,000 plus £100,000 in respect of her interest in the home. However, caution is required; in *Hewitson* (above), 'grave reservations' were expressed as to this decision.

DISABILITY

1.30   The court must have regard to 'any physical or mental disability of either of the parties to the marriage'.[77] This is another factor which overlaps with earning capacity or potential, and the position of disabled parties would be no different if this provision did not exist. There seems to be no other way in which disability has ever been regarded as a factor in itself.

CONTRIBUTIONS

1.31   The next s 25 factor is:

> 'the contributions which each of the parties has made or is likely in the foreseeable future to make to the welfare of the family, including any contribution by looking after the home or caring for the family.'[78]

The purpose of this subsection is, clearly, to try to reflect the value of each of the parties to the whole marriage, which is not an easy task. This factor may be subdivided into several categories.

Financial contributions

1.32   Contributions of a financial nature will include the earnings of both parties over the course of the marriage, any capital sums provided by them, for example for the acquisition of a house, and any inheritances which they have received from which the family has benefited. It also includes the value of a discounted purchase price for a former council house under the 'right to buy' scheme.

The court has a duty to make findings of fact where there is a dispute as to any financial contributions made by either party; any decision as to how available capital is to be divided to give effect to the s 25 criteria must start from an accurate assessment of what the parties' respective proprietary interests are.[79]

As to 'negative contributions', see para **1.35**.

In *White v White* the relevance of inherited wealth as a contribution was mentioned and for a time it was thought by some that this class of asset might fall outside the ambit of the normal division of assets. However, in *Norris v Norris*[80] Bennett J held that Lord Nicholls had not enunciated a guideline that inherited contributions should not be included in the pool of assets for

---

[77]   MCA 1973, s 25(2)(e).
[78]   MCA 1973, s 25(2)(f).
[79]   *M v B (Ancillary Proceedings: Lump Sum)* [1998] 1 FLR 53, CA, per Thorpe J at 58. See also *White v White* [1998] 2 FLR 310 and the comments at para **1.11**, and *A v A (Elderly Applicant: Lump Sum)* [1999] 2 FLR 969.
[80]   [2002] EWHC 2996 (Fam), [2003] 1 FLR 1142.

division. In theory, a spouse could claim more than half for this reason, but only in very limited and quite exceptional circumstances. Inherited property represented a contribution by one of the parties and was a factor to be taken into account.

This case was of some significance since it post-dated *Lambert v Lambert* and clearly reflects the thinking as to 'special contributions' in that case.[81] A similar conclusion was reached by Nicholas Mostyn QC in *GW v RW (Financial Provision: Departure from Equality)*.[82] Nevertheless, the fact that there might be room for more than one point of view on this issue was demonstrated by the decision of Munby J in *P v P (Inherited Property)*.[83] This was a case involving a family farm which had been in the husband's family for several generations. His Lordship held that fairness might demand a different approach if the inheritance were a pecuniary legacy which accrued during the marriage than if it were a landed estate which had been in one spouse's family for generations and had been brought into the marriage with an expectation that it would be retained in specie for future generations. In the instant case, the proper approach was to make an award based on the wife's reasonable needs for accommodation and income; to do more would be to tip the balance unfairly in her favour and unfairly against the husband.

1.33 The potential differences in judicial opinion at the highest level were revealed in the speeches of Lord Nicholls and Baroness Hale in *Miller/McFarlane*. *White v White* had already established that the contributions of the breadwinner are not to be favoured over those of the home-maker and child-carer. Both Lord Nicholls and Baroness Hale sought to deal with the vexed issue of the evaluation of special or exceptional contributions, such as, for example, those of an exceptionally gifted sportsman, musician or entrepreneur (these are the author's examples, not those of the court).

Lord Nicholls deprecated any lengthy and costly inquiry into such matters. The question was whether earnings of this character could be regarded as a 'special contribution', and thus as a good reason for departing from equality of division. The answer was that exceptional earnings were to be regarded as a factor pointing away from equality of division when, but only when, it would be inequitable to proceed otherwise. The wholly exceptional nature of the earnings must be, to borrow a phrase more familiar in a different context, obvious and gross.

Baroness Hale agreed, also equating contributions with conduct. The words she added are important and worth repeating.

---

[81] [2002] EWCA Civ 1685, [2003] 1 FLR 139, CA. Cases such as *M v M (Financial Provision: Valuation of Assets)* [2002] Fam Law 509 and *H v H (Financial Contributions: Special Contribution)* [2002] 2 FLR 1021 which arrive at the opposite conclusion may be distinguished and doubted for that reason.

[82] [2003] EWHC 611 (Fam), [2003] 2 FLR 108.

[83] [2004] EWHC 1364 (Fam), [2005] 1 FLR 576.

'Section 25(2)(f) of the 1973 Act does not refer to the contributions which each
has made to the parties' accumulated wealth, but to the contributions they have
made (and will continue to make) to the welfare of the family. Each should be seen
as doing their best in their own sphere. Only if there is such a disparity in their
respective contributions to the welfare of the family that it would be inequitable to
disregard it should this be taken into account in determining their shares.'

1.34 The difference between Lord Nicholls and Baroness Hale related to the
relevance of 'non-matrimonial property'. Lord Nicholls' approach was that
non-matrimonial property should be viewed as all property which the parties
bring with them into the marriage or acquire by inheritance or gift during the
marriage (plus perhaps the income or fruits of that property), while
matrimonial property should be viewed as all other property. The yardstick of
equality should apply generally to matrimonial property (although the shorter
the marriage, the smaller the matrimonial property is in the nature of things
likely to be). But the yardstick is not so readily applicable to non-matrimonial
property, especially after a short marriage, but in some circumstances even after
a long marriage.

Baroness Hale's approach took a more limited concep of matrimonial property,
as embracing 'family assets' (cf *Wachtel v Wachtel*[84]) and family businesses or
joint ventures in which both parties work (cf *Foster v Foster*[85]). In relation to
such property she agreed that the yardstick of equality may readily be applied.
However, she identified other 'non-business-partnership, non-family assets', to
which that yardstick may not apply with the same force particularly in the case
of short marriages; these included not merely (a) property which the parties
bring with them into the marriage or acquire by inheritance or gift during the
marriage (plus perhaps its income or fruits), but also (b) business or investment
assets generated solely or mainly by the efforts of one party during the
marriage.

Baroness Hale's view was that the source of assets may be taken into account
but that this would become less important with the passage of time; she points
out that the court is directed to take account of the length of the marriage. She
continued:

'If the assets are not "family assets", or not generated by the joint efforts of the
parties, then the duration of the marriage may justify a departure from the
yardstick of equality of division. As we are talking here of a departure from that
yardstick, I would prefer to put this in terms of a reduction to reflect the period of
time over which the domestic contribution has or will continue rather than in
terms of accrual over time.'

Baroness Hale concluded, on this issue:

'This is simply to recognise that in a matrimonial property regime which still starts
with the premise of separate property, there is still some scope for one party to

---

84   [1973] Fam 72 at 90, per Lord Denning MR.
85   [2003] EWCA Civ 565; [2003] 2 FLR 299, 305, para 19, per Hale LJ.

acquire and retain separate property which is not automatically to be shared equally between them. The nature and the source of the property and the way the couple have run their lives may be taken into account in deciding how it should be shared.'

Lord Mance approved this approach.

Given this approval, and the fact that Lord Hoffman expressly identified himself with Baroness Hale's speech and not with that of Lord Nicholls (Lord Hope favouring both equally), it could perhaps fairly be said that the true ratio of this case on this issue is that expressed by Baroness Hale and not that of Lord Nicholls. However, that was not an end of the debate as to 'exceptional' or 'special' contributions. When he gave his judgment in *Charman v Charman* at first instance[86] Coleridge J observed that:

'For the past nearly five years, since *White*, courts at every level have been wrestling with the question of whether or not in departing from equality and striving for fairness it is proper to take into account and give weight to exceptional wealth creation by one spouse. In reading and re-reading all the now familiar authorities, attempting to expose and explain the underlying principles, one is reminded of a frenzied butterfly hunter in a tropical jungle trying to entrap a rare and elusive butterfly using a net full of holes. As soon as it appears to have been caught it escapes again and the pursuit continues.'

The matter was considered in some detail when *Charman* reached the Court of Appeal for obvious reasons; this was a case involving very considerable assets (£138m) which it was common ground had almost entirely been generated by the exceptional and in every way 'special' efforts and ingenuity of the husband.[87] Giving the judgment of the court, Sir Mark Potter P said:

'It was inevitable, so it seems to us, that the notion of a special contribution should have "survived" the decision in *Miller* [as to which, see below]. The statutory requirement in every case to consider the contributions which each party has made to the welfare of the family, as well as those which each is likely to make to it, would be inconsistent with a blanket rule that their past contributions to its welfare must be afforded equal weight. Nevertheless the difficulty attendant upon a comparison of their different contributions and the danger of its infection by discrimination against the home-maker led the House in *Miller* heavily to circumscribe the situations in which it would be appropriate to find that one party had made a special contribution, in the sense of a contribution by one unmatched by the other, which, for the purpose of the sharing principle, should lead to departure from equality. In this regard the House was unanimous.'

The Court declined the invitation to identify a figure as a 'threshold' beyond which a special contribution would be appropriate, considering it dangerous to do so. Nevertheless, it was prepared to give guidance [90] as to 'the appropriate range of percentage adjustment to be made in cases in which the court is

---

[86] [2006] EWHC 1879 (Fam).
[87] For a similar case with a similar result see *Sorrell v Sorrell* [2005] EWHC 1717, [2006] 1 FLR 519.

satisfied that the principle requires departure from equality.' Even there, however, it was said that 'it is necessary however to bear in mind that fair despatch of some cases may require departure even from the range which we propose'.

The guidance offered was as follows:

1   The adjustment should be significant as opposed to token. The Court found it hard to conceive that where such a special contribution was established the percentages should be nearer equality that 55%–45%.

2   Equally, it should not be too great. The Court approved Coleridge J's comment that 'I think you need to be careful, after a very long marriage, to give a wife half of what you give the husband'. The judgment of the Court of Appeal continued:

> 'Arbitrary though it is, our instinct is the same, namely that, even in an extreme case and in the absence of some further dramatic feature unrelated to it, fair allowance for special contribution within the sharing principle would be most unlikely to give rise to percentages of division of matrimonial property further from equality than 66.6%–33.3%.'

Non-financial contributions

1.35   If the only contributions which the court could consider were financial, a wife and mother who had stayed at home to look after children would be at a distinct disadvantage. Thus it is that the court is directed to have regard to the value to the family of a non-working party. It may be that before the decision of the House of Lords in *White v White*[88] the guidance which was given as to how, if at all, such contributions should be weighed in the balance against financial contributions was not entirely clear. For example, it was held that it was wrong to make a distinction between cases where a wife makes actual financial contributions to the assets of the family and those in which her contribution is indirect.[89] However, in another, admittedly unusual, case,[90] it was held that, where there were ample assets and the wife had made a full contribution to the welfare of the family but had not contributed directly to the build-up of the family assets, the remarks in *Wachtel v Wachtel*,[91] to the effect that there should be a starting point of equality, should be confined to division of the family home and not to division of the family assets as a whole.

In *White v White*,[92] it was held that it is a principle 'of universal application' that there can be no discrimination between husband and wife in their

---

[88]   [2001] 1 AC 596, [2000] 2 FLR 981.
[89]   *Vicary v Vicary* [1992] 2 FLR 271, CA, cited with approval in *Conran v Conran* [1997] 2 FLR 615 by Wilson J.
[90]   *W v W (Judicial Separation: Ancillary Relief)* [1995] 2 FLR 259 (husband was 87, wife 78; wife's reasonable needs were limited).
[91]   [1973] Fam 72.
[92]   For the facts of the case, see para **1.48**.

respective roles. Different roles are assumed for many different reasons. Whatever the division of labour, fairness dictates that this should not prejudice either party when considering the statutory factors. There should be no bias in favour of the money-earner and against the homemaker and child-carer.

This principle was developed in *Lambert v Lambert*[93] . Here, judges were given clear guidance as to how to deal with issues of contributions. Any bias in favour of a breadwinner is an example of gender discrimination and therefore to be disapproved. 'The danger of gender discrimination resulting from a finding of special financial contribution is plain.'[94] The statutory requirement to consider all the s 25 factors does not require a detailed critical appraisal of the performance of each of the parties during the marriage. 'Couples who cannot agree division are entitled to seek a judicial decision without exposing themselves to intrusion, indignity, and possible embarrassment of such an appraisal.'[95]

Special financial contributions are dealt with above. However, it should not be forgotten that not all special contributions are financial. In *Charman v Charman*, above, it was pointed out at para [80] that:

> 'The notion of a special contribution to the welfare of the family will not successfully have been purged of inherent gender discrimination unless it is accepted that such a contribution can, in principle, take a number of forms; that it can be non-financial as well as financial; and that it can thus be made by a party whose role has been exclusively that of a home-maker.'

1.36 It is, perhaps, necessary to say again that no one factor is to be regarded as intrinsically more important than the others; the court must take an overall view.

In another unusual case,[96] it was said that the proper approach is to survey the wife's reasonable requirements and then place her contributions and all other factors in the balance, taking into account the nexus between the contributions and the creation of the resources.

Future contributions

1.37 The court must take account of the future as much as of the past. This will normally be relevant when one party is to care for the children of the family, and the longer the dependency the greater the significance of this factor. If one party is unable, for financial reasons, to make any significant contribution to the future welfare of the family, so that the burden will inevitably fall on the other party, this might well be a significant factor.

---

[93]   [2002] EWCA Civ 1685, [2003] 1 FLR 139.
[94]   Ibid, per Thorpe LJ at para 45.
[95]   Ibid, para 38.
[96]   *Conran v Conran* [1997] 2 FLR 615; unusual because of the size of the parties' wealth if for no other reason.

Since the advent of CSA 1991, and the virtual impossibility of contracting out of child support in most cases, the considerable sums which many 'non-resident parents' will have to pay is a future contribution which cannot be ignored.

CONDUCT

1.38   The court is directed to have regard to:

> 'the conduct of each of the parties, if that conduct is such that it would in the opinion of the court be inequitable to disregard it.'[97]

As has been emphasised before, no one factor is normally the sole determining factor in any application, and there are few examples of cases where conduct has been a major determining matter. Such examples as there are may be summarised as follows.

Financial conduct

1.39   Cases where it can be demonstrated that the behaviour of one party has had a clear (and, impliedly, detrimental) effect on the fortunes of the parties are the most usual examples of conduct having a real significance. In one case, the husband had dissipated the family capital, and the court held that he could not be allowed to fritter away assets and then claim as much of what was left as if he had behaved reasonably.[98] In another case, the husband, a farmer, had brought about financial disaster and his own bankruptcy; in the words of the judge he had 'obstinately, unrealistically and selfishly trailed on to eventual disaster, dissipating in the process not only his own money but his family's money, his friends' money, the money of commercial creditors unsecured and eventually his wife's money'.[99] Even so, he was not deprived of all entitlement but was restricted to the minimum sum needed to rehouse himself.

These decisions may perhaps be contrasted with another,[100] in which a wife had inherited her mother's estate and then sold part to her daughter at an undervalue, thereby depleting her own assets. The argument that this was 'financial conduct' was rejected, but the actions of the wife were held to be clearly relevant as one of the circumstances.

In another case, it was held that although the husband's conduct in relation to certain financial transfers was such that it would be inequitable to ignore it, the approach should be not to fix a sum as a penalty, but rather an evaluation based on all the relevant factors taken in the round.[101]

---

[97]   MCA 1973, s 25(2)(g).
[98]   *Martin v Martin* [1976] Fam 335.
[99]   *Beach v Beach* [1995] 2 FLR 160, per Thorpe J. See also *Le Foe v Le Foe and Woolwich plc* [2001] 2 FLR 970.
[100]   *Primavera v Primavera* [1992] 1 FLR 16, CA.
[101]   *H v H (Financial Relief: Conduct)* [1998] 1 FLR 971.

An unusual situation arose in *W v W*.[102] Both parties had agreed not to pursue allegations of conduct but the husband then sought to argue that, because of the wife's drinking, her contributions were 'negative'. Wilson J said that 'negative contributions' was an unhelpful oxymoron. Where a nil contribution or conduct were alleged, the allegations should be put in those terms.

Non-financial conduct

1.40   In previous editions of this book, a summary of what were believed to be the leading cases where conduct was found to be relevant were included. This task has now been made easier and more authoritative by the judgment of Stanley Burton J in *S v S*.[103] His Lordship had to consider whether or not the alleged conduct in that case should be taken into account. He was at pains to point out that he did not normally sit in the Family Division and so relied on the two expert counsel[104] appearing before him. He dealt with the position as follows:

'I have been told by Counsel that there are only rare cases in the reports where this has occurred. I have been taken to what I believe must be all of them. The examples given include:

(i)   *Armstrong v Armstrong* [1974] SJ 579: wife shoots husband with his shotgun with intent to endanger life.

(ii)   *Jones v Jones* [1976] Fam 8: husband attacks wife with a razor and inflicts serious injuries: there are financial consequences (wife rendered incapable of working).

(iii) *Bateman v Bateman* [1979] 2 WLR 377: wife twice inflicts stab wounds on her husband with a knife.

(iv)   *S v S* [1982] Fam Law 183: husband commits incest with children of the family.

(v)   *Hall v Hall* [1984] FLR 631: wife stabs husband in the abdomen with a knife.

(vi)   *Kyte v Kyte* [1987] 3 AER 1041: wife facilitates the husband's attempted suicide.

(vii) *Evans v Evans* [1989] 1 FLR 351: wife incites others to murder the husband.

(viii) *K v K* [1990] 2 FLR 225: Husband's serious drink problem and "disagreeable" behaviour led to the forced sale of the matrimonial home and serious financial consequences to the wife.

(ix)   *H v H* [1994] 2 FLR 801: serious assault and an attempted rape of wife by husband: and financial consequences because the consequent imprisonment of husband destroyed his ability to support her.

(x)   *A v A* [1995] 1 FLR 345: husband assaults the wife with a knife.

(xi)   *C v C* (Bennett J 12 December 2001 unreported): wife deliberately drugged husband to make him very sleepy and then while he was in a somnolent state placed a bag over his head, which she held in such a way that the husband could not breathe. Although it was found that the wife did not have an intent to kill, Bennett J concluded that the husband did believe that she was trying to kill him, and that her aim was to make him so believe.

---

[102]   [2001] Fam Law 656, Wilson J.
[103]   [2006] EWHC 2793.
[104]   Mr Nicholas Mostyn QC and Mr Philip Moor QC.

(xii) *Al-Khatib v Masry* [2002] 1 FLR 1053: husband guilty of "very grave" misconduct in abducting the children of the marriage in contempt of court.

(xiii) *H v H* [2006] 1 FLR 990: very serious assault by husband on wife with knife, leading to 12 years imprisonment for attempted murder and with financial consequences, namely destroying her Police career.'

His Lordship's comments on these cases were as follows:

'As will be seen, it is not suggested that there were any financial consequences from the conduct of which the Applicant complains in this case, which factor may have exacerbated, in the judgment of Scott Baker J, the facts in *K v K* referred to at (viii) above. However, that case apart, all of the conduct found in those cases appears of manifest seriousness. Apart from the statutory provision, and the words of Ormrod J in *Wachtel* quoted by Baroness Hale above, there is a certain amount of recurrent phraseology: "If the courts were in these circumstances not to discharge the order, the public might think that we had taken leave of our senses" (per Balcombe LJ at 355 in *Evans* at (vii) above): Sir Roger Ormrod in *Hall* at (v) above describes (at 632) the conduct as "gross and obvious" which has "nothing to do with the ordinary run of fighting and quarrelling in an unhappy marriage" and which the judge's "sense of justice required to be taken into account": Bennett J in *C* at (xi) above, asks whether "it would be repugnant to any sense of justice for the wife to receive any award at all". Mr Mostyn QC pointed to the words of Sir George Baker P in *W v W* [1976] Fam 107 at 110D when he referred to the sort of conduct which would cause the ordinary mortal to throw up his hands and say "... surely that woman is not going to get a full award": and, in the course of submissions, he suggested a test of applying what he called the "gasp factor".'

One case which was, perhaps surprisingly omitted from this pantheon of wrong-doing was *Clark v Clark*[105] which was described by Thorpe LJ as 'one of the most extraordinary marital histories that I have ever encountered' and 'as baleful as any to be found in the family law reports'. The wife was 36 years younger than the husband. At the date of the marriage, he was rich while her liabilities exceeded her assets. The marriage was never consummated. Over the 5-year marriage, she persuaded him to purchase a number of properties, most of which were vested in her sole name. In addition, she acquired shares, a racehorse, a Bentley and a boat. The husband was coerced into transferring a large house into the wife's name, and he was then forced to live as a virtual prisoner in part of the house while she occupied the larger part with her lover. He attempted suicide, and when he returned home he was again confined as a virtual prisoner, the wife removing his telephone and gate buzzer. He was eventually rescued by relatives.

The judge found that the wife had exercised undue influence over the husband, that this was a short marriage, that the husband's contributions had been enormous while hers were negligible and that her marital and litigation conduct must be condemned in the strongest terms. Nevertheless, he awarded her a lump sum of £552,500. Both parties appealed.

---

[105] [1999] 2 FLR 498, CA.

The wife's appeal was dismissed and the husband's appeal allowed. The judge had fallen into manifest error in allowing the wife £552,500. He had failed to reflect his findings on the wife's misconduct in his award; it would be hard to conceive of a case of graver marital misconduct. This was a rare case in which litigation misconduct should be reflected in the substantive award. However, to leave the wife with nothing was impracticable since that would have required her to make substantial repayments to the husband, and the lump sum was reduced to £125,000.

Conduct in the course of the proceedings

1.41 The conduct of the parties during and in relation to the proceedings may be a relevant factor. In *B v B (Real Property: Assessment of Interests)*,[106] it was held that a wife whose conduct in relation to discovery and dishonest statements had amounted to contempt as well as conduct which it was inequitable to disregard should have the award which she would otherwise have received reduced to take account of the conduct. However, this may be a decision which will rarely be followed. In another case,[107] where a wife had knowingly misrepresented her true financial position and failed in her duty to give full disclosure, Thorpe J held that, while accepting that such behaviour was conduct which it would be inequitable to disregard, this should be reflected in an order for costs rather than a reduction of the share of the assets.[108]

In *Al Khatib v Masry*[109] the husband had been highly obstructive and unco-operative in the wife's application for ancillary relief and the court observed that it would be difficult to imagine a worse case of litigation misconduct. The husband had also abducted the children to Saudi Arabia. It was thought that the husband's assets were at least £50m. The wife was awarded a lump sum of £10m, a Duxbury award of £5.5m and a 'fighting fund' for legal costs of £2.5m to assist her to recover the children.

Finally, in *M v M (Ancillary Relief: Conduct)* it was held that the husband's conduct both in respect of gambling and his disregard of court orders should not be disregarded. Such conduct should be taken into account in a broad way and not with mathematical precision and affected the order and not just the costs.

LOST BENEFITS

1.42 The court is directed to have regard to:

---

[106] [1988] 2 FLR 490.
[107] *P v P (Financial Relief: Non-disclosure)* [1994] 2 FLR 381.
[108] A similar result occurred in *T v T (Interception of Documents)* [1994] 2 FLR 1083 where a wife had obtained documents belonging to the husband by reprehensible means. See also *Tavoulareas v Tavoulareas* [1998] 2 FLR 418, CA.
[109] [2002] EWHC 108 (Fam), [2002] 1 FLR 1053.

'in the case of proceedings for divorce or nullity of marriage, the value to each of the parties to the marriage of any benefit which, by reason of the dissolution or annulment of the marriage, that party will lose the chance of acquiring.'[110]

This is the factor most frequently relied on when loss of pension benefits is an issue, and its significance is clear.

1.43 The Pensions Act 1995 amended the MCA 1973 to introduce a new s 25B which is concerned entirely with pensions. The original reference to pensions in s 25(2)(h) has been deleted, and the court is now directed to have regard to the value to each of the parties of any benefit which, by reason of the dissolution or annulment of the marriage, that party will lose the chance of acquiring.

Since pensions are now adequately covered elsewhere, it would seem that this is now to be a 'catch-all' provision, and it is difficult to think of circumstances which would be applicable to this subsection only and which would not be covered by some other provision.

As was seen above, pensions have been removed from the s 25(2) factors and given their own place in s 25B. Pensions is a very important subject which is considered in some detail in Chapter 10.

Here, it is only necessary to consider the requirement on the court to consider the subject; s 25B(1) in effect adds further s 25(2) factors to be considered in every case.

It is provided that the matters to which the court is to have regard under s 25(2) include:

(a)   in the case of paragraph (a) (ie when considering the income, means etc of the parties) any benefits under a pension scheme which a party to a marriage has or is likely to have, and

(b)   in the case of paragraph (h) (ie loss of benefits) any benefits under a pension scheme which, by reason of the dissolution or annulment of the marriage, a party to the marriage will lose the chance of acquiring.

It is also provided that, in relation to benefits under a pension scheme, the words 'in the foreseeable future' should be regarded as being deleted from s 25(2)(a).

The result of this is that, in every case, it is necessary to consider the benefits which either party may receive from a pension scheme, no matter how remote that event may seem. In the same way, the effect on the other party of the loss of any such pension benefits must be calculated.

---

[110]   MCA 1973, s 25(2)(h).

Section 25B(2) goes on to direct the court as to how it should consider dealing with loss of pension benefits. This is best considered in Chapter 10 on pensions.

AGREEMENTS

1.44 There is no specific s 25 factor which directs the court to have regard to an agreement made between the parties,[111] but such an agreement would be certainly one of the circumstances which the court must consider. The difficult question is the weight which the court should place on such an agreement. An initial important issue may be, of course, whether an alleged agreement is truly a binding agreement on the normal principles of the law of contract; an agreement reached as a result of fraud, duress, mistake or misrepresentation would clearly not be binding if made by 'strangers' and thus cannot be binding if made by spouses.

Subject to that qualification, the traditional statement of the law is that 'the wife cannot by her own covenant preclude herself from invoking the jurisdiction of the court or preclude the court from the exercise of that jurisdiction'.[112] The jurisdiction of the court cannot be excluded. However, this authority has been qualified in a number of respects.

The leading modern authority is *Edgar v Edgar*,[113] where Ormrod LJ said that 'in order to reach a just result' regard must be had to the conduct of both parties leading up to the agreement and to their subsequent conduct in consequence of it. The circumstances surrounding the making of the agreement were relevant, and Ormrod LJ highlighted the following:

– undue pressure from one side;

– exploitation of a dominant position to secure an unreasonable advantage;

– inadequate knowledge;

– possibly, bad legal advice;

– an important change of circumstances, unforeseen or overlooked at the time of making the agreement.

Ormrod LJ also stated the importance of the general proposition that:

---

[111] Although it has been suggested that it falls under the heading of conduct; *Brockwell v Brockwell* [1975] CAT 468, (1975) Fam Law 46, CA.

[112] *Hyman v Hyman* [1929] AC 601, HL, per Lord Hailsham LC at 614; see also *Sutton v Sutton* [1984] 1 All ER 168.

[113] [1980] 3 All ER 887, CA.

'formal agreements, properly and fairly arrived at with competent legal advice, should not be displaced unless there are good and substantial grounds for concluding that an injustice will be done by holding the parties to the terms of their agreement.'

1.45 In a later case,[114] where the wife, who was under great emotional strain and had received questionable legal advice, had agreed to relinquish her right to periodical payments, Ormrod LJ said that it was right to treat the case as quite different from *Edgar v Edgar*. There was no question of the wife getting what she required. If any independent bystander had been asked to consider the arrangement that was put forward at the time of the agreement, he would have been bound to say that it was an unfair arrangement as far as the wife was concerned.

The subject of bad legal advice was one of the issues in *B v B (Consent Order: Variation)*,[115] where the parties had incorporated their agreement (including dismissal of periodical payments after 7 years) in a consent order. Thorpe J held that the wife had received bad legal advice which was so manifestly bad and so manifestly the principal factor contributing to the consent order that the periodical payments order ought to be extended and enlarged. However, the position is different where there has been an order. In *Harris v Manahan*,[116] it was held that, while the question of bad legal advice clearly had a part to play (as part of 'all the circumstances'), and the court would approach the question of whether parties should be held to their agreement in the light of *Edgar v Edgar* and *Camm v Camm*, where there was a consent order the requirement of public policy that there be finality in litigation required that, save in the most exceptional case of the cruellest injustice, bad legal advice should not be a ground for interfering with a consent order.

1.46 In *G v G (Financial Provision: Separation Agreement)*,[117] the parties had signed a separation agreement by which the husband agreed to purchase a home and furniture for the wife and to pay her £30,000 p a until her youngest child was 18 and then £20,000 p a for life. The wife subsequently applied for the full range of ancillary relief. There was an issue as to the short duration of the marriage (as to which, see para **1.25**). As to the agreement, it was held that the separation agreement was the most important of the statutory factors, whether taken into account under 'all the circumstances' or as conduct. The agreement was not conclusive as to the outcome, but was persuasive as a starting point from which the other factors might be considered in the light of the circumstances. The most relevant questions to be asked were – how did the agreement come to be made? Did the parties themselves attach importance to it? Have the parties acted on it? The result was that the husband was ordered to pay the wife a lump sum of £240,000.

---

114   *Camm v Camm* (1983) FLR 577, CA.
115   [1995] 1 FLR 9.
116   [1997] 1 FLR 205, CA.
117   [2000] 2 FLR 18, Connell J.

In *X v X (Y and X intervening)*[118] minutes of a consent order had been agreed subject to decree nisi. After decree nisi, the wife sought to resile from the agreement. The husband was granted a summary order, the court holding that it would not lightly permit parties who had made an agreement to depart from it. A formal agreement, properly and fairly arrived at with competent legal advice, should be upheld by the court. A summary order is an order in terms of the minutes of order, without the need for a full hearing of the ancillary relief application.

1.47 Ante-nuptial agreements (ie agreements made before marriage purport-ing to govern the rights of the parties should the marriage be dissolved) have been considered in a number of cases,[119] and it seems clear that ante-nuptial agreements as a class are not specifically enforceable in English law. However, the existence of an agreement, and the weight to be given to it, are factors to be taken into account when the court exercises its discretion under s 25. The terms of an ante-nuptial agreement may be highly relevant when there is an issue of staying proceedings. In a recent case,[120] the husband had agreed in an ante-nuptial agreement to submit to the authority of the London Beth Din and to comply with its instructions in the event of a matrimonial dispute. In the event, he declined to do so, and specifically refused to obtain a Get (a Jewish divorce, without which the wife could not remarry in the Jewish faith). It was held that the court had no jurisdiction to enforce that agreement.

In *M v M (Pre-nuptial Agreement)*[121] the parties had made a pre-nuptial agreement in Canada. The wife had been advised not to sign the agreement but had insisted as she was pregnant. The husband's wealth, generated by him, was £7.5m, and the agreement provided for the wife to receive £275,000. After 5 years, the marriage broke down. It was held that it would be as unjust to the husband to ignore the agreement as to hold the wife strictly to it. The agreement was relevant as tending to guide the court to a more modest award than would otherwise have been the case. The wife's housing needs were £575,000 but she required periodical payments of £60,000 pa for 5 years. The award was therefore for £875,000 plus child maintenance. This was clearly significantly less than she would have been awarded had it not been for the agreement.

In the above case, the judge described the marriage as not a long marriage and took that into account. In *K v K (Ancillary Relief: Pre-nuptial Agreement)*[122] the marriage was definitely short, lasting only 14 months. Both parties had taken separate advice and made a pre-nuptial agreement under which the husband was to pay £100,000 increasing by 10% pa, plus child maintenance.

---

[118] [2002] 1 FLR 508.
[119] See eg *F v F (Ancillary Relief: Substantial Assets)* [1995] 2 FLR 45, *N v N (Foreign Divorce: Financial Relief)* [1997] 1 FLR 900, *S v S (Divorce: Staying Proceedings)* [1997] 2 FLR 100, and *N v N (Jurisdiction: Pre-Nuptial Agreement)* [1999] 2 FLR 745.
[120] *N v N (Jurisdiction: Pre-Nuptial Agreement)* (above).
[121] [2002] 1 FLR 654.
[122] [2003] 1 FLR 120.

His assets were about £25m. It was held that the wife should be held to the agreement as to capital; she had signed the agreement with understanding, the marriage was short and she had contributed nothing to the husband's wealth. However, periodical payments were different (the agreement had been silent on the point). Bringing up the child would require an enormous contribution from her, and she should receive £15,000 pa for herself, which should not be capitalised, and £15,000 pa for the child.

Perhaps the most interesting aspect of the case, which casts light on the law relating to short marriages as well as this topic, is that the judge ordered the husband to provide a home and furnishings for the child at a cost of £1.2m, which would revert to him in due course. In this way he treated the matter almost as if it had been an application under Sch 1 to the Children Act 1989, separating the interests of the child from those of the mother.

1.48 Whether or not an agreement to compromise litigation has been made and, if so, in what terms, may be in dispute. In *Xydhias v Xydhias*,[123] there were prolonged negotiations shortly before trial, which led to the wife asking for the trial to be vacated and for a short directions appointment. The wife applied successfully for an order in the terms of an agreement made between the parties, the husband failing in his purported withdrawal of all previous offers. The husband appealed, unsuccessfully, to the circuit judge and thence to the Court of Appeal. His appeal was dismissed.

It was held that it was a fundamental principle that an agreement for the compromise of an ancillary relief application did not give rise to an agreement enforceable in law; ordinary contractual principles did not apply. The award of ancillary relief was always fixed by the court. The court had a discretion in determining whether an accord had been reached, but if the court decided that agreement had been reached it might have to consider whether the terms of the agreement were vitiated by, for example, non-disclosure or one of the *Edgar v Edgar* factors.

In every case, the court must carry out its independent discretionary review under s 25. In this case, it was held that an agreement had been reached.

This development was extended in *Rose v Rose*[124] where, at the end of a financial dispute resolution (FDR) appointment, the judge was told that the parties had come to terms and it was left to counsel to draw up an agreed order. This draft order was agreed but the husband then sought to resile from it. On reference back to the judge, the judge refused to convert the agreement to an order. On appeal, an order was made in the terms of the agreement; it mattered not that the hearing had been an FDR appointment.

---

[123] [1999] 1 FLR 683, CA.
[124] [2002] EWCA Civ 208, [2002] 1 FLR 978.

Clearly, in the light of these decisions, when parties are negotiating at court and an agreement is reached, it is wise for the advocates to agree between themselves and record when a *Xydhias* agreement has been made.

SELF-SUFFICIENCY

1.49 So far, we have considered the factors which the court is directed to have in its mind when deciding whether, and if so, in what manner, to make an order for ancillary relief. No one factor is more important than any other; the court must weigh them all in its mind, and make a balanced judgment.

However, there is a further factor to which the court is directed to have regard, and that is the possibility of the parties achieving self-sufficiency. It has already been seen that, when considering the financial means of the parties, the court must consider what increase in the earning capacity of the parties it would be reasonable to expect them to acquire. This is reinforced by s 25A, which directs the court, when making a periodical payments order or secured periodical payments order, to consider whether the financial obligations of the parties to each other should be terminated as soon as the court considers it just and reasonable. In such circumstances, the court must also consider whether it should direct that no further application may be made.

1.50 There is therefore a positive obligation on the court to consider imposing a clean break in every case. Whether or not this will be the result depends on the circumstances of the case, and the position is, perhaps, not as clear as it might be. This is considered further in Chapter 2 at para **2.21** et seq.

EQUALITY AND FAIRNESS

1.51 Although s 25 prescribes the matters to which the court must have regard, it does not suggest or recommend any starting point, tariff or formula for deciding what proportion of the assets of the parties each should receive. This is in contrast to other jurisdictions, many of which contain prescriptions as to percentages to be awarded to each party, often depending on the length of the marriage. It is frequently argued by practitioners and academic commentators that the law of England and Wales should be amended to contain such guidelines. However, judges have continued to emphasise that such prescription is not possible within the terms of the statute, and that each case must be considered on its own merits against the background of consideration of the s 25 factors. What has been described as 'the search for principle' continues.

Having said that, guidance has been given in the two decisions of the House of Lords which are about to be considered, and it will be seen that, save in one important area (as to which see para **1.31**), there is general agreement as to certain important principles.

Neither the words 'fairness' nor 'equality' appear in the Matrimonial Causes Act. However, in *White v White*, Lord Nicholls, after recording the self-evident proposition that the court must act in a just and non-discriminatory way, set out the important principle that this means that the court must be fair, and that fairness implies equality. The six years which have elapsed between the decision of their Lordships' House in *White v White* (*White*) and *Miller v Miller* and *McFarlane v McFarlane* (*Miller/McFarlane*) have seen much discussion on the part of practitioners and judges as to what this means in various classes of case. These issues were raised in the judgments in *Charman v Charman* (*at first instance*) and *S v S*, the most significant post-*Miller/McFarlane* cases. However, they have now been considered further in the decision of the Court of Appeal in *Charman v Charman*, the effect of which will be considered below.

In this section we will consider the following-

1   The significance of *White v White*.

2   *Miller/McFarlane*.

3   Developments post *Miller/McFarlane*, in particular *Charman v Charman*.

White v White

1.52 Very few cases relating to ancillary relief reach the House of Lords. Family cases which get that far usually relate to children, particularly public law issues. When the financial dispute between Mr and Mrs White reached their Lordships in 2000[125] it was thought that this would be the final word on these matters for some considerable time. *White* set out guidelines for the determination of such cases which may be summarised as follows:

- The court must be fair. There can be no discrimination between husband and wife in their respective roles. Whatever the division of labour, fairness dictates that this should not prejudice either party when considering the statutory factors. There should be no bias in favour of the breadwinner as against the home-maker and child-carer.

- When carrying out the statutory exercise, the judge should always check his tentative views against the 'yardstick of equality of division'. Equality should only be departed from if, and to the extent that, there is good reason for doing so. This does not mean that there is a starting point or presumption of equality.

- The concept of reasonable requirements is erroneous. The statute refers to 'needs' but this is only one of the statutory factors.

---

[125]   *White v White* [2001] 1 AC 596.

However, this was not to be the last word and certain issues remained to trouble the courts, including the Court of Appeal. These issues may be summarised as essentially the search for fairness, and what fairness means. Given that the court must be fair, and given that the yardstick of equality is overriding but does not amount to a rigid regime of equality, what are the circumstances in which the court may be fair and at the same time depart from equal shares? Would this be appropriate where, for example, the marriage was short; if so, what constitutes a short marriage? Would it be appropriate where one party had created the wealth enjoyed by the couple by his or her exceptional contributions? If so, how exceptional would the contributions have to be? It would be inappropriate to recite here the cases in which these issues were discussed and sometimes contradictory answers given.[126] Running parallel with all this was academic criticism of the whole approach of the law of England and Wales.[127] This law is based on a discretionary approach, and even in recent times judges in the Court of Appeal have gone out of their way to emphasise that there is no formula which will apply to all cases; these matters have to be considered on a case-by-case basis.[128] The criticism made is that even on that basis, analysis of the cases reveals no rational pattern, and further, that this unpredictable case-by-case approach is unfair, since parties who wish to settle their disputes are given uncertain guidance and often have to risk large sums of money to achieve a result.

The combined appeals of *Miller v Miller* and *McFarlane v McFarlane* which were decided by the House in May 2006 therefore attracted widespread interest, both among family lawyers and in the popular press.

Miller and McFarlane

1.53 The House of Lords heard the appeals in *Miller v Miller* and *McFarlane v Macfarlane* (*Miller/McFarlane*) together because they clearly raised similar issues. Both were 'big money' cases, and both dealt with the issues arising out of *White* which are briefly outlined above. The facts in both cases need not be described here;[129] rather, the principles established or affirmed will be considered.

White v White re-affirmed

1.54 The two most important speeches were those of Lord Nicholls and Baroness Hale, who tried to set out a clear list of principles to be followed.

---

126 For a detailed analysis see R. Bird 'Dividing Marital Assets after Lambert' [2003] Fam Law 534. However, two decisions of Coleridge J repay careful reading, namely *H-J v H-J (Financial Provision: Equality)* [2002] 1 FLR 415, and *G v G (Financial Provision: Equal Division)* [2002] EWHC 1339 (Fam), [2002] 2 FLR 1143. In *Lambert v Lambert* [2002] EWCA Civ 1685, [2003] 1 FLR 139, CA Thorpe LJ said that Coleridge J was not wrong (ie he was right!) to find that '50/50 resonates with fairness' [para 38].
127 See eg R. Bailey-Harris [2003] Fam Law 386, and J. Eekelar [2003] Fam Law 828.
128 See eg Wall LJ in *Miller v Miller* [para 88].
129 For more detail see R. Bird 'Miller and McFarlane – The implications for Family Lawyers' (Family Law 2006).

They began with some fairly obvious but nonetheless important points; the court must be fair, and the statutory first consideration of the welfare of the children must be observed. The principles of *White v White*, such as fairness, non-discrimination and the yardstick of equality, were repeated and remain of the first importance.

Three principles: meeting needs, compensation and sharing

The House underlined the fact that financial relief is not a matter of taking from one party to give to the other, but is rather a matter of a proper and fair sharing of assets which both of them, in their interdependent and joint lives, have acquired.

The three principles which this case establishes and/or confirms as being the rationale for financial provision contained in the 1973 Act may be summarised as follows:

1   *Meeting the needs of the parties*
     Lord Nicholls said that mutual dependence begets mutual obligations of support. Fairness requires that the assets of the parties should be divided so as to meet their housing and financial needs.
     Baroness Hale said that the most common rationale for redistribution is that the relationship has generated needs which it is right that the other party should meet. Needs may arise as a result of one party having been a home-maker and child-carer, and needs generated by such a choice are 'a perfectly sound rationale for adjusting the parties respective resources in compensation'.

2   *Compensation*
     Lord Nicholls said that compensation is aimed at redressing any significant prospective disparity between the parties arising from the way they conducted their marriage. Baroness Hale described this as compensation for relationship-generated disadvantage, which goes beyond need.

3   *Sharing*
     Lord Nicholls sees sharing as derived from the basic concept of equality permeating a marriage. Husband and wife are equal partners in marriage. Baroness Hale described this as the sharing of the fruits of the matrimonial partnership.

These three principles may be taken as the foundation for any intellectual approach to the task of awarding financial provision. However, both Lord Nicholls and Baroness Hale made it clear that these are general principles and that they must be adapted to suit the requirements of a particular case. In particular, Lord Nicholls emphasised that equality applies 'unless there is good reason to the contrary. The yardstick of equality is to be applied as an aid, not a rule.'

Legitimate expectations and standard of living

1.55 The judge at first instance, and the Court of Appeal, had approved the concept of 'legitimate expectations'. The House strongly disapproved this concept; this could play no part in the decision-making process.

However, the importance of the standard of living of the parties during the marriage was affirmed, and this was one of the statutory factors prayed in aid by Lord Nicholls to justify the *Miller* award. For obvious reasons, it will only be important in cases where assets exceed needs, but this is an important reminder of the need to consider all the s 25 factors.

Application to smaller money cases

1.56 One of the problems with discussing decisions of the higher courts is that they normally involve very large amounts of money and rich parties. Practitioners will be more interested in whether or not they apply to the normal run of cases.

It must first be said that the *White v White* principles of fairness, non-discrimination and the yardstick of equality apply to all cases, big or small and regardless of the length of the marriage. However, Lord Nicholls makes it clear that while the approach has to be the same, the result will be different in cases where the needs exceed the assets because the funds are not available to take the matter further. It is worth repeating his words:

> 'When the marriage ends fairness requires that the assets of the parties should be divided primarily so as to make provision for the parties' housing and financial needs, taking into account a wide range of matters such as the parties' ages, their future earning capacity, the family's standard of living, and any disability of either party. Most of these needs will have been generated by the marriage, but not all of them. Needs arising from age or disability are instances of the latter.
>
> In most cases the search for fairness largely begins and ends at this stage. In most cases the available assets are insufficient to provide adequately for the needs of two homes. The court seeks to stretch modest finite resources so far as possible to meet the parties' needs. Especially where children are involved it may be necessary to augment the available assets by having recourse to the future earnings of the money-earner, by way of an order for periodical payments.'

Baroness Hale expressed similar views. An equal partnership does not always dictate equal sharing of the assets. One could interject there the view that, in lower value cases, it almost never does. As Baroness Hale, said, equal division may have to give way to the needs of one party or the children.

> 'Too strict an adherence to equal sharing and the clean break can lead to a rapid decrease in the primary carer's standard of living and a rapid increase in the breadwinner's. The breadwinner's unimpaired and unimpeded earning capacity is a powerful resource which can frequently repair any loss of capital after an unequal distribution.'

Baroness Hale adds that recognising this is one reason why English law has been successful in retaining a home for the children.

Other issues were discussed in this case, but they will considered under their separate subject-matter headings (see paras **1.25**, **1.31** and **1.38**).

Case law since Miller/McFarlane

1.57 Since the decision of the House of Lords in *Miller/McFarlane* the courts below have not been idle. Of particular interest were the decisions of Coleridge J at first instance in *Charman v Charman*, Stanley Burton J in *S v S* and Nicholas Mostyn QC, sitting as a deputy High Court Judge in *Rossi v Rossi*.[130] (*Charman* is also discussed under the heading of contributions (see para **1.31**)). To a large extent these decisions have been overtaken by the decision of the Court of Appeal in *Charman*, which will therefore form the major part of the analysis below.

1.58 In his judgment in *Rossi* (para 8) Mr Mostyn said that:

> 'It is clear that a number of issues arising from the opinions of the Law Lords in *Miller v Miller; McFarlane v McFarlane* [2006] UKHL 24, [2006] 2 WLR 1283, [2006] 1 FLR 1186 (*Miller*) will have to be worked out in future cases. For example, the question of whether compensation will be widely awarded (and if so for what compensable losses) or whether it will be confined to the exceptional case (as a number of comments appear to indicate) will, no doubt, be an early candidate for judicial interpretation. Equally demanding of early guidance will be the question of the application of the yardstick of equality to what Baroness Hale of Richmond and Lord Mance have characterised as 'non-business partnership, non-family assets', and whether or not departure therefrom in relation to such assets is confined to short marriage cases.'

He then went on to state his own view (at para 10):

> 'In all cases now a primary function of the court is to identify the matrimonial and non-matrimonial property. In relation to property owned before the marriage, or acquired during the marriage by inheritance or gift, there is little difficulty in characterising such property as non-matrimonial (provided it is not the former matrimonial home). The non-matrimonial property represents an unmatched contribution made by the party who brings it to the marriage justifying, particularly where the marriage is short, a denial of an entitlement to share equally in it by the other party'

1.59 He reviewed the earlier cases, culminating in *Miller/McFarlane*, and summarised the position as he saw it as follows:

> '**24.1** The statute requires all the assets to be valued at the date of trial.
> **24.2** For the purposes of establishing the matrimonial property in respect of which the yardstick of equality will "forcefully" apply the value of assets

---

[130] [2006] EWHC 1482 (Fam), [2007] 1 FLR 790.

brought into the marriage by gift and inheritance (other than the former matrimonial home), together with passive economic growth on those assets, should be excluded as non-matrimonial property.

24.3 Assets acquired or created by one party after (or during a period of) separation may qualify as non-matrimonial property if it can be said that the property in question was acquired or created by a party by virtue of his personal industry and not by use (other than incidental use) of an asset which has been created during the marriage and in respect of which the other party can validly assert an unascertained share. Obviously, passive economic growth on matrimonial property that arises after separation will not qualify as non-matrimonial property.

24.4 If the post-separation asset is a bonus or other earned income then it is obvious that if the payment relates to a period when the parties were cohabiting then the earner cannot claim it to be non-matrimonial. Even if the payment relates to a period immediately following separation I would myself say that it is too close to the marriage to justify categorisation as non-matrimonial. Moreover, I entirely agree with Coleridge J when he points out that during the period of separation the domestic party carries on making her non-financial contribution but cannot attribute a value thereto which justifies adjustment in her favour. Although there is an element of arbitrariness here, I myself would not allow a post-separation bonus to be classed as non-matrimonial unless it related to a period which commenced at least 12 months after the separation.

24.5 By this process the court should, without great difficulty, be able to separate the matrimonial and non-matrimonial property. The matrimonial property will in all likelihood be divided equally although there may be deviation from equal division: (a) if the marriage is short; and (b) part of the matrimonial property is "non-business partnership, non-family assets" (or if the matrimonial property is represented by autonomous funds accumulated by dual earners).

24.6 The non-matrimonial property is not quarantined and excluded from the court's dispositive powers. It represents an unmatched contribution by the party who brings it to the marriage. The court will decide whether it should be shared and, if so, in what proportions. In so deciding it will have regard to the reality that the longer the marriage the more likely non-matrimonial property will become merged or entangled with matrimonial property. By contrast, in a short marriage case non-matrimonial assets are not likely to be shared unless needs require this.

24.7 In deciding whether a non-matrimonial post-separation accrual should be shared and, if so, in what proportions, the court will consider, among other things, whether the applicant has proceeded diligently with her claim; whether the party who has the benefit of the accrual has treated the other party fairly during the period of separation; and whether the money-making party has the prospect of making further gains or earnings after the division of the assets and, if so, whether the other party will be sharing in such future income or gains and if so in what proportions, for what period, and by what means.'

1.60 In its judgment in *Charman v Charman*, the Court of Appeal did not specifically comment on Mr Mosttyn's analysis in detail so it remains to be seen whether his approach stands the test of time. However, in its judgment in

Charman, the Court dealt with several issues of considerable importance.[131]
The first of these how the yardstick of equality should be approached. In the
course of argument in that case, there has been debate as to whether a judge
should begin with some notion of equality and then, as it were, depart from it
where appropriate, or whether the various section 25 factors should be
considered with no preconceptions and then the provisional result compared
with the yardstick of equality. The Court dealt with this by reference to the new
concept of 'sharing' introduced in *Miller*, and it is worth quoting the passage
from the judgment of the Court in full. This begins at para [64] where it is said
that:

> '"The yardstick of equality of division", first identified by Lord Nicholls in White
> at p. 605G, filled the vacuum which resulted from the abandonment in that
> decision of the criterion of "reasonable requirements". The origins of the
> yardstick lay in s.25(2) of the Act, specifically in s.25(2)(f), which refers to the
> parties' contributions: see the preceding argument of Lord Nicholls at p. 605D-E.
> The yardstick reflected a modern, non-discriminatory conclusion that the proper
> evaluation under s.25(2)(f) of the parties' different contributions to the welfare of
> the family should generally lead to an equal division of their property unless there
> was good reason for the division to be unequal. It also tallied with the overarching
> objective: a fair result.
>
> [65] Although in *White* the majority of the House agreed with the speech of
> Lord Nicholls and thus with his description of equality as a "yardstick" against
> which tentative views should be "checked", Lord Cooke, at p. 615D, doubted
> whether use of the words "yardstick" or "check" would produce a result different
> from that of the words "guideline" or "starting point". In *Miller* the House clearly
> moved towards the position of Lord Cooke. Thus Lord Nicholls, at [20] and [29],
> referred to the "equal sharing principle" and to the "sharing entitlement"; those
> phrases describe more than a yardstick for use as a check. Baroness Hale put the
> matter beyond doubt when, referring to remarks by Lord Nicholls at [29], she said,
> at [144],
>
> > "I agree that there cannot be a hard and fast rule about whether one starts
> > with equal sharing and departs if need or compensation supply a reason to
> > do so, or whether one starts with need and compensation and shares the
> > balance."
>
> It is clear that the court's consideration of the sharing principle is no longer
> required to be postponed until the end of the statutory exercise. We should add
> that, since we take the "the sharing principle" to mean that property should be
> shared in equal proportions unless there is good reason to depart from such
> proportions, departure is not from the principle but takes place within the
> principle.'

---

[131] It is worth noting that this was a particularly strong court, consisting of the President, and
Thorpe and Wilson LJJ. It would be difficult to conceive a greater concentration of expertise in
this field. Moreover, the judgment was the judgment of the court, so there are no differences of
opinion to be analysed.

It seems therefore that sharing, which means equality and equal shares, is now more of a starting point than a yardstick.

The Court then amplified this to guidance to 'flesh out'[132] what the concepts of 'sharing, 'need' and 'compensation' set out in *Miller* actually meant. First, on the issue of what property falls to be shared, and whether there should be a category of 'matrimonial property, the Court said:

> '[66] We consider, however, the answer to be that, subject to the exceptions identified in *Miller*... the principle applies to all the parties' property but, to the extent that their property is non-matrimonial, there is likely to be better reason for departure from equality. It is clear that both in *White* at p.605 F-G and in *Miller* at [24] and [26] Lord Nicholls approached the matter in that way; and there was no express suggestion in *Miller*, even on the part of Baroness Hale, that in White the House had set too widely the general application of what was then a yardstick.'

The Court then dealt with the three principles enunciated in *Miller* as follows:

> '[70] Thus the principle of **need** requires consideration of the financial needs, obligations and responsibilities of the parties (s.25(2)(b)); of the standard of living enjoyed by the family before the breakdown of the marriage (s.25(2)(c)); of the age of each party (half of s.25(2)(d)); and of any physical or mental disability of either of them (s.25(2)(e)).

> [71] The principle of **compensation** relates to prospective financial disadvantage which upon divorce some parties face as a result of decisions which they took for the benefit of the family during the marriage, for example in sacrificing or not pursuing a career: per Lord Nicholls in *Miller* at [13], Lord Hope at [117] and Baroness Hale at [140]. But the principle goes wider than that. As long ago as 1976 this court decided that, where the marriage was short, it was relevant to consider whether a party had suffered financial disadvantage arising out of entry into it: see *S v. S* [1977] Fam 127 at 134C, albeit that the consideration was there directed to restriction rather than augmentation of the award. Equally, in respect of disadvantage arising out of exit from the marriage, s.25(2)(h) requires the court to consider any loss of possible pension rights consequent upon its dissolution. Even disadvantage of the type to which reference was made in the speeches in *Miller*, i.e. that stemming from decisions taken during the marriage, had been held in this court to be relevant before it became the driver for a principle of compensation: per Hale J (as she then was) in *SRJ v. DWJ (Financial Provision)* [1999] 2 FLR 176 at 182E and per Thorpe LJ in *Lambert v. Lambert* [2003] Fam 103 at 122G. In cases in which it arises, application of the principle of compensation is an appropriate contribution to the fair result.

> [72] The enquiry required by the principle of **sharing** is, as we have shown, dictated by reference to the contributions of each party to the welfare of the family (s.25(2)(f)); and, as we make clear in paragraph 85 below, the duration of the marriage (the other half of s.25(2)(d)) here falls to be considered. Also conveniently assigned to the sharing principle, no doubt dictating departure from equality, is the conduct of a party in the exceptional case in which it would be

---

[132] The author's term, not the court's.

inequitable to disregard it (s.25(2)(g)). [The husband's counsel] argued to the judge that the husband's generation of substantial wealth was not only a special contribution on his part to the welfare of the family but conduct which it would be inequitable to disregard. We think, however, that it is as unnecessarily confusing to present a case of contribution as a positive type of conduct as it is to present a case of conduct as a negative or nil type of contribution: see *W v. W* (2001) 31 Family Law 656.'

EQUALITY AND PERIODICAL PAYMENTS

1.61   The question of whether, and if so to what extent, equality should apply to periodical payments as opposed to capital has been debated since *White* and was the subject of the combined appeals of *McFarlane v McFarlane* and *Parlour v Parlour* [2004] EWCA (Civ) 872. The general principles enunciated by the House of Lords in *Miller/McFarlane* are discussed in detail above (paras **1.53** et seq). Here, the discussion is limited to equality and periodical payments, where the general thrust of the Court of Appeal's judgment was not disturbed, save in the important respect that the 5 year term imposed on Mrs McFarlane's order was removed.

Thorpe LJ put it like this: 'If the decision in *White v White* introduces the yardstick of equality for measuring a fair division of capital why should the same yardstick not be applied as the measure for the division of income?'

1.62   In the *Parlour* case, before Bennett J, the judge at first instance, the wife argued that she should receive the same proportion of the husband's income as that which had been agreed in respect of his capital, namely 37%. This would give her £444,000 per annum for herself and the three children. The husband contended for a global figure of £120,000 p a.

The wife's argument, in a nutshell, was that an earning capacity developed during marriage was a resource or thing of value which should be equitably shared, and that an award of periodical payments should not be confined to the wife's maintenance needs. The husband argued for restriction to reasonable needs.

Bennett J said that to confine periodical payments to needs or reasonable requirements would be a faulty exercise of discretion. That would apply only one matter in section 25(2) and ignore the rest. To award only 10% of the husband's income 'is thoroughly mean and would be unfair'. However, to award her £444,000 would be 'an unprincipled and unfair award'. The court 'must seek a way that does justice to the parties and which does not, so far as is possible, impose a glass ceiling on the one hand but which does not hand out capital on the other.'

1.63   In the *McFarlane* case, the first hearing was before District Judge Redgrave who found that the parties contributions to this long marriage had been different but of equal value. The wife's contributions had enabled the husband to create a working environment which had produced greater rewards, in respect of which she should have her fair share. It was unreasonable to expect the wife to take steps to improve her earning capacity in the foreseeable future.

The order made was for £250,000 per annum i.e. 33.18% of the husband's net income, to be index-linked. In the Court of Appeal Thorpe LJ commented [para 23] that 'implicit within the district judge's reasoning is first the conclusion that the wife should have the same opportunity as the husband to make provision for the years of retirement and second the conclusion that she should have the means with which to insure herself and the children against the risk of premature cessation of the husband's high professional earnings'.

The husband appealed on several grounds and the first appeal was heard by Bennett J who said: 'it is my judgment, with all due respect to the district judge, that, having given the wife an award from which she is likely to be able to save large sums of money and thereby accumulate capital, it is no answer to say, as she did, that it is a matter for the wife whether she chooses to make provision for pension and other matters.' He therefore chose to exercise his discretion afresh. He asked the question 'what figure should then be substituted for £250,000?' and answered 'the quantification of periodical payments is more an art than a science. The parameters of s 25 are so wide that it might be said that it is almost impossible to be 'scientific'. In my judgment, I would be doing justice to both parties if I award the wife £180,000 per annum by way of periodical payments.'

1.64 In the Court of Appeal, Thorpe LJ observed that 'the skeleton arguments prepared for the appeals … address the very general question: what should be the principles governing an award of periodical payments during joint lives or until remarriage in any case where the net income of the payer significantly exceeds what both parties need in order to meet their outgoings at the standard of living which the court has found to be appropriate.' As far as *McFarlane* was concerned, the Court decided that Bennett J had erred in interfering with the district judge's order which was therefore restored (applying *Cordle v Cordle*) subject only to the imposition of a 5 year term (subsequently removed by the House of Lords) and removal of the index-linking provision. In *Parlour*, Thorpe LJ observed that Mr Parlour, a professional footballer, might be nearing the end of his playing career and continued 'These considerations only underline the obvious need for a substantial proportion of the income in the present fat years to be stored up against the future famine. Again I conclude that it would be wrong in principle to leave the responsibility and opportunity to the husband alone. The wife's and the children's needs were put at £150,000 by the judge. To award her the global figure of £444,000 per annum sought by Mr Mostyn allows her and obliges her to lay-up £294,000 per annum as a reserve against the discharge of her periodical payments order. I would in this case order a four-year extendable term. Hopefully a clean break will be achievable then on an assessment of the husband's earning capacity at thirty-five years of age and the wife's independent fortune derived from the original capital settlement augmented by the substantial annual surplus built into her periodical payments order in the interim.'

1.65 The Court of Appeal was at pains to emphasise that the two cases before it were exceptional and outside the normal run of ancillary relief applications which come before the court. The exceptional factors were the very large incomes of the parties coupled with the fact that there was insufficient capital to provide a clean break now. One might also add the fact that the wives in both cases had no immediate prospect of improving their earning capacity and had to care for young children. The predominating factor therefore became how best to prepare for a clean break in years to come.

However, even if the effect of the judgment were limited to that class of case, it might still have a significant effect. As Thorpe LJ pointed out, there must be many high-earning professional couples who will find themselves in a similar financial situation.

1.66 One important lesson from the Court of Appeal's judgment is that periodical payments cannot be limited to the needs of the receiving party. To do so would be to concentrate on one section 25(2) factor to the exclusion of the others. This was upheld by the House of Lords decision. In his speech at para [31] Lord Nicholls said:

> 'There is nothing in the statutory ancillary relief provisions to suggest Parliament intended periodical payments orders to be limited to payments needed for maintenance. Section 23(1)(a) empowers the court, in quite general language, to order one party to the marriage to make to the other "such periodical payments, for such term, as may be specified in the order". In deciding whether, and how, to exercise this power the statute requires the court to have regard to all the circumstances of the case: s 25(1). The court is required to have particular regard to the familiar wide-ranging checklist set out in s 25(2). These provisions, far from suggesting an intention to restrict periodical payments to the one particular purpose of maintenance, suggest that the financial provision orders in s 23 were intended to be flexible in their application.

> [32] In particular, I consider a periodical payments order may be made for the purpose of affording compensation to the other party as well as meeting financial needs. It would be extraordinary if this were not so. If one party's earning capacity has been advantaged at the expense of the other party during the marriage it would be extraordinary if, where necessary, the court could not order the advantaged party to pay compensation to the other out of his enhanced earnings when he receives them. It would be most unfair if absence of capital assets were regarded as cancelling his obligation to pay compensation in respect of a continuing economic advantage he has obtained from the marriage.'

1.67 It has to be said that the judgments do not assist in deciding what proportion of the payer's income should be taken. In Parlour's case, the wife's submission was that the division of income should be in the same proportions as the division of capital and that submission succeeded. The wife had conceded that a departure from equality of capital was appropriate. One has to ask whether, if that concession had not been made and if the court had divided capital equally, the division of income would also have been equal.

Little help is derived from the *McFarlane* case because the Court of Appeal merely restored the district judge's order, on *Cordle* principles, and the district judge had not stated any particular principle in arriving at her figure of £250,000 per annum. Needs had been put at £128,000 and the eventual award was about one third of the husband's net income. Bennett J was similarly imprecise when he reduced the figure to £180,000 merely saying that he thought this would do justice to both parties. The imposition of a term is of course important.

In the Court of Appeal, Wall LJ was clearly unsure as to what, if any principle, should replace the emphasis on needs. He felt it necessary to fall back on the words of Ormrod LJ in *Martin v Martin* 26 years ago: 'the court should preserve, so far as it can, the utmost elasticity to deal with each case on its own facts. Therefore it is a matter of trial and error and imagination on the part of those advising clients.' This of course, was echoed by Thorpe LJ in *White v White* and *Parra v Parra*. Practitioners may therefore find it difficult to draw any more general lessons from this case than others in the past.

GUIDELINES IN CHILDREN ORDERS CASES

1.68   So far, the factors for the consideration of the court have been exclusively confined to orders between the parties to the marriage. When the court makes an order for a child, different criteria apply, and these are contained in s 25(3). These are considered further in Chapter 11, Children, at para **11.25**.

WHEN MAY ORDERS BE MADE?

1.69   An order for maintenance pending suit may be made at any time after the filing of the petition. Other orders, such as orders for periodical payments, a lump sum or property adjustment, may only be made on or after the grant of a decree.[133]

Interim capital provision is discussed further in Chapter 4, Lump Sum Orders, at para **4.5**.

The views of Mr Nicholas Mostyn QC, sitting as a deputy High Court Judge in *Rossi v Rossi*, as to whether there is a time limit on applications for ancillary relief are set out at para **1.59**. These statements have authority in the sense that they are from the High Court, but there may be room for doubt about whether they are universally shared.

---

[133]   MCA 1973, ss 22–24.

Jurisdiction

1.70 Jurisdiction to make orders for ancillary relief (except for those after a foreign decree – see Chapter 14) depends on the grant of a decree of divorce, nullity or judicial separation. Whether or not the court may make an order for ancillary relief is therefore the same question as whether it has jurisdiction to entertain the proceedings leading to the decree.

This is now governed by the EU Council Regulation on Jurisdiction and the Recognition and Enforcement of Judgments in Matrimonial Matters and in matters of Parental Responsibility for Joint Children (known as 'Brussels II') which came into force on 1 March 2001. This is binding on all EU Member States except Denmark and applies to all proceedings filed after 1 March 2001.

The Regulation deals with the jurisdiction of the court in matrimonial cases and in 'civil proceedings relating to parental responsibility for the children of both spouses'. As to matrimonial cases (eg divorce), Art 2 sets out a multiple choice of jurisdictional factors which do not have a hierarchy; ie no one factor is more important than any other. The factors are:

– both spouses' habitual residence;

– the last habitual residence of both spouses, one spouse still being habitually resident there;

– the respondent spouse's habitual residence;

– in cases of a joint application, either spouse's habitual residence;

– the applicant's habitual residence based on 12 months' residence immediately before the application;

– the applicant's habitual residence based on 6 months' residence immediately before the application coupled with nationality or (in the case of the UK or Ireland) domicile;

– the nationality of both the spouses or (in the case of the UK and Ireland) their domicile.

Where no Member State has jurisdiction under the above factors, jurisdiction is determined according to the laws of each State.

Where courts have concurrent jurisdiction, a court must defer to the court first seised of the case unless it needs to take protective measures in urgent cases. A court is seised of a case when the documents instituting the proceedings 'or other equivalent document' is lodged with the court, provided that steps are taken to serve it or, when it has to be served before issue, when it is received by the authority responsible for service.

1.71 Schedule 1 to the Domicile and Matrimonial Proceedings Act 1973 makes provision for a stay of proceedings where there are proceedings affecting the marriage in another jurisdiction. Such a stay may be obligatory (Sch 1, para 8) or discretionary (Sch 1, para 11).

Questions of jurisdiction can assume some importance in cases of ample means where it is thought that the approach of the courts of England and Wales may be more, or less, generous than that to be found elsewhere.[134]

---

[134] See eg *de Dampierre v de Dampierre* [1987] 2 FLR 300, HL; *W v W (Financial Relief: Appropriate Forum)* [1997] 1 FLR 257; *S v S (Divorce: Staying Proceedings)* [1997] 2 FLR 100; *Butler v Butler (Nos 1 and 2)* [1997] 2 FLR 311, CA; *C v C (Divorce: Stay of English Proceedings)* [2001] 1 FLR 624.

Chapter 2

PERIODICAL PAYMENTS

INTRODUCTION

2.1   Periodical payments can be distinguished from other forms of ancillary relief by the fact that they constitute a continuing obligation, normally an obligation to pay a weekly or monthly sum, as opposed to a once and for all payment such as a lump sum or a transfer of property. A further distinction is that they can be varied, whereas, with certain exceptions, the general principle is that there can be only one order for payment of a lump sum or transfer of property. This type of relief is what was once called, and which the layperson may still call, 'maintenance'.

Periodical payments ordered to be paid before decree absolute of divorce or decree of judicial separation are called maintenance pending suit.

DEFINITIONS

2.2   Periodical payments are not defined by FPR 1991. This is because they are a type of financial provision order, which is defined[1] as any of the orders mentioned in s 21(1) of MCA 1973. It is therefore to the statute that reference must be made.

2.3   One of the types of financial provision order contained in s 21(1)(a) is an order that a party must make, in favour of another person, such periodical payments, for such term, as may be specified (a 'periodical payments order').[2] This is the statutory authority for this type of order.

WHO MAY APPLY?

2.4   Only a party to the marriage or a child of the family may apply for periodical payments.[3] A party who has remarried cannot apply for periodical payments, even if the application is made before remarriage.[4] Orders for children are dealt with in Chapter 11.

---

[1]   FPR 1991, r 1.2(1).
[2]   MCA 1973, s 21(1)(a).
[3]   Heading to Part II of MCA 1973.
[4]   MCA 1973, s 28(3).

PROCEDURE

2.5   The procedure for applying for periodical payments is the same as for any other form of ancillary relief. Reference should therefore be made to Chapter 16.

GENERAL PRINCIPLES

2.6   As with any other form of ancillary relief, orders for periodical payments are rarely made in isolation; they are usually part of a combination of the various forms of relief, including lump sum, property adjustment and provision for children (whether made by the Child Support Agency or the court). When the court comes to decide whether or not an order for periodical payments should be made and, if so, in what sum, it must have regard to the needs of the parties and the ability of the paying party to meet the needs of the other party by these means. Such an exercise will normally be carried out after the court, at least notionally, has allocated the available capital. In particular, the court must have regard to the factors set out in s 25 of MCA 1973; these are considered in general terms in Chapter 1 at para **1.6** et seq. Case-law is perhaps of even more uncertain value in this field than when considering other forms of ancillary relief.[5]

However, one important principle has been established by the case of *McFarlane v McFarlane;*[6] for a detailed discussion see Chapter 1 **para 1.53** et seq. Here, it should be noted that the principle established was that periodical payments are not limited to maintenance, but can include provision for compensation and to reflect any capital imbalance between the parties.

Here we find the clear statement that periodical payments are not confined to maintenance nor the meeting of needs. They can be designed to enable one spouse to share in the future financial good fortune of the other and as a means of redressing capital imbalance. This is not the same as a lump sum by instalments, since the capital is not available at the time of the order. Rather, it recognises the kind of case where the fortunes of one party are likely to improve disproportionately to those of the other, and it would be unjust to the disadvantaged party not to allow her to share them.

However, before this is taken as a clear expression of principle, the words of caution expressed by Charles J in *H v H*.[7]

---

[5]   See e g *Sharpe v Sharpe* (1981) Fam Law 121, (1981) *The Times*, February 7.
[6]   [2006] 1 FLR 1186, HL.
[7]   [2007] EWHC 459 (Fam).

HOW DOES THE COURT MAKE ITS ORDERS?

2.7   Orders are made after consideration of the evidence and in the light of the factors in s 25. However, it would be logical to divide the reasoning process as follows:

−   whether an order for periodical payments should be made at all;

−   consideration of the amount of the order;

−   whether any order should be limited in time.

These will be considered in turn.

SHOULD THERE BE AN ORDER AT ALL?

2.8   Provided the party applying for periodical payments has not remarried, there is no absolute bar to an order being made. If the means of the parties are such that either the applicant does not need support or the respondent is unable to provide any support, an order would not normally be made. It may also be that, on consideration of all the factors, the court will decide that in the case before it the obligations of the parties to each other should be terminated and that there should be a clean break.[8]

However, provided both need and ability to pay can be demonstrated, the following matters may be relevant in making an initial decision as to whether an order should be made.

EARNING CAPACITY/POTENTIAL

2.9   The court is required to have regard to the financial means of the parties at the time or in the foreseeable future:

> '. . . including in the case of earning capacity any increase in that capacity which it would in the opinion of the court be reasonable to expect a party to the marriage to take steps to acquire.'[9]

The court may not, therefore, consider only the means of the parties at the time of the hearing. It is required to inquire into whether or not a party, particularly the applicant, could take reasonable steps to improve her position and even render herself self-sufficient.

---

[8]   For a detailed consideration of the clean break, see para **2.21** et seq.
[9]   MCA 1973, s 25(2)(a).

COHABITATION

2.10 A party who is cohabiting is not thereby precluded from applying for periodical payments. His or her financial position will clearly have to be considered in the light of the cohabitation, which will be one of the circumstances which the court is directed to consider. In some circumstances, cohabitation may be a source of considerable financial advantage; in others, quite the contrary. The principles have been lucidly set out as follows:

> 'First, cohabitation is not to be equated with marriage. In performing its functions under the Matrimonial Causes Act 1973 (as amended) . . . cohabitation is not to be given decisive weight. Secondly, cohabitation is, however, a relevant factor in that it bears upon the financial circumstances, particularly upon the assessment of the wife's financial needs. But to me it seems above all that the court should strive to discern the realities in determining what weight to give to the factor of cohabitation, particularly since the subjective presentation of the parties often seeks to disguise or distort the realities.'[10]

As to what constitutes cohabitation, it has been held[11] that, whilst it is impossible to produce a comprehensive list of criteria to determine the existence of cohabitation, relevant factors were living together in the same household; a sharing of daily life; stability and a degree of permanence; finances; a sexual relationship; children; intention and motivation, and the opinion of the reasonable person with normal perceptions.

The traditional statement of the law as set out above has been the subject of some judicial attack and it may be doubtful how long the present law will remain undisturbed. In *K v K (Periodical Payments: Cohabitation)*[12] Coleridge J referred to the 'social revolution' which has occurred and said that this should be recognised by the law. In the instant case he found that the cohabitation of the wife could not be ignored as a circumstance of the case and that the husband should be expected to support the wife for a shorter period than that envisaged by a previous consent order. However, he felt constrained by Court of Appeal authority from going further.

CONDUCT

2.11 Conduct of the parties is dealt with in more detail in Chapter 1 at para **1.34**. Here it may suffice to say that, although it is unusual for conduct to play a major part in ancillary relief, there may be rare cases in which the conduct of one party has been such as to disentitle him or her from any relief.

---

[10] *Atkinson v Atkinson* [1995] 2 FLR 356 per Thorpe J. See also *Hepburn v Hepburn* [1989] 1 FLR 373; *MH v MH* (1982) FLR 429; *Suter v Suter and Jones* [1987] Fam 111, and *Atkinson v Atkinson* [1988] 2 FLR 353 at 356 per Waterhouse J.

[11] In *Kimber v Kimber* [2000] 1 FLR 383. See also *Crake v Supplementary Benefits Commission* [1982] 1 All ER 498; *Re J (Income Support: Cohabitation)* [1995] 1 FLR 660.

[12] [2005] EWHC 2886 (Fam), [2006] 2 FLR 468.

LENGTH OF MARRIAGE

2.12 Special considerations arising from short marriages are considered in Chapter 1 at para **1.25**.

WHAT SHOULD BE THE AMOUNT OF THE ORDER?

2.13 It would be misleading to think that there is a conventional starting point for the quantification of a periodical payments order. Some older cases contain references to, for example, the 'one-third starting point'.[13] However, this is not now normally regarded as a proper approach.[14]

The only proper starting point is s 25. The particular factor which is normally important as an initial figure is the 'financial needs, obligations and responsibilities'[15] of the applicant party; these must be reduced to a figure which the court considers necessary to enable the applicant to live at a standard which is appropriate in the light of the other s 25 factors such as the standard of living during the marriage, the contributions of the parties and the length of the marriage. From this figure must be deducted the actual or potential income of that party; this will include non-means related State benefits such as retirement pension or child benefit, but not lone parent benefit. However, the ability of one party to increase her income by the proper use of State benefits cannot be overlooked. For example, working families tax credit is clearly an appropriate benefit for many working mothers on low incomes and should be applied for. It is available for families, including lone parents, who have one or more children, work more than 16 hours per week, and have savings of £8,000 or less. Applications are made to the Inland Revenue, who assess the sums payable.

2.14 Having ascertained the needs of the applicant party, the court must then assess the ability of the other party to meet those needs. This will involve consideration of that party's needs, obligations and responsibilities and all the other s 25 factors. It will also involve assessment of that party's financial means.

Clearly, one party cannot be ordered to pay money which he does not have. Nor should he normally be required to pay such sums as will reduce him to below subsistence level.[16] However, this is not inflexible, particularly where the court considers that the paying party has assumed obligations recklessly and without proper regard to his liability to the applicant and/or the children of the

---

[13] For a comparatively recent example, see *Sibley v Sibley* (1981) FLR 121, in which the principle did not seem to be challenged. See also, however, *Ward v Ward and Greene* (1980) FLR 368: 'the one-third rule is only a starting point'.

[14] See e g *Saunders v Saunders* (1980) FLR 121, per Brandon LJ:

[15] MCA 1973, s 25(2)(b).

[16] *Stockford v Stockford* (1982) FLR 58, CA.

family, or even where they have been assumed voluntarily.[17] In one recent case,[18] where the parties were comparatively affluent, Thorpe LJ observed that a 'conventional adjudication' would be to say that half the husband's net available income should be earmarked for the support of the wife and (two) children. This resulted in a figure of £20,000 from which it was necessary to deduct a Child Support Agency assessment of £7,500, the final sum being rounded down to £12,000 pa. However, this should not be taken as a 'rule' and perhaps is more akin to a maximum amount or even a starting point.

When calculating the incomes of the parties, the net figures (after income tax and national insurance contributions) are taken. Periodical payments are not taxable income in the hands of the recipient, nor is tax relief available on periodical payments orders.[19]

2.15 It is at this final stage that the court may wish to consider the proportion of the paying party's income which it is proposing to pay to the applicant and to consider the justice of the case in the round. Because of the essentially practical nature of this exercise, there are few reported cases on the appropriate proportion. It has been observed[20] that 'it has never been the custom in ancillary relief litigation to look with scrupulous care at the budget items of the prospective payer. Of course it is incumbent on the judge to cross-check to ensure that the adjudication that meets the applicant's needs is an adjudication which the respondent can afford'. It is difficult to improve on the reported words of Ormrod LJ in what is now a comparatively old case:[21]

> '. . . the court, in all cases, must apply the provisions of s 25 of the Matrimonial Causes Act 1973 . . . without superimposed judicial glosses . . . it becomes necessary to assess the actual impact of any order for periodical payments on the parties' respective financial means . . . The court must, therefore, look broadly at the overall position rather than enter upon a detailed investigation of household budgets. . . . In essence, it involves, working out . . . on the basis of [a] hypothetical order [the position of the parties] . . . The two figures [payer's and payee's positions as a result of the hypothetical order] can then be compared and related to the respective needs, and the hypothetical order adjusted accordingly. This is the "net effect" method . . .'

In all but the simplest cases, therefore, it is essential to prepare a 'net effect schedule' to demonstrate what will be the result of the order which is being proposed for each of the parties. This would involve starting with the net incomes from all sources for each party, making allowance for any tax changes which may occur as a result of the proposed order, and deducting (or adding, as the case may be) the amount of the proposed order. This will show the total income of each party if the order is made, and this figure can then be compared with each party's reasonable needs or requirements.

---

[17]   See *Campbell v Campbell* [1998] 1 FLR 828, CA.
[18]   *Scheeres v Scheeres* [1999] 1 FLR 241, CA.
[19]   See para **2.34**.
[20]   By Thorpe LJ in *Campbell v Campbell* (above).
[21]   *Stockford v Stockford* (above).

Once again, it should be noted that periodical payments are not limited to the maintenance of the receiving party (see **para 2.6**) though one has to say that the practical effect of this will only be felt in cases where the means of the parties are considerable.

SHOULD THE ORDER BE LIMITED IN DURATION?

2.16 Section 25A of MCA 1973 contains the statutory authority for the 'clean break'. This is considered as a topic in its own right at para **2.21**. Here, it should merely be noted that, in addition to s 25A(1) which requires the court to consider whether the financial obligations of the parties to each other should be terminated, s 25A(2) requires the court in every case where it makes a periodical payments order to consider whether it would be appropriate to require those payments to be made only for such term as would in the opinion of the court be sufficient to enable the party in whose favour the order is made to adjust without undue hardship to the termination of his or her financial dependence on the other party.

Further detail is contained at para **2.21** et seq.

MAINTENANCE PENDING SUIT

2.17 The jurisdiction to make an order for periodical payments depends on the grant of a decree. Any order for periodic maintenance before that time is called maintenance pending suit. Once a petition has been filed:

> 'the court may make an order for maintenance pending suit, that is to say, an order requiring either party to the marriage to make to the other such periodical payments for his or her maintenance and for such term, being a term beginning not earlier than the date of the presentation of the petition and ending with the date of the determination of the suit, as the court thinks reasonable.'[22]

There is no special law relating to this form of relief. The court must use the usual s 25 factors, the only difference being that the application will be normally to deal with a short-term position rather than the permanent situation.

M v M (Maintenance Pending Suit)[23] was a case where the parties were very rich. The judge awarded the wife maintenance pending suit of £330,000 p a, holding that in the instant case the court must have regard to the standards of the very rich and not to middle-class standards. He also held that a decision as to maintenance pending suit should not be taken as a pointer to the future.

---

[22]   MCA 1973, s 22.
[23]   [2002] EWHC 317 (Fam), [2002] 2 FLR 123.

In *TL v ML*[24] it was held that the sole criterion for determining an application for maintenance pending suit is 'reasonableness', ie fairness. It was emphasised that there should always be before the court a specific budget for the application for maintenance pending suit.

2.18 One of the problems of parties to matrimonial proceedings, particularly wives, is that they may be ineligible for public funding because of some modest accumulation of capital but have insufficient resources to pursue their rights against their spouse. This is made more acute when the spouse is wealthy, litigious or obstructive.[25] To some extent, this difficulty was overcome by the decision of Holman J in *A v A (Maintenance Pending Suit: Provision for Legal Fees)*.[26] Holman J ordered maintenance pending suit to include £4,000 per month towards legal costs, backdated to the discharge of the wife's certificate of public funding. He said that the costs of the matrimonial proceedings were not in a different category from other expenses; in fact, they were the wife's most urgent and pressing need. There was no authority excluding such an element as a matter of law. Holman J emphasised that the court should be cautious in including such a costs element in an order, and it may be noted that in this case the husband was of great wealth and the combined costs exceeded £350,000.

In *G v G (Maintenance Pending Suit: Costs)*[27] it was held that *A v A* was correctly decided and that maintenance pending suit could include an element for costs. The principle was further reinforced in *Minwalla v Minwalla* [2004] EWHC 2823 (Fam), [2005] 1 FLR 771.

In *Moses-Taiga v Moses-Taiga*[28] it was held that a costs element would only be included in an order for maintenance pending suit in an exceptional case. However, a more positive approach was given by the Court of Appeal in *Currey v Currey*.[29] Here, it was held that the principles applicable to determining whether support to meet legal costs should be given are no different whether under s 22 or under s 31 (variation applications). The initial overarching enquiry is into whether the applicant for a costs allowance can demonstrate that she cannot reasonably procure legal advice and representation by any other means. Thus, to the extent that she has assets, the applicant must demonstrate that they cannot reasonably be deployed whether directly or as means of raising a loan. She also has to demonstrate that she cannot reasonably procure legal services by offering a charge on ultimate capital recovery.

---

[24] [2005] EWHC 2680 (Fam), [2006] 1 FLR 1263.
[25] See *Sears Tooth v Payne Hicks Beach and Others* [1997] 2 FLR 116 at 118H–119A per Wilson J.
[26] [2001] 1 FLR 377.
[27] [2003] Fam Law 393.
[28] [2005] EWCA Civ 1013, [2006] 1 FLR 1074.
[29] [2006] EWCA Civ 1338, [2007] 1 FLR 946.

For the form of order, see below. For the general principles of costs see Chapter 17.

FORM OF ORDER

2.19   Precedents for orders for periodical payments will be found at Appendix A. Any order for periodical payments is for the joint lives of the parties, and is therefore discharged on the death of either.

The form of an order for maintenance pending suit including a costs element was consider in *TL v ML and Others*[30] where it was held that the order should be expressed as including a legal expenses component of, eg £50,000 payable at the rate of, eg £2,000 per month, upon the applicant undertaking to pay such legal expenses to her solicitors to be credited against any costs order which she may ultimately recover against the respondent.

TAX CONSIDERATIONS

2.20   Before the budget of 1988, tax relief was available on orders for periodical payments, and the computation of the fiscal benefits to be derived from various orders occupied much of the time of family lawyers. That fiscal regime was abolished by the Finance Act 1988, and the position until April 2000 was that recipients of periodical payments were no longer taxed on their receipts, and paying parties were allowed a flat rate annual sum by way of tax relief, or the actual sum paid, whichever was the lesser. From 6 April 2000, the position is different again. Tax relief on maintenance is largely abolished as from this date. Relief is retained only where one or both of the parties was aged 65 or over as at 5 April 2000. Relief under 'old orders' (ie those made before 30 June 1988) has also ended.

THE CLEAN BREAK

Introduction

2.21   When periodical payments were considered at para **2.1**, it was noted that the difference between that form of ancillary relief and the others is that periodical payments are a continuing form of relief whereas relief of a capital nature can normally be given only once. The standard form of order for periodical payments provides for payments during the joint lives of the parties and until the payee shall remarry. Periodical payments may therefore continue during the lifetime of the payer and may be varied at any time. Until the passage into law of MFPA 1984, it was possible to terminate the right of one

---

[30]   [2005] EWHC 2680 (Fam), [2006] 1 FLR 1263.

party to apply for periodical payments only by consent.[31] However, as a result of that statute, the provisions of which are now contained in s 25(2)(a) and s 25A of MCA 1973, it is now possible for the court to terminate the right to periodical payments without consent; this provision is generally known as the 'clean break'.

2.22 The meaning of the term 'clean break' is clear: once the break has occurred, neither party has any continuing financial claim on the other. When this change in the law occurred in 1984, it was generally considered to be an enlightened measure, and the desirability of a clean break in most cases has come to be regarded as axiomatic. During the period since then, judicial dicta have varied but it has seemed that the legal profession and the public generally have accepted, perhaps uncritically, the need for a clean break wherever possible. However, as will be seen, it may be that this has come about because of a failure to consider carefully the provisions of the statute.

Statutory provisions

2.23 The clean break provisions in MCA 1973 fall under four categories. The first of the changes effected in 1984 was that s 25(2)(a) was amended. This contains the statutory factors to which the court must have regard in respect of the means, including income, of the parties. The 1984 change was to add, after the reference to the income etc of the parties, the words:

> 'including in the case of earning capacity any increase in that capacity which it would in the opinion of the court be reasonable to expect a party to the marriage to take steps to acquire.'[32]

This may be taken, therefore, to represent the presumption of the desirability of self-sufficiency.[33]

2.24 Section 25A is more detailed. The second clean break provision is s 25A(1) which provides that whenever the court exercises any of its powers under ss 22A–24A, (except when making an interim order):

> 'it shall be the duty of the court to consider whether it would be appropriate so to exercise those powers that the financial obligations of each party towards the other will be terminated as soon after the grant of the decree as the court considers just and reasonable.'

2.25 Thirdly, s 25A(2) provides that where the court decides to make an order for periodical payments or secured periodical payments in 'favour' of a party to the marriage:

---

[31] See eg *Dipper v Dipper* [1981] Fam 31.
[32] MCA 1973, s 25(2)(a).
[33] Supported by some judicial dicta, eg Ward J in *B v B (Financial Provision)* [1990] 1 FLR 20.

'the court shall, in particular, consider whether it would be appropriate to require those payments to be made or secured only for such term as would in the opinion of the court be sufficient to enable the party in whose favour the order is made to adjust without undue hardship to the termination of his or her financial dependence on the other party.'

The fourth provision is s 25A(3), which contains the power to dismiss and prevent further applications. When the court exercises its powers under MCA 1973 to make an order for ancillary relief in favour of a party and considers that no continuing obligation should be imposed on either party to make or secure periodical payments in favour of the other, it may:

'. . . dismiss the application with a direction that the applicant shall not be entitled to make any future application in relation to that marriage for an order under section 23(1)(a) or (b) above.'

Summary of statutory provisions

2.26 The position may therefore be summarised as follows.

(1) When considering the earning capacity of either party, the court must consider whether it would be reasonable to expect that party to take steps to increase such capacity.[34]

(2) When making any order for ancillary relief (except an interim order), the court must consider whether the obligations of the parties to each other should be terminated.[35] If the court does come to that conclusion, the next paragraph is unnecessary.

(3) When it does decide to make an order for periodical payments or secured periodical payments the court must consider whether such order should be for a limited term only, such term being that which is sufficient to enable the receiving party to adjust without undue hardship to termination.[36]

(4) The above provisions are positive duties for the court. These matters must be considered in every case.

(5) This duty of the court must be exercised after consideration of all the factors contained in s 25. It is only after proper consideration of all those factors, that the court can come to an informed decision.

(6) When the court decides that there should be termination, it must effect this by the orders set out in s 25A(3).[37]

---

[34] MCA 1973, s 25(2)(a).
[35] Ibid, s 25A(1).
[36] Ibid, s 25A(2).
[37] Ibid, s 25A(3).

(7)   These provisions apply only to divorce and nullity cases. They do not apply to judicial separation.

Judicial guidance as to when a clean break is appropriate

2.27   As might have been expected, there have been many decided cases in which the court has given guidance on when a clean break is appropriate.[38] However, as will have been seen above, the decision which the court must make is not always one single issue. In many cases, the court will have to make two decisions:

(1)   whether the obligations of the parties towards each other should be terminated (the immediate clean break); and, if not,

(2)   whether they should be terminated at some future time (the delayed clean break).

These two possibilities are the subject of different, though sometimes overlapping, case-law.

When a delayed clean break is adopted, the separate question arises of whether a direction under s 28(1A) should be given and, if not, whether the term for periodical payments may be extended. These possibilities must be considered separately.

Should there be an immediate clean break?

2.28   At paras **2.32** and **2.33**, dicta from two cases will be considered. Like all fields of law, this is an evolving and constantly changing area and these cases contain the guidance which is most likely to predict accurately the approach of the higher courts. Accordingly, it may be that some of the earlier examples of the way in which the court has exercised its discretion will be of less importance than might previously have been the case, and those cases will, therefore, be summarised rather than set out in detail.

2.29   It is striking that s 25A(1) gives no guidance to the court as to how its discretion should be exercised. This is in contrast to s 25A(2) which seems to suggest that periodical payments should only be for a fixed term if, at the end of that term, the payee has adjusted without undue hardship to the loss of dependency. It might be thought that that test is also appropriate to s 25A(1), but that is not what the statute says.

---

[38]   See, eg *Waterman v Waterman* [1989] 1 FLR 380 (term order for 5 years when child would be 10, wife working as secretary, short marriage); *Suter v Suter and Jones* [1987] 2 FLR 232, CA (nominal order where wife with young children and uncertainties as to her future); *M v M (Financial Provision)* [1987] 2 FLR 1 (47-year-old wife, no prospect of self-sufficiency, no clean break); *Whiting v Whiting* [1988] 2 FLR 189 (wife self-sufficient, husband unemployed, no clean break; this is generally accepted to be an untypical decision).

Cases in which the principle of an immediate clean break has been approved by the court may be categorised as 'big money cases' and 'no money cases', 'intermediate cases' providing more of a problem.

Examples of the former are *Gojkovic v Gojkovic*,[39] and *F v F (Duxbury Calculation: Rate of Return)*.[40] These cases will be considered in more detail at Chapter 4, para **4.9** (big money cases) but it will be seen that the important factor was that it was possible to provide sufficient funds from ample capital resources to secure a fund from which the wife's income needs could be met for her lifetime. Accordingly, the rationale for the dismissal of all continuing claims in such cases seems to have been that true self-sufficiency could be achieved by an order for redistribution of capital.

2.30 In the 'no money' cases, such as *Ashley v Blackman*,[41] the rationale for the immediate clean break has been that there never was, and never would be any prospect of the husband paying periodical payments and so, for the achievement of certainty and the avoidance of further unnecessary litigation, an immediate clean break was the only sensible answer.

F v F (Clean Break: Balance of Fairness)[42] was a case involving assets of £3.48m which included shares in a family company worth £2.8m. The husband argued that the illiquidity of his company justified a departure from equality. After making orders to secure the wife's housing, Singer J ordered the husband to pay periodical payments of £75,000 p a. Here a clean break was neither feasible nor just. Where assets exceeded needs good reason must be found for departing from equality. The order for periodical payments would enable both parties to share in the results of the company's performance until a clean break was feasible.

It is, perhaps, in the intermediate cases that the courts have been placed in the most difficult position. In many such cases, it is clear that the income of the paying party (normally the husband) is such that a periodical payments order would cause hardship, while, at the same time, the income of the other party is not such as to entitle the court to find her to be self-supporting. There may have been a tendency, at least until the advent of CSA 1991, to make clean break orders where a matrimonial home was transferred to a mother so that children continued to live in the family home.[43] Nevertheless, there is clear authority that a direction under s 28(1A) prohibiting further applications should not be made where there are young children.[44] In *SRJ v DWJ (Financial*

---

[39] [1990] 1 FLR 140, CA.
[40] [1996] 1 FLR 833.
[41] [1988] 2 FLR 278.
[42] [2003] 1 FLR 847.
[43] See e g *Clutton v Clutton* [1991] 1 FLR 242 at 245 per Lloyd LJ.
[44] See *N v N (Consent Order: Variation)* [1993] 2 FLR 868 at 883 per Roch LJ for a clear statement of this principle. See also *Mawson v Mawson* [1994] 2 FLR 985 for a more mixed message (wife with young child, Thorpe J ordered term of 9 months but no s 28(1A) direction as this would not be appropriate where young child involved, complication because previous

Provision),[45] it was held that there is no presumption in favour of a clean break; in this case, there was a young child, and it was observed that it is difficult to achieve a financial clean break when there cannot be a personal clean break between the parties.

In another case,[46] where the husband had been ordered to pay periodical payments but had obstinately failed to do so, it was held that these developments demonstrated that the order made was not appropriate or practical, and that a clean break should be imposed to put an end to the expensive process of enforcement. It should, however, be noted that there were sufficient capital assets to enable the court to award a lump sum of the wife's capitalised maintenance requirements.

2.31 If the 'no money cases' are put to one side, it seems that the courts look to the test contained in s 25A(2) in order to make a decision under s 25A(1), an approach which is wholly reasonable even though it might seem not to be dictated by the words of the statute. This is not an insignificant point, since the two cases about to be considered were concerned with s 25A(2) and not s 25A(1). Nevertheless, the principles set out in the judgments of Ward LJ in these cases seem to establish authoritative guidelines for both subsections.

2.32 In *Flavell v Flavell*,[47] the court was concerned with a wife aged 54 who had a very limited earning capacity and no pension. The judge at first instance observed that it was not usually appropriate to provide for the termination of periodical payments in the case of a woman in her mid 50s, an opinion which Ward LJ endorsed with his approval. Ward LJ continued:

> 'The words of [s 25A(2)] do not impose more than an aspiration that the parties should achieve self-sufficiency. The power of the court to terminate dependency can, however, be exercised only in the event that adjustment can be made without undue hardship. There is, in my judgment, often a tendency for these orders to be made more in hope than in serious expectation. Especially in judging the case of ladies in their middle years the judicial looking into a crystal ball very rarely finds enough of substance to justify a finding that adjustment can be made without undue hardship. All too often, these orders are made without evidence to support them.'

2.33 Ward LJ gave further guidance in *C v C (Financial Relief: Short Marriage)*.[48] The facts of this case are unimportant save that it may be noted that, as its name suggests, it was concerned with a short marriage where the husband was comparatively wealthy. The judge at first instance had awarded the wife a lump sum and periodical payments of a level which, on appeal, was

---

agreement to which the parties should be held). See also *B v B (Mesher Order)* [2002] EWHC 3106 (Fam), [2003] 2 FLR 285 (no presumption of term order in short marriage).

[45] [1999] 2 FLR 176, CA.

[46] *Fournier v Fournier* [1998] 2 FLR 990, CA.

[47] [1997] 1 FLR 353, CA.

[48] [1997] 2 FLR 26, CA.

described as being 'at the top of the bracket' but which was nevertheless upheld. Ward LJ summarised the proper approach of the court as follows:

'(1)   The first task is to consider a clean break which pursuant to s 25A(1) requires the court to consider whether it would be appropriate to exercise its powers so that the financial obligations of each party towards the other will be terminated as soon after the grant of the decree as the court considers just and reasonable.'

It may be noted that no guidance is given as to how this exercise is to be carried out (see para **2.29**).

'(2)   If there is to be no clean break, and a periodical payments order is to be made, then the court must decide pursuant to s 25 what amount is to be ordered. The duration of the marriage is a factor relevant to the determination of quantum.

(3)   If a periodical payments order is made, whether for 5p per annum or whatever, the question is whether it would be appropriate to impose a term because in the absence of such a direction the order will endure for joint lives or until the remarriage of the payee: see s 28(1)(a).

(4)   The statutory test is this: is it appropriate to order periodical payments only for such a term as in the opinion of the court would be sufficient to enable the payee to adjust without undue hardship to the termination of financial dependence on the paying party?

(5)   What is appropriate must of necessity depend on all the circumstances of the case including the welfare of any minor child and the s 25 checklist factors, one of which is the duration of the marriage. It is, however, not appropriate simply to say, "this is a short marriage therefore a term must be imposed".

(6)   Financial dependence being evident from the very making of an order for periodical payments, the question is whether, in the light of all the circumstances of the case, the payee can adjust – and adjust without undue hardship – to the termination of financial dependence and if so when. The question is, can she adjust, not should she adjust. In answering that question, the court will pay attention not only to the duration of the marriage but to the effect the marriage and its breakdown and the need to care for any minor children has had and will continue to have on the earning capacity of the payee and the extent to which she is no longer in the position she would have been in but for the marriage, its consequences and its breakdown. It is highly material to consider any difficulties the payee may have in entering or re-entering the labour market, resuming a fractured career and making up any lost ground.

(7)   The court cannot form its opinion that a term is appropriate without evidence to support its conclusion. Facts supported by evidence must, therefore, justify a reasonable expectation that the payee can and will become self-sufficient. Gazing into the crystal ball does not give rise to such a reasonable expectation. Hope, with or without pious exhortations to end dependency, is not enough.

(8) It is necessary for the court to form an opinion not only that the payee will adjust, but also that the payee will have adjusted within the time that is fixed. The court may be in a position of such certainty that it can impose a deferred clean break by prohibiting an extension of the term pursuant to s 28(1A). If, however, there is any doubt about when self-sufficiency will be attained, it is wrong to require the payee to apply to extend the term. If there is uncertainty about the appropriate length of the term, the proper course is to impose no term but to leave the payer to seek the variation and if necessary go through the same exercise, this time pursuant to s 31(7)(a).'

Summary

2.34 These words have been quoted in full since they are likely to be studied by practitioners and courts for some time to come. Nevertheless, a short summary may assist. The proper approach is:

(a)   to consider whether an immediate clean break is appropriate. No guidance is given as to the principles to guide the court in this, but, by inference from the decided cases and by analogy with s 25(2), it would seem that the court should be satisfied that the payee is, or may become by order of the court, self-sufficient. (The court would also be entitled to take this view if there was no future possibility of any financial contribution by one party to the other);

(b)   if the court decides that an immediate clean break is not appropriate and that a periodical payments order (of whatever amount) should be made, the court must consider whether this should be for a finite term. The court may limit such an order only if satisfied that the payee will at the end of the term have adjusted to the termination of support without undue hardship. Such a conclusion may be reached only by evidence;

(c)   there seems to be no justification for an order for a fixed term without a direction that no further applications should be made. The requirements for both are identical;

(d)   where the court is in any doubt about the position, a deferred clean break order should not be made.

An important gloss has now been place on these words by the dicta of the House of Lords in *Miller/McFarlane* (see para **1.53** et seq). As previously discussed, the House held that periodical payments are not to be limited to maintenance but may include an element of compensation. Lord Nicholls put it in this way (paras [37]–[39]):

'[37] This statutory statement of principle raises a question of a similar nature to that affecting the whole of s 25. By s 25A(1) and (2) duties are imposed on the court but the court is left with a discretion. The court is required to "consider" whether it would be "appropriate" to exercise its powers in a particular way. But the section gives no express guidance on the type of circumstance which would render it inappropriate for the court to bring about a clean break.

[38] In one respect the object of s 25A(1) is abundantly clear. The subsection is expressed in general terms. It is apt to refer as much to a periodical payments order made to provide compensation as it is to an order made to meet financial needs. But, expressly, s 25A(1) is not intended to bring about an unfair result. Under s 25A(1) the goal the court is required to have in mind is that the parties' mutual financial obligations should end as soon as the court considers just and reasonable.

[39] Section 25A(2) is focused more specifically. It is concerned with the termination of one party's 'financial dependence' on the other 'without undue hardship'. These references to financial dependence and hardship are apt when applied to a periodical payments order making provision for the payee's financial needs. They are hardly apt when applied to a periodical payments order whose object is to furnish compensation in respect of future economic disparity arising from the division of functions adopted by the parties during their marriage. If the claimant is owed compensation, and capital assets are not available, it is difficult to see why the social desirability of a clean break should be sufficient reason for depriving the claimant of that compensation.'

The clean break on variation

2.35 It should be noted that the duty of the court to consider terminating financial dependency applies as much on a variation application as on an application for periodical payments.[49]

Direction under the Inheritance (Provision for Family and Dependants) Act 1975

2.36 Since a clean break order, whether immediate or deferred, is designed to terminate all continuing financial obligations between the parties, it would be illogical if this were to change on the death of one of the parties. Nevertheless, this could be the case in the absence of provision to the contrary, since a former spouse is among the class of persons on whom s 1(1)(b) of the Inheritance (Provision for Family and Dependants) Act 1975 confers the right to apply for financial relief from the estate of a deceased person.

Thus it is that s 15(1) of the 1975 Act provides that, on the grant of an order for divorce or separation or of a decree of nullity, or at any time thereafter, the court may, if it considers it just to do so and on the application of either party to the marriage, order that the other party shall not be entitled on the death of the applicant to apply for an order under the 1975 Act.

This is now a standard order which is made whenever a clean break order is made, and, normally, it would be justified. Nevertheless, it clearly requires

---

[49] *Fleming v Fleming* [2003] EWCA Civ 1841, [2004] 1 FLR 667. For variation generally see Chapter 13.

separate consideration by the court and a separate decision that the order is just must be made. There might be circumstances, such as the no money cases, in which an immediate clean break could be justified for pragmatic reasons but it would not necessarily follow that the right to apply under the 1975 Act should be prohibited. Further, such an order could be made only if one of the parties asked the court to do so.

Extension of terms

2.37 Where a direction is given under s 28(1A) of MCA 1973 that no further applications may be made, that is final and the court may not entertain an application for the term of a periodical payments order to be extended. This is not the case when a fixed-term order is made without such a direction. Arguably this should never happen, but it is possible for such orders to be made and the court has had to adjudicate on the position. The position is, in fact, quite simple. Provided the application to vary is made before the expiration of the term, the court has jurisdiction to entertain it.[50] However, if the term has expired, or the event on which the periodical payments were to cease has passed, the right to apply to vary is lost.[51]

Form of order

2.38 Precedents for the various clean break orders will be found in Appendix A.

> 'I can find no warrant for equating in this context remarriage with cohabitation, a word which itself presents problems of definition. . . . I do not consider that it is open to the courts to add a gloss to those existing provisions by equating cohabitation . . . with remarriage without sanction.'

In *Fleming v Fleming* [2003] EWCA Civ 1841, [2004] 1 FLR 667 it was held that Atkinson did not require re-visiting. The principle that cohabitation was not to be equated with remarriage was as sound as ever.

> '. . . we do not consider that the right approach to a case of this kind is to seek to apply the so-called one-third rule. The right approach is rather to consider the disposable income of each party apart from any order, and then to see what order will produce a redistribution of the disposable incomes which is fair and just in all circumstances.'

---

[50] *Richardson v Richardson* [1994] 1 FLR 286.
[51] Once the application is made, the hearing, and the order, can take place after the term has expired. See *Jones v Jones* [2000] 2 FLR 307, CA, disapproving *G v G (Periodical Payments: Jurisdiction)* [1997] 1 FLR 368, CA.

Chapter 3

SECURED PERIODICAL PAYMENTS

INTRODUCTION

3.1   Secured periodical payments are in some ways a curious hybrid, and are probably comparatively rare. The order incorporates an assessment of the amount of periodical payments which should be paid, with an order that they be secured, ie that security be provided for them, by some capital deposit.

The general principles on which orders for ancillary relief are made have already been considered, as have the detailed principles for assessment of the quantum of periodical payments. It is unnecessary to consider either here. Instead, it is proposed to consider the special circumstances which might give rise to an order for secured periodical payments and the practical consequences of such an order.

STATUTORY PROVISIONS

3.2   It is provided that:

> 'On granting a decree of divorce, a decree of nullity of marriage or a decree of judicial separation, or at any time thereafter (whether, in the case of a decree of divorce or nullity of marriage, before or after the decree is made absolute), the court may make . . .
>
> . . .
>
> (b) an order that either party to the marriage shall secure to the other to the satisfaction of the court, such periodical payments, for such term, as may be so specified.'[1]

It will be noted that this is one of the types of orders which can be made only after decree.

3.3   There are other statutory provisions concerning the procedure for making an order which will be considered below.

---

[1]   MCA 1973, s 23(1)(b).

NATURE OF THE ORDER

3.4   A precedent for the order will be found at Appendix A, precedent 9. It will be seen that the order requires the paying party to secure to the payee for a specified term the annual sum of periodical payments upon such security as may satisfy the court. The various elements of such an order are therefore as follows.

Secure

3.5   The order does not require the payer to make payments to the payee; it merely requires him to provide the fund out of which the payments may be made. In a leading case it was said that the order was 'an order to secure and nothing else. Under it the only obligation of the husband is to provide the security; having done that, he is under no liability. He enters into no covenant to pay and never becomes a debtor in respect of the payments'.[2]

The term

3.6   The court must specify the term, which may be for any term the court thinks fit, subject to certain statutory restrictions. It is provided that:

> 'in the case of a secured periodical payments order, the term shall begin not earlier than the date of the making of an application for the order, and shall be so defined as not to extend beyond the death or, where the order is made on or after the grant of such a decree [ie a decree of divorce or nullity], the remarriage of the party in whose favour the order is made.'[3]

The term must therefore be expressed to end on the death or remarriage of the payee. However, it may survive the death of the paying party.

If the court considers a limited term order with a 'clean break' direction appropriate, this can be incorporated into the order.

The amount to be secured

3.7   The quantum of the periodical payments will be assessed in the usual way.

The security

3.8   The fund to be provided is in the discretion of the court. The order will either specify the asset or order 'security to be agreed or referred to the district judge in default of agreement'. The asset provided will either be an

---

[2]   *Barker v Barker* [1952] P 184.
[3]   MCA 1973, s 28(1)(b).

income-producing asset such as a portfolio of securities or a non-income-producing asset. In the latter case, and sometimes in the former also, it is necessary to provide for sale to provide income.

An order imposing a general charge on all the husband's assets has been expressly disapproved by the Court of Appeal as 'sweeping and indiscriminate'.[4] It must be specific.

Although it has been said[5] that where there is ample free capital the whole of the order should be secured, it is necessary to have regard to all the circumstances of the case, including, in particular, the s 25 factors, and the order must be reasonable.

3.9 It is almost invariably necessary to require a deed to be lodged by the paying party as well as the asset itself, to give effect to the order. This would be necessary to ensure that the asset, which would remain vested in the name of the paying party, provides the payments to the payee. Where problems arise, the court may refer the matter to one of the conveyancing counsel of the court for settlement of a proper instrument to be executed by all parties.[6] Further, where the paying party refuses or neglects to execute the document, an order may be made for the district judge or some other person to sign on his behalf.[7]

The court also has power to order one party to lodge documents which are necessary for the preparation of the deed.[8]

WHEN WILL SUCH AN ORDER BE MADE?

3.10 The circumstances in which it might be appropriate to make an order for secured periodical payments can best be seen by considering the advantages to the payee of such an order. The principal advantage is that the payments are secure; the fund is there to make them safe and the payments will survive the death of the paying party or his bankruptcy or disappearance.

In order to be persuaded that this order is appropriate therefore, the court would normally have to come to the conclusion that there were dangers against which the payee needed protection and also, of course, that a capital fund was available for this purpose.

3.11 The nature of the problem was well illustrated by *Aggett v Aggett*.[9] The judge pointed out that the court was always reluctant to burden with security something which was the sole or main asset of the respondent, but on the other

---

4   *Barker v Barker* (above).
5   In *Shearn v Shearn* [1931] P 1.
6   MCA 1973, s 30.
7   Ibid.
8   Supreme Court Act 1981, s 39 and CCA 1984, s 38.
9   [1962] 1 All ER 190, CA.

hand the court was loath to leave a wife in circumstances in which it seemed clear that the husband might well leave her penniless. One had to consider whether the fears expressed on the wife's behalf were sufficiently cogent to justify making an order for security which would not be made if there was no reality in those fears.[10]

VARIATION AND AMENDMENT

3.12 The security may be varied or changed at any time; where this cannot be agreed the court may order a variation. Likewise, an order for secured provision may be varied by increasing or reducing the amount payable or by discharging it.[11] The order survives the death of the paying party, but can be varied after death in the light of the circumstances at the time. The fact that a wife has the benefit of a secured order does not prevent her from applying for provision from her former husband's estate.

---

[10]   See also *Shearn v Shearn* [1931] P 1; *Naish v Naish* (1916) 32 TLR 487.
[11]   See MCA 1973, s 31, and Chapter 13.

Chapter 4

LUMP SUM ORDERS

INTRODUCTION

4.1 A lump sum order is an order that one party pay to the other a sum of money. It is therefore to be contrasted with a property adjustment order, which requires the transfer of some specified real or personal property, and a periodical payments order which requires the payment of regular periodic (weekly, monthly or annual) sums by way of maintenance. An order for a lump sum is normally, therefore, a means of adjusting the capital resources of the parties on the dissolution of the marriage. The reasons for such an order might be various, but of course could only be based on the normal s 25(2) factors. Although in this chapter it is not intended to deal with housing needs and the matrimonial home,[1] it should be noted that in many cases the housing needs of one or both of the parties are the need which the order is intended to meet. Where a wife's capital claims have been fully resolved by a property adjustment order, the application for a lump sum should be dismissed so that both parties know that capital claims are not thereafter live between them.[2]

Unlike a periodical payments order, a lump sum order is intended to be a final order and, with certain limited exceptions, may be made only once.

4.2 As with most classes of relief, it would be unusual for only a lump sum order to be made. Most orders for ancillary relief contain a variety of types of order such as lump sum, periodical payments, property adjustment and so on. The exception to this might be where there are ample funds, and the purpose of the order is to fund continuing periodical payments for life; this would be known as a *Duxbury* order and this is considered below at para **4.14**.

Because of this factor, it has been thought appropriate to include in this chapter a section on so-called 'big money' cases. As will be seen, some of the principles to be observed in such cases are not confined to big money but have significance across the board.

By a process of logical extension, there will then follow a section of the special features which arise when one of the assets of the parties is a business.

---

[1]   See Chapter 5.
[2]   *Scheeres v Scheeres* [1999] 1 FLR 241.

STATUTORY PROVISION

4.3   A lump sum order is a financial provision order.[3] On granting a decree of
divorce, nullity or judicial separation or at any time thereafter the court may
make an order 'that either party to the marriage shall pay to the other such
lump sum as may be so specified'.[4] The powers of the court in this respect are
exercisable only after the grant of a decree. They are therefore classed as final
orders.

NUMBER OF LUMP SUMS

4.4   The statute refers to 'lump sum or sums'. This does not mean that more
than one lump sum order may be made, but rather that only one order may be
made, which order may provide for the payment of one or more lump sums.[5]
The order may also provide for payment by instalments, or for payment to be
deferred, and, in that event, for the payment of interest.[6] A lump sum payable
by instalments can be varied; for further details see Chapter 13.

4.5   With the limited exception mentioned below, there is at present no
provision for interim lump sums. After the decision of Waite J in *Barry v
Barry*,[7] it was thought that the court had the power to appropriate capital of
the parties to one or other of them on an interim basis, on the understanding
that the asset thereby acquired would be brought into account on the eventual
distribution of assets at the final hearing. This supposed power was developed
in other cases on the basis of the inherent jurisdiction of the court[8] and also the
court's powers to order sale under the Rules of the Supreme Court 1965 (RSC),
Ord 31, r 1, as applied by FPR 1991, r 2.64.[9]

This line of cases has been comprehensively demolished by the Court of
Appeal; in *Wicks v Wicks*,[10] each of the supposed bases of jurisdiction was
considered and, with regret, found wanting, and the law is therefore as it was
before *Barry v Barry* was decided. There is no way in which the court may order
an interim lump sum.

4.6   The court does, however, have limited powers to provide for payments of
sums of money on an interim basis for immediate needs. It is provided that:

---

3   MCA 1973, s 21(1)(c).
4   Ibid, s 23(1)(c).
5   *Coleman v Coleman* [1973] Fam 10.
6   MCA 1973, s 23(6). For an interesting example of an order to pay a lump sum by instalments
    see *R v R (Lump Sum Repayments)* [2003] EWHC 3197 (Fam), [2004] 1 FLR 928 where
    Wilson J ordered a husband to pay lump sums equivalent to the wife's obligations under a 20
    year repayment mortgage i.e. £30,000 forthwith and then 240 payments to cover the
    instalments.
7   [1992] Fam 140.
8   *F v F (Ancillary Relief: Substantial Assets)* [1995] 2 FLR 45.
9   *Green v Green* [1993] 1 FLR 326.
10 [1998] 1 FLR 470, per Ward LJ.

'an order under this section [s 23] that a party to a marriage shall pay a lump sum to the other party may be made for the purpose of enabling that other party to meet any liabilities or expenses reasonably incurred by him or her in maintaining himself or herself or any child of the family before making an application for an order under this section in his or her favour.'[11]

This is a little used provision, but its utility is clear. It could be used where for some reason a periodic order was inappropriate, but the applicant had some pressing need, for example some school fees, a council tax bill, or a major car repair which could not be met out of income. It would seem that the purpose for which the lump sum would be required must be limited to the maintenance of the applicant or a child, and so the subsection could not be used for major housing requirements; perhaps, however, it could be used to require the payment of a deposit on rented accommodation.

For an example (not an authority) of an order made under this subsection, see *Askew-Page v Page*.[12]

HOW ARE LUMP SUM ORDERS CALCULATED?

4.7   As always, it must be said that the only starting point for the court is the s 25 factors. There is no justification for taking any proportion of the assets as any kind of rule-of-thumb baseline.[13] The power to award a lump sum was, in fact, only introduced in 1970 and then incorporated into the MCA 1973. It may fairly be regarded as one of the most important developments in modern family law. In one of the early cases, it was emphasised that a lump sum was not simply another way of quantifying maintenance; the court might take into account all the factors laid down in the Act. It was essential that the court should retain complete flexibility of approach in the light of the circumstances of the case, present, past, and insofar as one could make a reliable estimate, future.[14]

4.8   In another case,[15] Thorpe J held that the discretionary power of the court to adjust capital shares between the parties should not be exercised unless there is a manifest need for intervention upon the application of the s 25 criteria. In particular, the idea that an applicant was entitled to a 'nest egg' against a 'rainy day' was expressly disapproved; any specific award of capital must have an evidential justification.[16] Whether this guidance survives *White v*

---

[11]   MCA 1973, s 23(3)(a).
[12]   [2001] Fam Law 794, Bath County Court, HHJ Meston QC.
[13]   See eg *Potter v Potter* (1983) FLR 331, CA.
[14]   *Trippas v Trippas* [1973] Fam 134, CA. See also *Hobhouse v Hobhouse* [1999] 1 FLR 961, CA.
[15]   *H v H (Financial Provision: Capital Allowance)* [1993] 2 FLR 335.
[16]   Disapproving *Re Besterman dec'd* [1984] Ch 458. But see *A v A (Financial Provision)* [1998] 2 FLR 180, where Singer J 'rounded up' the appropriate provision.

White[17] and the subsequent cases culminating in *Miller/McFarlane* (as to which, see below and Chapter 1) entirely unscathed is at the least debatable and probably unlikely.

The conventional wisdom set out above is now subject to several qualifications arising out of the decisions of the House of Lords in *White v White*[18] and *Miller/McFarlane*.[19] Both these cases, and the legal position arising from them, are considered in detail in Chapter 1 at para **1.47** et seq and reference should be made to that section of this book. However, some further comments can be added in the context of lump sums and will now be set out.

First, it is necessary to bear in mind the fundamental distinction between those cases where assets do not exceed needs and those where they do. For the sake of clarity, the latter can be referred to as 'big money cases'.

Cases where assets do not exceed needs

4.9   In this class of case, the function of the court, with the help of the practitioner, is to manage scarce funds so that the most pressing needs of the parties are met. By definition, there is not enough money to go round and so the court has to apply a 'hierarchy of needs'. Where there is a child, the first consideration will normally be to try to provide a home for the parent with care and the child. Where there are sufficient funds, the court will then try to make such order as enables the non-resident parent to rehouse himself or herself.

This will normally take up most of the parties' funds, but if any money is left over the court will then consider any item for which a need is proved.

BIG MONEY CASES

4.10   Cases involving assets surplus to needs are fundamentally different from the cases considered above. It is still necessary to be guided by the s 25 factors but with the addition of the 'yardstick of equality'. By definition, there are sufficient funds to meet the needs of the parties. The role of the court is therefore now to achieve a just result in the light of s 25 and reference should be made to the section on the post *White* and *Miller/McFarlane* position in Chapter 1.

As to what constitutes a 'big money' case, it is interesting (and, perhaps surprising) that in *D v D (Lump Sum: Adjournment of Application)*[20] Connell J considered that a case where the total assets were £700,000 and the husband earned £230,000 pa net was such a case on the ground that the available assets clearly exceeded the parties' needs for housing and income.

---

17   [2000] 2 FLR 981, HL.
18   [2000] 2 FLR 981.
19   [2006] 1 FLR 1186, HL.
20   [2001] 1 FLR 633.

4.11 There will now be considered two particular aspects of this class of case, namely the 'millionaire's defence' and *Duxbury* funds.

The millionaire's defence

4.12 The fact that an approach based on a mathematical proportion is even less appropriate in big money cases than is normally the case is underlined by a number of decisions establishing what is known as 'the millionaire's defence'. This so-called defence, or argument, is to the effect that since the means of the paying party are such as to enable the payer to meet any award which the court could conceivably make based on the payee's reasonable requirements, it is unnecessary to give detailed and possibly costly disclosure of the full extent of the payer's means. This is also known as the '*Thyssen* defence', after the parties in the leading case on the point.[21] There, the husband deposed in his affidavit to very substantial and complicated assets worth over £400m, and concluded by saying, 'I would meet any order the court decides to make in relation to the financial dispute between the petitioner and myself'. The wife applied for detailed discovery, designed to support her assertion that the husband's wealth was, in reality, in excess of £1,000m. It was held that, since there was more than ample wealth to make a very substantial financial order to support the wife in luxury for the rest of her life, and the largest award which could be made would not be significantly increased by proof of a larger fortune, the limited discovery which had been offered was all that was reasonably necessary.

4.13 This decision was followed in another case in which the assets of the husband were 'only' £8m.[22] However, it is not to be taken as carte blanche for a less than careful or conscientious approach. In another case[23] in which the assets of the husband were between £150m and £200m, it was held that, while a restrictive approach to the wife's questionnaire was justified, this did not entitle the husband to refuse reasonably framed questions designed to establish the broad realities of the case and to illuminate issues as to past dealings. The death blow to the millionaires' defence might seem to have been delivered by the dicta of Thorpe LJ in *Parlour v Parlour* and *Mcfarlane v Mcfarlane* (as to which see para **1.59**); his Lordship said: 'We were told by the Bar that a practice has grown up for substantial earners to decline any statement of their needs on the grounds that they can afford any order that the court is likely to make. These appeals must put an end to that practice.'

The *Duxbury* fund

4.14 As was mentioned above, one of the characteristics of big money cases is that there is normally sufficient liquid capital to provide a fund of money from which one party's income for life can be derived. A well-settled practice has now been established by which, once a payee's reasonable income needs have been established, a calculation can be made to quantify the capital sum

---

21 *Thyssen-Bornemisza v Thyssen-Bornemisza (No 2)* [1985] FLR 1069.
22 *B v B (Discovery: Financial Provision)* [1990] 2 FLR 180.
23 *F v F (Ancillary Relief: Substantial Assets)* [1995] 2 FLR 45.

required to fund that income for life on an inflation-proof basis. This is based on a computer program into which it is necessary to feed such information as the age of the recipient, and certain assumptions as to tax bands, inflation and so on are made.

The best guidance as to the weight to be placed on such calculations is to be found not in the case from which the calculation derives its name[24] but in the words of Ward J in *B v B (Financial Provision)*.[25] Here it was pointed out that, as a result of the observations made in *Preston v Preston*,[26] accountants had devised a computer program which could calculate the lump sum which, if invested on the assumptions as to life expectancy, rates of inflation, return on investment, growth of capital, incidence of income tax, will produce enough to meet the recipient's needs for her life. Ward J concluded that, if their calculation were accepted as no more than a tool for the judge's use, it was a very valuable help to him in many cases.[27]

4.15 In other cases[28] it has been emphasised that a *Duxbury* calculation cannot by itself provide the answer as to the sum to which a wife is entitled, and that there is a danger that it might be regarded as having achieved a status far beyond that which it had in the original case. There are also obvious uncertainties in trying to calculate the rate of return for any investment over a long period.

It has been said that '*Duxbury* is a tool and not a rule', and that 'the utility of the *Duxbury* methodology depends in part upon the skill of the user. It must be applied with flexibility, with a due recognition of its limitations and with intelligent perception of special features which are capable of being incorporated within the computer programme'.[29]

It was held in one case[30] that a *Duxbury* calculation was not appropriate because the wife had a life expectancy in excess of 40 years.

It would therefore be wrong to treat the result of a *Duxbury* calculation as being anything other than the probable best guess as to the sum which needs to be provided. There is room for argument over the method used and whether the

---

24   *Duxbury v Duxbury* [1987] 1 FLR 7.
25   [1990] 1 FLR 20.
26   [1982] Fam 17, [1981] 3 WLR 619, CA.
27   For background information on the origins of the computer program, see also the article by its originator Mr Timothy Lawrence at [1990] Fam Law 12.
28   See *F v F (Duxbury Calculation: Rate of Return)* [1996] 1 FLR 833; *Gojkovic v Gojkovic* [1992] Fam 40 at p 48E; *Vicary v Vicary* [1992] 2 FLR 271 at p 278B.
29   Per Thorpe LJ in *White v White* [1998] 2 FLR 310. See also *A v A (Elderly Applicant: Lump Sum)* [1999] 2 FLR 969 and *G v G (Financial Provision: Separation Agreement)* [2000] 2 FLR 8, Connell J.
30   *Fournier v Fournier* [1998] 2 FLR 990, CA.

whole basis of the *Duxbury* calculation should be changed.[31] The court is greatly assisted by such calculations and they should be regarded as indispensable in appropriate cases.[32]

For some time the courts were troubled by the so-called '*Duxbury* paradox', arising from the fact that, when a *Duxbury* calculation was appropriate, the older (and possibly more deserving) spouse recovered a lower amount than a younger spouse, because the calculation is based, in part, on life expectancy. This paradox was to some extent made easier by the comments of Lord Nicholls in *White v White*,[33] where it was said that the proper application of the 'yardstick of equality' would resolve the problem in any event.

BUSINESS CASES

4.16 Many cases involving lump sums and, a fortiori, substantial amounts of money, are cases where one of the assets is a business owned by one or both of the parties. Where the business is a 'private' business, ie one in which the parties themselves have a controlling interest and which provides the source of the family's prosperity, particular considerations arise. The court has two essential functions in such cases. The first is to establish a value for the parties' interests in the business, as part of its duty under s 25(2)(a). The second is to decide how that value should be reflected in the final distribution.

4.17 As to the issue of valuation, it should be remembered that, until very recently, the conventional wisdom was that the court will avoid making any final order the effect of which would be that the business would have to be sold against the will of the party wishing to continue in the business; in most cases, the business would be regarded as the provider of income, now and in the future, and not as a source of liquid capital. It follows that any valuation should not be in the same detail as would be employed by someone wishing to buy the company but rather to establish a reasonably accurate figure for the income which the business could generate, and its eventual value as, for example, the source of a pension annuity.

4.18 There was a wealth of authority to establish this point. In *Potter v Potter*[34] there had been extensive and costly accountancy evidence to establish a precise value of a small business; the judge then awarded the wife one-third of the value of the assets. On appeal it was pointed out that the valuation of a business in these circumstances was a 'necessarily hypothetical exercise because the only way that it can be done is for those valuing it to assume that the business would be sold and that, of course, is the one thing which is not going

---

[31]   See 'Is Duxbury misleading? Yes, it is' at [2001] Fam Law 747.
[32]   While expert advice may be needed in complicated cases, an indispensable source of information, giving helpful tables etc is the publication *At a Glance*, published and annually updated by the Family Law Bar Association.
[33]   [2000] 2 FLR 981, HL. See also paras **1.48** and **4.10**.
[34]   (1983) FLR 331, CA.

to happen and very rarely does happen'. Such a valuation was 'an almost wholly irrelevant consideration', and the proper approach was to take the wife's reasonable needs and balance them against the husband's ability to pay.

In another case,[35] where there was a family company with a value of £1.2m to £1.5m, it was said that all that was required was 'the broadest evaluation of the company's worth to enable the court to decide the wife's reasonable requirements'. If there was liquidity in the company which could be realised to meet her requirements then the final order would take that liquidity into account; if there was none, in the sense that the company (the source of the breadwinner's income) would be damaged, then the court should look elsewhere.

This decision was cited in *Evans v Evans*[36] in support of one of the propositions laid down for the guidance of the profession in these cases. It was emphasised that, while it may be necessary to obtain a broad assessment of the value of a shareholding in a private company, it is inappropriate to undertake an expensive and meaningless exercise to achieve a precise valuation of a private company which will not be sold.

It must be said that it is now necessary to approach these cases with a degree of caution. *White v White* has introduced a new set of principles, particularly in cases of substantial assets, and in *N v N (Financial Provision: Sale of Company)*,[37] it was said that the older authorities disapproving the sale of the golden goose might no longer apply. The same judge (Coleridge J) held, in *R v R (Financial Relief: Company Valuation)*[38] that the valuation of companies was more of an art than a science.[39]

4.19 These warnings must, however, still be borne in mind, as must the point that the value of one of the assets is only one (even if the most important) factor which the court will take into account in the s 25 exercise. Nevertheless, the court does still have the duty to place some value on a business, and the following comments are designed to offer some guidance as to how that might be approached.

Businesses can of course take a variety of forms. What is to follow is not concerned with shares in publicly quoted companies, since their value is a matter of public record and should cause no difficulty. Here, we are concerned with sole traders, partnerships, and limited companies.

The only exceptions to the principle that a detailed and precise valuation is inappropriate would be where one party was likely in the near future to convert

---

[35] *P v P (Financial Provision)* [1989] 2 FLR 241.
[36] [1990] 1 FLR 319.
[37] [2001] 2 FLR 69, Coleridge J. See para **1.51**.
[38] [2005] 2 FLR 365.
[39] For an interesting example of valuation of a minority interest in a company, see the decision of Charles J in *A v A* [2004] EWHC 2818 (Fam), [2006] 2 FLR 115.

his or her interest in the business into a liquid form, for example by sale, retirement or takeover, or where the wife had acquired a quantifiable interest in the business, for example by a direct financial contribution or by working in the business.[40] Perhaps the best test as to the latter point would be to ask whether the wife would be able to prove some beneficial interest in the business if she were a stranger and not involved in matrimonial proceedings; if this were the case, she would be entitled to an interest in the business in her own right, and not only as part of the s 25 exercise, and a more detailed examination might be appropriate.[41]

4.20 If any valuation of the business is to be carried out with a view to relying on it in court proceedings or advice to a client, it will at some stage become necessary to instruct an accountant. A lawyer who relied on his or her own expertise for such a purpose would be in grave danger of an action for negligence. Nevertheless, there are several reasons why the family lawyer should be familiar with methods of valuation. First and foremost, such knowledge enables the lawyer to scrutinise the evidence of experts, to understand the terms which are used, and, if necessary, to challenge it. It is the court which makes the final decision as to such issues, and lawyers must be able to make intelligent and informed submissions to the court, based on an understanding of what the experts have been saying. Secondly, when a case is at an early stage, the lawyer should be able to make a provisional estimate of what a business is likely to be worth, with a view to advising the client and deciding how to conduct the application.

4.21 The value of any business is normally what a willing purchaser would pay for it on an arm's length basis. There are three bases of valuation which an interested purchaser would normally use; these are the asset basis, the dividend yield basis, and the earnings basis. Frequently, a calculation is done on each of these bases and then the results compared to obtain a cross-checked final result.

The asset basis produces the figure which would be obtained if the assets were sold and the business closed down. The problem for the family lawyer with this basis is that the book value of the assets as shown in the balance sheet is almost invariably wrong and of no assistance in calculating the market value of the assets. Expert valuation of the assets is therefore essential, but it would also be necessary to take account of the legal and other costs involved in closing down a business. For the reasons given above, businesses are rarely closed down to provide a lump sum, so, in addition to being the most difficult, this basis of valuation is unlikely to be the one finally relied on by the court.

4.22 The dividend yield basis is equally unlikely to provide a final answer. It gives the value to a potential purchaser who is principally interested in the dividend income from the company. It involves dividing the gross dividend by

---

[40] See eg *Gojkovic v Gojkovic* [1990] 1 FLR 140, CA.
[41] See *White v White* [1998] 2 FLR 310, CA.

the required rate of return to give a value per share. It is therefore necessary to select the rate of return required. This method is usually employed as a cross-check on the result of a calculation on the earnings basis.

The earnings basis of valuation is therefore likely to be the most useful starting point. It involves first establishing the maintainable earnings of the business. This figure will be derived from one or more sources; one would be the most recent year's gross profits. Another would be the average of the last 3 years' gross profits. These could then be compared to obtain the final figure. This figure must then be adjusted to take account of such matters as inappropriate payments of various kinds (eg adding back excessive remuneration or pension contributions) and tax at the current rate must then be deducted.

The figure for maintainable earnings must then be multiplied by the P/E (profits : earnings) ratio appropriate for that type of business. This ratio can be obtained from the FT Actuaries Share Index, published daily, which should be rounded down to the nearest whole number. The resulting figure may then have to be discounted to take account of the size of the business. As a rough rule of thumb, if maintainable earnings are in excess of £1m, no discount need be applied. If the earnings are between £500,000 and £1m, a discount factor of 90% is appropriate, £250,000 to £500,000 would attract a discount of 80%, £100,000 to £250,000, 66%, and less than £100,000, 50%.

It is important to note that a discount factor of, say, 66% means that the result of maintainable earnings multiplied by the P/E ratio is then multiplied by 66%.

Finally, some discount to take account of control, or, rather, lack of control may be necessary. Where the person whose interest is being assessed has more than a 75% interest in the business, no discount need be made. Where it is less than 10%, a discount factor of 45% is appropriate, ie the figure obtained as a result of the last calculation is multiplied by 45%. A holding of 10% to 25% would attract 55%, 25% to 49% would attract 65%, 50% would attract 75%, and 51% to 75% would attract 85%.

4.23   To be able to carry out the calculations as above, or to instruct an expert, certain documents are necessary, and should be obtained at an early date. At the very least the last 3 years' accounts must be obtained; these will enable a preliminary valuation to be done. If an expert is to be instructed he will say what he wants, but this will include the Memorandum and Articles of Association of a company, shareholders' agreements, and internal documents relating to business plans and forecasts, board minutes and cash-flow projections.

Once again, it should be emphasised that the family lawyer should not try to be his or her own expert witness nor to rely on what has been said above as anything other than a guide to help find a way through the thickets of a complicated field. Nevertheless, if it succeeds in giving that limited amount of help, it should prove useful.

4.24 As was said at para **4.16**, after ascertaining the value of the parties' interests in a business, the court must then decide what to do with those figures. The facts of *White v White*[42] and its general relevance have already been considered at paras **1.11** and **1.48**. In the Court of Appeal, Thorpe LJ said that the dominant feature of the case was that from first to last the parties traded as equal partners. Had the partnership been dissolved by the death of either party, the extent of the estate of the deceased partner would have been established according to the law of partnership. Equally, the wife was entitled to her share on dissolution by mutual agreement. Later in the judgment, he said that where the parties had during marriage elected for a financial regime which made each financially independent, one gain might be said to be that they may thereby have obviated the need to embark upon ancillary relief litigation in the event of divorce.

In the light of these principles, Thorpe LJ said that the first fundamental issue was what was the financial worth of the parties on the immediate dissolution of the partnership; the second was whether the court should exercise its powers under s 23 or s 24 to increase the wife's share; the third was, if no, whether the court should exercise its powers to reduce the wife's share. He concluded by saying that 'it offends my sense of fairness that a wife who has worked for over 30 years equally and not nominally in partnership should exit with anything less than her legal entitlement in the absence of extraordinary features'.

Butler-Sloss LJ agreed, adding that there would of course be partnership cases where the starting point for the spouses would have to be adjusted upwards or downwards in the circumstances of the individual case, particularly where there were children. Where the spouses were shown to be genuine partners, the dissolution of their partnership both in marriage and in business ought not to require the intervention of the courts.

4.25 As is now well known, the decision of the Court of Appeal was not upset by the House of Lords, but the dicta of Lord Nicholls suggest that in certain respects the reasoning of the lower court was not to be accepted.[43] As to this specific issue, the House of Lords did not disagree with Thorpe LJ in principle, but expressed the hope that, in the light of the yardstick of equality, it would not be necessary to have a prolonged investigation of the parties' interests in most cases. See also the section on Fairness at paras **1.51** et seq.

TAX CONSIDERATIONS

4.26 Since this is not a textbook on revenue law, only the briefest mention is to be made of this subject; however, it is important that family lawyers should be aware of the tax implications of any proposed order. This will normally involve taking expert advice.

---

[42] [1998] 2 FLR 310, CA.
[43] See Chapter 1 at para **1.48**.

The simplest explanation of this topic is that the sale or transfer of any asset, other than the sole or principal residence of a person, may attract capital gains tax. The tax is on the gain between acquisition and disposal, subject to 'indexation'. When spouses are separated, and assets are sold by one of them to provide a lump sum, tax is, in principle, payable on the gain achieved by the sale. When a matrimonial home, in which both parties have continued to live, is transferred to one of them, the private residence exemption should apply. This also applies even where the transferor has left the home, provided the transferee has continued to live in it.

Before the court can decide whether to order a lump sum payment which is to be funded by the sale of assets, therefore, the tax implications of any sale must be ascertained, and the net effect of these incorporated in the calculations leading to the order.

Chapter 5

TRANSFER OF PROPERTY ORDERS AND HOUSING NEEDS

INTRODUCTION

5.1 Transfer of property orders and housing needs are both topics which, clearly, have to be considered. It has been thought appropriate to combine them in one chapter because of the obvious overlapping nature of the subjects. Nevertheless, it should be remembered that the meeting of housing needs is not the sole purpose of a transfer of property order.

A transfer of property order is an order that one party transfer to the other some property. In most cases this will be real property, such as land or a dwelling-house. However, personal property such as shares, chattels, or even the matrimonial dog may also be the subject of a transfer of property order. The essential nature of the order is that an identifiable and specific item of property is ordered to be transferred; it therefore differs from a lump sum order, which provides for the payment of a sum of money.

5.2 The housing needs of the parties are, almost invariably, a high priority in any ancillary relief application. In many cases, particularly in the lower financial range, the matrimonial home is the sole or principal asset, and the whole case revolves around the housing needs of the parties and their children. The significance of this will be explored in more detail in para **5.6** et seq.

The subject of transfers of tenancy will be considered at para **5.21** et seq. A tenancy may be the subject of a transfer of property order, but there may also be an application pursuant to Part IV of the Family Law Act 1996 (FLA 1996).

The wording of transfer of property orders may be particularly important, and is considered in some detail at para **5.10** et seq.

STATUTORY PROVISION

5.3   A transfer of property order is a type of property adjustment order,[1] the other two types being settlement of property orders and variation of settlement; the latter two are dealt with elsewhere. This is the most common form of property adjustment order.

It is provided that:

> 'on granting a decree of divorce, a decree of nullity of marriage or a decree of judicial separation or at any time thereafter (whether, in the case of a decree of divorce or of nullity of marriage, before or after the decree is made absolute) the court may make . . .
>
> (a)   an order that a party to the marriage shall transfer to the other party, to any child of the family or to such person as may be specified in the order for the benefit of such a child such property as may be so specified, being property to which the first-mentioned party is entitled, either in possession or reversion.'[2]

It will be noted that the order may be made only on or after the grant of a decree; there is no provision for interim orders. It will also be seen that the court may make 'an order'; the court may not make more than one order, although it may, of course, provide for the transfer of more than one item of property in the same order.

Clearly, the person ordered to transfer may only transfer property which he is entitled to transfer, ie that which he owns. However, this may include property in which he has a joint interest (eg with the applicant) or a reversionary interest.

The provisions as to children are considered in more detail in Chapter 11.

RULES

5.4   There are certain requirements in the rules which are specific to transfer of property orders; these are considered in more detail in Chapter 16.

THE BASIS ON WHICH ORDERS ARE MADE

5.5   As always, it must be said that the only basis on which the court makes any order for ancillary relief is the consideration and balancing of the factors in MCA 1973, s 25, and the position is no different in relation to transfer of property orders. The proper approach to ancillary relief is dealt with in more

---

[1]   MCA 1973, s 21(2)(a).
[2]   Ibid, s 24(1)(a).

detail in Chapter 1 and need not be considered in such detail here. Nevertheless, the question of housing needs is usually important, and it is therefore appropriate to consider that as a preliminary matter.

5.6   In one leading case,[3] Thorpe LJ said that it was one of the paramount considerations in applying the s 25 criteria to endeavour to stretch what was available to cover the need of each party for a home, particularly where there were young children involved. Obviously the primary carer needed whatever was available to make a main home for the children, but it was of importance, albeit of lesser importance, that the other party should have a home of his own where the children could enjoy their contact time with him. In any case, where there was, by stretch and a degree of risk-taking, the possibility of a division to enable both parties to rehouse themselves, that was an exceptionally important consideration and one which would almost invariably have a decisive impact on the outcome. In the instant case, the resources were available to make a division which would, just about, enable each to rehouse and the judge's order, which had awarded the husband a lump sum of an insufficient size, was set aside and a larger sum awarded.

5.7   This is an important restatement of, and compelling authority for, a general principle which the courts have normally striven to observe. That the need for a roof over one's head is one of the most basic human needs is a principle which hardly needs restating, and housing must, therefore, be one of the most important financial needs to be met pursuant to s 25(2)(b). However, it has also been emphasised[4] that the statement of the desirability of the non-caring parent having his or her accommodation should not be elevated into a rigid rule of law; there was no rule of law that each party must be able to purchase a property, and each case depends on its own facts.

Sometimes, when assets are severely limited, the needs of one party have to give way to the needs of the family as a whole and the requirement to treat the welfare of the children as the first consideration pursuant to s 25(1). A home for the minor children is normally the principal requirement. However, that does not always mean that they should continue to occupy the former matrimonial home; that may be a desirable objective in many cases, but where they could be satisfactorily rehoused in cheaper accommodation, thereby releasing capital for the rehousing of the non-carer, that is an option which should be adopted.

Each case will, of course, turn on its own facts. Ability to borrow is an important feature of such cases, and is regarded as a resource under s 25(2)(a).

5.8   The fact that one party (and the children) have to occupy a particular property does not always mean that that party is entitled to the sole ownership of that property. In the following section the various options for the court are

---

3   *M v B (Ancillary Proceedings: Lump Sum)* [1998] 1 FLR 53, CA.
4   In *Piglowska v Piglowski* [1999] 2 FLR 763, HL.

considered, and clearly an outright transfer is not always appropriate. Where a property could be sold after the children had ceased to need it as their residence and some capital released for the non-carer, this is an option which the court should consider. This might be attractive where the non-carer was going to be under a continuing obligation to pay periodical payments as well as sacrificing all his capital. However, the factors which might persuade a court to the contrary view are:

–   the desire of most parties for finality;

–   the undesirability in some cases of maintaining a link between the non-carer and the carer;

–   uncertainty as to the future ability of the carer to rehouse himself or herself once the children had gone;

–   the value of the property in question;

–   the length of time which was likely to elapse before the property could be sold; and

–   the fact that ownership of a property, particularly one of modest value, is not always a markedly superior position to that of someone entitled to reasonably secure rented accommodation.

5.9   When assessing housing needs, the court must take account of the effect of its proposed order on those directly affected by its decision; in one case,[5] that was described as 'the court's primary if not exclusive concern'. In that case the judge had held that he should not make an order which might be regarded as usurping the role of the local housing authority, but on appeal this was held to be an incorrect approach. Phillips LJ said that he did not see how the court could perform its duty without taking into account what would happen to those deprived of the right to live in the matrimonial home. However, he went on to say that this necessarily involved having regard to the effect of the local authority housing policy, and he did not think it correct to describe the effect of such an approach as being to manipulate housing lists or to usurp the function of the council.

The fact that one party may be eligible for local authority housing is therefore a valid consideration, although, once again, each case will turn on its own facts.

TYPES OF TRANSFER OF PROPERTY ORDERS

5.10   Once the court has decided the overall scheme of its disposition this must be incorporated into an order, and in many cases the order might take a variety

---

5   *Jones v Jones* [1997] 1 FLR 27, CA.

of forms. In this section it is intended to set out the various types of order which may be made. Some of these orders, while being property adjustment orders, would properly fall under the heading of settlement of property or variation of settlement orders; however, for convenience, they are all set out here. Forms of order will be found at Appendix A.

5.11 Although it may seem simplistic to make this point, it is extremely important for the practitioners to have seen the deeds or land certificate to the property well before the application is heard. The information which lay clients give about ownership of property is not always accurate and it is important to be aware of the exact nature of the title and any incumbrances.

As a final preliminary point, it should be noted that there are many references in the text and elsewhere to trusts for sale of land. As a result of the Trusts of Land and Appointment of Trustees Act 1996 (TLATA 1996), trusts for sale have been replaced by trusts of land. The wording of any orders now made will therefore have to reflect that change.

Outright transfer

5.12 The simplest form of order which can be made is for one party to transfer to the other his or her estate or interest (whether sole or joint) in a property.[6] When the property to be transferred is mortgaged, the order would have to provide either for the simultaneous redemption of the mortgage (eg by a separate order for payment of a lump sum for this purpose), or for the transfer to be subject to the existing charge (this would be the case even if the order did not provide for it). A mortgagee cannot prevent a transfer, but if the property were merely transferred subject to the charge, the property would be at risk if the terms of the mortgage were not observed and the transferor would continue to be liable under the mortgage covenants.

This frequently has to be the position. However, an order in these circumstances should normally also contain an undertaking by the transferee to perform the obligations of the mortgage and to indemnify the transferor against liability under the mortgage.

5.13 A possible variation of this type of outright transfer order would be to transfer in return for some consideration. This consideration could take the form of a cash payment, or the discharge of the transferor's obligation to pay periodical payments by a clean break order.[7] The latter order might be appropriate where the value of the property transferred was roughly equivalent to the value of the lost benefits. It might also be appropriate where it was clear that the transferor would be unable to make any significant contribution to the support of the transferee, and it was important for the transferee (and any

---

6   As was done in *Hanlon v Hanlon* [1978] 1 WLR 592, CA. If the house were to be sold, neither party could rehouse themselves on 50% of the proceeds. The husband was earning significantly more and it was better that the parties knew where they stood.

7   As in *Mortimer v Mortimer-Griffin* [1986] 2 FLR 315, CA.

children) to have settled accommodation. In *Lawrence v Bertram (Judgment on Preliminary Issue)*[8] it was held that the court had jurisdiction to order a transfer of property on condition that the transferee pay the transferor a fixed sum.

In the absence of other factors, it would not be appropriate where the value of the interest transferred was significantly less than the lost benefits. The desire of the transferee for certainty should not obscure the need for her advisers to have regard to the circumstances in which a clean break order is inappropriate.[9]

Similarly, a potential transferor should be aware that, even if the transferee's right to periodical payments can be extinguished, the same does not apply to the children, and even if a mother undertook not to claim for the children this would not be binding on the Child Support Agency.

Transfer subject to charge

5.14   An order may provide for the transfer to one party of a property, subject to a charge in favour of the transferor for payment of a sum of money. Such a payment would be required either on a fixed date[10] or on the occurrence of a certain event or the first of certain events, such as the death or remarriage of the transferee, the children attaining their majority or ceasing full-time education or some other event.[11] The payment to be made could be expressed as a fixed monetary amount, but it is more common, and normally preferable, for it to be a percentage of the gross or net proceeds of sale.[12]

Orders frequently provide for the enforcement of the charge on the remarriage or cohabitation of the transferee. Where there are dependent children, this should be subject to the proviso that any enforcement on this ground should be subject to the leave of the court. In any event, the provision as to cohabitation is liable to raise problems, since cohabitation may be difficult to define and, even if proved, may not endure. Perhaps a better form of words would be: 'if any adult person other than the [transferee] and the children of the family occupies the property as his or her home for a period, whether continuous or cumulative, in excess of six months save with the written consent of the [transferor]'.

An order that the property 'stand charged' with payment of a certain sum on terms is valid and will be recognised by the Land Registry. However, this may be a less desirable form of order than the alternative which is to order the transfer in return for the delivery to the transferor of a charge duly executed by the transferee, such charge to be in a form agreed between the solicitors for the

---

8   *Croydon County Court* [2004] Fam Law 323. This is a decision of a circuit judge in a county court and is therefore only a persuasive authority but there seems no reason to doubt it.
9   See generally Chapter 2, para **2.28**.
10   *Knibb v Knibb* [1987] 2 FLR 396.
11   As in *Hector v Hector* [1973] 1 WLR 1122, CA.
12   See *McDonnell v McDonnell* (1976) 120 SJ 87, CA.

parties and, in default of agreement, to be settled by the district judge. The parties and, in default, the court, then retain some control over the terms on which the transferee occupies the property.

5.15 A brief but not exhaustive list of the possible problems which should be eliminated by a properly drawn charge is as follows.

(a) The right to redeem. In the absence of this, a mortgagee entitled to e g 30% of the net proceeds of sale could insist on a sale of the property.

(b) Provision for determination of the value of the property in the event of dispute, e g by a chartered surveyor.

(c) A bare charge for moneys on demand entitles the chargee to possession of the property without proof of breach of any term. Even where this does not apply, a chargee is entitled to take possession on breach, e g if the charge is not redeemed on the fixed date. The charge should be so drawn as to prevent either of these possibilities.

(d) Where there is no prior mortgage, or that mortgage is redeemed, the chargee is entitled to hold the deeds. This might not be desirable in many post-matrimonial situations.

(e) Unless there is express power to tack, the chargor cannot raise any further money on the security of the property. The power to lease should also be restricted.

(f) The right to move house and transfer the charge to another property, e g during the minority of the children should be considered.

Mesher orders

5.16 A *Mesher* order, so called after the eponymous case,[13] is essentially a postponement of the exercise of a trust for sale until a named event occurs; this is normally connected with the children of the family. In the case itself, the order was for the matrimonial home to be held on trust for sale for the parties in equal shares, and that the house be not sold for so long as the child of the family was under the age of 17 or until further order.[14] The wife was to live there rent-free but had to pay the outgoings, and capital repayments of the mortgage were to be shared equally. Strictly speaking, it is a settlement order rather than a transfer of property order.

Such an order may be amended to take account of the circumstances of a particular case. For example, the 'trigger event' for sale of the house could be

---

[13] *Mesher v Mesher and Hall* [1980] 1 All ER 126, CA.

[14] 'Until further order' entitles the court to make an order for earlier sale, if appropriate, but not to postpone the sale; see *Carson v Carson* [1983] 1 WLR 285, CA, and *Norman v Norman* (1983) FLR 446.

expressed as the first of various occurrences including the death or remarriage of the carer spouse, the children continuing in full-time education, or further order; the division of the proceeds of sale could be other than equal; and the occupying party could be required to pay an occupation rent.[15]

5.17 Some of the comments on orders for transfer subject to chargeback set out at para **5.14** apply equally to *Mesher* orders. The orders can also be refined to provide for the exclusive occupation of the home by the occupying party.[16] However, there are more fundamental objections to *Mesher* orders which cannot always be met by different wordings, and whether the court's objectives could be met by other means should always be considered.

One reason why a *Mesher* order might be unsuitable would be the undesirability in a particular case of the parties remaining joined together in property ownership. However, the principal objection to these orders is the state of uncertainty in which the parties might be left. When these orders were more fashionable, there were many cases in which 'the chickens came home to roost' a number of years later, and it was found that one or even both parties were unable to rehouse themselves from the available funds.[17]

In *B v B (Mesher Order)*[18] it was held that a *Mesher* order was inappropriate where there was a young child, and the commitment of the mother to child rearing would mean that her ability to generate capital would be much less than that of her husband. The result would be inequality of outcome which was discriminatory and unacceptable. This is an interesting gloss on the meaning of equality in the post-*White* and *Lambert* world.

With that in mind, and in the light of the requirement for the court to strive to make such order as will enable both parties to rehouse themselves, it can be said that it would now be unusual for the court to make a *Mesher* order unless it were satisfied, by credible evidence, either that the eventual net proceeds of sale would be sufficient to provide for both parties, or that, for some reason, this was not necessary or desirable.

5.18 In summary, therefore, there may well be cases in which a *Mesher* order would be suitable, but in most cases an alternative form of order will probably be preferable.

---

[15] As in *Harvey v Harvey* (1982) FLR 141, CA.
[16] See *Allen v Allen* [1986] 2 FLR 265, CA.
[17] See *Mortimer v Mortimer-Griffin* [1986] 2 FLR 315, CA; *Carson v Carson* (above); *Norman v Norman* (above); *Thompson v Thompson* [1985] FLR 863, CA.
[18] [2002] EWHC 3106 (Fam), [2003] 2 FLR 285.

Martin orders

5.19 A *Martin* order[19] is, in effect, a refinement of a *Mesher* order. It provides for the postponement of the trust for sale and for the division of the net proceeds when sold, but also provides for the property to be settled on the occupying party for life or until remarriage or voluntary removal. Such orders have been further refined to provide for the occupying party to pay an occupation rent,[20] or for the right of occupation to terminate on the wife's cohabitation. A more sophisticated form of order was that in *Chamberlain v Chamberlain*[21] where it was ordered that the property should not be sold until every child of the family had ceased to receive full-time education or thereafter without leave of the court or with the consent of the parties.

Martin orders are clearly appropriate where the justice of the case demands that one party be entitled to occupy a property for as long as he or she wishes, but it is not intended to deprive the other party of his or her capital entitlement for ever and even in the event of the other party's death.

Other orders

5.20 The orders set out above are the principal types of orders made for transfer of property and/or settlement of property. It should not be forgotten that the court may also order the immediate sale of a property and the division of the net proceeds of sale in whatever proportions appear appropriate in suitable cases.

An interesting case involving transfer of shares in a company is *C v C (Company Shares)*[22] where Coleridge J held that, where a wife had played a part, and wished to continue to play a part in the future of a company, there had to be a compelling reason why she should not be entitled to do so. Where the wife had made out a sensible case for holding shares, the court should, in fairness, accede to it.

TRANSFER OF TENANCY

5.21 When the interest or estate which the parties to an ancillary relief application have in a property is a tenancy and not ownership of the property, different considerations arise from those already considered. In principle, the court must deal with the application in the same way as any other, namely by application of the s 25 factors. However, there are additional matters to be borne in mind.

---

[19] Named after *Martin v Martin* [1978] Fam 12, CA. See also *Bateman v Bateman* [1979] Fam 25; *Clutton v Clutton* [1991] 1 FLR 242, CA.

[20] *Harvey v Harvey* (above).

[21] [1973] 1 WLR 1557, CA.

[22] [2003] 2 FLR 493.

Perhaps, at the outset, it should be made clear that most of the tenancies which will be the subject of an application will be local authority or social housing tenancies. This is because most tenancies in the private sector are now shorthold tenancies which are likely to contain a covenant against assignment (as to which, see para **5.22**) or to be of so short a period as not to be worth transferring.

5.22 It has been held[23] that a tenancy is 'property' for the purposes of s 24(1)(a) and is therefore capable of being transferred pursuant to an order. There are two ways in which such an order may be obtained, and the choice will depend on the terms of the tenancy.

While the court has jurisdiction to make an order for transfer of a tenancy under s 24(1)(a), it should not exercise its discretion to do so when its order would be rendered ineffective by a covenant against assignment or where it would interfere with the statutory duties and discretion of a local housing authority.[24] If, therefore, there is a covenant against assignment, so that the tenant has contractually agreed not to assign, it has been said that it is doubtful that the court would transfer the tenancy.[25]

However, this statement may be subject to doubt, at least as far as council tenants are concerned, since in another decision of the Court of Appeal[26] it was described as out of date on the ground that, since the Housing Act 1980, council tenants had security of tenure and even the right to buy.

In any event, the position would be different where the local housing authority had expressly declined to become involved on behalf of either party but made it clear that it had no objection to transfer.

5.23 In a case where s 24 could not be invoked, an application for transfer of tenancy may be made under FLA 1996, Sch 7. This empowers the court to order the transfer of a protected or statutory tenancy, a statutory tenancy within the meaning of the Rent (Agriculture) Act 1976, a secure tenancy within the meaning of the Housing Act 1985, s 79, or an assured tenancy or assured agricultural tenancy within the meaning of Part I of the Housing Act 1988. In the case of spouses, past or present, the court has jurisdiction to make an order whenever it has power to make a property adjustment order.

It will be noted that shorthold tenancies are not included in the list of tenancies which may be transferred. However, secure tenancies are included, and the Act provides a procedure for allowing landlords to be heard and provides a checklist for the guidance of the court. It is for this reason that it can be said

---

23   *Thompson v Thompson* [1976] Fam 25, CA.
24   See *Regan v Regan* [1977] 1 WLR 84; *Hale v Hale* [1975] 1 WLR 931. See also *Newlon Housing Trust v Alsulaimen* [1997] 1 FLR 914, CA.
25   Most recently in *Newlon Housing Trust v Alsulaimen* (above).
26   *Jones v Jones* [1997] 1 FLR 27, CA.

that even where there is a covenant against assignment, the court has jurisdiction to consider an application under this statute.

5.24 The procedure for applying for a transfer of tenancy under FLA 1996, Sch 7 is set out in FPR 1991, r 3.6(7)–(9).[27] Application is made by originating application supported by affidavit and not as the Standard FLA forms.

TAX IMPLICATIONS

5.25 This topic has been considered at para **4.26**.

---

[27] Applied by FPR 1991, r 3.8(14).

Chapter 6

SETTLEMENT OF PROPERTY ORDERS AND VARIATION OF SETTLEMENTS

INTRODUCTION

6.1   As was seen in Chapter 5, when dealing with transfer of property orders, settlement of property orders and transfer of property orders are both types of property adjustment order and, to a large extent, overlap. For example, a *Mesher* order,[1] often regarded as a typical transfer of property order, is in reality a settlement of property order. The distinction is, for most purposes, immaterial, and in Chapter 5 the general principles governing the making of all such orders involving property were considered. In this chapter, therefore, it is proposed to consider only the special characteristics of settlement orders and also the subject of variation of settlement.

STATUTORY PROVISION

6.2   The power to order settlement of property or variation of settlement is contained in s 24 of MCA 1973 which provides that on granting a decree of divorce, a decree of nullity of marriage, or a decree of judicial separation or at any time thereafter (whether, in the case of a decree of divorce or of nullity of marriage, before or after the decree is made absolute) the court may make one or more of the following orders, that is to say:

'(b)   an order that a settlement of such property as may be so specified, being property to which a party to the marriage is so entitled, be made to the satisfaction of the court for the benefit of the other party to the marriage and of the children of the family or either or any of them;

(c)   an order varying for the benefit of the parties to the marriage and of the children of the family or either or any of them any ante-nuptial or post-nuptial settlement (including such a settlement made by will or codicil) made on the parties to the marriage, other than one in the form of a pension arrangement (within the meaning of section 25D . . .);

(d)   an order extinguishing or reducing the interest of either of the parties to the marriage under any settlement, other than one in the form of a pension arrangement (within the meaning of section 25D . . .).'[2]

---

[1]   *Mesher v Mesher and Hall* [1980] 1 All ER 126, CA.
[2]   MCA 1973, s 24(1).

6.3   These orders are, therefore, only capable of being made after decree. There is no provision for any interim relief of this nature.

WHAT IS A SETTLEMENT?

6.4   This is considered in more detail at para **6.9**.

6.5   With the exception of *Mesher* and *Martin*[3] -type orders, settlement orders are quite rare today. The reason for this is the comparatively sophisticated range of orders of other kinds available under the statute, and the fact that settlements of land are unusual in any circumstances in contemporary conditions. It is therefore not proposed to spend much time considering the requirements for settlement orders.

6.6   It should be noted that the power to settle is not limited in any way. When, therefore, the court considers that a settlement order is appropriate, it may do so in a wide variety of ways.[4] Since, with the exception of *Mesher* or *Martin* orders, this will be quite unusual, it is not proposed to consider the matter further here.

VARIATION OF SETTLEMENT

6.7   As has been seen, the statute confers on the court wide jurisdiction to vary or discharge settlements. This was once an important part of the court's jurisdiction on marriage breakdown, but has become comparatively rare. When marriage settlements were common and the court had restricted powers, the power to vary the settlement was clearly significant. Now that such settlements are less common and, in any event, the court enjoys wide discretionary powers, it is unusual for the court to have to exercise this branch of its jurisdiction. A modern example of a case in which the court would have had no means of providing for a party (in terms of pension provision) except by way of variation of settlement is *Brooks v Brooks*, considered at para **6.10**.

6.8   Having said that, it must also be said that the approach of the court when dealing with such applications must be exactly the same as in any other ancillary relief application. The s 25 factors must be observed, and the interest of either party under a settlement is one of the assets to be brought into the calculations under s 25(2)(a). It will be for the court to consider the settlement in the light of the overall picture, and to decide how, if at all, it should be varied.

6.9   The first matter to be proved is, of course, that there is an ante-nuptial or post-nuptial settlement. The court interprets the term 'settlement' in a liberal

---

3   *Martin v Martin* [1976] Fam 335.
4   For an example, see *Tavoulareas v Tavoulareas* [1998] 2 FLR 418, CA.

manner and is not constrained by conveyancing concepts. The form is not the most important element; settlements can range from the strict settlement which would be easily recognised by a chancery lawyer to a mere covenant to pay periodic amounts. The settlement may be contained in a separation agreement, a will or codicil, or any document.

What is important is that the settlement provide for the financial benefit of one of the spouses and with reference to their married state.[5] A mere gift between spouses, or by a third party to a spouse, does not of itself create a settlement. An agreement to pay sums of money to a spouse after the marriage came to an end has been held to lack the required nuptial element.[6]

6.10 In *Brooks v Brooks*,[7] the parties had married in 1977 and in 1980 the husband's company set up a non-contributory pension scheme for him. It included the right for him to elect on retirement to give up a portion of his pension to provide on his death a deferred pension to his spouse or other person financially dependent on him. It was held that this was a post-nuptial settlement which the court could vary. The significance of *Brooks v Brooks* in terms of pensions has now diminished due to the effect of the Welfare Reform and Pensions Act 1999 (WRPA 1999) (see Chapter 10, para **10.4**).

In his speech, Lord Nicholls conceded the wide interpretation given to 'settlement' and said that the disposition must be one which makes some form of continuing provision for both or either of the parties to the marriage, with or without provision for their children. A disposition which conferred an immediate, absolute interest in an item of property would not constitute a settlement; in such a case, the appropriate remedy (if remedy were needed) would be a property transfer order or property settlement order. The authorities had consistently given a wide meaning to settlement in this context and had spelled out no precise limitation. A disposition which created interests in succession in specified property would cause no difficulty, nor where such interests were concurrent but discretionary. Concurrent joint interests, such as where parties to a marriage hold the matrimonial home as joint tenants or tenants in common, were 'near the borderline' but there was (rightly) authority[8] for holding this to be within the scope of the section. Income provision from settled property would readily qualify, and it was 'only a short step' to include income provision which took the form of an obligation by one party to the marriage to make periodical payments to the other.

6.11 In *Charamalous v Charamalous*[9] it was held that, provided it existed at the date of the order, the court has jurisdiction under section 24(1)(c) to vary a settlement that, at the date it was made, was ante or post-nuptial, notwithstanding that, prior to the date of the order, the features that made it

---

5 *Prescott (formerly Fellowes) v Fellowes* [1958] P 260, CA.
6 *Young v Young* [1962] P 27, CA.
7 [1996] 1 AC 375, [1995] 2 FLR 13, HL.
8 In *Brown v Brown* [1959] P 86.
9 [2004] 2 FLR 1093, CA.

nuptial had been removed. In this case the Court accorded primacy to the ancillary relief regime over the trust regime and emphasised the incapacity of individuals to elect out of it. The nuptial character or otherwise of a settlement was held to be a question of fact.

6.12 The powers of the court to vary the settlement are wide:

–   the capital or income can be given to either party or to the children;[10]

–   the interest of a party under the settlement can be extinguished;

–   the settlement may be terminated; the property contained in the settlement may be resettled.[11]

When the property contained in the settlement is the matrimonial home, the various options adopted in transfer of property orders may be employed. The court has the power to require separate representation of children where there may be a conflict of interest,[12] and other third parties must be given the right to be heard.[13] It has been held that, on an application under this section the court has power to remove a trustee.[14]

In the older cases it was held that the court would not interfere with the terms of a settlement more than was necessary to do justice between the parties.[15] Clearly, today the court has wide powers of redistribution, and is more prepared to intervene in the parties' affairs than was once the case. Nevertheless, in a 1989 case[16] dealing with a post-nuptial settlement, Ewbank J said that his first consideration was the welfare of the children and the second consideration was that he should not interfere with the settlement more than was necessary for the purposes of the s 25 factors. In another more recent case[17] involving a lump sum (and not variation of settlement), Thorpe J said that the discretionary powers of the court to adjust capital shares between the parties should not be exercised unless there was a manifest need for intervention upon the application of the s 25 criteria; it might be said that this statement of principle echoes the older cases on this subject and is equally valid in this context.

---

[10]   See e g *E v E* [1990] 2 FLR 233; *Jump v Jump* [1883] 8 PD 159.

[11]   *Bacon v Bacon* [1947] P 151.

[12]   FPR 1991, r 2.57.

[13]   Ibid, r 2.59(3).

[14]   *E v E (Financial Provision)* [1990] 2 FLR 233, per Ewbank J; for a different, albeit older, view, see *Compton v Compton and Hussey* [1960] P 201.

[15]   See e g *Smith v Smith and Graves* (1887) 12 PD 102; *Ulrich v Ulrich and Felton* [1968] 1 All ER 67; *Egerton v Egerton* [1949] 2 All ER 238, CA.

[16]   *E v E* [1990] 2 FLR 233.

[17]   *H v H (Financial Provision: Capital Allowance)* [1993] 2 FLR 335 at p 348.

Chapter 7

ORDERS FOR SALE

INTRODUCTION

7.1   The effect of an order for ancillary relief is frequently that property must be sold. This may happen as a direct result of the order, for example if the former matrimonial home is to be sold, or perhaps when some asset has to be sold to provide a lump sum for one of the parties. This chapter will consider briefly the types of order for sale which may be made and the law and practice involved.

ORDER FOR SALE UNDER SECTION 24A OF MCA 1973

7.2   Statutory power of sale is provided by s 24A which provides that:

> 'Where the court makes under section 23 or 24 of this Act a secured periodical payments order, an order for the payment of a lump sum or a property adjustment order, then, on making that order or at any time thereafter, the court may make a further order for the sale of such property as may be specified in the order, being property in which or in the proceeds of sale of which either or both of the parties to the marriage has or have a beneficial interest, either in possession or reversion.'[1]

7.3   This power of sale is, therefore, ancillary to the principal capital order which has been made, and is only exercisable if such an order has been made.[2] An order for a lump sum, property adjustment or secured provision takes effect only on decree absolute, so no order could be made under this section to take effect before that time.[3] Subject to that proviso, the order may be made either at the same time as making the principal order or at any time thereafter; however, it must be the case that the court could not make such an order if the principal order had been complied with.

The order may contain a provision that it shall not take effect until the occurrence of an event specified by the order or the expiration of a period so specified. The court has, therefore, considerable discretion as to the terms which it imposes.

---

[1]   MCA 1973, s 24A(1).
[2]   *Thompson v Thompson* [1986] Fam 38.
[3]   MCA 1973, s 24A(3).

7.4   Section 24A also contains further provisions ancillary to the power to order sale. It is provided that any order for sale may contain such consequential or supplementary provisions as the court thinks fit and, without prejudice to the generality of those provisions, may include:

> '(a)   provision requiring the making of a payment out of the proceeds of sale of the property to which the order relates, and
> (b)   provision requiring any such property to be offered for sale to a person or class of persons specified in the order.'[4]

The order could, therefore, for example, require the sale of a property owned by the respondent, and the payment of a lump sum from the proceeds of sale with the balance to be paid to the respondent; or the sale of a jointly owned former matrimonial home, with a requirement that one of the parties to the marriage and his or her cohabitant be entitled to bid. It is not uncommon for such orders to provide that the property be sold for the best offer received in excess of a certain figure.

What the order cannot do is require payments to third parties such as creditors who have no connection with the property or the sale thereof;[5] it would be proper to include an order for payment of estate agents' charges but not for payment of debts owed by the parties.

7.5   When the property in respect of which sale is sought is owned jointly by one of the parties and a third party, it is provided that:

> 'before deciding whether to make an order under this section in relation to that property, it shall be the duty of the court to give that other person an opportunity to make representations with respect to the order; and any representations made by that other person shall be included among the circumstances to which the court is required to have regard under section 25(1) . . .'[6]

It follows from this that the court must direct service of all relevant proceedings on the third party; procedure for this is considered in more detail at Chapter 16, para **16.9**. In *Ram v Ram (No 2)* [2004] EWCA Civ 1684, [2005] 2 FLR 75 it was held that the court's power under s 24A is limited to property in which either or both of the parties has or have a beneficial interest in possession or reversion. Thus, where a bankruptcy order has been made and the property therefore vested in the tree, the bankrupt has no beneficial interest even after his discharge.

---

[4]   MCA 1973, s 24A(2).
[5]   *Burton v Burton* [1986] 2 FLR 419.
[6]   MCA 1973, s 24A(6).

HOW IS JURISDICTION EXERCISED?

7.6 There is no separate set of guidelines applicable to orders under s 24A. An order under this section is an order to which s 25 applies, and the exercise of the court's discretion will be governed by the usual s 25 factors. An order under s 24A may be made if the court considers it necessary to do so to achieve its purpose pursuant to s 25.

INTERIM ORDERS

7.7 There is no power to make an interim order for sale under s 24A or, indeed, under any other provision. This is considered in more detail at Chapter 4, para **4.5**.

ORDERS UNDER RSC ORDER 31, RULE 1

7.8 RSC Ord 31, r 1 provides that:

'where, in any cause or matter in the Chancery Division relating to any land, it appears necessary or expedient for the purposes of the cause or matter that the land or any part thereof should be sold, the court may order that land or part to be sold and any party bound by the order and in possession of that land or part, or in receipt of the rents and profits thereof, may be compelled to deliver up such possession or receipt to the purchaser or to such other person as the court may direct.

In this order, "land" includes any interest in, or right over, land.'

By FPR 1991, r 2.64(3):

'RSC Order 31, rule 1 (power to order sale of land) shall apply to applications for ancillary relief as it applies to causes and matters in the Chancery Division.'

7.9 It may be thought that, in view of the specific and wide powers contained in s 24A, this provision is unnecessary to found jurisdiction to order sale. Nevertheless, the power is there if needed. The real usefulness of this provision probably lies in the fact that it enables the court to require one party with an interest in a property to vacate it before sale; this might be necessary where one party occupied the property and was obstructing sale.[7]

7.10 It has been held that RSC Ord 31, r 1 does not permit the court to order an interim sale of a property pending the final resolution of an application for ancillary relief.[8]

---

[7] As was the case in *Crosthwaite v Crosthwaite* [1989] 2 FLR 86, CA, the decision in which case was probably responsible for the introduction of FPR 1991, r 2.64(3).

[8] *Wicks v Wicks* [1998] 1 FLR 470, CA.

THE TRUSTS OF LAND AND APPOINTMENT OF TRUSTEES ACT 1996

7.11 Under s 30 of the Law of Property Act 1925 (LPA 1925), when property was held on trust for sale (which was always the case when jointly owned) either trustee could apply to the court for an order for sale, which would be granted unless, for example, it could be found that the purposes for which the trust was established (such as the provision of a family home) had not been fulfilled. Section 30 has now been repealed by the Trusts of Land and Appointment of Trustees Act 1996 (TLATA 1996) and, for the purposes of this chapter, the important part of this statute is s 14 which permits the court to order sale.

The difference between s 14 and LPA 1925, s 30 is that there is now no presumption as to an order for sale. Instead, the court is directed by s 15 to have regard to various matters such as the intentions of the persons who created the trust, the purposes for which the property is held, the welfare of any minor occupying the property, and the interests of any secured creditor.

7.12 It is unlikely that it will be necessary to make an application under s 14 in the course of an application for ancillary relief. Nevertheless, the statutory powers exist, and it may be necessary to have them in mind as a fall-back position in some situations.[9]

For further discussion in the context of insolvency, see Chapter 12, para **12.20**.

---

[9]   See the discussion at Chapter 4, para **4.5**.

Chapter 8

AVOIDANCE OF DISPOSITION AND OTHER INJUNCTIONS

INTRODUCTION

8.1   The course of an application for ancillary relief does not always run smoothly. Sometimes, orders are not obeyed, parties are less than frank, and, in extreme cases, there may be a concerted effort to defeat the just entitlement of one of the parties by the other party. The court therefore has to have powers to overcome such stratagems.

These powers may be summarised as follows:

(a)   the power to prevent or set aside a disposition under s 37 of MCA 1973;

(b)   a similar power under the inherent jurisdiction of the court;

(c)   the power to grant a freezing injunction;

(d)   the power to grant a search order.

8.2   These powers and remedies will be considered in turn. The first is by far the most common.

APPLICATIONS UNDER MCA 1973, SECTION 37 FOR AN AVOIDANCE OF DISPOSITION ORDER

8.3   It is provided that:

'Where proceedings for financial relief are brought by one person against another, the court may, on the application of the first-mentioned person—

(a)   if it is satisfied that the other party to the proceedings is, with the intention of defeating the claim for financial relief, about to make any disposition or to transfer out of the jurisdiction or otherwise deal with any property, make such order as it thinks fit for restraining the other party from so doing or otherwise for protecting the claim;

(b)   if it is satisfied that the other party has, with that intention, made a reviewable disposition and that if the disposition were set aside financial relief or different financial relief would be granted to the applicant, make an order setting aside the disposition;

(c)   if it is satisfied, in a case where an order has been obtained under any of the provisions mentioned in subsection (1) above by the applicant against the other party, that the other party has, with that intention, made a reviewable disposition, make an order setting aside the disposition;

and an application for the purposes of paragraph (b) above shall be made in the proceedings for the financial relief in question.'[1]

8.4   Section 37(2) refers to s 37(1) which is a definition section. There, it is provided that, for the purposes of s 37:

'. . . "financial relief" means relief under any of the provisions of sections 22, 23, 24, 24B, 27, 31 (except subsection (6)) and 35 above, and any reference in this section to defeating a person's claim for financial relief is a reference to preventing financial relief from being granted to that person, or to that person for the benefit of a child of the family, or reducing the amount of any financial relief which might be so granted, or frustrating or impeding the enforcement of any order which might be or has been made at his instance under any of those provisions.'[2]

Issues arising out of these provisions will now be considered in turn.

Two types of remedy

8.5   Section 37 gives the right to apply for two distinct remedies. The first, which is pre-emptive, is the power of the court to prevent a disposition before it has been made. Thus, for example, a spouse who threatened to transfer assets to another person, or to squander some asset, could be ordered not to do so; banks or other financial institutions can be served with copies of any order made which would normally have the result of freezing transactions.

The second is the power to undo or set aside any disposition which has been made. Where a spouse transfers assets to another with the intention of putting them out of reach of the court, the person to whom the assets were transferred can be ordered to transfer them back so that they may form part of the funds available for distribution between the parties. This provision itself falls into two categories, namely the power to set aside in anticipation of an ancillary relief hearing, and the power to set aside at or after the hearing.

Separate factors obviously govern these two remedies, but there are a number of common factors which will be considered.

---

[1]   MCA 1973, s 37(2).
[2]   Ibid, s 37(1).

The requirement for an application for ancillary relief

8.6 Section 37 is best regarded as a remedy ancillary to an application for ancillary relief; there cannot be a free-standing s 37 application. Subsection (2) begins by requiring that financial proceedings are brought by one person against another, and there can be no application under s 37 unless this has happened. Where the applicant is a petitioner, or a respondent who has filed an answer, the prayer for ancillary relief contained in the petition or answer will be deemed sufficient for this purpose, although it would normally be considered right to require a Form A to have been issued; s 37 is a discretionary remedy, and the court would not normally think it right to make an order unless satisfied that the application for financial relief was to proceed.

The application for financial relief may be filed at court at the same time as the s 37 application. In cases of urgency, the court will accept an undertaking to file the application by a fixed date.

8.7 'Financial relief' is defined by s 37(1) as, in effect, an application for either a financial provision order, a property adjustment order, an order for maintenance pending suit, an order on the ground of neglect to maintain, or a variation order.

Only the applicant can apply

8.8 After reciting the need for an application for financial relief by one person against another, s 37(2) sets out the remedies which may be granted 'on the application of the first mentioned person', ie the applicant for financial relief. A respondent to such an application who had made no prayer for ancillary relief in an answer would have no right to apply under s 37. This is perhaps a formal hurdle only because all the respondent would have to do would be to file a notice of application, but the point should be noted.

What is a 'disposition'?

8.9 The section provides that 'disposition' does not include provision made by will or codicil, but that it does include any conveyance, assurance or gift of property of any description, whether made by an instrument or otherwise.[3] Apart from this, no attempt is made to define the term, but clearly it includes any act, deed or transaction which has the effect of transferring ownership or possession from one person to another. It has been held to include a legal charge on real property.[4] It has also been held that failure to deal with property, as opposed to a positive dealing, is not a disposition.[5] A notice to quit a periodic tenancy is not a disposition and cannot be set aside under s 37.[6]

---

[3] MCA 1973, s 37(6).
[4] *Whittingham v Whittingham* [1979] Fam 9, CA.
[5] *Crittenden v Crittenden* [1990] 2 FLR 361, CA.
[6] *Newlon Housing Trust v Alsulaimen* [1998] 2 FLR 690, HL.

'With the intention of defeating the claim for financial relief'

8.10   The court must be satisfied that, in the case of a pre-emptive application, the disposition or transfer is to be made, or, in the case of a post-disposition or transfer application, has been made, with the intention of defeating the applicant's claim for financial relief. The onus of proof is on the applicant, and if this burden is not discharged the order cannot be made. However, it has been held that the question which the judge must ask himself is whether he is 'satisfied', and that it is inappropriate to add tests such as 'beyond reasonable doubt' or 'on the balance of probabilities'.[7]

To some extent, the task of the applicant is made easier by s 37(1) which goes some way to defining 'defeating the claim'. Here, it is said that this means any of the following:

(a)   preventing (any) financial relief from being granted to the applicant, either for herself or for a child;

(b)   reducing the amount of any financial relief which might otherwise be granted;

(c)   frustrating or impeding the enforcement of any order for financial relief which might be made or which has been made.[8]

The court will therefore have to find that one of these results is more likely than not to happen if an order is not made.

8.11   This leaves the question of proving 'intention'. Where it is found that one of the outcomes set out above is likely to occur, the court would have no difficulty in deducing that the respondent to the application intended that to happen. A person is deemed to intend the normal consequences of his actions, and where, for example, the inevitable result of a transfer of a property to someone else would be that the funds available for distribution between the spouses would be diminished, it would almost inevitably have to be found that the transferor had intended that consequence.

Different factors might arise where there could be more than one reason for the disposition or transfer, particularly where it could also be said that the funds available for distribution would not be diminished. For example, a person whose livelihood depended on the sale and purchase of assets should not be prevented from trading for no other reason than a pending ancillary relief application, and a person involved in any business should not be subjected to unusual and unreasonable restrictions. In the context of marriage breakdown, it is not unusual for the parties to be both deeply suspicious of each other and resentful of any interference with their normal activities. The court has to

---

[7]   *K v K (Avoidance of Reviewable Disposition)* (1983) FLR 31, CA.
[8]   MCA 1973, s 37(1).

distinguish these cases from those where there is evidence that some deliberate attempt to defeat the claim is being or has been made.[9]

Special considerations in applications to set aside dispositions

8.12 As has already been mentioned, the power to set aside a disposition is distinct from the power to prevent a disposition. Clearly, once a disposition or transfer has been made, it may be that third parties have acquired rights in the property concerned, and different considerations arise from those when it is sought to prevent a disposition from taking place. The various relevant factors will now be considered.

Reviewable dispositions

8.13 For a disposition or transfer to be set aside, it has to be 'reviewable'. This term is defined by the section. First, it is provided that:

> 'any disposition made by the other party to the proceedings for financial relief in question (whether before or after the commencement of those proceedings) is a reviewable disposition for the purposes of subsection (2)(b) and (c) above unless it was made for valuable consideration (other than marriage) to a person who, at the time of the disposition, acted in relation to it in good faith and without notice of any intention on the part of the other party to defeat the applicant's claim for financial relief.'[10]

8.14 The significance of this is that it will be presumed that any disposition is reviewable unless the respondent to the application (and the transferee) can establish all the matters mentioned, namely:

(a)   valuable consideration (for this purpose, marriage does not count);

(b)   transferee acting in good faith;[11]

(c)   transferee without any notice of transferor's intention to defeat applicant's claim.

The onus will therefore be on the respondent or transferee to satisfy the court of these matters. This applies to any transfer or disposition which the respondent has made.[12]

---

[9]   See *Smith v Smith* (1973) Fam Law 80; the court must be satisfied that a disposition is in fact about to take place, and also that its intention is to defeat the applicant's claim. There is no general power to freeze a party's assets pending the hearing of an application for financial relief.

[10] MCA 1973, s 37(4).

[11] See *Whittingham v Whittingham* [1979] Fam 9, CA; at the very least lack of good faith involves lack of honesty, and may require something akin to fraud.

[12] There is no general rule that anyone acquiring an interest in property from someone he knows to be divorced thereby has notice of an application for financial relief. However, the facts may indicate constructive notice. A bank may be under an obligation to make inquiries, and a lender who knows that an aspirant borrower has been involved in divorce proceedings is

Presumption of intention to defeat claim in some cases

8.15   The section goes further. It is provided that:

> 'Where an application is made under this section with respect to a disposition
> which took place less than three years before the date of the application or with
> respect to a disposition or other dealing with property which is about to take place
> and the court is satisfied—
>
> (a)   in a case falling within subsection (2)(a) or (b) above, that the disposition or
>   other dealing would (apart from this section) have the consequence, or
> (b)   in a case falling within subsection (2)(c) above, that the disposition has had
>   the consequence,
>
> of defeating the applicant's claim for financial relief, it shall be presumed, unless
> the contrary is shown, that the person who disposed of or is about to dispose of or
> deal with the property did so, or, as the case may be, is about to do so, with the
> intention of defeating the applicant's claim for financial relief.'[13]

8.16   This subsection therefore erects a further hurdle which the respondent or
transferee must cross. Where the disposition was either less than 3 years before
the application, or, in the case of an application to prevent a disposition, has
not yet been made, and it is established to the satisfaction of the court that its
effect will be to defeat the applicant's claim for financial relief (as defined in
s 37(1): see para **8.7**) it will be presumed that the intention was or is to defeat
the claim for financial relief unless the respondent is able to prove the contrary.

Consequential directions

8.17   When an order is made setting aside a disposition, the court must give
consequential directions as it thinks fit for giving effect to the order, including
directions requiring the making of any payments or the disposal of any
property.

How will the court exercise its discretion?

8.18   Even if the court finds in favour of the applicant on the issues of
intention to defeat the claim etc, the position remains that the court 'may' make
an order under s 37; the final disposal is subject to the discretion of the court.
Clearly, each case will turn on its own facts, and, as always, the factors set out
in s 25 apply.

In deciding whether or not to grant an order under s 37(2)(a) (a pre-emptive
order), and assuming that the intention on the part of the respondent had been

---

obliged to ask him whether his spouse has any potential interest in a property sought to be
charged; however, it is under no obligation to verify information given by the borrower unless
the spouse is in occupation of the property. See *Whittingham v Whittingham* (above); *B v B
(P Ltd Intervening) (No 2)* [1995] 1 FLR 374, CA.
[13]   MCA 1973, s 37(5).

proved, the court would normally feel obliged to make an order unless it could be demonstrated that the disposition or transfer need not affect the final result because there would be more than enough capital left to provide for any order which the court could conceivably make.

In deciding whether or not to set aside a disposition, the same consideration will apply, but the court will also have to weigh up the hardship which would be caused to the transferee if the disposition were set aside against that which would be caused to the applicant if it were not set aside.

Foreign property

8.19 It has been held that an order under s 37 can be granted even though the property in question is outside England and Wales.[14] The court might, in the exercise of its discretion, decline to make any order which would be unenforceable, but that would not per se prevent an application being made and an order granted in appropriate cases.

Procedure

8.20 Some of the procedural requirements, such as the fact that the applicant must have applied for financial relief, have already been considered above. The general subject of procedure is considered in detail in Chapter 16, and need not be considered here. It seems that the procedure for applying for an order under s 37 has not been affected by the 1999 rule changes.

It should be noted, however, that r 2.62(2) of FPR 1991 provides that any application for an avoidance of disposition order shall, if practicable, be heard at the same time as any[15] related application for ancillary relief. This would not be possible in the case of an interim emergency application to prevent a transaction. The final disposal of the s 37 application should be at the same time as the application for financial relief.

In the case of an application under s 37(2)(b) or (c), a copy of the Form A, together with a copy of the affidavit in support, must be served on the person in whose favour the disposition is alleged to have been made.[16]

8.21 When an application is made ex parte for an order to prevent a disposition, the applicant's representative must produce a draft of the order sought. When the application is being made in a county court, this order must be in Form N16A of County Court Rules 1981 (CCR). If an ex parte order is made, the court will fix a date for the application to be considered on notice to the respondent at the earliest date.

---

[14]   *Hamlin v Hamlin* [1986] 1 FLR 61, CA.
[15]   The word 'any' is perhaps superfluous since there cannot be an application under s 37 without an application for financial relief.
[16]   FPR 1991, r 2.59(3)(b).

Forms

8.22 Suggested draft orders will be found in Appendix A.

APPLICATIONS FOR AVOIDANCE OF DISPOSITION UNDER THE INHERENT JURISDICTION OF THE COURT

8.23 As has been seen, s 37 contains a series of requirements which the court must find to have been fulfilled before an order under that section may be made. However, there may be occasions when, although the evidence might not support a positive finding under s 37, the justice of the case demands that some injunctive relief be granted. In such circumstances, it has been held that the court is not powerless, since it may invoke its inherent jurisdiction. Whether or not a county court enjoys any inherent jurisdiction may be a matter for debate. The practice in the Principal Registry is that applications invoking the inherent jurisdiction are transferred to the High Court and heard by a judge.

In *Shipman v Shipman*[17] it was held that, although the requirements of s 37 (including in particular the intention to defeat the wife's claim) could not be met, the court had an inherent jurisdiction to freeze assets which might be put beyond the reach of the applicant; in deciding whether or not to exercise its discretion in favour of the applicant, the court was not bound by the many restrictions and safeguards which must be observed when granting a worldwide freezing injunction (as to which see **8.26** et seq).

8.24 Another example of the court's ability to grant an injunction to preserve the status quo is provided by the decision of Thorpe J in *Poon v Poon*.[18] In that case, the parties were directors and shareholders of a family company. Proceedings for ancillary relief were pending, and the wife proposed to remove the husband from his position in the company and replace him with her current boyfriend; she was in a position to do this since other members of her family were also shareholders. Thorpe J said that, pending a final hearing, every effort was made to preserve the status quo. Although the company was a separate entity, it was not an entity in which any other individual or non-family member had any interest; it was unthinkable that the wife should be allowed to proceed to emasculate the husband's interest. Accordingly, an injunction was granted restraining the wife from placing her proposals before the general meeting.

8.25 However, a word of caution may be in order. The inherent jurisdiction of the court was considered by the Court of Appeal in *Wicks v Wicks*,[19] a case which dealt with a different issue, namely the power of the court to order an

---

[17] [1991] 1 FLR 250, Anthony Lincoln J; see also *Roche v Roche* (1981) Fam Law 243, CA, and *Walker v Walker* (1983) FLR 455.
[18] [1994] 2 FLR 857.
[19] [1998] 1 FLR 470, CA; discussed in more detail at Chapter 4, para **4.5**.

interim sale of property, and it was held that, for that purpose at least, the court did not have inherent jurisdiction. Ward LJ pointed out that the inherent jurisdiction related to the procedural and not the substantive law. In the instant case:

> 'Under the cloak of ensuring fair play, the judge was in fact making orders affecting the parties' substantive rights, and that must be governed by the general law and rules, not by resort to a wide judicial discretion derived from the court's inherent jurisdiction. . . . The reality [in *Wicks*] is that the wife is seeking the enforcement of rights which the Matrimonial Causes Act 1973 does not grant her. She wants an order for sale before s 24A allows the court to order it.'

It remains to be seen whether these comments as to the inherent jurisdiction will ever be used to overturn the line of authorities referred to in this section, or, indeed, whether it would be held that these injunctions affected the substantive rather than the procedural rights of the parties. For the time being the decisions remain good law, and at least one of them is a decision of the Court of Appeal. However, the possibility of development should not be ignored.

FREEZING INJUNCTIONS

8.26 Freezing injunctions were originally called *Mareva* injunctions after the name of the vessel in the leading case on the subject.[20] Although this was a mercantile case, the principles laid down are applicable to family cases, and the Practice Direction referred to below is specifically referable to the Family Division.

The essence of such an injunction is that the respondent to the application is forbidden to remove from the jurisdiction of the court (ie from England and Wales) funds or property until the trial of the action or matter. The onus is on the applicant to show that it is likely that she will recover a capital sum or property at the final hearing and that there is a danger that the court's order may be emasculated by the respondent removing funds out of the court's reach.

8.27 The statutory basis is s 37 of the Supreme Court Act 1981 (SCA 1981). This is applied to county courts by County Courts Act 1984 (CCA 1984), s 38. The county court, therefore, has jurisdiction in a family matter,[21] but under normal circumstances a freezing injunction, particularly where the issues are contested, should be transferred to the High Court.[22] A freezing injunction may be worldwide (ie applying to assets outside the jurisdiction) or limited to assets within the jurisdiction.

---

[20] *Mareva Cia Naviera SA v International Bulkcarriers SA, The Mareva* [1980] 1 All ER 213n, CA.

[21] See MFPA 1984, s 32.

[22] *Practice Direction (Family Business: Distribution of Business)* [1992] 3 All ER 151.

8.28 The law and practice relating to freezing injunctions is clearly both complicated and of a specialist nature, and it is not proposed to say more in detail about it in this book. However, essential material is contained in the Practice Direction to the Civil Procedure Rules 1998 (CPR), Part 25 on ex parte freezing injunctions and search orders, which is clearly required reading for anyone contemplating such an application.

SEARCH ORDERS

8.29 Similar comments to those contained in the previous paragraph apply to search orders. These orders were originally called *Anton Piller* orders after the eponymous case[23] in which they were first made, were of mercantile or commercial origin, and have been adapted for use in family proceedings.[24] Such orders now have a statutory basis in s 7 of the Civil Procedure Act 1997. The Practice Direction referred to in the previous paragraph also governs practice and procedure in these cases. A suggested form for a search order will be found in Appendix A, Precedent 3.

8.30 A search order may be granted where it appears that the respondent to the application has in his possession documents or other material relevant to the application for financial relief, that he has not disclosed them, and that there is a real possibility that he may destroy them before an application can be made inter partes. The order is therefore always made ex parte, and its effect is that the applicant or her agent is empowered to enter the respondent's premises and to seize and remove documents or material of the classes specified in the order. By s 7 of the 1997 Act, an order may be made against 'any person'.

The order is, therefore, extremely drastic and has been described as being 'at the extremity of the court's powers'.[25] Such orders are therefore rarely made, and where it eventually appears that the search was fruitless, severe penalties in costs will be inflicted on the applicant.[26]

8.31 An application for a search order made in county court proceedings must be transferred to the High Court.

---

[23] *Anton Piller KG v Manufacturing Processes Ltd* [1976] Ch 55, [1976] 1 All ER 779, CA.

[24] See *Emanuel v Emanuel* [1982] 2 All ER 342; *Kepa v Kepa* (1983) FLR 515.

[25] *Anton Piller KG v Manufacturing Processes Ltd* (above), per Ormrod LJ.

[26] As in *Burgess v Burgess* [1996] 2 FLR 34.

Chapter 9

CONSENT ORDERS

INTRODUCTION

9.1   Not all applications for ancillary relief result in a final contested hearing. Some applications are agreed from the outset; some become agreed in the course of the proceedings but before the final hearing, and yet more are settled at the doors of the court. The principles applicable to these different classes of case are the same, but there are differences in procedure.

A consent order is defined by MCA 1973 as 'an order in the terms applied for to which the respondent agrees';[1] in effect, it is an order which both parties to the application for financial relief ask the court to make without hearing evidence or argument. Before considering the procedural steps necessary for a consent order and the requirements to be observed when drafting such an order, it will be necessary to consider the duty of the court on such occasions, and the general principles applicable to applications for consent orders.

Finally, while appeals and other applications to set aside are dealt with elsewhere, it seems appropriate in this chapter to deal with the separate question of the circumstances in which a consent order may be set aside.

THE DUTY OF THE COURT

9.2   It is a fundamental principle of family law in England and Wales that the rights of the parties are not finally declared until the court has made an order endorsing their agreement; any attempt to oust the jurisdiction of the court is likely to fail, and the parties cannot know that their agreement is final until the court has made an order incorporating its terms.[2]

It is a further fundamental principle that the court has a duty to scrutinise and approve whatever agreement is put before it. The position was authoritatively established in *Livesey (formerly Jenkins) v Jenkins*,[3] where the position as to consent orders was summarised as follows:

---

[1]   MCA 1973, s 33A(3).
[2]   *Pounds v Pounds* [1994] 1 FLR 775, CA. See also Chapter 1, para **1.40** as to agreements generally.
[3]   [1985] AC 424, HL.

–   the jurisdiction of the court to make orders for financial relief is derived entirely from statute, namely MCA 1973;

–   the function of the court when making such orders is exactly the same when the application is by consent as when the hearing is contested;

–   s 25 of MCA 1973 prescribes a list of matters to which the court is required to have regard;

–   it follows that the court must consider the merits of any consent application in the light of the s 25 factors, and only make the order if it appears to be just and reasonable.

The position was well set out in a later case,[4] where it was said that in consent applications for ancillary relief:

> 'the court does not act, it has been said, as a rubber stamp. The judge will be concerned, whether the order be made by consent or imposed after argument, to be satisfied that the criteria of ss 25 and 25A of the Matrimonial Causes Act 1973 have been duly applied.'

Having said that, it should also be said that the function of the court is not to scrutinise the agreed terms and evidence in the same way as it would on a defended hearing.[5] It is submitted that the court's role is limited to satisfying itself that the proposed order is within the band of reasonable discretion and that it does not, on the face of it, offend any obvious principle. For a case where there was a dispute as to whether an agreement had been made at all, see *Xydhias v Xydhias*[6] discussed at para **1.44**.

9.3   It follows from what has been said that the court cannot perform its statutory functions unless it has the information and material on which to base its assessment. When the question of setting aside consent orders is considered below, the importance of full and frank disclosure will become apparent; this was one of the major issues in *Livesey v Jenkins*. Another important result of that case was that it became necessary to establish procedures to give the court the required information when it was considering a consent application, and this will now be considered.

INFORMATION REQUIRED BY THE COURT

9.4   After some uncertainty following *Livesey v Jenkins* as to what would be required by the court in order to carry out its investigations, statutory authority was provided by s 33A of MCA 1973. This provides that:

---

4   *Pounds v Pounds* [1994] 1 FLR 775, CA.
5   Ibid.
6   [1999] 1 FLR 683, CA.

'on an application for a consent order for financial relief the court may, unless it has reason to think that there are other circumstances into which it ought to inquire, make an order in the terms agreed on the basis only of the prescribed information furnished with the application.'[7]

'Prescribed' means prescribed by rules of court, and these are to be found in FPR 1991, r 2.61. This provides that there must be lodged with the application two copies of a draft of the order sought, and a Statement of Information which shall include:

'(a) the duration of the marriage, the age of each party and of any minor or dependent child of the family;

(b) an estimate in summary form of the approximate amount of value of the capital resources and net income of each party and of any minor child of the family;

(c) what arrangements are intended for the accommodation of each of the parties and any minor child of the family;

(d) whether either party has remarried or has any present intention to marry or to cohabit with another person;

(dd) where the order includes provision to be made under s 24B, 25B or 25C of the Act of 1973, a statement confirming that the person responsible for the pension arrangement in question has been served with the documents required by rule 2.70(11) and that no objection to such an order has been made by that person within 14 days from such service;

(e) where the terms of the order provide for a transfer of property, a statement confirming that any mortgagee of the property has been served with notice of the application and that no objection to such a transfer has been made by the mortgagee within 14 days from such service; and

(f) any other especially significant matters.'[8]

EXCEPTIONS TO THE GENERAL RULE

9.5 There are two sets of circumstances in which it is not necessary to comply fully with the requirements of FPR 1991, r 2.61. First, where the application is for variation of periodical payments or interim periodical payments only, it is only necessary to file a statement giving the information as to net income under subpara (b) above.[9]

Secondly, when all or any of the parties attend the hearing of an application for financial relief, the court may dispense with the lodging of a statement of information and give directions for the information which would otherwise be required to be given in such a manner as it thinks fit.[10] This would apply when the application was settled on the day of the hearing or at a very late stage and

---

[7] MCA 1973, s 33A(1).
[8] FPR 1991, r 2.61(1).
[9] Ibid, r 2.61(2).
[10] Ibid.

the parties or their representatives were present; the court would normally require only to be told of the prescribed matters.

It is important to make the point that there are no other circumstances in which the r 2.61 statement may be dispensed with; it certainly is not acceptable for parties or their advisers to send the court a consent order with an invitation to read the Forms E or other evidence on the court file, however recent that evidence may be.

PRACTICE ON APPLYING FOR A CONSENT ORDER

9.6   The information required by FPR 1991, r 2.61 was reduced into a practice form by Registrar's Directions of 17 February 1986 and 5 January 1990.[11] This form is now prescribed as Form M1 in Appendix A to the FPR 1991; copies are available from law stationers.

When an application is made for a consent order, therefore, the following documents are required to be filed at court:

(a)   the consent notice of application in Form A, endorsed with the signatures of both parties;

(b)   two copies of the draft order, one of which must be signed by the respondent;

(c)   Form M1, duly completed.

When there are solicitors on record, they must sign the documents on behalf of their client; it is a matter for them as to whether they obtain the signature of their client also. It should be remembered that the court's jurisdiction to make certain orders, such as property adjustment orders and lump sum orders, arises only on or after the grant of a decree. There is therefore little point in applying for such orders until after decree. However, the court may be invited to approve terms of settlement and to leave the order on the court file, and this is acceptable to most courts,[12] with the proviso that the time period between the approving of the order and the making of the order should not be very long. Where any appreciable delay does occur, the court might well require updated information.

NOTES ON DRAFTING CONSENT ORDERS

9.7   It is clearly important that all orders should be correctly drafted. This is more than usually important in the case of consent orders. In the first place, the

---

[11]   [1990] 1 FLR 234.
[12]   *Pounds v Pounds* [1994] 1 FLR 775, CA.

drafting of the order is in the hands of the parties' advisers, who therefore assume responsibility for the order and any defects in it. In the second place, in most cases of a consent order, the application is considered by the court in the absence of the parties, and any matter which requires amendment or further inquiry by the court results in delay and, probably, additional cost for the lay client.[13]

The following paragraphs include common causes of query by the court.

The distinction between matters which may be ordered and those which may not

9.8   In *Livesey v Jenkins* it was pointed out that the powers of the court in respect of financial relief are entirely statutory; if the power to make a certain order cannot be identified in MCA 1973, that order cannot be made.

> 'When a consent order is drafted it is essential that all its terms should come clearly within the court's powers conferred on it by sections 23 and 24 of the Act of 1973.'[14]

Having said that, frequently there are matters of fact which the parties wish to have recorded, or agreements which are essential to the proper performance of the overall arrangement which the parties have made which cannot be brought within the terms of the statute but which, nevertheless, should appear in the order. One of the most common reasons for rejection of a consent order is a failure on the part of the draftsman to recognise the difference between the various parts of the order.

The distinction which must be made is between recitals of fact, recitals of agreement, undertakings, and orders. These will be considered in turn.

Recitals of fact

9.9   Most of the important factual matters, such as the declared means of the parties, will have been set out in the Form M1 filed pursuant to FPR 1991, r 2.61, so it should not normally be necessary to recite detailed facts in the preamble to the order itself. Nevertheless, there are certain matters which it may be thought helpful for the court to have on the face of the order (eg that the former matrimonial home has been sold and the proceeds divided in certain proportions). There may also be important matters which have been in dispute, and which the party agreeing to compromise wishes to have placed on record unambiguously, so that if it later appeared that any such recited matter was not true it would be easier for that party to establish that he or she was misled.

---

[13]   For an example of the problems which can be caused by lack of care in a drafting order, see *McGladdery v McGladdery* [1999] 2 FLR 1102.

[14]   *Livesey v Jenkins* [1984] AC 424, HL, per Lord Brandon.

Recitals of agreement

9.10 An agreement should be recited in the preamble to the order if it is an integral part of the overall settlement between the parties, but is not a matter which could properly be worded as an undertaking (as to which, see below). This might be the case, for example, where one party agreed that the other should be given the conduct of a sale, or be allowed to occupy premises until sale. It would also be the case where one party agreed to indemnify the other in respect of liability under a contract. In the event of a breach of any such agreement, the remedy of the aggrieved party would be to institute separate proceedings for breach of contract rather than trying to enforce the order in the preamble to which the agreement was recited.

Another useful recital of agreement (or of the existence of an agreement) would arise when the parties had made a written agreement for the support of a child pursuant to s 8(5) of CSA 1991.[15]

Undertakings

9.11 The difference between an agreement and an undertaking is that in the case of an undertaking the person giving the undertaking is making a promise to the court and not to the other party. The expectation is therefore that the court would be able to punish any breach of undertaking, for example by committal to prison.

In *Livesey v Jenkins*, Lord Brandon drew the distinction between obligations which could be the subject of an order of the court and those which could not, pointed out that the latter should be drawn as undertakings, and observed that 'such undertakings are, needless to say, enforceable as effectively as direct orders'.[16] This statement clearly has the unanimous authority of the highest court and must be taken to be correct. Nevertheless, the position is not entirely free from doubt, and it may be that not all undertakings are as easily enforceable as has been suggested.

9.12 Until the decision of the Court of Appeal in *Mubarak v Mubarak*,[17] there was no doubt that an undertaking by one party to pay money to the other party is capable of being enforced by judgment summons.[18] For further discussion of the present position, see para **19.9** et seq. It is possible that this remedy could extend to an undertaking to pay money to a third party, for example an undertaking to discharge a debt. Beyond that, however, the position is not free from doubt.[19]

---

[15] See also the Child Maintenance (Written Agreements) Order 1993, SI 1993/620; but note para **11.16** and **11.19**.
[16] [1984] AC 424, HL.
[17] [2001] 1 FLR 698.
[18] *Symmons v Symmons* [1993] 1 FLR 317.
[19] For some of the rival views on the matter, see articles by Bird at [1990] Fam Law 420, and Moor and Mostyn at [1992] Fam Law 233. The author has been assured by counsel of some

It would certainly be wise for those drafting undertakings to ensure that they were worded in terms as unambiguous as possible, and to consider in all cases whether they might be better expressed as agreements. Although there is currently no authority for what is about to be said, it is suggested that good practice might require a person giving an undertaking to sign personally the consent application and to include a statement that he/she recognised that breach of the undertaking could result in proceedings for contempt.

Dismissal of claims, and clean break orders

9.13 This is mentioned only for the purpose of underlining what was said on the subject of the clean break in Chapter 2. The justification for a clean break is one of the most common reasons for inquiry and delay in the making of consent orders. The court must ask itself in every case whether, if the case were being considered on a contested basis, the claims of the parties would be dismissed. In Chapter 2 at para **2.28** et seq, it is suggested that it may be that the Court of Appeal, by its dicta in recent decisions, has reminded courts that a clean break should certainly not be imposed as a matter of course, and only after careful consideration to ensure that the statutory criteria are met.

Some common faults

9.14 Most of the possible pitfalls have been suggested above. However, care should also be taken to ensure that all dates for the commencement of certain actions, and all matters of detail such as mortgage account or insurance policies are inserted; if there are blank spaces left in a form of order this will cause delay.

It is important that the prescribed Statement of Information should be completed in full.

While not, strictly speaking, a fault, one matter which is frequently not provided for is interest on any overdue sum ordered to be paid. It would avoid doubt if this were always included.

APPLICATIONS TO SET ASIDE CONSENT ORDERS

9.15 Since an order made by consent is made with the express agreement of the parties, there are clearly only limited grounds on which it might be set aside; an appeal cannot lie on the merits of the order, in the usual way. Any appeal against a consent order has, therefore, to attack the fundamental basis of the order, and there are four recognised ways of doing this. They are by alleging:

(a)   non-disclosure of some essential matter;

---

eminence that he secured an order for the committal of a man who broke his undertaking to give his wife a Get; there is no reason to doubt this, but there seems to be no reported authority on the point.

(b)   fraud or misrepresentation;

(c)   supervening events which invalidate the whole basis of the order;

(d)   undue influence.

These possibilities will be considered in turn, with (a) and (b) being considered together since, as will be seen, they are essentially variations on the same basic allegation, namely that the respondent to the application has in some way misled the applicant.

The two means of attacking a consent order are applications for leave to appeal out of time and applications to set aside the order; the first is made by the normal appellate route from the court which made the order, while the second is made to the court which made the order.[20] It would seem that the former is more appropriate in the case of events occurring after the date of the order while the latter would be appropriate in the case of non-disclosure or fraud.

Non-disclosure, fraud and misrepresentation

9.16   The duty of full and frank disclosure has already been mentioned above, and was one of the principal issues in *Livesey (formerly Jenkins) v Jenkins.*[21] In that case the parties had settled their litigation by means of a consent order, but the wife had omitted to tell her former husband, or even her own solicitors, that she was intending to remarry; that remarriage was a significant matter and something which she should have disclosed. In his speech, Lord Brandon emphasised that the parties were under the same obligation as to complete disclosure in cases of consent orders as in contested proceedings, and said that in order to do justice to the husband it was necessary to set the order aside.

This decision confirmed a number of earlier decisions, notably *Robinson v Robinson (Disclosure)*,[22] where it was held that there was a duty on litigants in matrimonial proceedings to make full and frank disclosure of their property and financial resources; the power to set aside orders was not limited to cases of fraud and mistake but extended to material non-disclosure.

In *Vicary v Vicary*,[23] a consent order was made on the basis that the husband's assets, including his shares in a private company, were £430,000. He did not disclose the fact that negotiations were taking place for the sale of the company, and, shortly thereafter, he sold his shares for £2.8m. The order was set aside.[24]

---

[20]   For a flow chart of the means by which an application to set aside an order may be made, see *B-T v B-T (Divorce Procedure)* [1990] 2 FLR 1 per Ward J, set out in Appendix A, Precedent 33.

[21]   See para **9.2**.

[22]   (1983) FLR 102, CA.

[23]   [1992] 2 FLR 271, CA.

[24]   See also *Thompson v Thompson* [1991] 2 FLR 530, CA.

In *Rose v Rose*[25] a consent order was made in August 2001. At an FDR hearing the wife had claimed that her relationship with a boyfriend had cooled. However, the husband subsequently adduced evidence to show that they had planned to buy a house in Italy and spend part of each year there. He applied to set aside the consent order, but the wife successfully applied for a summary order striking out his application. It was held that the operative date for non-disclosure was the date of the order. On that date the husband had been aware of the relationship and had chosen not to cross-examine her on it. Even if the husband were able to prove non-disclosure, it was utterly unlikely that the wife's interest would be confined to a life interest in property as he now suggested.

It was also emphasised in *Livesey v Jenkins* that not every example of non-disclosure would result in the order being set aside. Orders will not be set aside if the disclosure would not have made any substantial difference to the order which the court would have made:

> 'It will only be in cases where the absence of full and frank disclosure has led to the court making, either in contested proceedings or by consent, an order that is substantially different from the order which would have been made if such disclosure had taken place that a case for setting aside can possibly be made good.'[26]

Parties who applied on trivial grounds would be penalised in costs. In another case, the fact that there is no jurisdiction to vary a lump sum order nor to award a second lump sum was advanced to support the point that consent orders should not lightly be set aside.[27]

It was emphasised in *Rose v Rose* that a delay of one year in making an application of this kind is 'wholly unreasonable'.[28]

9.17 In *Robinson v Robinson*,[29] Ormrod LJ expressed the view that, while applications to set aside could be made by means of either a new action or an appeal to a higher court, there was much convenience in an application to the judge who made the original order who could determine the application and then go on, as the Court of Appeal could not, to make a new order in appropriate cases.

New or supervening circumstances

9.18 As has already been said, there is no jurisdiction to vary a lump sum order or property adjustment order on the ground of new circumstances or

---

25 [2003] EWHC 505 (Fam), [2003] 2 FLR 197. For the circumstances leading up to the consent order see Chapter 1, para **1.44**.
26 *Livesey v Jenkins* [1984] AC 424, HL, per Lord Brandon.
27 *Redmond v Redmond* [1986] 2 FLR 173.
28 A point repeated in *Shaw v Shaw* [2002] EWCA Civ 1298, [2002] 2 FLR 1204, CA.
29 (1983) FLR 102, CA. For a similar statement, see *Fournier v Fournier* [1998] 2 FLR 990, CA, per Lord Woolf MR.

otherwise. Nevertheless, some procedure has to exist to deal with the kind of case where the whole factual basis on which the order was made has disappeared.

In *Barder v Caluori*,[30] a consent order was made by which the husband was ordered to transfer his interest in the former matrimonial home to the wife. One of the principal reasons for this order was that the wife had the care of the children. Shortly thereafter, the wife killed the children and herself. On appeal to the House of Lords, the principal issue was whether leave to appeal out of time should have been granted, but the reasons given in the speech of Lord Brandon may be applied to an application to the judge at first instance. Lord Brandon said that the court might properly exercise its discretion to grant leave to appeal out of time from an order for financial provision or property transfer on the ground of new events provided four conditions were met. These conditions were:

(1)   that new events have occurred since the making of the order which invalidate the basis or fundamental assumption upon which the order was made, so that, if leave to appeal out of time were given, the appeal would be certain, or very likely, to succeed;

(2)   that the new events should have occurred within a relatively short time of the order having been made. While that time could not be precisely defined, Lord Brandon thought it extremely unlikely that it could be as long as a year, and that in most cases it would be no more than a few months;

(3)   that the application should be made reasonably promptly in the circumstances of the case;

(4)   that the grant of leave should not prejudice third parties who have acquired in good faith and for valuable consideration interests in property which is the subject matter of the order.

9.19   Inevitably, circumstances change after orders are made, and it must be emphasised that the courts will not set aside an order merely on the ground that things are now different from how they appeared at the time of the order.[31] It seems that there are several common grounds for such applications which may conveniently be summarised as follows.

1. Disputes as to the value of an asset

9.20   The position was summarised in *Cornick v Cornick*.[32] Where an asset which was correctly valued at the time of the order changes value within a

---

[30]   [1988] AC 20, sub nom *Barder v Barder (Caluori Intervening)* [1987] 2 FLR 480, HL.
[31]   See e g *McGladdery v McGladdery* [1999] 2 FLR 1102.
[32]   [1994] 2 FLR 530.

relatively short period because of the natural processes of price fluctuation, leave to appeal should not be granted (and the order should not be set aside).

Where a wrong value was placed on an asset at the time of the order and, had this been known, a different order would have been made, provided that this was not the fault of the person alleging the mistake, leave to appeal may be granted (and the order set aside).

Where something unforeseen and unforeseeable has occurred since the date of the order which has altered the value of the assets so dramatically as to bring about a substantial change in the balance of the assets brought about by the order, then, provided the other 3 *Barder* conditions are met, the *Barder* principles may apply. The circumstances in which these conditions might apply are rare.[33]

9.21 At a time of rapid fluctuation of property prices, it is natural that there should be second thoughts about the wisdom of some consent orders. However, it will always be necessary to show that the facts fall within the principles set out above. For example, in one case[34] the Court of Appeal granted leave to appeal out of time on the ground that the actual value of a house was so much lower than the agreed valuation that the applicant could not be rehoused on the division of the proceeds of sale originally agreed. In another,[35] the division of the proceeds of sale would have been enough to rehouse the parties had the husband not 'disgracefully' delayed the sale by more than three years, and leave to appeal was granted on the basis that the fundamental assumption underlying the order, namely that the wife would be able to rehouse herself, had been falsified. However, in another case,[36] where the value of a house at the time of the order was £340,000 and at the time of the hearing of the application for leave to appeal 3 years later £250,000, leave to appeal was refused.

In *Kean v Kean*[37] a consent order was made in 2000 on the basis that the property was worth £500,000 to £550,000. No formal valuation was obtained. In the summer of 2001 the property was sold for £765,000 and the wife sought leave to appeal out of time. This application was refused on the ground that the estimate of the value was not a basis of, nor a fundamental assumption underlying the agreement. It was not certain that the court would have made a different order if the true value had been known. Moreover, the wife had to take some responsibility since she had been advised to take separate advice and had refused.

---

[33] See e g *Middleton v Middleton* [1998] 2 FLR 821, CA.
[34] *Heard v Heard* [1995] 1 FLR 970, CA.
[35] *Hope-Smith v Hope-Smith* [1989] 2 FLR 56, CA.
[36] *B v B (Financial Provision: Leave to Appeal)* [1994] 1 FLR 219. See also, for a contrary decision, *Heard v Heard* [1995] 1 FLR 970, CA.
[37] [2002] 2 FLR 28.

2. Remarriage or cohabitation

9.22 It has been seen above that in *Livesey v Jenkins* the fact that the wife failed to disclose to the husband her intention to remarry undermined the basis on which the order was made and was sufficient to enable the court to set it aside. This will, of course, not always be the case.[38] In another case,[39] where the wife had remarried since the order, it was held that the fact of her remarriage did not affect her entitlement to capital and this would have been the case even if she had been remarried at the time of the order. It is therefore necessary to demonstrate that the basis on which the order was made has been falsified before the application will stand any chance of success. See also para **9.16**.

In *Williams v Lindley*[40] a consent order of 70/30 in favour of a wife had been made after the wife had denied any relationship with a certain man. Soon thereafter she married the man in question. A circuit judge refused the husband's application for a re-hearing but this was allowed by the Court of Appeal. It was held that the main foundation of the wife's case had been undermined, and Thorpe LJ added that, when approaching the 'supervening event', greater flexibility was needed; the court should move away from rigid prescription and reconsideration of all the s 25 factors was necessary.

3. Death

9.23 The same principles apply in the case of the death of a party. It might be thought that where the basis of an order was the provision of a home for one party, the death of that party would invalidate the whole order, but that would be an over-simplistic view of the law. Death was, clearly, the background to *Barder v Caluori*, considered at para **9.18**, and the principles set out there need not be repeated.

In *Amey v Amey*,[41] there had been an agreement between the parties which they intended to have approved by means of a consent order. However, before they could do so, the wife died. The husband sought to set aside the agreement. It was held that the mere fact of the wife's death was not sufficient; the agreement had been a fair distribution of assets on the basis of the wife's entitlement, and the only ground for setting it aside would be if the death had undermined the fundamental assumptions on which the order was made.

In *Barber v Barber*,[42] an order was made for the wife to have more than half the proceeds of sale of the former matrimonial home on the assumption that, though she was ill, she had at least 5 years to live. She died 3 months after the order was made. The order was set aside in part, on the ground that its fundamental basis had been invalidated. It was held that the proper approach

---

[38]   See eg *Cook v Cook* [1988] 1 FLR 521, CA.
[39]   *B v B (Financial Provision: Leave to Appeal)* (above).
[40]   [2005] EWCA Civ 103, [2005] 2 FLR 710.
[41]   [1992] 2 FLR 89.
[42]   [1993] 1 FLR 476, CA.

was to start again and make an order on the basis of what the court would have done had it known at the date of the order what it now knew. This followed the decision of the court in *Smith v Smith (Smith and Others Intervening)*,[43] which established similar principles.

In *Reid v Reid*[44] the facts were that a consent order had awarded the wife £99,000 on a clean break basis. She had disclosed the fact that she suffered from ill-health. Fifteen days after decree absolute she died. The husband sought leave to appeal out of time. The court held that her death 2 months after the order was a new event and attracted *Barder* principles. It was not reasonably foreseeable; the husband's needs had not been fully met by the order and the wife's death had invalidated the parties' perceptions of her needs. The husband would receive a lump sum of £37,000; the executor's arguments based on entitlement and contributions were not appropriate where assets were very limited.

4. Other matters

9.24 For the sake of completeness, reference should be made to *Crozier v Crozier*,[45] where an application was made to set aside a clean break order with nominal maintenance for a child on the ground that the Child Support Agency, which had come into being since the making of the order, seemed likely to require the husband to pay a substantial amount by way of child maintenance. The application was refused, partly on the ground that parties could never agree to contract out of liability for a child.

In *S v S (Ancillary Relief: Consent Order)*[46] a consent order was made for a payment of £800,000 to the wife on a clean break basis one month before the House of Lords decision in *White v White*. The wife applied to set aside the order on the ground of a supervening event. The application was dismissed. It was held that, while a change in the law could be a supervening event, it must be unforeseeable. At the time of the order, the House was considering its judgment, and a change in the law was foreseeable.

FORMS

9.25 Some standard precedents for use as preambles to consent orders will be found in Appendix A, Precedent 31.

---

[43] [1991] 2 FLR 432, CA.
[44] [2004] 1 FLR 736 Wilson J.
[45] [1994] 1 FLR 126.
[46] [2002] 1 FLR 992.

Chapter 10

PENSIONS

INTRODUCTION

10.1 After the matrimonial home, a pension fund is, for many people, the most substantial financial investment they will ever make. It is also a resource which is most likely to be lost to one party, usually the wife, on divorce if no action is taken; in most cases a wife will lose the ability to enjoy with her husband not only the benefits of the lump sum and regular payments which he will receive on retirement but also the protection of the benefits which the pension scheme will confer on his death. It appears that, as a matter of government policy, the value of the State retirement pension may diminish in relative terms in the future and that people will be encouraged to make their own pension provision to supplement and even, perhaps, to replace the State scheme.

Pensions are therefore of the highest importance when dealing with financial relief. However, the present law on the subject is complicated and can only be understood if explained in terms of its evolution.

10.2 The various ways in which a pension has been and (in some cases) may in the future be dealt with by the court may be summarised as follows:

(1)   variation of settlement (*Brooks v Brooks*[1]);

(2)   as a general resource under MCA 1973, s 25B and s 25C (offsetting);

(3)   attachment under MCA 1973, ss 25B–25D;

(4)   pension sharing.

It must be emphasised that not all these possibilities are available in every case; indeed, it is virtually certain that all the possibilities will *not* be available. Each case must be examined carefully on its own facts.

In the final section of this chapter (para **10.66** et seq), the various types of remedy now available will be compared.

---

[1]   [1995] 2 FLR 13, HL.

There is one further possibility which must be examined, namely loss of pension as an example of hardship enabling a party to defend certain divorce proceedings under MCA 1973, s 10. This is considered in more detail at para **10.15**.

Procedural aspects will be considered in more detail in Chapter 16. However, it should be noted here that the introduction of Form P has made ascertaining the value of a pension more straightforward. In *Martin-Dye v Martin-Dye*[2] (see para **10.8**) Thorpe LJ summarised the position at paras [68] and [69] of his judgment as follows:

> 'The difficulties that have been encountered in the present case should hopefully not recur. The Family Proceedings (Amendment) No (5) Rules 2005 came into force on the 5 December 2005. Rule 118(F)(i) introduces Form P which should be used in every case where a pension is significant and where a pension sharing order might be made. It can be used on a voluntary basis if the scheme member signs to give his authority on the first page or can be ordered to be completed by the court, probably at the first direction appointment. The commencement date for this new practice is set by r 123, the effect of which, in my opinion, makes the new form available for use in any case where a Form A was filed after the 5 December 2005.
>
> The virtue of Form P is that it directs the attention of the professions to the information which is required for the just disposal of the claim, whether by consent or by order of the court. That information includes the value of the pension and the valuation method to be used.'

VARIATION OF SETTLEMENT

10.3   As was seen in Chapter 6, the court has the power under s 24(1)(c) to make an order:

> 'varying for the benefit of the parties to the marriage and of the children of the family or either or any of them any ante-nuptial or post-nuptial settlement (including such a settlement made by will or codicil) made on the parties to the marriage . . .'[3]

In *Brooks v Brooks*,[4] one of the central issues was whether the pension scheme which formed the object of the application was 'nuptial'. The House of Lords held that, in making that decision, the scheme must be looked at in the round and in the context of the circumstances then subsisting. Something more than a scheme in which all the benefits were payable to the husband was required, even if, in a broad sense, the benefits could be described as family assets.

10.4   This class of remedy has been considered only in brief detail for two reasons. First, it was only applicable to a very limited number of cases.

---

[2]   [2006] EWCA Civ 681, [2006] 2 FLR 901, CA.
[3]   MCA 1973, s 24(1)(c).
[4]   [1995] 2 FLR 13, HL.

Secondly, and more importantly, this type of variation of settlement application has been abolished by WRPA 1999. This remedy is therefore no longer available.

PENSIONS AS A RESOURCE: MCA 1973, SECTIONS 25B AND 25C

10.5 Sections 25B to 25D were inserted by the Pensions Act 1995[5] and have been in force since 1 August 1996. They apply to petitions filed after 1 July 1996, and do not apply, for example, where the petition was filed before that date but an answer or cross-petition was filed after that date.[6]

The contents of these provisions may be summarised as follows:

–   s 25B prescribes the matters to which the court is to have regard in respect of pensions, and confers new powers to make orders directed to the trustees of pensions schemes;

–   s 25C empowers the court to order a lump sum to be paid from a pensions scheme;

–   s 25D provides for 'earmarking' (now known as 'attachment').

Matters to which the court must have regard

10.6 It is provided that the matters to which the court is to have regard under s 25(2) include:

'(a)   in the case of paragraph (a) [ie the financial resources of the parties] any benefits under a pension arrangement which a party to the marriage has or is likely to have, and

(b)   in the case of paragraph (h) [ie the value to the parties of any benefit to be lost by reason of the divorce or annulment] any benefits under a pension arrangement which by reason of the dissolution or annulment of the marriage, a party to the marriage will lose the chance of acquiring,

---

[5]   Section 166.

[6]   This led to the possibility that a husband wishing to avoid the effect of MCA 1973, ss 25B–25D (eg as to attachment – see **10.17**) might have filed a petition before 1 July 1996, thereby preventing his wife from reaping the advantage of the provision. However, it seems that there would be no reason why a wife, faced with that position, should not issue her own petition after 1 July 1996; there is nothing in FPR 1991 to prevent this. The court would then have to give directions as to how the two petitions were to proceed. See the article by Catherine Hallam at [1997] Fam Law 267. This should no longer be a problem.

and, accordingly, in relation to benefits under a pension arrangement, section 25(2)(a) above shall have effect as if "in the foreseeable future" were omitted.'[7]

Section 25(2)(a) requires the court to have regard to the financial resources which a party has 'or is likely to have in the foreseeable future'. The specific disapplication of these words means that the court is required to have regard to any pension benefit which either party is likely to have at any time, however far in the future; however, as will be seen, the fact that the court takes such matters into account does not in itself prescribe any particular method of dealing with them. A pension fund is, thus, a resource like any other and must be included in any list of assets supplied to the court.[8]

Paragraph (h), referred to in s 25B(1)(b), refers to 'the value to each of the parties . . . of any benefit which, by reason of the divorce or annulment of the marriage, that party will lose the chance of acquiring'. Section 25B(1)(b) therefore makes specific what was implied in s 25(2)(h), namely that the court must look at the value of lost benefits, and the most significant aspect of this will normally be lost widow's benefits. These will be considered at para **10.12**.

10.7 Having noted that the benefits under a pension must be taken into account, the following questions arise:

(1)   How are the benefits to be valued for the purpose of the s 25 calculation?

(2)   When will they be sufficiently significant to have an effect on the order?

Valuation

10.8   The starting point for any discussion of this topic must be the comment of Thorpe LJ in *Martin-Dye v Martin-Dye*[9] . In the course of his judgment, his Lordship observed:

'Thus it is the remarkable and regrettable fact that the parties have engaged well known specialist counsel and incurred costs of over half a million pounds on two hearings in the court below which were distorted by the failure to cite and focus on the method of valuation of pensions in payment provided by the regulation in force.'

The lawyers had failed to note that the regulations to be addressed were no longer the 1996 regulations, but those referred to below which had been passed into law in 2000.

---

[7]   MCA 1973, s 25B(1).
[8]   See Form E, para 2.16.
[9]   [2006] 2 FLR 901, CA.

The 1973 Act[10] provides for regulations to be made for the value of any benefits under a pension scheme to be calculated and verified for the purpose of orders under s 23. These regulations are contained in the Divorce etc (Pensions) Regulations 2000 (referred to as the 'Pensions Regulations 2000')[11] and the Pensions on Divorce etc (Provision of Information) Regulations 2000 (referred to as the 'Information Regulations 2000'),[12] and may be summarised as follows:

(1)　The value of pension benefits shall be valued on a date to be specified by the court between one year before the date of petition and the date of order.[13]

The significance of this is not only that any direction by the court should specify the date for valuation but also that, strictly speaking, the court should be invited to specify such a date in all cases.

(2)　If the party is an active member of an occupational pension scheme the value shall be the cash equivalent to which he would have acquired a right under s 94(1)(a) of the Pension Schemes Act 1993 if his pensionable service had terminated at the specified date;[14] if he is a deferred member of such a scheme the value shall be the cash equivalent of his rights acquired at termination of his pensionable service.[15]

(3)　If the party is a member of a personal pension scheme the value shall be the cash equivalent to which he would have acquired a right under s 94(1)(b) of the Pension Schemes Act 1993 if he had made an application under s 95(1) at the specified date.[16]

The significance of the references to the 1993 Act is that ss 93–101 of that Act provide for the right of persons in occupational and personal pension schemes to take a 'cash equivalent transfer value' (CETV), and for the method of calculating and taking such value. The CETV is by far the most common form of valuation to be used in cases involving pensions, and includes the value of the member's payment on retirement, the lump sum payable on retirement, the lump sum payable on death after leaving active service but before retirement, the lump sum payable on death after retirement, and the spouse's pension payable on the member's death. It does not include death in service benefits, future expectations nor discretionary benefits.

---

[10]　MCA 1973, s 25D(2)(e).
[11]　SI 2000/1123.
[12]　SI 2000/1048.
[13]　Pensions Regulations 2000, reg 3(1)(a).
[14]　Information Regulations 2000, reg 3(3).
[15]　Ibid, reg 3(4).
[16]　Ibid, reg 3(5).

(4) Managers of pension schemes must provide a CETV to a party on request or when ordered within the period of 3 months beginning with the date of the request.[17]

(5) When asked, the managers must specify what proportion of the CETV is attributable to any pension or other periodical payments to which a spouse of the member would or might become entitled in the event of the member's death.[18]

10.9 Although the CETV is the conventional method of valuation, it is not the only one, and this method is not without its critics. It is sometimes argued that in defined contribution or money purchase schemes the CETV is likely to be less than the actual value of the fund accrued for the member due to certain costs being deducted. In final salary and defined benefit schemes, the CETV may be considerably less than the true value of the lost benefits as the scheme actuary may adopt conservative assumptions to protect the remaining scheme members.

The court cannot, in principle, depart from the CETV method of valuation, but it may be persuaded to take other matters into account, provided they were supported by expert evidence. In particular, evidence of matters not included in the CETV, such as death in service benefits or discretionary benefits, might be admissible, as might evidence as to future expectations where is seemed that the CETV provided an inadequate indication as to its value.

10.10 Valuation of a pension in payment is a more open question. As was seen at para **10.9**, the court has a complete discretion. One answer might be to do a *Duxbury* calculation.[19] It should also be noted that there is no prescribed method of valuation of either future pension rights or death in service benefits.

What weight is to be attached to the value of the benefits?

10.11 Having established the value of the benefits, normally by a CETV, what does the court do with it? What figure is to be brought into the 'pot' or calculation? In *H v H*,[20] the pension had been earned over 13 years of service. Only seven of those years were years of cohabitation. Thorpe J said that it was more important to look to 'the value of what has been earned during cohabitation than to look to the prospective value of what may be earned over the course of the 25 or 30 years between separation and retirement age'. In *Hedges v Hedges*,[21] where the pension was not payable for 20 years, Mustill LJ said 'I note the existence of this sum, but it seems to me that the time when it will fall to hand is so remote that it has little relevance except as a piece of background'.

---

[17] Information Regulations 2000, reg 2.
[18] Ibid, reg 5.
[19] See Chapter 4 at para **4.14**.
[20] *H v H (Financial Provision: Capital Allowance)* [1993] 2 FLR 335, FD.
[21] [1991] 1 FLR 196, CA.

In *Milne v Milne*[22] (decided well before the recent statutory changes, but of some value nevertheless), after a 33-year marriage where the husband was a member of a pension scheme and had up to 10 years still to serve, the wife was awarded a lump sum equivalent to one-half of the amount to which the husband or his estate should become entitled under the scheme, provided she was still surviving at that time.

In a more recent case,[23] the wife argued for a *Milne v Milne* type order, but this argument was rejected; in principle this was the kind of case in which such an order might have been appropriate but the practicalities were such that in reality this would be of little benefit to the wife.

Both these cases were decided before the coming into force of ss 25B–25D, but that does not detract from their force since, as has been seen, the new provisions provide new mechanisms but do not prescribe the weight which the court is to place on the information which it receives. The principles to be derived from these cases may be as follows.

(1)   Where the parties are comparatively young, and the pension will not become payable for many years, the value of the pension is likely to be academic. The parties are under a duty to obtain the information, and the court has the duty to consider it, but it will probably not be a matter of great relevance. How far ahead a pension must be to be disregarded is debatable. In *Hedges v Hedges*, the period was 20 years, and it may be that anything in excess of that period would not be relevant. However, each case must turn on its own facts, and it would be difficult to prescribe with any degree of accuracy a period of less than 20 years which in itself rendered a pension irrelevant.

(2)   When the value of a pension is to be taken into account, the principle enunciated by Thorpe J in *H v H* should be followed; the CETV should be divided by the number of years' service so far and then multiplied by the number of years of cohabitation. Use of the term 'cohabitation' may be potentially misleading. As used by Thorpe J in this case, it referred to the years from the date of the marriage to separation, and does not seem to have been intended to include any pre-marital cohabitation; whether such extra-marital cohabitation could be held to be relevant must remain a matter for speculation.

Should the value of the pension be aggregated with the other assets for the purpose of the s 25 exercise or for some apportionment of assets? In *Maskell v Maskell*[24] it was held that to do so would be incorrect. Thorpe LJ observed (para [6]) that the judge had made:

---

[22]   [1981] 2 FLR 286, CA, following *Priest v Priest* (1980) 1 FLR 189.
[23]   *SRJ v DWJ (Financial Provision)* [1999] 2 FLR 176, CA.
[24]   [2003] 1 FLR 1138, CA.

'... the seemingly somewhat elementary mistake of confusing present capital with a right to financial benefits on retirement, only 25% of which maximum could be taken in capital terms, the other 75% being taken as an annuity stream. He simply failed to compare like with like. I have a grave anxiety that the district judge made the same mistake ...'

Further guidance was given in *Martin-Dye v Martin-Dye* (see para **10.8**). In his judgment Dyson LJ said:

'But I do not read Thorpe LJ as saying that, as a matter of law, it is never open to the court to aggregate the value of pensions with that of other assets and distribute the resultant total value between the parties. Examples of where such an approach might be appropriate could be where the parties have pensions in payment which are of approximately equal value and/or where the value of the pensions is small in comparison with that of the other assets. It will all depend in the particular circumstances of the case.'

Both Thorpe LJ and Dyson LJ agreed that it was artificial to regard pensions as being the same as other assets. In the words of Dyson LJ:

'It seems to me that in a case such as this the better course is to take the pensions out of the assets altogether and to make a pension-sharing order. This reflects the reality that the pensions are in truth non-transferable income streams and are quite different in kind from the other assets owned by the parties. In my judgment, it is artificial to say that the pensions are capital assets valued at £940,000 (husband) and £100,000 (wife). The reality is that the sole value of their pensions to the parties is that they produce gross incomes of £37,840 and £5,818 respectively. In my judgment, the judge below, in effect, mischaracterised the pensions as being, or being equivalent to, capital assets.'

Although the pensions in the case were pensions in payment, the comments of Thorpe LJ may be taken to be relevant to all pensions. His Lordship saw the matter as follows:

'Our focus is upon pensions in payment and cash equivalent benefits. They are to be characterised as "other financial resources" within the s 25(2)(a) classification. For they do not sit comfortably in the category of "property", since they are unrealisable and non-transferable. Nor do they sit comfortably in the category of "income" because, although purely an income stream, the income does not derive from future endeavour but from past employment or contribution which will generally have been effected during the years of marriage.

This case provides a useful example of this analysis. The "property" consists of the houses and the investments. The "income" is the receipts anticipated from the parties continuing endeavours, the wife in her livery business and the husband in his fitted kitchen business. The "other financial resources" are their respective pensions in payment.'

Loss of widow's pension rights

10.12 On divorce or annulment of marriage, the party who is not a pension scheme member (normally the wife) is liable to lose two classes of benefits. The first, namely loss of the chance of sharing in the benefits payable under the scheme on retirement, has already been considered. The second is just as important for many wives; this is loss of the benefits of a widow's pension in the event of a husband's death. As has been seen, the court is specifically directed to have regard to the benefits under a pension scheme which a party to the marriage will lose the chance of acquiring.[25]

10.13 The value of the lost benefits should be comparatively simple to ascertain, since an obligation is imposed on managers or trustees of a pension scheme to specify what proportion of the CETV is attributable to any pension or other periodical payments to which a spouse of the member would be or might become entitled in the event of the member's death.[26] However, once again, the CETV method may be criticised on the ground that the proportion specified will represent only the estimated cost of providing a pension to an average widow of the member and presupposes termination of service as at the date of valuation. By contrast, s 25(2)(h) clearly requires consideration of the potential loss in the event that service is completed to normal retirement date. There may therefore be scope for expert evidence to supplement the CETV information in appropriate cases.

10.14 Having established a figure for the value of the lost benefits, the next calculation is that of the sum which might be paid to compensate the wife for the loss of the chance of acquiring the widow's pension. This figure will be the sum which she would need to buy an annuity which would come into payment on her husband's death.[27] Both these figures should therefore be available for the use of the court.

However, it should not be supposed that a lump sum of this nature will be awarded as a matter of right in all cases. Where the value of the lost benefits is taken into account it will normally be as part of a greater lump sum which takes account of other matters, and any award will only be made after consideration of all the s 25 factors.

10.15 There is another area in which loss of widow's benefits is highly relevant, namely a divorce suit which is defended on the ground of grave financial hardship.[28] All that has been said so far is equally applicable to that class of case.

---

[25] MCA 1973, s 25(2)(h).
[26] Information Regulations 2000, reg 2.
[27] Tables for calculating the value of the lost benefits and of the cost of a replacement annuity will be found at table 16 of *At a Glance*. These should be used as a guide.
[28] Under MCA 1973, s 5.

In such cases, if a respondent wife establishes a prima facie case of grave financial hardship, it is for the husband to make proposals to mitigate the hardship; if he does not do so, the petition must be dismissed. However, it would be wrong to suppose that a wife is entitled to be compensated pound for pound for what she will lose in consequence of the divorce; she has to show, not that she will lose something by being divorced but that she will suffer grave financial hardship, which is a very different thing.[29]

It has been held that the proper approach for the court is first to determine whether it has been established that grave financial hardship will result from the divorce and secondly to decide whether in all the circumstances the marriage should be dissolved.[30] In many cases, the issue may be whether the husband is, in fact, in a position to do anything to remedy the hardship; the availability of State benefits will also be relevant.[31]

In another case[32] where the husband was a serving police officer, after a long marriage it was held that the husband's proposals came nowhere near mitigating the hardship; the hearing was adjourned generally to enable the parties to negotiate further.

What orders may be made?

10.16 There are separate sections below on orders directed to the pension fund member to commute, and attachment orders. For the sake of completeness, here it need only be said that, apart from those orders, the usual order to be made which reflects a pension element will be a 'standard' lump sum order against the pension fund member. Lump sum orders are discussed generally in Chapter 4.

ATTACHMENT (FORMERLY EARMARKING) ORDERS

10.17 One of the principal innovations of the changes introduced by the Pensions Act 1995 and now found in MCA 1973, ss 25B–25D is the concept of what was then called earmarking and is now called attachment. An attachment order is an order directed to the persons responsible for the pension arrangement requiring them to pay to the party who is not the pension fund member sums which would normally have gone to the member. It is important to note that attachment is not a separate head of relief. It is made under MCA 1973, s 23 and will be either a periodical payments order, whether deferred or not, or a deferred lump sum order.[33]

29　*Le Marchant v Le Marchant* [1977] 1 WLR 559, CA.
30　*Jackson v Jackson* [1993] 2 FLR 848, CA.
31　Ibid.
32　*K v K (Financial Relief: Widow's Pension)* [1997] 1 FLR 35, FD.
33　MCA 1973, s 25B(2) and (3), as amended by WRPA 1999.

It is also important to note that, although the court 'may' make an attachment order, it is obliged to consider making such an order whenever one party has or is likely to have a benefit under a pension scheme.[34] Attachment orders may, therefore, be of a capital or income nature; the court's powers are also strengthened by the power to order a person entitled to a benefit to commute all or part of those benefits.

10.18 The relevant statutory provisions, which apply whenever, having regard to any benefits under a pension scheme, the court determines to make an order under s 23, are as follows:

'(4)   To the extent to which the order [ie the s 23 order] is made having regard to any benefits under a pension arrangement, the order may require the person responsible for the pension arrangement in question, if at any time any payment in respect of any benefits under the arrangement becomes due to the party with pension rights, to make a payment for the benefit of the other party.

(5)   The order must express the amount of any payment required to be made by virtue of subsection (4) as a percentage of the payment which becomes due to the party with pension rights.

(6)   Any such payment by the person responsible for the arrangement—
    (a)   shall discharge so much of his liability to the party with pension rights as corresponds to the amount of the payment, and
    (b)   shall be treated for all purposes as a payment made by the party with pension rights in or towards the discharge of his liability under the order.

(7)   Where the party with pension rights has a right of commutation under the arrangement, the order may require him to exercise it to any extent; and this section applies to any payment due in consequence of commutation in pursuance of the order as it applies to other payments in respect of benefits under the arrangement.'[35]

10.19 The remaining statutory provisions are concerned exclusively with lump sums due under the pension scheme on death; they apply whenever the benefits which the party with pension rights has or is likely to have under a pension scheme include any lump sum payable in respect of his death. In such cases, the court may:

'(a)   if the person responsible for the pension arrangement in question has power to determine the person to whom the sum, or any part of it, is to be paid, require him to pay the whole or part of that sum, when it becomes due, to the other party,

(b)   if the party with pension rights has power to nominate the person to whom the sum or any part of it is to be paid, require the party with pension rights to nominate the other party in respect of the whole or part of that sum,

(c)   in any other case, require the person responsible for the pension arrangement in question to pay the whole or part of that sum, when it

---

[34]   MCA 1973, s 25B(2).
[35]   Ibid, s 25B(4)–(7), as amended by WRPA 1999.

becomes due, for the benefit of the other party instead of to the party to whom, apart from the order, it would be paid.'[36]

The effect of all these provisions may now be considered.

Summary of attachment provisions

10.20 As mentioned above, these provisions came into force on 1 August 1996, and are only available for petitions filed on or after 1 July 1996 and in respect of applications made on or after 1 August 1996. The position may be summarised as follows.

(1) When the court makes an attachment order, whether by way of periodical payments or lump sum, it can order the trustees or managers (now known as 'the person responsible') to pay it on the husband's behalf.

(2) Payments of periodical payments are taxable in the hands of the recipient. This distinguishes them from 'normal' periodical payments.

(3) A periodical payments attachment order is in reality no more than an attachment of earnings order against the pension fund.

(4) A periodical payments attachment order may be deferred, ie may be ordered to be paid at some future date. It will therefore be, in effect, a deferred attachment order against the fund.

(5) A periodical payments attachment order will end on the death of either party, and is fully variable; this might mean that it could be varied before it had ever been paid.

(6) When the court is considering making a lump sum attachment order to be paid from pension benefits, it can require the pension fund member to exercise any commutation rights which he may enjoy. This can be for part or all of the benefits, and would be accompanied by an order requiring the trustees or managers to pay the commuted sum to the other party. However, a defect in the provisions is that the court cannot order the member to take his pension at any particular time.

(7) The court can order a lump sum attachment order from death benefits, and can force the member to nominate the other party to receive such death benefits.

(8) All lump sum attachment orders are variable.[37] In this, they are in stark contrast to other lump sum orders. It remains to be seen what the effect of this will be; for example, it might be argued that the remarriage of a wife

---

[36] MCA 1973, s 25C(2), as amended by WRPA 1999.
[37] Ibid, s 31(2)(dd).

in whose favour such an order had been made would be ground for variation, particularly if her new husband was a man of means.

Judicial guidance on attachment orders

10.21 The first important case on the earmarking provisions (as they were then called) was the decision of Singer J in *T v T (Financial Relief: Pensions)*.[38] The facts were comparatively simple. H was 46, W was 47, and the childless marriage had lasted for 17 years. Joint assets were £186,000, and H had in his sole name between £90,000 and £100,000. The judge observed 'with regret' that costs of about £60,000 had been incurred. It was agreed that this was not a clean break case. W did not work but the judge ascribed to her an earning capacity of £5,000 p a. H's income was £109,000 p a, with the possibility of a bonus.

10.22 Singer J first made the following orders. W's housing needs were for a house costing £175,000, and there were no other capital requirements (except for pension). Her income requirements were £22,000 p a. The judge therefore made an order for her to receive £175,000, and £22,000 until mid-1999, by which time she should have realised her earning potential and the order could be reduced to £5,000 p a. This was to be an order unlimited in duration, and W retained her rights under the Inheritance (Provision for Family and Dependants) Act 1975.

Singer J then considered how, if at all, the approach which he had adopted so far should be effected or revised in the light of the new powers of the court under ss 25B, 25C and 25D.

10.23 Singer J rejected the first argument advanced by W that the new provisions manifested an intention on the part of the legislature to require, and not just enable, a spouse in W's position to be compensated for her actual and potential loss of pension benefits.

The statute required the court 'in particular' to 'have regard' to the pension benefits etc, and to consider how the pension considerations 'should affect' the terms of the order it intended to make; that formulation in no way precluded the court from giving the answer 'not at all' to that question.

10.24 He also rejected as unsustainable W's next submission that the orders which could be made against pension providers were distinct from the other orders which could be made under s 23, and that one consequence of this was that an earmarking maintenance order would not terminate on W's remarriage.

10.25 W then sought an order that, from the date when H began to draw his pension, the trustees should pay to W a proportion of H's pension to reflect the

---

[38]   [1998] 1 FLR 107.

duration of the marriage by reference to the period over which the pension was paid (this would have meant an order for one-half of three-fifths of the pension).

Singer J declined to adopt this approach. It was impossible to preduct now what on ordinary principles would be the quantum of W's maintenance entitlement in 2011. In any event, 2011 was a notional date since H could delay taking his pension for up to a further 15 years; the court had no control over that, and could earmark payments which become due but had no power to interfere in when that was to be. Either party could apply to vary any earmarking order even before it came into effect. If no earmarking order were made now, the court would be in just as effective a position if consideration of the quantum and form of the appropriate order were left until the time H took his pension. In the circumstances, the judge saw no advantage in making an order for deferred periodical payments now, and many pitfalls if he did.

10.26 W then argued that she should receive additional provision to compensate for the potential loss of widow's pension she would receive if H predeceased her after commencing to draw his pension. Singer J took account of the fact that W might be expected to outlive H by 4 years after his assumed death at the age of 74; he was therefore being asked to fix a sum certain to be payable in 13 years' time to reflect a potential loss of what 4 years' worth of widow's pension started in 2025 or 2026 might be. He declined to make H pay the price of this element of W's potential pension loss. Far more fairly, it would be open to W in such circumstances to raise claims against his estate.

10.27 Finally, W sought an order under s 25C(1) for payment in respect of the lump sum which would be made in the event of H's death in service. Singer J acceded to this request, in part because the death in service benefits which could be earmarked for her might very well not fall into H's estate.

10.28 A similar result was reached in *Burrow v Burrow*.[39] The assets in this case were the former matrimonial home, which had a net equity of £425,000, the husband's 98% shareholding in the family building business, and the husband's interest in the pension fund worth £267,712. The district judge made orders that the wife receive £349,500 from the proceeds of sale of the home and periodical payments for herself and the children, and then made an earmarking order for 50% of the pension fund both as to capital and the annuity fund. On appeal, Cazalet J removed all provision relating to the annuity fund. He said that the provisions of MCA 1973, ss 25B–25D do not create any entitlement in the sense of an accrued right to pension sharing. In determining whether to make an earmarking order and, if so, the quantum, the court must simply exercise its discretion under the s 25 criteria. Adopting that approach, it had been wrong to make the earmarking order against the annuity fund, having regard to the disadvantages in making the order well before any sums were due to become payable under it. It was open to either party to apply for variation of

---

[39] [1999] 1 FLR 508, FD.

periodical payments. However, the order earmarking 50% of the capital fund could stand since it appropriately reflected the wife's contribution both within the family and the building up of assets as well as being a future benefit which would otherwise be lost to her.

Procedure

10.29 An important procedural point is that attachment orders must be specifically applied for.[40] If there is no such application, the court should not make an order. This is not mere pedantry, because the rules[41] require notice of the application to be given to the trustees or managers of the scheme.

The persons responsible for a pension scheme must furnish certain information to a member seeking it where the member is the petitioner or respondent in proceedings for divorce, nullity of marriage of judicial separation and:

(a) has requested the information and has not previously received information for the purpose of the proceedings; or

(b) has been required by the court to request the information.

The information which the person responsible is obliged to supply is, in effect, the CETV. This must be valued at a date to be chosen by the person responsible and must be within 3 months beginning with the date of the request. The valuation must be supplied not more than 10 working days after the valuation.[42]

10.30 The effect of this is, therefore, that the scheme member must apply for the information from the person responsible, and those acting for him should ensure that this is done. When he fails to do so, an order can be obtained from the court requiring him to do so.[43]

Armed forces pensions

10.31 It was previously the case that pensions payable by virtue of the Army Act 1955 and comparable legislation relating to the other services were not susceptible to orders of the court.[44] The effect of these provisions has now been abrogated by the WRPA 1999.

---

[40] Family Proceedings (Amendment No 2) Rules 1996, SI 1996/1674, r 3. See also FPR 1991, r 2.61A(3).

[41] FPR 1991, r 2.70(4).

[42] Pensions Regulations 2000, reg 4(3).

[43] FPR 1991, r 2.70(2).

[44] See e g *Roberts v Roberts* [1986] 2 FLR 152, FD; *Happe v Happe* [1990] 2 FLR 212, CA.

PENSION SHARING

10.32 Pension sharing has been enacted by the WRPA 1999 and came into force on 1 December 2000. This completes the armoury of powers relating to pensions enjoyed by the court; pension sharing is an alternative to the other options available as described above (with the exception of *Brooks v Brooks* orders).

Pension sharing is available only in respect of petitions for divorce or nullity of marriage (not judicial separation) filed after 1 December 2000.

It has been held[45] that where both parties sought to rescind a decree nisi to enable a fresh petition containing a prayer for a pension sharing order to be presented, the application should be granted. Parties were entitled consensually to arrange their affairs to their best advantage. However, it has also been held[46] that where one party objected, rescission could not be allowed.

What is pension sharing?

10.33 WRPA 1999, s 29 applies, and pension sharing occurs when a pension sharing order made under MCA 1973, s 21A takes effect.[47] Section 21A provides that a pension sharing order is an order which:

(a) provides that one party's:
    (i) shareable rights under a specified pension arrangement, or
    (ii) shareable State scheme rights,
    be subject to pension sharing for the benefit of the other party; and

(b) specifies the percentage value to be transferred.

It should be noted that WRPA 1999, s 28 also provides certain other events when pension sharing will come about but, since these were all contingent on the coming into force of the Family Law Act 1996, they have all become otiose.

10.34 It will be seen that MCA 1973, s 21A contemplates two classes of pension rights, namely 'shareable rights under a specified pension arrangement' and 'shareable State scheme rights'. There are therefore two types of pension to be considered, which may crudely be classed as private pensions and State pensions.

WRPA 1999, s 29(1) applies to private pensions, and provides that on the application of that section (ie on the taking effect of a pension sharing order):

---

45 In *S v S (Rescission of Decree Nisi: Pension Sharing Provision)* [2002] 1 FLR 457.
46 In *H v H (Pension Sharing: Rescission of Decree Nisi)* [2002] 2 FLR 116. See also *Rye v Rye* [2002] 2 FLR 981.
47 WRPA 1999, s 28(1)(a).

(a)   the transferor's shareable rights under the relevant arrangement become subject to a debit of the appropriate amount, and

(b)   the transferee becomes entitled to a credit of that amount as against the person responsible for that arrangement.

This therefore describes the effect of a pension sharing order for any pension other than a State pension.

WRPA 1999, s 48(1) applies to State pensions, and provides that pension sharing occurs on the making of a pension sharing order. On the making of such an order, s 49 applies; the effect of this is that:

(a)   the transferor becomes subject, for the purposes of Part II of the Social Security Contributions and Benefits Act 1992 (contributory benefits), to a debit of the appropriate amount, and

(b)   the transferee becomes entitled, for those purposes, to a credit of that amount.[48]

This describes the effect of pension sharing in respect of State pensions.

10.35 A number of the key concepts of pension sharing have already emerged and these, together with some others, must be considered in detail. These are:

–   shareable rights;

–   shareable State scheme rights;

–   shared additional pension;

–   pension arrangement;

–   person responsible;

–   pension debit;

–   pension credit;

–   implementation period.

These will now be considered in turn.

---

[48]   WRPA 1999, s 49(1).

Shareable rights

10.36 A person's shareable rights under a pension arrangement are any rights that person has under the arrangement, other than rights of a description specified by regulations made by the Secretary of State (for Social Security).[49] Pension sharing is available in respect of shareable rights in any pension arrangement (other than an excepted public service pension scheme; such an excepted scheme would have to be designated as such by the responsible Minister).[50]

In practical terms, therefore, the pension entitlement of most people will be vulnerable to an application for pension sharing.

Shareable State scheme rights

10.37 Not all State pensions are shareable. A person's shareable State scheme rights are defined as:

(a) that person's entitlement or prospective entitlement to a Category A retirement pension by virtue of s 44(3)(b) of the Social Security Contributions and Benefits Act 1992 (earnings-related additional pensions), and

(b) that person's entitlement or prospective entitlement to a pension under s 55A of that Act (shared additional pension).[51]

The first category comprises what are normally known as State Earnings Related Pension Schemes (SERPS). The basic State pension is not susceptible to pension sharing.

Shared additional pension is defined below.

Shared additional pension

10.38 This is the description to be given to a pension derived from a pension credit from shareable State scheme rights; a person who obtains a pension sharing order against another person's State scheme rights has a shared additional pension. The significance of the definition in (b) above is therefore merely that such a pension would itself be susceptible to an application for pension sharing made by a (subsequent) spouse.

---

[49] WRPA 1999, s 27(2).
[50] Ibid, s 27(1) and (2).
[51] Ibid, s 47(2).

Pension arrangement

10.39 'Pension arrangement' is defined as:

(a)   an occupational pension scheme;

(b)   a personal pension scheme;

(c)   a retirement annuity contract;

(d)   an annuity or insurance policy purchased, or transferred, for the purpose of giving effect to rights under an occupational pension scheme or a personal pension scheme; and

(e)   an annuity purchased or entered into for the purpose of discharging liability in respect of a pension credit.[52]

This definition covers most, if not all, private pensions.

Person responsible

10.40 On many occasions throughout the Act, obligations are placed on the person responsible for the pension arrangement. This term replaces 'trustees or managers' of the arrangement.

Pension credit and pension debit

10.41 A pension credit is what the person in whose favour a pension sharing order has been made actually receives. The order must specify the percentage value to be transferred,[53] and this is a percentage of the cash equivalent of the (transferee's) relevant benefits on the valuation day,[54] defined as such day within the implementation period (as to which, see below) as the person responsible may specify to the parties in writing.[55]

10.42 This requires a little explanation. The first stage of valuation of a pension benefit is when the court decides what that value is at the hearing. It is provided[56] that, for the purpose of the court's functions when exercising any of its powers under Part II of MCA 1973, benefits under a pension arrangement must be calculated as set out in reg 3 of the Information Regulations 2000. Of more immediate relevance to the courts and to practitioners are the additional provisions[57] that:

(a)   the benefits must be valued at a date to be specified by the court;

---

[52]   WRPA 1999, s 26(1).
[53]   MCA 1973, s 21A(1)(b).
[54]   WRPA 1999, s 29(2).
[55]   Ibid, s 29(7).
[56]   By the Pensions Regulations 2000, reg 3(1).
[57]   Information Regulations 2000, reg 3(1)(a)–(c).

(b)   such date must be not earlier than one year before the date of the petition and not later than the date on which the court is exercising its power;

(c)   in determining the value, the court may have regard to information furnished by the person responsible for the pension arrangement pursuant to any of the provisions set out in reg 3(2).

From this, the following points may be made. First, the court must specify at some stage a date on which the benefits are to be valued and must then, presumably, state that date in whatever final order is made. Secondly, the court must exercise its discretion in deciding when that date is to be, but it cannot go back earlier than one year before the petition.

However, the person responsible has then to decide a date within the implementation period for the application of the proportion stated in the order (eg 50%) to the pension benefits, and the credit will be the percentage on that date.

Thirdly, the court 'may have regard' to information from the pension scheme. It is difficult to see how the court could do otherwise, but it should be noted that there is here no prohibition of additional evidence, for example from actuaries. The court would be bound to regard the valuation given by the scheme as being the correct CETV figure, but it would be entitled also to take the view that this was a low figure (analogous to a surrender value on a life policy) which might not accurately reflect the true value to the member of all the benefits under the scheme.

10.43 When the pension arrangement is an occupational scheme and the transferor is still in pensionable service the relevant benefits are those to which he would have been entitled if he had retired immediately before the transfer day;[58] otherwise, the benefits are those to which he was entitled, including future benefits, immediately before the transfer day.[59] The pension debit is, in effect, the value of his pension which the transferor loses by virtue of the pension sharing.

Implementation period

10.44 Persons responsible for pension arrangements have to be given a period of time in which to effect the pension sharing and transfer the pension credit to the transferee. This is known as the implementation period and is 4 months beginning with the day on which the order takes effect or the day on which the person responsible receives the order and prescribed information, whichever be the later.[60] The prescribed information is contained in reg 5 of the Information Regulations 2000 and includes such matters as dates of birth, national insurance numbers, and names and addresses.

---

[58]   WRPA 1999, s 29(4).
[59]   Ibid, s 29(5).
[60]   Ibid, s 34(1).

Summary so far

10.45 It has been seen above that pension sharing in respect of pensions other than State pensions is essentially quite simple. The court specifies the percentage of the transferor's pension which is to be transferred to the transferee. The person responsible for the pension arrangement has 4 months from notification to effect the transfer, and nominates a day within that period for the valuation of the transferor's rights. He then credits the transferee with the appropriate amount and debits the transferor with the same amount. Three further matters remain to be considered. They are:

(1)   the ways in which the pension credit may be applied;

(2)   how sharing of shareable State scheme rights is effected;

(3)   the effect on a shared additional pension.

These will be considered in turn.

How can a pension credit be used?

10.46 The basic position relating to the rights of the transferee is dealt with in WRPA 1999, Sch 5, which bears the heading 'Pension credits: mode of discharge'. The Schedule consists of the obligations of the persons responsible for the pension arrangement, ie the fund manager or trustees, and sets out the ways in which such persons may discharge their obligations. Liability in respect of a pension credit may not be discharged otherwise than in accordance with Sch 5.[61]

The nature of the obligations depend on the kind of pension scheme in question.

10.47 The intention behind the provisions in WRPA 1999 is that, where the scheme is a funded occupational scheme or a personal pension scheme, the person responsible for the scheme should first offer to discharge its liability to the transferee for the pension credit by making a transfer payment to a suitable scheme or arrangement of the transferee's choice. This can include conferring rights on the transferee within the scheme (an internal transfer). The transferee will be invited to make a choice as to the destination of the pension credit, and if no choice is made within a specified period, the person responsible will decide.

10.48 Accordingly, para 1(2) of Sch 5 provides that the trustees or managers of the scheme from which a pension credit derives may discharge their liability in respect of the credit by conferring appropriate rights under that scheme on the person entitled to the credit:

---

[61]   WRPA 1999, s 32.

(a)   with his consent; or

(b)   in accordance with regulations made by the Secretary of State.

In other words, the internal transfer may be effected only if the transferee agrees or if regulations so provide.

'Appropriate rights' are defined as rights which are conferred with effect from and including the day on which the order or provision under which the credit arises takes effect, and whose value, when calculated in accordance with regulations, equals the amount of the credit.[62]

10.49 It is then provided[63] that the trustees or managers may discharge their liability by paying the amount of the pension credit to 'the person responsible for a qualifying arrangement with a view to acquiring rights under that arrangement for the person entitled to the credit', ie to another pension scheme, providing certain conditions are met. These are that:

(a)   'the qualifying arrangement is not disqualified as a destination for the credit';

The arrangements which would or might be disqualified are set out in para 7 of the Schedule.

(b)   'the person responsible for that arrangement is able and willing to accept payment in respect of the credit';

(c)   'payment is made with the consent of the person entitled to the credit or in accordance with regulations made by the Secretary of State'.

Where the person entitled to the credit does not consent, transfer may only be made in accordance with regulations. The detail of such regulations is now contained in the Pension Sharing (Implementation and Discharge of Liability) Regulations 2000.[64]

It is also provided that no account will be taken of the consent of the person entitled to credit unless it is given after receipt of notice in writing of an offer to make a payment to another scheme as an external transfer, or it is not withdrawn within 7 days of receipt.[65] What this seems to mean is that the person responsible must offer to make an external transfer (presumably to a destination of the transferee's choice), and any consent given may not be acted on for 7 days after receipt.

---

[62]   WRPA 1999, Sch 5, para 5.
[63]   Ibid, Sch 5, para 1(3).
[64]   SI 2000/1053.
[65]   WRPA 1999, Sch 5, para 1(4).

10.50 Schedule 5, para 2 relates to occupational pension schemes which are not funded and which are public service pension schemes. With one exception, the person responsible may only provide benefits under the scheme, by way of internal transfer;[66] external transfer is not permitted. The exception occurs when the scheme is closed to new members, in which case the transferee may be offered membership of an alternative public service scheme which has been specified by regulations.[67]

10.51 When the person responsible has to specify another scheme, he must secure that appropriate rights are conferred on the person entitled to the credit by the person responsible for the alternative scheme, and must require them to take such steps as may be required.[68]

10.52 Schedule 5, para 3 applies when the pension credit is derived from an occupational pension scheme which is not funded and which is not a public service pension scheme. Here, the person responsible has choice, but the choice of the transferee is limited. The person responsible 'may discharge their liability in respect of the credit by conferring appropriate rights under that scheme [ie the transferor's scheme] on the person entitled to the credit';[69] this would be an internal transfer. The person responsible has, therefore, the absolute right to do this and the transferee has no choice.

However, the person responsible may transfer the credit externally, subject to certain conditions, namely:

(a)   the proposed destination is not disqualified; this has been considered at para **10.50** above;

(b)   the person responsible for the arrangement proposed as the destination is able and willing to accept payment in respect of the credit;

(c)   payment is made with the consent of the person entitled to the credit or in accordance with regulations.[70]

If the person entitled to credit does not consent, therefore, the transfer may only be made by the authority of regulations. For the detail, see the Pension Sharing (Implementation and Discharge of Liability) Regulations 2000.

10.53 Schedule 5, para 4 is limited to pension credits which derive from a retirement annuity contract, an annuity or insurance policy purchased or transferred for the purpose of giving effect to rights under an occupational pension scheme or a personal pension scheme, or an annuity purchased or entered into for the purpose of discharging liability in respect of a pension

---

[66]   WRPA 1999, Sch 5, para 2(2).
[67]   Ibid, Sch 5, para 2(3) and (4).
[68]   Ibid, Sch 5, para 2(4).
[69]   Ibid, Sch 5, para 3(2).
[70]   Ibid, Sch 5, para 3(3).

credit.[71] The person responsible for the scheme may discharge his obligations by an external transfer in exactly the same way as a person responsible for a funded occupational scheme or a personal pension scheme. The pension arrangement may discharge its obligations by entering into a policy of insurance or an annuity contract with the transferee, provided the transferee consents and the arrangement is not disqualified as a destination.[72] However, it is also provided that the pension arrangement may discharge its obligation by assuming an obligation to provide an annuity even if the transferee does not consent, if this is permitted by regulations.[73]

10.54 Schedule 5, para 8 provides for the amount of a pension credit which derives from an occupational pension scheme and which is to be the subject of an external transfer to be reduced when the scheme which is subject to the minimum funding requirement under the Pensions Act 1995, s 56 is underfunded on the valuation day. For the purposes of this provision, the valuation day is the day by reference to which the cash equivalent on which the pension credit depends falls to be calculated.[74]

10.55 It is also provided that when a person's shareable rights have become subject to a pension debit, and the person responsible for the pension arrangement makes a payment (presumably to the scheme member) without knowing of that debit, the amount of the credit shall be of such lesser amount as may be determined by regulations.[75] It is intended in this way to protect a scheme against loss arising out of a bona fide payment made in ignorance because of a late notification of a debit.

10.56 Schedule 5, para 10 provides for an increase of the amount of a pension credit where payment is made after the end of the implementation period (as to which, see para **10.44**). This is intended to compensate the transferee for delay on the part of the scheme. This is governed by regulations, but the method of compensation will be the award of interest. The detail is contained in the Pension Sharing (Pension Credit Benefit) Regulations 2000.[76]

Sharing of State scheme rights

10.57 The creation of State scheme pension debits and credits is governed by WRPA 1999, s 49(1). It is provided[77] that this section applies on the taking effect of any of the events set out in s 45, and that then:

'(a) the transferor becomes subject, for the purposes of Part II of the Contributions and Benefits Act (contributory benefits), to a debit of the appropriate amount, and

---

[71] WRPA 1999, Sch 5, para 4(1).
[72] Ibid, Sch 5, para 4(2).
[73] Ibid, Sch 5, para 4(3) and (4).
[74] Ibid, Sch 5, para 8(3).
[75] Ibid, Sch 5, para 9.
[76] SI 2000/1054.
[77] WRPA 1999, s 49(1).

(b)   the transferee becomes entitled, for those purposes, to a credit of that amount.'

10.58 Essentially, therefore, the transferor's additional pension is reduced by the amount of the debit, and the transferee becomes entitled to an additional pension in her own right based on the pension credit. The effect is set out in detail in Sch 6, which inserts a new s 45B into the Social Security Contributions and Benefits Act 1992.

Regulations govern the calculation of the cash equivalent (see para **10.42**). It is provided that, in determining prospective entitlement to a Category A retirement pension for the purposes of this section, only tax years before the year in which the transfer day falls will be taken into account.[78]

10.59 The amount of the reduction of the additional pension caused by pension sharing depends on the age of the transferor on the transfer day. If a person becomes subject to the debit in or after 'the final relevant year', that is to say the tax year immediately before he reaches pensionable age,[79] the additional pension will be reduced by 'the appropriate weekly amount';[80] this is a weekly amount which is of an actuarially equivalent value to the State scheme debit.[81] Assuming, therefore, that pensionable age is 65, this provision would apply when the debit took effect, not earlier than the tax year in which the transferor attained the age of 65.

Where the debit is made 'before the relevant year', ie before the tax year immediately before the transferor attains pensionable age, the additional pension will be reduced by 'the appropriate weekly amount multiplied by the relevant revaluation percentage'.[82] This means the weekly amount referred to above, multiplied by the earnings factor percentage for the relevant tax year specified in the latest annual Revaluation of Earnings Factor Order.

10.60 The new ss 55A–55C of the Social Security Contributions and Benefits Act 1992, inserted by WRPA 1999, Sch 6, deal with the meaning of 'shared additional pension'. This term is significant in two respects. First, pension sharing may occur in relation to a shared additional pension, so it is necessary for an applicant to know exactly what it is. Secondly, the effect on a shared additional pension of pension sharing (one might say 'further pension sharing') must be considered.

10.61 A person becomes entitled to a shared additional pension if he is:

(a)   over pensionable age, and

---

[78]   WRPA 1999, s 46(5).
[79]   Social Security Contributions and Benefits Act 1992, s 45B(8) (as amended by WRPA 1999, Sch 6).
[80]   Ibid, s 45B (as amended by WRPA 1999, Sch 6, para 2).
[81]   This is the effect of s 45B(4).
[82]   Social Security Contributions and Benefits Act 1992, s 45B(3) (as amended).

(b)   entitled to a State scheme pension credit.[83]

The entitlement cannot, therefore, arise until the person concerned (the transferee under the pension sharing) attains pensionable age. For the avoidance of doubt, it should be noted that the transferor need not yet have attained pensionable age, and could be younger than the transferee; the original pension sharing arrangement would have been calculated on the basis of his accrued entitlement.

The requirement for a State scheme pension credit is obvious; there must have been a pension sharing arrangement.

10.62 It is provided that a person's entitlement to a shared additional pension will continue throughout his life.[84] Once the pension is in payment, it will be increased by the same percentage as other pensions on an annual basis. Where a person's entitlement to a shared additional pension is deferred, the rate of his shared additional pension is increased by a formula contained in the new s 55C(2).

Pension sharing in respect of a shared additional pension

10.63 Having considered the significance of the shared additional pension in the most common case, namely a person (normally a wife) acquiring by means of pension transfer a share in her former spouse's SERPS entitlement, it is now necessary to consider the further circumstances in which this may be relevant. These arise out of the fact that a shared additional pension acquired in this conventional way may itself be the subject of pension sharing in favour of a subsequent former spouse.

10.64 It is provided that the weekly amount of a shared additional pension will be reduced in any case where:

(a)   the pensioner has become subject to a State scheme pension debit; and

(b)   the debit is to any extent referable to the pension.[85]

This assumes that the pensioner (the transferor) is entitled to a shared additional pension. It is contemplated that the pension debit may have occurred before the pensioner attains pensionable age since the same formula as that set out at para **10.59** is used to calculate the weekly rate of the reductions.[86]

---

[83]   Social Security Contributions and Benefits Act 1992, s 55A(1).
[84]   Ibid, s 55A(2).
[85]   Ibid, s 55B(1).
[86]   See s 55B(2)–(4).

COMPARISON OF THE VARIOUS TYPES OF REMEDY

10.65 Before considering the question of how the court's armoury of powers should be deployed, the more fundamental question of what the court is trying to do in any particular case will have to be considered. The value of any benefits or potential benefits under the pension arrangement must first be ascertained; this has to be by way of the CETV, but evidence may be admissible to show that the CETV figure understates the true value.

Once the value is known, that figure is considered together with the values of the other assets and liabilities. What does the court do next?[87]

10.66 Pensions are part of the overall exercise to be performed under s 25. It used to be said that there was no intrinsic reason why the property rights of parties should be disturbed and that redistribution in itself was not the purpose of the litigation. Such a confident statement is no longer possible, and the reader is referred to the section on equality and fairness at para **1.47** et seq. It is suggested that the court will now be concerned with equality of outcome where pensions are concerned and that overall fairness is likely to be an increasing preoccupation.

10.67 Assuming that the husband in most cases is the pension scheme member and that the wife has little or no pension provision, most cases will be approached on the basis of first considering whether or not the wife's reasonable needs include a need for pension provision. It is submitted that this is normally by no means the most pressing need, and the need for housing for the wife (and any dependent children) and her need for income would have been considered as the first priorities. However, assuming those needs to have been met, either from the wife's own resources or from redistribution of the assets, the pension position must be considered.

10.68 It is assumed that, in the kind of case in which pensions are relevant, the husband has some pension rights. It must further be assumed that his own needs for housing, income etc have been met; in most cases it would clearly be wrong, for example, to provide the funds for the wife to rehouse herself, to leave the husband with no adequate provision for housing and then to seek to attack his pension which might be the only asset or security he had left.

Given those assumptions, the pension needs of the wife would have to be considered. In considering these, the following questions would be relevant.

(1) How old is the wife? It seems to be generally accepted that the younger the parties (particularly the wife), and the longer the time before retirement, the less relevant is the pension issue. Quite how long this period has to be

---

[87] In what follows, the present author, by a different route, has come to roughly the same conclusions as those contained in an article entitled 'Pensions on divorce – Compensation or needs?' by Catherine Hallam and David Salter in [1997] Fam Law 608. A careful reading of that article is recommended.

to make it irrelevant is debatable.[88] Clearly, a wife aged under 30, perhaps even under 35, would find it difficult to mount a successful attack on a husband's pension. Equally clearly, a wife aged over 50 would have little problem. Between those ages exists an area of uncertainty and potential for litigation.

(2)   How old is the husband and how soon will the pension become payable? This question may be particularly relevant when there is a significant discrepancy in the parties' ages.

(3)   In the light of all the circumstances of the case, what are the wife's reasonable needs? In the context of pensions, these needs might be subdivided into need for income after the retirement of the husband or after his death, and need for capital after his retirement or death. Where there is an order for periodical payments without limit, clearly there will be a need for a continuing source of income; this might be met by means of periodical payments or by a one-off capital payment. The position of the wife if the husband dies must be considered.

10.69 Having decided what the needs of the wife are, what is available must be considered; it is, of course, necessary to remember that the husband is entitled to a pension as well, so that his needs must be considered unless it seems that he will be able to provide adequately for himself from other assets. The needs of the wife might be met by one of the orders now to be considered.

In *Maskell v Maskell*[89] it was held that comparing present capital with a right to future benefits on retirement was not a like-for-like comparison. The judge had confused present capital with a right to future financial benefits: only 25% could be taken as capital and the remainder as an annuity stream. This was an elementary mistake.

Offsetting

10.70 Offsetting will only be appropriate where there are sufficient other assets to provide a fund to meet the wife's needs or such of her needs as it is reasonable to cater for in the context of the parties' overall financial position. Ideally, a *Duxbury* fund[90] which would be sufficient to provide the wife's income and capital needs for life would serve this purpose, but it may be that a less ambitious amount of money would suit individual cases. Offsetting might be appropriate where the parties were comparatively young, and the wife's lack of pension was not yet serious, but where the husband had some pension provision it might be thought that it would be wrong to interfere with his pension entitlement but that the wife should have some additional capital to recognise her lack of provision.

---

[88]   See eg *H v H (Financial Provision: Capital Allowance)* [1993] 2 FLR 335 and *Hedges v Hedges* [1991] 1 FLR 196.
[89]   [2001] EWCA Civ 858, [2003] 1 FLR 1138.
[90]   See *B v B (Discovery: Financial Provision)* [1990] 2 FLR 180, per Ward J.

Attachment for income purposes (s 25B(4))

10.71 This would be appropriate where a pension in payment was, either now or at some time in the future, to be attached to provide periodical payments. In effect, this would be equivalent to an attachment of earnings order against the pension fund. Clearly it would be inappropriate where the parties wished there to be a clean break. It would also be dependent on the husband surviving, since it would cease on his death. It would always be liable to variation in the event of a change of circumstances of either party.

Attachment for a capital sum (s 25B(4))

10.72 This would be the case where the wife was to receive a deferred lump sum from the husband's pension entitlement. It might be appropriate where there was insufficient capital when the s 23 order was made and the only way to secure the money was from the pension fund. It would suffer from similar defects to an income order, particularly the fact that it may be varied, save that it would be possible to have a clean break.

Capital from commuted lump sum benefits (s 25B(7))

10.73 This is, in effect, a device to secure a deferred lump sum and to compel the husband to make the capital fund available.

Attachment of death in service benefits (s 25C(2)(a))

10.74 This category of relief would be appropriate where the wife was financially dependent on the husband, either for her own periodical payments or for payments in respect of the children (whether direct or through CSA 1991). On the death of the husband before retirement, any lump sum payable on his death, or part thereof, would be paid to the wife. By s 25C(2)(b), the husband could be compelled to nominate the wife as the person to receive all or part of the benefits, and, by s 25C(2)(c), any trust of a retirement annuity contract could be overridden to secure payment for the wife.

This class of order is also liable to be varied.

A pension sharing order

10.75 A pension sharing order would be most appropriate where it was intended that the parties should have a clean break and it was thought desirable to provide the wife with a share of the husband's pension entitlement to give her a pension fund of her own, or the base for such a fund. It would be possible for there to be a periodical payments order in addition to a pension sharing order in appropriate cases, but it would not be possible to make any form of attachment order so that, for example, there could be no protection as to death in service benefits. The advantage of a pension sharing order would be that, subject to appeal, it could not be varied and it would survive the respondent's death, so that the pension credit transferred to the wife would be hers for life.

There would be, therefore, distinct advantages to a pension sharing order, but it might not be appropriate for a mother with young dependent children who wished to protect her income in the event of the husband's premature death. It would be highly appropriate for the wife who wanted a clean break in every sense of the term and wished to take her pension and go.

10.76 Since the onset of the availability of pension sharing orders, some problems have arisen in practice. One of the major problems is concerned with valuation and implementation.

The court has to carry out its valuation at a date to be specified by the court, being a date which is not earlier than one year before the date of the petition and not later than the date of the order.[91] This will be the date of the CETV adopted by the court or the parties. However, the pension fund must implement the order at a time of its choice within four months after service of the order. It may well be that the valuation used by the court or the parties to arrive at the proportions in which the pension will be shared will be many months old at the date of implementation, with the almost inevitable result that the share which is actually transferred will not be the precise amount which the court or the parties earlier had in mind.

One distinguished authority[92] suggests that this difficulty might be overcome by adopting as the wording for the share to be transferred: 'whatever percentage (not being greater than 100%) shall yield a transfer of £x at the valuation day specified by the person responsible for [relevant arrangements] for the purpose of the WRPA 1999, s 29'. Clearly this proposal has its attractions and, if accepted by the relevant arrangement, would be very useful. However, it is known that the Society of Pensions Consultants has reservations about the proposal, principally on the ground that it does not comply with the legislation; it is argued that a fixed amount may not be stated in orders made in England and Wales. It seems there is no consensus as to a solution.

Pensions and insolvency

10.77 For the position when a person entitled to a pension is made bankrupt see Chapter 12, para **12.14**. See also the next section.

The Pension Protection Fund

10.78 The Pension Protection Fund (PPF) was established by the Pensions Act 2004, Part 2, and came into force on 6 April 2005. Its purpose is to provide some compensation to pension scheme members whose schemes are under-funded or insolvent and who therefore run the risk of losing the benefits to which they would otherwise be entitled under the scheme. The PPF is in effect an insurance scheme to mitigate the effects of such under-funding or insolvency, but it must be emphasised that it not yet universally available. The

---

[91] Divorce etc (Pensions) Regulations 2000, reg 3.
[92] David Salter *Pension Sharing in Practice* (Family Law, 2nd edn, 2003) at p 44.

PPF has also, from September 2005, assumed responsibility for the Fraud Compensation Fund established under the Pensions Act 2004, ss 182–189.

Whether or not a particular pension scheme which is under-funded is covered by the PPF is potentially complicated and beyond the scope of this book. However, family practitioners must be alert to the possibility of a claim against the Fund.[93]

10.79 To take account of the PPF a new s 25E has been inserted into the Matrimonial Causes Act. This provides as follows:

'(1) The matters to which the court is to have regard under section 25(2) include –

(a)   in the case of paragraph (a), any PPF compensation to which a party to the marriage is or is likely to be entitled, and

(b)   in the case of paragraph (h), any PPF compensation which, by reason of the dissolution or annulment of the marriage, a party to the marriage will lose the chance of acquiring entitlement to,

and, accordingly, in relation to PPF compensation, section 25(2)(*a*) shall have effect as if "in the foreseeable future" were omitted.

(2) Subsection (3) applies in relation to an order under section 23 so far as it includes provision made by virtue of section 25B(4) which –

(a)   imposed requirements on the trustees or managers of an occupational pension scheme for which the Board has assumed responsibility in accordance with Chapter 3 of Part 2 of the Pensions Act 2004 (pension protection) or any provision in force in Northern Ireland corresponding to that Chapter, and

(b)   was made before the trustees or managers of the scheme received the transfer notice in relation to the scheme.

(3) The order is to have effect from the time when the trustees or managers of the scheme receive the transfer notice –

(a)   as if, except in prescribed descriptions of case –
   (i)   references in the order to the trustees or managers of the scheme were references to the Board, and
   (ii)   references in the order to any pension or lump sum to which the party with pension rights is or may become entitled under the scheme were references to any PPF compensation to which that person is or may become entitled in respect of the pension or lump sum, and

(b)   subject to such other modifications as may be prescribed.

(4) Subsection (5) applies to an order under section 23 if –

---

[93]   For a more detailed account of the PPF and the way it operates, see David Salter 'Pension Protection Fund and the Family Lawyer' [2007] Fam Law 135.

(a)   it includes provision made by virtue of section 25B(7) which requires the party with pension rights to exercise his right of commutation under an occupational pension scheme to any extent, and

(b)   before the requirement is complied with the Board has assumed responsibility for the scheme as mentioned in subsection (2)(a).

(5) From the time the trustees or managers of the scheme receive the transfer notice, the order is to have effect with such modifications as may be prescribed.

(6) Regulations may modify section 25C as it applies in relation to an occupational pension scheme at any time when there is an assessment period[94] in relation to the scheme.

(7) Where the court makes a pension sharing order in respect of a person's shareable rights under an occupational pension scheme, or an order which includes provision made by virtue of section 25B(4) or (7) in relation to such a scheme, the Board subsequently assuming responsibility for the scheme as mentioned in subsection (2)(*a*) does not affect –

(a)   the powers of the court under section 31 to vary or discharge the order or to suspend or revive any provision of it, or

(b)   on an appeal, the powers of the appeal court to affirm, reinstate, set aside or vary the order.

(8) Regulations may make such consequential modifications of any provision of, or made by virtue of, this Part as appear to the Lord Chancellor necessary or expedient to give effect to the provisions of this section.'

Subsection (9) goes on to set out various definitions.

10.80 The Family Proceedings (Amendment) (No 2) Rules 2006[95] have amended the FPR to take account of the PPF. A new rule 2.70A provides as follows:

'2.70A.—(1) This rule applies where—

(a)   rule 2.70 applies; and

(b)   the party with pension rights or the civil partner with pension rights ("the member") receives or has received notification in compliance with the Pension Protection Fund (Provision of Information) Regulations 2005[3] ("the 2005 Regulations") —

(i)   from the person responsible for the pension arrangement, that there is an assessment period in relation to the pension arrangement; or

(ii)   from the Board that it has assumed responsibility for the pension arrangement or part of it.

---

[94]   The assessment period is the period after a 'qualifying insolvency event' during which the scheme's assets and liabilities are valued to determine whether it is necessary for the PPF to assume responsibility for the scheme.

[95]   SI 2006/2080.

(2) If the person responsible for the pension arrangement notifies or has notified the member that there is an assessment period in relation to the pension arrangement, the member must send to the other party or civil partner—

(a) a copy of the notification; and
(b) a copy of the valuation summary,

in accordance with paragraph (3).

(3) The member must send the documents referred to in paragraph (2)—

(a) if available, when he sends the information received under rule 2.70(2); or
(b) otherwise, within 7 days of receipt.

(4) If—

(a) the pension arrangement is in an assessment period; and
(b) the Board notifies the member that it has assumed responsibility for the pension arrangement, or part of it,

the member must—

(i) send a copy of the notification to the other party or civil partner within 7 days of receipt; and
(ii) comply with paragraph (5).

(5) Where paragraph (4) applies, the member must —

(a) within 7 days of receipt of the notification, request the Board in writing to provide a forecast of his compensation entitlement as described in the 2005 Regulations; and
(b) send a copy of the forecast of his compensation entitlement to the other party or civil partner within 7 days of receipt.

(6) In this rule—

(a) in a matrimonial cause, all words and phrases defined in section 25E(9) of the Act of 1973 have the meanings assigned by that subsection;
(b) in a civil partnership cause, all words and phrases defined in paragraph 37 of Schedule 5 to the Act of 2004 have the meanings assigned by that paragraph; and
(c) "valuation summary" has the meaning assigned to it by the 2005 Regulations.

(7) Paragraph (18) of rule 2.70 shall apply to this rule as it applies to rule 2.70.'

Chapter 11

CHILDREN

INTRODUCTION

11.1 Any attempt to describe the significance of children in ancillary relief cases is bound to result in a somewhat muddled account. The welfare of any minor children of the family is the first consideration of the court,[1] but this does not mean that their interests take precedence over those of the adults in the case; the meaning of the 'first consideration' is considered in more detail in Chapter 1 at para **1.8**. It certainly does not mean that the court must make orders for the support of children before it may deal with their parents; indeed, as will be seen, in most cases the court is precluded by statute from doing so.

11.2 The complicating factor in cases involving children is the CSA 1991, which is intended to provide support for most children. It will, therefore, be necessary to consider the principles of this Act at the outset, after which the principles for dealing with those cases in which the court has jurisdiction will be examined.

THE CHILD SUPPORT ACT 1991

11.3 Until the coming into force of the CSA 1991 the only way to obtain financial support for a child was an application to the court, and few people would have supposed that any other method was appropriate. This position has been almost entirely changed by the 1991 Act, the effect of which may be summarised as follows.

(a) In cases involving 'natural' children (ie children of both parties, whether by birth or adoption) jurisdiction to make orders for financial support is removed from the courts and vested in the Child Support Agency.[2] The Agency assumes responsibility for the enforcement and collection of any maintenance required to be paid.

(b) A person with the care of children is described as 'the person with care' and the other parent is the 'non-resident parent' (formerly the 'absent parent').[3] A child is only subject to the Act if he is a 'qualifying child', ie a

---

[1]   MCA 1973, s 25(1).
[2]   CSA 1991, s 8(3).
[3]   Ibid, s 3.

child of the person with care and the non-resident parent who lives with the person with care, and where all three are habitually resident in the UK.

(c)   Child maintenance is calculated under the Act according to a formula prescribed by the Act. In the original version of the formula there was no room for discretion or variation; indeed, one of the purposes of the Act was to depart from what was described as the 'discredited discretionary system' adopted by the courts. When it was found that this resulted in hardship, attempts were made to make the formula more flexible, but the principle that all jurisdiction must be derived from the Act remains.

(d)   There are two types of applications for assessment (now called a 'maintenance calculation') under the Act. The most significant of these, and, it may be argued, the type of case for which the whole system was designed, is where the person with care is in receipt of income support. Here, the Secretary of State may require her to make an application under s 6, and may exact penalties if she does not co-operate. The other type of application is made under s 4 by the person with care herself when she is not in receipt of benefit.

11.4   This is not the place for a detailed examination of the principles of the 1991 Act.[4] Instead, the following matters will be considered:

(a)   the basic principles of the formula;

(b)   exceptions to the Act.

It should be emphasised that the formula was changed as from March 2003. The pre-2003 formula was outlined in the previous edition of this book and will not be repeated here.

The significance of the Act in relation to cases to which it does not apply and in which the court has jurisdiction will be considered at para **11.28**.

Finally, by way of introduction, it should be said that the government has announced that the formula and, indeed, the functions of the Child Support Agency, are to be changed yet again. There is to be a public consultation ending in the summer of 2007, followed by a White Paper and, presumably, legislation, in the autumn of 2007. It seems, therefore, that this particular experiment with the lives and well-being of separated spouses and their children has not yet run its course.

---

[4]   For a comprehensive account, see Bird *Child Support – The New Law* (Family Law, 2002). For a practical guide to calculating child support assessments see Bird *Child Support Calculation Kit 2003/2004* (Family Law).

Basic principles of the formula from March 2003

11.5 As was mentioned at para **11.4**, as from the beginning of March 2003 the formula then existing was changed, and Sch 1, Part 1 to the 1991 Act was amended to contain the new formula. The parents are now called 'the parent with care' (PWC) and 'the non-resident parent' (NRP). What used to be the 'maintenance assessment' is now the 'maintenance calculation'. The essential features of the new formula are that the income of the PWC is ignored and the calculation is based entirely on the income of the NRP, being a percentage of that income depending on the number of children. However, as always with child support, the calculation is more complex than might appear to be the case, and the stages through which the calculation must go are outlined below.

11.6

(1) No child maintenance is payable when the NRP has a net income of below £5 or his income is of a prescribed description (eg students and prisoners).

(2) When the NRP's net income is £100 per week or less, or he receives any benefit, pension or allowance prescribed for this purpose, or he or his partner receive any benefit prescribed for this purpose, and the nil rate does not apply, the flat rate of £5 per week applies.

(3) Where the NRP has a partner who is also an NRP, and the partner is a person with respect to whom a maintenance calculation is in force, and the NRP or his partner receive any benefit prescribed for this purpose, the nil rate applies.

(4) When neither the nil rate nor a flat rate applies, and the NRP's net income is between £100 and £200 per week, the reduced rate applies.[5]

(5) When none of the previous categories is applicable, the basic rate applies. This is a percentage of the net weekly income of the NRP and is 15% where there is one qualifying child, 20% for two children and 25% for three or more.

(6) Income of the NRP exceeding £2,000 per week is ignored. The maximum sum payable under a maintenance calculation is therefore £500 per week, but the provisions as to applications to the court for 'top-up' orders are maintained.

(7) When the NRP or his partner has 'relevant other children', ie children other than qualifying children in respect of whom the NRP or his partner receives child benefit, an allowance is made in respect of the NRP's income before the maintenance calculation is made. These percentages are the same as those set out in (5) above. For example, if there were three

---

[5] Reduced rate is defined in the CSA 1991, Sch 1, para 3.

qualifying children and the NRP had a net income of £300 per week and two relevant other children, 20% or £60 would be notionally deducted from his income, leaving £240 as the basis of the maintenance calculation. He would have to pay 25% of this sum, namely £60 per week. No account is taken of the income of the partner.

(8)	Where the NRP has more than one qualifying child, living with different PWCs, the rate of maintenance liability is divided by the number of qualifying children and shared among the PWCs according to the number of qualifying children living with that PWC.

(9)	The amount of the maintenance calculation may be reduced if the NRP has one or more qualifying children with him for more than a certain number of nights per annum. The amount of decrease in respect of each child is as follows:

Number of nights with NRP	*Fraction to subtract*
52 to 103	One-seventh
104 to 155	Two-sevenths
156 to 174	Three-sevenths
175 or more	One half

If the PWC is providing for more than one qualifying child of the NRP, the applicable decrease is the sum of the appropriate fractions in the table divided by the number of qualifying children. If the applicable fraction is one half in relation to any qualifying child in the care of the PWC, the total amount payable to the PWC is then to be further decreased by £7 for each such child. Finally, if the application of these provisions would reduce the weekly amount of child support payable by the NRP to the PWC to less than £5 per week, the NRP has to pay £5 per week.

WHEN MAY APPLICATIONS BE MADE TO THE COURT?

11.7	As was explained above, one of the principal features of the 1991 Act is that it is intended that the jurisdiction of the court shall be excluded and replaced by that of the Secretary of State. In *R (Kehoe) v Secretary of State for Work and Pensions*[6] it was held that the intention of the 1991 Act was to replace – except as expressly retained by the Act itself – any pre-existing rights of either a child or parent to periodical payments for the maintenance of that child. The applicant mother had no right that she could exercise against the father and accordingly she could not assert that she had an arguable civil right that entitled her under Article 6(1) HRA to a determination by the court. However,

---

[6]	[2004] EWCA Civ 225, [2004] 1 FLR 1132. Upheld on appeal at [2005] UKHL 48, [2005] 2 FLR 1249, HL. The PWC had no right she could enforce against the NRP apart from judicial review. The maintenance obligation was enforceable only by the Secretary of State.

the Act itself contains various exceptions to this principle, and further exceptions have been provided for as a result of the Agency's inability to handle all the tasks originally intended for it. These may be summarised as follows.

(a) Cases where the Secretary of State does not have jurisdiction

11.8 The Secretary of State has jurisdiction only where the child is under 18 years of age and is the natural or adopted child of a person with care and a non-resident parent, and all three are habitually resident in the UK. It follows that stepchildren, children aged over 18, and cases where any one of the parties or child are not habitually resident are excluded from the jurisdiction of the Secretary of State and fall within the jurisdiction of the court.

(b) Applications to the court permitted by the Act

11.9 The Act allows applications to the court to be made in addition to a calculation by the Secretary of State in certain cases.

(i) 'Topping up', ie when the maximum amount payable under the formula has been reached; in such cases the court may make an order for such additional amount as is appropriate.[7]

(ii) Additional educational expenses. An order may be made 'solely for the purposes of requiring the person making or securing the making of periodical payments fixed by the order to meet some or all of the expenses incurred in connection with the provision of . . . instruction or training'.[8] The most obvious way in which this might be used is to obtain an order for the payment of school fees, but the provision is not limited to this.

(iii) Disabled or blind children. Where a disability living allowance is paid to or in respect of a child, or no such allowance is paid but the child is disabled, an order may be made solely for the purpose of requiring the person making the payments 'to meet some or all of any of the expenses attributable to the child's disability'.[9]

In the case of (i) above, it is a prerequisite that a maintenance calculation has been made. This is not necessary in the two other cases.

(c) Certain consent orders

11.10 A court may make an order where 'a written agreement (whether or not enforceable) provides for the making, or securing, by a non-resident parent of the child of periodical payments to or for the benefit of the child; and the

---

7   CSA 1991, s 8(6).
8   Ibid, s 8(7).
9   Ibid, s 8(8). By s 8(9), a child is disabled if he is blind, deaf or dumb or is substantially and permanently handicapped by illness, injury, mental disorder or congenital deformity or such other disability as may be prescribed.

maintenance order which the court makes is, in all material respects, in the same terms as that agreement'.[10] In order to be satisfied of its jurisdiction, therefore, the court may need to see a copy of the written agreement.

It should also be noted that the CSA 1991 provides that 'nothing in this Act shall be taken to prevent any person from entering into a maintenance agreement'.[11]

(d) Capital orders

11.11 There is nothing in the CSA 1991 to prevent a lump sum order or a property adjustment order in favour of a child (but see para **11.29**).

(e) Applications under 'transitional provisions'

11.12 It was always envisaged that the Agency would not be able to take on all cases immediately and that there would have to be a phased take up. What began as transitional provisions seem to have achieved a degree of permanence, but there seems little point in summarising the position further since, with the advent of the new formula, this will be a diminishing problem.

(f) Variation and duration of orders

11.13 As was noted above, the court has jurisdiction to make orders for child maintenance where there is no maintenance calculation in effect and the parties have agreed the terms of such order in writing. Such an order, once made, may be varied. Until the coming into force of the new provisions in 2003, this prevented any application for a maintenance calculation under s 4 of the 1991 Act. The position after implementation of the new provisions is different. By s 4(10) of the 1991 Act, as amended by the Child Support, Pensions and Social Security Act 2000 (CSPSSA 2000), the Secretary of State may make a maintenance calculation, provided that one year has elapsed from the date of the order. Advisers should therefore be aware that any agreement made and reflected in a consent order may last only for one year, and the message would seem to be that orders should, as far as possible, be in terms similar to those of a maintenance calculation.

APPLICATIONS TO THE COURT

11.14 For the purposes of this book, it will be assumed that any application to the court in respect of children will be made under the provisions of MCA 1973. For the sake of completeness, however, it should be noted that, where the court has jurisdiction, applications may be made under the provisions of Sch 1 to the Children Act 1989. The principles governing the exercise of the court's discretion under the 1989 Act are virtually identical to those under MCA 1973.

---

[10]   CSA 1991, s 8(5).
[11]   Ibid, s 9(2).

Jurisdiction

11.15 The powers of the court to make financial provision orders and property adjustment orders have been set out in the chapters applicable to each of the various forms of relief (eg periodical payments, lump sum, etc). It will be noted that in each case the court has jurisdiction to make an order of the kind described for the benefit of a child of the family. 'Child of the family' is defined as, in relation to the parties to a marriage:

'(a) a child of both those parties; and
(b) any other child, not being a child who is placed with those parties as foster parents by a local authority or voluntary organisation, who has been treated by both of those parties as a child of their family.'[12]

Age limits

11.16 The basic principle is that 'no financial provision order and no order for a transfer of property under section 24(1)(a) . . . shall be made in favour of a child who has attained the age of eighteen'.[13] It is also provided that the term specified in any order for periodical payments or secured periodical payments in favour of a child:

'(a) shall not in the first instance extend beyond the date of the birthday of the child next following his attaining the upper limit of the compulsory school age . . . unless the court considers that in the circumstances of the case the welfare of the child requires that it should extend to a later date; and
(b) shall not in any event, subject to subsection (3) below, extend beyond the date of the child's eighteenth birthday.'[14]

11.17 Section 29(3) will be considered below. However, the principle is that no order may be made in respect of a child who is aged over 18, or which extends beyond the age of 18. Moreover, any periodic order for a child should not extend beyond the child's seventeenth birthday unless the court considers that the welfare of the child requires such an order.

However, there is an exception to this principle. It is provided that the limitations on orders for children aged over 18 or extending beyond that age shall not apply:

'if it appears to the court that—

(a) the child is, or will be, or if an order were made without complying with either or both of those provisions would be, receiving instruction at an educational establishment or undergoing training for a trade, profession or vocation, whether or not he is also, or will also be, in gainful employment; or

---

[12]   MCA 1973, s 52(1).
[13]   Ibid, s 29(1).
[14]   Ibid, s 29(2).

(b)   there are special circumstances which justify the making of an order without complying with either or both of those provisions.'[15]

The effect of this is that when a child is, or will be, in education or training, whether full-time or part-time, an order may be made for or to him. 'Special circumstances' are not defined, but would probably include cases where the 'child' was unable to be self-sufficient because of some mental or physical disability.

11.18 The usual wording of an order for a child under the age of 17 is that the payments continue 'until the said child shall attain the age of seventeen years or ceases full-time education if later or further order'.

Principles on which the court exercises its jurisdiction

11.19 When the court exercises its jurisdiction in respect of a child, it is directed to have regard in particular to the following matters:

'(a)   the financial needs of the child;
(b)   the income, earning capacity (if any), property and other financial resources of the child;
(c)   any physical or mental disability of the child;
(d)   the manner in which he was being and in which the parties to the marriage expected him to be educated or trained;
(e)   the considerations mentioned in relation to the parties to the marriage in paragraphs (a), (b), (c) and (e) of subsection (2).'[16]

The matters referred to in (e) are the income, capital, etc, of each of the parties, their needs, obligations and responsibilities, the standard of living enjoyed by the family and any mental or physical disability of either party.

11.20 In addition to the matters prescribed above, when the court is exercising its powers against a party to the marriage in favour of a child of the family who is not the child of that party, the court is directed to have regard:

'(a)   to whether that party assumed any responsibility for the child's maintenance, and, if so, to the extent to which, and the basis upon which, that party assumed such responsibility and to the length of time for which that party discharged such responsibility;
(b)   to whether in assuming and discharging such responsibility that party did so knowing that the child was not his or her own;
(c)   to the liability of any other person to maintain the child.'[17]

---

[15]   MCA 1973, s 29(3).
[16]   Ibid, s 25(3).
[17]   Ibid, s 25(4).

Periodic orders for children

11.21 The quantification of an order for periodical payments for a child must be approached on the same basis as any other periodical payments order, ie by assessing the reasonable needs and requirements of the child in the light of the statutory factors set out above and then determining the ability of the parents to provide for such needs and requirements. Both parents have an obligation to provide for a child, and the court would normally expect this obligation to be regarded as a prior responsibility by both of them. However, this principle must be tempered by the recognition of the fact that the 'non-resident parent' has to maintain himself and discharge any proper responsibilities which he may have assumed; the latter may include a new family.[18] In one case it was said that:

> 'The respondent husband is entitled to order his life in such a way as will hold in reasonable balance the responsibilities to his existing family which he carries into his new life, as well as his proper aspirations for that new future. In all life, for those who are divorced as well as for those who are not divorced, indulging one's whims or even one's reasonable desires must be held in check by the constraints imposed by limited resources and compelling obligations.'[19]

11.22 Whatever view is eventually taken of the parents' ability to pay, it is normally necessary to make a provisional assessment of the child's needs. In many cases, the formula prescribed by CSA 1991 will assist as a starting point, and a 'child support calculation' is always useful in such cases. Indeed, in *E v C (Child Maintenance)*,[20] where a family proceedings court had declined to vary an order for £5 per week against a father who was unemployed and in receipt of benefit, Douglas Brown J allowed the appeal and observed that the justices would have done well to consider what a child support assessment would have been (in the instant case it would have been a nil assessment). While that assessment would not have been binding on the court, it would have been strongly persuasive. It was the practice of professional judges to ask about a child support assessment, and it would be helpful for justices to do likewise.

Support for this view is now to be found in *GW v RW (Financial Provision: Departure from Equality)*,[21] a case involving very substantial assets. It was held that, in fixing a child maintenance award in a case where the Agency lacked jurisdiction, the appropriate starting point was almost invariably the figure thrown up by the new child support rules.

This case is, therefore, authority for considering what a child support calculation would be in all cases involving a child. It could not be the last word, since the court is bound by s 25(3) and (4) and not by CSA 1991 when dealing with children's cases, but it would at least be a useful starting point. It is suggested that these principles supersede the earlier practice of adopting

---

[18] See eg *R v R* [1988] 1 FLR 89, CA.
[19] *Delaney v Delaney* [1990] 2 FLR 457, CA, at 461 per Ward J.
[20] [1996] 1 FLR 472.
[21] [2003] EWHC 611 (Fam), [2003] 2 FLR 108, Nicholas Mostyn QC.

income support figures (in lower income cases) or the National Foster Care Association recommendations (in cases of greater affluence) as a starting point.

Capital provision for children

11.23 As was observed when the exceptions to CSA 1991 were being considered, there is nothing in the Act to prevent a lump sum order or property adjustment order in favour of a child, even when a child support calculation is in force. However, it must be said that such orders are rare, since it is difficult to show that a child, as distinct from the parent with whom he lives, has a need or reasonable requirement for capital. There is, in principle, no justification for the children to expect to share in their parents' capital assets on or after the dissolution of marriage,[22] although settlement orders may be made in exceptional cases.[23]

An example of a capital order for children in somewhat unusual circumstances is *V v V (Child Maintenance)*,[24] where the father, having invited the judge to determine the level of child maintenance, then refused to consent to the judge's proposed order. The judge awarded the children lump sums, saying that, in those circumstances, it was right to seek to reflect the balance of the provision in another form of order.

The cases brought under the Children Act 1989, Sch 1 in which property has been ordered to be transferred for the benefit of children support this general proposition. Such cases have been brought when the parents have not been married and so the parent with care (normally the mother) has been unable to apply for provision in her own right.[25] The orders for transfer of capital to provide a home have all provided for the property to be held on trust until the majority of the child and then to return to the transferor. In *Phillips v Peace*[26] it was held that in an application under Sch 1 only one settlement of property order could be made.

An interesting insight into financial provision for a child is provided by *K v K (Ancillary Relief: Pre-nuptial Agreement)*.[27] This case is considered in more detail at para **1.43**, but the important point is that, after a short marriage where there had been a pre-nuptial agreement, the wife was held to her agreement as to capital. However, the judge also ordered the husband to provide a home and furnishings for the mother and child at a cost of £1.2m (to revert to him in due course) and £15,000 pa for the child.

---

[22]   *Lilford (Lord) v Glyn* [1979] 1 All ER 441; *Kiely v Kiely* [1988] 1 FLR 248, CA.

[23]   See e g *Tavoulareas v Tavoulareas* [1998] 2 FLR 418, CA.

[24]   [2001] 2 FLR 799, Wilson J.

[25]   See e g *A v A (Minor: Financial Provision)* [1994] 1 FLR 657; *T v S (Financial Provision for Children)* [1994] 2 FLR 883; *Phillips v Peace* [1996] 2 FLR 230; *J v C (Child: Financial Provision)* [1999] 1 FLR 152. For the position where the mother was a joint owner of the house see *Re B (Child: Property Transfer)* [1999] 2 FLR 418.

[26]   [2004] EWHC 3180 (Fam), [2005] 2 FLR 1212.

[27]   [2003] 1 FLR 120.

Given this decision, the decision of the Court of Appeal in *Re P (Child: Financial Provision)*[28] is also of interest, although it was clearly a most unusual case. Here, the parties were not married and the child was aged 2 years. The father was described as 'fabulously rich'. The court decided that a home in central London was appropriate and ordered the father to provide £1m for this purpose, £100,000 for decoration and furnishing, and £70,000 pa periodical payments, on the basis that the father undertook to pay school fees. The Court of Appeal gave further guidance as to the quantum of financial support for children in *F v G (Child: Financial Provision)*.[29] It was held that, although standard of living is not a factor which appears in Children Act, Sch 1 para 4(1), it is clearly among the totality of circumstances which the court must hold in view. The extent to which the unit of primary carer and child have become accustomed to a particular level of lifestyle can impact legitimately on an evaluation of a child's needs. The remainder of the case is an interesting example of the way the court may exercise its discretion but, as each case is fact-specific, no further comment need be made here.

In *W v J (Child: Variation of Periodical Payments)*[30] it was held that there was no jurisdiction to make an order for increased periodical payments for a child to cover legal costs to be incurred in forthcoming litigation between the parties.

School fees

11.24 As was seen above, provision for school fees or other educational expenses is an area where the court always retains jurisdiction, whether or not a child support calculation has been or might be made. Since the Finance Act 1988, there has been no tax advantage to be gained by any particular form of order. A form of order will be found at Appendix A, precedent 12.

In *T V T (Financial Provision:Private Education)*[31] the husband applied to be relieved of his obligation under a Consent Order to pay school fees. The application was dismissed and the husband ordered to pay £254,680.71 lump sum for fees. Bennett J held that he could afford to do so even if he had to sell some assets. This would still leave him securely housed.

However, sub nom *Tracey v Tracey*,[32] the Court of Appeal allowed in part the husband's appeal. This was allowed on the facts, important information not having been before Bennett J, and the lump sum was reduced. However, the principle was not affected.

For the general position as to tax, see Chapter 2, para **2.20**.

---

28 [2003] EWCA Civ 837, [2003] 2 FLR 865.
29 [2004] EWHC 1848 (Fam), [2005] 1 FLR 261.
30 [2003] EWHC 2657 (Fam), [2004] 2 FLR 300.
31 [2005] EWHC 2119 (Fam), [2006] 1 FLR 903.
32 [2006] EWCA Civ 734, [2007] 1 FLR 196.

INTERIM APPLICATIONS

11.25 The situation may (indeed, frequently does) arise in which a parent with the care of a child, normally the mother, is left without any support for a child, and, whether or not she seeks to recover any periodical payments or maintenance payment suit for herself, wishes to obtain support for a child. In many such cases the provisions of CSA 1991 prohibit her from applying to the court for an order for the child, but the Child Support Agency may well take many months to deal with any application under s 4.

11.26 In such cases, there is nothing to prevent the court from making an order for the mother which includes support for the child. Such an order has to be expressed as remaining in force 'until a child support calculation is made'. When the order is made up partly of the mother's maintenance and partly the child's, the court would add the words 'whereupon this order shall be reduced by the amount of any such calculation'. Such an order would not be possible where the mother had remarried. Indeed, any such order is only legitimate where there is a genuine and substantial amount of spousal support in the order; where the order in reality relates only to children, it is not legitimate.[33]

---

[33] *Dorney-Kingdom v Dorney-Kingdom* [2000] 2 FLR 855, CA.

Chapter 12

INSOLVENCY AND RIGHTS OF CREDITORS

INTRODUCTION

12.1 In this chapter it is intended to consider the effect on the parties of the bankruptcy of one of them. It also seems convenient at this point to consider the position of one or both of the parties when a creditor has a charge, whether by virtue of a mortgage deed or a charging order, over the matrimonial home. The two situations are different, but the effect on the party who is not insolvent or the object of the judgment or charge may seem to be similar; a third party is perceived to wish to deprive that party of what she regards as hers.

THE INSOLVENCY ACT 1986 AND SALE OF THE MATRIMONIAL HOME

12.2 When a person becomes bankrupt, the whole of his estate vests in his trustee in bankruptcy,[1] who is then under an obligation to realise the bankrupt's assets for the benefit of the creditors. One of the assets will be any property in which the bankrupt has a legal or beneficial interest, and this will frequently include the matrimonial home. If a property is held by the bankrupt and another as joint tenants, the bankruptcy severs the joint tenancy;[2] the result of this is that the trustee and the other co-owner hold the property as tenants in common in equal shares. Where the property was held as tenants in common, the trustee holds the share which the bankrupt previously held.

12.3 The trustee is then in the position of any joint owner in the sense that he may apply to the court for an order for sale, previously under s 30 of the Law of Property Act 1925 (LPA 1925) and now under s 14 of the Trusts of Land and Appointment of Trustees Act 1996 (TLATA 1996).[3] However, the trustee is in a different position from other joint owners because the Insolvency Act 1986 (IA 1986) prescribes the duties of the court in such circumstances. It is provided[4] that, on application for an order for sale, the court shall make such order:

---

[1]   IA 1986, s 306.
[2]   *Re Gorman (A Bankrupt)* [1990] 2 FLR 284.
[3]   As to when time begins to run for the purposes of the Limitation Act 1980, s 20(1), see *Gotham v Doodes* [2006] EWCA Civ 1080, [2007] 1 FLR 373; the right to receive the money could not predate an order for sale. Until the order for sale, the charge is merely a deferred charge.
[4]   By IA 1986, s 336(4).

'as it thinks just and reasonable having regard to—

(a)   the interests of the bankrupt's creditors,
(b)   the conduct of the spouse or former spouse, so far as contributing to the bankruptcy,
(c)   the needs and financial resources of the spouse or former spouse,
(d)   the needs of any children, and
(e)   all the circumstances of the case other than the needs of the bankrupt.'

It will be seen that the court is afforded a certain degree of discretion when considering such applications. However, this may be more apparent than real since it is further provided[5] that when the application is made more than one year after the bankruptcy the court 'shall assume, unless the circumstances of the case are exceptional, that the interests of the bankrupt's creditors outweigh all other considerations'.

12.4   The result of these provisions is that applications for orders for sale are rarely made before one year has elapsed, and, when they are eventually made, there is little or no dispute that an order must be made. It is clearly difficult to prove that the circumstances of a particular case are exceptional, and the courts have accepted the clear intention of the insolvency legislation which puts the interests of the creditors to the forefront. In one case,[6] the fact that the wife and children would be rendered homeless was described as 'not an exceptional circumstance. It is a normal circumstance and is the result, the all too obvious result, of a husband having conducted the financial affairs of the family in a way that has lead to bankruptcy'. In another case, Hoffmann J decided that, since the half share which the bankrupt's wife would receive would not be sufficient to rehouse her and the children, the order for sale and possession should not be enforced until the youngest child was 16 years old. The Court of Appeal allowed the trustee's appeal and said that an order for immediate sale should have been made. The eviction of the wife, with all the consequent problems, was not exceptional but was 'one of the melancholy consequences of debt and improvidence with which every society has been familiar'.[7] A similar result was reached in *Barca v Mears*[8] but it should be noted that in that case the learned judge said that the *Re Citro* approach might be incompatible with Convention rights and might need re-examining in light of the European Convention.

12.5   However, it is not impossible to prove exceptional circumstances.[9] In *Re Holliday*,[10] the husband had presented his own petition in bankruptcy as a tactical move to defeat his wife's claims. No creditors were pressing and he was

---

5   By IA 1986, s 336(5).
6   *Re Lowrie (A Bankrupt)* [1981] 3 All ER 353.
7   *Re Citro (A Bankrupt)* [1991] Ch 142, CA.
8   [2004] EWHC 2170 (Ch).
9   For another example of the application of the relevant principals leading to an order for sale, see the judgment of Lawrence Collins J in *Dean v Stout* [2005] EWHC 3315 (Ch), [2006] 1 FLR 725.
10   [1981] 3 All ER 353.

in a position to discharge his debts out of income. The judge postponed sale for 5 years. In *Re Bailey*,[11] although an order for sale was made, it seems to have been accepted that if a house had been specially converted to meet the needs of a disabled child, the circumstances could properly be described as exceptional.

In *Judd v Brown*,[12] the fact that the wife was suffering from cancer and had to undergo a course of chemotherapy was held to be an exceptional circumstance and the trustee's application for an order for sale was refused. A slightly different result was reached in *Re Raval (A Bankrupt)*,[13] where the bankrupt's wife suffered from schizophrenia and it was thought that 'adverse life events' might cause a relapse. The former matrimonial home was the only asset but there was a substantial equity. Possession was suspended for one year.

In *Re Bremner*,[14] the bankrupt husband was aged 79, suffering from cancer, and unlikely to survive more than 6 months. It was held that the wife's need to care for him was distinct from the husband's needs and was exceptional; sale was deferred with marketing not to begin until 3 months after the husband's death.

An example to the contrary is *Donohoe v Ingram*[15] where the bankrupt's partner applied for sale to be postponed on the ground that the home was needed for the children and the creditors would be paid in full by 2017. It was held that the case was not sufficiently similar to Holliday to permit a deviation from the usual *Re Citro* approach.

12.6 The position of a spouse who has no legal or beneficial interest in the home is different from that of the spouse with such an interest, in that when the house is sold she will recover nothing. However, in terms of her right of occupation, her position is very similar. A spouse with no legal or beneficial interest has matrimonial home rights,[16] which include the right not to be evicted save by order of the court. A former spouse has similar rights provided an order to that effect has been made before decree absolute.[17] A trustee in bankruptcy who wishes to obtain a possession order must apply to the court having jurisdiction in the bankruptcy.[18] The factors which the court must take into account are those already set out above where the spouse is a joint owner. In *Byford v Butler*[19] it was held that a wife who had continued to live in the former matrimonial home after the bankruptcy was entitled to credit for mortgage interest paid, subject to the trustee's right to set off occupation rent.

---

[11] [1977] 1 WLR 278.
[12] [1998] 2 FLR 360.
[13] [1998] 2 FLR 718.
[14] [1999] 1 FLR 912. See also *Claughton v Charalamabous* [1999] 1 FLR 740, CA (the court must make a value judgment and look at all the circumstances); the process leaves little scope for interference by an appellate court.
[15] [2006] 2 FLR 1084.
[16] FLA 1996, s 30.
[17] Ibid, s 33(5).
[18] IA 1986, s 336(3).
[19] [2004] 1 FLR 56.

12.7 Finally, in this section, the position of a bankrupt spouse who has the care of children must be considered. A person who has a beneficial interest in a property, has been adjudged bankrupt, and who has living with him in the property any person under the age of 18 has the right not to be evicted without order of the court.[20] On an application for sale made by a trustee, the court must have regard to 'the interests of the creditors, to the bankrupt's financial resources, to the needs of the children, and to all the circumstances of the case other than the needs of the bankrupt'.[21] There is a similar provision in respect of applications made one year after the bankruptcy to that set out above.[22]

Effect of bankruptcy on order for financial relief

12.8 All that has been said so far in this chapter assumes that the bankruptcy has pre-dated any order for financial relief; once the bankruptcy occurs, there is normally little point in considering such applications, and the provisions of the IA 1986 apply. What must now be considered is the position when a bankruptcy order is made after an order for financial relief has been made, and what, if any, effect the bankruptcy will have on the order and its implementation.

The answer to this will depend on the type of order which has been made, and each must be considered in turn.

Property adjustment orders

12.9 The court has no jurisdiction to make a property adjustment order against a bankrupt spouse.[23]

A common danger which may be encountered by a party in whose favour a property adjustment order has been made is that the transaction, ie the transfer of property pursuant to the order, may be set aside on an application by the trustee in bankruptcy. The trustee has the right to apply to the court[24] for an order to set aside any transaction 'at an undervalue' made within a specified period before the day of the presentation of the bankruptcy petition. The fact that the transfer has been made pursuant to an order of the court does not prevent it from being the object of such an application.[25]

However, in *Mountney v Treharne*,[26] where the court had ordered the transfer of a house to the wife but a bankruptcy order was made in respect of the husband before the transfer was signed, it was held that the order had the effect of conferring on the wife an equitable interest in the property at the moment it

---

[20]   IA 1986, s 337(2).
[21]   Ibid, s 337(5).
[22]   Ibid, s 337(6).
[23]   *McGladdery v McGladdery* [1999] 2 FLR 1102.
[24]   Under IA 1986, s 339.
[25]   MCA 1973, s 39.
[26]   [2002] EWCA Civ 1174, [2002] 2 FLR 930, CA.

took effect, ie on decree absolute. The trustee in bankruptcy therefore took the property subject to the wife's equitable interest.[27] For the position in a similar case involving pension policies see para **12.15**.

The specified period is 5 years unless it can be shown that the other party was not insolvent at the date of the transaction and that he did not become insolvent because of it, in which case it is 2 years.[28]

12.10 Whether or not a transaction was at an undervalue will depend on the facts of the case. For example, if it could be shown that a former husband and wife had agreed to transfer the property of one of them to the other in an attempt to defeat creditors, and had obtained an order of the court to that effect, it is virtually certain that the transaction would be set aside. On the other hand, it was thought that, if an order for transfer of property were made for the housing of a spouse and children in the normal way and after consideration of the s 25 factors, it might be difficult to establish that the transaction was at an undervalue and that this might also be the case where the property transferred was on a clean break basis, and in settlement of all a wife's claims including her right to periodical payments.

However, this may have been clarified by the decision in *Hill and another v Haines*.[29] Here, in the proceedings for ancillary relief, the district judge had ordered, inter alia, that the husband transfer to the wife all his interest in the former matrimonial home. The husband was subsequently adjudged bankrupt. Following the bankruptcy , trustees of the bankrupt were appointed and they applied for an order to set aside the transfer of property pursuant to s 339 of the Insolvency Act 1986. The application was refused and the trustees appealed against the refusal of their application. They submitted that the transfer was a transaction at an undervalue either under s 339(3)(a) or (c) of the Act in view of the fact that the property adjustment order had not involved the respondent giving consideration and certainly not such that could be measured in money or money's worth within the meaning of s 339(3)(c). The wife submitted that a transferee under a transfer made pursuant to a property transfer order was to be regarded as having given consideration equivalent to the value of the property being transferred, unless the case was an exceptional one where it could be demonstrated that the property transferred was obtained by fraud or some broadly similar exceptional circumstance. The appeal was allowed. It was held that the district judge had been wrong to conclude that the transfer of the property pursuant to the order made in favour of the respondent by the matrimonial court was not a transaction at an undervalue. The transaction had been at an undervalue by application of s 339(3)(a) of the Act and in any event on an application of s 339(3)(c).

The judge held that agreeing to dismissal of claims in return for a transfer did not in itself amount to giving good consideration and it might seem that he

---

[27] This would not have been the case had decree absolute not been pronounced.
[28] See IA 1986, s 341.
[29] [2007] EWHC 1012 (Ch), [2007] All ER (D) 72 (May).

went so far as to say that a transfer in these circumstances where no actual consideration is given would always be at an undervalue. It may well be that there will be an appeal, but in any event the case illustrates the difficulties when dealing with a case where one of the parties is actually or potentially bankrupt.

12.11 Any disposition of property made by a bankrupt between the date of the presentation of the petition and the date of the bankrupt's property vesting in the trustee is void unless made with the consent of the court or subsequently ratified by the court.[30]

Lump sum orders

12.12 The point made in para **12.11** should be noted; for these purposes, a lump sum payment would be a disposition of property. Subject to that point, the issues arising as to lump sums are:

(a)   whether or not a lump sum could be set aside by the court on the trustee's application;

(b)   whether it can be enforced against a bankrupt's estate;

(c)   irrespective of (b), whether an order will be made against a bankrupt's estate.

12.13 As to the first point, it would seem that, for the lump sum to be successfully attacked by the trustee, it would have to constitute a preference.[31] When a bankrupt has given a preference within the time specified by the IA 1986, the court may make such order as is necessary to restore the position to what it would have been had the preference not been made.[32] The specified times are the same as those applicable to transfers at an undervalue (see para **12.9**). The fact that the lump sum had been paid pursuant to an order of the court would not prevent it from being classed as a preference.[33]

There is no mention in the IA 1986 of a lump sum constituting a transfer at an undervalue, and no authority as to whether this might be possible.

12.14 The second point may arise when a lump sum order has been made and the paying party then becomes bankrupt (or, as may be the case, is already bankrupt). Any obligation arising under an order made in family or domestic proceedings is not provable in bankruptcy.[34] The effect of this is that, so long as the bankrupt remains bankrupt, the order cannot be enforced against his estate. However, it also follows that the order survives the bankruptcy and may be enforced after the bankrupt's discharge, or during the bankruptcy by other

---

[30]   IA 1986, s 284(1).
[31]   For example, see *Trowbridge v Trowbridge* [2003] 2 FLR 231.
[32]   IA 1986, s 340(1) and (2).
[33]   Ibid, s 340(6).
[34]   Insolvency Rules 1986, r 12.3(2)(a). See also *Woodley v Woodley (No 2)* [1993] 2 FLR 477, CA.

methods, for example a judgment summons. Prior to 2005 it was held that even though a lump sum order cannot be proved in a bankruptcy, there is no reason in principle why an unpaid lump sum should not found a bankruptcy petition.[35] However, by virtue of the Insolvency (Amendment) Rules 2005 (SI 2005/527), with effect from 1 April 2005 lump sum and costs orders made within family proceedings are provable in bankruptcy.

12.15 In *Re Nunn (Bankruptcy: Divorce: Pension Rights)*[36] the husband was ordered to pay one half of the lump sums which he would receive under his pension policies. He was then made bankrupt. It was held that the wife had no rights as against the trustee in bankruptcy; the court lacked jurisdiction to make an order for payment in any form which created an equitable interest or security.

12.16 Finally, the jurisidiction of the court to make an order against an undischarged bankrupt must be considered. In view of what has been said above, there will be little point in such an application in most cases. However, there is no reason in principle why such an order should not be made; the only restriction is that the court must consider the bankrupt's ability to pay.[37] In one case,[38] it was shown that there would be a substantial surplus in the bankruptcy, and an order for a lump sum of £450,000 was upheld. The only caveat was that the judge must have a clear picture of the assets and liabilities of the bankrupt so that he can determine what assets the bankrupt will have in the foreseeable future.

12.17 The fact that a spouse seeks a bankruptcy order in order to defeat a claim for ancillary relief is not a matter which the court may take into account under s 37 of the MCA 1973. In such a case, the appropriate remedy is to apply to the bankruptcy court for an annulment of the bankruptcy.[39]

Periodical payments orders

12.18 Orders for periodic maintenance for a spouse or child are probably the class of order for financial relief which is most vulnerable to attack after bankruptcy. After bankruptcy, the income of the bankrupt may be claimed by the trustee as part of the bankrupt's estate.[40] The court may make an income payments order, which requires the bankrupt to make payments from his

---

[35] *Russell v Russell* [1998] 1 FLR 936; *Wheatley v Wheatley* [1999] 2 FLR 205 (where the husband's repeated failures to pay and the presence of other creditors made the strategy justifiable). For the position in a voluntary arrangement, see *Re Bradley-Hole (A Bankrupt)* [1995] 2 FLR 838 and *Re A Debtor; JP v A Debtor* [1999] 1 FLR 926. For the position where bankruptcy is based on a foreign order, see *Cartwright v Cartwright (No 2)* [2002] EWCA Civ 931, [2002] 2 FLR 610, CA.

[36] [2004] 1 FLR 1123.

[37] *Woodley v Woodley (No 2)* (above).

[38] *Hellyer v Hellyer* [1996] 2 FLR 579, CA.

[39] *F v F (Divorce: Insolvency: Annulment of Bankruptcy Order)* [1994] 1 FLR 359. See also *Couvaras v Wolf* [2002] 2 FLR 107.

[40] IA 1986, s 307(1).

income to the trustee for the benefit of the creditors;[41] this order may continue to have effect after discharge from bankruptcy.[42]

When assessing the amount of an income payments order, the court must leave the bankrupt with sufficient to meet the reasonable domestic needs of the bankrupt and his family, defined in this context as the persons who are living with the bankrupt and are dependent on him.[43] It is therefore not difficult to see that any order for periodical payments made before bankruptcy is at great risk of not being paid in full or even at all once the paying party is made bankrupt.

An order for periodical payments or maintenance pending suit is not provable in the bankruptcy.[44] Similarly, although an order for costs made in ancillary relief proceedings is a 'bankruptcy debt' within the meaning of s 382(1) of the IA 1986, it has been held that it would be difficult to envisage any circumstances in which the court could properly make a bankruptcy order based on such an unprovable debt.[45] On the other hand, an order in favour of a bankrupt may be claimed by the trustee by way of an application for an income payments order.[46]

THE RIGHTS OF THIRD-PARTY CREDITORS

12.19 In general, while the court must take account of the proper liabilities of either party when performing the s 25 exercise,[47] it does not have to put the interests of creditors before those of the parties to the marriage and the children. There is no jurisdiction to make an order for payment to any person other than the parties or a child.

The only exception to this general rule is the position of a creditor which has a secured interest over any property which is the object of an application by either party. When procedure is considered in Chapter 16, it will be seen that a mortgagee or chargee is one of the persons who must be served with notice of any application for a property adjustment order, and who have the right to be heard on the application. This is not normally a situation which causes difficulty, since the court would not order transfer of any property if the transferee was unable to maintain the mortgage payments from some source of funds, whether private or public.

---

41   IA 1986, ss 310(1) and 385(1).
42   Ibid, ss 310(5) and 280(2)(c).
43   Ibid, ss 310(2) and 385(1).
44   Insolvency Rules 1986, r 12.3(2)(a).
45   *Levy v Legal Services Commission* [2001] 1 FLR 435, CA. See also *Wehmeyer v Wehmeyer* [2001] 2 FLR 84.
46   IA 1986, ss 310(1) and 283(1)(b).
47   MCA 1973, s 25(2)(b).

12.20 However, some difficulties have arisen and may arise when either a mortgagee has a charge which is repayable on demand, or is a creditor which has obtained a charging order to secure a judgment debt. The position is most difficult when only one of the parties is liable in respect of the judgment debt and the charging order is over that party's interest in a jointly owned property and a dispute arises as to whether the interests of the non-liable party and the family or those of the creditor are to have precedence. Such a dispute will not normally arise on the application for the charging order itself, but more commonly arises on an application for an order for sale or on an application to vary the charging order.

In *Harman v Glencross and Another*,[48] it was held first that, in such a case, the application for the charging order to be varied should be transferred to the Family Division (or to the Divorce County Court), so that the court might be fully apprised of all the circumstances of the case. The court should strike a balance between the creditor's normal expectation that an order enforcing a money judgment lawfully obtained would be made, and the hardship to the wife and children that such an order could entail. Where, as in this case, the wife's right of occupation would not be adequately protected under LPA 1925, s 30, an order with *Mesher*-type terms would normally be appropriate.

It was also said in this case that where the application for the charging order to be made absolute is heard before the commencement of divorce proceedings, the court should normally make the order sought. Where the charging order nisi has been made after the filing of the petition, the court considering the application for the charging order absolute should bear in mind that the court is holding the balance not only between the wife and the husband but also between the wife and the judgment creditor, and should make only such order as is necessary to protect the wife's right to occupy the home.

12.21 In another case,[49] it was held that there was no automatic predominance for either claim. Every case depended on striking a fair balance between the normal expectations of the creditor and the hardship to the wife and children if an order were made. The use of the term 'hardship' necessarily implied that there would be instances in which a wife and/or children would be compelled, in the interests of justice to the judgment creditor, to accept a provision for their accommodation which fell below the level of adequacy. The court, having weighed all the circumstances, was required to make only such orders as might be necessary to protect the wife's right to occupy the home, albeit not on a permanent basis.

By virtue of the TLATA 1996, trusts are no longer trusts for sale and the court should therefore be able to take a more balanced view of competing interests.[50]

---

[48] [1984] FLR 652, FD.

[49] *Austin-Fell v Austin-Fell and Midland Bank* [1989] 2 FLR 497.

[50] See *Mortgage Corporation v Shaire* [2000] 1 FLR 973. For a recent example of the disadvantaged position of a spouse as against the creditors of a bankrupt, see *Ram v Ram, Ram and Russell* [2004] EWCA Civ 1452, [2005] 2 FLR 63.

This issue was argued on behalf of a wife in *Bank of Ireland Mortgages v Bell and Bell*[51] where a judge at first instance had refused to order the sale of a property on the application of the creditor on the grounds that it had been purchased as a family home, was occupied by the wife and son, and the wife was in poor health. On appeal, it was held that while s 15 of TLATA 1996 had given scope for some change to the court's previous practice, a powerful consideration was whether a creditor was receiving proper recompense for being kept out of his money of which repayment was overdue. Here, the house had ceased to be the family home when the husband left, the son was nearly 18 and the wife's ill-health might at best have justified only postponement of the sale. Sale was ordered.

---

51 [2001] 2 FLR 809, CA.

Chapter 13

VARIATION

INTRODUCTION

13.1 The orders which may be made under MCA 1973 may be divided into those which can be reconsidered and, if appropriate, changed or varied, and those which are 'final orders' and which cannot normally be changed. With certain limited exceptions, only periodic orders can be varied. The general principle of MCA 1973 is that a capital order cannot be varied, save as to detail.

The statutory powers to vary are contained in s 31 of MCA 1973, which must be considered in detail. There is some case-law as to the way the courts should approach such cases, and this must also be considered.

STATUTORY PROVISIONS

What orders can be varied?

13.2 Section 31 begins by defining the types of order to which it applies. Since s 31 is intended to be a comprehensive code, it may be taken that unless an order appears in the list of orders in s 31(2), it cannot be varied.

It is provided that:

'This section [ie s 31] applies to the following orders, that is to say—

(a) any order for maintenance pending suit and any interim order for maintenance;
(b) any periodical payments order;
(c) any secured periodical payments order;
(d) any order made by virtue of section 23(3)(c) or 27(7)(b) above (provision for payment of a lump sum by instalments);
(dd) any deferred order made by virtue of section 23(1)(c) (lump sums) which includes provision made by virtue of—
      (i)   section 25B(4), or
      (ii) section 25C,
      (provision in respect of pension rights);
(e) any order for a settlement of property under section 24(1)(b) or for a variation of settlement under section 24(1)(c) or (d) above, being an order made on or after the grant of a decree of judicial separation;
(f) any order made under section 24A(1) above for the sale of property;

(g)   a pension sharing order under section 24B above which is made at a time before the decree has been made absolute.'[1]

13.3   The powers of the court in respect of each of these types of order are set out in s 31(1). It is provided that:

'Where the court has made an order to which this section applies, then, subject to the provisions of this section and of section 28(1A) above, the court shall have power to vary or discharge the order or to suspend any provision thereof temporarily and to revive the operation of any provision so suspended.'

Section 28(1A) is the section of the Act which empowers the court to direct that no further applications may be made. The reference to s 28(1A) therefore reminds the court that, when such a direction has been given, the order may not be varied.

13.4   The principles observed by the court when considering an application will be set out at para **13.11** et seq. First, however, some particular considerations applicable to certain types of orders must be considered.

Capital orders

13.5   As was seen above, lump sum orders and property adjustment orders cannot be varied and they are not included in the list of variable orders in s 31(2). Little more need be said, save that when any dispute arises as to the precise meaning of an order, the question which must be asked is whether the order was intended to be, and can reasonably be construed as being, a final resolution of all issues between the parties. Where that is the case, and the order is in effect a lump sum order, property adjustment order or settlement of property order, it must be a final order and cannot be varied.[2]

Maintenance pending suit and periodical payments

13.6   When an order of this type is varied the court has power to remit any arrears which have accrued.[3] It may also, of course, either increase or decrease the rate of payment or discharge the order.

Since November 1998, the court has also enjoyed the valuable power[4] to substitute a lump sum order or property adjustment order when it discharges a periodical payments order and also, where the petition was filed on or after 1 December 2000, to make a pension sharing order. This in effect allows the court to capitalise maintenance. When substituting a lump sum order on discharging a periodical payments order, the court is not limited to a

---

[1]   MCA 1973, s 31(2).
[2]   See *Dinch v Dinch* [1987] 2 FLR 162, HL; *Peacock v Peacock* [1991] 1 FLR 324; *Hill v Hill* [1998] 1 FLR 198, CA.
[3]   MCA 1973, s 31(2A).
[4]   Ibid, s 31(7A) and (7B), introduced by FLA 1996, Sch 8, para 7; the remedy established by *S v S* [1987] 1 FLR 71 is now therefore obsolete.

mathematical calculation of the capital equivalent of the ongoing periodical payments but may consider what lump sum would be fair in all the circumstances.[5] The court may also order that no further applications may be made for periodical payments, secured periodical payments, or an extension of any term granted by the court.

In *Pearce v Pearce*[6] Thorpe LJ summarised his general conclusions on this issue as follows.

(1)   On dismissing an entitlement to future periodical payments, the court's function is not to reopen capital claims but to substitute for the periodical payments order such other order or orders as will both fairly compensate the payee and at the same time complete the clean break.

(2)   In surveying what substitute order or orders should be made, first consideration should be given to the option of carving out of the payor's pension funds a pension for the payee equivalent to the discharged periodical payments order.

When the court decides to vary or discharge a periodical payments order or secured periodical payments order it may direct that the variation or discharge shall not take effect until the expiration of such period as may be specified in the order.[7]

Secured periodical payments

13.7   The comments made above apply equally to secured periodical payments. There is also a provision[8] to deal with the position where a person liable to make secured payments has died. In principle, an order for secured periodical payments survives the death of the paying party; his obligation was to provide the security for the payments, and these will continue after his death.[9] It is therefore provided that the person entitled to payments or the personal representatives of the deceased may apply for an order for the proceeds of sale of a property to be used for securing the payments, but, save with leave of the court, no such application may be made later than 6 months after the date on which representation in regard to the deceased's estate is taken out.

Lump sum payable by instalments

13.8   As has already been said, in principle, a lump sum order cannot be varied. The provision in s 31(2) is limited to the question of payment by instalments. It only applies when the court's original order provided for

5   *Cornick v Cornick (No 3)* [2001] 2 FLR 1240, Charles J.
6   [2003] EWCA Civ 1054, [2003] 2 FLR 1144.
7   MCA 1973, s 31(10).
8   Ibid, s 31(6).
9   See Chapter 3, para **3.12**.

payment by instalments rather than by one single payment. The power of the court is, therefore, to reduce or increase the size of the instalments or to change the frequency of the payments. In practice, of course, the court could render a lump sum order ineffective by so reducing the instalments that it would never be paid, but this would be unusual.

Provision in respect of pension rights

13.9 Pensions are dealt with in detail in Chapter 10. The types of orders which are covered by s 31(2)(dd) are, first, orders under s 25B(4) which enable the court to 'attach' a pension lump sum, and secondly, orders under s 25C which contains a similar power including the power to compel the trustees or a party with pension rights to nominate the other party as the payee. The essential nature of these provisions is that a deferred order is made requiring the trustees of a pension scheme to make a payment or payments out of the scheme to the party who is not the scheme member at some future date.

The effect of this provision is that the court may vary any such order, whether it is of a periodic or capital nature at any time after the order is made. This might be before the order had come into effect.

It is provided that, in respect of these types of orders, s 31 shall cease to apply on the death of either of the parties to the marriage.[10]

Settlement of property or variation of settlement

13.10 The powers of the court under s 31 in relation to these types of orders are limited[11] to orders made in judicial separation proceedings and also to applications:

'made in proceedings—

(a)   for the rescission of the decree of judicial separation by reference to which the order was made, or
(b)   for the dissolution of the marriage in question.'

This provision therefore recognises that a decree of judicial separation leaves the parties still married to each other. If the decree itself is rescinded, any justification for the order must fall away, and if the marriage is dissolved, the court has wider powers as to a clean break, and the position may need to be reconsidered.

---

[10]   MCA 1973, s 31(2B).
[11]   Ibid, s 31(4).

THE PRINCIPLES ON WHICH THE COURT EXERCISES ITS DISCRETION

13.11 The principles which govern the exercise of the court's discretion are contained in s 31(7) and fall into three parts. First, it is provided that:

> 'the court shall have regard to all the circumstances of the case, first consideration being given to the welfare while a minor of any child of the family who has not attained the age of eighteen . . .'[12]

This provision requires little comment. The meaning of 'the first consideration' has already been considered at Chapter 1, para **1.8**.

Secondly, it is provided that:

> 'the circumstances of the case shall include any change in any of the matters to which the court was required to have regard when making the order to which the application relates.'[13]

Thirdly, it is provided that:

> 'in the case of a periodical or secured periodical payments order made on or after the grant of a decree of divorce or nullity of marriage, the court shall consider whether in all the circumstances and after having regard to any such change it would be appropriate to vary the order so that payments under the order are required to be made or secured only for such further period as will in the opinion of the court be sufficient . . . to enable the party in whose favour the order was made to adjust without undue hardship to the termination of those payments.'[14]

Then, in a provision which applies only to secured periodical payments, it is also provided that:

> 'in a case where the party against whom the order was made has died, the circumstances of the case shall also include the changed circumstances resulting from his or her death.'[15]

The clean break on variation applications

13.12 The significance of the reference to termination of payments is clear. On a variation application, the court must perform the same task of inquiry into whether or not there should be a clean break as would be performed on an original application. The principles of the clean break are considered in detail in Chapter 2, para **2.21** et seq and need not be considered further here, save to

---

[12]   MCA 1973, s 31(7).
[13]   Ibid.
[14]   Ibid, s 31(7)(a).
[15]   Ibid, s 31(7)(b).

say that the courts have adopted a variety of approaches to the termination of payments on a variation application, depending on the circumstances of the case.[16] (See also para **13.6**.)

In *Fleming v Fleming*[17] it was held that on an application for variation the court was under a duty to consider terminating financial dependence provided such outcome could be achieved without undue hardship and that this principle was much enhanced where there was a previous term order.

Changes in circumstances

13.13 The court must consider all the circumstances including any change there may have been in any of the matters to which it was originally directed to have regard under s 25. The requirement to have regard to all the circumstances therefore dictates a complete review of all relevant matters; the changes since the order was made are merely one of the aspects to be considered. It is not correct merely to look at what has changed since the order was made.[18]

Having said that, it is inevitable that the court will require some change in the circumstances before it varies an order; otherwise, a dissatisfied litigant could apply repeatedly for variation as a method of appeal or challenge. The starting point must be that the order was correctly made. In a case[19] involving variation of a consent order, it was said that 'the court should not adopt an approach which differs radically from the approach taken by the parties themselves in assessing quantum of maintenance when the original order was made'; the same could be said of the approach adopted by the court in a contested case.

13.14 In *Primavera v Primavera*,[20] the husband was ordered to pay the wife periodical payments of £10,000 pa less tax, and a lump sum of £72,000. The wife was a beneficiary of her mother's estate, part of which was a house. The wife agreed to sell her share of the house to one of her daughters for the district valuer's valuation, which was considerably less than the true value, with the result that she received much less than she would otherwise have done. She applied to vary her periodical payments, and Booth J increased the order to £28,000 pa. The husband was a wealthy man. On appeal, Booth J's conclusion that there was no reason why the wife should not have regarded the inheritance as hers to do with as she wished was upheld. However, it was emphasised that an important factor was that the husband was wealthy and well able to pay the increased order; the position might be very different where the parties were of more modest means and the inheritance would have made a material difference to the total means of both parties.

---

[16] See e g *Morris v Morris* [1985] FLR 1176; *Sandford v Sandford* [1986] 1 FLR 412; *Richardson v Richardson (No 2)* [1994] 2 FLR 1051; *Ashley v Blackman* [1988] Fam 85; *Jones v Jones* [2000] 2 FLR 307 (see para **2.36**).
[17] [2004] 1 FLR 667.
[18] *Lewis v Lewis* [1977] 3 All ER 992, CA.
[19] *Boylan v Boylan* [1988] 1 FLR 282 per Booth J.
[20] [1991] 1 FLR 16, CA.

It was also held that, although financial mismanagement by a party was not a relevant factor in this case, it could well be a relevant circumstance in an appropriate case.

PROCEDURE

13.15 An application to vary is contained within the definition of 'ancillary relief'.[21] There are therefore no separate rules applicable to such an application, and it should be conducted according to the normal rules applicable to ancillary relief.[22]

FORMS OF ORDER

13.16 Forms of order for variation applications will be found at Appendix A, Precedent 32.

VARIATION SUBJECT TO CONDITIONS

13.17 In *Mubarak v Mubarik* [2004] EWCA 1158 (Fam), [2004] 2 FLR 932 the husband applied to vary. He was in default of earlier orders and had been found to be dishonest. It was held that *Hadkinson v Hadkinson* [1952] P 285 was still good law and was an important discretionary power of last resort – see also *Corbett v Corbett* [2003] EWCA Civ 559 [2003] 2 FLR 385. The court could impose conditions on the husband proceeding with his application. It must consider–

(a)   whether the husband was in contempt;

(b)   whether he caused an impediment to the course of justice;

(c)   whether there was any other effective way of securing justice;

(d)   whether the contempt was wilful;

(e)   whether it was appropriate to impose conditions and if so what would be appropriate.

---

[21]   FPR 1991, r 1.2(1).
[22]   See Chapter 16.

Chapter 14

MISCELLANEOUS APPLICATIONS

INTRODUCTION

14.1 In this chapter, it is intended to deal with certain types of application which, although they must be mentioned, do not merit a chapter to themselves. They are:

(a) applications under MCA 1973, s 27;

(b) applications under MCA 1973, s 10(2);

(c) alteration of agreements.

APPLICATIONS UNDER MCA 1973, SECTION 27

14.2 The marginal note to s 27 of MCA 1973 reads 'Financial provision in cases of neglect to maintain', and the section is intended to provide a remedy for financial relief exercisable by courts exercising family jurisdiction. The essential difference from the other types of relief described in this book is that the exercise of the jurisdiction conferred by s 27 does not depend on the grant of a decree of divorce, nullity or judicial separation nor even the filing of a petition. It is a 'free-standing' remedy, and the application is by way of an originating application.

14.3 Before 1970, applications to neglect to maintain were quite common, but for some time, s 27 has been little used. It was thought that it might assume a more prominent role when FLA 1996 came into force but that is now, at most, an academic possibility.

14.4 It is provided that either party to a marriage may apply to the court for an order on the ground that the other party:

'(a) has failed to provide reasonable maintenance for the applicant, or
(b) has failed to provide, or to make a proper contribution towards, reasonable maintenance for any child of the family.'[1]

---

[1] MCA 1973, s 27(1).

Jurisdiction to make the order is the same as in other matrimonial causes.[2]

The orders which the court may make in favour of the applicant are orders for periodical payments, secured periodical payments, and a lump sum.[3] There is jurisdiction to make similar orders for a child, but the effect of CSA 1991, s 8 reduces the value of those provisions. The court may also make a lump sum order for the purpose of enabling any liabilities or expenses to be met;[4] this is a similar provision to that contained in s 23(3).[5] The court also has jurisdiction to make interim orders.[6]

14.5 In deciding whether or not the respondent has failed to provide reasonable maintenance for the applicant, and, if so, what order to make, the court is directed to:

> '. . . have regard to all the circumstances of the case including the matters mentioned in section 25(2) above and where an application is also made under this section in respect of a child of the family who has not attained the age of eighteen, first consideration shall be given to the welfare of the child while a minor.'[7]

The court has therefore to take account of the usual s 25 factors.[8] Since the marriage has not yet been dissolved, the termination of the parties' financial dependence on each other does not arise.

14.6 There are few authorities under the modern law to indicate how the courts exercise their discretion; this may be because s 27 has been little used, and also, perhaps, because when used the orders are often only of temporary duration. The duty of both parties to a marriage to maintain each other is an established part of English law;[9] what is reasonable will depend on the circumstances of the case.

The wording of the statute was changed in 1978,[10] the old formula of 'wilful neglect to maintain' being replaced by the present 'failure to maintain'. It had been held that the common law rule that a husband has no duty to maintain a wife who has committed adultery which he has not connived at, nor by his conduct conduced to, applied to the duty to provide reasonable maintenance under s 27.[11] However, it is thought that the change in the wording of the statute, which omits the word 'wilful' and introduces some general guidelines,

---

2   Ibid, s 27(2). See Chapter 1, para **1.61**.
3   Ibid, s 27(6).
4   Ibid, s 27(7).
5   See Chapter 4, para **4.6**.
6   MCA 1973, s 27(5).
7   Ibid, s 27(3).
8   See Chapter 1.
9   *Northrop v Northrop* [1968] P 74, CA.
10   By Domestic Proceedings and Magistrates' Courts Act 1978, s 63(1); see also MFPA 1984, s 4.
11   *Gray v Gray* [1976] Fam 324; *Newmarch v Newmarch* [1978] Fam 79.

means that the law is no longer simply a procedure for enforcing the common law duty to maintain, and therefore that the rule that adultery is a bar no longer applies.[12]

14.7 Applications under s 27 are made by filing an originating application in Form M19.[13] At the same time, the applicant must file an affidavit giving the formal details of the marriage as would be given in a petition, details of the applicant's means and the respondent's means so far as the applicant is aware, and details of the alleged failure to maintain.[14] The respondent must file an affidavit in reply within 14 days. The application then proceeds as if it were an application for ancillary relief.[15]

APPLICATIONS UNDER MCA 1973, SECTION 10(2)

14.8 In 1969, for the first time, the law of divorce was changed to allow 'no fault' divorce.[16] For the first time, a divorce could be granted on the ground that the parties had lived apart for 2 years and the respondent consented to the grant of a decree, or that they had lived apart for 5 years even though the respondent did not consent to the grant of a decree; in the latter case, an 'innocent party' could be divorced against her will. These provisions are now s 1(2)(d) and (e) of the 1973 Act.

Because of these then novel provisions, it was thought right to include in the legislation special protection for respondents in such cases, and this protection survives unchanged in the modern law as s 10(2). The only significant advantage which can be obtained by an application under s 10(2) as opposed to a conventional application for ancillary relief is that the filing of the notice of application prevents the grant of decree absolute,[17] which can, in appropriate cases, be postponed until proper provision has been made.

When an application under s 10(2) is made, it is common to apply for ancillary relief in the usual way at the same time.

14.9 The section therefore applies where the court has granted a decree nisi under s 1(2)(d) or (e) and the respondent applies for her financial position to be considered; when the decree was also on the basis of one of the other facts in s 1 the section does not apply.[18] The application must clearly be made before decree absolute or it will lose its purpose.

---

[12] This certainly was the intention of the Law Commission; see Law Com No 77, paras 2.15, 9.11, and 9.24(c).
[13] FPR 1991, r 3.1(1).
[14] Ibid, r 3.1(3).
[15] Ibid, r 3.1(10).
[16] Divorce Reform Act 1969, s 2.
[17] MCA 1973, s 10(3).
[18] Ibid, s 10(2).

It is provided that the court hearing the application:

> 'shall consider all the circumstances, including the age, health, conduct, earning capacity, financial resources and financial obligations of each of the parties, and the financial position of the respondent as, having regard to the divorce, it is likely to be after the death of the petitioner should the petitioner die first . . .'[19]

The statute imposes two duties on the court: first, to consider the age, health and general financial position of the parties and any issue of conduct which may be relevant, and, secondly, to consider what the position of the respondent would be if the petitioner died first. Section 10(3) then continues:

> '. . . and, subject to subsection (4) below, the court shall not make the decree absolute unless it is satisfied—
>
> (a)   that the petitioner should not be required to make any financial provision for the respondent, or
> (b)   that the financial provision made by the petitioner for the respondent is reasonable and fair or the best that can be made in the circumstances.'

14.10 The court must, therefore, satisfy itself either that no financial provision need be made, or that the provision made is fair and reasonable, or the best in the circumstances. The latter case (best in the circumstances) would apply where the provision made was inadequate but there were insufficient funds to do better.

As indicated, there is provision for exception made in s 10(4) which provides that the court may, if it thinks fit, make the decree absolute notwithstanding the requirements of s 10(3), if:

> '(a)   it appears that there are circumstances making it desirable that the decree should be obtained without delay, and
> (b)   the court has obtained a satisfactory undertaking from the petitioner that he will make such financial provision for the respondent as the court may approve.'[20]

Both parts of this requirement must be met before the court could act under s 10(4).

14.11 As was said in the introduction to this part, the only separate usefulness of s 10(2) is to hold up decree absolute until all financial matters have been concluded. When the person in need of protection is the petitioner, an application under s 10(2) is unnecessary as well as impossible. In *Wickler v Wickler*,[21] where the respondent applied for decree absolute under s 9(2) of MCA 1973, the petitioner having failed to apply, it was held that the court had power to refuse the application unless and until he complied with orders as to

---

[19]   Ibid, s 10(3).
[20]   MCA 1974, s 10(4).
[21]   [1998] 2 FLR 326, Bracewell J.

ancillary relief. There always will be a residue of cases where a respondent feels that the only way to ensure proper relief is to make an application under s 10(2); these will nearly always be cases where she will lose all rights under the husband's pension scheme on the grant of decree absolute.[22]

14.12 An application under s 10(2) is made by filing notice in Form B.[23] At this stage, no evidence in support is necessary since the application proceeds as if Form B were Form A and the application becomes an application for financial relief.

ORDERS FOR ALTERATION OF AGREEMENTS DURING LIFETIMES OF PARTIES

14.13 Section 35 of MCA 1973 applies where there is a maintenance agreement subsisting, and each of the parties is, for the time being, either domiciled in or resident in England and Wales.[24] In those circumstances, either party may apply to the court for an order making such alterations in the agreement:

'(i)   by varying or revoking any financial arrangements contained in it, or

(ii)   by inserting in it financial arrangements for the benefit of one of the parties to the agreement or a child of the family,

as may appear to that court to be just having regard to all the circumstances, including, if relevant, the matters mentioned in section 25(4) above; and the agreement shall have effect thereafter as if any alteration made by the order had been made by agreement between the parties and for valuable consideration.'[25]

Section 25(4) refers to the liability of a step-parent. This is the only specific s 25 factor to be mentioned. Otherwise, the court must consider all the circumstances.

14.14 Before it can make such an order, the court must be satisfied either:

'(a)   that by reason of a change in the circumstances in the light of which any financial arrangements contained in the agreement were made or, as the case may be, financial arrangements were omitted from it (including a change foreseen by the parties when making the agreement), the agreement should be altered so as to make different, or, as the case may be, so as to contain, financial arrangements, or

(b)   that the agreement does not contain proper financial arrangements with respect to any child of the family.'[26]

---

22   For examples, see *Cumbers v Cumbers* [1975] 1 All ER 1, CA; *Grigson v Grigson* [1974] 1 All ER 748, CA; *Garcia v Garcia* [1991] 3 All ER 451, CA.

23   FPR 1991, r 2.45(1).

24   MCA 1973, s 35(1).

25   MCA 1973, s 35(2).

26   Ibid, s 35(2).

The second provision may now be of little effect due to CSA 1991.

14.15 There are other matters of detail in the section. It should be noted that application may be made to a magistrates' court under s 35, provided the parties are resident in England and Wales and at least one of the parties resides in the area of that court.[27] The powers of the magistrates are limited to issues of periodical payments.[28]

14.16 Application under s 35 is made by originating application containing the information required by Form M21.[29] An affidavit must be filed with the application, and the respondent should file an affidavit within 14 days of service.[30] The application will normally be heard by the district judge.

---

[27]   Ibid, s 35(3).
[28]   Ibid.
[29]   FPR 1991, r 3.2(1).
[30]   Ibid, r 3.2(3) and (4).

Chapter 15

FINANCIAL RELIEF AFTER OVERSEAS DIVORCE

INTRODUCTION

15.1 The various forms of financial relief described in this book, with the exception of applications under s 27 of MCA 1973, all depend on the grant of a decree of divorce, nullity or judicial separation (or at least the filing of a petition for such relief). Without a petition and, in the case of a final order, a decree, the court can do nothing. The type of relief about to be described in this chapter is different, in that the basis for jurisdiction is an overseas divorce or other order. There are two stages in such applications. First, the court must grant leave to apply. Secondly, the court will adjudicate on the application; in this case, the relief it may grant is practically identical to that which would be granted after a decree of the English and Welsh courts.

JURISDICTION

15.2 It is provided that an application for financial relief may be made where:

'(a) a marriage has been dissolved or annulled, or the parties to a marriage have been legally separated, by means of judicial or other proceedings in an overseas country, and
(b) the divorce, annulment or legal separation is entitled to be recognised as valid in England and Wales.'[1]

Remarriage of the applicant is a bar to an application in relation to that marriage.[2]

15.3 The classes of divorce etc which would be recognised as valid are those set out in the Recognition of Divorces and Legal Separations Act 1971, ss 2–6.

15.4 Jurisdiction therefore depends on the existence of a divorce etc which would be recognised and on the requirements of MFPA 1984, s 15, which provides that the court shall have jurisdiction if any of the following three jurisdictional requirements are satisfied:

---

[1]   MFPA 1984, s 12(1).
[2]   Ibid, s 12(2).

(1)   domicile of either party at the date of application for leave or as at the divorce etc;

(2)   the habitual residence of either party for one year ending with either the application for leave or the divorce etc;

(3)   either party having, at the date of the application for leave, a beneficial interest in possession in a dwelling-house in England and Wales which was at some time in the marriage a matrimonial home of the parties to the marriage.

15.5   If the proposed respondent is domiciled in a contracting State within the meaning of the Civil Jurisdiction and Judgments Act 1982,[3] a further complication may arise. The general theme of the 1982 Act is that a respondent who is in a contracting State must be sued there. However, the Act does not apply to rights in property arising out of a matrimonial relationship, nor to maintenance.

APPLICATIONS FOR LEAVE

15.6   The first step the applicant must take is to apply for leave, and it is provided that the court shall not grant leave unless it considers that there is substantial ground for the making of an application for such an order.[4] Clearly, the court would first have to be satisfied that it had jurisdiction, as explained above. However, that would not be an end of the matter, since s 16 provides that:

> 'the court shall consider whether in all the circumstances of the case it would be appropriate for such an order to be made by a court in England and Wales, and if the court is not satisfied that it would be appropriate the court shall dismiss the application.'[5]

There follows a list of the matters to which the court must have particular regard. These include:

–   the connection which the parties have with England and Wales, the country where the divorce etc was granted, or any other country;

–   the financial benefit which the applicant or a child has or is likely to have received in the foreign proceedings;

–   the financial relief awarded by any foreign court and the likelihood of any such order being complied with;

---

3   Most countries in western Europe are contracting States.
4   MFPA 1984, s 13.
5   Ibid, s 16(2).

– the right to apply in any other jurisdiction;

– availability of property in this country;

– length of time since divorce etc.[6]

15.7 Applications under these provisions can be made only to the High Court in the Principal Registry; they cannot be made elsewhere. The application for leave is made ex parte to a judge. The applicant must file an originating summons in Form M25, supported by an affidavit which gives the particulars required by FPR 1991.[7] Since the application is made ex parte, it follows that the respondent is entitled to apply to set the order aside if he is aggrieved by it.

The application for leave is a crucial step. The court has to be satisfied as to the 'substantial ground for the making of an application', and if, on the application for leave, it is clear that if leave were granted the substantive application would fail, leave should not be granted.[8] The burden is on the person bringing the application for leave, and it was held, in a case where there had been a connection with England before the marriage but the connection with the foreign jurisdiction was now stronger, that leave should not be granted.[9]

It has been held that the mischief which the Act was designed to redress is a narrow one, and does not include the case of a foreign court of competent jurisdiction making an order which has neither been appealed nor impugned.[10] While there is no absolute rule of law that leave will not be granted where the sole motive is to enforce a foreign order, in practice leave will only rarely be granted in such circumstances.[11] Leave was refused in one case where the wife, wisely or unwisely, had allowed the breakdown of her marriage to be referred to the courts in France; she was not to be allowed to relitigate here an issue which had been taken to its conclusion there.[12] In another case, it was held that it was essential to demonstrate that the applicant was suffering some injustice before the court could find that there was a substantial ground[13] but in a later decision of the Court of Appeal it was said that the judge had gone too far and his decision should not be followed.[14]

---

[6]   Ibid, s 16(2)(a)–(i).
[7]   Rule 3.17.
[8]   *Holmes v Holmes* [1989] Fam 47, CA.
[9]   *Z v Z (Financial Provision: Overseas Divorce)* [1992] 2 FLR 291.
[10] *Hewitson v Hewitson* [1995] Fam 100, CA.
[11] *Jordan v Jordan* [1999] 2 FLR 1069, CA.
[12] *M v M (Financial Provision after Foreign Divorce)* [1994] 1 FLR 399.
[13] *N v N (Foreign Divorce: Financial Relief)* [1997] 1 FLR 900, per Cazalet J.
[14] *Jordan v Jordan* (above).

ORDERS WHICH MAY BE MADE

15.8   Once the vital step of obtaining leave has been taken (and assuming that the order granting leave is not set aside), the applicant may proceed with the application for financial relief. The powers of the court are contained in ss 14, and 17 to 26 of MFPA 1984. Broadly speaking, the court has power to make all the types of order it could make if the divorce etc had been granted in England and Wales, including avoidance of disposition. The matters to which the court must have regard are contained in s 18, and are similar to those in s 25.

Examples of cases where substantive orders have been made after the grant of leave are found in two recent cases. In *A v S (Financial Relief After Overseas US Divorce and Financial Proceedings)*[15] the parties had been divorced in Texas, and the Texan court had made an order in financial proceedings awarding the wife almost nothing, based on the Texan doctrine of community of property. Before the marriage, the wife lived in a house in England which the husband had purchased for her occupation; after the marriage she had moved to live with him in Texas. The Texan court ordered her to leave the house in England to which she had returned, and she applied for relief in the English court. Bodey J held that extreme caution had to be exercised when a mature foreign jurisdiction had already adjudicated and there was also a problem because the wife had repeatedly lied in the Texan proceedings. Nevertheless, there was an injustice which could be remedied by the application of the discretionary approach, and the wife had a real need for financial help. It was only appropriate to intervene to the minimum extent necessary so as to remedy the injustice perceived. The wife was awarded £60,000.

In *M v L (Financial Relief After Overseas Divorce)*[16] there had been a 30-year delay between divorce and the application. The fact that the divorce had been in South Africa was anomalous, since the case should always have been an English one. The wife had remained dependent on the husband through voluntary payments. Coleridge J declined to divide the husband's capital on modern principles, but made an award of periodical payments based on what it would be reasonable for her to have in all the circumstances.

The procedure is contained in FPR 1991, r 3.18, and applications continue to have to be made to a judge in the Principal Registry.

---

[15]   [2003] 1 FLR 431.
[16]   [2003] 2 FLR 425.

Chapter 16

PROCEDURE

INTRODUCTION

16.1 Until 5 June 2000, there were two sets of rules governing the procedure for an application for ancillary relief. Depending on the court in which an application was issued, the first, which might be described as the standard procedure, was that contained in FPR 1991, rr 2.52 to 2.70. This applied in all courts except 'pilot courts'.

The second code was established by the 'pilot scheme', and applied only to certain courts (called 'pilot courts'). From 5 June 2000, the pilot scheme, as amended, became the standard procedure applicable to all courts and to all applications for ancillary relief commenced after 5 June 2000.

ISSUE OF PROCEEDINGS

16.2 Applicants for ancillary relief may be classified into:

(a) those who have included a prayer for ancillary relief in a petition or answer;

(b) petitioners who have not included such a prayer in their petition;

(c) respondents.

Those in class (a) may apply for ancillary relief in the manner described in para **16.5** et seq.[1] Those in class (b) must apply for leave to make the application.[2] If the decree nisi has not yet been pronounced, the appropriate method to apply for leave is to apply to the district judge for leave to amend the petition by including such a prayer. The amended petition must then be re-served on the respondent unless he has already consented to the application. When the application to the court is for a consent order for ancillary relief, leave is not required.[3]

---

[1]   FPR 1991, r 25.3(1).
[2]   FPR 1991, r 2.53(2).
[3]   Ibid, r 2.53(2)(b).

If the application is made after decree nisi, it must be made on notice to the respondent by filing Form A, supported by an affidavit explaining why the petition contained no such prayer. The application may be made at the trial of the application,[4] but, for obvious reasons, it is preferable to make the application well in advance.

The reasons for the omission may be many and various. It may have been a simple mistake; the respondent may have promised to support the petitioner and then failed to do so; circumstances may have changed since the filing of the petition. Leave is not to be granted as of right; some reason must be given.[5]

16.3 The principle behind the rule requiring the prayer in the petition is that a respondent is entitled to know from the outset what claims are being made against him. It follows that the most likely reason why leave would be refused would be that the respondent had been led to believe that there would be no such claim, that such a belief was reasonable in the circumstances, and that he had acted to his detriment on the strength of this belief.[6] In such circumstances, the longer the delay on the part of the applicant the greater the chance of a refusal of leave.

However, refusal of leave is uncommon. The applicant has a statutory right to apply, and should not be deprived of this by some technical defect. It has been held[7] that the court ought not to refuse leave in any case where it seems that the applicant has a seriously arguable case for ancillary relief; accordingly, any affidavit in support of the application should, in addition to dealing with the reason for the omission, deal with the applicant's means, the respondent's means insofar as the applicant is aware of them, and the general merits of the case.

16.4 A respondent who has not filed an answer or even an acknowledgement of service has an unfettered right to be heard on any question of ancillary relief.[8] This would include making an application.

16.5 Subject to what has been said above, either the petitioner or the respondent may apply for ancillary relief. The persons who may apply for ancillary relief for a child are set out in r 2.54, and include parents and others who might normally be regarded as being in loco parentis and also any child of the family who has been given leave to intervene in the cause for the purpose of applying for ancillary relief.[9] Where the application is for a variation of settlement, the court must, unless it is satisfied that the proposed variation does

---

[4]   FPR 1991, r 2.53(2)(a).
[5]   *Marsden v Marsden* [1973] 2 All ER 851.
[6]   As in *Marsden v Marsden* (above).
[7]   *Chatterjee v Chatterjee* [1976] Fam 199, CA.
[8]   FPR 1991, r 2.52.
[9]   Ibid, r 2.54(1)(f).

not adversely affect the rights of the child or children concerned, direct that the children be separately represented on the application.[10]

THE OVERRIDING OBJECTIVE

16.6 Rule 2.51B contains a statement of the overriding objective, a concept familiar to those who have read the CPR but which, until now, has been absent from, or at least unexpressed in, ancillary relief procedure. It is provided that the ancillary relief rules are 'a procedural code with the overriding objective of enabling the court to deal with cases justly'.[11] The rule then proceeds to state what dealing with a case justly includes, emphasising saving expense, proportionality, expedition and fairness, and provides that both the court and the parties must further the overriding objective.[12] In particular, the court is required to further the overriding objective 'by actively managing cases';[13] this includes identifying issues, regulating disclosure, helping settlement, fixing timetables and giving appropriate directions.[14]

16.7 Many of the essential characteristics of the current rules are encapsulated in the overriding objective. The full text of the rules is set out in Appendix B and should be studied since, in the event of any dispute as to the way in which the rules should be interpreted, the overriding objective would be a legitimate source of guidance and is likely to be referred to quite regularly.

ISSUE OF APPLICATION

16.8 Notice of application is made by filing Form A. An application under MCA 1973, s 10(2) is made in Form B.[15] Where the applicant requests an order which includes provision by virtue of MCA 1973, s 25B or s 25C (attachment of pensions – see Chapter 10, para **10.17**), the terms of the order requested must be specified in the notice in Form A.[16] It will be noted that, except in s 10(2) applications, the parties are referred to as 'the applicant' and 'the respondent'; a respondent to the main suit may be the applicant in the ancillary relief application.

At this stage, no affidavit or other evidence is filed. Instead, the parties receive a notice in Form C which informs them of the date of the first appointment (FA) and the requirements as to the filing of evidence. The court allocates a date for hearing of the FA not less than 12 weeks and not more than 16 weeks

---

10   FPR 1991, r 2.57(1).
11   Ibid, r 2.51B(1).
12   Ibid, r 2.51B(2).
13   Ibid, r 2.51B(5).
14   Ibid 1991, r 2.51B(6).
15   Ibid, r 2.61A(1) and r 2.45.
16   Ibid, r 2.61A(3).

after the date of issue.[17] The documents must then be served on the respondent to the application by the court (not the applicant) within 4 days.[18]

SERVICE AND PARTIES

16.9　Once the Form A has been issued, the court serves it on the other party within 4 days of the date of issue.[19] The documents are sent either to the solicitors who are on the record as acting for the other party[20] or to the party in person where no solicitor is acting for him.[21] In certain circumstances, service may also be effected by DX or fax.[22] When the application is for a variation of settlement, a copy of the application must be served by the applicant on the trustees of the settlement and the settlor if living.[23] In the case of an application for avoidance of disposition, the same documents must be sent by the applicant to the person in whose favour the disposition is alleged to have been made.[24]

When the application is for a property adjustment order, a copy of the application must be served by the applicant on any mortgagee or other person of whom particulars are given in the form. It is not necessary to serve a copy of the evidence in support, but any person so served may apply to the court, within 14 days after service, for a copy of the applicant's Form E.[25]

Sometimes it is necessary to join other parties, for example persons with whom the respondent jointly owns property. RSC Ord 15, r 6(2)(b) allows the joinder of 'any person between whom and any party . . . there may exist a question or issue arising out of . . . any relief or remedy claimed'; this applies in family proceedings in the High Court and county courts because there is no other provision in the FPR 1991 or County Court Rules 1984 (CCR). A determination made in ancillary relief proceedings is binding on a third person who has been joined as a party.[26]

16.10　Where an affidavit or document contains an allegation of adultery or of an improper association with a named person, then, if the court so directs, it must be endorsed with a notice in Form M14, and a copy of the affidavit or of such part thereof as the court may direct, endorsed as aforesaid, shall be served on that person by the person who files the affidavit, and the person against

---

17　FPR 1991, r 2.61A(4).
18　Ibid.
19　Ibid, rr 2.55 and 2.58(1).
20　Ibid, r 10.2.
21　Ibid, r 10.3.
22　See ibid, r 10.2(1), and RSC Ord 65, r 5(2b).
23　Ibid, r 2.59(3)(a).
24　Ibid, r 2.59(3)(b).
25　Ibid, r 2.59(4).
26　*Tebbut v Haynes* [1981] 2 All ER 238, CA.

whom the allegation is made shall be entitled to intervene in the proceedings by applying for directions under r 2.62(5) within 7 days of the service of the affidavit on him.[27]

The court has a discretion as to whether to make an order for service on a named person, and one of the problems about this rule is that it is frequently overlooked until the trial of the application, by which time, in most cases, it would not be cost-effective to do anything about it. The intention of the rule, clearly, is that anyone whose name is mentioned in an affidavit is entitled to know about it and to have the opportunity to deny what is said. Difficulties could be avoided if the following procedure were adopted.

(1) The person drafting the document should be satisfied that it really is necessary to name the person concerned. This might be necessary where it was alleged that the other party was cohabiting and that this had some relevance to the issues but, even then, unless the cohabitation was in dispute it would not be necessary to name the other party.

(2) Where a person is named, a copy of the affidavit, or of the relevant part, should be sent to him or her or to any solicitors acting, with a letter asking if the named person wishes to be formally served or to make any representations.

(3) After the time specified in the letter has elapsed, a letter should be sent to the district judge pointing out the relevant passage in the affidavit, informing the court of any reply from the named person, and asking for a direction under r 2.60.

SPECIAL RULES RELATING TO PENSIONS

16.11 Detailed changes to the procedure relating to pensions have been made by the Family Proceedings (Amendment) (No 5) Rules 2005[28] which apply to all cases where Form A is issued on or after 5 December 2005. Since pensions play a part in most cases, even though they may not be the main issue, these rules are important and must be carefully adhered to.

The new rule 2.70 provides as follows:

'2.70 Pensions

(1) This rule applies where an application for ancillary relief has been made, or notice of intention to proceed with the application has been given, in Form A, or an application has been made in Form B, and the applicant or respondent has or is likely to have any benefits under a pension arrangement.

---

[27] FPR 1991, r 2.60(1).
[28] SI 2005/2922.

(2)   When the court fixes a first appointment as required by rule 2.61A(4)(a),

        (a)   in a matrimonial cause, the party with pension rights, and

        (b)   in a civil partnership cause, the civil partner with pension rights,

        shall within seven days after receiving notification of the date of that appointment, request the person responsible for each pension arrangement under which he has or is likely to have benefits to furnish the information referred to in regulation 2(2) of the Pensions on Divorce etc (Provision of Information) Regulations 2000.

(3)   Within seven days of receiving information under paragraph (2) the party with pension rights or civil partner with pension rights, as the case may be, shall send a copy of it to the other party or civil partner, together with the name and address of the person responsible for each pension arrangement.

(4)   A request under paragraph (2) above need not be made where the party with pension rights or the civil partner with pension rights is in possession of, or has requested, a relevant valuation of the pension rights or benefits accrued under the pension arrangement in question.'

This rule should be read in conjunction with the new rule 2.61D which provides that:

'(2)   At the first appointment the district judge –

        ...

        (f)   may –

                ...

               (iii)   in a matrimonial cause, in a case where an order for ancillary relief is requested that includes provision to be made under section 24B, 25B or 25C of the Act 1973, direct any party with pension rights to file and serve a Pension Inquiry Form (Form P), completed in full or in part as the court may direct;'

16.12 The vital part of all this is the Pension Enquiry Form – the new Form P. Reference should be made to Chapter 10, para **10.03** where the guidance of Thorpe LJ as to the use of the new Form is set out in detail. Form P is intended to provide a cheaper and more cost-effective procedure than what previously prevailed.

FILING OF EVIDENCE

16.13 Evidence is given by each party completing Form E. These forms must be filed at court and simultaneously exchanged not less than 35 days before the date of the FA.[29] Form E is a comprehensive document which requires the parties to set out full details of the marriage, their children, their property and income and financial needs and obligations, and enables them to depose as to any specific MCA 1973, s 25 matter (such as contributions) on which they

---

[29]   FPR 1991, r 2.61B(1) and (2).

rely.[30] Form E is a sworn document. It is intended that the information contained in Form E will be all the information which the court will need in the majority of cases.

Form E must have attached to it any documents required by the form itself and any other documents necessary to clarify or explain any of the information contained in the form.[31] It may not annex or exhibit any other documents.[32] At this stage, no further evidence or documents may be requested, filed or served.[33]

16.14 Those familiar with the Form E, which was in use during the pilot scheme, will recognise that the documents which are now required to be annexed are considerably more extensive than was previously the case. One of the reasons for this is that, in relatively simple cases, it should be possible to use the FA as a Financial Dispute Resolution (FDR) appointment (see para **16.26**) but this cannot happen where one side is waiting for important documents from the other; given the rule that no voluntary discovery may be given before the FA, it was found during the pilot scheme period that parties were frequently not in a position to settle a case at the FA. It is hoped that the new provisions, which require the annexation of all documents which might be relevant in a standard case, will remove any problems in this respect.

16.15 Form E therefore requires the annexation of the following documents:

– any property valuation obtained within the last 6 months (paras 2.1 and 2.2);

– bank or building society statements for the past 12 months for any account held (para 2.3);

– surrender value quotations in respect of any life insurance policies (para 2.5);

– the last 2 years' accounts and any other document used as a basis for valuation of business assets (para 2.14) and for income from business (para 2.20);

– any valuation of pension rights actually available (para 2.16);

– the last three payslips and most recent P60 (para 2.18).

This list is a useful summary of requirements to hand to clients in an ancillary relief case at an early stage. It has been held that:

---

[30] For a complete list, see Form E itself in FPR 1991, App 1A, set out at Appendix B of this book.
[31] FPR 1991, r 2.61B(3).
[32] Ibid, r 2.61B(4).
[33] Ibid, r 2.61B(6).

'solicitors advising the makers of Forms E have, as officers of the court, an important responsibility to ensure that true and realistic figures are inserted in a Form E. And deponents have a greater responsibility to ensure that their Forms E are truthful and honest. The rubric at the beginning of the Form . . . is not mere window dressing'.[34]

16.16 The fairly strict limits imposed by the rule can clearly cause difficulties when one party fails to co-operate; disclosure of the Forms E must be simultaneous, and if the date of the FA is drawing near there may seem to be insufficient time to prepare the case. The date of the FA may be vacated only with permission of the court,[35] and the courts are generally slow to permit any variation in the timetable.

In these circumstances, the applicant's solicitor should immediately apply ex parte to the district judge for an order that the respondent file and exchange his Form E within, say, 4 days of the service of the order upon him. If this does not produce the desired result, it may be that there will be no alternative to seeking an adjournment of the FA at the FA itself; in such circumstances, there is no reason why the court should not assess the wasted costs and order the respondent to pay them within 14 days.

16.17 Where a party is unavoidably prevented from sending any document required by Form E, he must at the earliest opportunity serve copies of that document on the other party and file a copy with the court together with a statement explaining the failure to send it with Form E.[36]

OTHER DOCUMENTS TO BE SERVED

16.18 At least 14 days before the hearing of the FA, each party must file at court and serve on the other an important series of documents, designed to clarify the case and narrow the issues.[37] These are as follows:

–   a concise statement of the issues between the parties (see para **16.17**);

–   a chronology;

–   either a questionnaire setting out by reference to the statement of issues any further information or documents requested or a statement that no such information is requested;

–   notice in Form G (see para **16.23**).

---

[34]   *W v W (Financial Provision: Form E)* [2003] EWHC 2254 (Fam), [2004] 1 FLR 494.
[35]   FPR 1991, r 2.61A(5).
[36]   Ibid, r 2.61B(5).
[37]   Ibid, r 2.61B(7).

The importance of these documents will be seen when they are considered in turn.

THE STATEMENT OF APPARENT ISSUES

16.19 One of the documents which both parties must file at court and serve on each other before the hearing of the FA is the statement of apparent issues. This is an important document, and, in a well-prepared case, should be the central document for the district judge at the FA, since the principal purpose of that hearing is to define the issues in the case. It is essential, therefore, that the parties and their advisers should have contemplated the issues and committed their thoughts to writing before the FA. The Forms E of both parties will have concluded by stating the terms of the order which each party seeks, and it should therefore be possible to identify the issues in the case.

16.20 It would be a mistake to set out a laborious list of each and every issue on which the parties do not agree. For example, it would be unnecessary to record that 'the wife asserts that the cost of her gas and electricity is £800 per annum whereas the husband says it should be only £550 per annum', or that 'the wife says that the husband has an improper relationship with Mrs X, but the husband denies this'.

Proper issues might read, for example:

–   'The wife asserts that the matrimonial home should be transferred to her, to provide a home for her and the children; the husband says that the wife's housing needs can be met by a lump sum payment of £x which should be paid to her from the proceeds of sale of the home.'

–   'The husband states that there should be a clean break on payment to the wife of £x and says that the wife could acquire an earning capacity of £y per annum and make herself self-sufficient within 12 months. The wife says that her earning capacity is uncertain and unpredictable, and that, in any event, as long as the children are of school age, there should be no dismissal of her claims.'

–   'The wife asserts that her separate capital amounts to £z, acquired in the following manner [brief details] and that this is the minimum sum which should be paid to her before consideration of the s 25 factors. The husband denies this claim, and says that the majority of the wife's notional capital came from him or his family.'

16.21 It is unnecessary to continue at great length. The importance of the statement of apparent issues, and the requirement on the parties to formulate these in a manner which will enable the court to use the statement as the foundation of its deliberations, is obvious.

QUESTIONNAIRES AND REQUESTS FOR DOCUMENTS

16.22 It is of the essence of the current procedure that no disclosure of documents may be sought or given after the issue of the application and before the FA, except as provided for under the rule.[38] The intention of the rule is that the 35 days between the exchange of the Forms E and the FA shall be taken up with deciding what further information and documents are needed, and formulating the questionnaire and request for documents. The questionnaire and request for documents must be filed at court and served on the other party not later than 7 days before the hearing of the FA.[39] At the same time, it is necessary to file and serve a statement of the apparent issues between the parties and confirmation that all relevant persons have been served.[40]

It is important to note that care should be taken with the questionnaire and request for documents, since it is provided that, following the FA, no party shall be entitled to seek further documents save with leave of the court.[41] It is therefore intended that the district judge at the FA shall deal comprehensively and finally with all issues of disclosure and questionnaires, and those orders will be based on the requests before him.

As to service, it should be noted that the applicant has the same obligations to serve mortgagees and persons responsible for pension schemes, for example, as under the amended FPR 1991.

THE FIRST APPOINTMENT

16.23 The FA is conducted by the district judge. The parties to the case must attend every hearing in addition to the lawyers unless the court otherwise directs.[42] By now, the Forms E, questionnaires, requests for documents, and statements of apparent issues should be on the court file, and the district judge should have read them in advance.

The other vital document which each party must produce at the FA is the 'written estimate of the solicitor and client costs hitherto incurred on his behalf'.[43] This document (as updated) must be produced at every hearing, and this is the first of these occasions. It should have been agreed with the client in advance, and is an open statement, the contents of which the district judge should state publicly in the presence of the parties.

16.24 The objective of the district judge at the FA is defined in r 2.61D(1) as 'defining the issues and saving costs'. Definition of the issues has already been

---

[38]   FPR 1991, r 2.61B(6).
[39]   Ibid, r 2.61B(7).
[40]   Ibid, r 2.61B(8).
[41]   Ibid, r 2.61D(3).
[42]   Ibid, r 2.61D(5).
[43]   Ibid, r 2.61F.

discussed above. The district judge's specific duties are set out in r 2.61D(2)(a)–(f). He must decide to what extent questionnaires should be answered and documents produced, direct valuations and expert evidence, and decide whether any further evidence is required from the parties (for example, on issues as to contributions). In all this, he will be guided by his definition of what the issues in the case are to be and by the overriding objective.

16.25 Having declared what the issues are to be, and directed the filing of the further evidence necessary to bring the issues on for hearing, the district judge must then consider the future progress of the case. This will involve a decision as to whether the FA is to be treated as the FDR appointment.[44] Both parties should have filed and served Form G indicating whether or not they will be in a position to proceed to FDR there and then, but, even where they have not done so, the district judge may inquire as to whether this is possible. When the FA is to be so treated, he will conduct the FDR hearing (as to which see para **16.26**) and then, if necessary, direct the final hearing. If FDR is not dealt with there and then, he will direct an FDR appointment and a final hearing shortly thereafter, unless he thinks the case suitable for mediation or out-of-court private negotiation.[45] In directing the final hearing, the district judge must determine the judicial level at which the case will be heard, ie either by district judge, High Court judge or (more rarely) circuit judge.

EXPERT EVIDENCE

16.26 Wherever practicable, expert evidence should be by an expert instructed jointly by the parties. It is provided that CPR, rr 35.1–35.14 relating to expert evidence (with appropriate modifications), except CPR, rr 35.5(2) and 35.8(4)(b), apply to all ancillary relief proceedings.[46] The two exceptions relate to an inappropriate reference to the fast track and the right of the expert to seek directions from the court, but, with those exceptions, what are now the general rules of court relating to experts apply. Therefore, for example, the court has the duty to restrict expert evidence to that which is reasonably required, experts owe an overriding duty to the court, parties may put written questions to experts, and the court may direct a meeting of experts.

Expert evidence may be called only with leave of the court, although many courts have a form of standard directions which includes a provision for expert evidence where the value of any property being the subject matter of the application is in dispute. The following guidance given by Booth J in the old case of *Evans v Evans* still applies.[47]

(1) Wherever possible, valuations of properties should be obtained from a single valuer jointly instructed by both parties. Where each party instructs

---

[44] FPR 1991, r 2.61D(2)(f)(ii).
[45] Ibid, r 2.61D(2)(d).
[46] Ibid, r 2.61C.
[47] [1990] 1 FLR 319.

a valuer, reports should be exchanged and the valuers should meet in an attempt to resolve any differences between them or otherwise to narrow the issue.

(2)   While it may be necessary to obtain a broad assessment of the value of a shareholding in a private company, it is inappropriate to undertake an expensive and meaningless exercise to achieve a precise valuation of a private company which will not be sold.[48]

(3)   All professional witnesses should be careful to avoid a partisan approach and should maintain proper professional standards.

In *N v C (Property Adjustment Order: Surveyor's Negligence)*,[49] Thorpe LJ said that the practice of delegating not only the valuer but the choice of valuer to the appropriate profession (eg the president of the RICS) no longer applied. Today, the practice is still to delegate the valuation (to a single valuer) but not the choice of valuer. The court, having given the parties the opportunity to make representations, appoints a specific expert to determine value in default of agreement. The expert's valuation cannot be absolute and above challenge, and the order appointing him will contain an express or implied liberty to apply as to implementation. If either party subsequently conceived that the determination was vitiated by fraud, collusion, bias, mistake or negligence, it must be open to that party to raise that assertion on liberty to apply and then to seek to support it by evidence, always at risk as to costs.

16.27 Guidance as to the practice to be followed when instructing an expert was given by the President's Ancillary Relief Advisory Group in the *Best Practice Guide for Instructing a Single Joint Expert* (the *Best Practice Guide*) in December 2002.[50]

What follows is a summary of the *Best Practice Guide*.

(1)   Where expert evidence is sought to be relied on, parties should if possible agree on a single joint expert (SJE) whom they can jointly instruct.[51]

(2)   Before instructions are given, the parties should establish the SJE's availability, fees, and expertise. They should also agree between themselves the proportions in which the SJE's fees are to be shared.

(3)   When the court directs a report from an SJE, the order should:
       (a)   identify the SJE;
       (b)   specify the task to be performed;
       (c)   provide for instructions in a joint letter;

---

[48]   See also *P v P (Financial Provision)* [1989] 2 FLR 241.
[49]   [1998] 1 FLR 63, CA.
[50]   [2003] 1 FLR 573.
[51]   See *President's Practice Direction of 25 May 2000* [2000] 1 FLR 997.

(d) specify the time for sending the joint letter, the date for the report and the dates for written questions to be sent and answered;

(e) make any provision as to fees which are appropriate.

(4) Supplementary instructions to the SJE should not be given unless both parties agree or the court sanctions them.

(5) Communications by the SJE must be addressed to both parties.

(6) Any meeting with the SJE must be proportionate and should be with both parties and/or their advisers.

In *Martin-Dye v Martin-Dye*[52] Thorpe LJ held that where proportionate the court should be ready to act on the recommendations of the *Fifth Report from the Social Security Committee of Session 1997–98 on Pensions on Divorce*, HC 869 (TSO, October 1998), para 47, for instruction of an expert in a case requiring a bespoke valuation; in such a case it would usually be appropriate for the court to direct valuation by a single joint expert. This guidance relates to pensions but it is submitted that it has wider application and is relevant to all forms of valuation.

THE FINANCIAL DISPUTE RESOLUTION HEARING

16.28 The FDR appointment was one of the innovations of the pilot scheme and now the amendments introduced to the FPR 1991 by the Family Proceedings (Amendment No 2) Rules 1999[53] (the 1999 Rules). Its purpose is to give the parties an opportunity to put their fundamental positions to the district judge and to each other, and for the district judge to make such comments as he or she may consider to be helpful, and it is hoped that this process may facilitate a settlement. It is normally helpful for solicitors and/or counsel and their clients to arrive at court some time before the appointed time to enable them to negotiate. This is frequently a process which continues over the course of a day.

The FDR appointment is a privileged occasion; it must be treated as a meeting held for the purposes of discussion and negotiation[54] and the fact that without prejudice offers must be filed at court does not make them admissible in evidence if they would not otherwise be admissible.[55] The district judge who conducts the FDR appointment must have no further involvement with the matter other than to conduct any further FDR appointment.[56]

---

[52] [2006] EWCA Civ 681, [2006] 2 FLR 901.
[53] SI 1999/3491.
[54] FPR 1991, r 2.61E(1).
[55] Ibid, r 2.61E(4).
[56] Ibid, r 2.61E(2).

There is no reason why, in a case which is likely to be tried by a judge, such a judge should not conduct the FDR appointment. A judge who has dealt with an FDR which has led to a consent order is not thereafter precluded from dealing with an application to vary that order.[57]

16.29 Not later than 7 days before the FDR appointment, the applicant must file at court details of all offers, proposals and responses thereto; at the end of the appointment, all such documents must be returned.[58] At the appointment, the parties must, of course, file their up-to-date written costs estimates.

It is provided by the rule that 'parties attending the appointment shall use their best endeavours to reach agreement on the matters in issue between them'.[59] The role of the district judge is, essentially, to ensure that the parties have a full opportunity to exchange offers and counter-offers and to encourage them to reach a settlement. It is not part of a district judge's duties to mediate between the parties, if for no other reason than that he or she may lack mediation skills. However, this is not to say that the district judge does not have a creative role to play. It is now generally accepted that the district judge should indicate to the parties how he or she sees the case, and what he or she thinks are the principal issues. The district judge may choose not to predict the likely outcome (although many district judges will assume this burden) but is likely to indicate how he or she would approach the case and try to eliminate what he or she sees as any unrealistic expectations. In essence, the FDR appointment is designed for settlement seeking.

In *Rose v Rose*[60] the parties had reached agreement at an FDR appointment and gone away to prepare a draft order, which was subsequently agreed. The husband then sought to resile from the agreement. On appeal, it was held that the fact that the agreement was made at an FDR appointment made no difference and the order should be made. An FDR appointment should not be restricted.

16.30 At the conclusion of the FDR appointment, if an agreement is reached, the district judge may make a consent order.[61] The appointment may be adjourned for a further FDR appointment if that seems likely to assist the parties, or the district judge may give directions to lead to the final hearing. This may include the filing of evidence, which should only be necessary in a limited number of cases; all the financial information should have been contained in the Forms E and replies to questionnaires, and where there is a particular issue, the court may have directed the filing of sworn statements limited to those issues. It might seem, therefore, that a further narrative statement of the evidence-in-chief which a party intends to give would, in the run-of-the-mill case, be contrary to the spirit of the new rules and constitute a

---

[57] *G v G* [2006] EWHC 1993 (Fam), [2007] 1 FLR 237.
[58] FPR 1991, r 2.61E(3).
[59] Ibid, r 2.61E(6).
[60] [2002] 1 FLR 978, CA.
[61] FPR 1991, r 2.61E(8).

return to the old narrative affidavit, and that it should only be necessary in a case which is likely to be lengthy and complex. In *W v W (Ancillary Relief: Practice)*,[62] Wilson J said that it would be desirable in cases of greater wealth for the evidence to be broadened by narrative affidavits but, it is submitted, this decision does not detract from the generality of what has been said above.

16.31 One of the principal reasons why cases involving substantial assets reach a final hearing and cannot be resolved before is that there is a genuine dispute as to the amount of the assets, coupled with allegations of lack of good faith and failure to disclose. In *OS v DS (Oral Disclosure: Preliminary Hearing)*[63] Coleridge J devised a novel procedure for resolving issues at an early stage. At a directions appointment he ordered a 3 day preliminary/oral discovery hearing, to take oral evidence and resolve questions of joinder. This enabled the judge to make findings and resolved the issues with great savings of costs and court time. It is unlikely that this procedure will be used in more than a small proportion of cases but it remains a useful tool to bear in mind in appropriate cases.

THE FINAL HEARING

16.32 In most respects, once the final hearing is reached, the differences between the 1991 Rules and the 1999 Rules end, and the hearing is exactly like any other ancillary relief hearing. In particular, the former practice as to bundles, skeleton arguments, etc, applies (see *Practice Direction of 10 March 2000 (Family Proceedings: Court Bundles)*[64] in Appendix B). There are three exceptions. First, as has already been seen, the district judge who conducted the FDR appointment may not hear the application. Secondly, not less than 14 days before the hearing, the applicant must file with the court and serve on the other party a concise statement setting out the nature and amount of the orders which he or she proposes to invite the court to make, and the respondent must reply within 7 days thereafter. No privilege attaches to these documents, so they are open offers.[65] These documents are then before the court and should focus the scope of the hearing. Thirdly, the 1999 Rules contain much more elaborate provisions as to costs. Full details of these provisions will be found in Chapter 17.

INSPECTION APPOINTMENTS

16.33 A problem which frequently arises is that one of the parties to the case, or a third party, fails to produce for inspection some document which is potentially important for the preparation of the application. To solve this

---

[62] [2000] Fam Law 473.
[63] [2004] EWHC 2376 (Fam), [2005] 1 FLR 675.
[64] [2000] 1 FLR 536.
[65] FPR 1991, r 2.69E(1) and (2).

problem, it is now provided that any party may apply to the court for an order that any person attends an appointment (an 'inspection appointment') before the court and produces any documents to be specified or described in the order, the production of which appears to the court to be necessary for disposing fairly of the application for ancillary relief or for saving costs.[66] This provision, which was previously called a 'production appointment' has been described as 'an extraordinarily useful addition to the range of powers available to the court', with the caveat that 'the very breadth of the power does, however, present opportunity for abuse'.[67] The provision enables the court to exercise a wide discretion, and should be directed to saving costs or achieving a just result.

The rule is principally invoked against third parties, since, as was seen above, a party to the application may be ordered to produce documents and this can, if necessary, be enforced by penal sanctions. The rule is, therefore, principally useful when trying to obtain documents from a third party against whom, normally, an order may not be made in the proceedings. The most common classes of persons against whom orders are sought are the cohabitant of one of the parties, and some person or body (such as a bank, or business partner) with whom the other party has a financial relationship.

16.34 The first stage in obtaining an inspection order is to apply to the district judge, on notice to the other party[68] but not the person against whom the order is sought. The notice of application should specify the order sought, with details of the documents to be disclosed, and should be supported by an affidavit sworn by the applicant or his or her solicitor setting out all factual matters relied upon. It will normally be the case that the other party has refused or failed to produce the evidence which is sought, and the affidavit should give particulars of this refusal or failure.

The court will bear in mind that, when the documents sought are the personal documents of the third party, he or she is entitled to privacy and should not normally be required to disclose them to others. The court must, therefore, be satisfied that there is prima facie evidence that the documents relate to a relevant issue in the proceedings and that the evidence which they will provide cannot be obtained in any other way. For example, it is frequently the case that the means of a cohabitant are irrelevant, and in such a case it would be necessary to show that the financial positions of the cohabitant and the other party were so interlinked as to make it necessary to see the cohabitant's documents.

16.35 It is provided that no person shall be compelled by an order under r 2.62(7) to produce any document at an inspection appointment which he

---

[66]   FPR 1991, r 2.62(7).

[67]   *B v B (Production Appointment: Procedure)* [1995] 1 FLR 913, per Thorpe J.

[68]   Applications should normally be on notice, except where there is a legitimate anxiety that notice might lead to the destruction or invasion of the document: *B v B (Production Appointment: Procedure)* (above).

could not be compelled to produce at the hearing of the application for ancillary relief.[69] In *Frary v Frary*,[70] the husband cohabited with a wealthy woman with whom he said he had no financial relationship and who did not support him. On appeal, a production order was set aside. It was observed that r 2.62(7) did not change the law but merely brought forward the time at which a witness might be compelled to attend court. In this case, the applicant had no intention of calling the third party, neither she nor the respondent had made any secret of their relationship and there was no particular relevance in the precise limits of the third party's means. There was nothing to make it a proper exercise of the court's discretion to order the appellant, a stranger to the proceedings, to attend and be examined at the trial or to produce documents.

On the other hand, in *D v D (Production Appointment)*,[71] the husband's attempts to obtain proper disclosure of the wife's considerable means had been obstructed and frustrated. Thorpe J made a production order requiring the wife's accountant to attend and produce his files, such disclosure being on a broad basis in view of the earlier obstructions and having the effect of overriding any professional privilege.

In *M v M (Ancillary Relief: Conduct: Disclosure)*[72] it was held that the existing case-law on disclosure against a third party had been strengthened rather than weakened by Article 8 ECHR.

16.36 When an inspection order is made, the person concerned is directed to attend court and to produce any documents named in the order. Such a person is entitled to be legally represented at the appointment.[73]

INTERIM ORDERS

16.37 A problem which may arise is that an applicant for ancillary relief is in urgent need of interim support and cannot wait for up to 14 weeks for the FA. It is therefore provided that a party may apply at any stage of the proceedings for an order for maintenance pending suit, interim periodical payments or an interim variation order.[74] It is implicit that such an application can be made only where a full application for ancillary relief is pending, so one or other party must have issued Form A. The application for an interim order is made by filing a notice of application, and the day fixed for the hearing must be not less than 14 days after the issue of the application, notice of which must be served forthwith on the other party.[75]

---

[69]   FPR 1991, r 2.62(8).
[70]   [1993] 2 FLR 696.
[71]   [1995] 2 FLR 497.
[72]   [2006] Fam Law 923.
[73]   FPR 1991, r 2.62(9).
[74]   Ibid, r 2.69F(1).
[75]   Ibid, r 2.69F(2) and (3).

When, as will normally be the case, the application is made before the filing of Forms E, the applicant must file with the court and serve on the other party a draft of the order requested and a short sworn statement explaining why the order is necessary and giving the necessary information about his or her means.[76] Not less than 7 days before the hearing, the other party must file and serve a short sworn statement about his or her means unless he or she has already filed Form E.[77]

VARIATION APPLICATION

16.38 A variation application pursuant to MCA 1973, s 31 is an application for ancillary relief and therefore falls to be dealt with in exactly the same way as any other application, by the filing of Form A and Forms E and the fixing of an FA and FDR. This will be the procedure to be adopted in the majority of variation cases since, clearly, the court will need to know the whole financial position of a party even where only periodical payments are in dispute.

However, there may be a limited number of cases where there genuinely can be no point in requiring lengthy disclosure of means, for example where an increase in the amount payable under an old order for a child is the only issue. In these circumstances, it is submitted that, after Form A has been issued, application could be made for an interim order and the procedure set out in para **16.34** adopted. Once a determination had been made at the interim hearing, the court could be invited to make the order a final order to dispose of the application and to vacate the FA. In this way, time and costs could be saved.

It is emphasised, however, that this procedure would only be appropriate in the simplest cases.

THE PROTOCOL

16.39 One of the innovations of the CPR, which govern civil proceedings other than family proceedings, is the introduction of protocols which govern how practitioners deal with the preparation of cases up to the issue of proceedings. These protocols have the force of law in the sense that the court may refer to them once proceedings have been issued when deciding whether or not various orders should be made and when deciding issues of costs.

The Lord Chancellor's Advisory Group recommended that there should be a protocol in respect of ancillary relief applications and this recommendation was accepted by the Lord Chancellor. A copy of the protocol will be found

---

[76]   FPR 1991, r 2.69F(4).
[77]   Ibid, r 2.69F(5).

annexed to the Practice Direction of 25 May 2000[78] set out in Appendix B, and this protocol is required reading for all practitioners. In particular, the following points should be noted.

–   Where there is pre-action disclosure and inspection it must be dealt with cost-effectively and in line with the overriding objective.

–   While there is sometimes an advantage in preparing disclosure before proceedings are commenced, solicitors must bear in mind the objective of controlling costs and in particular the costs of disclosure of documents.

–   Solicitors should consider at an early stage and keep under review whether mediation would be appropriate.

–   Proportionality must be borne in mind at all times.

–   Parties should seek to clarify their claims and identify the issues as soon as possible.

–   Wherever possible, valuations should be by a joint valuer.

THE PRACTICE DIRECTION OF 25 MAY 2000

16.40 The President has signed a Practice Direction to govern the procedure for applications made after 5 June 2000.[79] This is set out at Appendix B.

---

[78]   *Practice Direction of 25 May 2000 (Ancillary Relief Procedure)* [2000] 1 FLR 997.
[79]   Ibid.

Chapter 17

COSTS

INTRODUCTION

17.1 In all forms of litigation, the incidence of costs is one of the primary considerations and causes of concern for the lay client. When lawyers are instructed, they have to be paid, and in the absence of any order to the contrary, the client has to pay. A client who is successful in most forms of civil litigation expects to recover his or her costs from the unsuccessful party; when he or she does so, the unsuccessful party has a double burden to pay, but the successful party rarely recovers all costs and normally still has something to pay. In short, while costs may be an area of the law which the intelligent client can understand, it will rarely bring much satisfaction.

17.2 If what has been said applies to all litigation, the problems caused thereby are magnified in family cases and, in particular, in ancillary relief. The average litigant, pursuing, for example, an action for damages or a boundary dispute, normally has a choice as to whether to proceed with the action or abandon it, and this decision can be taken on rational grounds. The person caught up in a dispute as to the occupation of the family home, or the financial support of the other party usually has no such choice. Family disputes go to the heart of most people's lives, in both a financial and an emotional sense, and when, as is the case in most run-of-the-mill disputes, something as intimate as a person's home is involved, it is difficult if not impossible for the litigants to adopt a detached approach.

17.3 If these general comments are applied to the particular problems in ancillary relief, the most common difficulty faced by the parties and by the court is that the money which is paid to lawyers is money which the parties can normally ill afford to lose, since it is needed for meeting the needs and reasonable requirements of the parties and their children. The court frequently has to face the difficulty of being asked to make an order for costs which will upset a finely balanced distribution of property which it has taken care to work out; if the order for costs is not made, the party who has behaved unrealistically may benefit, but if it is made the whole basis of the order may disappear. Two overriding considerations emerge from this. The first is that the parties must be made and kept aware of the economic facts of their case, and the second is that the lawyers involved must ensure that the case is conducted in the most cost-effective manner consistent with the interests of the client. The problems inherent in family litigation have led to the sweeping changes in the general principles of costs which are described in para **17.4** et seq.

This chapter is not going to deal in detail with the rules as to assessment of costs (previously known as 'taxation'). The minutiae of such matters are best left to more specialist publications. Instead, the matters to be considered are those which have most direct relevance to the subject of ancillary relief. They are:

(a) some general principles of costs;

(b) the effect of the FPR 1991, including the effect on *Calderbank* offers;

(c) the Practice Direction dated 28 March 1988;[1] and

(d) aspects of funded services (previously legal aid).

SOME GENERAL PRINCIPLES OF COSTS

17.4 Previous editions of this book have contained a detailed account of the elaborate system of rules and case law which governed costs in ancillary relief cases. This body of law is now obsolete, save in respect of applications made before 3 April 2006.[2] With effect from 3 April 2006 the Family Proceedings (Amendment) (No 6) Rules 2005[3] have effect, and the 1991 rules have been amended accordingly. (The detail of which applications are governed by these changes is complicated – see para **17.6**).

The general rule

17.5 Rule 2.71(1) makes it clear that this rule contains discrete and self-contained provisions as to costs in ancillary relief proceedings by providing that CPR r 44.3(1)–(5) (ie those rules which govern costs in other civil proceedings and provide, inter alia, that costs are in the discretion of the court and normally follow the event) shall not apply to ancillary relief proceedings.[4] CPR r 44.3(6)–(9) continue to apply to ancillary relief proceedings but those rules relate to the mechanics of assessment of costs and not the principles governing the award of costs.

17.6 Rule 2.71(4)(a) begins by providing that 'the general rule in ancillary relief proceedings is that the court will not make an order requiring one party to pay the costs of another party;... but...'

As will be seen, the rule continues and will make an exception to that general principle but it is worth pausing at this point to reinforce the general effect of the rule. The general principle with which all lawyers are familiar and which governs other civil proceedings, namely that the 'loser' pays the costs of the

---

[1] *Registrar's Direction (Ancillary Relief: Costs Estimates)* [1988] 1 FLR 452.
[2] Interested readers should refer to the 5th edition.
[3] SI 2005/352.
[4] See para **1.3** for definition of 'ancillary relief'.

'winner' no longer applies to ancillary relief. There are many reasons for this change of legislative position, which cannot all be considered here. However, the principal reasons for the change were first, the difficulty in many cases of establishing which party was the winner and which the loser; second, the fact that breakdown of marriage and the need to re-order family assets should be regarded as a misfortune falling on both parties rather than the fault of either of them; thirdly, the award of costs subsequent to the main substantive order in any particular case frequently distorted the intentions of the order itself. It might also be said that previous attempts to improve the rules relating to costs, as detailed in the 5th edition of this book, had led to an extremely complicated and self-contradictory set of rules.

The general rule, therefore, is that each party will bear his or her costs. The way the court will treat such costs is dealt with at para **17.14**.

Exceptions to the general rule

17.7   Rule 2.71(4)(b) contains the exception to the general rule and provides:

> 'the court may make such an order at any stage of the proceedings where it considers it appropriate to do so because of the conduct of a party in relation to the proceedings (whether before or during them).'

The matters to which the court must have regard in deciding whether or not to make such an order are then set out, but at this stage the following points should be noted. First, the only matter which may trigger an order for costs is 'the conduct of a party'. Second, it is only conduct 'in relation to the proceedings' which will be taken into account. 'Conduct' in the general sense, as considered at para **1.38** et seq, is not to be taken into account. This conduct may therefore be described as 'litigation misconduct'.

Third, the court may order costs 'at any stage of the proceedings'. Applications for costs orders may therefore be made at any stage where it seems appropriate.

17.8   Rule 2.71(5) then sets out the matters which should guide the court, as follows:

> (5)   In deciding what order (if any) to make under paragraph (4)(b), the court must have regard to—
>   (a)   any failure by a party to comply with these Rules, any order of the court or any practice direction which the court considers relevant;
>   (b)   any open offer to settle made by a party;
>   (c)   whether it was reasonable for a party to raise, pursue or contest a particular allegation or issue;
>   (d)   the manner in which a party has pursued or responded to the application or a particular allegation or issue;
>   (e)   any other aspect of a party's conduct in relation to the proceedings which the court considers relevant; and
>   (f)   the financial effect on the parties of any costs order.'

Examples of the operation of these rules might be as follows.

Failure to comply with rules, orders etc

17.9 Obvious examples of this would be failure to file Form E on time, or failure to comply with an order as to information, which led to a further application to the court.

Open offers

17.10 This rule must be read with the rule as to offers to settle contained in rule 2.71(6); 'no offer to settle which is not an open offer to settle shall be admissible at any stage of the proceedings...'. (There is an exception to this which relates to FDR appointments only and is not relevant here.)

The only offers which may be considered are therefore open offers, ie the open position of a party revealed to the court in the course of the proceedings. The previous jurisprudence as to 'Calderbank letters' is now firmly abolished and out of date.

It must be emphasised that this is not intended to bring in the old 'winner gets his costs' provision by the back door. However, there remains some uncertainty as to when a court might think it appropriate to make an order for costs in reliance on this part of the rule. The following tentative suggestions are made with the intention of helping to clarify the position but it must be emphasised that these are suggestions only and that only judicial decisions will give accurate guidance.

(a) There is clearly every incentive to parties to make their positions clear by means of open offers to settle. Such offers to settle could be revised or amended in the light of changing developments.

(b) Such offers should not normally be made until disclosure is complete. A party against whom a costs order is sought could reasonably argue that he or she was not in a position to decide whether or not to accept an offer until all relevant information was available and that, if any order was to be made, it should only be in respect of work done after that date.

(c) It is not intended that any party who fails to beat an open offer made by the other will automatically be liable to costs. The general rule remains that there will be no order as to costs. Presumably the court will take account of whether or not the 'unsuccessful' party made any open offer and, if so, the gap between the open positions of the parties and the stage at which any offer was made. Although the rule avoids the use of the term 'unreasonable', one cannot avoid the conclusion that reasonableness may be a factor. It may well be that, where one party has throughout made a reasonable offer, or a series of reasonable offers to settle which the other has ignored, and the final result accords with the offers made, the court will feel entitled to condemn the unsuccessful party in costs.

This does not mean that 'without prejudice' offers cannot continue to be made. No doubt this will be the case and such offers will remain a useful part of the procedure. It does mean, however, that such offers will not be admissible in any arguments as to costs.

Whether reasonable to raise or pursue allegations or issues and the manner in which allegations or issues were pursued or responded to

17.11 The significance of these two provisions is fairly clear. A party who raises an issue of, eg conduct, or alleged concealed assets, and pursues the issue in the face of all the evidence, is going to be liable to pay the other party's additional costs incurred in dealing with such issues. In the same way, a party who causes the other party unnecessary work by failing to provide the necessary information or to concede an obvious issue is also exposing himself to a liability for costs.

Any other aspect of conduct in relation to the proceedings which the court considers relevant

17.12 This is a 'catch-all' provision, and means that the other matters mentioned in sub-rule (5) are not exclusive. One can only say that for such conduct to be 'caught' by this provision, it would presumably be necessary for it to have increased the costs which the other party had to pay.

The financial effect on the parties of a costs order

17.13 The significance of this is that, even if the court decided it was appropriate to make a costs order, it must still take account of what the financial consequences of such an order would be. For example, where the court decided that a parent should have a property or sum of money to provide a home for children, and that to make a costs order, however, richly deserved, would have the effect of making it impossible for that parent to provide the home, it might well decide that it should not make the costs order.

How will costs be treated?

17.14 Given that the general rule is that each party bears his or her own costs, and that costs are a necessary part of life, the question of how the court will deal with the costs is of great importance. Costs still due should presumably be regarded as a debt due from the client, and, in order to be fair, it is arguable that costs already paid should be added back (as was done in *Leadbeater v Leadbeater*).[5]

---

[5]   [1985] FLR 789.

Useful guidance has been given by Wilson LJ in *Currey v Currey*,[6] where he said that the proper treatment of liabilities for costs will generally be to regard them as debts to be considered when the judge is making his substantive award, with an allowance for costs (eg a lump sum on account of costs – see para **17.23**) being fully consonant with the thrust of the new rules to cater for costs at an earlier stage than hitherto.

Generally, when preparing schedules of assets for a final or interim hearing, it will be proper to include the total amount of costs paid by and still due from a party as a liability of that party.

Procedure

17.15 Procedural requirements as to the new costs rules are contained in a new rule 2.61F which provides as follows:

> '(1) Subject to paragraph (2), at every hearing or appointment each party must produce to the court an estimate in Form H of the costs incurred by him up to the date of that hearing or appointment.
>
> (2) Not less than 14 days before the date fixed for the final hearing of an application for ancillary relief, each party must (unless the court directs otherwise) file with the court and serve on each other party a statement in Form H1 giving full particulars of all costs in respect of the proceedings which he has incurred or expects to incur, to enable the court to take account of the parties' liabilities for costs when deciding what order (if any) to make for ancillary relief.'

This rule is supplemented by paragraph 3 of the President's Practice Direction as to costs dated, which provides as follows:

> 'The new rules require the completion of Forms H1 and H2. Form H1 is to be used at interim hearings so that the court has available to it a realistic estimate of the costs incurred to date. Form H2 is for use at a final hearing to provide the court with accurate details of the costs which the party has incurred, or expects to incur, in relation to the proceedings. The purpose of this form is to enable to court to take account of the impact of each party's costs liability on their financial situations. Parties should ensure that the information contained in these forms is as full and accurate as possible.'

Forms H1 and H2 will be found at Appendix B. The purpose of these forms, which require much more detail than their predecessors, is to enable parties to justify what they tell the court about their liability for costs and to enable the court to examine such submissions. They are therefore very important and should be taken far more seriously than were the previous costs estimates.

---

6   [2006] EWCA Civ 1338, [2007] 1 FLR 946.

17.16 New provisions are made relating to the First Appointment (FDA) and to the FDR appointment (generally, see Chapter 16). Rule 2.61D sets out the responsibilities of the district judge at the FDA, which now include a new sub-rule 2.61D(2)(e) as follows:

'[the district judge]

> (e) in considering whether to make a costs order under rule 2.71(4), must have particular regard to the extent to which each party has complied with the requirement to send documents with Form E;'

It should also be noted that the rule as to the admissibility of without prejudice offers does not apply at the FDR appointment. Therefore, when parties comply with rule 2.61E(3) which requires them to file details of offers and counter-offers seven days before the FDR, this includes without prejudice offers and counter-offers.

17.17 When a party intends to apply for an order for costs against the other party, he or she must follow paragraph 4 of the President's Practice Direction which reads as follows:

> 'Parties who intend to seek a costs order against another party in proceedings to which rule 2.71 of the Family Proceedings Rules 1991 applies should ordinarily make this plain in open correspondence or in skeleton arguments before the date of the hearing. In any case where summary assessment of costs awarded under rule 2.71 of the Family Proceedings Rules 1991 would be appropriate parties are under an obligation to file a statement of costs in CPR Form N260 (see CPR Practice Direction supplementing Parts 43 to 48 (Costs), Section 13 and paragraph 6 below).'

This is self-explanatory. The complete Practice Direction will be found at Appendix B.

Transitional provisions

17.18 The rules contain convoluted provisions as to when the new rules take effect. Rule 10 of the Amendment Rules provides as follows:

> '(1) The 1991 Rules shall apply to—
>> (a) an application for ancillary relief made in a petition or answer before these Rules come into force;
>> (b) an application for ancillary relief made in Form A before these Rules come into force (no such application having been made in the petition or answer); or
>> (c) an application under section 10(2) of the Matrimonial Causes Act 1973 or an application under section 48(2) of the Civil Partnership Act 2004 made in Form B before these Rules come into force,
>> as if these Rules had not been made.
> (2) The 1991 Rules shall also apply to an application of a kind mentioned in paragraph (1) which is made after these Rules come into force but is heard

by the court at the same time as an application to which paragraph (1) applies, as if these Rules had not been made.'

The meaning seems to be as follows:

(a) Where a Petition or Answer which includes a prayer for ancillary relief dates from before 3 April 2006, the new costs rules do not apply.

(b) The same applies to an application where Form A dates from before 3 April 2006.

(c) The new rules apply to all other applications, save where an application which is 'caught' by 1 or 2 above is heard at the same time as an application which is not so 'caught'.

It is to be hoped that judges will be sufficiently robust, and practitioners sufficiently realistic, to adopt the spirit of the new rules even where the letter of the law indicated that they do not apply.

The basis of assessment

17.19 Although the detail of this subject is not to be considered, practitioners must know which of the various (and potentially confusing) regimes of assessment applies to ancillary relief cases.

17.20 CPR, Part 44 contains certain provisions as to principle which must be considered.

There are two bases of assessment, namely the standard basis and the indemnity basis.[7] Unless otherwise specified, assessment is on the standard basis.[8] In funded cases, assessment is always on the standard basis. When the order for costs is on the inter partes basis with no funded element involved, the court may order costs on the indemnity basis, but this is unusual. The difference between the two bases is that on the standard basis the taxing officer must resolve any doubt in favour of the paying party, whereas on the indemnity basis the taxing officer must award all costs save where they are found to be unreasonable in amount or where they were unreasonably incurred.[9]

Generally speaking, indemnity costs are more generous and are more likely to reflect the actual cost to the client, and are frequently awarded when the court wishes to demonstrate its disapproval of some action by the paying party which has led to the order for costs. However, it has been emphasised that to make a

---

[7] CPR, r 44.4(1).
[8] Ibid, r 44.4(4).
[9] Ibid, r 44.4(2) and (3).

full indemnity order against a party 'is a Draconian thing to do',[10] and it would be rare for the whole costs of an application to be on that basis.

What use should the court make of costs estimates?

17.21 In *Leadbeater v Leadbeater*,[11] Balcombe J was given the information as to the parties' costs and posed the following question: 'the question of principle which arises here is how should I treat these costs in estimating the assets of the parties and in particular those of the wife in finding out what she has available for her needs?' His Lordship adopted the following formula: there should be added back into a party's assets what had already been paid by that party on account of costs, less only such part of those costs as would never be recoverable inter partes (ie solicitor and own client costs) and any costs which might be recovered on taxation as inter partes costs. Any future liability for costs should be omitted from that party's liabilities except such part as might properly never be recoverable. The justification for this approach was that if, in estimating the wife's present capital position and, in particular, what money she had available to buy a house, the money which she had already spent on costs was not included in her assets and her future liability for costs was included, the court would be anticipating the order as to costs which it might make.

This decision was followed in an appeal from a district judge's order where the district judge had awarded the husband a lump sum to meet his housing needs and declined to make an order for costs in favour of the wife, even though her *Calderbank* offer equalled if not exceeded the award, on the ground that it would defeat a settlement which would meet the husband's needs. Singer J allowed the appeal as to costs. The district judge had not conducted the exercise recommended and authorised by Balcombe J in *Leadbeater v Leadbeater*, and had therefore fallen into error.[12]

However, in *Wells v Wells*,[13] the Court of Appeal observed, per curiam, that the *Leadbeater* practice had been introduced on the premise that the assessment of an applicant's needs without both adding back payments made and disregarding liability for unpaid costs incurred and to be incurred would effectively anticipate the costs order that would eventually be made. However, in the modern world, few, if any, litigate on credit and solicitors require to be in funds at all stages. Judges must not lose sight of this reality. The *Leadbeater* mechanism should never be automatic and was probably most useful in cases where one party had paid money out and the other had obtained security, or where the court suspects some element of contrivance or artificiality in the arrangements set up by one party.

---

[10] *H v H (Clean Break: Non-disclosure: Costs)* [1994] 2 FLR 309, a case where the husband had been criticised for lack of disclosure, but the judge thought that justice could be done by making a standard basis order.
[11] [1985] FLR 789.
[12] *A v A (Costs Appeal)* [1996] 1 FLR 14.
[13] [2002] 2 FLR 97, CA.

17.22 Before the introduction of the new costs rules it was often thought that the relevance of *Leadbeater* was limited, and, as has been seen, it was frequently not followed. However, it is now suggested that the new costs rules have given the decision a new lease of life. Since the costs incurred and yet to be incurred by a party are regarded as a debt or obligation of that party or, where paid, have reduced the capital available to that party, it is necessary to take them into account in some way, and the mechanism suggested in *Leadbeater* has the virtue of a logical approach and may assist the court to arrive at a fair result.

LUMP SUM ORDERS AS TO COSTS

17.23 When one party is ordered to pay the costs of the other party, the normal order is for those costs to be assessed if not agreed. In *Leary v Leary*,[14] the judge found that the long duration and complexity of the application for ancillary relief had been due to the husband's failure to disclose his financial situation and concluded that the wife should be indemnified against the costs incurred as a result of the husband's action. In order to prevent further delay and litigation arising out of taxation, she ordered the husband to pay to the wife a lump sum of £31,000 under the provisions of RSC Ord 62, r 9, that sum being based on an itemised schedule of costs prepared by the wife's solicitors in accordance with the Practice Direction. The Court of Appeal dismissed the husband's appeal. RSC Ord 62, r 9(4) conferred on the court unlimited discretion to award a gross sum to avoid protracted taxation proceedings. It was necessary to warn the parties of the court's intention to act in this way. There was no justification for the suggestion that the court should only use Ord 62, r 9 in simple cases or cases involving small amounts, provided the court exercised its discretion in a judicial manner according to the facts of each individual case. While this decision pre-dated the provisions for summary assessment and other provisions now found in the CPR, there is no reason to think that the principle established by this case has changed.

It should be noted that where the court has ordered one party to pay costs, it may order an amount to be paid before the costs are assessed (CPR 44.3(7)).

ASPECTS OF FUNDED SERVICES

The statutory charge

17.24 A party who is in receipt of what used to be called legal aid and is now called 'funded services' is not exempt from the financial implications of costs. Where any property is recovered or preserved for an assisted person, the Legal Services Commission has a statutory charge over such property,[15] and the

---

[14]   [1987] 1 FLR 384.
[15]   Access to Justice Act 1999, s 10(7). See also the Community Legal Service (Financial) Regulations 2000, SI 2000/516, Part III.

client's solicitor must inform the Regional Director of the property which has been recovered or preserved.[16] The client must therefore be made aware at all stages that all costs incurred under the funded services may fall to be deducted from any property, or the proceeds of any property, recovered by him or her.

The Commission may, subject to conditions, agree to defer enforcing the statutory charge in certain circumstances.[17] However, it must be satisfied that the property recovered is to be used as a home, or used to purchase a home, for the applicant or his or her dependants, and, to avoid any doubt as to this, a certificate must be incorporated in the order to that effect.

Precedents for such a certificate will be found at Appendix A, within Precedents 13 and 14.

Orders for costs against clients in receipt of funded services and against the Commission

17.25 A party who is not in receipt of funded services may sometimes be at a disadvantage when he is opposed by a funded client, since the fact that the client is funded usually means that his or her resources are limited. The Access to Justice Act 1999, s 11 therefore established a procedure under which, in certain circumstances, such a party might apply for costs against the funded client or even against the Commission. An order for costs against the Commission could be obtained by a party who was not funded and who was the respondent to the proceedings where all the following conditions applied:

(a) a costs order had been made against the funded party client and the amount of costs which that party was required to pay was less than the full costs;

(b) the proceedings were instituted by the funded client, and the court was satisfied that the non-funded party will suffer severe financial hardship if the order were not made;

(c) in any case, the court was satisfied that it was just and equitable in the circumstances that provision should be made out of public funds.[18]

17.26 The detail as to procedure was contained in regulations[19] and was fairly detailed. The protection afforded to the funded party was described as 'costs protection'. The regulations in fact combined the two areas described above, namely protection of the funded client (costs protection) and the ability of the non-funded party to seek an order against the Commission.

---

[16] Community Legal Service (Costs) Regulations 2000, SI 2000/441, reg 20(1)(a).
[17] Community Legal Service (Financial) Regulations 2000, reg 52(1).
[18] Community Legal Service (Cost Protection) Regulations 2000, SI 2000/824, reg 5.
[19] Community Legal Service (Costs) Regulations 2000, Part II.

This procedure is now a matter of history in most cases. By the Community Legal Service (Costs Protection) (Amendment) Regulations 2005[20] 'cost protection' has been abolished in respect of certificates granted or amended after 25 July 2005. The effect of this is that the funded party now has no protection and is at risk in respect of costs in the same way as a non-funded party.

17.27 What is less clearly established is the question of the right of the non-funded party to seek an order against the Commission; no regulations governing this issue have ever been brought into effect. However, the regulations which govern costs against the Commission[21] (which are still in force) begin by providing[22] that they 'apply only where cost protection applies'. Given that cost protection no longer exists, it must follow that Part II of the regulations no longer has any effect. Whether this was the intention of those responsible for the regulations, or whether it is an unintended consequence is unclear, but the practical effect does seem to be clear.

However, this leaves the issue of what, if anything, s 11 of the Access to Justice Act 1999 now means. This section has not been repealed, and so is still good law. It provides, in effect, that, except in prescribed circumstances, an order for costs against a funded party may not exceed the amount which it is reasonable for the funded party to pay having regard to all the circumstances including financial circumstances and conduct. By s 11(3) regulations may be made to govern the procedure, but, as has been seen, there are no longer any such regulations and there are no 'prescribed circumstances'. It is submitted that the fact that there are now no regulations cannot mean that s 11 has no effect, so presumably, if and when a court has to consider an application for costs against a funded party it will be guided by s 11 and no other provisions.

What is clear, however, is that the non-funded party cannot now seek an order against the Commission.

ORDERS FOR PAYMENTS ON ACCOUNT OF COSTS

17.28 See Chapter 2, para **2.18** for orders for maintenance pending suit which may include provision for costs. See also para **17.31** as to payments on account.

WASTED COSTS ORDERS

17.29 Provision for wasted costs orders is made in SCA 1981, s 51(6) and (7) whereby costs incurred as result of any improper, unreasonable or negligent act or omission on the part of any legal or other representative may be visited on

---

[20]   SI 2005/2006.
[21]   Community Legal Service (Costs) Regulations 2000 Part II.
[22]   At reg 5.

that individual or firm. The procedure is contained in CPR, r 48.7 and the Practice Direction to Part 48. Generally, a court will deal with a wasted costs application in two stages; first, a determination as to whether there is material before it which might lead to a wasted costs order, and then a second stage after notice to show cause has been given to the legal representative.

In *B v B (Wasted Costs: Abuse of Process)*,[23] Wall J held that there were circumstances in family proceedings which may render it appropriate to hear applications for wasted costs orders in the course of the proceedings and to dispense with the two-stage process.

PRECEDENTS FOR ORDERS FOR COSTS

17.30 See Appendix A, Precedent 45 for precedents for orders for costs.

---

[23]   [2001] 1 FLR 843. In this case, Wall J ordered the wasted costs of an unmeritorious appeal to be apportioned as to 75% to counsel and 25% to the solicitors.

Chapter 18

APPEALS

INTRODUCTION

18.1 The appeals to be considered in this chapter are appeals in cases of ancillary relief. These are therefore appeals from district judge to circuit judge or High Court judge, and from the latter to the Court of Appeal.

IMPORTANT: It is possible that the procedure outlined in this chapter will be changed in the foreseeable future.

FROM DISTRICT JUDGE TO JUDGE (COUNTY COURT)

18.2 Appeal lies without leave from district judge to circuit judge in a divorce county court. Notice of appeal must be lodged within 14 days of the decision under appeal, and ideally should state briefly the ground for the appeal.[1] When the notice of appeal is lodged more than 14 days from the date of the decision, leave to appeal is required; this application must be made to the circuit judge.

18.3 Until recently it has been the duty of the appellant to request notes of evidence from the district judge at the earliest opportunity where it is thought that they will be relevant. It is also the duty of the appellant to prepare a note of the judgment (save where the judgment was in writing), agree it with the respondent, and submit it to the district judge for approval. The notes and the judgment would then form part of the bundle to be placed before the judge on the hearing of the appeal.[2] Where the appellant acts in person, the solicitor for the respondent should assume these responsibilities.[3]

The preparation of notes of evidence may be a burdensome task, particularly in a long case, and the parties must certify that they are necessary for the purposes of the appeal. The district judge may ask the parties whether notes are necessary if the facts as contained in the judgment are agreed. It may only be necessary to have a transcript of the notes where it is alleged that the evidence did not support the findings of fact. Moreover, now that all hearings before district judges are recorded, it seems more sensible for appellants to

---

[1] FPR 1991, r 8.1.
[2] *Practice Direction of 21 February 1985* [1985] FLR 355.
[3] Ibid.

request a complete transcript of the hearing and it is unlikely that a judge would agree to spend the time approving his notes when the simpler solution of a transcript was available.

18.4 Until 2001, appeals to the judge from the district judge were conducted as a rehearing on the principles established in *Marsh v Marsh*,[4] but this changed first as a result of the Court of Appeal's decision in *Cordle v Cordle*[5] where it was held that the previous practice as to family appeals must give way to the philosophy of the CPR and the Access to Justice Act 1999. It was said to be inappropriate in 2001 that appeals in ancillary relief proceedings from a district judge to a circuit judge should be by way of a rehearing and not by way of a review. Where it was sought to adduce additional evidence on such an appeal, that should be dealt with under the normal principles appropriate to the more liberal traditions of family proceedings, giving the judge discretion to admit evidence if appropriate. However, such discretion should be exercised sparingly. In *Cordle v Cordle*, since it had not been demonstrated that the district judge had fallen into any error, his order should be restored.

However, the Court of Appeal's attempt to reform the procedure for appeals was soon seen to have run foul of the rules, in particular FPR 1991, r 8.1, and it was realised that the rules would have to be amended to bring about the changes which were thought desirable. Accordingly, r 8.1(3)[6] now provides that in an appeal in respect of an ancillary relief order:

(a)   the appeal shall be limited to a review of the decision or order of the district judge unless the judge considers that in the circumstances of the case it would be in the interests of justice to hold a rehearing;

(b)   oral evidence or evidence which was not before the district judge may be admitted if in all the circumstances of the case it would be in the interests of justice to do so, irrespective of whether the appeal was by way of review or rehearing.

18.5 As to who should hear the appeal, in principle until very recently any circuit judge could do so, although in practice only 'ticketed' judges should have done so. However, the Court of Appeal experienced frequent problems with this, and as a result of a report by the Family Appeals Review Group, a consultation paper on appeals was issued by the DCA in the autumn of 2004 and it was thought that this would lead to rule changes in April 2005. Unfortunately, this has proved not to be the case and it seems that this proposal has been abandoned for the time being.

18.6 Under certain circumstances, an appeal in a case which has previously been heard in a county court may be transferred to the High Court when it

---

4   [1993] 1 FLR 467, CA.
5   [2001] EWCA Civ 1791, [2002] 1 FLR 207, CA.
6   As substituted by the Family Proceedings (Amendment) Rules 2003, SI 2003/184.

appears to the district judge, whether on the application of a party or otherwise, that the appeal raises a difficult or important question whether of law or otherwise.[7]

FROM DISTRICT JUDGE TO JUDGE (HIGH COURT)

18.7 Notice of appeal must be lodged within 5 days and served within 5 days thereafter.[8] Although the comments as to notes of evidence, judgment and principles to be observed, as set out above, are not provided for in the rules, common sense suggests that they should be applied.

FROM DISTRICT JUDGE TO JUDGE (PRINCIPAL REGISTRY)

18.8 Although for all purposes the Principal Registry is a divorce county court, all appeals from district judges are in practice heard by judges of the Family Division as if they were in the High Court. Procedurally, the requirements are the same as for an appeal in a county court.

FROM CIRCUIT JUDGE OR HIGH COURT JUDGE TO COURT OF APPEAL

18.9 An appeal lies only with permission of the judge, or, if refused, with permission of the Court of Appeal.[9] The appeal notice must be filed at the Court of Appeal within either the time directed by the lower court or, where no such direction was given, 14 days of the decision of the lower court.[10]

The procedure for lodging documents and the requirements as to skeleton arguments, etc, are beyond the scope of this book, but will be found in CPR Part 52 and its corresponding Practice Direction, PD52.

---

[7]   CPR Practice Direction to Part 52 – Appeals.
[8]   RSC Ord 58, r 1.
[9]   CPR, r 52.3.
[10] Ibid, r 52.4(2).

Chapter 19

ENFORCEMENT

INTRODUCTION

19.1 In this chapter, it is intended to give an outline of the types of enforcement available in respect of orders for ancillary relief and the practical details of how to proceed in the most common types of enforcement.

19.2 Although many of the rules as to these matters are contained in the RSC and the CCR, Part VII of the FPR 1991 contains some particular rules governing enforcement of orders for the payment of money in family cases which to some extent modify the other sets of rules. In particular, FPR 1991, r 7.1 contains general provisions applicable to all cases.

A particular rule which must be observed, and is an essential starting point for enforcement, is that which provides that:

> 'Before any process is issued for the enforcement of an order made in family proceedings for the payment of money to any person, an affidavit shall be filed verifying the amount due under the order and showing how that amount is arrived at.'[1]

It might be added that it would be good practice to exhibit to the affidavit a sealed copy of the order which it is sought to enforce; sometimes, enforcement is sought in courts other than those which made the order, and it is necessary to prove that the order has been made.

19.3 A further preliminary point relating to enforcement of orders for periodical payments is that leave of the court is required for the enforcement of arrears which are more than 12 months old.[2] When this is the case, the affidavit should depose as to the amount which has been in arrears for more than 12 months and the reasons for the delay.

Finally, because the FPR have not been amended to take account of the CPR, enforcement is still governed by the RSC and CCR which are rapidly becoming historical memories for most people.

---

[1]   FPR 1991, r 7.1(1).
[2]   MCA 1973, s 32.

EXECUTION

19.4 Execution is the seizure and sale of the debtor's goods, and takes the form of a writ of fiere facias in the High Court and a warrant of execution in the county court. The appropriate provisions are RSC Ord 47 and CCR Ord 26.

For the purposes of a warrant of execution, the Principal Registry is, in effect, treated as a county court.[3]

CHARGING ORDERS

19.5 This process is governed by the Charging Orders Act 1979, RSC Ord 50 and CCR Ord 31. Process may be issued in the High Court in respect of maintenance orders of the High Court or other orders of the High Court where the sum to be enforced is over £5,000; otherwise, the county court has exclusive jurisdiction.

The procedure is that a charging order nisi is obtained by filing the affidavit in support, and then a date is fixed for the hearing of the inter partes application for a charging order absolute. A charging order is most commonly granted over real property, but can be granted over shares, funds in court or other forms of property.

A charging order nisi must be served on any joint owner and on any known creditor, who is then entitled to be heard at the inter partes hearing. Once a charging order has been made, it is a security for the debt and the person in whose favour the order was made is in the position of a mortgagee. Any further enforcement has to be by way of an application for an order for sale.[4]

The court has no power to make a charging order on a debtor's entitlements under a pension scheme, as the debtor would have no beneficial interest under the trusts of the scheme.[5]

GARNISHEE ORDER (NOW THIRD PARTY DEBT ORDER)

19.6 The rules are contained in RSC Ord 47 and CCR Ord 30. A third party debt order directs someone who owes money to the debtor (such as a bank, where the account is in credit, or a trade debtor) to make the payment to the creditor. As with a charging order, the procedure is that an order nisi is granted

---

3   FPR 1991, r 7.1(3).
4   See TLATA 1996, s 14, and CCR Ord 31, r 4.
5   *Field v Field* [2003] 1 FLR 376.

upon the filing of the affidavit in support and an inter partes hearing is then fixed for the application for the final order.

ATTACHMENT OF EARNINGS

19.7 The primary authority for attachment of earnings orders is the Attachment of Earnings Act 1971, and the rules are contained in CCR Ord 27. CCR Ord 27, r 17 has particular relevance to maintenance orders. Although attachment of earnings is normally used to enforce orders for periodical payments, it can be used, for example, to recover an unpaid lump sum over a period of time. The essential features of an attachment of earnings order are that the court fixes a normal deduction rate (the weekly or monthly sum to be deducted from the debtor's earnings by his employer), and a protected earnings rate (the sum which the debtor must be allowed to keep). An attachment of earnings order is normally made in respect of earnings, but it can be used to deduct payments from a pension.

When the order to be enforced was made by a divorce county court, application for an attachment of earnings order must be made to that court.[6]

19.8 Attachment of earnings is unique among forms of enforcement in that a court which makes an order for periodical payments may make an attachment of earnings order at the same time, even if, as must be the case, no arrears have arisen.[7]

JUDGMENT SUMMONS

19.9 The power of the court to make an order on a judgment summons derives from the Debtors Act 1869, s 5[8] and CCA 1984, s 147(1). Proceedings may be issued in the High Court in respect of High Court orders and otherwise in the county court. Procedure in the High Court is governed by FPR 1991, r 7.5 and in the county court by CCR Ord 28. FPR 1991, r 7.4 applies generally.

Proceedings in respect of High Court orders may be issued in the Principal Registry, a District Registry or a divorce county court.[9] Orders of a divorce county court may be enforced in this way in any divorce county court of the applicant's choice.[10] Application is made by filing Form M16 with an affidavit of arrears.[11]

---

[6]   CCR Ord 27, r 17(2).
[7]   Maintenance Enforcement Act 1991, s 1, and CCR Ord 27, r 17(4).
[8]   Subject to Administration of Justice Act 1970, s 11.
[9]   FPR 1991, r 7.4(2)(a).
[10] Ibid, r 7.4(2)(b).
[11] Ibid, r 7.4(3).

19.10 Judgment summonses must be heard by a judge.[12] The order which is made, if the application is successful, is committal, which may be suspended.[13]

It has always been the case that a committal order should only be made where there is a contumacious debtor who has or has had the means to pay and whose conduct is therefore a contempt. However, the whole position of judgment summonses was thrown into disarray by the decision of the Court of Appeal in *Mubarak v Mubarak*,[14] where it was held that the procedure as it existed was incompatible with the Human Rights Act 1998 (HRA 1998) since, in effect, it presumed the guilt of the debtor and required him to show cause why he should not be punished. Because of this, the President issued a Practice Direction dated 16 March 2001,[15] which is contained in Appendix B, the effect of para 2 of which is that the proceedings must be 'HRA 1998 compliant'.

These developments have given rise, first, to the removal of the provision that proof of the debtor's means may be given by summoning him to give evidence on oath[16] and secondly, to a new version of FPR 1991, r 7.4, the important parts of which may be summarised as follows.

(1) The judgment summons must be in (the new) Form M17 and must be served with copies of the evidence on which the applicant relies (r 7.4(5)).

(2) The debtor may not be compelled to give evidence (r 7.4(7C)).

(3) No person may be committed unless the judgment creditor proves:
    (i) that the debtor has or has had since the date of the order the means to pay the sum in respect of which he has made default; and
    (ii) that the debtor has refused or failed or neglected to pay that sum (r 7.4(7B)).

(4) Any committal order may be suspended on terms as to payment (r 7.4(10)).

(5) If the court decides that the original order would have been varied if the debtor had made an application for that purpose, the court may make a new order for payment of the amount due under the original order either at a specified time or by instalments (r 7.4(9)).

In *Corbett v Corbett*[17] the Court of Appeal held that the judge below had plainly overlooked the opportunity to vary the order. As a matter of pragmatic management, the court must ensure that any application for variation, which

---

[12]   Debtors Act 1869, s 5(1).
[13]   CCR Ord 28, r 7.
[14]   [2001] 1 FLR 698.
[15]   *President's Direction (Committal Applications and Proceedings in which a Committal Order may be made)* [2001] 1 FLR 949.
[16]   Effected by the Civil Procedure (Modification of Enactments) Order 2002.
[17]   [2003] EWCA Civ 559, [2003] 2 FLR 385.

includes full investigation of both means and good faith, precedes the determination of the judgment summons.

19.11 Although a judgment summons is principally a means of enforcing a periodical payments order, it has also been used when there was a breach of an order to pay money into court pending an application for a lump sum.[18] It also seemed previously to be the most effective way to enforce an undertaking for the payment of money.[19]

19.12 A 'Hadkinson order', so called after the decision in *Hadkinson v Hadkinson*[20] is an order which permits the court to impose terms on a party who is in contempt and wishes to be heard on a subsequent application. The court will decide, in the exercise of its discretion, and in the light of the circumstances of the particular case, whether the interests of justice are best served by hearing a party in contempt or by refusing to do so.

A helpful recent example is the latest stage in the long-running litigation of *Mubarak v Mubarik*.[21] Here, Bodey J held that breach of a matrimonial order to pay money was in itself a contempt of court, and there was no requirement that the non-payment be shown to be culpable. Culpability only came in when the court was exercising its discretion as to whether and, if so, how, to act on the contempt. The imposition of terms did not violate Article 8 ECHR provided the test of proportionality was properly applied on a case-by-case basis.

In the instant case, Bodey J imposed terms which included the contemnor accepting that he was bound by the court's decision and making payments to cover the wife's costs.

APPOINTMENT OF A RECEIVER

19.13 A receiver may be appointed by the court by way of equitable execution whenever this is 'just and convenient'.[22] Procedure is governed by RSC Ord 30 and CCR Ord 32. Application may be made at trial or at any time.

When an order is made, or application for an order has been made, an injunction may be granted in support of the order or application.

---

18 *Graham v Graham* [1992] 2 FLR 406, CA.
19 *Symmons v Symmons* [1993] 1 FLR 317.
20 [1952] P 285; see also *Baker v Baker (No 2)* [1997] 1 FLR 148; *Mubarak v Mubarik* [2004] EWHC 1158 (Fam), [2004] 2 FLR 932; *Motorola Credit Corp v Uzan* [2003] EWCA Civ 752, [2004] 1 WLR 113.
21 [2006] EWHC 1260 (Fam), [2007] 1 FLR 722.
22 SCA 1981, s 37(1) and CCA 1984, s 38 but see *Field v Field* [2003] FLR 376.

REGISTRATION OF ORDER IN A MAGISTRATES' COURT

19.14 An order for periodical payments made in a divorce county court may be registered for purposes of enforcement in a magistrates' court.[23] Once registration has been effected, any application to vary the amount of the order (as opposed to, for example, its duration) must be made in a magistrates' court.[24]

Procedure is governed by FPR 1991, r 7.23. Application is made by completing and filing Form M33. An order for registration of an interim order or nominal order will not normally be made.

THE MAINTENANCE ENFORCEMENT ACT 1991

19.15 This Act has already been mentioned in connection with attachment of earnings. It should also be noted that, whenever the court makes a periodical payments order[25] or at any time thereafter,[26] it may direct that payment of the order be made in a specified manner such as by standing order or by direct debit.[27] This power may be exercised on application of either party or of the court's own motion.[28]

To enforce payment by this method, the court may order the paying party to open a bank account.[29]

EXECUTION OF DOCUMENTS BY NOMINATED PERSON

19.16 Sometimes, when an order is made for the transfer of property, the person ordered to transfer fails to do so. In those circumstances, the court may order that some other person execute the document on his behalf.[30] The proposed nominee is frequently the district judge but this need not be so; a partner in the applicant's firm of solicitors would be a more convenient person. Application for such an order may be made when the order for transfer is made,

---

[23] Maintenance Orders Act 1958, s 2(1).
[24] Ibid, s 4(5).
[25] Maintenance Enforcement Act 1991, s 1(1).
[26] Ibid, s 1(3).
[27] Ibid, s 1(4), (5).
[28] Ibid, s 1(3).
[29] Ibid, s 1(6).
[30] SCA 1981, s 39; CCA 1984, s 38.

but, if it is not, it must be made on notice to the other party, supported by an affidavit as to the facts of the case. This remedy should always be used rather than an application to commit.[31]

SEQUESTRATION

19.17 Sequestration is a drastic method of enforcing an order to do an act (such as a payment of money, or transfer of property) within a specified time. The effect of the issue of a writ of sequestration is that the property of the defaulting party is bound by the sequestration until the money is paid or the act otherwise performed. Sequestration is in fact a means of punishing a contempt.

Procedure is governed by RSC Ord 46, r 5, and CCA 1984, s 38 (there are no separate county court rules relating to sequestration). Application must be made to a judge; in the High Court, application is made in the Family Division, and it is suggested that county court applications should be made to a divorce county court.

There are several reported examples of the use of sequestration in family cases.[32]

COMMITTAL

19.18 Save in the case of judgment summons, committal is rarely used for the enforcement of orders for ancillary relief. Where another method exists, it is normally adopted.

Nevertheless, there may be occasions when no other remedy is available or appropriate. Application in the High Court is made by summons.[33] Application in the county court is made by notice to show cause in Form N78.[34] Both applications should be supported by affidavit. In all cases, a copy of the order which is alleged to have been disobeyed must have been personally served on the defaulter.

---

[31] *Danchevsky v Danchevsky* [1975] Fam 17.
[32] *Sansom v Sansom* (1879) 4 PD 69; *Birch v Birch* (1883) 8 PD 163; *Hyde v Hyde* (1888) 13 PD 166; *Romilly v Romilly* [1964] P 22.
[33] FPR 1991, r 7.2(1) and RSC Ord 52, r 6.
[34] CCR Ord 29, r 1(4A).

RECIPROCAL ENFORCEMENT

19.19 Maintenance and other orders may be registered for enforcement in some other jurisdictions. The reader will find the relevant procedural material in FPR 1991, rr 7.16–7.39 and the following outline may help.

19.20 In this section, the principles and practice of reciprocal enforcement – that is to say the enforcement in the courts of England and Wales of 'family finance orders' made in other jurisdictions – will be discussed. The enforcement in other jurisdictions of orders made in England and Wales is not considered, due to the detail required. The reader is referred to FPR 1991, r 7.16 et seq. Here, only 'incoming' orders made in other jurisdictions wil be considered.

19.21 Even within the limited compass of this section, it has to be said that the picture is complicated and potentially confusing. This stems from the fact that enforcement may take place pursuant to several different treaties and sets of international obligations which, to some extent, overlap. It has also to be said that the courts in which enforcement takes place are not always best equipped to deal with cases involving complicated international issues.

The various types of enforcement of incoming orders will now be considered.

Registration of a maintenance order made in a European UN Convention country

19.22 These orders are enforced pursuant to Part II of the Maintenance Orders (Reciprocal Enforcement) Act 1972 (MO(RE)A 1972). Orders made in France may be registered for enforcement under these provisions. The orders are limited to maintenance orders and will be registered as if they had been made here under 'the relevant Act', ie under the Children Act 1989 in the case of children's orders and under the Domestic Proceedings and Magistrates' Courts Act 1978 otherwise.

An application for enforcement sent by a UN Convention country is first sent to the Lord Chancellor, who sends it to the clerk to the justices for the petty sessional (magistrates' court) division in which the respondent (the paying party) lives. A date for hearing is then fixed on notice to the respondent. The court then hears the application and makes an order under the relevant Act, so that the obligation to pay is, in effect, incorporated in an order of that court. The court decides how payment should be made after hearing representations from the paying party.

Once the court has made an order under the relevant Act, the respondent may apply to that court for variation or revocation of the order, and the application will be dealt with under the powers to vary or revoke contained in the relevant Act. This can lead to the original order proving of no effect. This must be contrasted with the position of the applicant who, if she wishes to vary the order, has to apply to the court of the Convention country.

The court may not transfer to the High Court or a county court any order relating to children only.

Registration of a maintenance order made in an EU or EFTA country

19.23 These orders are registered pursuant to the Civil Jurisdiction and Judgments Act 1982 (CJJA 1982). The distinction between this process and that set out above is that the order is 'registered'; there is no new order made under any 'relevant Act'. As before, the foreign country ('the contracting State') sends a certified copy of the judgment and a request for enforcement to the Lord Chancellor, who sends it to the magistrates' court for the area where the paying party resides or has assets. When the paying party does in fact reside or have assets in that area, the order is registered by the clerk without a hearing and becomes enforceable as if it were a magistrates' maintenance order.

There is a process of appeal against registration or refusal to register, and the order cannot be enforced until the appeal process has been completed. Power to vary is limited to variations of the method of payment. Any other application to vary must be made in the original contracting State. France is, of course, an EU country.

Enforcement of a judgment or order (not being a maintenance order) made in an EU or EFTA country

19.24 These orders are enforced pursuant to the CJJA 1982 and CJJA 1991, and are orders other than maintenance orders. In practice, they are limited to lump sum orders which are capitalised maintenance and orders for costs, since rights in property arising out of a matrimonial relationship are excluded from enforcement by Art 1 of the Brussels Convention on Jurisdiction and the Enforcement of Judgments in Civil and Commercial Matters 1968.

The application is made direct to the Principal Registry of the Family Division, and is considered without a hearing by a district judge. If the application is granted, the order is registered for enforcement and an order is served on the debtor, who has a right of appeal limited to the issue of whether the order should have been registered. The order may then be enforced in the same way as any other monetary judgment of the High Court.

Registration of a maintenance order made in a European Hague Convention country

19.25 These orders are registered pursuant to MO(RE)A 1972. France is a Hague Convention country. The application is sent by the Convention country to the Lord Chancellor, who forwards it to the clerk to the justices for the magistrates' court area where the payer lives. If it appears that the payer lives in that area, the order is registered and becomes enforceable as if it were a maintenance order of that court. Once registration has taken place, either party may apply to that court for a variation.

19.26 For the sake of completeness, it should be said that there are other provisions to deal with the enforcement of orders made elsewhere, eg in Commonwealth countries, but these are not considered here.

Chapter 20

THE IMPACT OF THE HUMAN RIGHTS ACT 1998

INTRODUCTION

20.1 The enactment of the Human Rights Act 1998 (HRA 1998) means that all areas of the law of England and Wales are now subject to the overriding duty to comply with the provisions of the European Convention for the Protection of Human Rights and Fundamental Freedoms ('the Convention') which has applied to most of the rest of Europe since 1950. Family law, and ancillary relief in particular, is not exempt from this general requirement. The purpose of this chapter is not to provide a detailed examination of all the implications of the HRA 1998[1] but rather to draw attention to some of the major points which may impinge on the law and practice of ancillary relief.

20.2 The structure of this chapter will therefore be to examine the following matters:

(a) the principal provisions of the HRA 1998;

(b) the parts of the Convention which may affect ancillary relief;

(c) the likely effect in practice of these provisions.

THE PRINCIPAL PROVISIONS OF THE HRA 1998

20.3 In this section it is proposed to consider the following:

– duties of the court in respect of Convention rights;

– declarations of incompatibility;

– acts of 'public authorities';

– remedies available.

---

[1] For such a detailed examination, see Swindells et al *Family Law and the Human Rights Act 1998* (Jordans, 1999).

Before doing so, however, two key terms must be defined. 'Convention rights' means:[2]

> 'the rights and fundamental freedoms set out in—
>
> (a) Articles 2 to 12 and 14 of the Convention,
> (b) Articles 1 to 3 of the First Protocol, and
> (c) Articles 1 and 2 of the Sixth Protocol,
>
> as read with Articles 16 to 18 of the Convention.'

'Protocol' means:[3]

> 'a protocol to the Convention—
>
> (a) which the United Kingdom has ratified; or
> (b) which the United Kingdom has signed with a view to ratification.'

Application and interpretation of Convention rights

20.4 HRA 1998, s 3 provides that, so far as possible, primary legislation and subordinate legislation must be read and given effect in a way which is compatible with the Convention rights. The overall effect is clear: domestic legislation must be read and interpreted in such a way as to give effect to and not to go against the letter or the spirit of Convention rights. The courts are directed as to their duties in this respect. A court or tribunal determining any question which has arisen in connection with a Convention right must take into account any:

(a) judgment, decision, declaration or advisory opinion of the European Court of Human Rights (ECHR),

(b) opinion of the Commission (ie the European Commission of Human Rights, now incorporated in the new ECHR) given in a report adopted under Art 31 of the Convention,

(c) decision of the Commission in connection with Art 26 or Art 27(2) of the Convention, or

(d) decision of the Committee of Ministers taken under Art 46 of the Convention,

whenever made or given, so far as, in the opinion of the court or tribunal, it is relevant to the proceedings in which that question has arisen.[4]

---

[2]   HRA 1998, s 1(1).
[3]   Ibid, s 1(5).
[4]   Ibid, s 2(1).

20.5 The duty of the court is therefore clear. Convention rights govern and have an overriding effect on the way the courts exercise their jurisdiction and, in deciding what Convention rights mean or imply, the court is given a menu of possible sources of law.

Declaration of incompatibility

20.6 Circumstances may arise in which a court finds it impossible to give effect to Convention rights because of the clear meaning of domestic law. In those circumstances, normally domestic law will prevail; the court may not strike down primary legislation, but may strike down delegated legislation provided the terms of the parent statute do not make that impossible.[5] However, that need not be an end of the matter. Whenever a court (as defined below) decides that a provision of the law of England and Wales is incompatible with a Convention right, it may make a declaration of that incompatibility.[6] This will not affect the validity, continuing operation or enforcement of the provision and is not binding on the parties to the proceedings in which it is given,[7] so that nothing will change in the instant case. However, it is thought that such a declaration would lead Parliament to change, or to consider changing, the offending provision.

Because of the potential importance of a declaration of incompatibility, this power is reserved to the High Court and above.[8]

Acts of public authorities

20.7 The HRA 1998 provides that it is unlawful for a public authority to act in a way which is incompatible with a Convention right.[9] This is of more significance than might first appear because 'public authority' includes a court or tribunal as well as 'any person certain of whose functions are functions of a public nature'.[10] It is therefore unlawful for a court to disregard, breach, or act otherwise than in accordance with, Convention rights. Acting unlawfully in this context would, therefore, include, in the case of a court, failing to have regard to s 3 (the obligation to read and give effect to domestic legislation in a way which is compatible with Convention rights) and failing to interpret Convention rights in accordance with s 2 (see para **20.4**).

The individual who claims that a court or other body has acted unlawfully has, therefore, a right of action.

---

5   'Rights Brought Home: The Human Rights Bill' (Cm 3782) ('White Paper'), paras 2.13 and 2.15.
6   HRA 1998, s 4(2).
7   Ibid, s 4(6).
8   Ibid, s 4(5).
9   Ibid, s 6(1).
10   Ibid, s 6(3).

Remedies available

20.8 A person who claims that a public authority has acted or proposes to act in a way which is unlawful by virtue of these provisions must either bring proceedings against the authority in the 'appropriate court or tribunal' or rely on the Convention rights in 'any legal proceedings'.[11] 'Appropriate court or tribunal' means such court as may be determined by rules of court;[12] in the case of the public authority being a court, it is most likely that such proceedings will have to be by way of judicial review.

As to reliance on the Convention in 'any legal proceedings', it would seem that this means that the Convention rights may be relied on in argument in the proceedings in which the court has acted, or threatens to act, unlawfully. It is also specifically provided[13] that 'legal proceedings' includes an appeal against a decision of a court or tribunal; an unlawful act by a court could therefore constitute a ground of appeal.

If proceedings are brought by way of judicial review, an applicant will be taken to have a sufficient interest in relation to the unlawful act only if he or she is, or would be, a victim of the unlawful act.[14]

PARTS OF THE CONVENTION WHICH MAY AFFECT ANCILLARY RELIEF

20.9 In the section above, we have considered, in brief outline only, the way in which the HRA 1998 incorporates the Convention into the law of England and Wales. In this section, those Convention rights which may affect ancillary relief will be set out and briefly described. It must be borne in mind that the Convention covers all aspects of law and, by its nature, includes such matters as the right to life and liberty which do not normally impinge on ancillary relief applications. Nevertheless, as will be seen, there are several Convention rights which may have a profound effect on this area of law.

20.10 The rights guaranteed by the Convention which may concern family law in general, and ancillary relief in particular, are as follows:

– the right to a fair trial (Art 6);

– the right to respect for private and family life, home and correspondence (Art 8);

– the right to marry and found a family (Art 12);

---

11 HRA 1998, s 7(1).
12 Ibid, s 7(2).
13 By ibid, s 7(6).
14 Ibid, s 7(4).

– freedom from discrimination in the field of Convention rights (Art 14);

– the right to property (Art 1 of the First Protocol).

These will be considered in turn. It should be noted that Art 5 of the Seventh Protocol, which provides for equality of rights of spouses, has been omitted from HRA 1998. However, this may only be a temporary omission, and in view of its potential importance for ancillary relief, this Convention right will also be discussed.

The right to a fair trial

20.11 Article 6 of the Convention provides that 'everyone is entitled to a fair and public hearing within a reasonable time by an independent and impartial tribunal established by law'. This is one of the most important Convention rights for obvious reasons; the rule of law, which underpins the whole Convention, would be impossible without it.

The following points emerge from this.

– The individual must have right of access to a court.

– The proceedings must be fair.

– Any hearing must be within a reasonable time.

– The tribunal must be independent and impartial.

– The hearing, and pronouncement of any decision, must be in public.

20.12 Although it is impossible to deal with this topic in more than outline, it may be helpful to consider briefly how the guarantee of a 'fair hearing' has been interpreted. The following principles have been developed.

– The concept of 'equality of arms' has emerged. Each party must be afforded a reasonable opportunity to present his case, including his evidence, under conditions which do not place him at a substantial disadvantage vis-à-vis his opponent.[15]

– Both parties must have access to all evidence.[16]

– No one may be required to incriminate himself.[17]

– Reasons for any judgment must be given.

---

[15] *Dombo Beheer BV v The Netherlands* (1994) 18 EHRR 213, para 33.
[16] See *Bönisch v Austria* (1985) 9 EHRR 191, where it was held that there was inequality between a court appointed expert and an expert for one of the parties.
[17] See e g *Saunders v UK* (1996) 23 EHRR 313, para 71.

This Article has already had an effect. In *Mubarak v Mubarak*,[18] the applicant had issued a judgment summons against her former husband for the non-payment of a lump sum order. An order was made against the husband by the judge at first instance. The husband appealed and in his judgment Brooke LJ observed that the HRA 1998, which had then been in force for 2 months:

> 'is doing work of considerable value in shining light into some of the dustier corners of our law. The experience of this case shows, at any rate to my satisfaction, that corners do not get much dustier than those inhabited by section 5 of the Debtors Act 1869 and the prescribed procedures under that Act.'

His Lordship referred to the new CPR Practice Direction – Committal Applications, which provided that the burden of proof was that the allegation be proved beyond reasonable doubt. It was not clear that that applied to judgment summonses, but Brooke LJ (and the court) emphasised that in order to comply with Art 6, it would have to do so. The husband's appeal was allowed and the President has now issued a Practice Direction to govern the judgment summons procedure in future[19] (see Chapter 19, para **19.10**).

Respect for private and family life

20.13 Article 8 provides that everyone has the right to respect for his private and family life, his home and his correspondence. The essential object of Art 8 is 'to protect the individual against arbitrary action by the public authorities';[20] it will be remembered that a court is a 'public authority'. It has also been held that 'respect for private life must also comprise to a certain degree the right to establish and develop relationships with other human beings'.[21]

The right to a home has been held to be a right to occupy a home and not to be expelled or evicted.[22] Telephone tapping has been held to be a violation of Art 8.[23]

The right to marry and found a family

20.14 Article 12 states that 'men and women of marriageable age have the right to marry and to found a family, according to the national laws governing the exercise of this right'. This is an absolute right in that the State has no right to interfere with it.[24] However, the exercise of the right to marry is subject to the national laws of the contracting States.[25]

---

18 [2001] 1 FLR 698, CA.
19 *President's Direction of 16 March 2001 (Committal Applications and Proceedings in which a Committal Order may be made)* [2001] 1 FLR 949.
20 *Kroon v The Netherlands* (1994) 19 EHRR 263.
21 *Niemitz v Germany* (1993) 16 EHRR 97.
22 *Wiggins v UK* Application No 7456/76, (1978) 13 DR 40.
23 *Klass v Germany* (1979–80) 2 EHRR 214.
24 *X v UK* Application No 6564/74, (1975) 2 DR 105.
25 *F v Switzerland* (1987) 10 EHRR 411.

The right to freedom from discrimination

20.15 Article 14 provides that 'the enjoyment of the rights and freedoms set forth in this Convention shall be secured without discrimination on any ground such as sex, race, colour, language, religion, political or other opinion, national or social origin, association with a national minority, property, birth or other status'.

The right to property

20.16 Article 1 of the First Protocol provides that 'every natural person or legal person is entitled to the peaceful enjoyment of his possessions. No one shall be deprived of his possessions except in the public interest and subject to the conditions provided for by law and by the general principles of international law'.

The right to property is therefore guaranteed by the Protocol.

Equality of rights of spouses

20.17 Article 5 of the Seventh Protocol provides that 'spouses shall enjoy equality of rights and responsibilities of a private law character between them, and in their relations with their children, as to marriage, during marriage, and in the event of its dissolution. This Article shall not prevent States from taking such measures as are necessary in the interests of children'.

As was mentioned above, this Article has not been included in the HRA 1998, although it may well be included in the future. Its implications are discussed below.

THE EFFECT OF HRA 1998 IN PRACTICE

20.18 Perhaps the most interesting result of the HRA 1998 in relation to ancillary relief will be when Art 5 of the Seventh Protocol (Equality of Rights of Spouses) is introduced into domestic law; this has not yet happened but it may only be a matter of time. It is thought that the principal reason for its omission was the potential difficulties which the Government foresaw while the law of ancillary relief remained in its present state.[26] As shown in Chapter 21, during 1996 ministers expressed an interest in amending MCA 1973, s 25 to provide for some statement of equality as a starting point. In 1998, this issue was referred to the Lord Chancellor's Advisory Group, whose unanimous advice was that the existing law should not be changed.

Whatever the future shape of domestic legislation, it is clearly possible that Art 5, if incorporated into domestic law, could provide a fruitful source of litigation and argument. It is difficult to speculate as to what the result of such

---

[26] 'Rights Brought Home: The Human Rights Bill' (Cm 3782), para 4.15.

litigation would be, or as to the degree to which the ECHR would arrive at different conclusions from the courts of England and Wales. One possible difference of approach might arise from argument as to whether 'equality' means 'equality of outcome' although this argument was firmly rejected as a possibility in *Cowan v Cowan*.[27]

20.19 Turning to provisions which have been included in HRA 1998, the right to property under Art 1 of the First Protocol might give rise to some argument. The right to peaceful enjoyment of property may be interfered with when, for example, a property adjustment order is made. However, it is also provided that contracting States may control the use of property in accordance with the general interest by enforcing such laws as they deem necessary for the purpose, and there seem to be no reported cases which give any guidance as to how Art 1 might affect ancillary relief.

20.20 The right to a fair trial (Art 6) will clearly have an effect on ancillary relief. Some of the general implications have already been discussed at para **20.12**. One issue which will have to be faced is the requirement for a public hearing and the public pronouncement of judgment; were this adopted, procedure would have to change. It might be that cases will continue to be heard in chambers with only the judgment being given in public, and, even then, it seems that it might be permissible for the parties to be referred to merely by their initials. Only time will tell.

It might also be argued that the obligation on parties to give full and frank disclosure could, in some cases, constitute a breach of the freedom from self-incrimination; again, we must await developments.

20.21 Finally, there are many examples in this book of cases where the court has had to consider the application of the ECHR to ancillary relief cases. The reader will find these at the appropriate places, but examples are *Mubarak v Mubarik*,[28] *Nicholls v Lan*,[29] *R (Kehoe) v Secretary of State for Work and Pensions*,[30] and *Barca v Mears*.[31]

---

27   [2001] EWCA Civ 679, [2001] 2 FLR 192, CA (as to which, see Chapter 1, para **1.52**).
28   [2006] EWHC 1260 (Fam), [2007] 1 FLR 722.
29   [2006] EWHC 1255 (Ch), [2007] 1 FLR 744.
30   [2005] UKHL 48, [2005] 2 FLR 1249, HL.
31   [2004] EWHC 2170 (Ch), [2005] 2 FLR 1.

Chapter 21

THE PROCEEDS OF CRIME ACT 2002

INTRODUCTION

21.1 Family lawyers have always had a potential difficulty in deciding what to do when it appeared that their client was involved in some illegal activity. Conflicting duties to the client, the court, their profession and the administration of justice have meant that difficult decisions have had to be made.

These dilemmas have been made more urgent by the coming into force of the Proceeds of Crime Act 2002 (POCA 2002). In one sense, POCA 2002 removes some of the dilemmas in that the lawyer's duties are now more clearly defined. However, these duties impose burdens on the family lawyer which are new, and it is the purpose of this chapter to alert the reader to the potential difficulties.

It must be emphasised that this chapter is not an exhaustive analysis of the whole of POCA 2002. It is merely intended to alert the family lawyer to the most obvious consequences of the Act in the hope that the traps may be recognised in practice.

THE PURPOSE OF POCA 2002

21.2 POCA 2002 is designed to help to fight organised crime. The philosophy behind the Act is that if the Crown can intercept and recover the proceeds of crime, thereby depriving the wrongdoer of the benefits of criminal activities, the incentive to crime will be diminished. Until now, it has been possible for the Crown Court to make confiscation orders, but that has been dependent on a criminal conviction. The court may exercise its powers under POCA 2002 without a criminal conviction and according to the civil standard of proof – the balance of probabilities. In this way, it is hoped, the process will be made more efficient and quick and criminals will no longer be able to enjoy the fruit of their labours.

POCA 2002 is also to some extent a codifying Act, which incorporates the former Drugs Trafficking Offences Act 1986.

As will be seen below, POCA 2002 is drafted in wide terms and the problem for the family lawyer (or any other kind of lawyer) is that provisions intended to defeat large-scale crime may have the unintended effect of 'catching' much smaller and possibly less heinous transactions; there is no de minimis level and every transaction, however small, which might come within the ambit of the Act can give rise to offences being committed.

MONEY LAUNDERING

21.3   Money laundering is dealt with in Part 7 of POCA 2002. It is one of the key concepts of the Act and the part which is most likely to impinge on the family lawyer. As its name implies, laundering occurs where the proceeds of crime are cleaned up and made apparently legitimate. This may be done, for example, by placing tainted money into the economy; cash may be paid to a solicitor for a purpose which fails, such as the purchase of a house, and is then repaid to the original payor by a solicitor's cheque. The first appearance of the money in the payor's accounts is the solicitor's cheque, which would not attract attention.

Money may also be layered, which means that it would be a part of a series of transactions designed to obscure the origin of the money. Finally, the money may be integrated legitimately into the economy, for example by being used to purchase a legitimate business.

Tax evasion is a criminal offence and is the crime which is most likely to taint money which is used in the family law context. Where the fortunes of parties to ancillary relief have been augmented by historic tax evasion, and those fortunes are to be divided between the parties at the conclusion of the proceedings, the lawyers may well find that they are caught by the Act.

The detail about money laundering will be contained in the Money Laundering Regulations 2003 (the Regulations).[1]

OFFENCES UNDER POCA 2002

21.4   A person commits an offence if he:

(1)   conceals, disguises, converts, transfers or removes criminal property from England and Wales (s 327);

(2)   enters into an arrangement which he knows, or suspects, will assist someone to acquire, retain, use or control criminal property by or for another person (s 328);

(3)   acquires, uses or has possession of criminal property (s 329);

---

[1]   SI 2003/3075.

(4) fails to disclose a known or suspected money laundering offence; this includes the position where the defendant merely has reasonable grounds to suspect; this applies in the 'regulated sector' (s 330);

(5) fails to disclose a money laundering offence; this applies to a nominated officer in the regulated sector (s 331);

(6) fails to disclose a money laundering offence as soon as practicable after the information comes to him; this applies to other nominated officers;

(7) 'tips off' after a s 337 or s 338 disclosure has been made so as to prejudice an investigation (s 333).

Defences and/or exceptions to the various offences are contained in ss 330(6) and (7) and 338.

21.5 Criminal property is the benefit from criminal conduct or something which represents the benefit (in whole or in part and whether directly or indirectly), and the person concerned knows or suspects that it constitutes or represents such a benefit.

Criminal conduct is conduct which is an offence in any part of the UK or would be an offence if it happened in the UK; this is the case even if it is legal in the jurisdiction in which it is done. This definition therefore covers all crimes, including crimes committed abroad, irrespective of by whom they were committed or the date on which they were committed. As an example of a potential difficulty, the United States of America can choose to apply its domestic legislation with extra-territorial effect, with the result that a case with a US connection may give rise to offences in respect of acts done in the UK which are not criminal in the UK.

21.6 Reporting must be made to the National Criminal Intelligence Service (NCIS). Once the report is made the solicitor or barrister cannot continue to act unless NCIS give the appropriate consent. NCIS has 7 working days in which to give this consent, but if consent is refused there is a further period of 31 days during which a restraint order may be applied for.

21.7 The duty to report is set out above. However, equally important is the duty not to tell the client that the report has been made. If a person makes an internal or external report and tells the client or anyone else that he has made a report or that there is an investigation he commits an offence. Note, however, that no offence of tipping off can be committed if no report has been made. Merely asking questions of the client to find out more information is not tipping off.

If a lawyer receives the information (leading him to suspect an offence) in privileged circumstances, he does not have to report. Privilege attaches to confidential communications made between a solicitor and his client in connection with the giving of legal advice or in connection with or in contemplation of legal proceedings and for the purpose of such proceedings. Privilege provides a defence to failure to report or tipping off. However, it would then be impossible for the lawyer to continue to act.

21.8 Solicitors are part of the regulated sector if they provide legal services which involve participation in a financial or real property transaction, whether by assisting in the planning or execution of transactions or otherwise by acting for or on behalf of a client.

JUDICIAL GUIDANCE AS TO THE OPERATION OF POCA 2002

21.9 The uncertainties about the effect on the legal profession of POCA 2002 led to a prompt application to the High Court in *P v P (Ancillary Relief: Proceeds of Crime)*[2] and the President handed down her judgment on 8 October 2003. This judgment was intended to give constructive guidance to the profession and its contents will be summarised below. However, as will be seen, this judgment has been to some extent overtaken by the judgment of the Court of Appeal in *Bowman v Fels* which is also summarised below.

(a) Whether and in what circumstances it is permitted to act in relation to an arrangement

21.10 There are a variety of ways in which a legal professional might become 'concerned in' an arrangement. It could not be the case that the offence under s 328 can only be committed at the point of execution of the arrangement. The act of negotiating an arrangement would equally amount to being 'concerned in' the arrangement.

The President said that the duties under s 328 of a barrister or solicitor engaged in family litigation are straightforward. There is nothing in that section to prevent a solicitor or barrister from taking instructions from a client. However, if having taken instructions the solicitor or barrister knows or suspects that he or she or his or her client will become involved in an arrangement that might involve the acquisition, retention, use or control of criminal property, then an authorised disclosure should be made and the appropriate consent sought under s 335. Therefore, if it seems to the solicitor or barrister that there are grounds for suspicion that any arrangement being sought from the court or negotiated between the parties is contrary to the requirements of s 328(1), then authorisation should be sought. It would seem that the position as set out above would apply equally to ss 327 and 329.

---

[2]   [2003] EWHC 2260 (Fam), [2004] 1 FLR 193.

The President's view was that issues of legal professional privilege did not seem to arise under ss 327, 328 or 329 and there was no professional privilege exemption in these sections.

21.11 The effect of s 335 was that a person may make a disclosure, generally but not necessarily, to NCIS seeking consent to continue taking steps in relation to an arrangement. The person must not take any further steps in relation to the arrangement, until the person either:

(1)   receives from NCIS notice of consent within 7 working days from the next working day after the disclosure is made ('the notice period' – s 335(5)), in which case the person may resume acting in relation to the arrangement (by virtue of s 335(3)); or

(2)   hears nothing from NCIS within the notice period, in which case the person is treated as having deemed consent to resume acting in relation to the arrangement (by virtue of s 335(3)); or

(3)   receives from NCIS notice of refusal of consent within the notice period, in which case the person must not act in relation to the arrangement for the duration of the moratorium period of 31 days starting with the day on which the person receives the refusal notice (by virtue of s 335(4)). Once the moratorium period has expired the person may resume acting in relation to the arrangement.

In practice, the longest possible time for which a person could be prevented from taking steps in relation to an arrangement, after sending a notice to the NCIS, would be 31 days plus 7 working days.

21.12 The President said that the consent procedures in ss 335 and 338 apply to those persons who make the authorised disclosure. So, for example, if a solicitor makes an authorised joint disclosure on behalf of himself, counsel and his client, then all three will be protected from prosecution. Indeed, where the solicitor acts for the innocent party, it would be sensible as a matter of practice for solicitors to make an authorised disclosure. If a solicitor is disclosing suspicions about his own client, it may, of course, be a different matter.

21.13 It was important for the legal profession to take into account that the Act makes no distinction between degrees of criminal property. An illegally obtained sum of £10 is no less susceptible to the definition of 'criminal property' than a sum of £1m. Parliament clearly intended this to be the case. The President said that whatever may be the resource implications, the legal profession would appear to be bound by the provisions of the Act in all cases, however big or small. If this approach is scrupulously followed by the legal advisers, the result is likely to have a considerable and potentially adverse impact upon the NCIS and would create serious consequential delays in listing and hearing family cases, including child cases.

(b) Whether and in what circumstances a legal adviser, having made an authorised disclosure, is permitted to tell others of this fact

21.14 Section 93D of the Criminal Justice Act 1988 (now repealed) contained a prohibition against tipping off in relation to criminal investigations of money laundering. In *Governor and Company of the Bank of Scotland v A Ltd*[3] the Court of Appeal considered the meaning of the legal professional exemption contained in s 93D(4) of the Criminal Justice Act 1988, a provision dealing with 'tipping off' in almost identical terms to s 333. In that case, the bank suspected that the moneys held in a client's account had been obtained by fraud. Lord Woolf CJ at para [7] of the judgment of the court said:

'During argument there was discussion as to the extent of the defence provided by s 93D(4). Mr Crow helpfully drew our attention to the similarity between the language of s 93D(4) and the scope of legal professional privilege. Based on this assistance, we conclude that the subsection broadly protects a legal adviser when that adviser is engaged in activities which attract legal professional privilege.'

The President said that passage would appear to support the protection given to members of the legal profession in carrying out their duties to their clients.

21.15 The President said that sections 333 and 342 specifically recognise a legal adviser's duty in ordinary circumstances to make the relevant disclosures, even where the result would be to tip off their client, where to do so would fall within the ambit of being in connection with the giving of legal advice or with legal proceedings actual or contemplated. A central element of advising and representing a client must be the duty to keep one's client informed and not to withhold information from him or her.[4] Since the function of the Act is to regulate the proceeds of criminal behaviour, it is clear that in every circumstance where a solicitor believes an authorised disclosure to the NCIS is necessary there will be at least a suspicion of criminal purpose. If, as the NCIS suggests, ss 333(4) and 342(5) bite every time a party who is suspected of holding a criminal purpose is given notice that a disclosure has been or will be made to the NCIS (ie is 'tipped off'), then the legal professional exemptions in ss 333(3) and 342(4) would be rendered meaningless. Sections 333(4) and 342(5) must have some purpose and the interpretation suggested by the NCIS cannot be correct. The exemption is lost if a disclosure to a client is made 'with the intention of furthering a criminal purpose'. The natural meaning of those words would seem to be clear. The approach which the House of Lords took to the construction of the word 'held' in *R v Central Criminal Court ex parte Francis & Francis*[5] should not be transposed into this context in relation to the word 'made', nor would it be necessary or proper to attempt to do so. Whereas the purpose of holding documents can be tainted by the intention of any number of people (including client and third parties), the intention of a legal

---

[3]   [2001] EWCA Civ 52, [2001] 1 WLR 754.
[4]   *Halsbury's Law of England* (above), paras 148–149.
[5]   [1989] 1 AC 346.

adviser in choosing to make a disclosure would seem to belong to the adviser alone. The context and purpose of this particular s of the POCA 2002 is distinguishable from that in *Francis*, not least because the Act has specifically underlined the duty of disclosure by legal advisers.

The president observed that even though the client's criminal intent disqualified him from claiming privilege, it did not disqualify him from his entitlement to be consulted by his lawyer without falling foul of the tipping off rules.

There might well be instances where a solicitor's disclosure to a client is in breach of s 333(4) or s 342(5), because the solicitor makes the disclosure with an improper purpose. In such a case the legal professional exemption would, of course, be lost. The President could not give a blanket guarantee to all family practitioners that they would never lose the protection of the exemption. But unless the requisite improper intention is there, the solicitor should be free to communicate such information to his or her client or opponent as is necessary and appropriate in connection with the giving of legal advice or acting in connection with actual or contemplated legal proceedings.

21.16 The President recognised that the conclusion she had reached might cause some difficulty to the investigating authorities. The time lines set out in ss 328, 335 and 338 are independent from the provisions of ss 333 and 342. Having complied with the obligations under s 328, there is nothing in the statute to require a solicitor to delay in informing his client. Either he is entitled to do so forthwith by virtue of the s 333(3) exemption, or if s 333(4) or s 342(5) bite, he is not entitled to do so at all. There is no middle ground.

Good practice

21.17 The President was, however, concerned that the purpose of the Act be respected, and that as a matter of good practice (as opposed to statutory obligation) the investigation authorities should be permitted time to do their job without frustration. In most cases, she could not see why a delay of, at most, 7 working days before informing a client would generally cause particular difficulty to the solicitor's obligations to his client or his opponent. Where appropriate consent is refused and a 31-day moratorium is imposed, best practice would suggest that the legal adviser and the NCIS (or other relevant investigating body) try to agree on the degree of information which can be disclosed during the moratorium period without harming the investigation. In the absence of agreement, or in other urgent circumstances where even a short delay in disclosure would be unacceptable (such as where a hearing or FDR is imminent, or orders for discovery require immediate compliance), the guidance of the court may be sought.

21.18 The Court of Appeal in *C v S and others*[6] set out a procedure to be followed where compliance with an order for disclosure of information in civil

---

[6]   [1999] 2 All ER 343.

proceedings might reveal money laundering and cause the financial institution to be in breach of tipping off provisions under s 93D of the Criminal Justice Act 1988 (as amended). In *Governor and Company of the Bank of Scotland v A Ltd*[7] the Court of Appeal suggested a similar procedure whereby the bank in that case could have made an application to the court naming the Serious Fraud Office as respondent. The application could be held in private and there would be no question of serving the customer since he would not be a party. The procedures suggested by the Court of Appeal in those two cases might usefully be adapted to the family financial proceedings where a disclosure has been made. Since the purpose of such an application is to protect the legal advisers and, in some cases, the client, the President could not see how one can impose an obligation on the NCIS to be the applicant (although the NCIS would however also be entitled to approach the court if it wished to do so). It would be appropriate for the legal advisers to make the application without notice to the other side, making the NCIS the respondent to the application. It would be an application, however, within the ambit of the existing court proceedings and there did not seem to be any difficulty at the moment in the court making any appropriate order, including, if in the High Court, declarations. In the present case the President granted declarations since the situation was entirely new and she did so to clarify the situation. It would not seem to be necessary for the court generally to grant declarations, but rather to deal with the practical consequences of the authorised disclosure to the NCIS. The application would be heard in private and the court should direct that any mechanical recording of the proceedings should not be disclosed or transcribed without the leave of the judge.

The President reminded legal advisers that it would not seem to be necessary to make repeated disclosures on the same facts, unless it is proposed to enter into a new arrangement or a variation of the same arrangement. Each time a further disclosure is made, time will start running again for 7 days or possibly 7 plus 31 days.

21.19 The President's judgment in *P v P* was not appealed. However, the same issues came to be considered by the Court of Appeal in *Bowman v Fels* and to some extent the guidance given by the President was modified.

Lord Justice Brooke, giving the judgment of the Court, said that on this appeal the Court was invited to determine whether s 328 meant that as soon as a lawyer acting for a client in legal proceedings discovered or suspected anything in the proceedings that might facilitate the acquisition, retention, use or control (usually by his own client or his client's opponent) of 'criminal property', he must immediately notify NCIS of his belief if he was to avoid being guilty of the criminal offence of being concerned in an arrangement which he knew or suspected facilitated such activity (by whatever means). This particular appeal focused on the applicability or otherwise of s 328 in a case where information

---

7   [2001] EWCA Civ 52, [2001] 1 WLR 754.

comes to the attention of the lawyer for one of the parties in the course of legal proceedings and leads him to know or, more likely, suspect that the other party has engaged in money laundering

21.20 The central issue on this appeal was whether s 328 applied to the ordinary conduct of legal proceedings or any aspect of such conduct – including, in particular, any step taken to pursue proceedings and the obtaining of a judgment. A question not directly raised by the facts of the appeal, but which his Lordship thought it would not be sensible to ignore, was whether the section applied to any consensual steps taken or settlement reached during legal proceedings.

The fact that s 328 (unlike article 7) applied to any person gave rise to the argument that s 328 applied to lawyers conducting legal proceedings. But there was a general problem about this argument which existed as much under the directives as under the more expanded domestic law.

21.21 After an exhaustive examination of the issues, his Lordship on behalf of the Court concluded that the proper interpretation of s 328 was that it was not intended to cover or affect the ordinary conduct of litigation by legal professionals. That included any step taken by them in litigation from the issue of proceedings and the securing of injunctive relief or a freezing order up to its final disposal by judgment. The Court did not consider that either the European or the United Kingdom legislator could have envisaged that any of these ordinary activities could fall within the concept of 'becoming concerned in an arrangement which ... facilitates the acquisition, retention, use or control of criminal property'.

Summarising the position, Brooke LJ said that legal proceedings were a state-provided mechanism for the resolution of issues according to law. Everyone had the right to a fair and public trial in the determination of his civil rights and duties which is secured by article 6 of the European Convention on Human Rights. Parliament could have intended that proceedings or steps taken by lawyers in order to determine or secure legal rights and remedies for their clients should involve them in 'becoming concerned in an arrangement which ... facilitates the acquisition, retention, use or control of criminal property', even if they suspected that the outcome of such proceedings might have such an effect.

21.22 Brooke LJ went on to consider what the position would be if the court were wrong in its conclusion on the central issue. The question would remain whether on its true construction s 328 had the effect of overriding legal professional privilege and the terms on which lawyers were permitted to have access to documents disclosed in the litigation process. He therefore proceeded to apply to the interpretation of s 328 certain principles that were used to interpret English Acts of Parliament when there was not a European perspective. He observed that there was nothing in the language of s 328 to suggest that Parliament expressly intended to override legal professional privilege.

After further consideration, his Lordship said that the Court was of the firm opinion that it would require much clearer language than is contained in s 328 and its ancillary sections before a Parliamentary intention could be gleaned to the effect that a party's solicitor is obliged, in breach of this implied duty to the court, and in breach of the duty of confidence he owes to his own client as his litigation solicitor, to disclose to NCIS a suspicion he may have that documents disclosed under compulsion by the other party evidence one of the matters referred to in s 328. It followed that on this narrower issue the court was satisfied that even if, contrary to its primary view, s 328 was to be interpreted as including legal proceedings within its purview, it could not be interpreted as meaning either that legal professional privilege was to be overridden or that a lawyer was to breach his duty to the court by disclosing to a third party external to the litigation documents revealed to him through the disclosure processes.

DISTRIBUTION OF 'TAINTED' FUNDS

21.23 The issue of whether or not funds tainted by criminal activities of which the applicant spouse was aware and which are subject to possible confiscation may be distributed in ancillary relief proceedings was considered in *Customs and Excise Commissioners v A and another; A v A*,[8] and *CPS v Richards and Richards.*[9] The general rule was established that such assets should not ordinarily, as a matter of justice and public policy, be distributed in ancillary relief proceedings. That was not to say that the court is deprived of jurisdiction under the Matrimonial Causes Act 1973 nor that that are no circumstances in which such an order could be justified.

---

8   [2002] EWCA Civ 1039.
9   [2006] EWCA Civ 849.

Chapter 22

FUTURE DEVELOPMENTS

INTRODUCTION

22.1 Family law is likely to change in significant respects throughout the next few years, and the purpose of this chapter is to alert the reader to the probable shape of things to come. Most of the changes to be discussed have been anticipated to some extent in the preceding chapters, but there are others which are still somewhat speculative.

REFORM OF MCA 1973, SECTION 25

22.2 During the parliamentary passage of the FLA 1996, the then Lord Chancellor announced his intention of considering whether anything could be learned from the Scottish system of ancillary relief with a view to improving the system in England and Wales. This statement aroused little attention, but it became clear that these ideas were being pursued when the then parliamentary secretary in the Lord Chancellor's Department, Mr Geoffrey Hoon, announced, at the annual conference of the Solicitors Family Law Association in 1998 that the Government was giving favourable consideration to adopting the Scottish concept of a presumption of equal sharing of matrimonial property (as defined in the Family Law (Scotland) Act 1985), and making pre-nuptial contracts enforceable, subject to various safeguards. This gave rise to some debate, although the only formal consultation which the Government carried out was to invite the Lord Chancellor's Advisory Group on Ancillary Relief to comment. In the event, the Advisory Group advised against amendment of s 25 in this way, and no more came of the proposal. It is impossible to say that it will never be revisited.

The decisions of the House of Lords in *White v White* and *Miller/McFarlane* (as to which see Chapter 1, paras **1.51** et seq) do not seem to have stopped the calls for a more predictable and formulaic approach. No doubt conscious of this continuing debate, in *Charman v Charman*[1] the Court of Appeal added a postscript entitled 'Changing the Law'. At the end of a lengthy review of the history, the Court identified the new problems which have arisen as follows:

---

[1]   [2007] EWCA Civ 503 at para [106] et seq.

'[116] However a social change that was not perhaps recognised in that decision was the extent to which the origins and the volume of big money cases were shifting. Most of the big money cases pre *White* involved fortunes created by previous generations. The removal of exchange control restrictions in 1979, a policy that offered a favourable tax regime to very rich foreigners domiciled elsewhere, and a new financial era dominated by hedge-funds, private equity funds, derivative traders and sophisticated off-shore structures meant that very large fortunes were being made very quickly. These socio-economic developments coincided with a retreat from the preference of English judges for moderation. The present case well illustrates that shift. At trial Mr Pointer achieved for his client an award of £48 million. Before us he freely conceded that he could not have justified an award of more than £20 million on the application of the reasonable requirements principle. Thus, in very big money cases, the effect of the decision in *White* was to raise the aspirations of the claimant hugely. In big money cases the *White* factor has more than doubled the levels of award and it has been said by many that London has become the divorce capital of the world for aspiring wives. Whether this is a desirable result needs to be considered not only in the context of our society but also in the context of the European Union of which we are a singular Member State, in the sense that we are a common law jurisdiction amongst largely Civilian fellows and that in the determination of issues ancillary to divorce we apply the lex fori and decline to apply the law more applicable to the parties.

[117] In the case of *Cowan* the need for legislative review in the aftermath of the case of *White* was articulated: see paragraphs 32, 41 and 58. Undoubtedly the decision in *White* did not resolve the problems faced by practitioners in advising clients or by clients in deciding upon what terms to compromise.

[118] However this court adopted a cautious approach both in *Cowan* and in the later case of *Lambert*. In his submission Mr Singleton drew attention to an article by Joanna Miles in International Journal of Law, Policy and the Family 19 (2005) 242. He told us that he had incorporated the article in his argument for Mrs McFarlane in the House of Lords. The article criticises the earlier decision of this court in the conjoined appeals of *McFarlane* and *Parlour* [2005] Fam 171 for having declined the opportunity to identify principles underpinning the exercise of judicial discretion under the Act of 1973. The article is particularly interesting in that it demonstrates that the principles discussed in the article (needs, entitlement and compensation), were subsequently the principles identified by the House of Lords in deciding the conjoined appeals of *Miller* and *McFarlane*.'

Later, in relation to the European aspects, the Court had this to say:

'[124] Any harmonisation within the European region is particularly difficult, given that the Regulation Brussels I is restricted to claims for maintenance and the Regulation Brussels II Revised expressly excludes from its application the property consequence of divorce. In the European context this makes sense because in Civilian systems the property consequences of divorce are dealt with by marital property regimes. Almost uniquely our jurisdiction does not have a marital property regime and it is scarcely appropriate to classify our jurisdiction as having a marital regime of separation of property. More correctly we have no regime, simply accepting that each spouse owns his or her own separate property during the marriage but subject to the court's wide distributive powers in prospect upon a decree of judicial separation, nullity or divorce. The difficulty of harmonising our law concerning the property consequences of marriage and divorce and the law of the Civilian Member States is exacerbated by the fact that our law has so far given little status to pre-nuptial contracts. If, unlike the rest of Europe, the property consequences of divorce are to be regulated by the principles of needs, compensation and sharing, should not the parties to the marriage, or the projected marriage, have at the least the opportunity to order their own affairs otherwise by a nuptial contract? The White Paper, "Supporting Families", not only proposed specific reforms of section 25 but also to give statutory force to nuptial contracts. The government's subsequent abdication has not been accepted by specialist practitioners. In 2005 Resolution published a well argued report urging the government to give statutory force to nuptial contracts. The report was subsequently fully supported by the Money and Property Sub-Committee of the Family Justice Council.'

The Court recommended research by the Law Commission, and particularly stressed the need to reform the law to include the enforceability of pre-nuptial contracts.[2]

However, it seems doubtful that Parliament would want to embark on the time-consuming and unpredictable task of family law reform and it is a safe prediction that there will be no legislative changes until at least after the next general election.

There may also be a ECHR dimension to this issue which is discussed further in Chapter 20.

ENFORCEMENT

22.3 The Advisory Group has also made quite wide-ranging proposals for the reform of the procedure relating to enforcement of family financial orders, which were approved by public consultation. In previous editions of this book it was stated that it was thought that implementation of the recommendations was imminent. However, hopes were dashed and, for some time it seemed that this statement was hopelessly optimistic. However, it now seems that when the rules of court are changed and harmonised (see para **22.4**) the recommendations of the Working Party may well be included. Perhaps, therefore, a degree of cautious optimism may be in order.

HARMONISATION OF RULES OF COURT

22.4 For some time work has been proceeding on the harmonisation of the Family Proceedings Rules with the Civil Procedure Rules (and the consequent

---

2   Though it has to be said that this would not have achieved very much in *Charman*. When the parties married they had no money and would, no doubt, have agreed equal sharing at that stage.

final abolition of the RSC and CCR which are at present incorporated in the FPR.) There have been several false dawns and it may be tempting fate to be too confident, but it can be said that the intention of government is now that the new harmonised rules will be brought into effect in the autumn of 2008.

Chapter 23

A SUMMING UP

INTRODUCTION

23.1 Throughout this book, a number of recurring themes have appeared. One of the problems of writing any book of this kind is that the separate chapters on individual topics may appear to the reader to be self-contained, whereas the lessons to be learned from many of them apply across the board and should be borne in mind generally. Nevertheless, it would be irksome for the reader if the same messages were driven home in every chapter.

For these reasons, it has been thought appropriate to include in this final chapter the principal matters which anyone involved in an ancillary relief application should have in mind. First, the generally accepted principles on which the courts decide these matters will be outlined, with accompanying references as to where a longer exposition may be found. Then, some of the practical lessons for the conduct of an application will be considered.

THE PRIMACY OF THE STATUTE

23.2 Applications for ancillary relief are governed by s 25 of MCA 1973, which is a self-contained code which directs the court's attention to certain specified factors. Decided cases are of some assistance, but they can never replace the words of the statute.

23.3 Subject to the 'first consideration' of the welfare of the minor children, no single factor within s 25 is intrinsically more important than the others. All of them must be considered. In most cases, the facts of the case will mean that there is a 'gravitational pull' towards one or more factors which assume particular significance, but this does not mean that all the factors should not be borne in mind.

THE IMPORTANCE OF FINDING THE FACTS

23.4 Notwithstanding what was said above, no case can proceed without accurate findings under s 25(2)(a). Until the income and capital of each of the parties is ascertained, the court cannot begin to consider whether the assets should be redistributed in accordance with any of the other factors. When determining the facts, the usual rules of evidence apply. The fact that a hearing is in chambers and may seem relatively informal should not deceive a practitioner or litigant into thinking that the court will make findings of fact on less than the normal civil standard of proof.

23.5 The court will be concerned, where this is relevant, to decide what is and is not 'matrimonial property', ie property acquired during the marriage (or any relevant period of pre-marital cohabitation) which is neither property inherited by either of the parties nor property which they owned well before the marriage or relevant period of cohabitation. However, it must be emphasised that this does not mean that such property is then excluded from the calculations. Generally speaking, the longer the marriage the less inclined a court will be to hive off any particular asset. Moreover, in cases where assets are not sufficient to meet the needs of both parties and one party has a greater need than the other, it is unlikely that this aspect of the matter will be decisive.

NO MATHEMATICAL STARTING POINT

23.6 There is no 'one-third rule' nor any other fractional starting point. When a judge has decided how the assets of the parties should be divided (if at all) in accordance with the s 25 factors, he may cross-check his proposals by considering the proportions of the joint assets which each party would have, but there is no absolute proportion with which either party must be left. The yardstick of equality (see below) is a useful cross-check at the end of the calculation to ensure fairness. However, having said that, it is a reasonable inference from the judgment of the Court of Appeal in *Charman v Charman*[1] that the concept of 'sharing' derived from *Miller v Miller* implies equal sharing and that this is now considerably more of a starting point than once it was.

REASONABLE NEEDS AND ABILITY TO PROVIDE

23.7 The reasonable needs as to capital and income of both parties must be considered. These will vary in every case, but will depend on the age and health of the parties in the light of the history of the marriage, and the responsibilities which they both have, particularly to children of the family. How far these needs can be met will depend on the means available.

THE IMPORTANCE OF HOUSING

23.8 The most important requirement for most people is to be housed, and the primary task of the court in average income and capital cases should be to ensure that both are housed. Where there are dependent children, the housing

---

[1] [2007] EWCA Civ 503, [2007] All ER (D) 425 (May) at [65]. See also the discussion in Chapter 1 paras **1.51** et seq.

of the parent with the care of the children must come first, even if this means that the other party is not rehoused as he would wish. However, rehousing of a parent with children does not mean that that parent must live in the former matrimonial home. The housing of the other parent is an important priority also, and where a parent and children can be adequately rehoused in cheaper accommodation with a proportion of the proceeds of sale, to enable the other parent to be rehoused, this should be done.

NO REDISTRIBUTION FOR ITS OWN SAKE

23.9 When either or both parties have capital, there is no presumption that it must be redistributed. Redistribution is only appropriate if required to do justice between the parties in the light of the s 25 factors. However, this must be balanced against what is said in the next paragraph.

THE YARDSTICK OF EQUALITY

23.10 When the court has performed its statutory functions of investigating all the s 25 factors, it must first arrive at a provisional and tentative view as to what is required before comparing that provisional view with what the result would be on the basis of equal division. If the provisional view does not approximate to equal division, the court must be able to articulate and express reasons, based on the s 25 criteria, as to why it should not do so. Where there are no such reasons, equality should prevail.

SELF-SUFFICIENCY

23.11 The court must have regard to the possibility of self-sufficiency and a clean break in every case. Nevertheless, a clean break should not be imposed where the evidence does not suggest that self-sufficiency will be achieved.

PENSIONS NOT A SEPARATE REGIME

23.12 The only reason for making the following point is the recent date of the legislative changes. Pensions are not a separate form of assets which must be re-allocated according to some discrete code. The extent to which the court will consider pensions relevant, and make orders in respect of them, will depend entirely on the application of the s 25 factors.

SOME PRACTICAL HINTS ON PREPARING A CASE

23.13 Practitioners acting for a party to ancillary relief proceedings should bear in mind all that has been said above. The following practical questions emerge and should be asked in every case.

(a) What are the assets and incomes of both parties?

(b) What are the needs of the parties? In particular:
   (i) Where will the parent with care of a child (if any) live?
   (ii) Where will the other party live?

(c) What are the income needs of the parties, in particular your client? Be realistic; do not merely compile a wish-list. What will it cost him or her to live?

(d) How can these needs be met? Can your client support himself or herself? Are there other sources of funds?

(e) What is the position as to pensions?

(f) Can there be a clean break?

(g) Having considered all the s 25 factors, is there some particular factor which is relevant to this case?

(h) Finally, what would be the position if there were equal division? Is there some s 25 factor which makes equal division unjust?

APPENDICES

Appendix A

PRECEDENTS

1 Example of request for documents

[*Heading*]

Request for documents

1. Please provide accounts for the XYZ Co Ltd for the last three accounting years and any six-monthly draft accounts in respect of the period since the last prepared accounts.

2. Please supply copy bank statements in respect of every account in the Respondent's name or in respect of which the Respondent is a Signatory, whether solely or jointly with any other person, for the past 12 months and identify all credits and all debits over £250.

3. In respect of expenses on company business please supply copies of I.T. Form P 11D for the past two years.

4. The Respondent alleges in paragraph _____ of Form E that he owes [*name*] the sum of £_____. Please supply any memorandum of this debt and give full details of when it was incurred, for what purpose, whether any sums have been repaid and the Respondent's intentions as to repayment.

5. In connection with the Respondent's purchase of the property [*address*] please state the source of the deposit and legal fees and provide a copy of the application for a mortgage from the ABC Building Society.

6. Please disclose the Respondent's passport(s) since 2000.

7. Please state the cost of the Respondent's holiday in Bermuda in September 1997, state where the money came from and provide any documentation in existence with regard to it. Identify any payments in respect of that holiday in bank accounts or credit card accounts. In the absence of any such identifications state why none such exist.

8. In 1994 the Respondent's loan account with the XYZ Co Ltd stood at £10,741. Explain the source of this and account for any fluctuations since.

9. Please disclose all correspondence and any other relevant documentation with respect to the investigation by the Inland Revenue of the XYZ Co Ltd in 2001.

10. What connection has the Respondent with the DEF Finance Co with offices at [*address*]?

11. Please state the means of the Co-respondent [*or name of other person with whom Respondent is living*], his/her income and capital and assets.

2   Order for inspection appointment pursuant to FPR 1991, rule 2.62(7)

[*Heading*]

Upon hearing Counsel/the solicitor for the Applicant and Counsel/solicitor for the Respondent.

It is ordered that the Applicant/Respondent [*or* Miss G. H.] do attend the District Judge in chambers at [*address of court*] on [*day*], [*date*] at [*time*] and produce for inspection the documents specified or described in the schedule hereto.

And it is further ordered that the costs of this application be [as the court thinks fit].

THE SCHEDULE

[*set out the documents to be produced*]

3   Search order – discovery by order permitting entry of premises and search for documents

[*Heading*]

Upon hearing counsel for the Applicant on an *ex parte* application and upon reading the affidavit of _____ sworn the _____ day of [*month and year*].

And the Applicant by her counsel undertaking:

(1)   to serve this order together with a copy of the affidavit of [*the affidavit referred to above*] by a solicitor of the Supreme Court;

(2)   to abide by any order this court may make as to damages in case this court shall hereafter be of opinion that the Respondent shall have suffered any by reason of this order which the petitioner ought to pay;

(3)   to notify the Respondent or the person on whom this order is served by the solicitor of the Supreme Court who serves this order upon them that they may seek legal advice and to explain fairly and in everyday language the meaning or effect thereof;

(4)   [*any necessary undertaking to issue proceedings, eg to issue a summons to set aside an order allegedly obtained by deception or non-disclosure or the like*].

And the solicitors for the Applicant by counsel for the Applicant being their counsel for this purpose undertaking that all documents obtained as a result of this order will be retained in their safe custody until further order.

It is ordered that the Respondent or such person as shall appear to be in charge of the premises at [*address*] do forthwith permit the person who shall serve this order upon him, together with such persons not exceeding two as may be duly authorised by the Applicant, to enter the premises at [*address*] at any hour between 8 o'clock in the forenoon and 8 o'clock in the evening for the purpose of:

(a)   looking for and inspecting any of the following:

(i)   all documents relating to the Respondent's earnings, income and capital from [*date*] to date;

(ii)   all documents relating to the sale by the Respondent and the proceeds of sale of shares in any company and of any capital asset including [*description of asset*];

(iii)   all bank statements and building society passbooks and documents related thereto including pass books, cheque stubs, paid cheques and paying-in books;

(iv)   all documents relating to the purchase by the Respondent of [*description of asset allegedly purchased*] including documents relating to provision of the purchase price;

(b)   taking into the Applicant's solicitors' custody all and any of the above-mentioned documents and of making copies of the same and it is ordered that the respondent and/or the person or person appearing for the time being to be in charge of the premises aforesaid do produce forthwith to the person serving this order all of the documents referred to in the above orders.

Liberty to apply.

4 Ex parte order permitting entry to premises and search for assets and documents

[*Heading*]

[*Undertakings by Applicant by counsel as in Precedent 3*]

And the solicitors for the Applicant by counsel for the Applicant being their counsel for this purpose undertaking that all property and documents inspected or obtained as a result of this order will be retained in their safe custody, save only that any precious metals, jewels or jewellery, watches [*add other specific items or classes of items that the search relates to*] may be released into the custody of [*name*] a jeweller for the purpose of valuing the same on the premises to which this order relates.

It is ordered that the Respondent do forthwith permit the person who shall serve this order upon him, together with such other persons not exceeding two in number as may be duly authorised by the Applicant, to enter the premises at [*address*] at any hour between 8 o'clock in the forenoon and 8 o'clock in the evening for the purpose of:

(a)   looking for and inspecting any of the following: (i) all jewels, semi-precious stones, amber, agate or similar, precious metals and alloys thereof, jewellery and similar valuable items, watches [*continue with specific items or classes of items to be searched for*]; (ii) all money; (iii) all documents relating to [*define according to circumstances*];

(b)   taking into the Applicant's solicitors' custody all and any of the above-mentioned documents and of making copies of the same and thereafter returning the originals to the Respondent's solicitors.

And it is further ordered that the Respondent do produce forthwith to the person serving this order all of the property and documents referred to herein and do open for inspection by the person serving this order any safe, cupboard, cabinet drawer and/or room at the said premises that is or appears to be locked.

Liberty to apply, costs reserved.

Dated the _____ day of [*month and year*].

GENERAL NOTE

Based on the order in *Kepa v Kepa* (1983) FLR 515.

5 Maintenance pending suit order

[*Heading*]

It is ordered that the Respondent do pay or cause to be paid to the Applicant as from the _____ day of [*month and year*] maintenance pending suit at the rate of £100 per week payable weekly.

Dated the _____ day of [*month and year*].

GENERAL NOTE

Commencement date of order. This will usually be the date of the filing of the petition (it cannot be earlier). See MCA 1973, s 22.

Termination of order. The order will cease when the suit ceases to be pending, i e when a decree of judicial separation is made; when a decree nisi of divorce or nullity is made absolute or when the petition is dismissed.

Variation. The order is variable under MCA 1973, s 31; the words 'until further order' are customarily not inserted as it is most often the case that the order is intended to subsist for only a short time.

Order combined with periodical payments. Where, at the hearing of the application for maintenance pending suit, the court has jurisdiction to make an order for periodical payments, i e after decree nisi but before decree absolute, then, provided application has been duly made, the District Judge may make an order for maintenance pending suit and also for periodical payments (or interim periodical payments) to run from the date when the decree nisi is made absolute. The court can only consider periodical payments after a decree nisi has been pronounced and accordingly such a combined order can only be asked for where the hearing is after decree nisi and before decree absolute.

5A Order for maintenance pending suit to include a costs element

It is ordered that the Respondent do pay or cause to be paid to the Applicant as from the _____ day of [*month and year*] maintenance pending suit at the rate of £3,000 per month payable monthly, such sum to include a legal expenses component of £50,000 payable at the rate of £2,000 per month, upon the applicant undertaking to pay such legal expenses to her solicitors to be credited against any costs order which she may ultimately recover against the respondent.

6 Order for maintenance payments to be paid by standing order

And it is further ordered:

(1)   That the said Maintenance pending suit/Periodical payments be paid by means of standing order to the Applicant's account at ABC Bank Plc, _____ Branch, account number 12345.

(2)   That the Respondent forthwith give to his Bankers authority for payments of £ _____ per week/month to be made from his account to the Applicant's account no 12345 with ABC Bank Plc, _____ branch, on the _____ day of each month until further order of this court without the need for any further authority by the Respondent.

(3)   That the application for an order pursuant to section 1(5) of the Maintenance Enforcement Act 1991 be adjourned for 21 days to enable the Respondent to open a bank account.

(4)   The court being satisfied that the Respondent has failed without reasonable excuse to open an account out of which payments under this order may be made, that the Respondent do within 7 days from the date of this order [*or* from the order of service of this order] open such an account.

GENERAL NOTE

See para **19.14**.

7   Periodical payments order for spouse

[*Heading*]

It is ordered that the above-named Respondent do make or cause to be made to the above-named Applicant as from the _____ day of [*month and year*] periodical payments for herself during their joint lives until [the _____ day of [*month and year*] or such earlier date as] he/she shall remarry or further order at the rate of £5,500 per annum payable monthly.

[And it is further ordered that the Applicant shall not be entitled to apply under section 31 of the Matrimonial Causes Act 1973 for an extension of the term specified above.]

Dated the _____ day of [*month and year*].

8   Order directing cessation of order made in magistrates' court

[*Heading*]

It is ordered, pursuant to section 28(1) of the Domestic Proceedings and Magistrates' Courts Act 1978, that the order of the _____ Magistrates dated the _____ day of [*month and year*] [insofar as the same relates to periodical payments for the Applicant *and/or* the child (*name in full*)] do cease to have effect from the _____ day of [*month and year*].

GENERAL NOTE

The county court and the High Court may order that a magistrates' court order made under Part 1 of the 1978 Act do cease to have effect (excluding an order for a lump sum under s 2 thereof). A county court or High Court order may implicitly supersede or revoke a magistrates' court order without specifically directing that it ceases to have effect.

9   Secured periodical payments order

[*Heading*]

It is ordered that the above-named Respondent do secure to the above-named Applicant for her life until [the _____ day of [*month and year*] or such earlier date as] she shall remarry or further order as from the _____ day of [*month and year*] the annual sum of £5,000 upon [*here state the nature of the securities or if they are not agreed or fixed at the time of making the order use the words* 'security to be agreed or referred to a District Judge in default of agreement'] and that in default of agreement as to the form of deed between the parties it be referred to conveyancing counsel of the High Court to settle the necessary deed or deeds.

[And it is further ordered that the Applicant shall not be entitled to apply under section 31 of the Matrimonial Causes Act 1973 for an extension of the term specified above.]

Dated the _____ day of [*month and year*].

10   Periodical payments order to child

[*Heading*]

It is ordered that the above-named Respondent do make to [*name of child in full*] as from the _____ day of [*month and year*] periodical payments until he/she shall attain the age of 17 years or further order at the rate of £25 per week payable weekly.

Dated the _____ day of [*month and year*].

GENERAL NOTE

Note the limitation on the power of the court, see para **11.3**.

11   Order to parent or other person for child

[*Heading*]

It is ordered that the above-named Respondent do make to [*name of payee*] as from the _____ day of [*month and year*] periodical payments for the child [*name in full*] until he/she shall attain the age of 17 years or further order at the rate of £25 per week payable weekly.

Dated the _____ day of [*month and year*].

12   Order to include payment of school fees

[*Heading*]

It is ordered that the Respondent do pay or cause to be paid [to the child (*name in full*)] or [to the Applicant for the child (*name in full*)] as from the _____ day of [*month and year*] [until he/she shall attain the age of 17 years] *and/or* [he/she shall cease to receive full time education] [whichever is the later/earlier] or until further order periodical payments [for himself/herself]:

(a) of an amount equivalent to the school fees (but not the extras in the school bill) *or* (including (*specified extra*)) at the school the said child attends for each financial year (by way of three payments on _____ and _____ and _____) (payable monthly); together with

(b) the sum of £ _____ per annum payable monthly in respect of the general maintenance of the said child.

And it is further ordered that payment of the school fees to the [Headmaster *or* Bursar *or* School Secretary] shall be a sufficient discharge of the Respondent's liability to pay to the Applicant for the said child the said school fees.

13 Lump sum orders

[Heading]

A. For Spouse or Former Spouse

It is ordered that the Respondent do, within 28 days from the date of this order, pay to the Applicant a lump sum of £25,000.

or

It is ordered that the Respondent do pay to the Applicant a lump sum of £25,000 by instalments as follows: £5,000 within 14 days from the date of this order; a further £10,000 on December 1, 2000 and the balance of £10,000 on March 1, 2001 and that the said instalments of £10,000 do carry interest at _____ per cent as from the date of this order until the dates when they are respectively due to be paid.

And it is further ordered that the said instalments of £10,000 be secured by a charge to be effected on the property [*address*].

or

It is ordered that the Respondent do pay to the Applicant within 12 months from today a lump sum of £50,000 and that the lump sum shall carry interest at the rate of _____ per cent as [from the date three months] from today until the date 12 months from today when the said sum is due to be paid.

or

(*where the payee is a funded person and the Court has ordered that the lump sum is to be used for the purpose of purchasing a home for himself or his dependants.*)

It is ordered that the Respondent do, within 28 days from the date of this order, pay to the Applicant a lump sum of £75,000.

And it is certified for the purposes of regulation 21 of the Community Legal Service (Costs) Regulations 2000 that the lump sum of £75,000 has been ordered to be paid to enable the Applicant to provide a home for herself (and her dependants).

B. For or To Child

It is ordered that the Respondent do within 28 days from the date of this order [pay to the Applicant for the benefit of the child of the family (*name of child in full*) a lump sum of £5,000] *or* [pay to the child of the family (*name of child in full*) a lump sum of £5,000] [*insert details as to instalments, security and interest, if appropriate, as in A. above*].

C. For Spouse or Child under MCA 1973, s 23(3) – Urgent Application

It is ordered pursuant to section 23(3) of the Matrimonial Causes Act 1973 that the above-named Respondent do pay, within (*specified time*) from today, [to the Applicant] *or* [to the Applicant for the benefit of the child (*name in full*)] *or* [to the child (*name in full*)] the sum of £1,250 for the purpose of enabling [the Applicant]/[the said child] to meet liabilities (and/or expenses) reasonably incurred in maintaining [herself]/[the said child].

Dated the _____ day of [*month and year*].

GENERAL NOTE

An order under MCA 1973, s 23(3) may be made before applying for a lump sum order under s 23(1)(c) or (f). It is essentially a provision to enable a payment to be ordered to cover liabilities which cannot otherwise be met where such provision is urgently required. See para **4.60**.

Lump sum for legally assisted person's home. The Community Legal Service (Costs) Regulations 2000, reg 21 provides for the deferment of the statutory charge, in respect of the assisted person's costs, over money recovered or over property recovered or preserved by order of the court or by agreement, if by the order or agreement the money recovered or the property is to be used to purchase a home for the assisted person or his dependants.

14   Order to transfer property to assisted person with direction that it be used as a home for funded person or his dependants

It is ordered that the Respondent do, within 28 days from today, transfer to the Applicant the property known as and situate at [*address*]; [*add any conditions such as* 'subject to the existing mortgage with the XYZ Building Society; the Applicant undertaking to indemnify the Respondent for any liability thereunder'].

And it is certified for the purposes of the Community Legal Service (Costs) Regulations 2000 that the property [*address*] has been preserved/recovered for the Applicant for use as a home for herself (and her dependants).

GENERAL NOTE

See General Note to Precedent 13.

15   *Mesher* order – house in joint names – party to be allowed to live there until child attains a certain age

[*Heading*]

It is ordered that the property [*address*] be held upon trust to hold the net proceeds of sale and rents and profits until sale in equal shares, provided that as long as the child [*name in full*] be under the age of 17 years or until further order the house be not sold; the Applicant to be at liberty to live there rent-free paying and discharging all rates, taxes and outgoings, including mortgage interest and indemnifying the Respondent therefor; and repayments of capital to be borne in equal shares.

Dated the _____ day of [*month and year*].

GENERAL NOTE

This precedent is based upon that in *Mesher v Mesher and Hall* [1980] 1 All ER 126, CA. The case was decided in 1973. The words 'or until further order' have been inserted as they or the words 'liberty to apply' or other words of more particular intent allow for a prior application for the sale of the property if circumstances so justify although not permitting an application to postpone sale after the term specified in the order. In such respect, the order is not variable.

The reference to 'trust for sale' has been omitted, see para **5.11**.

16 A more elaborate form of *Mesher*-type order

[*Heading*]

It is ordered that the trust [for sale] upon which the Parties presently hold the property [*address*] be varied forthwith to provide that the Applicant and the Respondent do hold the said property [*or* It is ordered that the Respondent do transfer into the joint names of the Applicant and Respondent the property [*address*] to hold the same] upon trust as tenants in common in equal shares upon the statutory trusts for sale declared by the Law of Property Act 1925 and upon the following terms and conditions:

(a) the property not to be sold without the prior written consent of both Parties or without the leave of the court until either (i) the child of the family [*name in full*] reaches the age of 18 years or completes her full-time education, whichever shall later occur; or (ii) the remarriage of the Applicant, whichever shall first occur;

(b) the Applicant to be solely responsible for payment of all interest due under a subsisting mortgage upon the said property in favour of the ABC Building Society and to be responsible for half of the instalments of capital repayments due under the said mortgage;

(c) the Respondent to be responsible for one half of the instalments of capital repayments due under the said mortgage;

(d) the Parties to be equally liable and responsible for insuring the said property and for structural repairs upon the said property; in the event of any dispute in relation thereto, such dispute to be referred to arbitration by a surveyor/valuer appointed by agreement between the Parties' solicitors and in default of agreement as to the surveyor/valuer to be appointed by the President of the Royal Institution of Chartered Surveyors;

(e) the Applicant to be responsible for all decorative repairs to the said property;

(f) the Applicant to have exclusive possession of the said property until sale;

(g)   in the event of the Applicant wishing to move to another property prior
       to the aforesaid property being sold in pursuance of the foregoing terms
       and conditions, she be at liberty to sell and re-invest the proceeds of sale
       in another property, subject to clause (a) above (the consent of the
       Respondent not to be withheld unreasonably), which said property to be
       held upon the same trusts and the same terms and conditions and any
       surplus arising on the acquisition thereof to be divided equally between
       the parties;
(h)   the Applicant to have the right, at the end of the period in which she has
       exclusive possessions under the terms of this order, to purchase the
       Respondent's interest at a valuation to be agreed or, in default of
       agreement, to be determined by a valuer nominated by the President of
       the Royal Institution of Chartered Surveyors.

Liberty to apply as to implementation of this order.

Dated the _____ day of [*month and year*].

GENERAL NOTE

See also Precedent 22 where the post-nuptial settlement created by the purchase of the matrimonial
home in joint names (both having contributed) is varied to provide that the trust continues subject
to terms set out in the order.

See also Precedent 13 and General Note to Precedent 13 for appropriate wording where property
transferred to a funded applicant, or preserved for him, is to be used to house him and his
dependants with the property being charged in favour of the Legal Services Commission in respect
of his costs.

17   *Mesher*-type order with provisions for extended right of occupation and for occupant to pay rent from a specified date

[*Heading*]

It is ordered:

(1)   that the property [*address*] be transferred by the Respondent into the joint
       names of the Applicant and Respondent on trust;
(2)   that upon sale the net proceeds of sale be divided in the proportion of
       two-thirds to the Applicant and one-third to the Respondent;
(3)   that such sale be postponed in any event until the youngest child of the
       family shall attain the age of 18 years or completes his full-time education
       whichever shall be the later;
(4)   that thereafter the said sale shall continue to be postponed during the
       lifetime of the Applicant or until she consents to such sale: provided that
       if she has remarried before the date referred to in clause (3) hereof, or
       remarries or cohabits with another man, thereafter the said property shall
       be sold forthwith and the proceeds of sale divided in accordance with the
       terms of clause (2) hereof;
(5)   that the Applicant be responsible, subject to the provisions of this clause,
       for all outgoings including mortgage repayments until the sale of the
       property from the date of this order, and to pay to the Respondent from
       the date referred to in clause (3) hereof, such sum by way of occupation

rent of the premises as may be agreed, or in default, determined by the District Judge of the _____ County Court in respect of his interest in the said property; the said occupation rent shall be one-third of such sum as represents a fair rent.

GENERAL NOTE

Based on the order in *Harvey v Harvey* [1982] 2 WLR 283, [1982] 1 All ER 693, CA. The terms of this order permit the Applicant to continue to live in the property for as long as it is reasonable for her to do so.

18 Order for transfer of property to applicant and charge imposed in favour of respondent in a fixed sum

[Heading]

It is ordered that the Respondent do transfer to the Applicant all his interest both legal and beneficial in the property *[address]* within *[specified time]* from today and that as from the date of transfer as aforesaid the said property do stand charged in favour of the Respondent for the sum of £ _____; such charge not to be enforced until (a) the death of the Applicant; (b) the sale of the property; or (c) the date when the youngest child of the family attains the age of _____ years whichever is the soonest.

Dated the _____ day of *[month and year]*.

GENERAL NOTE

Based on the order in *Hector v Hector* [1973] 1 WLR 1122, [1973] 3 All ER 1070, CA. The order would be improved by the addition of a further qualification to the period of prohibition for enforcement of the charge to allow an earlier enforcement if circumstances warranted, eg 'such charge not to be enforced without leave of the court until (a) . . . (etc)'.

In *McDonnell v McDonnell* [1976] 1 WLR 34, the Court of Appeal held that an order giving a spouse a proportion of the value of the matrimonial home was to be preferred to a charge for a fixed amount. A charge for a fixed sum may be appropriate if the period for which it will be deferred is known to be short.

19 Alternative order for transfer of property to applicant and charge imposed in favour of respondent in a proportion

It is ordered that the Respondent do transfer to the Applicant all his interest both legal and beneficial in the property *[address]* within [eg 28 days] on condition that the Applicant deliver in return a charge over the said property executed by her for [eg 25%] of the gross/net proceeds of sale of the said property such charge to be in a form to be agreed between the solicitors for the Applicant and Respondent and in default to be settled by the District Judge and to be enforceable only on the first of the following events, namely:

[adapt a Mesher *or* Martin *order as the circumstances require]*.

20 Suggested form of charge

HM Land Registry

Land Registration Acts 1925–1986

COUNTY AND DISTRICT

TITLE NUMBER

PROPERTY

DATE

In pursuance of an order of District Judge in the Divorce Registry/ _____
_____ County Court dated _____ in proceedings between the Mortgagor and
[*name of the husband*] bearing Number of Matter _____:

1. AB of [*address*] (hereinafter called 'the Mortgagor') hereby covenant with
BB of [*address*] (hereinafter called 'the husband') to pay to the husband on the
occurrence of the first of the events below mentioned [*or* on the _____ day of
[*month and year*] (hereinafter called 'the specified dates') the secured amount as
hereinafter defined:

(i)   The remarriage of the Mortgagor
(ii)   The death of the Mortgagor
(iii)   The sale of the property charged by this deed
(iv)   The child of the family [*name in full*] attaining the age of 17 years or
        ceasing full time education or training whichever be the later
(v)   The further order of the Court

[*or, as the case may be. The specified dates will of course be the 'trigger events' as
set out in the Court order*].

2. The secured amount shall be [*as ordered by the Court, eg* x *per cent of the
gross or net proceeds of sale of the property, stating which sums are to be
deducted in calculating net proceeds of sale. The charge might profitably include
the right of the Mortgagor to redeem at a time other than one of the specified
dates without sale and for the value of the property to be determined by an
independent valuer in that event, should the parties not agree as to value*].

3. The husband will not before the first to happen of the specified dates call in
the husband's share or any part thereof provided always that notwithstanding
and without prejudice to the provisions hereof the power of sale applicable to
this charge shall for the protection of a purchaser be deemed to arise on the
date hereof.

4. The Mortgagor as beneficial owner hereby charges by way of legal mortgage
the land comprised in the title above referred to (hereinafter called 'the
property') with payment to the husband of the secured amount [*add, if
appropriate*, subject to the charge dated *etc*]

5. The Mortgagor further covenants with the husband that the Mortgagor:

(a)   will duly and punctually pay the instalments in respect of the said charge
       in favour of the XYZ Building Society
(b)   will at all times keep the property insured in accordance with the
       covenant contained in the first mortgage.

[*Add any further provisions thought appropriate, eg covenants to repair, the right
to substitute the charge to a new property*.]

SIGNED AS A DEED by
AB in the presence of:

GENERAL NOTE

This form of charge is suggested as suitable in many cases, as merely to order a charge to be executed can cause further problems since the parties may not agree on the terms of the charge. Precedent 19 enables the court to specify in the order as many of the terms of the charge as seems necessary, e g the fact that it will or will not bear interest, who is to be responsible for insurance and repairs, and so on. This can make a form of order very unwieldy and it is suggested that if the form of charge is left to be agreed between the parties with liberty to apply to the District Judge to settle the form of charge or any of its terms, this may be the better solution; this should not be necessary where the order is by consent since all these matters should have been agreed beforehand.

In extreme cases, the District Judge may refer the settling of the charge to conveyancing counsel.

21 Order for sale and for possession

[And] it is [further] ordered that:

(1) The property known as [*address*] be sold.
(2) The Applicant's/Respondent's solicitors have conduct of the sale.
(3) The net proceeds of sale after deduction of all sums due to mortgagees, estate agents, charges and the proper solicitor's costs of sale be divided as to _____ per cent to the _____ and per cent _____ to the _____ [*or* £ _____ to the _____ and the balance to the _____].
(4) Liberty to apply for further directions as to the conduct of the sale.

And it is further ordered that the Applicant/Respondent do deliver possession of the said property to the Respondent/Applicant and vacate the same on the _____ day of [*month and year*].

GENERAL NOTE

Section 24A of MCA 1973 enables the court to make an order for sale on making a property adjustment order or at any time thereafter. Paragraph (3) of the order above would only be necessary when the proportions had not been stated earlier in the order.

FPR 1991, r 2.64(3) provides that RSC Ord 31, r 1 applies to applications for ancillary relief. By Ord 31, r 1, the Court may order any land to be sold 'and any party bound by the order and in possession of that land or part, or in receipt of the rents and profits thereof, may be compelled to deliver up such possession or receipt to the Purchaser or to such other person as the court may direct'. In any case where an order for sale is made, therefore, an order for possession should be considered if it is thought that one of the parties who is in possession may be reluctant to leave.

22 Order varying settlement created by purchase in joint names (both having contributed) to the effect that the trust for sale continues on terms set out – M*esher*-type provision with power to substitute property

[*Heading*]

It is ordered that the post-nuptial settlement comprised in the transfer dated _____ whereby the freehold property [*address*] registered at HM Land Registry under Title number _____ was transferred to the Applicant and the Respondent as tenants in common in equal shares be and the same is hereby varied so that the trust thereby created is and continues henceforth subject to the terms set out in the schedule to this order.

SCHEDULE

(a) In this Schedule 'the trust period' shall mean the period beginning at the date of this order and continuing so long as the Applicant shall have the care and control of the children _____ and _____ or either of them or until the death of the Applicant or until the remarriage of the Applicant or until the last survivor of the said children attains the age of 17 (whichever shall first occur) or until such other date as the Applicant and the Respondent may jointly by deed appoint.

(b) In this Schedule 'the property' shall mean the freehold property known as _____ registered at HM Land Registry under Title Number _____ and where the context admits any dwelling or flat purchased in substitution for the property pursuant to paragraph (h) hereof.

(c) The Trustees shall be the Applicant and/or such other persons as may from time to time during the trust period be appointed by the Applicant and the Respondent jointly (or in default of agreement by the Court) in addition to or in substitution for either or both of them.

(d) The Trustees shall not sell the property during the trust period so long as the Applicant resides and is entitled to reside therein without the Applicant's consent in writing.

(e) During the trust period the net income of the property shall be held upon trust for the Applicant absolutely.

(f) During the trust period the Applicant shall pay all rates and other outgoings payable in respect of the property and keep the same in good repair and condition and insured in the names of the Trustees against such risks and in such amount as the Trustees shall from time to time reasonably require.

(g) During the trust period:

(i)   the Applicant shall be entitled and the Trustees shall permit the Applicant to occupy the property or any part thereof as her residence rent-free;

(ii) so long as the Applicant occupies the property as aforesaid and herself remains a Trustee the Trustees shall at her request delegate to the Applicant (upon terms that the Applicant consents to use her best endeavours at her expense to obtain possession from any tenants prior to her ceasing to reside in the property) the powers of and incidental to leasing any parts of the property not occupied by her in respect of weekly or monthly lettings at rack rent she receiving all rents arising therefrom without being required to account for the same to the Trustees.

But save as aforesaid the Trustees shall not delegate their powers and shall not without the consent of the Applicant and the Respondent in writing create any lease of or charge mortgage or otherwise encumber the property.

(h) If during the trust period the Applicant shall at any time request the Trustees to sell the property or any other property purchased pursuant to this paragraph then provided the Applicant shall have used her best endeavours as aforesaid to ensure sale with vacant possession the Trustees shall sell the same as soon as reasonably practicable thereafter and shall at the like request of the Applicant apply all or any part of the net proceeds of sale in or towards the purchase of another freehold dwellinghouse or flat selected by the Applicant and any dwellinghouse or flat so purchased shall be assured to the Trustees upon trust for sale upon the same terms as the property as varied by this Order.

(i)   Any proceeds of sale of the property not required for the purchase of another property pursuant to paragraph (g) hereof shall be invested by the Trustees during the trust period in or upon the acquisition or security of any property of whatsoever nature and wheresoever situate to the intent that the Trustees shall have the same full and unrestricted power of investing in all respects as if they were absolutely entitled thereto beneficially.

(j)   In the event of the Respondent dying before the expiration of the trust period the rights and powers hereby reserved to him shall be exerciseable by his personal representatives.

Dated the _____ day of [*month and year*].

23   Order for variation of settlement (pensions)

[*Order as approved by Wilson J*]

1.   The trusts of the pension scheme called 'The XYZ Pension Scheme' ('the Scheme') established by Interim Trust Deed dated [. . .] and presently governed by a Trust Deed dated [. . .] between H Limited (1) and the Respondent and others (2) be varied so as to provide as follows:

(a)   £107,000 of the funds of the Scheme forthwith be allocated to provide benefits for the Petitioner; being such sum as will with effect from _____ (being the date of the Petitioner's 60th birthday) and for her lifetime provide the Petitioner with an annuity per annum of an amount equal to £9,900 increased in line with increases in the Retail Prices Index from [*date of order*] on terms that the annuity will itself increase annually in course of payment during the Petitioner's lifetime in line with increases in the Retail Prices Index ('the Pension') and on further terms that:

(i)   The Petitioner will have the right to effect commutation to a lump sum of such part of the Pension as may be permitted by the Inland Revenue; and

(ii)   Subject to the consent of the Inland Revenue, the Petitioner will be entitled to take an immediate transfer of the whole of such proportion of the funds of the Scheme to a personal pension scheme or occupational pension scheme (as defined in section 1 of the Pension Schemes Act 1993) of her choice; and

(iii)   If the Inland Revenue do not give the consent sought in (ii) above, the Petitioner will have the right to effect a commutation to a lump sum of such part of the Pension as may be permitted by the Inland Revenue, such lump sum then being paid from the funds of the Scheme; and the trustees of the Scheme will secure the Pension and future increases on it with effect from [. . .] (after making reasonable allowances for any commutation) with an annuity contract or policy (effected with the UK office or branch of an insurance company nominated by the trustees and consented to by the Petitioner (such consent not to be unreasonably withheld, and the court to be the sole arbiter of any issue as to whether consent is or is not being unreasonably withheld) to which Part II of the Insurance Companies Act 1982 applies and which is authorised by or under section 3 or 4 of that Act to carry on ordinary long term insurance business as defined in that Act) which contains such limitation on benefits and dealing as may be required by the Inland Revenue.

(b)   the trustees of the scheme shall not exercise any powers of amendment vested in them so as to deprive the petitioner of the pension specified in (a) above.

GENERAL NOTE

Because of the effect of WRPA 1999, such orders will be of reduced interest (see para **10.4**). The term 'applicant' has therefore not been substituted for 'petitioner'.

24   *Martin*-type order – house in joint names – party to be allowed to live there for life

[*Heading*]

It is ordered that the property [*address*] be held by the Applicant and the Respondent upon trust for themselves as beneficial tenants in common and to divide the net proceeds of sale of the said property between themselves in equal shares such sale to be postponed until after the death or remarriage of the Applicant or until her voluntary removal therefrom whichever event first occurs and until such sale the Applicant shall have liberty to occupy the said property provided that the Applicant regularly and duly pays all instalments of capital and interest in respect of the mortgage on the said property to the ABC Building Society falling due after the [*specified date*] and the Respondent paying all instalments before that date.

Dated the _____ day of [*month and year*].

GENERAL NOTE

Based on the order in *Martin v Martin* [1978] Fam 12, [1977] 3 All ER 762, CA.

25   Order for transfer on payment and provision for sale in default

[*Heading*]

It is ordered:

(a)   that on or before [*date*] the Applicant do transfer to the Respondent all his interest, both legal and beneficial, in the property [*address*] and that the Respondent on such transfer do pay to the Applicant the sum of £ _____.

(b)   that in the event that the said transfer shall not be completed by [the said date] the property be placed on the market for sale at the best price obtainable; the Applicant's solicitors to have the conduct of the sale and conveyancing and the net proceeds of sale, that is to say, the sum remaining after discharge of the mortgage to the ABC Building Society, estate agents costs of sale including VAT and the legal costs and disbursements including VAT, be divided equally between the Applicant and Respondent.

And it is recorded that, in the event of the said transfer being completed by [the said date] the Respondent undertakes to indemnify the Applicant against all liability under the mortgage to the ABC Building Society.

Dated the _____ day of [*month and year*].

26 Order dismissing claims to periodical payments, etc

[*Heading*]

It is ordered that the Applicant's application(s) for periodical payments [and a lump sum *and/or* a property adjustment order] do stand dismissed.

And it is directed that the Applicant shall not be entitled to make any further application in relation to the marriage of the Applicant and the Respondent for an order under section 23(1)(a) or (b) of the Matrimonial Causes Act 1973.

[And it is further ordered that neither party/the Applicant/the Respondent shall (not) on the death of the other party/ the Respondent/the Applicant be entitled to apply for an order under section 2 of the Inheritance (Provision for Family and Dependants) Act 1975.]

Dated the _____ day of [*month and year*].

27 Order for execution of contract or conveyance on behalf of person refusing to do so or who cannot be found

[*Heading*]

It is ordered under and by virtue of section 39 of the Supreme Court Act 1981 [applied by virtue of section 38 of the County Courts Act 1984] that [*name and/or description of person nominated*] do sign the conveyance of [the contract for the sale of] the property [*address*] to [*name*] at the price of £ _____ on behalf of the Respondent.

Dated the _____ day of [*month and year*].

ENDORSEMENT ON TRANSFER OR CONTRACT

Signed, Sealed and Delivered by [*name and description*] on behalf of [*name*] pursuant to order made [*date*] under section 39 of the Supreme Court Act 1981 [applied by virtue of section 38 of the County Courts Act 1984] in the presence of:

[*Signature, description and address of witness*]

28 Injunction under MCA 1973, section 37 – interim injunction made ex parte (high court)

[*Heading*]

Upon hearing counsel/solicitor for the Applicant and upon reading the affidavit of _____ sworn on [*date*] and the Applicant undertaking by her counsel to abide by any order the court may make as to damages in case the court shall hereafter be of opinion that the Respondent shall have sustained any by reason of this order which the Applicant ought to pay.

It is ordered and directed that the Respondent by himself, his agents or servants or otherwise be restrained, and an interim injunction until further order or until the hearing of the Applicant's summons (application) before District Judge [*name*] at [*address of court*] at 10.30 am on [*date*] is hereby granted restraining him from disposing of, transferring out of the jurisdiction or otherwise dealing with any monies received by him or receivable by him in respect of the estate of [*name*] deceased save the action of placing any such monies in either a bank deposit account or in a building society account in England. [*Or such other order as may be appropriate.*] Liberty to the Respondent to apply to discharge or vary this order on 48 hours' notice to the solicitor for the Applicant. Costs reserved.

Dated the _____ day of [*month and year*].

GENERAL NOTE

The action in respect of which the respondent to the application is enjoined and restrained from taking is, of course, merely an example and the precedent may be adapted to suit the purpose of the application. This is a form which may be used in the High Court. For the position in the county courts and divorce registry where the suit is not in the High Court, see Precedent 30.

29 Order setting aside disposition

[*Heading*]

It is ordered that the transfer by [*name*] the Respondent to [*name*] the Co-respondent of the property [*address*] [registered under title number _____ at HM Land Registry] on [*date*] be set aside and that the Co-respondent do within _____ days from the date hereof transfer the said property into the name of the Respondent.

GENERAL NOTE

If the transferee is not a party to the suit he or she will normally be added to the title of orders relating to avoidance of disposition proceedings as a respondent or defendant.

30   General form of injunction

In the	
	County Court
Case No. Always quote this	
Plaintiff's Ref	
Defendant's Ref	

Between _____ ☐ Plaintiff
☐ Applicant
☐ Petitioner
(Tick whichever applies)
and _____ ☐ Defendant
☐ Respondent

To⁽¹⁾
of⁽²⁾

For completion by the Court
Issued on

Seal

If you do not obey this order you will be guilty of contempt of court and you may be sent to prison

(1) The name of the person the order is directed to

On the   of   20
the court considered an application for an injunction

The Court ordered that⁽¹⁾

(2) The address of the person the order is directed to

is forbidden (whether by himself or by instructing or encouraging any other person)⁽³⁾

(3) The terms of the restraining order. If the defendant is a limited company, delete the words in brackets and insert 'whether by its sevants, agents, officers or otherwise'

This order shall remain in force until (the   of   20   at   o'clock unless before then it is revoked by a) further order of the court

And it is ordered that⁽¹⁾

shall⁽⁴⁾

(4) The terms of any orders requiring acts to be done

(5) Enter time (and place) as ordered	on or before[5]
(6) The terms of any other orders costs etc	It is further ordered that[6]

(7) Use when the order is temporary or ex parte otherwise delete

Notice of further hearing[7]

The court will re-consider the application and whether the order should continue at a further hearing

at

on   the   day   of

(8) Delete if order made on notice

20   at   o'clock

If you do not attend at the time shown the court may make an injunction order in your absence

You are entitled to apply to the court to re-consider the order before that day[8]

If you do not fully understand this application you should go to a Solicitor, Legal Advice Centre or a Citizen's Advice Bureau

---

The Court Office at
is open from 10 am to 4 pm Mon–Fri. When corresponding with the court, address all forms and letters to the Chief Clerk and quote the case number

---

GENERAL NOTE

This is the general form of injunction in Form N16 which must be used. The Marginal Notes act as a useful checklist.

For examples of the kind of orders which may be granted, see the precedents immediately preceding this.

31   Examples of agreements and undertakings to be recited in preambles to consent orders

(i) As to matrimonial home

(a)   The Applicant/Respondent undertaking to the court to continue to discharge the mortgage on the property [*address*] and the outgoings thereon, namely charges for rates, water rates, gas, electricity, insurance and telephone pending suit.

(b)   The Applicant/Respondent having agreed that the Respondent/Applicant be at liberty to reside in the property [*address*] until its sale, as provided for in the order hereunder, and not to let or share or part with possession of the basement flat in the property otherwise than by a letting or parting with possession which does not give the tenant or occupier any security of tenure under the Rent Acts and, save as aforesaid, not to let or share or part with possession or occupation of the property except with the written permission of the [*other party*], such permission not to be withheld unreasonably.

(ii) As to insurances

(a) The Applicant/Respondent undertaking to the court to provide private medical insurance for the (other party and/or children) to provide benefits not less than those that exist under the policy funded by his employer (or alternatively to procure that the said children remain covered under his employer's said policy).

(b) The Applicant/Respondent undertaking to the court to undergo such medical examination as may be required by an insurance company to enable the Respondent/Applicant to insure his/her life.

(c) The Applicant/Respondent undertaking to the court to maintain the policy with the ABC Insurance Co PLC being number _____ maturing on [*date*] and to provide the Respondent/Applicant annually on January 1, in each year with proof of the maintenance of the said policy.

(iii) As to companies

(a) The Applicant/Respondent undertaking to the court that he/she will, for the consideration of £1 transfer to the Respondent/Applicant or to whomsoever he/she may direct or nominate his/her one share in the ABCD Co Ltd and resign his/her directorship therein and he/she hereby acknowledges that he/she has no claim against the said company.

(b) The Applicant/Respondent undertaking to the court to indemnify the _____ in respect of any capital gains tax liability consequent upon the transfer to him/her of the _____'s shareholding in the ABCD Co Ltd and in respect of any other tax liability that may be suffered by the _____ arising from the _____'s involvement in and work for the said Co.

(iv) As to children

(a) The Applicant/Respondent undertaking to the court to reimburse the _____ in respect of any expenditure on behalf of the children he/she incurs at the _____'s request.

(b) The Applicant/Respondent undertaking to the court to provide each year a return air ticket to enable the child of the family [*name in full*] to visit him in [*country*] for access on dates to be agreed each year by the parties.

(c) The Applicant/Respondent undertaking to the court to provide one-third of the increased cost of the school fees beyond the level of such fees at the date hereof in respect of the children.

(v) As to Jewish Gets

(a) The Applicant/Respondent hereby undertaking to the court

(i)   to apply [within _____ weeks of this order *or* within _____ weeks from the date of the [decree nisi *or* decree absolute]] to the London Beth Din (Court of the Chief Rabbi) for a religious divorce (*Get*), and

(ii)   thereafter to take all such steps as are directed by the Court of the Chief Rabbi to complete the *Get*, such completion to take place not later than [_____ weeks *or* _____ months] from the date of application to the Court of the Chief Rabbi; costs thereof to be [borne by the [Applicant]/[Respondent] *or* shared equally].

(b) The Applicant/Respondent hereby undertaking to the court, upon application by the Respondent/Applicant to the London Beth Din (Court of the Chief Rabbi) for a religious divorce (*Get*), to take all such steps as are directed by the Court of the Chief Rabbi to complete the *Get*, such completion to take place not later than _____ months from the date of application to the Court of the Chief Rabbi; costs thereof to be [borne by the [Applicant]/[Respondent] *or* shared equally].

NOTE

There is considerable debate about whether and if so how, undertakings are enforceable. There is authority (see chapter 9) that undertakings to pay money are enforceable by way of judgment summons or third party debt orders. Whatever the true position may be, it is submitted that the position can only be made more clear if the party giving the undertaking expressly states in the application for the order that he/she accepts his/her obligations by reason of the undertaking and signs such acknowledgment.

Such acknowledgment might read as follows-

'I [full name] understand that the undertakings which I have given to the court as set out above are enforceable against me in the same way as orders of the court, and that breach of an order to pay money is a contempt of court'

32 Variation of orders

[*Heading*]

1. It is ordered that the order herein dated the _____ day of [*month and year*] be varied and that, as from the _____ day of [*month and year*], the Respondent do pay [*continue as in such precedent as may be appropriate, setting out the terms of the new provision for maintenance pending suit or periodical payments*].

Part of prior order only to be varied
2. It is ordered that the order herein dated the _____ day of [*month and year*] insofar as it relates to periodical payments for the Applicant be varied and that as from [*continue as in above precedent*].

Dated the _____ day of [*month and year*].

Arrears remitted under s 31(2A) of MCA 1973
3. And it is ordered that the arrears outstanding at the date of this order under the said order dated _____ be and the same are hereby remitted [as to £ _____] *or* [as to arrears accrued due prior to [*date*]].

33   Setting aside orders for ancillary relief

Type of Order	*Appeal*	*Fresh Action*	*Rehearing**
1. County Court District Judge by consent	Yes: without leave. Fresh evidence admissible without leave. Hearing *de novo*	Yes	Yes: apply to District Judge
2. High Court District Judge by consent	As above	As above	No
3. County Court Judge by consent	Yes: but only with leave of the Judge. Needs leave of CA to admit fresh evidence	As above	Yes: apply to the Judge
4. High Court Judge by consent	As above	As above	No
5. County Court District Judge after contested hearing	Yes: without leave. Fresh evidence admissible. Hearing *de novo*	As above	Maybe not
6. High Court District Judge after contested hearing	As above	As above	No
7. County Court Judge after contested hearing	Yes: but with leave of the Judge or the CA. Needs leave to admit fresh evidence	As above	Maybe not
8. High Court Judge	As above	As above	No

* So far as rehearings are concerned, see CCR Ord 37, r 1. The doubt expressed in categories 5 and 7 above stems from the possible interpretation of the words in CCR Ord 37, r 1 'when no error of the court at the hearing is alleged'.

GENERAL NOTE

Light has been shed on the appropriate procedure to be adopted when it is sought to set aside an order for ancillary relief by reason of alleged non-disclosure of material information by Ward J in *B-T v B-T* [1990] 2 FLR 1. The procedure depends upon whether the order was made in the High Court or in a county court and whether it was made by a district judge or by a judge. The applicability of three possible avenues to achieve setting aside is set out in the following table adapted from Ward J's judgment.

34 Undertaking to request commencement of pension on stipulated date and with sufficient benefits to meet order

AND UPON the [Applicant/Respondent] undertaking to the court:

EITHER
[*Occupational pension scheme*]

to request the commencement of [his/her] pension under the _____ pension scheme [forthwith]/[upon [his/her] ceasing employment with any employer participating in the said scheme]/[on [*date*]]/[upon [his/her] attaining the age of _____ years] in such a form that there will be a sufficient [net annuity]/[sum available for commutation] payable under the terms of the said scheme to meet the requirements of paragraph _____ of this order

OR
[*Personal/pension/retirement annuity contract*]

to take any benefits under [his/her] pension policy with _____ [forthwith]/[no earlier than [his/her] _____ birthday]/[no later than [his/her] _____ birthday]/[on [*date*]] in such a form that there will be a sufficient [net annuity]/[sum available for commutation] payable under the terms of the said pension policy to meet the requirements of paragraph _____ of this order

35 Undertaking not to frustrate attachment order – personal pension/retirement annuity contract

AND UPON the [Applicant/Respondent] undertaking to the court not to draw any benefits from [his/her] [personal pension policy]/[retirement annuity contract] with [*company*] [by way of income withdrawal]/[in such form] so as to frustrate the provisions of paragraph _____ of this order without the written consent of the [Respondent/Applicant].

36 Undertaking as to death benefits (occupational pension scheme)

AND UPON the [Applicant/Respondent] undertaking to the court that [he/she] will within _____ days from the date of this order irrevocably nominate and keep nominated

EITHER

the [Respondent/Applicant] [provided that [he/she] shall not have remarried at the date of the [Applicant's/Respondent's] death]/[for so long as the periodical payments order contained in paragraph _____ below shall subsist]

OR

the child of the family [*name*] [for so long as the periodical payments order contained in paragraph _____ below shall subsist]

BOTH

to receive [£ _____]/[_____% of the lump sum payable] in the event of [his/her] death under the [Applicant's/Respondent's] pension scheme with _____ [or such scheme of which [he/she] may from time to time be a member] and to provide upon request by the [Respondent/Applicant] written evidence of receipt by the person responsible for such scheme or schemes of the said nomination.

37   Clean break recital: attachment order

AND UPON the Applicant and the Respondent agreeing that the nominal order for periodical payments in favour of the [Applicant/Respondent] contained in paragraph _____ of this order is intended solely to preserve the entitlement of the [Applicant/Respondent] to periodical payments upon the retirement of the [Respondent/Applicant] as provided for by paragraph [*attached periodical payments order*] of this order and that the [Applicant/Respondent] will not apply to the court to vary the said nominal order save that the [Applicant/Respondent] shall be at liberty to apply to vary the order for periodical payments contained in paragraph [*attached periodical payments order*] of this order during the subsistence of the said nominal order in the event of a reduction in benefits within the meaning of the Divorce etc (Pensions) Regulations 1996, reg 7 [*or* the Divorce etc (Pensions) Regulations 2000, reg 5] [*or as appropriate*].

38   Non-attached deferred lump sum order from pension

The [Applicant/Respondent] do pay or cause to be paid to the [Respondent/Applicant] a lump sum [of £ _____]/[equal to _____% of the [maximum] lump sum payable to the [Applicant/Respondent] upon [his/her] retirement under the terms of [the _____ pension scheme]/[[his/her] pension with _____]/[such scheme of which [he/she] may from time to time be a member]] within _____ days of receipt by the [Applicant/Respondent] of the said lump sum WITH THE PROVISO that the [Respondent/Applicant] shall be alive and shall not have remarried at the date of the [Applicant's/Respondent's] retirement.

39   Attached periodical payments order

(a)   As from [the date of this order]/[the [Respondent's/Applicant's] retirement under the terms of [his/her] pension with [*pension provider*]]/[the date the [Applicant/Respondent] first draws benefits under [his/her] personal pension with [*pension provider*]] the person responsible for the said pension do pay to the [Applicant/Respondent] on behalf of the [Respondent/Applicant] periodical payments at the rate of [£ _____]/[_____% of [his/her] net pension payable under the terms of the said pension] payable monthly [in advance] [to be increased annually on the anniversary of this order [in accordance with the Retail Prices Index subject to a maximum of _____% per annum]/[by the percentage of any increase in the amount of pension payable to the [Respondent/Applicant] under the terms of the said pension]/[in accordance with the following formula _____] during joint lives and during the period of payment of the [Respondent's/Applicant's] pension payable under the terms of the said pension until the [Applicant/Respondent] shall remarry or further order].

(b) Any such payment by the person responsible for the said pension shall be treated pursuant to the Matrimonial Causes Act 1973, s 25B(6) for all purposes as a payment by the [Respondent/Applicant] as the party with pension rights in or towards [his/her] liability under the terms of this order and such payment shall be appropriated from the pension to be paid to the [Respondent/Applicant] which shall be reduced accordingly.

40 Attached lump sum order

(a) The person responsible for the [Applicant's/Respondent's] pension scheme with _____ do pay or cause to be paid to the [Respondent/Applicant] on behalf of the [Applicant/Respondent] a lump sum [of £ _____]/[equal to _____% of the maximum amount capable of commutation in accordance with the said pension scheme's approval by the Inland Revenue to the [Applicant/Respondent]] within _____ days of [his/her] [retirement]/[taking of benefits] under the terms of the said pension scheme WITH THE PROVISO THAT the [Respondent/Applicant] shall be alive and shall not have remarried at the date of the [Applicant's/Respondent's] retirement or taking of benefits under the terms of the said pension scheme;

(b) Any such payment by the person responsible for the said pension shall be treated pursuant to the Matrimonial Causes Act 1973, s 25B(6) for all purposes as a payment made by the [Applicant/Respondent] as the party with pension rights in or towards [his/her] liability under the terms of this order and shall be appropriated from the lump sum or pension to be paid to the [Applicant/Respondent] which shall be reduced accordingly.

GENERAL NOTE

A commutation order will also be required: see Precedent 41.

41 Commutation order

The [Applicant/Respondent] do upon commencement of payment of [his/her] pension scheme with _____ commute [the maximum amount capable of commutation in accordance with the said pension scheme's approval by the Inland Revenue]/[_____% of the maximum amount capable of commutation in accordance with the said pension schemes approval by the Inland Revenue]/[£ _____] to a lump sum under the terms of the said pension scheme.

42 Death benefits attachment order under MCA 1973, section 25C (occupational pension scheme)

(a)   The person responsible for the _____ pension scheme do pay or cause to be paid to the [Applicant/Respondent] on behalf of the [Respondent/ Applicant] [£ _____]/[[_____% of] the lump sum payable] in the event of [his/her] death under the terms of the said pension scheme [WITH THE PROVISO THAT the [Applicant/Respondent] shall be alive and not have remarried at the date when the said sum becomes payable].

(b)   Any such payment by the person responsible for the said pension scheme shall be treated pursuant to the Matrimonial Causes Act 1973, s 25B(6) for all purposes as a payment made by the [Respondent/Applicant] as the party with pension rights in or towards [his/her] liability under the terms of this order.

43 Death benefits attachment order under MCA 1973, section 25C (personal pension/retirement annuity contract)

(a)   The [Respondent/Applicant] do nominate within _____ from the date of this order in respect of any sum payable in the event of [his/her] death prior to drawing any benefits other than income withdrawals pursuant to the Finance Act 1995, s 58 and Sch 11 under [his/her] [personal pensions]/[retirement annuity contract] number _____ with [*pension provider*]

[*either*]

the [Respondent/Applicant] [provided that [he/she] shall be alive and not have remarried at the date of the [Applicant's/Respondent's] death]/[for so long as the periodical payments order contained in paragraph _____ below shall subsist]

[*or*]

the child of the family [name] [for so long as the periodical payments order contained in paragraph _____ below shall subsist]

[*both*]

to receive [£ _____/[_____%] of the said sum]

(b)   Any such payment by the person responsible for the said pension scheme shall be treated pursuant to the Matrimonial Causes Act 1973, s 25B(6) for all purposes as a payment made by the [Respondent/Applicant] as the party with pension rights in or towards his liability under the terms of this order.

44 Pension sharing/attachment order

[*Heading as appropriate*]

[It is ordered that]

Provision is made in favour of the [Applicant/Respondent] by way of [pension sharing *and/or* pension attachment] in accordance with the [annex/annexes] to this order.

FORM: P3

PENSION INQUIRY FORM

Information needed when a Pension Sharing Order or Pension Attachment Order may be made

(insert details of pension scheme here)
TO:
of
Reference Number:

A. To be completed by Pension Scheme member or policy holder:	
Name of pension scheme member or policy holder:	
Address:	
Reference:	.... Signature of Pension Scheme member or policy holder (The scheme member's signature is necessary to authorise the release of the requested information, unless a court order requiring the information is attached to this form.)

2. Solicitors details:
  Address:
  Reference:
  Tel:	

3. Address to which the form should be sent once completed if different from 2 above.	

B. To be completed by the Pension Arrangement.

This section deals with information required to be provided under the Pensions on Divorce etc (Provision of Information) Regulations 2000 SI1048/2000, Regulations 2 and 3 and Rule 2.70(2) of the Family Proceedings Rules 1991 as amended). If a request for a Cash Equivalent Transfer Value has been made, the pension arrangement has 3 months to provide the information or 6 weeks if notified that the information is needed in connection with matrimonial proceedings, or such shorter time as notified by the court. Otherwise, the information should be provided within one month or such shorter time as notified by the court.

If this information has already been prepared in a standard form please send this instead.

1. (a)	Please confirm that you have already provided a valuation of the member's pension rights to the scheme member or to the Court.	Yes	☐	No	☐
(b)	If the answer to (a) is no, details of the CETV quotation should be attached and the date on which it was calculated.				
2. Provide a statement summarising the way in which the valuation referred to above has been or will be calculated.					
3. State the pension benefits included in the valuation referred to in B1 above.					
4. (a)	Does the person responsible for the pension arrangement offer scheme membership to the person entitled to a pension credit?	Yes	☐	No	☐
(b)	If yes, does this depend on Employer and/or trustee approval?	Yes	☐	No	☐
5. If the answer to 4(a) is yes, what benefits are available to the person with the pension credit?					

6. *Charging Policy*				
Does the arrangement charge for providing information or implementing a pension sharing order?	Yes	☐	No	☐
If so, please:				
– provide a list of charges; – indicate when these must be paid; and – whether they can be paid directly from benefits held in the scheme or policy, or the pension credit.				

C. To be completed by the pension arrangement.

This information is required to be provided by the pension arrangement under the Pension on Divorce (Provision of Information) Regulations 2000 S.I. 1048, Regulation 4 within 21 days of being notified that a pension sharing order may be made. If such notification has not already been given, please treat this document as notification that such an order may be made. Alternatively the Court may specify a date by which this information should be provided.

If this information has already been prepared in a standard form please send this instead.

1. The full name of the pension arrangement and address to which a pension sharing order should be sent.				
2. In the case of an occupational pension scheme only, is the scheme winding up? If so:	Yes	☐	No	☐
– when did the winding up commence? and – give the name and address of the trustees who are dealing with the winding up				
3. In the case of an occupational pension scheme only, assuming that a calculation of the member's CETV was carried out on the day the pension scheme received notification that a pension sharing order may be made, would that CETV be reduced?	Yes	☐	No	☐
4. As far as you are aware, are the member's rights under the pension scheme subject to any of the following:				
– a pension sharing order	Yes	☐	No	☐
– a pension attachment order made under s 23 of the Matrimonial Causes Act 1973 (England and Wales), s 12 A(2) or (3) of the Family Law (Scotland) Act 1985 or under art 25 of the Matrimonial Causes (Northern Ireland) Order 1978	Yes	☐	No	☐
– a forfeiture order	Yes	☐	No	☐
– a bankruptcy order	Yes	☐	No	☐
– an award of sequestration on a member's estate or the making of the appointment on his estate of a judicial factor under section 41 of the Solicitors (Scotland) Act 1980	Yes	☐	No	☐
5. Do the member's rights include rights which are not shareable by virtue of regulation 2 of the Pension Sharing (Valuation) Regulations 2000? If so, please provide details.	Yes	☐	No	☐
6. Does the pension arrangement propose to levy additional charges specified in Regulation 6 of the Pensions on Divorce (Charging) Regulations 2000? If so, please provide the scale of the additional charges likely to made.	Yes	☐	No	☐
7. Is the scheme member a trustee of the pension scheme?	Yes	☐	No	☐
8. If a pension sharing order is made, will the person responsible for the pension arrangement require information regarding the scheme member's state of health before implementing the pension sharing order?	Yes	☐	No	☐
9. Does the person responsible for the pension sharing arrangement require any further information other than that contained in regulation 5 of the Pensions on Divorce etc (Provision of Information Regulations) 2000, before implementing any Pension Sharing Order? If so, specify what.	Yes	☐	No	☐

D. To be completed by the pension arrangement.	
The following information should be provided if the scheme member requests it or the Court orders it pursuant to its powers under the Pensions on Divorce etc (Provision of Information) Regulations 2000, SI 1048/2000. Please note that pension arrangements may make an additional charge for providing this information.	
1. Disregarding any future service or premiums that might be paid and future inflation, what is the largest lump sum payment that the member would be entitled to take if s/he were to retire at a normal retirement age?	
2. What is the earliest date on which the member has the right to take benefits , excluding retirement on grounds of ill health?	
3. Are spouse's benefits payable?	Yes ☐ No ☐
4. What lump sum would be payable on death at the date of completion of this form?	
5. What proportion of the member's pension would be payable as of right to the spouse of the member if the member were to die (a) before retirement; and (b) after retirement, disregarding any future service or premiums that might be paid and future inflation.	
6. Is the pension in payment, drawdown or deferment? If so, which?	
7. Please provide a copy of the scheme booklet.	

DATE: . ...

FORM: P1

Pension Sharing Annex under Section 24B of the Matrimonial Causes Act 1973 (Rule 2.70 (14) FPR 1991)	In the *(County Court) *(Principal Registry of the Family Division) Case No. Always quote this Transferor's Solicitor's Reference Transferee's Solicitor's Reference

The marriage of   and

Take Notice that:

On   the Court

made a pension sharing order under Part IV of the Welfare Reform and Pensions Act 1999.
[varied] [discharged] an order which included provision for pension sharing under Part IV of the Welfare Reform and Pensions Act 1999 and dated

This annex to the order provides the person responsible for the pension arrangement with the information required by virtue of the Family Proceedings Rules 1991 as amended.

A. *Transferor's Details* (i) The full name by which the Transferor is known (ii) All names by which the Transferor has been known (iii) The Transferor's date of birth (iv) The Transferor's address (v) The Transferor's National Insurance Number	
B. *Transferee's Details* (i) The full name by which the Transferee is known (ii) All names by which the Transferee has been known (iii) The Transferee's date of Birth (iv) The Transferee's address (v) The Transferee's National Insurance Number (vi) If the Transferee is also a member of the pension scheme from which the credit is derived, or a beneficiary of the same scheme because of survivor's benefits, the membership number	
C. *Details of the Transferor's Pension Arrangement* (i) Name of the arrangement (ii) Name and address of the person responsible for the pension arrangement: (iii) Policy Reference Number: (iv) If appropriate, such other details to enable the pension arrangement to be identified: (v) The specified percentage of the member's CETV to be transferred:	 ____ . _____%
D. *Pension Sharing Charges* It is directed that:	* The pension sharing charges be apportioned between the parties as follows: or * The pension sharing charges be paid in full by the Transferor. (*Delete as appropriate)

E. Where no Form M1 (Statement of Information for a Consent Order) is filed, the parties certify that they have received the information required by Regulation 4 of the Pensions on Divorce (Provision of Information) Regulations 2000 and that information is attached on Form P3 and that it appears from that information that there is power to make an order including provision under s.24B Matrimonial Causes Act 1973 (pension sharing).	
F. In cases where the transferee has a choice of an internal or external transfer, if the transferee has indicated a preference, indicate what this is.	☐ Internal Transfer ☐ External Transfer
G. *In the case of external transfer only (recommended but optional information)* (i) The name of the qualifying arrangement which has agreed to accept the pension credit. (ii) The address of the qualifying arrangement (iii) If known, the transferee's membership or policy number in the qualifying arrangement and reference number of the new provider (iv) The name, or title, business address, phone and fax numbers and email address of the person who may be contacted in respect of the discharge of liability for the pension credit on behalf of the Transferee. (This may be an Independent Financial Advisor, for example, if one is advising the Transferee or the new pension scheme itself.) (v) Please attach a copy of the letter from the qualifying arrangement indicating its willingness to accept the pension credit.	
Please complete boxes H to J where applicable	
H. Where the credit is derived from an occupational scheme which is being wound up, has the Transferee indicated whether he wishes to transfer his pension credit rights to a qualifying arrangement?	☐ Yes ☐ No
I. Where the pension arrangement has requested details of the Transferor's health, has that information been provided?	☐ Yes ☐ No
J. Where the pension arrangement has requested further information, has that information been provided?	☐ Yes ☐ No

Note: Until the information requested in A, B, (and as far as applicable G, H, I & J) is provided the Pension Sharing Order cannot be implemented although it may be made. Even if all the information requested has been provided, further information may be required before implementation can begin. If so, reasons why implementation cannot begin should be sent by the Pension arrangement to the transferor and transferee within 21 days of receipt of the Pension Sharing Order and this annex.
THIS ORDER TAKES EFFECT FROM the date on which the Decree Absolute of Divorce or nullity is made or if later, either

a. 21 days from the date of this Order, unless an Appeal has been lodged, in which case
b. the effective date of the Order determining that appeal.

To the person responsible for the pension arrangement:
Take notice that you must discharge your liability within the period of 4 months beginning with the later of:

–   the day on which this order takes effect; or
–   the first day on which you are in receipt of –

        (a) the pension sharing order including this annex properly completed (and where appropriate any attachments);
        (b) the decree nisi and absolute of divorce or nullity of marriage;
        (c) the information contained in G, including any further information requested; and
        (d) payment of all outstanding charges requested by the pension scheme.

To the court

You must send the following documents to the person responsible for the pension arrangement (as set out in box C above), within 7 days of the making of decree absolute of divorce or nullity of marriage or the making of the order, whichever is the later.

- A copy of the decree of divorce or nullity of marriage;
- A copy of the certificate under the Family Proceedings Rules 1991, rule 2.51 that the decree has been made absolute; and
- A copy of the order, or the order varying or discharging that order, including any annex to that order relating to that pension arrangement but no other annex to that order.

45 Orders for costs

[It is ordered that]

(1) The [Respondent/Applicant] pay to the [Applicant/Respondent] the costs of the application for ancillary relief [from *date*] [limited to the issue of, eg, the existence or extent of his interest in ABC Ltd] to be the subject of detailed assessment if not agreed [assessed in the sum of £ _____ to be paid by *date*].

(2) The [Respondent/Applicant] pay to the [Applicant/Respondent] the costs of the application for ancilliary relief on the indemnity basis from [*date*] to be the subject of detailed assessment if not agreed and interest on those costs from [*date*] until payment at the rate of [*a rate not exceeding 10% above base rate*].

NOTE

This is a general form of order for costs. The first words in brackets would apply where, for example, the receiving party had made an offer on a certain date which had 'beaten' the order made. The second set of words would apply where one party had succeeded on one important issue, or acted unreasonably in relation thereto.

Appendix B

LEGISLATION

1. MATRIMONIAL CAUSES ACT 1973

(1973 c. 18)

PART II
FINANCIAL RELIEF FOR PARTIES TO MARRIAGE AND CHILDREN OF FAMILY

Financial provision and property adjustment orders

21 *Financial provision and property adjustment orders* **[Financial provision orders, property adjustment orders and pension sharing orders]**

(1) The financial provision orders for the purposes of this Act are the orders for periodical or lump sum provision available (subject to the provisions of this Act) under section 23 below for the purpose of adjusting the financial position of the parties to a marriage and any children of the family in connection with proceedings for divorce, nullity of marriage or judicial separation and under section 27(6) below on proof of neglect by one party to a marriage to provide, or to make a proper contribution towards, reasonable maintenance for the other or a child of the family, that is to say —

    (a) any order for periodical payments in favour of a party to a marriage under section 23(1)(a) or 27(6)(a) or in favour of a child of the family under section 23(1)(d), (2) or (4) or 27(6)(d);

    (b) any order for secured periodical payments in favour of a party to a marriage under section 23(1)(b) or 27(6)(b) or in favour of a child of the family under section 23(1)(e), (2) or (4) or 27(6)(e); and

    (c) any order for lump sum provision in favour of a party to a marriage under section 23(1)(c) or 27(6)(c) or in favour of a child of the family under section 23(1)(f), (2) or (4) or 27(6)(f);

and references in this Act (except in paragraphs 17(1) and 23 of Schedule 1 below) to periodical payments orders, secured periodical payments orders, and orders for the payment of a lump sum are references to all or some of the financial provision orders requiring the sort of financial provision in question according as the context of each reference may require.

(2) The property adjustment orders for the purposes of this Act are the orders dealing with property rights available (subject to the provisions of this Act) under section 24 below for the purpose of adjusting the financial position of the parties to a marriage and any children of the family on or after the grant of a decree of divorce, nullity of marriage or judicial separation, that is to say —

(a) any order under subsection *(1)(a)* of that section for a transfer of property;

(b) any order under subsection *(1)(b)* of that section for a settlement of property; and

(c) any order under subsection *(1)(c)* or *(d)* of that section for a variation of settlement.

[(1) For the purposes of this Act, a financial provision order is —

(a) an order that a party must make in favour of another person such periodical payments, for such term, as may be specified (a 'periodical payments order');

(b) an order that a party must, to the satisfaction of the court, secure in favour of another person such periodical payments, for such term, as may be specified (a 'secured periodical payments order');

(c) an order that a party must make a payment in favour of another person of such lump sum or sums as may be specified (an 'order for the payment of a lump sum').

(2) For the purposes of this Act, a property adjustment order is —

(a) an order that a party must transfer such of his or her property as may be specified in favour of the other party or a child of the family;

(b) an order that a settlement of such property of a party as may be specified must be made, to the satisfaction of the court, for the benefit of the other party and of the children of the family, or either or any of them;

(c) an order varying, for the benefit of the parties and of the children of the family, or either or any of them, any marriage settlement, other than one in the form of a pension arrangement (within the meaning of section 25D below);

(d) an order extinguishing or reducing the interest of either of the parties under any marriage settlement, other than one in the form of a pension arrangement (within the meaning of section 25D below).

(3) For the purposes of this Act, a pension sharing order is an order which —

(a) provides that one party's —
    (i) shareable rights under a specified pension arrangement, or
    (ii) shareable state scheme rights,
    be subject to pension sharing for the benefit of the other party, and

(b) specifies the percentage value to be transferred.

(4) Subject to section 40 below, where an order of the court under this Part of this Act requires a party to make or secure a payment in favour of another person or to transfer property in favour of any person, that payment must be made or secured or that property transferred —

(a) if that other person is the other party to the marriage, to that other party; and

(b) if that other person is a child of the family, according to the terms of the order —

(i) to the child; or
(ii) to such other person as may be specified, for the benefit of that child.

(5) References in this section to the property of a party are references to any property to which that party is entitled either in possession or in reversion.

(6) Any power of the court under this Part of this Act to make such an order as is mentioned in subsection (2)(b) to (d) above is exercisable even though there are no children of the family.

(7) In subsection (3) —

(a) the reference to shareable rights under a pension arrangement is to rights in relation to which pension sharing is available under Chapter I of Part IV of the Welfare Reform and Pensions Act 1999, or under corresponding Northern Ireland legislation, and
(b) the reference to shareable state scheme rights is to rights in relation to which pension sharing is available under Chapter II of Part IV of the Welfare Reform and Pensions Act 1999, or under corresponding Northern Ireland legislation.

(8) In this section —

'marriage settlement' means an ante-nuptial or post-nuptial settlement made on the parties (including one made by will or codicil);
'party' means a party to a marriage; and
'specified' means specified in the order in question.]

Amendments—Prospectively substituted, together with s 21A, by new s 21, by the Family Law Act 1996, s 15, Sch 2, para 2 (as amended by the Welfare Reform and Pensions Act 1999, s 84(1), Sch 12, Pt I, paras 64, 65(1)–(8)), for transitional provisions see s 66(2), Sch 9, para 5 thereof.

21A Pension sharing orders

(1) For the purposes of this Act, a pension sharing order is an order which —

(a) provides that one party's —
(i) shareable rights under a specified pension arrangement, or
(ii) shareable state scheme rights,
be subject to pension sharing for the benefit of the other party, and
(b) specifies the percentage value to be transferred.

(2) In subsection (1) above —

(a) the reference to shareable rights under a pension arrangement is to rights in relation to which pension sharing is available under Chapter I of Part IV of the Welfare Reform and Pensions Act 1999, or under corresponding Northern Ireland legislation,
(b) the reference to shareable state scheme rights is to rights in relation to which pension sharing is available under Chapter II of Part IV of the Welfare Reform and Pensions Act 1999, or under corresponding Northern Ireland legislation, and
(c) 'party' means a party to a marriage.

Amendments—Section inserted by Welfare Reform and Pensions Act 1999, s 19, Sch 3, paras 1, 2; prospectively substituted, together with s 21, by new s 21, by the Family Law Act 1996, s 15, Sch 2, para 2 (as amended by the Welfare Reform and Pensions Act 1999, s 84(1), Sch 12, Pt I, paras 64, 65(1)–(8)); for transitional provisions see s 66(2), Sch 9, para 5 thereof.

Ancillary relief in connection with divorce proceedings etc

22 Maintenance pending suit

On a petition for divorce, nullity of marriage or judicial separation, the court may make an order for maintenance pending suit, that is to say, an order requiring either party to the marriage to make to the other such periodical payments for his or her maintenance and for such term, being a term beginning not earlier than the date of the presentation of the petition and ending with the date of the determination of the suit, as the court thinks reasonable.

Amendments—Section prospectively repealed with savings by the Family Law Act 1996, s 66(3), Sch 10.

[22A Financial provision orders: divorce and separation]

[(1) On an application made under this section, the court may at the appropriate time make one or more financial provision orders in favour of —

    (a)   a party to the marriage to which the application relates; or

    (b)   any of the children of the family.

(2) The 'appropriate time' is any time —

    (a)   after a statement of marital breakdown has been received by the court and before any application for a divorce order or for a separation order is made to the court by reference to that statement;

    (b)   when an application for a divorce order or separation order has been made under section 3 of the 1996 Act and has not been withdrawn;

    (c)   when an application for a divorce order has been made under section 4 of the 1996 Act and has not been withdrawn;

    (d)   after a divorce order has been made;

    (e)   when a separation order is in force.

(3) The court may make —

    (a)   a combined order against the parties on one occasion,

    (a)   separate orders on different occasions,

    (c)   different orders in favour of different children,

    (d)   different orders from time to time in favour of the same child,

but may not make, in favour of the same party, more than one periodical payments order, or more than one order for payment of a lump sum, in relation to any marital proceedings, whether in the course of the proceedings or by reference to a divorce order or separation order made in the proceedings.

(4) If it would not otherwise be in a position to make a financial provision order in favour of a party or child of the family, the court may make an interim

periodical payments order, an interim order for the payment of a lump sum or a series of such orders, in favour of that party or child.

(5) Any order for the payment of a lump sum made under this section may —

(a) provide for the payment of the lump sum by instalments of such amounts as may be specified in the order; and

(b) require the payment of the instalments to be secured to the satisfaction of the court.

(6) Nothing in subsection (5) above affects —

(a) the power of the court under this section to make an order for the payment of a lump sum; or

(b) the provisions of this Part of this Act as to the beginning of the term specified in any periodical payments order or secured periodical payments order.

(7) Subsection (8) below applies where the court —

(a) makes an order under this section ('the main order') for the payment of a lump sum; and

(b) directs —

(i) that payment of that sum, or any part of it, is to be deferred; or

(ii) that that sum, or any part of it, is to be paid by instalments.

(8) In such a case, the court may, on or at any time after making the main order, make an order ('the order for interest') for the amount deferred, or the instalments, to carry interest (at such rate as may be specified in the order for interest) —

(a) from such date, not earlier than the date of the main order, as may be so specified;

(b) until the date when the payment is due.

(9) This section is to be read subject to any restrictions imposed by this Act and to section 19 of the 1996 Act.]

Amendments—Section prospectively inserted with savings by the Family Law Act 1996, s 15, Sch 2, para 3.

[22B Restrictions affecting section 22A]

[(1) No financial provision (1) order, other than an interim order, may be made under section 22A above so as to take effect before the making of a divorce order or separation order in relation to the marriage, unless the court is satisfied —

(a) that the circumstances of the case are exceptional; and

(b) that it would be just and reasonable for the order to be so made.

(2) Except in the case of an interim periodical payments order, the court may not make a financial provision order under section 22A above at any time while the period for reflection and consideration is interrupted under section 7(8) of the 1996 Act.

(3) No financial provision order may be made under section 22A above by reference to the making of a statement of marital breakdown if, by virtue of section 5(3) or 7(9) of the 1996 Act (lapse of divorce or separation process), it has ceased to be possible —

(a)   for an application to be made by reference to that statement; or

(b)   for an order to be made on such an application.

(4) No financial provision order may be made under section 22A after a divorce order has been made, or while a separation order is in force, except —

(a)   in response to an application made before the divorce order or separation order was made; or

(b)   on a subsequent application made with the leave of the court.

(5) In this section, 'period for reflection and consideration' means the period fixed by section 7 of the 1996 Act.]

Amendments—Section prospectively inserted with savings by the Family Law Act 1996, s 15, Sch 2, para 3.

23 *Financial provision orders in connection with divorce proceedings etc* [Financial provision orders nullity]

(1) On granting a decree of divorce, a decree of nullity of marriage or a decree of judicial separation or at any time thereafter (whether, in the case of a decree of divorce or of nullity of marriage, before or after the decree is made absolute), the court may make any one or more of the following orders, that is to say —

(a)   an order that either party to the marriage shall make to the other such periodical payments, for such term, as may be specified in the order;

(b)   an order that either party to the marriage shall secure to the other to the satisfaction of the court such periodical payments, for such term, as may be so specified;

(c)   an order that either party to the marriage shall pay to the other such lump sum or sums as may be so specified;

(d)   an order that a party to the marriage shall make to such person as may be specified in the order for the benefit of a child of the family, or to such a child, such periodical payments, for such term, as may be so specified;

(e)   an order that a party to the marriage shall secure to such person as may be so specified for the benefit of such a child, or to such a child, to the satisfaction of the court, such periodical payments, for such term, as may be so specified;

(f)   an order that a party to the marriage shall pay to such person as may be so specified for the benefit of such a child, or to such a child, such lump sum as may be so specified;

subject, however, in the case of an order under paragraph (d), (e) or (f) above, to the restrictions imposed by section 29(1) and (3) below on the making of financial provision orders in favour of children who have attained the age of eighteen.

(2) The court may also, subject to those restrictions, make any one or more of the orders mentioned in subsection (1)(d), (e) and (f) above —

> *(a)* in any proceedings for divorce, nullity of marriage or judicial separation, before granting a decree; and
>
> *(b)* where any such proceedings are dismissed after the beginning of the trial, either forthwith or within a reasonable period after the dismissal.

(3) Without prejudice to the generality of subsection (1)(c) or (f) above —

> *(a)* an order under this section that a party to a marriage shall pay a lump sum to the other party may be made for the purpose of enabling that other party to meet any liabilities or expenses reasonably incurred by him or her in maintaining himself or herself or any child of the family before making an application for an order under this section in his or her favour;
>
> *(b)* an order under this section for the payment of a lump sum to or for the benefit of a child of the family may be made for the purpose of enabling any liabilities or expenses reasonably incurred by or for the benefit of that child before the making of an application for an order under this section in his favour to be met; and
>
> *(c)* an order under this section for the payment of a lump sum may provide for the payment of that sum by instalments of such amount as may be specified in the order and may require the payment of the instalments to be secured to the satisfaction of the court.

(4) The power of the court under subsection (1) or (2)(a) above to make an order in favour of a child of the family shall be exercisable from time to time; and where the court makes an order in favour of a child under subsection (2)(b) above, it may from time to time, subject to the restrictions mentioned in subsection (1) above, make a further order in his favour of any of the kinds mentioned in subsection (1)(d), (e) or (f) above.

(5) Without prejudice to the power to give a direction under section 30 below for the settlement of an instrument by conveyancing counsel, where an order is made under subsection (1)(a), (b) or (c) above on or after granting a decree of divorce or nullity of marriage, neither the order nor any settlement made in pursuance of the order shall take effect unless the decree has been made absolute.

(6) Where the court —

> *(a)* makes an order under this section for the payment of a lump sum; and
>
> *(b)* directs —
>
>> *(i)* that payment of that sum or any part of it shall be deferred; or
>>
>> *(ii)* that the sum or any part of it shall be paid by instalments,

the court may order that the amount deferred or the instalments shall carry interest at such rate as may be specified by the order from such date, not earlier than the date of the order, as may be so specified, until the date when payment of it is due.

[(1) On or after granting a decree of nullity of marriage (whether before or after the decree is made absolute), the court may, on an application made under this section, make one or more financial provision orders in favour of —

(a)   either party to the marriage; or

(b)   any child of the family.

(2) Before granting a decree in any proceedings for nullity of marriage, the court may make against either or each of the parties to the marriage —

(a)   an interim periodical payments order, an interim order for the payment of a lump sum, or a series of such orders, in favour of the other party;

(b)   an interim periodical payments order, an interim order for the payment of a lump sum, a series of such orders or any one or more other financial provision orders in favour of each child of the family.

(3) Where any such proceedings are dismissed, the court may (either immediately or within a reasonable period after the dismissal) make any one or more financial provision orders in favour of each child of the family.

(4) An order under this section that a party to a marriage must pay a lump sum to the other party may be made for the purpose of enabling that other party to meet any liabilities or expenses reasonably incurred by him or her in maintaining himself or herself or any child of the family before making an application for an order under this section in his or her favour.

(5) An order under this section for the payment of a lump sum to or for the benefit of a child of the family may be made for the purpose of enabling any liabilities or expenses reasonably incurred by or for the benefit of that child before the making of an application for an order under this section in his favour to be met.

(6) An order under this section for the payment of a lump sum may —

(a)   provide for the payment of that sum by instalments of such amount as may be specified in the order; and

(b)   require the payment of the instalments to be secured to the satisfaction of the court.

(7) Nothing in subsections (4) to (6) above affects —

(a)   the power under subsection (1) above to make an order for the payment of a lump sum; or

(b)   the provisions of this Act as to the beginning of the term specified in any periodical payments order or secured periodical payments order.

(8) The powers of the court under this section to make one or more financial provision orders are exercisable against each party to the marriage by the making of —

(a)   a combined order on one occasion, or

(b)   separate orders on different occasions,

but the court may not make more than one periodical payments order, or more than one order for payment of a lump sum, in favour of the same party.

(9) The powers of the court under this section so far as they consist in power to make one or more orders in favour of the children of the family —

(a)   may be exercised differently in favour of different children; and

(b)   except in the case of the power conferred by subsection (3) above, may be exercised from time to time in favour of the same child; and

(c)   in the case of the power conferred by that subsection, if it is exercised by the making of a financial provision order of any kind in favour of a child, shall include power to make, from time to time, further financial provision orders of that or any other kind in favour of that child.

(10) Where an order is made under subsection (1) above in favour of a party to the marriage on or after the granting of a decree of nullity of marriage, neither the order nor any settlement made in pursuance of the order takes effect unless the decree has been made absolute.

(11) Subsection (10) above does not affect the power to give a direction under section 30 below for the settlement of an instrument by conveyancing counsel.

(12) Where the court —

(a)   makes an order under this section ('the main order') for the payment of a lump sum; and

(b)   directs —

     (i)   that payment of that sum or any part of it is to be deferred; or

     (ii)   that that sum or any part of it is to be paid by instalments,

it may, on or at any time after making the main order, make an order ('the order for interest') for the amount deferred or the instalments to carry interest at such rate as may be specified by the order for interest from such date, not earlier than the date of the main order, as may be so specified, until the date when payment of it is due.

(13) This section is to be read subject to any restrictions imposed by this Act.]

Amendments—Administration of Justice Act 1982, s 16; section prospectively substituted with savings by the Family Law Act 1996, s 15, Sch 2, para 4.

[23A Property adjustment orders: divorce and separation]

[(1) On an application made under this section, the court may, at any time mentioned in section 22A(2) above, make one or more property adjustment orders.

(2) If the court makes, in favour of the same party to the marriage, more than one property adjustment order in relation to any marital proceedings, whether in the course of the proceedings or by reference to a divorce order or separation order made in the proceedings, each order must fall within a different paragraph of section 21(2) above.

(3) The court shall exercise its powers under this section, so far as is practicable, by making on one occasion all such provision as can be made by way of one or more property adjustment orders in relation to the marriage as it thinks fit.

(4) Subsection (3) above does not affect section 31 or 31A below.

(5) This section is to be read subject to any restrictions imposed by this Act and to section 19 of the 1996 Act.]

Amendments—Welfare Reform and Pensions Act 1999, s 19, Sch 3, paras 1, 3; section prospectively inserted with savings by the Family Law Act 1996, s 15, Sch 2, para 5.

[23B Restrictions affecting section 23A]

[(1) No property adjustment order may be made under section 23A above so as to take effect before the making of a divorce order or separation order in relation to the marriage unless the court is satisfied —

(a)   that the circumstances of the case are exceptional; and

(b)   that it would be just and reasonable for the order to be so made.

(2) The court may not make a property adjustment order under section 23A above at any time while the period for reflection and consideration is interrupted under section 7(8) of the 1996 Act.

(3) No property adjustment order may be made under section 23A above by virtue of the making of a statement of marital breakdown if, by virtue of section 5(3) or 7(5) of the 1996 Act (lapse of divorce or separation process), it has ceased to be possible —

(a)   for an application to be made by reference to that statement; or

(b)   for an order to be made on such an application.

(4) No property adjustment order may be made under section 23A above after a divorce order has been made, or while a separation order is in force, except —

(a)   in response to an application made before the divorce order or separation order was made; or

(b)   on a subsequent application made with the leave of the court.

(5) In this section, 'period for reflection and consideration' means the period fixed by section 7 of the 1996 Act.]

Amendments—Section prospectively inserted with savings by the Family Law Act 1996, s 15, Sch 2, para 5.

24 *Property adjustment orders in connection with divorce proceedings etc*
[Property adjustment orders: nullity of marriage]

(1) On granting a decree of divorce, a decree of nullity of marriage or a decree of judicial separation or at any time thereafter (whether, in the case of a decree of divorce or of nullity of marriage, before or after the decree is made absolute), the court may make any one or more of the following orders, that is to say —

(a)   an order that a party to the marriage shall transfer to the other party, to any child of the family or to such person as may be specified in the order for the benefit of such a child such property as may be so specified, being property to which the first-mentioned party is entitled, either in possession or reversion;

(b) an order that a 'settlement' of such property as may be so specified, being
     property to which a party to the marriage is so entitled, be made to the
     satisfaction of the court for the benefit of the other party to the marriage
     and of the children of the family or either or any of them;

(c) an order varying for the benefit of the parties to the marriage and of the
     children of the family or either or any of them any ante-nuptial or
     post-nuptial settlement (including such a settlement made by will or
     codicil) made on the parties to the marriage, other than one in the form
     of a pension arrangement (within the meaning of section 25D below);

(d) an order extinguishing or reducing the interest of either of the parties to
     the marriage under any such settlement, other than one in the form of a
     pension arrangement (within the meaning of section 25D below);

subject, however, in the case of an order under paragraph (a) above, to the
restrictions imposed by section 29(1) and (3) below on the making of orders for a
transfer of property in favour of children who have attained the age of eighteen.

(2) The court may make an order under subsection (1)(c) above notwithstanding
that there are no children of the family.

(3) Without prejudice to the power to give a direction under section 30 below for
the settlement of an instrument by conveyancing counsel, where an order is made
under this section on or after granting a decree of divorce or nullity of marriage,
neither the order nor any settlement made in pursuance of the order shall take
effect unless the decree has been made absolute.

[(1) On or after granting a decree of nullity of marriage (whether before or after
the decree is made absolute), the court may, on an application made under this
section, make one or more property adjustment orders in relation to the
marriage.

(2) The court shall exercise its powers under this section, so far as is practicable,
by making on one occasion all such provision as can be made by way of one or
more property adjustment orders in relation to the marriage as it thinks fit.

(3) Subsection (2) above does not affect section 31 or 31A below.

(4) Where a property adjustment order is made under this section on or after
the granting of a decree of nullity of marriage, neither the order nor any
settlement made in pursuance of the order is to take effect unless the decree has
been made absolute.

(5) That does not affect the power to give a direction under section 30 below for
the settlement of an instrument by conveyancing counsel.

(6) This section is to be read subject to any restrictions imposed by this Act.]

Amendments—Welfare Reform and Pensions Act 1999, s 19, Sch 3, paras 1, 3; section prospectively
substituted with savings by the Family Law Act 1996, s 15, Sch 2, para 6.

24A Orders for sale of property

(1) Where the court makes under *section 23 or 24 of this Act* [any of
sections 22A to 24 above] a secured periodical payments order, an order for the

payment of a lump sum or a property adjustment order, then, on making that order or at any time thereafter, the court may make a further order for the sale of such property as may be specified in the order, being property in which or in the proceeds of sale of which either or both of the parties to the marriage has or have a beneficial interest, either in possession or reversion.

(2) Any order made under subsection (1) above may contain such consequential or supplementary provisions as the court thinks fit and, without prejudice to the generality of the foregoing provision, may include —

   (a)   provision requiring the making of a payment out of the proceeds of sale of the property to which the order relates, and
   (b)   provision requiring any such property to be offered for sale to a person, or class of persons, specified in the order.

(3) Where an order is made under subsection (1) above on or after the grant of a decree of *divorce or* nullity of marriage, the order shall not take effect unless the decree has been made absolute.

(4) Where an order is made under subsection (1) above, the court may direct that the order, or such provision thereof as the court may specify, shall not take effect until the occurrence of an event specified by the court or the expiration of a period so specified.

(5) Where an order under subsection (1) above contains a provision requiring the proceeds of sale of the property to which the order relates to be used to secure periodical payments to a party to the marriage, the order shall cease to have effect on the death or re-marriage of, or formation of a civil partnership by, that person.

(6) Where a party to a marriage has a beneficial interest in any property, or in the proceeds of sale thereof, and some other person who is not a party to the marriage also has a beneficial interest in that property or in the proceeds of sale thereof, then, before deciding whether to make an order under this section in relation to that property, it shall be the duty of the court to give that other person an opportunity to make representations with respect to the order; and any representations made by that other person shall be included among the circumstances to which the court is required to have regard under section 25(1) below.

Amendments—Sections inserted by Matrimonial Homes and Property Act 1981, s 7 and Civil Partnership Act 2004, s 261(1), Sch 27, para 42; amended by Matrimonial and Family Proceedings Act 1984, s 46(1), Sch 1, para 11; para (1) words in square brackets prospectively substituted with savings by the Family Law Act 1996, s 66(1), (3), Sch 8, para 8, Sch 10.

24B Pension sharing orders in connection with divorce proceedings etc

(1) On granting a decree of divorce or a decree of nullity of marriage or at any time thereafter (whether before or after the decree is made absolute), the court may, on an application made under this section, make one or more pension sharing orders in relation to the marriage.

(2) A pension sharing order under this section is not to take effect unless the decree on or after which it is made has been made absolute.

(3) A pension sharing order under this section may not be made in relation to a pension arrangement which —

  (a)   is the subject of a pension sharing order in relation to the marriage, or
  (b)   has been the subject of pension sharing between the parties to the marriage.

(4) A pension sharing order under this section may not be made in relation to shareable state scheme rights if —

  (a)   such rights are the subject of a pension sharing order in relation to the marriage, or
  (b)   such rights have been the subject of pension sharing between the parties to the marriage.

(5) A pension sharing order under this section may not be made in relation to the rights of a person under a pension arrangement if there is in force a requirement imposed by virtue of section 25B or 25C below which relates to benefits or future benefits to which he is entitled under the pension arrangement.

[24B Pension sharing orders: divorce

(1) On an application made under this section, the court may at the appropriate time make one or more pension sharing orders.

(2) The 'appropriate time' is any time —

  (a)   after a statement of marital breakdown has been received by the court and before any application for a divorce order or for a separation order is made to the court by reference to that statement;
  (b)   when an application for a divorce order has been made under section 3 of the 1996 Act and has not been withdrawn;
  (c)   when an application for a divorce order has been made under section 4 of the 1996 Act and has not been withdrawn;
  (d)   after a divorce order has been made.

(3) The court shall exercise its powers under this section, so far as is practicable, by making on one occasion all such provision as can be made by way of one or more pension sharing orders in relation to the marriage as it thinks fit.

(4) This section is to be read subject to any restrictions imposed by this Act and to section 19 of the 1996 Act.]

Amendments—Section inserted by Welfare Reform and Pensions Act 1999, s 19, Sch 3, paras 1, 4; prospectively substituted, together with ss 24BA, 24BB and 24BC, for s 24B (as inserted by the Welfare Reform and Pensions Act 1999, s 19, Sch 3, paras 1, 4), by the Family Law Act 1996, s 15, Sch 2, para 6A (as inserted by the Welfare Reform and Pensions Act 1999, s 84(1), Sch 12, Pt I, paras 64, 65(1), (9)).

[24BA Restrictions affecting section 24B]

[(1) No pension sharing order may be made under section 24B above so as to take effect before the making of a divorce order in relation to the marriage.

(2) The court may not make a pension sharing order under section 24B above at any time while the period for reflection and consideration is interrupted under section 7(8) of the 1996 Act.

(3) No pension sharing order may be made under section 24B above by virtue of a statement of marital breakdown if, by virtue of section 5(3) or 7(9) of the 1996 Act (lapse of divorce process), it has ceased to be possible —

   (a)   for an application to be made by reference to that statement, or
   (b)   for an order to be made on such an application.

(4) No pension sharing order may be made under section 24B above after a divorce order has been made, except —

   (a)   in response to an application made before the divorce order was made, or
   (b)   on a subsequent application made with the leave of the court.

(5) A pension sharing order under section 24B above may not be made in relation to a pension arrangement which —

   (a)   is the subject of a pension sharing order in relation to the marriage, or
   (b)   has been the subject of pension sharing between the parties to the marriage.

(6) A pension sharing order under section 24B above may not be made in relation to shareable state scheme rights if —

   (a)   such rights are the subject of a pension sharing order in relation to the marriage, or
   (b)   such rights have been the subject of pension sharing between the parties to the marriage.

(7) A pension sharing order under section 24B above may not be made in relation to the rights of a person under a pension arrangement if there is in force a requirement imposed by virtue of section 25B or 25C below which relates to benefits or future benefits to which he is entitled under the pension arrangement.

(8) In this section, 'period for reflection and consideration' means the period fixed by section 7 of the 1996 Act.]

Amendments—Prospectively substituted, together with ss 24B, 24BB and 24BC, for s 24B (as inserted by the Welfare Reform and Pensions Act 1999, s 19, Sch 3, paras 1, 4), by the Family Law Act 1996, s 15, Sch 2, para 6A (as inserted by the Welfare Reform and Pensions Act 1999, s 84(1), Sch 12, Pt I, paras 64, 65(1), (9)).

[24BB Restrictions affecting section 24B]

[(1) On or after granting a decree of nullity of marriage (whether before or after the decree is made absolute), the court may, on an application made under this section, make one or more pension sharing orders in relation to the marriage.

(2) The court shall exercise its powers under this section, so far as is practicable, by making on one occasion all such provision as can be made by way of one or more pension sharing orders in relation to the marriage as it thinks fit.

(3) Where a pension sharing order is made under this section on or after the granting of a decree of nullity of marriage, the order is not to take effect unless the decree has been made absolute.

(4) This section is to be read subject to any restrictions imposed by this Act.]

Amendments—Prospectively substituted, together with ss 24B, 24BA and 24BC, for s 24B (as inserted by the Welfare Reform and Pensions Act 1999, s 19, Sch 3, paras 1, 4), by the Family Law Act 1996, s 15, Sch 2, para 6A (as inserted by the Welfare Reform and Pensions Act 1999, s 84(1), Sch 12, Pt I, paras 64, 65(1), (9)).

[24BC Restrictions affecting section 24BB]

[(1) A pension sharing order under section 24BB above may not be made in relation to a pension arrangement which —

    (a)   is the subject of a pension sharing order in relation to the marriage, or
    (b)   has been the subject of pension sharing between the parties to the marriage.

(2) A pension sharing order under section 24BB above may not be made in relation to shareable state scheme rights if —

    (a)   such rights are the subject of a pension sharing order in relation to the marriage, or
    (b)   such rights have been the subject of pension sharing between the parties to the marriage.

(3) A pension sharing order under section 24BB above may not be made in relation to the rights of a person under a pension arrangement if there is in force a requirement imposed by virtue of section 25B or 25C below which relates to benefits or future benefits to which he is entitled under the pension arrangement.]

Amendments—Prospectively substituted, together with ss 24B, 24BA and 24BB, for s 24B (as inserted by the Welfare Reform and Pensions Act 1999, s 19, Sch 3, paras 1, 4), by the Family Law Act 1996, s 15, Sch 2, para 6A (as inserted by the Welfare Reform and Pensions Act 1999, s 84(1), Sch 12, Pt I, paras 64, 65(1), (9)).

24C Pension sharing orders: duty to stay

(1) No pension sharing order may be made so as to take effect before the end of such period after the making of the order as may be prescribed by regulations made by the Lord Chancellor.

(2) The power to make regulations under this section shall be exercisable by statutory instrument which shall be subject to annulment in pursuance of a resolution of either House of Parliament.

Amendments—Section inserted by Welfare Reform and Pensions Act 1999, s 19, Sch 3, paras 1, 4.

24D Pension sharing orders: apportionment of charges

If a pension sharing order relates to rights under a pension arrangement, the court may include in the order provision about the apportionment between the parties of any charge under section 41 of the Welfare Reform and Pensions Act 1999 (charges in respect of pension sharing costs), or under corresponding Northern Ireland legislation.

Amendments—Section inserted by Welfare Reform and Pensions Act 1999, s 19, Sch 3, paras 1, 4.

25 Matters to which court is to have regard in deciding how to exercise its powers under ss 23, 24 and 24A

(1) It shall be the duty of the court in deciding whether to exercise its powers under *section 23, 24, 24A or 24B* [any of sections 22A to 24BB] above and, if so, in what manner, to have regard to all the circumstances of the case, first consideration being given to the welfare while a minor of any child of the family who has not attained the age of eighteen.

(2) As regards the exercise of the powers of the court under *section 23(1)(a), (b) or (c)*, [section 22A or 23 above to make a financial provision order in favour of a party to a marriage or the exercise of its powers under section 23A,] 24 [, 24A or 24B [, 24B or 24BB]] above in relation to a party to the marriage, the court shall in particular have regard to the following matters —

   (a)   the income, earning capacity, property and other financial resources which each of the parties to the marriage has or is likely to have in the foreseeable future, including in the case of earning capacity any increase in that capacity which it would in the opinion of the court be reasonable to expect a party to the marriage to take steps to acquire;

   (b)   the financial needs, obligations and responsibilities which each of the parties to the marriage has or is likely to have in the foreseeable future;

   (c)   the standard of living enjoyed by the family before the breakdown of the marriage;

   (d)   the age of each party to the marriage and the duration of the marriage;

   (e)   any physical or mental disability of either of the parties to the marriage;

   (f)   the contributions which each of the parties has made or is likely in the foreseeable future to make to the welfare of the family, including any contribution by looking after the home or caring for the family;

   (g)   the conduct of each of the parties[, whatever the nature of the conduct and whether it occurred during the marriage or after the separation of the parties or (as the case may be) dissolution or annulment of the marriage], if that conduct is such that it would in the opinion of the court be inequitable to disregard it;

(h) *in the case of proceedings for divorce or nullity of marriage*, the value to each of the parties to the marriage of any benefit *(for example, a pension)* which, by reason of the dissolution or annulment of the marriage, that party will lose the chance of acquiring.

(3) As regards the exercise of the powers of the court under *section 23(1)(d), (e) or (f), (2) or (4)* [section 22A or 23 above to make a financial provision order in favour of a child of the family or the exercise of its powers under section 23A,], 24 or 24A above in relation to a child of the family, the court shall in particular have regard to the following matters —

(a) the financial needs of the child;
(b) the income, earning capacity (if any), property and other financial resources of the child;
(c) any physical or mental disability of the child;
(d) the manner in which he was being and in which the parties to the marriage expected him to be educated or trained;
(e) the considerations mentioned in relation to the parties to the marriage in paragraphs (a), (b), (c) and (e) of subsection (2) above.

(4) As regards the exercise of the powers of the court under *section 23(1)(d), (e) or (f), (2) or (4), 24 or 24A* [any of sections 22A to 24A] above against a party to a marriage in favour of a child of the family who is not the child of that party, the court shall also have regard —

(a) to whether that party assumed any responsibility for the child's maintenance, and, if so, to the extent to which, and the basis upon which, that party assumed such responsibility and to the length of time for which that party discharged such responsibility;
(b) to whether in assuming and discharging such responsibility that party did so knowing that the child was not his or her own;
(c) to the liability of any other person to maintain the child.

[(5) In relation to any power of the court to make an interim periodical payments order or an interim order for the payment of a lump sum, the preceding provisions of this section, in imposing any obligation on the court with respect to the matters to which it is to have regard, shall not require the court to do anything which would cause such a delay as would, in the opinion of the court, be inappropriate having regard —

(a) to any immediate need for an interim order;
(b) to the matters in relation to which it is practicable for the court to inquire before making an interim order; and
(c) to the ability of the court to have regard to any matter and to make appropriate adjustments when subsequently making a financial provision order which is not interim.]

Amendments—Substituted by Matrimonial and Family Proceedings Act 1984, s 3; amended by Welfare Reform and Pensions Act 1999, s 19, Sch 3, paras 1, 5(a, b); Pensions Act 1995, s 166(2); paras (1), (2) words prospectively substituted with savings by the Family Law Act 1996, s 66(1),

Sch 8, Pt I, para 9(2), (3)(aa) (as amended/inserted by the Welfare Reform and Pensions Act 1999, s 84(1), Sch 12, Pt I, paras 64, 66(1), (2)(a), (b)); paras (2–4): words prospectively substituted with savings by the Family Law Act 1996, s 66(1), Sch 8, para 9(3)(a); (4), (5); paras (2)(g), (5) words prospectively inserted with savings by the Family Law Act 1996, s 66(1), Sch 8, para 9(3)(b); (6); para (2)(h), words prospectively repealed with savings by the Family Law Act 1996, s 66(1), (3), Sch 8, para 9(3)(c), Sch 10.

25A Exercise of court's powers in favour of party to marriage on decree of divorce or nullity of marriage

(1) *Where on or after the grant of a decree of divorce or nullity of marriage the court decides to exercise its powers under section 23(1)(a), (b) or (c), 24, 24A or 24B above in favour of a party to the marriage* [If the court decides to exercise any of its powers under any of sections 22A to 24BB above in favour of a party to a marriage (other than its power to make an interim periodical payments order or an interim order for the payment of a lump sum)], it shall be the duty of the court to consider whether it would be appropriate so to exercise those powers that the financial obligations of each party towards the other will be terminated as soon after the grant of *the decree* [a divorce order or decree of nullity] as the court considers just and reasonable.

(2) Where the court decides in such a case to make a periodical payments or secured periodical payments order in favour of a party to the marriage, the court shall in particular consider whether it would be appropriate to require those payments to be made or secured only for such term as would in the opinion of the court be sufficient to enable the party in whose favour the order is made to adjust without undue hardship to the termination of his or her financial dependence on the other party.

(3) *Where on or after the grant of a decree of divorce or nullity of marriage an application is made by a party to the marriage for a periodical payments or secured periodical payments order in his or her favour, then, if the court considers that no continuing obligation should be imposed on either party to make or secure periodical payments in favour of the other, the court may dismiss the application with a direction that the applicant shall not be entitled to make any future application in relation to that marriage for an order under section 23(1)(a) or (b) above*

[If the court —

    (a)   would have power under section 22A or 23 above to make a financial provision order in favour of a party to a marriage ('the first party'), but

    (b)   considers that no continuing obligation should be imposed on the other party to the marriage ('the second party') to make or secure periodical payments in favour of the first party,

it may direct that the first party may not at any time after the direction takes effect, apply to the court for the making against the second party of any periodical payments order or secured periodical payments order and, if the first party has already applied to the court for the making of such an order, it may dismiss the application.

(3A) If the court —

(a) exercises, or has exercised, its power under section 22A at any time before making a divorce order, and

(b) gives a direction under subsection (3) above in respect of a periodical payments order or a secured periodical payments order,

it shall provide for the direction not to take effect until a divorce order is made.]

Amendments—Inserted by Matrimonial and Family Proceedings Act 1984, s 3; substituted by Welfare Reform and Pensions Act 1999, s 19, Sch 3, paras 1, 6; para (1) words prospectively substituted with savings by the Family Law Act 1996, s 66(1), Sch 8, Pt I, para 10(2), (3) (as amended by the Welfare Reform and Pensions Act 1999, s 84(1), Sch 12, Pt I, paras 64, 66(1), (3)); paras (3), (3A) prospectively substituted with savings, for para (3) as originally enacted, by the Family Law Act 1996, s 66(1), Sch 8, para 10(4).

25B Pensions

(1) The matters to which the court is to have regard under section 25(2) above include —

(a) in the case of paragraph (a), any benefits under a pension arrangement which a party to the marriage has or is likely to have, and

(b) in the case of paragraph (h), any benefits under a pension arrangement which, by reason of the dissolution or annulment of the marriage, a party to the marriage will lose the chance of acquiring,

and, accordingly, in relation to benefits under a pension arrangement, section 25(2)(a) above shall have effect as if 'in the foreseeable future' were omitted.

(2) (*repealed*)

(3) The following provisions apply where, having regard to any benefits under a pension arrangement, the court determines to make an order under *section 23* [section 22A or 23] above.

(4) To the extent to which the order is made having regard to any benefits under a pension arrangement, the order may require the person responsible for the pension arrangement in question, if at any time any payment in respect of any benefits under the arrangement becomes due to the party with pension rights, to make a payment for the benefit of the other party.

(5) The order must express the amount of any payment required to be made by virtue of subsection (4) above as a percentage of the payment which becomes due to the party with pension rights.

(6) Any such payment by the person responsible for the arrangement —

(a) shall discharge so much of his liability to the party with pension rights as corresponds to the amount of the payment, and

(b) shall be treated for all purposes as a payment made by the party with pension rights in or towards the discharge of his liability under the order.

(7) Where the party with pension rights has a right of commutation under the arrangement, the order may require him to exercise it to any extent; and this

section applies to any payment due in consequence of commutation in pursuance of the order as it applies to other payments in respect of benefits under the arrangement.

(7A) The power conferred by subsection (7) above may not be exercised for the purpose of commuting a benefit payable to the party with pension rights to a benefit payable to the other party.

(7B) The power conferred by subsection (4) or (7) above may not be exercised in relation to a pension arrangement which —

    (a)   is the subject of a pension sharing order in relation to the marriage, or

    (b)   has been the subject of pension sharing between the parties to the marriage.

(7C) In subsection (1) above, references to benefits under a pension arrangement include any benefits by way of pension, whether under a pension arrangement or not.

[(8) If a pensions adjustment order under subsection (2)(c) above is made, the pension rights shall be reduced and pension rights of the other party shall be created in the prescribed manner with benefits payable on prescribed conditions, except that the court shall not have the power —

    (a)   to require the trustees or managers of the scheme to provide benefits under their own scheme if they are able and willing to create the rights for the other party by making a transfer payment to another scheme and the trustees and managers of that other scheme are able and willing to accept such a payment and to create those rights; or

    (b)   to require the trustees or managers of the scheme to make a transfer to another scheme —

        (i)   if the scheme is an unfunded scheme (unless the trustees or managers are able and willing to make such a transfer payment); or

        (ii)   in prescribed circumstances.

(9) No pensions adjustment order may be made under subsection (2)(c) above —

    (a)   if the scheme is a scheme of a prescribed type, or

    (b)   in prescribed circumstances, or

    (c)   insofar as it would affect benefits of a prescribed type.]

Amendments—Section inserted by Pensions Act 1995, s 166; amended by Welfare Reform and Pensions Act 1999, ss 21, 88, Sch 4, para 1, Sch 13, Pt I; para (3) words prospectively substituted with savings by the Family Law Act 1996, s 66(1), Sch 8, para 1; paras (8), (9) prospectively inserted with savings by the Family Law Act 1996, s 16(3).

25C Pensions: lump sums

(1) The power of the court under *section 23* [section 22A or 23] above to order a party to a marriage to pay a lump sum to the other party includes, where the benefits which the party with pension rights has or is likely to have under a

pension arrangement include any lump sum payable in respect of his death, power to make any of the following provision by the order.

(2) The court may —

(a)   if the person responsible for the pension arrangement in question has power to determine the person to whom the sum, or any part of it, is to be paid, require him to pay the whole or part of that sum, when it becomes due, to the other party,

(b)   if the party with pension rights has power to nominate the person to whom the sum, or any part of it, is to be paid, require the party with pension rights to nominate the other party in respect of the whole or part of that sum,

(c)   in any other case, require the person responsible for the pension arrangement in question to pay the whole or part of that sum, when it becomes due, for the benefit of the other party instead of to the person to whom, apart from the order, it would be paid.

(3) Any payment by the person responsible for the arrangement under an order made under *section 23* [section 22A or 23] above by virtue of this section shall discharge so much of his liability in respect of the party with pension rights as corresponds to the amount of the payment.

(4) The powers conferred by this section may not be exercised in relation to a pension arrangement which —

(a)   is the subject of a pension sharing order in relation to the marriage, or

(b)   has been the subject of pension sharing between the parties to the marriage.

Amendments—Section inserted by Pensions Act 1995, s 166; amended by Welfare Reform and Pensions Act 1999, s 21, Sch 4, para 2; paras (1), (3) words prospectively substituted with savings by the Family Law Act 1996, s 66(1), Sch 8, para 11.

25D Pensions: supplementary

(1) Where —

(a)   an order made under *section 23* [section 22A or 23] above by virtue of section 25B or 25C above imposes any requirement on the person responsible for a pension arrangement ('the first arrangement') and the party with pension rights acquires rights under another pension arrangement ('the new arrangement') which are derived (directly or indirectly) from the whole of his rights under the first arrangement, and

(b)   the person responsible for the new arrangement has been given notice in accordance with regulations made by the Lord Chancellor,

the order shall have effect as if it had been made instead in respect of the person responsible for the new arrangement.

(2) The Lord Chancellor may by Regulations —

(a)   in relation to any provision of sections 25B or 25C above which authorises the court making an order under *section 23* [section 22A or 23] above to require the person responsible for a pension arrangement to make a payment for the benefit of the other party, make provision as to the person to whom, and the terms on which, the payment is to be made, or prescribe the rights of the other party under the pension scheme,

(aa)   make such consequential modifications of any enactment or subordinate legislation as appear to the Lord Chancellor necessary or expedient to give effect to the provisions of section 25B; and an order under this paragraph may make provision applying generally in relation to enactments and subordinate legislation of a description specified in the order,

(ab)   make, in relation to payment under a mistaken belief as to the continuation in force of a provision included by virtue of section 25B or 25C above in an order under *section 23* [section 22A or 23] above, provision about the rights or liabilities of the payer, the payee or the person to whom the payment was due,

(b)   require notices to be given in respect of changes of circumstances relevant to such orders which include provision made by virtue of sections 25B and 25C above,

(ba)   make provision for the person responsible for a pension arrangement to be discharged in prescribed circumstances from a requirement imposed by virtue of section 25B or 25C above,

(c),   (d) (*repealed*)

(e)   make provision about calculation and verification in relation to the valuation of —
       (i)   benefits under a pension arrangement, or
       (ii)   shareable state scheme rights,
       for the purposes of the court's functions in connection with the exercise of any of its powers under this Part of this Act.

(2A) Regulations under subsection (2)(e) above may include —

(a)   provision for calculation or verification in accordance with guidance from time to time prepared by a prescribed person, and

(b)   provision by reference to regulations under section 30 or 49(4) of the Welfare Reform and Pensions Act 1999.

(2B) Regulations under subsection (2) above may make different provision for different cases.

(2C) Power to make regulations under this section shall be exercisable by statutory instrument which shall be subject to annulment in pursuance of a resolution of either House of Parliament.

(3) In this section and sections 25B and 25C above —

'occupational pension scheme' has the same meaning as in the Pension Schemes Act 1993;

'the party with pension rights' means the party to the marriage who has or is
likely to have benefits under a pension arrangement and 'the other party'
means the other party to the marriage;
'pension arrangement' means —

- (a)   an occupational pension scheme,
- (b)   a personal pension scheme,
- (c)   a retirement annuity contract,
- (d)   an annuity or insurance policy purchased, or transferred, for the
purpose of giving effect to rights under an occupational pension
scheme or a personal pension scheme, and
- (e)   an annuity purchased, or entered into, for the purpose of
discharging liability in respect of a pension credit under
section 29(1)(b) of the Welfare Reform and Pensions Act 1999 or
under corresponding Northern Ireland legislation;

'personal pension scheme' has the same meaning as in the Pension Schemes
Act 1993;
'prescribed' means prescribed by regulations;
'retirement annuity contract' means a contract or scheme approved under
Chapter III of Part XIV of the Income and Corporation Taxes Act 1988;
'shareable state scheme rights' has the same meaning as in *section 21A(1)*
[section 21(3)] above; and
'trustees or managers', in relation to an occupational pension scheme or a
personal pension scheme, means —

- (a)   in the case of a scheme established under a trust, trustees of the
scheme, and
- (b)   in any other case, the managers of the scheme.

(4) In this section and sections 25B and 25C above, references to the person
responsible for a pension arrangement are —

- (a)   in the case of an occupational pension scheme or a personal pension
scheme, to the trustees or managers of the scheme,
- (b)   in the case of a retirement annuity contract or an annuity falling
within paragraph (d) or (e) of the definition of 'pension arrangement'
above, the provider of the annuity, and
- (c)   in the case of an insurance policy falling within paragraph (d) of the
definition of that expression, the insurer.

Amendments—Section inserted by Pensions Act 1995, s 166; amended by Welfare Reform and
Pensions Act 1999, s 21, Sch 4, para 3; paras (1)(a), (2)(a), (ab), (3) words prospectively substituted
with savings by the Family Law Act 1996, s 66(1), Sch 8, Pt I, para 11 (as amended by the Welfare
Reform and Pensions Act 1999, s 84(1), Sch 12, Pt I, paras 64, 66(1), (4)); paras (2)(a), (aa), (4A)
words and paragraphs prospectively inserted with savings by the Family Law Act 1996, s 16(4)(a).

25E The Pension Protection Fund

(1) The matters to which the court is to have regard under section 25(2)
include —

- (a)   in the case of paragraph (a), any PPF compensation to which a party
to the marriage is or is likely to be entitled, and

(b)   in the case of paragraph (h), any PPF compensation which, by reason of the dissolution or annulment of the marriage, a party to the marriage will lose the chance of acquiring entitlement to,

and, accordingly, in relation to PPF compensation, section 25(2)(a) shall have effect as if 'in the foreseeable future' were omitted.

(2) Subsection (3) applies in relation to an order under section 23 so far as it includes provision made by virtue of section 25B(4) which —

(a)   imposed requirements on the trustees or managers of an occupational pension scheme for which the Board has assumed responsibility in accordance with Chapter 3 of Part 2 of the Pensions Act 2004 (pension protection) or any provision in force in Northern Ireland corresponding to that Chapter, and

(b)   was made before the trustees or managers of the scheme received the transfer notice in relation to the scheme.

(3) The order is to have effect from the time when the trustees or managers of the scheme receive the transfer notice —

(a)   as if, except in prescribed descriptions of case —
    (i)   references in the order to the trustees or managers of the scheme were references to the Board, and
    (ii) references in the order to any pension or lump sum to which the party with pension rights is or may become entitled under the scheme were references to any PPF compensation to which that person is or may become entitled in respect of the pension or lump sum, and

(b)   subject to such other modifications as may be prescribed.

(4) Subsection (5) applies to an order under section 23 if —

(a)   it includes provision made by virtue of section 25B(7) which requires the party with pension rights to exercise his right of commutation under an occupational pension scheme to any extent, and

(b)   before the requirement is complied with the Board has assumed responsibility for the scheme as mentioned in subsection (2)(a).

(5) From the time the trustees or managers of the scheme receive the transfer notice, the order is to have effect with such modifications as may be prescribed.

(6) Regulations may modify section 25C as it applies in relation to an occupational pension scheme at any time when there is an assessment period in relation to the scheme.

(7) Where the court makes a pension sharing order in respect of a person's shareable rights under an occupational pension scheme, or an order which includes provision made by virtue of section 25B(4) or (7) in relation to such a scheme, the Board subsequently assuming responsibility for the scheme as mentioned in subsection (2)(a) does not affect —

(a)   the powers of the court under section 31 to vary or discharge the order or to suspend or revive any provision of it, or

(b) on an appeal, the powers of the appeal court to affirm, reinstate, set aside or vary the order.

(8) Regulations may make such consequential modifications of any provision of, or made by virtue of, this Part as appear to the Lord Chancellor necessary or expedient to give effect to the provisions of this section.

(9) In this section —

'assessment period' means an assessment period within the meaning of Part 2 of the Pensions Act 2004 (pension protection) (see sections 132 and 159 of that Act) or an equivalent period under any provision in force in Northern Ireland corresponding to that Part;

'the Board' means the Board of the Pension Protection Fund;

'occupational pension scheme' has the same meaning as in the Pension Schemes Act 1993;

'prescribed' means prescribed by regulations;

'PPF compensation' means compensation payable under Chapter 3 of Part 2 of the Pensions Act 2004 (pension protection) or any provision in force in Northern Ireland corresponding to that Chapter;

'regulations' means regulations made by the Lord Chancellor;

'shareable rights' are rights in relation to which pension sharing is available under Chapter 1 of Part 4 of the Welfare Reform and Pensions Act 1999 or any provision in force in Northern Ireland corresponding to that Chapter;

'transfer notice' has the same meaning as in section 160 of the Pensions Act 2004 or any corresponding provision in force in Northern Ireland.

(10) Any power to make regulations under this section is exercisable by statutory instrument, which shall be subject to annulment in pursuance of a resolution of either House of Parliament.

Amendments—Section inserted by the Pensions Act 2004, s 319(1), Sch 12, para 3.

26 Commencement of proceedings for ancillary relief etc

(1) *Where a petition for divorce, nullity of marriage or judicial separation has been presented, then, subject to subsection (2) below, proceedings for maintenance pending suit under section 22 above* [If a petition for nullity of marriage has been presented, then, subject to subsection (2) below, proceedings], for a financial provision order under section 23 above, or for a property adjustment order may be begun, subject to and in accordance with rules of court, at any time after the presentation of the petition.

(2) Rules of court may provide, in such cases as may be prescribed by the rules —

(a) that applications for any such relief as is mentioned in subsection (1) above shall be made in the petition or answer; and

(b) that applications for any such relief which are not so made, or are not made until after the expiration of such period following the presentation of the petition or filing of the answer as may be so prescribed, shall be made only with the leave of the court.

Amendments—Para (1), words prospectively substituted with savings by the Family Law Act 1996, s 66(1), Sch 8, para 12.

Financial provision in case of neglect to maintain

27 Financial provision orders etc in case of neglect by party to marriage to maintain other party or child of the family

(1) Either party to a marriage may apply to the court for an order under this section on the ground that the other party to the marriage (in this section referred to as the respondent) —

(a)   has failed to provide reasonable maintenance for the applicant, or

(b)   has failed to provide, or to make a proper contribution towards, reasonable maintenance for any child of the family.

(2) The court shall not entertain an application under this section unless —

(a)   the applicant or the respondent is domiciled in England and Wales on the date of the application; or

(b)   the applicant has been habitually resident there throughout the period of one year ending with that date; or

(c) the respondent is resident there on that date.

(3) Where an application under this section is made on the ground mentioned in subsection (1)(a) above, then, in deciding —

(a)   whether the respondent has failed to provide reasonable maintenance for the applicant, and

(b)   what order, if any, to make under this section in favour of the applicant,

the court shall have regard to all the circumstances of the case including the matters mentioned in section 25(2) above, and where an application is also made under this section in respect of a child of the family who has not attained the age of eighteen, first consideration shall be given to the welfare of the child while a minor.

(3A) Where an application under this section is made on the ground mentioned in subsection (1)(b) above then, in deciding —

(a)   whether the respondent has failed to provide, or to make a proper contribution towards, reasonable maintenance for the child of the family to whom the application relates, and

(b)   what order, if any, to make under this section in favour of the child,

the court shall have regard to all the circumstances of the case including the matters mentioned in section 25(3)(a) to (e) above, and where the child of the family to whom the application relates is not the child of the respondent, including also the matters mentioned in section 25(4) above.

(3B) In relation to an application under this section on the ground mentioned in subsection (1)(a) above, section 25(2)(c) above shall have effect as if for the reference therein to the breakdown of the marriage there were substituted a reference to the failure to provide reasonable maintenance for the applicant, and in relation to an application under this section on the ground mentioned in subsection (1)(b) above, section 25(2)(c) above (as it applies by virtue of section 25(3)(e) above) shall have effect as if for the reference therein to the breakdown of the marriage there were substituted a reference to the failure to provide, or to make a proper contribution towards, reasonable maintenance for the child of the family to whom the application relates.

(4) (*repealed*)

(5) Where on an application under this section it appears to the court that the applicant or any child of the family to whom the application relates is in immediate need of financial assistance, but it is not yet possible to determine what order, if any, should be made on the application, the court may make an interim order for maintenance, that is to say, an order requiring the respondent —

(a)   to make to the applicant until the determination of the application such periodical payments as the court thinks reasonable, or

(b)   to pay to the applicant such lump sum or sums as the court thinks reasonable.

(6) *Where on an application under this section the applicant satisfies the court of any ground mentioned in subsection (1) above, the court may make any one or more of the following orders, that is to say —*

(*a*)   *an order that the respondent shall make to the applicant such periodical payments, for such term, as may be specified in the order;*

(*b*)   *an order that the respondent shall secure to the applicant, to the satisfaction of the court, such periodical payments, for such term, as may be so specified;*

(*c*)   *an order that the respondent shall pay to the applicant such lump sum as may be so specified;*

(*d*)   *an order that the respondent shall make to such person as may be specified in the order for the benefit of the child to whom the application relates, or to that child, such periodical payments, for such term, as may be so specified;*

(*e*)   *an order that the respondent shall secure to such person as may be so specified for the benefit of that child, or to that child, to the satisfaction of the court, such periodical payments, for such term, as may be so specified;*

(*f*)   *an order that the respondent shall pay to such person as may be so specified for the benefit of that child, or to that child, such lump sum as may be so specified;*

subject, however, in the case of an order under paragraph (d), (e) or (f) above, to the restrictions imposed by section 29(1) and (3) below on the making of financial provision orders in favour of children who have attained the age of eighteen. [Subject to the restrictions imposed by the following provisions of this Act, if on an application under this section the applicant satisfies the court of any ground mentioned in subsection (1) above, the court may make one or more financial provision orders against the respondent in favour of the applicant or a child of the family.]

(6A) An application for the variation under section 31 of this Act of a periodical payments order or secured periodical payments order made under this section in favour of a child may, if the child has attained the age of sixteen, be made by the child himself.

(6B) Where a periodical payments order made in favour of a child under this section ceases to have effect on the date on which the child attains the age of sixteen or at any time after that date but before or on the date on which he attains the age of eighteen, then if, on an application made to the court for an order under this subsection, it appears to the court that —

(a)   the child is, will be or (if an order were made under this subsection) would be receiving instruction at an educational establishment or undergoing training for a trade, profession or vocation, whether or not he also is, will be or would be in gainful employment; or

(b)   there are special circumstances which justify the making of an order under this subsection,

the court shall have power by order to revive the first mentioned order from such date as the court may specify, not being earlier than the date of the making of the application, and to exercise its power under section 31 of this Act in relation to any order so revived.

(7) Without prejudice to the generality of subsection *(6)(c) or (f)* [(6)] above, an order under this section for the payment of a lump sum —

(a)   may be made for the purpose of enabling any liabilities or expenses reasonably incurred in maintaining the applicant or any child of the family to whom the application relates before the making of the application to be met;

(b)   may provide for the payment of that sum by instalments of such amount as may be specified in the order and may require the payment of the instalments to be secured to the satisfaction of the court.

(8) *(repealed)*

Amendments—Domicile and Matrimonial Proceedings Act 1973, s 6(1); Domestic Proceedings and Magistrates' Courts Act 1978, ss 63, 89(2)(b), Sch 3; Matrimonial and Family Proceedings Act 1984, s 4, Sch 1, para 12; Family Law Reform Act 1987, s 33(1), Sch 2, para 52; para (5) figures and words prospectively inserted, para (6) and words in para (7) prospectively substituted with savings by the Family Law Act 1996, s 66(1), Sch 8, para 13(2–4).

Additional provisions with respect to financial provision and property adjustment orders

28 Duration of continuing financial provision orders in favour of party to marriage, and effect of remarriage or formation of civil partnership

(1) Subject *in the case of an order made on or after the grant of a decree of a divorce or nullity of marriage* to the provisions of sections 25A(2) above and 31(7) below, the term to be specified in a periodical payments or secured periodical payments order in favour of a party to a marriage shall be such term as the court thinks fit, except that the term shall not begin before or extend beyond the following limits, that is to say —

(a) *in the case of a periodical payments order, the term shall begin not earlier than the date of the making of an application for the order, and shall be so defined as not to extend beyond the death of either of the parties to the marriage or, where the order is made on or after the grant of a decree of divorce or nullity of marriage, the remarriage of, or formation of a civil partnership by the party in whose favour the order is made; and*

(b) *in the case of a secured periodical payments order, the term shall begin not earlier than the date of the making of an application for the order, and shall be so defined as not to extend beyond the death or, where the order is made on or after the grant of such a decree, the remarriage of, or formation of a civil partnership by the party in whose favour the order is made.*

[(a) a term specified in the order which is to begin before the making of the order shall begin no earlier —

    (i) where the order is made by virtue of section 22A(2)(a) or (b) above, unless sub-paragraph (ii) below applies, than the beginning of the day on which the statement of marital breakdown in question was received by the court;

    (ii) where the order is made by virtue of section 22A(2)(b) above and the application for the divorce order was made following cancellation of an order preventing divorce under section 10 of the 1996 Act, than the date of the making of that application;

    (iii) where the order is made by virtue of section 22A(2)(c) above, than the date of the making of the application for the divorce order; or

    (iv) in any other case, than the date of the making of the application on which the order is made;

(b) a term specified in a periodical payments order or secured periodical payments order shall be so defined as not to extend beyond —

    (i) in the case of a periodical payments order, the death of the party by whom the payments are to be made; or

    (ii) in either case, the death of the party in whose favour the order was made or the remarriage of that party following the making of a divorce order or decree of nullity.]

(1A) *Where a periodical payments or secured periodical payments order in favour of a party to a marriage is made on or after the grant of a decree of divorce or nullity of marriage,* [At any time when —

(a) the court exercises, or has exercised, its power under section 22A or 23 above to make a financial provision order in favour of a party to a marriage,

(b) but for having exercised that power, the court would have power under one of those sections to make such an order, and

(c) an application for a divorce order or a petition for a decree of nullity of marriage is outstanding or has been granted in relation to the marriage,]

the court may direct that that party shall not be entitled to apply under section 31 below for the extension of the term specified in the order.

[(1B) If the court —

(a) exercises, or has exercised, its power under section 22A at any time before making a divorce order, and

(b) gives a direction under subsection (1A) above in respect of a periodical payments order or a secured periodical payments order

it shall provide for the direction not to take effect until a divorce order is made.]

(2) Where a periodical payments or secured periodical payments order in favour of a party to a marriage is made otherwise than *on or after the grant of a decree of divorce or nullity of marriage* [at such a time as is mentioned in subsection (1A)(c) above], and the marriage in question is subsequently dissolved or annulled but the order continues in force, the order shall, notwithstanding anything in it, cease to have effect on the remarriage of, or formation of a civil partnership by, that party, except in relation to any arrears due under it on the date of the remarriage or formation of the civil partnership.

(3) If after the grant of *a decree* [an order or decree] dissolving or annulling a marriage either party to that marriage remarries whether at any time before or after the commencement of this Act or forms a civil partnership, that party shall not be entitled to apply, by reference to the grant of *that decree* [that order or decree], for a financial provision order in his or her favour, or for a property adjustment order, against the other party to that marriage.

Amendments—Matrimonial and Family Proceedings Act 1984, s 5(1–3); paras (1)(a–b), (2), (3) words inserted by the Civil Partnership Act 2004, s 261(1), Sch 27, para 43(1–5); para (1) words prospectively repealed, with savings, by the Family Law Act 1996, s 66(3), Sch 10; paras (1)(a–b), (1A), (2), (3) prospectively substituted, with savings, by the Family Law Act 1996, s 15, Sch 2, para 7(1) and s 66(1), Sch 8, para 14(2), (4–5); para (1B) prospectively inserted with savings by the Family Law Act 1996, s 66(1), Sch 8, para 14(3).

29 Duration of continuing financial provision orders in favour of children, and age limit on making certain orders in their favour

(1) Subject to subsection (3) below, no financial provision order and no order for a transfer of property under *section 24(1)(a)* [such as is mentioned in section 21(2)(a)] above shall be made in favour of a child who has attained the age of eighteen.

[(1A) The term specified in a periodical payments order or secured periodical payments order made in favour of a child shall be such term as the court thinks fit.

(1B) If that term is to begin before the making of the order, it may do so no earlier than —

(a) in the case of an order made by virtue of section 22A(2)(a) or (b) above, except where paragraph (b) below applies, the beginning of the day on which the statement of marital breakdown in question was received by the court;

(b) in the case of an order made by virtue of section 22A(2)(b) above where the application for the divorce order was made following cancellation of an order preventing divorce under section 10 of the 1996 Act, the date of the making of that application;

(c) in the case of an order made by virtue of section 22A(2)(c) above, the date of the making of the application for the divorce order; or

(d) in any other case, the date of the making of the application on which the order is made.]

(2) The term to be specified in a periodical payments or secured periodical payments order in favour of a child *may begin with the date of the making of an application for the order in question or any later date or a date ascertained in accordance with subsection (5) or (6) below but —*

(a) shall not in the first instance extend beyond the date of the birthday of the child next following his attaining the upper limit of the compulsory school age (construed in accordance with section 8 of the Education Act 1996) unless the court considers that in the circumstances of the case the welfare of the child requires that it should extend to a later date; and

(b) shall not in any event, subject to subsection (3) below, extend beyond the date of the child's eighteenth birthday.

(3) Subsection (1) above, and paragraph (b) of subsection (2), shall not apply in the case of a child, if it appears to the court that —

(a) the child is, or will be, or if an order were made without complying with either or both of those provisions would be, receiving instruction at an educational establishment or undergoing training for a trade, profession or vocation, whether or not he is also, or will also be, in gainful employment; or

(b) there are special circumstances which justify the making of an order without complying with either or both of those provisions.

(4) Any periodical payments order in favour of a child shall, notwithstanding anything in the order, cease to have effect on the death of the person liable to make payments under the order, except in relation to any arrears due under the order on the date of the death.

(5) Where —

(a) a *maintenance assessment* [maintenance calculation] ('the *current assessment'* [current calculation]) is in force with respect to a child; and

(b) an application is made under Part II of this Act for a periodical payments or secured periodical payments order in favour of that child —

(i) in accordance with section 8 of the Child Support Act 1991, and

(ii) before the end of the period of 6 months beginning with the making of the *current assessment* [current calculation],

the term to be specified in any such order made on that application may be expressed to begin on, or at any time after, the earliest permitted date.

(6) For the purposes of subsection (5) above, 'the earliest permitted date' is whichever is the later of —

(a) the date 6 months before the application is made; or

(b) the date on which the *current assessment* [current calculation] took effect or, where successive *maintenance assessments* [maintenance calculations] have been continuously in force with respect to a child, on which the first of *those assessments* [those calculations] took effect.

(7) Where —

(a) a *maintenance assessment* [maintenance calculation] ceases to have effect *or is cancelled* by or under any provision of the Child Support Act 1991; and

(b) an application is made, before the end of the period of 6 months beginning with the relevant date, for a periodical payments or secured periodical payments order in favour of a child with respect to whom that *maintenance assessment* [maintenance calculation] was in force immediately before it ceased to have effect *or was cancelled,*

the term to be specified in any such order made on that application may begin with the date on which that *maintenance assessment* [maintenance calculation] ceased to have effect *or, as the case may be, the date with effect from which it was cancelled,* or any later date.

(8) In subsection (7)(b) above —

(a) where the *maintenance assessment* [maintenance calculation] ceased to have effect, the relevant date is the date on which it so ceased; *and*

(b) *where the maintenance assessment was cancelled, the relevant date is the later of —*

(i) *the date on which the person who cancelled it did so, and*

(ii) *the date from which the cancellation first had effect.*

Amendments—Matrimonial and Family Proceedings Act 1984, s 5; SI 1993/623; Education Act 1996, Sch 37, Pt II, para 136; paras (5–8) prospective amendments (except in relation to certain cases) see s 86(2) Child Support, Pensions and Social Security Act 2000, s 26, Sch 3, para 3(1), (2)(a–d) and s 85, Sch 9, Pt I; para (1): words prospectively substituted with savings by the Family Law Act 1996, s 66(1), Sch 8, para 15; paras (1A), (1B) inserted with savings by the Family Law Act 1996, s 15, Sch 2, para 7(2) and para (2) words prospectively repealed with savings by the Family Law Act 1996, s 66(3), Sch 10; words and paras (5)–(8) inserted by SI 1993/623, art 2, Sch 1, paras 1, 2.

30 Direction for settlement of instrument for securing payments or effecting property adjustment

Where the court decides to make a financial provision order requiring any payments to be secured or a property adjustment order —

(a)   it may direct that the matter be referred to one of the conveyancing counsel of the court for him to settle a proper instrument to be executed by all necessary parties; and

(b)   where the order is to be made in proceedings for *divorce*, nullity of marriage *or judicial separation* it may, if it thinks fit, defer the grant of the decree in question until the instrument has been duly executed.

Amendments—Words prospectively repealed with savings by the Family Law Act 1996, s 66(3), Sch 10.

Variation, discharge and enforcement of certain orders etc

31 Variation, discharge etc of certain orders for financial relief

(1) Where the court has made an order to which this section applies, then, subject to the provisions of this section and of section 28(1A) above, the court shall have power to vary or discharge the order or to suspend any provision thereof temporarily and to revive the operation of any provision so suspended.

(2) This section applies to the following orders [under this Part of this Act], that is to say —

(a)   any *order for maintenance pending suit and any* interim order for maintenance;

(b)   any periodical payments order;

(c)   any secured periodical payments order;

[(d)   an order for the payment of a lump sum in a case in which the payment is to be by instalments;]

(dd)   any deferred order made by virtue of section 23(1)(c) [21(1)(c)] (lump sums) which includes provision made by virtue of —

(i)   section 25B(4), or

(ii)   section 25C,

(provision in respect of pension rights);

[(de)   any other order for the payment of a lump sum, if it is made at a time when no divorce order has been made, and no separation order is in force, in relation to the marriage;]

(e)   *any order for a settlement of property under section 24(1)(b) or for a variation of settlement under section 24(1)(c) or (d) above, being an order made on or after the grant of a decree of judicial separation;* [any order under section 23A of a kind referred to in section 21(2)(b),(c) or (d) which is made on or after the making of a separation order;

(ea) any order under section 23A which is made at a time when no divorce order has been made, and no separation order is in force, in relation to the marriage;]

(f) any order made under section 24A(1) above for the sale of property;

[(fa) a pension sharing order under section 24B which is made at a time when no divorce order has been made, and no separation order is in force, in relation to the marriage;]

(g) a pension sharing order under section *24B* [24BB] above which is made at a time before the decree has been made absolute.

(2A) Where the court has made an order referred to in subsection (2)(a), (b) or (c) above, then, subject to the provisions of this section, the court shall have power to remit the payment of any arrears due under the order or of any part thereof.

(2B) Where the court has made an order referred to in subsection (2)(dd)(ii) above, this section shall cease to apply to the order on the death of either of the parties to the marriage.

(3) The powers exercisable by the court under this section in relation to an order shall be exercisable also in relation to any instrument executed in pursuance of the order.

(4) The court shall not exercise the powers conferred by this section in relation to an order *for a settlement under section 24(1)(b) or for a variation of settlement under section 24(1)(c) or (d)* [referred to in subsection (2)(e)] above except on an application made in proceedings —

(a) *for the rescission of the decree of judicial separation by reference to which the order was made, or*

(b) *for the dissolution of the marriage in question [on an application for a divorce order in relation to the marriage].*

(4A) In relation to an order which falls within paragraph [(de), (ea), (fa) or] (g) of subsection (2) above ('the subsection (2) order') —

(a) the powers conferred by this section may be exercised —
   (i) only on an application made before the subsection (2) order has or, but for paragraph (b) below, would have taken effect; and
   (ii) only if, at the time when the application is made, the decree has not been made absolute; and

(b) an application made in accordance with paragraph (a) above prevents the subsection (2) order from taking effect before the application has been dealt with.

[(4AA) No variation —

(a) of a financial provision order made under section 22A above, other than an interim order, or

(b) of a property adjustment order made under section 23A above, shall be made so as to take effect before the making of a divorce order or separation order in relation to the marriage, unless the court is satisfied that the circumstances of the case are exceptional, and that it would be just and reasonable for the variation to be so made.

(4AB) No variation of a pension sharing order under section 24B above shall be made so as to take effect before the making of a divorce order in relation to the marriage.]

(4B) No variation of a pension sharing order [under section 24BB above] shall be made so as to take effect before the decree is made absolute.

(4C) The variation of a pension sharing order prevents the order taking effect before the end of such period after the making of the variation as may be prescribed by regulations made by the Lord Chancellor.

(5) Subject to subsections (7A) to (7G) below and without prejudice to any power exercisable by virtue of subsection (2)(d), (dd), (e) or (g) above or otherwise than by virtue of this section, no property adjustment order or pension sharing order shall be made on an application for the variation of a periodical payments or secured periodical payments order made (whether in favour of a party to a marriage or in favour of a child of the family) under *section 23* [section 22A or 23] above, and no order for the payment of a lump sum shall be made on an application for the variation of a periodical payments or secured periodical payments order in favour of a party to a marriage (whether made under *section 23* [section 22A or 23] or under section 27 above).

(6) Where the person liable to make payments under a secured periodical payments order has died, an application under this section relating to that order (and to any order made under section 24A(1) above which requires the proceeds of sale of property to be used for securing those payments) may be made by the person entitled to payments under the periodical payments order or by the personal representatives of the deceased person, but no such application shall, except with the permission of the court, be made after the end of the period of six months from the date on which representation in regard to the estate of that person is first taken out.

(7) In exercising the powers conferred by this section the court shall have regard to all the circumstances of the case, first consideration being given to the welfare while a minor of any child of the family who has not attained the age of eighteen, and the circumstances of the case shall include any change in any of the matters to which the court was required to have regard when making the order to which the application relates, and —

    (a)   in the case of a periodical payments or secured periodical payments order made *on or after the grant of a decree of divorce or nullity of marriage, the court shall consider* [in favour of a party to a marriage, the court shall, if the marriage has been dissolved or annulled, consider] whether in all the circumstances and after having regard to any such change it would be appropriate to vary the order so that payments under the order are required to be made or secured only for such further period as will in the opinion of the court be sufficient (in the light of any proposed exercise by the court, where the marriage has been dissolved, of its powers under subsection (7B) below) to enable the party in whose favour the order was made to adjust without undue hardship to the termination of those payments;

(b)   in a case where the party against whom the order was made has died, the circumstances of the case shall also include the changed circumstances resulting from his or her death.

(7A) Subsection (7B) below applies where, after the dissolution of a marriage, the court —

(a)   discharges a periodical payments order or secured periodical payments order made in favour of a party to the marriage; or

(b)   varies such an order so that payments under the order are required to be made or secured only for such further period as is determined by the court.

(7B) The court has power, in addition to any power it has apart from this subsection, to make supplemental provision consisting of any of —

(a)   an order for the payment of a lump sum in favour of a party to the marriage;

(b)   one or more property adjustment orders in favour of a party to the marriage;

(ba) one or more pension sharing orders;

(c)   a direction that the party in whose favour the original order discharged or varied was made is not entitled to make any further application for —

(i)   a periodical payments or secured periodical payments order, or

(ii) an extension of the period to which the original order is limited by any variation made by the court.

(7C) An order for the payment of a lump sum made under subsection (7B) above may —

(a)   provide for the payment of that sum by instalments of such amount as may be specified in the order; and

(b)   require the payment of the instalments to be secured to the satisfaction of the court.

(7D) Section 23(6) above applies where the court makes an order for the payment of a lump sum under subsection (7B) above as it applies where the court makes such an order under section 23 above.

(7E) If under subsection (7B) above the court makes more than one property adjustment order in favour of the same party to the marriage, each of those orders must fall within a different paragraph of section 21(2) above.

(7F) Sections 24A and 30 above apply where the court makes a property adjustment order under subsection (7B) above as they apply where it makes such an order under section 24 above.

[(7FA) Section 24B(3) above applies where the court makes a pension sharing order under subsection (7B) above as it applies where the court makes such an order under section 24B above.]

(7G) *Subsections (3) to (5) of section 24B* [Section 24BA(5) to (7)] above apply in relation to a pension sharing order under subsection (7B) above as they apply in relation to a pension sharing order under *that section* [section 24B above].

(8) The personal representatives of a deceased person against whom a secured periodical payments order was made shall not be liable for having distributed any part of the estate of the deceased after the expiration of the period of six months referred to in subsection (6) above on the ground that they ought to have taken into account the possibility that the court might permit an application under this section to be made after that period by the person entitled to payments under the order; but this subsection shall not prejudice any power to recover any part of the estate so distributed arising by virtue of the making of an order in pursuance of this section.

(9) In considering for the purposes of subsection (6) above the question when representation was first taken out, a grant limited to settled land or to trust property shall be left out of account and a grant limited to real estate or to personal estate shall be left out of account unless a grant limited to the remainder of the estate has previously been made or is made at the same time.

(10) Where the court, in exercise of its powers under this section, decides to vary or discharge a periodical payments or secured periodical payments order, then, subject to section 28(1) and (2) above, the court shall have power to direct that the variation or discharge shall not take effect until the expiration of such period as may be specified in the order.

(11) Where —

    (a)   a periodical payments or secured periodical payments order in favour of more than one child ('the order') is in force;

    (b)   the order requires payments specified in it to be made to or for the benefit of more than one child without apportioning those payments between them;

    (c)   a *maintenance assessment* [maintenance calculation] ('*the assessment* [the calculation]') is made with respect to one or more, but not all, of the children with respect to whom those payments are to be made; and

    (d)   an application is made, before the end of the period of 6 months beginning with the date on which *the assessment* [the calculation] was made, for the variation or discharge of the order,

the court may, in exercise of its powers under this section to vary or discharge the order, direct that the variation or discharge shall take effect from the date on which *the assessment* [the calculation] took effect or any later date.

(12) Where —

(a) an order ('the child order') of a kind prescribed for the purposes of section 10(1) of the Child Support Act 1991 is affected by a *maintenance assessment* [maintenance calculation];

(b) on the date on which the child order became so affected there was in force a periodical payments or secured periodical payments order ('the spousal order') in favour of a party to a marriage having the care of the child in whose favour the child order was made; and

(c) an application is made, before the end of the period of 6 months beginning with the date on which the *maintenance assessment* [maintenance calculation] was made, for the spousal order to be varied or discharged,

the court may, in exercise of its powers under this section to vary or discharge the spousal order, direct that the variation or discharge shall take effect from the date on which the child order became so affected or any later date.

(13) For the purposes of subsection (12) above, an order is affected if it ceases to have effect or is modified by or under section 10 of the Child Support Act 1991.

(14) Subsections (11) and (12) above are without prejudice to any other power of the court to direct that the variation or discharge of an order under this section shall take effect from a date earlier than that on which the order for variation or discharge was made.

(15) The power to make regulations under subsection (4C) above shall be exercisable by statutory instrument which shall be subject to annulment in pursuance of a resolution of either House of Parliament.

Amendments—Matrimonial Homes and Property Act 1981, s 8(2); Administration of Justice Act 1982, s 51; Matrimonial and Family Proceedings Act 1984, s 6; SI 1993/623; Pensions Act 1995, s 166(3); Family Law Act 1996, s 66(1), Sch 8, para 16(5)(a), (6)(b), (7); Welfare Reform and Pensions Act 1999, s 19, Sch 3, paras 1, 7; paras (11), (11)(c), (d), (12)(a), (c) prospectively amended by Child Support, Pensions and Social Security Act 2000, ss 26, 86(2), Sch 3, para 3(1), (3)(a), (b); paras (7D), (7F) SI 1998/2572; paras (2), (2)(a), (2)(d), (2)(dd), (2)(de), (2)(e), (ea), (4), (4)(a), (b), (5), (7)(a) prospectively amended with savings by the Family Law Act 1996, s 66(1), (3), Sch 8, 10 para 16(2)(a–e), (3), (3)(a), (5)(b), (6)(a); paras (2)(fa), (g), (4A), (4AA), (4AB), (4B), (7FA), (7G) prospectively amended with savings by the Family Law Act 1996, s 66(1), Sch 8, Pt I, para 16(2)(f), (g), (3A), (4), (4A), (8), (9) (as inserted by the Welfare Reform and Pensions Act 1999, s 84(1), Sch 12, Pt I, paras 64, 66(1), (5), (6), (8), (9).

[31A Variation etc following reconciliations]

[(1) Where, at a time before the making of a divorce order —

(a) an order ('a paragraph (a) order') for the payment of a lump sum has been made under section 22A above in favour of a party,

(b) such an order has been made in favour of a child of the family but the payment has not yet been made, or

(c) a property adjustment order ('a paragraph (c) order') has been made under section 23A above,

the court may, on an application made jointly by the parties to the marriage, vary or discharge the order.

(2) Where the court varies or discharges a paragraph (a) order, it may order the repayment of an amount equal to the whole or any part of the lump sum.

(3) Where the court varies or discharges a paragraph (c) order, it may (if the order has taken effect) —

    (a)   order any person to whom property was transferred in pursuance of the paragraph (c) order to transfer —
        (i)   the whole or any part of that property, or
        (ii)   the whole or any part of any property appearing to the court to represent that property,
        in favour of a party to the marriage or a child of the family; or
    (b)   vary any settlement to which the order relates in favour of any person or extinguish or reduce any person's interest under that settlement.

(4) Where the court acts under subsection (3) it may make such supplemental provision (including a further property adjustment order or an order for the payment of a lump sum) as it thinks appropriate in consequence of any transfer, variation, extinguishment or reduction to be made under paragraph (a) or (b) of that subsection.

(5) Sections 24A and 30 above apply for the purposes of this section as they apply where the court makes a property adjustment order under section 23A or 24 above.

(6) The court shall not make an order under subsection (2), (3) or (4) above unless it appears to it that there has been a reconciliation between the parties to the marriage.

(7) The court shall also not make an order under subsection (3) or (4) above unless it appears to it that the order will not prejudice the interests of —

    (a)   any child of the family; or
    (b)   any person who has acquired any right or interest in consequence of the paragraph (c) order and is not a party to the marriage or a child of the family.]

Amendments—Section prospectively inserted with savings by the Family Law Act 1996, s 15, Sch 2, para 8.

[31B Discharge of pension sharing orders on making of separation order]

[Where, after the making of a pension sharing order under section 24B above in relation to a marriage, a separation order is made in relation to the marriage, the pension sharing order is discharged.]

Amendments—Section prospectively inserted with savings by the Family Law Act 1996, s 66(1), Sch 8, Pt I, para 16A (as inserted by the Welfare Reform and Pensions Act 1999, s 84(1), Sch 12, Pt I, paras 64, 66(1), (10)).

32 Payment of certain arrears unenforceable without the leave of the court

(1) A person shall not be entitled to enforce through the High Court or any county court the payment of any arrears due under *an order for maintenance*

pending suit, an interim order for maintenance or any financial provision order [any financial provision order under this Part of this Act or any interim order for maintenance] without the leave of that court if those arrears became due more than twelve months before proceedings to enforce the payment of them are begun.

(2) The court hearing an application for the grant of leave under this section may refuse leave, or may grant leave subject to such restrictions and conditions (including conditions as to the allowing of time for payment or the making of payment by instalments) as that court thinks proper, or may remit the payment of the arrears or of any part thereof.

(3) An application for the grant of leave under this section shall be made in such matters as may be prescribed by rules of court.

Amendments—Paragraph (1) words prospectively substituted with savings by the Family Law Act 1996, s 66(1), Sch 8, para 17.

33 Orders for repayment in certain cases of sums paid under certain orders

(1) Where on an application made under this section in relation to an order to which this section applies it appears to the court that by reason of —

    (a)   a change in the circumstances of the person entitled to, or liable to make, payments under the order since the order was made, or

    (b)   the changed circumstances resulting from the death of the person so liable,

the amount received by the person entitled to payments under the order in respect of a period after those circumstances changed or after the death of the person liable to make payments under the order, as the case may be, exceeds the amount which the person so liable or his or her personal representatives should have been required to pay, the court may order the respondent to the application to pay to the applicant such sum, not exceeding the amount of the excess, as the court thinks just.

(2) *This section applies to the following orders, that is to say —*

    (a)   any order for maintenance pending suit and any interim order for maintenance;
    (b)   any periodical payments order; and
    (c)   any secured periodical payments order.

[This section applies to the following orders under this Part of this Act —

    (a)   any periodical payments order;
    (b)   any secured periodical payments order; and
    (c)   any interim order for maintenance, so far as it requires the making of periodical payments.]

(3) An application under this section may be made by the person liable to make payments under an order to which this section applies or his or her personal representatives and may be made against the person entitled to payments under the order or her or his personal representatives.

(4) An application under this section may be made in proceedings in the High Court or a county court for —

(a)   the variation or discharge of the order to which this section applies, or

(b)   leave to enforce, or the enforcement of, the payment of arrears under that order;

but when not made in such proceedings shall be made to a county court, and accordingly references in this section to the court are references to the High Court or a county court, as the circumstances require.

(5) The jurisdiction conferred on a county court by this section shall be exercisable notwithstanding that by reason of the amount claimed in the application the jurisdiction would not but for this subsection be exercisable by a county court.

(6) An order under this section for the payment of any sum may provide for the payment of that sum by instalments of such amount as may be specified in the order.

Amendments—Paragraph (2) prospectively substituted with savings by the Family Law Act 1996, s 66(1), Sch 8, para 18.

Consent orders

33A Consent orders for financial provision on property adjustment

(1) Notwithstanding anything in the preceding provisions of this Part of this Act, on an application for a consent order for financial relief the court may, unless it has reason to think that there are other circumstances into which it ought to inquire, make an order in the terms agreed on the basis only of the prescribed information furnished with the application.

(2) Subsection (1) above applies [(subject, in the case of the powers of the court under section 31A above, to subsections (6) and (7) of that section)] to an application for a consent order varying or discharging an order for financial relief as it applies to an application for an order for financial relief.

(3) In this section —

'consent order', in relation to an application for an order, means an order in the terms applied for to which the respondent agrees;
'order for financial relief' means *an order under any of sections 23, 24, 24A, 24B or 27 above* [any of the following orders under this Part of this Act, that is to say, any financial provision order, any property adjustment order, any pension sharing order, any order for the sale of property or any interim order for maintenance], and
'prescribed' means prescribed by rules of court.

Amendments—Section inserted by Matrimonial and Family Proceedings Act 1984, s 7; amended by Welfare Reform and Pensions Act 1999, s 19, Sch 3, paras 1, 8; para (2): words prospectively inserted with savings by the Family Law Act 1996, s 66(1), Sch 8, para 19(2); para (3), definition 'order for financial relief' words prospectively substituted with savings by the Family Law Act 1996, s 66(1), Sch 8, Pt I, para 19(3) (as amended by the Welfare Reform and Pensions Act 1999, s 84(1), Sch 12, Pt I, paras 64, 66(1), (11)).

Maintenance agreements

34 Validity of maintenance agreements

(1) If a maintenance agreement includes a provision purporting to restrict any right to apply to a court for an order containing financial arrangements, then —

  (a)   that provision shall be void; but

  (b)   any other financial arrangements contained in the agreement shall not thereby be rendered void or unenforceable and shall, unless they are void or unenforceable for any other reason (and subject to sections 35 and 36 below), be binding on the parties to the agreement.

(2) In this section and in section 35 below —

  'maintenance agreement' means any agreement in writing made, whether before or after the commencement of this Act, between the parties to a marriage, being —

    (a)   an agreement containing financial arrangements, whether made during the continuance or after the dissolution or annulment of the marriage; or

    (b)   a separation agreement which contains no financial arrange-ments in a case where no other agreements in writing between the same parties contains such agreements;

  'financial arrangements' means provisions governing the rights and liabilities towards one another when living separately of the parties to a marriage (including a marriage which has been dissolved or annulled) in respect of the making or securing of payments or the disposition or use of any property, including such rights and liabilities with respect to the maintenance or education of any child, whether or not a child of the family.

35 Alteration of agreements by court during lives of parties

(1) Where a maintenance agreement is for the time being subsisting and each of the parties to the agreement is for the time being either domiciled or resident in England and Wales, then, subject to subsection (3) below, either party may apply to the court or to a magistrates' court for an order under this section.

(2) If the court to which the application is made is satisfied either —

  (a)   that by reason of a change in the circumstances in the light of which any financial arrangements contained in the agreement were made or, as the case may be, financial arrangements were omitted from it (including a change foreseen by the parties when making the agreement), the agreement should be altered so as to make different, or, as the case may be, so as to contain, financial arrangements, or

    (b)   that the agreement does not contain proper financial arrangements with respect to any child of the family,

then subject to subsections (3), (4) and (5) below, that court may by order make such alterations in the agreement —

    (i)   by varying or revoking any financial arrangements contained in it, or

    (ii)   by inserting in it financial arrangements for the benefit of one of the parties to the agreement or of a child of the family,

as may appear to that court to be just having regard to all the circumstances, including, if relevant, the matters mentioned in section 25(4) above; and the agreement shall have effect thereafter as if any alteration made by the other had been made by agreement between the parties and for valuable consideration.

(3) A magistrates' court shall not entertain an application under subsection (1) above unless both the parties to the agreement are resident in England and Wales and *at least one of the parties is resident within the commission area for which the court is appointed* the court acts in, or is authorised by the Lord Chancellor to act for, a local justice area in which at least one of the parties is resident, and shall not have power to make any order on such an application except —

    (a)   in a case where the agreement includes no provision for periodical payments by either of the parties, an order inserting provision for the making by one of the parties of periodical payments for the maintenance of the other party or for the maintenance of any child of the family;

    (b)   in a case where the agreement includes provision for the making by one of the parties of periodical payments, an order increasing or reducing the rate of, or terminating, any of those payments.

(4) Where a court decides to alter, by order under this section, an agreement by inserting provision for the making or securing by one of the parties to the agreement of periodical payments for the maintenance of the other party or by increasing the rate of the periodical payments which the agreement provides shall be made by one of the parties for the maintenance of the other, the term for which the payments or, as the case may be, the additional payments attributable to the increase are to be made under the agreement as altered by the order shall be such term as the court may specify, subject to the following limits, that is to say —

    (a)   where the payments will not be secured, the term shall be so defined as not to extend beyond the death of either of the parties to the agreement or the remarriage of, or formation of a civil partnership by, the party to whom the payments are to be made;

    (b)   where the payments will be secured, the term shall be so defined as not to extend beyond the death or remarriage of , or formation of a civil partnership by, that party.

(5) Where a court decides to alter, by order under this section, an agreement by inserting provision for the making or securing by one of the parties to the

agreement of periodical payments for the maintenance of a child of the family or by increasing the rate of the periodical payments which the agreement provides shall be made or secured by one of the parties for the maintenance of such a child, then, in deciding the term for which under the agreement as altered by the order the payments, or as the case may be, the additional payments attributable to the increase are to be made or secured for the benefit of the child, the court shall apply the provisions of section 29(2) and (3) above as to age limits as if the order in question were a periodical payments or secured periodical payments order in favour of the child.

(6) For the avoidance of doubt it is hereby declared that nothing in this section or in section 34 above affects any power of a court before which any proceedings between the parties to a maintenance agreement are brought under any other enactment (including a provision of this Act) to make an order containing financial arrangements or any right of either party to apply for such an order in such proceedings.

[(7) Subject to subsection (5) above, references in this Act to any such order as is mentioned in section 21 above shall not include references to any order under this section.]

Amendments—Matrimonial and Family Proceedings Act 1984, s 46(1), Sch 1, para 13; Access to Justice Act 1999, s 106, Sch 15, Pt V; para (3) words substituted by the Courts Act 2003, s 109(1), Sch 8, para 169; para (4)(a), (b) words inserted by the Civil Partnership Act 2004, s 261(1), Sch 27, para 44; para (7) prospectively inserted with savings by the Family Law Act 1996, s 66(1), Sch 8, para 20.

36 Alteration of agreements by court after death of one party

(1) Where a maintenance agreement within the meaning of section 34 above provides for the continuation of payments under the agreement after the death of one of the parties and that party dies domiciled in England and Wales, the surviving party or the personal representative of the deceased party may, subject to subsections (2) and (3) below, apply to the High Court or a county court for an order under section 35 above.

(2) An application under this section shall not, except with the permission of the High Court or a county court, be made after the end of the period of six months from the date on which representation in regard to the estate of the deceased is first taken out.

(3) A county court shall not entertain an application under this section, or an application for permission to make an application under this section, unless it would have jurisdiction by virtue of section 22 of the Inheritance (Provision for Family and Dependants) Act 1975 (which confers jurisdiction on county courts in proceedings under that Act if the value of the property mentioned in that section does not exceed £5,000 or such larger sum as may be fixed by order of the Lord Chancellor) to hear and determine proceedings for an order under section 2 of that Act in relation to the deceased's estate.

(4) If a maintenance agreement is altered by a court on an application made in pursuance of subsection (1) above, the like consequences shall ensue as if the

alteration had been made immediately before the death by agreement between the parties and for valuable consideration.

(5) The provisions of this section shall not render the personal representatives of the deceased liable for having distributed any part of the estate of the deceased after the expiration of the period of six months referred to in subsection (2) above on the ground that they ought to have taken into account the possibility that a court might permit an application by virtue of this section to be made by the surviving party after that period; but this subsection shall not prejudice any power to recover any part of the estate so distributed arising by virtue of the making of an order in pursuance of this section.

(6) Section 31(9) above shall apply for the purposes of subsection (2) above as it applies for the purposes of subsection (6) of section 31.

(7) Subsection (3) of section 22 of the Inheritance (Provision for Family and Dependants) Act 1975 (which enables rules of court to provide for the transfer from a county court to the High Court or from the High Court to a county court of proceedings for an order under section 2 of that Act) and paragraphs (a) and (b) of subsection (4) of that section (provisions relating to proceedings commenced in county court before coming into force of order of the Lord Chancellor under that section) shall apply in relation to proceedings consisting of any such application as is referred to in subsection (3) above as they apply in relation to proceedings for an order under section 2 of that Act.

Amendments—Inheritance (Provision for Family and Dependants) Act 1975, ss 18 and 26.

Miscellaneous and supplemental

37 Avoidance of transactions intended to prevent or reduce financial relief

(1) For the purposes of this section 'financial relief' means relief under any of the provisions of sections *22, 23, 24, 24B, 27, 31 (except subsection (6))* [22A to 24BB, 27, 31 (except subsection (6)), 31A] and 35 above, and any reference in this section to defeating a person's claim for financial relief is a reference to preventing financial relief from being granted to that person, or to that person for the benefit of a child of the family, or reducing the amount of any financial relief which might be so granted, or frustrating or impeding the enforcement of any order which might be or has been made at his instance under any of those provisions.

(2) Where proceedings for financial relief are brought by one person against another, the court may, on the application of the first-mentioned person —

    (a)   if it is satisfied that the other party to the proceedings is, with the intention of defeating the claim for financial relief, about to make any disposition or to transfer out of the jurisdiction or otherwise deal with any property, make such order as it thinks fit for restraining the other party from so doing or otherwise for protecting the claim;

    (b)   if it is satisfied that the other party has, with that intention, made a reviewable disposition and that if the disposition were set aside financial relief or different financial relief would be granted to the applicant, make an order setting aside the disposition;

(c)   if it is satisfied, in a case where an order has been obtained under any of the provisions mentioned in subsection (1) above by the applicant against the other party, that the other party has, with that intention, made a reviewable disposition, make an order setting aside the disposition;

and an application for the purposes of paragraph (b) above shall be made in the proceedings for the financial relief in question.

(3) Where the court makes an order under subsection (2)(b) or (c) above setting aside a disposition it shall give such consequential directions as it thinks fit for giving effect to the order (including directions requiring the making of any payments or the disposal of any property).

(4) Any disposition made by the other party to the proceedings for financial relief in question (whether before or after the commencement of those proceedings) is a reviewable disposition for the purposes of subsection (2)(b) and (c) above unless it was made for valuable consideration (other than marriage) to a person who, at the time of the disposition, acted in relation to it in good faith and without notice of any intention on the part of the other party to defeat the applicant's claim for financial relief.

(5) Where an application is made under this section with respect to a disposition which took place less than three years before the date of the application or with respect to a disposition or other dealing with property which is about to take place and the court is satisfied —

(a)   in a case falling within subsection (2)(a) or (b) above, that the disposition or other dealing would (apart from this section) have the consequence, or

(b)   in a case falling within subsection (2)(c) above, that the disposition has had the consequence,

of defeating the applicant's claim for financial relief, it shall be presumed, unless the contrary is shown, that the person who disposed of or is about to dispose of or deal with the property did so or, as the case may be, is about to do so, with the intention of defeating the applicant's claim for financial relief.

(6) In this section 'disposition' does not include any provision contained in a will or codicil but, with that exception, includes any conveyance, assurance or gift of property of any description, whether made by an instrument or otherwise.

(7) This section does not apply to a disposition made before 1 January 1968.

Amendments—Welfare Reform and Pensions Act 1999, s 19, Sch 3, paras 1, 9; para (1) words prospectively substituted with savings by the Family Law Act 1996, s 66(1), Sch 8, Pt I, para 21 (as amended by the Welfare Reform and Pensions Act 1999, s 84(1), Sch 12, Pt I, paras 64, 66(1), (12))

38 Orders for repayment in certain cases of sums paid after cessation of order by reason of remarriage or formation of civil partnership

(1) Where —

    (a)   a periodical payments or secured periodical payments order in favour of a party to a marriage (hereafter in this section referred to as 'a payments order') has ceased to have effect by reason of the remarriage of, or formation of a civil partnership by, that party, and

    (b)   the person liable to make payments under the order or his or her personal representatives made payments in accordance with it in respect of a period after the date of the remarriage or formation of the civil partnership in the mistaken belief that the order was still subsisting,

the person so liable or his or her personal representatives shall not be entitled to bring proceedings in respect of a cause of action arising out of the circumstances mentioned in paragraphs (a) and (b) above against the person entitled to payments under the order or her or his personal representatives, but may instead make an application against that person or her or his personal representatives under this section.

(2) On an application under this section the court may order the respondent to pay to the applicant a sum equal to the amount of the payments made in respect of the period mentioned in subsection (1)(b) above or, if it appears to the court that it would be unjust to make that order, it may either order the respondent to pay to the applicant such lesser sum as it thinks fit or dismiss the application.

(3) An application under this section may be made in proceedings in the High Court or a county court for leave to enforce, or the enforcement of, payment of arrears under the order in question, but when not made in such proceedings shall be made to a county court; and accordingly references in this section to the court are references to the High Court or a county court, as the circumstances require.

(4) The jurisdiction conferred on a county court by this section shall be exercisable notwithstanding that by reason of the amount claimed in the application the jurisdiction would not but for this subsection be exercisable by a county court.

(5) An order under this section for the payment of any sum may provide for the payment of that sum by instalments of such amounts as may be specified in the order.

(6) The designated officer for a magistrates' court to whom any payments under a payments order are required to be made, and the collecting officer under an attachment of earnings order made to secure payments under a payments order, shall not be liable —

    (a)   in the case of the designated officer, for any act done by him in pursuance of the payments order after the date on which that order ceased to have effect by reason of the remarriage of , or formation of a civil partnership by, the person entitled to payments under it, and

(b)   in the case of the collecting officer, for any act done by him after that date in accordance with any enactment or rule of court specifying how payments made to him in compliance with the attachment of earnings order are to be dealt with,

if, but only if, the act was one which he would have been under a duty to do had the payments order not so ceased to have effect and the act was done before notice in writing of the fact that the person so entitled had remarried or formed a civil partnership was given to him by or on behalf of that person, the person liable to make payments under the payments order or the personal representatives of either of those persons.

(7) In this section 'collecting officer', in relation to an attachment of earnings order, means the officer of the High Court, the registrar of a county court or the designated officer for a magistrates' court to whom a person makes payments in compliance with the order.

Amendments—Access to Justice Act 1999, s 90, Sch 13, para 82(1), 2; section heading and paras (1)(a), (b), (6), (6)(a) words inserted by the Civil Partnership Act 2004, s 261(1), Sch 27, para 45(1), (2)(a), (b), (3)(a), (b), (4); paras (6), (6)(a), (7) words substituted by the Courts Act 2003, s 109(1), Sch 8, para 170(1), (2)(a), (b), (3).

39 Settlement etc made in compliance with a property adjustment order may be avoided on bankruptcy of settlor

The fact that a settlement or transfer of property had to be made in order to comply with a property adjustment order shall not prevent that settlement or transfer from being a transaction in respect of which an order may be made under section 339 or 340 of the Insolvency Act 1986 (transfers at an undervalue and preferences).

Amendments—Insolvency Act 1985, s 235, Sch 8, para 23; Insolvency Act 1986, s 439(2), Sch 14.

40 Payments etc under order made in favour of person suffering from mental disorder

[(1)] Where the court makes an order under this Part of this Act requiring payments (including a lump sum payment) to be made, or property to be transferred, to a party to a marriage and the court is satisfied that the person in whose favour the order is made *is incapable, by reason of mental disorder within the meaning of the Mental Health Act 1959, of managing and administering his or her property and affairs* [('P' lacks capacity (within the meaning of the Mental Capacity Act 2005) in relation to the provisions of the order.]then, subject to any order, direction or authority made or given in relation to *that person under Part VIII of that Act*, [P under that Act], the court may order the payments to be made, or as the case may be, the property to be transferred, to *such persons having charge of that person as the court may direct.*[such person ('D') as it may direct].

[(2) In carrying out any functions of his in relation to an order made under subsection (1), D must act in P's best interests (within the meaning of that Act).]

Amendments—Mental Capacity Act 2005, s 67(1), Sch 6,para19, subsection (1) renumbered, subsection (1) prospectively substituted, and subsection (2) prosepectively inserted.

40A Appeals relating to pension sharing orders which have taken effect

(1) Subsections (2) and (3) below apply where an appeal against a pension sharing order is begun on or after the day on which the order takes effect.

(2) If the pension sharing order relates to a person's rights under a pension arrangement, the appeal court may not set aside or vary the order if the person responsible for the pension arrangement has acted to his detriment in reliance on the taking effect of the order.

(3) If the pension sharing order relates to a person's shareable state scheme rights, the appeal court may not set aside or vary the order if the Secretary of State has acted to his detriment in reliance on the taking effect of the order.

(4) In determining for the purposes of subsection (2) or (3) above whether a person has acted to his detriment in reliance on the taking effect of the order, the appeal court may disregard any detriment which in its opinion is insignificant.

(5) Where subsection (2) or (3) above applies, the appeal court may make such further orders (including one or more pension sharing orders) as it thinks fit for the purpose of putting the parties in the position it considers appropriate.

(6) Section 24C above only applies to a pension sharing order under this section if the decision of the appeal court can itself be the subject of an appeal.

(7) In subsection (2) above, the reference to the person responsible for the pension arrangement is to be read in accordance with section 25D(4) above.

Amendments—Section inserted by Welfare Reform and Pensions Act 1999, s 19, Sch 3, paras 1, 10.

2. FAMILY PROCEEDINGS RULES 1991, SI 1991/1247

. . .

Ancillary relief

2.51 Indorsement and certificate of final order

(1) Where a conditional order is made final, the proper officer shall make an indorsement to that effect on the order, stating the precise time at which it was made final.

(2) On a conditional order being made final, the proper officer shall send to the petititoner and respondent a copy of the order in Form M9A or M10A

whichever is appropriate making the conditional order final, authenticated by the seal of the civil partnership proceedings county court or registry from which it is issued.

(3) A central index of final orders shall be kept under the control of the principal registry and any person shall be entitled to require a search to be made of that index, and to be furnished with a certificate of the result of the search, on payment of the prescribed fee.

(4)A certificate in Form M9A or M10A that a conditional order has been made final shall be issued to any person requiring it on payment of the prescribed fee.

Amendments—Inserted by SI 2005/2922.

2.51B Application of ancillary relief rules

(1) The procedures set out in rules 2.51D to 2.71 ('the ancillary relief rules') apply to —

    (a)   any ancillary relief application,
    (b)   any application under section 10 (2) of the Act of 1973, and
    (c)   any application under section 48 (2) of the Act of 2004.

(2) In the ancillary relief rules, unless the context otherwise requires:

    ' applicant' means the party applying for ancillary relief;
    'respondent' means the respondent to the application for ancillary relief;
    'FDR appointment' means a Financial Dispute Resolution appointment in accordance with rule 2.61E.

Amendments—Inserted by SI 1999/3491;amended by SI 2005/2922; SI 2006/352.

2.51C Application under section 6 of the Gender Recognition Act 2004

(1) This rule applies to an application made under section 6(1) of the Gender Recognition Act 2004 in respect of full gender recognition certificate issued by a court under section 5(1) of that Act.

(2) The application must be made to the court which issued the certificate, unless otherwise directed,

(3) Where the applicant is —

    (a)   the person to whom the certificate was issued, the Secretary of State must be a respondent.
    (b)   the Secretary of State, the person to whom the certificate was issued must be a respondent.

(4) Where the court issues a corrected gender recognition certificate under section 6(4) of the Gender Recognition Act 2004, the proper officer must send a copy of the corrected certificate to the Secretary of State.

Amendments—Inserted by SI 2005/559; amended by SI 2005/2922.

2.51D The overriding objective

(1) The ancillary relief rules are a procedural code with the overriding objective of enabling the court to deal with cases justly.

(2) Dealing with a case justly includes, so far as is practicable –

- (a) ensuring that the parties are on an equal footing;
- (b) saving expense;
- (c) dealing with the case in ways which are proportionate –
  - (i) to the amount of money involved;
  - (ii) to the importance of the case;
  - (iii) to the complexity of the issues; and
  - (iv) to the financial position of each party;
- (d) ensuring that it is dealt with expeditiously and fairly; and
- (e) allotting to it an appropriate share of the court's resources, while taking into account the need to allot resources to other cases.

(3) The court must seek to give effect to the overriding objective when it –

- (a) exercises any power given to it by the ancillary relief rules; or
- (b) interprets any rule.

(4) The parties are required to help the court to further the overriding objective.

(5) The court must further the overriding objective by actively managing cases.

(6) Active case management includes –

- (a) encouraging the parties to co-operate with each other in the conduct of the proceedings;
- (b) encouraging the parties to settle their disputes through mediation, where appropriate;
- (c) identifying the issues at an early date;
- (d) regulating the extent of disclosure of documents and expert evidence so that they are proportionate to the issues in question;
- (e) helping the parties to settle the whole or part of the case;
- (f) fixing timetables or otherwise controlling the progress of the case;
- (g) making use of technology; and
- (h) giving directions to ensure that the trial of a case proceeds quickly and efficiently.

Amendments—Inserted by SI 1999/3491; SI 2005/2922.

2.52 Right to be heard on ancillary questions

A respondent may be heard on any question of ancillary relief without filing an answer and whether or not he has returned to the court office an acknowledgement of service stating his wish to be heard on that question.

Amendments—SI 1999/3491, rr 2, 3.

2.53 Application by petitioner or respondent for ancillary relief

(1) Any application by a petitioner, or by a respondent who files an answer claiming relief, for —

(a)   an order for maintenance pending suit,

(aa) an order for maintenance pending outcome of proceedings,

(b)   a financial provision order,

(c)   a property adjustment order,

(d)   a pension sharing order,

shall be made in the petition or answer, as the case may be.

(2) Notwithstanding anything in paragraph (1), an application for ancillary relief which should have been made in the petition or answer may be made subsequently —

(a)   by leave of the court, either by notice in Form A or at the trial, or

(b)   where the parties are agreed upon the terms of the proposed order, without leave by notice in Form A.

(3) An application by a petitioner or respondent for ancillary relief, not being an application which is required to be made in the petition or answer, shall be made by notice in Form A.

Amendments—SI 1999/3491; rr 2, 3, 7; SI 2000/2267, r 5(2); SI 2005/2922.

2.54 Application by parent, guardian etc for ancillary relief in respect of children

(1) Any of the following persons, namely —

(a)   a parent or guardian of any child of the family,

(b)   any person in whose favour a residence order has been made with respect to a child of the family, and any applicant for such an order,

(c)   any other person who is entitled to apply for a residence order with respect to a child,

(d)   a local authority, where an order has been made under section 31(1)(a) of the Act of the Act of 1989 placing a child in its care,

(e)   the Official Solicitor, if appointed the guardian ad litem of a child of the family under rule 9.5, and

(f)   a child of the family who has been given leave to intervene in the cause for the purpose of applying for ancillary relief,

may apply for an order for ancillary relief as respects that child by notice in Form A.

(2) In this rule 'residence order' has the meaning assigned to it by section 8(1) of the Act of 1989.

Amendments—SI 1999/3491, rr 2, 3, 7; SI 2005/2922.

2.55 *(revoked)*

Amendments—SI 1999/3491, rr 2, 3, 8.

2.56 (*revoked*)

Amendments—SI 1999/3491, rr 2, 3, 8.

2.57 Children to be separately represented on certain applications

(1) Where an application is made to the High Court or a designated county court for an order for a variation of settlement, the court shall, unless it is satisfied that the proposed variation does not adversely affect the rights or interests of any children concerned, direct that the children be separately represented on the application, either by a solicitor or by a solicitor and counsel, and may appoint the Official Solicitor or other fit person to be guardian ad litem of the children for the purpose of the application.

(2) On any other application for ancillary relief the court may give such a direction or make such appointment as it is empowered to give or make by paragraph (1).

(3) Before a person other than the Official Solicitor is appointed guardian ad litem under this rule there shall be filed a certificate by the solicitor acting for the children that the person proposed as guardian has no interest in the matter adverse to that of the children and that he is a proper person to be such guardian.

Amendments—SI 1999/3491, rr 2, 3; SI 2005/2922.

2.58 (*revoked*)

Amendments—SI 1999/3491, rr 2, 3, 8.

2.59 Evidence on application for property adjustment or avoidance of disposition order

(1) (*revoked*)

(2) Where an application for a property adjustment order or an avoidance of disposition order relates to land, the notice in Form A shall identify the land and —

    (a)   state whether the title to the land is registered or unregistered and, if registered, the Land Registry title number; and

    (b)   give particulars, so far as known to the applicant, of any mortgage of the land or any interest therein.

(3) Copies of Form A and of Form E completed by the applicant shall be served on the following persons as well as on the respondent to the application, that is to say —

    (a)   in the case of an application for an order for a variation of settlement, the trustees of the settlement and the settlor if living;

    (b)   in the case of an application for an avoidance of disposition order, the person in whose favour the disposition is alleged to have been made;

and such other persons, if any, as the district judge may direct.

(4) In the case of an application to which paragraph (2) refers, a copy of Form A shall be served on any mortgagee of whom particulars are given pursuant to that paragraph; any person so served may apply to the court in writing, within 14 days after service, for a copy of the applicant's Form E.

(5) Any person who —

    (a)   is served with copies of Forms A and E pursuant to paragraph (3), or

    (b)   receives a copy of Form E following an application made in accordance with paragraph (4),

may, within 14 days after service or receipt, as the case may be, file a statement in answer.

(6) A statement filed under paragraph (5) shall be sworn to be true.

Amendments—SI 1992/456 rr 12, 13; SI 1999/3491, rr 2, 3, 9(1), (2), (3), (9(4)(a), (b), (5)(a–c), (6).

2.60 Service of statement in answer

(1) Where a form or other document filed with the court contains an allegation of adultery or of an improper association with a named person ('the named person'), the court may direct that the party who filed the relevant form or document serve a copy of all or part of that form or document on the named person, together with Form F.

(2) If the court makes a direction under paragraph (1), the named person may file a statement in answer to the allegations.

(3) A statement under paragraph (2) shall be sworn to be true.

(4) Rule 2.37(3) shall apply to a person served under paragraph (1) as it applies to a co-respondent.

Amendments—SI 1999/3491, rr 2, 3, 10.

2.61 Information on application for consent order for financial relief

(1) Subject to paragraphs (2) and (3), there shall be lodged with every application for a consent order under any of sections 23, 24 or 24A of the Act of 1973,or Parts 1,2 and 3 of Schedule 5 to the Act of 2004, two copies of a draft of the order in the terms sought, one of which shall be indorsed with a statement signed by the respondent to the application signifying his agreement, and a statement of information (which may be made in more than one document) which shall include —

    (a)   the duration of the marriage or civil partnership the age of each party and of any minor or dependent child of the family;

    (b)   an estimate in summary form of the approximate amount of value or the capital resources and net income of each party and of any minor child of the family;

    (c)   what arrangements are intended for the accommodation of each of the parties and any minor child of the family;

(d) whether either party has subsequently married or formed a civil partnership or has any present intention to do so or to cohabit with another person;

(dd) where the order includes provision to be made under section 25B or 25C of the Act of 1973, or under paragraphs 25 or 26 of Schedule 5 to the Act of 2004, a statement confirming that the person responsible for the pension arrangement in question has been served with the documents required by rule 2.70(11) and that no objection to such an order has been made by that person within 21 days from such service;

(e) where the terms of the order provide for a transfer of property, a statement confirming that any mortgagee of that property has been served with notice of the application and that no objection to such a transfer has been made by the mortgagee within 14 days from such service; and

(f) any other especially significant matters.

(2) Where an application is made for a consent order varying an order for periodical payments paragraph (1) shall be sufficiently complied with if the statement of information required to be lodged with the application includes only the information in respect of net income mentioned in paragraph (1)(b) (and, where appropriate, a statement under paragraph (1)(dd)), and an application for a consent order for interim periodical payments pending the determination of an application for ancillary relief may be made in like manner.

(3) Where all or any of the parties attend the hearing of an application for financial relief the court may dispense with the lodging of a statement of information in accordance with paragraph (1) and give directions for the information which would otherwise be required to be given in such a statement to be given in such a manner as it sees fit.

Amendments—SI 1996/1674, r 4(1); SI 2000/2267, r 6(b), (c); SI 1999/3491, rr 2, 3; SI 2003/2839, r 3; SI 2005/2922, r 1(2), r 50(c); SI 2006/2080, r 1(1).

2.61A Application for ancillary relief

(1) A notice of intention to proceed with an application for ancillary relief made in the petition or answer or an application for ancillary relief must be made by notice in Form A.

(2) The notice must be filed —

(a) if the case is pending in a designated county court, in that court; or

(b) if the case is pending in the High Court, in the registry in which it is proceeding.

(3) Where the applicant requests an order for ancillary relief that includes provision to be made by virtue of section 24B, 25b or 25C of the Act of 1973 or under paragraphs 15,25 or 26 of Schedule 5 to the Act of 2004 the terms of the order requested must be specified in the notice in Form A.

(4) Upon the filing of Form A the court must —

(a)	fix a first appointment not less than 12 weeks and not more than 16 weeks after the date of the filing of the notice and give notice of that date;

(b)	serve a copy on the respondent within 4 days of the date of the filing of the notice.

(5) The date fixed under paragraph (4) for the first appointment, or for any subsequent appointment, must not be cancelled except with the court's permission and, if cancelled, the court must immediately fix a new date.

Amendments—Inserted by SI 1999/3491, rr 2, 3, 11; amended by SI 2000/2267, r 7; SI 2005/2922.

2.61B Procedure before the first appointment

(1) Both parties must, at the same time, exchange with each other, and each file with the court, a statement in Form E, which —

(a)	is signed by the party who made the statement;
(b)	is sworn to be true; and
(c)	contains the information and has attached to it the documents required by that Form.

(2) Form E must be exchanged and filed not less than 35 days before the date of the first appointment.

(3) Form E must have attached to it —

(a)	any documents required by Form E; . . .
(b)	any other documents necessary to explain or clarify any of the information contained in Form E;. . .
(b)	any documents furnished to the party producing the form by a person responsible for a pension arrangement, either following a request under rule 2.70(2) or as part of a 'relevant valuation' as defined in rule 2.70(4); and
(d)	any notification or other document referred to in paragraphs (2), (4) or (5) of rule 2.70A which has been received by the party producing the form.

(4) Form E must have no documents attached to it other than the documents referred to in paragraph (3).

(5) Where a party was unavoidably prevented from sending any document required by Form E, that party must at the earliest opportunity —

(a)	serve copies of that document on the other party, and
(b)	file a copy of that document with the court, together with a statement explaining the failure to send it with Form E.

(6) No disclosure or inspection of documents may be requested or given between the filing of the application for ancillary relief and the first appointment, except —

(a)	copies sent with Form E, or in accordance with paragraph (5); or
(b)	in accordance with paragraph (7).

(7) At least 14 days before the hearing of the first appointment, each party must file with the court and serve on the other party —

- (a)   a concise statement of the issues between the parties;
- (b)   a chronology;
- (c)   a questionnaire setting out by reference to the concise statement of issues any further information and documents requested from the other party or a statement that no information and documents are required;
- (d)   a notice in Form G stating whether that party will be in a position at the first appointment to proceed on that occasion to a FDR appointment.

(8) *(revoked)*

(9) At least 14 days before the hearing of the first appointment, the applicant must file with the court and serve on the respondent, confirmation of the names of all persons served in accordance with rule 2.59(3) and (4), and that there are no other persons who must be served in accordance with those paragraphs.

Amendments—Inserted by SI 1999/3491, rr 2, 3, 11; amended by SI 2000/2267, r 8(a–c); SI 2006/2080.

2.61C Expert evidence

CPR rules 35.1 to 35.14 relating to expert evidence (with appropriate modifications), except CPR rules 35.5(2) and 35.8(4)(b), apply to all ancillary relief proceedings.

Amendments—Inserted by SI 1999/3491, rr 2, 3, 11.

2.61D The first appointment

(1) The first appointment must be conducted with the objective of defining the issues and saving costs.

(2) At the first appointment the district judge —

- (a)   must determine —
  - (i)   the extent to which any questions seeking information under rule 2.61B must be answered, and
  - (ii)   what documents requested under rule 2.61B must be produced, and give directions for the production of such further documents as may be necessary;
- (b)   must give directions about —
  - (i)   the valuation of assets (including, where appropriate, the joint instruction of joint experts);
  - (ii)   obtaining and exchanging expert evidence, if required; and
  - (iii) evidence to be adduced by each party and, where appropriate, about further chronologies or schedules to be filed by each party;
- (c)   must, unless he decides that a referral is not appropriate in the circumstances, direct that the case be referred to a FDR appointment;

(d)   must, where he decides that a referral to a FDR appointment is not appropriate, direct one or more of the following —
    (i)   that a further directions appointment be fixed;
    (ii)   that an appointment be fixed for the making of an interim order;
    (iii) that the case be fixed for final hearing and, where that direction is given, the district judge must determine the judicial level at which the case should be heard;
    (iv)   that the case be adjourned for out-of-court mediation or private negotiation or, in exceptional circumstances, generally;

(e)   in considering whether to make a costs order under rule 2.71(4) must have particular regard to the extent to which each party has complied with the requirement to send documents with Form E; and

(f)   may —
    (i)   make an interim order where an application for it has been made in accordance with rule 2.69F returnable at the first appointment;
    (ii)   having regard to the contents of Form G filed by the parties, treat the appointment (or part of it) as a FDR appointment to which rule 2.61E applies;
    (iii) in a matrimonial cause, in a case where an order for ancillary relief is requested that includes provision to be made under section 24B, 25B or 25C of the Act of 1973, direct any party with pension rights to files and serve a Pension Inquiry Form (Form P),completed in full or in part as the court may direct;

(3) After the first appointment, a party is not entitled to production of any further documents except in accordance with directions given under paragraph (2)(a) above or with the permission of the court.

(4) At any stage —

(a)   a party may apply for further directions or a FDR appointment;
(b)   the court may give further directions or direct that the parties attend a FDR appointment.

(5) Both parties must personally attend the first appointment unless the court orders otherwise.

Amendments—Inserted by SI 1999/3491, rr 2, 3, 11; amended by SI 2003/184, r 5(a), (b); amended by SI 2005/2922; SI 2006/352.

2.61E The FDR appointment

(1) The FDR appointment must be treated as a meeting held for the purposes of discussion and negotiation and paragraphs (2) to (9) apply.

(2) The district judge or judge hearing the FDR appointment must have no further involvement with the application, other than to conduct any further FDR appointment or to make a consent order or a further directions order.

(3) Not later than 7 days before the FDR appointment, the applicant must file with the court details of all offers and proposals, and responses to them.

(4) Paragraph (3) includes any offers, proposals or responses made wholly or partly without prejudice, but paragraph (3) does not make any material admissible as evidence if, but for that paragraph, it would not be admissible.

(5) At the conclusion of the FDR appointment, any documents filed under paragraph (3), and any filed documents referring to them, must, at the request of the party who filed them, be returned to him and not retained on the court file.

(6) Parties attending the FDR appointment must use their best endeavours to reach agreement on the matters in issue between them.

(7) The FDR appointment may be adjourned from time to time.

(8) At the conclusion of the FDR appointment, the court may make an appropriate consent order, but otherwise must give directions for the future course of the proceedings, including, where appropriate, the filing of evidence and fixing a final hearing date.

(9) Both parties must personally attend the FDR appointment unless the court orders otherwise.

Amendments—Inserted by SI 1999/3491, rr 2, 3, 11.

2.61F Costs

(1) subject to paragraph (2), at every court hearing or appointment each party must produce to the court an estimate in Form H of the costs incurred by him up to the date of that hearing or appointment.

(2) Not less than 14 days before the date fixed for the final hearing of an application for ancillary relief, each party must (unless the court directs otherwise) file with the court and serve on each other party a statement in Form H1 giving full particulars of all costs in respect of the proceedings which he has incurred or expects to incur, to enable the court to take account of the parties' liabilities for costs when deciding what order (if any) to make for ancillary relief.

Amendments—Inserted by SI 1999/3491, rr 2, 3, 11; amended by SI 2006/352, r 5.

2.62 Investigation by district judge of application for ancillary relief

(1) *(revoked)*

(2) An application for an avoidance of disposition order shall, if practicable, be heard at the same time as any related application for financial relief.

(3) *(revoked)*

(4) At the hearing of an application for ancillary relief the district judge shall, subject to rules 2.64, 2.65 and 10.10 investigate the allegations made in support of and in answer to the application, and may take evidence orally and may at any stage of the proceedings, whether before or during the hearing, order the

attendance of any person for the purpose of being examined or cross-examined and order the disclosure and inspection of any document or require further statements.

(4A) A statement filed under paragraph (4) shall be sworn to be true.

(5) (*revoked*)

(6) (*revoked*)

(7) Any party may apply to the court for an order that any person do attend an appointment (an 'inspection appointment') before the court and produce any documents to be specified or described in the order, the inspection of which appears to the court to be necessary for disposing fairly of the application for ancillary relief or for saving costs.

(8) No person shall be compelled by an order under paragraph (7) to produce any document at an inspection appointment which he could not be compelled to produce at the hearing of the application for ancillary relief.

(9) The court shall permit any person attending an inspection appointment pursuant to an order under paragraph (7) above to be represented at the appointment.

Amendments—SI 1999/3491, rr 2, 3, 12(1), (2)(a), (b), (3), (4)(a), (b), (5), (6).

2.63 (*revoked*)

Amendments—SI 1999/3491, rr 2, 3, 13.

2.64 Order on application for ancillary relief

(1) Subject to rule 2.65 the district judge shall, after completing his investigation under rule 2.62, make such order as he thinks just.

(2) Pending the final determination of the application, and subject to rule 2.69F, the district judge may make an interim order upon such terms as he thinks just.

(3) RSC Order 31, rule 1 (power to order sale of land) shall apply to applications for ancillary relief as it applies to causes and matters in the Chancery Division.

Amendments—SI 1999/3491, rr 2, 3, 14.

2.65 Reference of application to judge

The district judge may at any time refer an application for ancillary relief, or any question arising thereon, to a judge for his decision.

Amendments—SI 1999/3491, rr 2, 3.

2.66 Arrangements for hearing of application etc by judge

(1) Where an application for ancillary relief or any question arising thereon has been referred or adjourned to a judge, the proper officer shall fix a date, time

and place for the hearing of the application or the consideration of the question and give notice thereof to all parties.

(2) The hearing or consideration shall, unless the court otherwise directs, take place in chambers.

(3) In a matrimonial cause, where the application is proceeding in a divorce county court which is not a court of trial or is pending in the High Court and proceeding in a district registry which is not in a divorce town, the hearing or consideration shall take place at such court of trial or divorce town as in the opinion of the district judge is the nearest or most convenient.

For the purposes of this paragraph the Royal Courts of Justice shall be treated as a divorce town.

(3A) In a civil partnership cause, where an application is proceeding in a civil partnership proceedings county court which is not a court of trial or pending in the High Court and proceeding in a district registry which is not in a dissolution town, the hearing or consideration shall take place at such court of trial or dissolution town as in the opinion of the district judge is the nearest or most convenient.

For the purposes of this paragraph the Royal Courts of Justice shall be treated as a dissolution town.

(4) In respect of any application referred to him under this rule, a judge shall have the same powers to make directions as a district judge has under these rules.

Amendments—Inserted by SI 1999/3491, rr 2, 3, 15; amended by SI 2005/2922.

2.67 Request for periodical payments order at same rate as order for maintenance pending suit

(1) Where at or after the date of a decree nisi of divorce or nullity of marriage or a conditional order of dissolution or nullity of civil partnership an order for maintenance pending suit or outcome of proceedings, as the case may be, is in force, the party in whose favour the order was made may, if he has made an application for an order for periodical payments for himself in his petition or answer, as the case may be, request the district judge in writing to make such an order (in this rule referred to as a 'corresponding order') providing for payments at the same rate as those provided for by the order for maintenance pending suit or outcome of proceedings.

(2) Where such a request is made, the proper officer shall serve on the other spouse or civil partner, as the case may be, a notice in Form I requiring him, if he objects to the making of a corresponding order, to give notice to that effect to the court and to the applicant within 14 days after service of the notice on Form I.

(3) If the other spouse or civil partner does not give notice of objection within the time aforesaid, the district judge may make a corresponding order without further notice to that spouse or civil partner and without requiring the

attendance of the applicant or his solicitor, and shall in that case serve a copy of the order on the applicant as well as on the other spouse or civil partner, as the case may be.

Amendments—Inserted by SI 1999/3491, rr 2, 3, 16; amended by SI 2005/2922.

2.68 Application for order under section 37(2)(a) of Act of 1973 or paragraph 74(2) of Schedule 5 to Act of 2004.

(1) An application under section 37(2)(a) of the Act of 1973 [or paragraph 74(2) of Schedule 5 to the Act of 2004] for an order restraining any person from attempting to defeat a claim for financial provision or otherwise for protecting the claim may be made to the district judge.

(2) Rules 2.65 and 2.66 shall apply, with the necessary modifications, to the application as if it were an application for ancillary relief.

Amendments—Inserted by SI 1999/3491, rr 2, 3; amended by SI 2005/2922.

2.69 (*revoked*)

Amendments—Inserted by SI 1992/2067, r 5; substituted by SI 1999/3491, rr 2, 3, 17; revoked by SI 2006/352, r 6.

2.69A (*revoked*)

Amendments—Substituted for r 2 69 by SI 1999/3491, rr 2, 3, 17; revoked by SI 2003/184, rr 2(b), (6).

2.69B (*revoked*)

Amendments—Substituted for r 2 69 by SI 1999/3491, rr 2, 3, 17; revoked by SI 2006/352, r 6.

2.69C (*revoked*)

Amendments—Substituted for r 2 69 by SI 1999/3491, rr 2, 3, 17; revoked by SI 2003/184, rr 2(b), 7.

2.69D (*revoked*)

Amendments—Substituted for r 2 69 by SI 1999/3491, rr 2, 3, 17; amended by SI 2003/184, rr 2(c), 8(2), (3); revoked by SI 2006/352, r 6.

2.69E Open proposals

(1) Not less than 14 days before the date fixed for the final hearing of an application for ancillary relief, the applicant must (unless the court directs otherwise) file with the court and serve on the respondent an open statement which sets out concise details, including the amounts involved, of the orders which he proposes to ask the court to make.

(2) Not more than 7 days after service of a statement under paragraph (1), the respondent must file with the court and serve on the applicant an open statement which sets out concise details, including the amounts involved, of the orders which he proposes to ask the court to make.

Amendments—Substituted for r 2 69 by SI 1999/3491, rr 2, 3, 17.

2.69F Application for interim orders

(1) A party may apply at any stage of the proceedings for an order for maintenance pending suit, or outcome of proceedings, as the case may be, interim periodical payments or an interim variation order.

(2) An application for such an order must be made by notice of application and the date fixed for the hearing of the application must be not less than 14 days after the date the notice of application is issued.

(3) The applicant shall forthwith serve the respondent with a copy of the notice of application.

(4) Where an application is made before a party has filed Form E, that party must file with the application and serve on the other party, a draft of the order requested and a short sworn statement explaining why the order is necessary and giving the necessary information about his means.

(5) Not less than 7 days before the date fixed for the hearing, the respondent must file with the court and serve on the other party, a short sworn statement about his means, unless he has already filed Form E.

(6) A party may apply for any other form of interim order at any stage of the proceedings with or without notice.

(7) Where an application referred to in paragraph (6) is made with notice, the provisions of paragraphs (1) to (5) apply to it.

(8) Where an application referred to in paragraph (6) is made without notice, the provisions of paragraph (1) apply to it.

Amendments—Substituted for r 2 69 by SI 1999/3491, rr 2, 3, 17; amended by SI 2005/2922.

2.70 Pensions

(1) This rule applies where an application for ancillary relief has been made, or notice of intention to proceed with the application has been given, in Form A, or an application has been made in Form B, and the applicant or respondent has or is likely to have any benefits under a pension arrangement.

(2) When the court fixes a first appointment as required by rule 2.61A(4)(a),

    (a)   in a matrimonial cause, the party with pension rights, and
    (b)   in a civil partnership cause, the civil partner with pension rights,

shall within seven days after receiving notification of the date of that appointment, request the person responsible for each pension arrangement under which he has or is likely to have benefits to furnish the information referred to in regulation 2(2) of the Pensions on Divorce etc (Provision of Information) Regulations 2000.]

(3) Within seven days of receiving information under paragraph (2) the party with pension rights or civil partner with pension rights, as the case may be, shall

send a copy of it to the other party or civil partner, together with the name and address of the person responsible for each pension arrangement.

(4) A request under paragraph (2) above need not be made where the party with pension rights or the civil partner with pension rights is in possession of, or has requested, a relevant valuation of the pension rights or benefits accrued under the pension arrangement in question.

(5) In this rule, a relevant valuation means a valuation of pension rights or benefits as at a date not more than twelve months earlier than the date fixed for the first appointment which has been furnished or requested for the purposes of any of the following provisions —

    (a)   the Pensions on Divorce etc (Provision of Information) Regulations 2000;

    (b)   regulation 5 of and Schedule 2 to the Occupational Pension Schemes (Disclosure of Information) Regulations 1996 and regulation 11 of and Schedule 1 to the Occupational Pension Schemes (Transfer Value) Regulations 1996;

    (c)   section 93A or 94(1)(a) or (aa) of the Pension Schemes Act 1993;

    (d)   section 94(1)(b) of the Pension Schemes Act 1993 or paragraph 2(a) (or, where applicable, 2(b)) of Schedule 2 to the Personal Pension Schemes (Disclosure of Information) Regulations 1987.

(6) Upon making or giving notice of intention to proceed with an application for ancillary relief which includes a request for a pension sharing order, or upon adding a request for such an order to an existing application for ancillary relief, the applicant shall send to the person responsible for the pension arrangement concerned a copy of Form A.

(7) Upon making or giving notice of intention to proceed with an application for ancillary relief which includes an application for a pension attachment order, or upon adding a request for such an order to an existing application for ancillary relief, the applicant shall send to the person responsible for the pension arrangement concerned —

    (a)   a copy of Form A;

    (b)   an address to which any notice which the person responsible is required to serve on the applicant under the Divorce etc (Pensions) Regulations 2000 or the Dissolution etc (Pensions) Regulations 2005, as the case may be, is to be sent;

    (c)   an address to which any payment which the person responsible is required to make to the applicant is to be sent; and

    (d)   where the address in sub-paragraph (c) is that of a bank, a building society or the Department of National Savings, sufficient details to enable payment to be made into the account of the applicant.

(8) A person responsible for a pension arrangement on whom a copy of a notice under paragraph (7) is served may, within 21 days after service, require the party or civil partner with the pension rights, as the case may be, to provide him with a copy of section 2.13 of his Form E; and that party or civil partner must then provide that person with the copy of that section of the statement

within the time limited for filing it by rule 2.61B(2), or 21 days after being required to do so, whichever is the later.

(9) A person responsible for a pension arrangement who receives a copy of section 2.13 of Form E as required pursuant to paragraph (8) may within 21 days after receipt send to the court, the applicant and the respondent a statement in answer.

(10) A person responsible for a pension arrangement who files a statement in answer pursuant to paragraph (9) shall be entitled to be represented at the first appointment, and the court must within 4 days of the date of filing of the statement in answer give the person notice of the date of the first appointment.

(11) Where the parties have agreed on the terms of an order and the agreement includes a pension attachment order, then unless service has already been effected under paragraph (7), they shall serve on the person responsible for the pension arrangement concerned —

   (a)   the notice of application for a consent order under rule 2.61(1);
   (b)   a draft of the proposed order under rule 2.61(1), complying with paragraph (13) below; and
   (c)   the particulars set out in sub-paragraphs (b), (c) and (d) of paragraph (7) above.

(12) No consent order under paragraph (11) shall be made unless either —

   (a)   the person responsible has not made any objection within 21 days after the service on him of such notice; or
   (b)   the court has considered any such objection

and for the purpose of considering any objection the court may make such direction as it sees fit for the person responsible to attend before it or to furnish written details of his objection.

(13) An order for ancillary relief, whether by consent or not, which includes a pension sharing order or a pension attachment order, shall —

   (a)   in the body of the order, state that there is to be provision by way of pension sharing or pension attachment in accordance with the annex or annexes to the order; and
   (b)   be accompanied by an annex in Form P1 (Pension Sharing annex) or Form P2 (Pension Attachment annex) as the case may require; and if provision is made in relation to more than one pension arrangement there shall be one annex for each pension arrangement.

(14) *(revoked)*

(15) *(revoked)*

(16) A court which makes, varies or discharges a pension sharing order or a pension attachment order], shall send[, or direct one of the parties to send, to the person responsible for the pension arrangement concerned —

   (a)   a copy of —

(i)   in a matrimonial cause, the decree of divorce, nullity of marriage or judicial separation; or

(ii)   in a civil partnership cause, the conditional order of dissolution, nullity of civil partnership or the order of separation;

(b) in the case of —

(i)   divorce or nullity of marriage, a copy of the certificate under rule 2.51 that the decree has been made absolute; or

(ii)   dissolution or nullity of civil partnership, a copy of the order making the conditional order final under rule 2.51A; and

(c) a copy of that order, or as the case may be of the order varying or discharging that order, including any annex to that order relating to that pension arrangement but no other annex to that order.

(17) The documents referred to in paragraph (16) shall be sent —

(a) in a matrimonial cause, within 7 days after —

(i)   the making of the relevant pension sharing or pension attachment order; or

(ii)   the decree absolute of divorce or nullity or decree of judicial separation,

whichever is the later; and

(b) in a civil partnership cause, within 7 days after —

(i)   the making of the relevant pension sharing or pension attachment order; or

(ii)   the final order of dissolution or nullity or order of separation,

whichever is the later.

(18) In this rule —

(a) in a matrimonial cause, all words and phrases defined in sections 25D(3) and (4) of the Act of 1973 have the meanings assigned by those subsections;

(ab) in a civil partnership cause, all words and phrases defined in paragraphs 16(4) to (5) and 29 of Schedule 5 to the Act of 2004 have the meanings assigned by those paragraphs;

(b) all words and phrases defined in section 46 of the Welfare Reform and Pensions Act 1999 have the meanings assigned by that section;

(c) 'pension sharing order' means —

(i)   in a matrimonial cause, an order making provision under section 24B of the Act of 1973; and

(ii)   in a civil partnership cause, an order making provision under paragraph 15 of Schedule 5 to the Act of 2004; and

(d) 'pension attachment order' means —

(i)   in a matrimonial cause, an order making provision under section 25B or 25C of the Act of 1973; and

(ii)   in a civil partnership cause, an order making provision under paragraph 25 and paragraph 26 of Schedule 5 to the Act of 2004.

Amendments—Inserted by SI 1996/1674, r 5; substituted by SI 2000/2267, r 9; amended by SI 2001/821, r 10; SI 2003/184, r 9; SI 2005/2922.

2.71–2.77 (*revoked*)

Amendments—SI 1999/3491.

PART III
OTHER MATRIMONIAL ETC PROCEEDINGS

3.1 Application in case of failure to provide reasonable maintenance

(1) Every application under section 27 of the Act of 1973 or under Part 9 of Schedule 5 to the Act of 2004 shall be made by originating application in Form M19.

(2) The application may be made

(a)   in the case of an application under the Act of 1973, to any divorce county court, and

(b)   in the case of an application under the Act of 2004, to any civil partnership proceedings county court,

and there shall be filed with the application an affidavit by the applicant and also a copy of the application and of the affidavit for service on the respondent.

(3) The affidavit shall state —

(a)   the same particulars regarding the marriage or the civil partnership as the case may be, the court's jurisdiction, the children and the previous proceedings as are required in the case of a petition by sub-paragraphs (a), (c), (d), (f) and (i) of paragraph 1 of Appendix 2;

(b)   particulars of the respondent's failure to provide reasonable maintenance for the applicant, or, as the case may be, of the respondent's failure to provide, or to make a proper contribution towards, reasonable maintenance for the children of the family; and

(c)   full particulars of the applicant's property and income and of the respondent's property and income, so far as may be known to the applicant.

(4) A copy of the application and of the affidavit referred to in paragraph (2) shall be served on the respondent, together with a notice in Form M20 with Form M23A.

(5) Subject to paragraph (6), the respondent shall, within 14 days after the time allowed for sending the acknowledgement of service, file an affidavit stating —

(a)   whether the alleged failure to provide, or to make proper contribution towards, reasonable maintenance is admitted or denied, and, if denied, the grounds on which he relies;

(b)   any allegation which he wishes to make against the applicant; and

(c)   full particulars of his property and income, unless otherwise directed.

(6) Where the respondent challenges the jurisdiction of the court to hear the application he shall, within 14 days after the time allowed for sending the acknowledgement of service, file an affidavit setting out the grounds of the challenge; and the obligation to file an affidavit under paragraph (5) shall not

arise until 14 days after the question of jurisdiction has been determined and the court has decided that the necessary jurisdiction exists.

(7) Where the respondent's affidavit contains an allegation of adultery or of an improper association with a person named, the provisions of sub-paragraphs (4) to (7) of paragraph 4 of Appendix 4 (which deal with service on, and filing of a statement in answer by, a named person) shall apply.

(8) If the respondent does not file an affidavit in accordance with paragraph (5), the court may order him to file an affidavit containing full particulars of his property and income, and in that case the respondent shall serve a copy of any such affidavit on the applicant.

(9) Within 14 days after being served with a copy of any affidavit filed by the respondent, the applicant may file a further affidavit as to means and as to any fact in the respondent's affidavit which is disputed, and in that case the applicant shall serve a copy on the respondent.

No further affidavit shall be filed without leave.

(10) The following provisions shall apply to applications under section 27 of the Act of 1973 and Part 9 of Schedule 5 to the Act of 2004 —

(a) rule 10.10 with such modifications as may be appropriate and as if the application were an application for ancillary relief; and

(b) paragraphs 5 to 9 of Appendix 4.

Amendments—SI 1999/3491, rr 2, 21; SI 2005/559, r 10; SI 2005/2922, r 58(a).

3.2 Application for alteration of maintenance agreement during lifetime of parties

(1) An application under section 35 of the Act of 1973 or under paragraph 69 of Schedule 5 to the Act of 2004 for the alteration of a maintenance agreement shall be made by originating application containing, unless otherwise directed, the information required by Form M21.

(2) The application may be made —

(a) in the case of an application under the Act of 1973, to any divorce county court, and

(b) in the case of an application under the Act of 2004, to any civil partnership proceedings county court,

and may be heard and determined by the district judge.

(3) There shall be filed with the application an affidavit by the applicant exhibiting a copy of the agreement and verifying the statements in the application and also a copy of the application and of the affidavit for service on the respondent.

(4) A copy of the application and of the affidavit referred to in paragraph (3) shall be served on the respondent, together with a notice in Form M20 with Form M23A attached.

(5) The respondent shall, within 14 days after the time limited for giving notice of intention to defend in Form M23A, file an affidavit in answer to the application containing full particulars of his property and income and, if he does not do so, the court may order him to file an affidavit containing such particulars.

(6) A respondent who files an affidavit under paragraph (5) shall at the same time file a copy which the proper officer shall serve on the applicant.

Amendments—SI 2005/559, rr 10, 11; SI 2005/2922, r 59(a), 59(b).

3.3 Application of alteration of maintenance agreement after death of one party

(1) An application under section 36 of the Act of 1973 or under paragraph 73 of Schedule 5 to the Act of 2004 for the alteration of a maintenance agreement after the death of one of the parties shall be made —

   (a) in the High Court, by originating summons out of the principal registry or any district registry, or
   (b) in a county court, by originating application,
   in Form M22.

(2) There shall be filed in support of the application an affidavit by the applicant exhibiting a copy of the agreement and an official copy of the grant of representation to the deceased's estate and of every testamentary document admitted to proof and stating —

   (a) whether the deceased died domiciled in England and Wales;
   (b) the place and date of the marriage between the parties to the agreement, or the place at and date on which they formed their civil partnership, as the case may be;
   (c) the name of every child of the family and of any other child for whom the agreement makes financial arrangements, and —
      (i)   the date of birth of each such child who is still living (or, if it be the case, that he has attained 18) and the place where and the person with whom any such minor child is residing,
      (ii) the date of death of any such child who has died since the agreement was made;
   (d) whether there have been in any court any, and if so what, previous proceedings with reference to the agreement or to the marriage or civil partnership, as the case may be, or to the children of the family or any other children for whom the agreement makes financial arrangements, and the date and effect of any order or decree made in such proceedings;
   (e) whether there have been in any court any proceedings by the applicant against the deceased's estate under the Inheritance (Provision for Family and Dependants) Act 1975 or any Act repealed by that Act and the date and effect of any order made in such proceedings;
   (f) in the case of an application by the surviving party, the applicant's means;

(g) in the case of an application by the personal representatives of the deceased, the surviving party's means, so far as they are known to the applicants, and the information mentioned in sub-paragraphs (a), (b) and (c) of rule 3.4(4);

(h) the facts alleged by the applicant as justifying an alteration in the agreement and the nature of the alteration sought;

(i) if the application is made after the end of the period of six months from the date on which representation in regard to the deceased's estate was first taken out, the grounds on which the court's permission to entertain the application is sought.

(3) CCR Order 48, rules 3(1), 7 and 9 shall apply to an originating application under the said section 36 as they apply to an application under section 1 of the Inheritance (Provision for Family and Dependants) Act 1975.

(4) In this rule and the next following rule 'the deceased' means the deceased party to the agreement to which the application relates.

Amendments—SI 2005/2922, r 60(a), 60(b).

. . .

PART VII
ENFORCEMENT OF ORDERS

Chapter 1. General

7.1 Enforcement of order for payment of money etc

(1) Before any process is issued for the enforcement of an order made in family proceedings for the payment of money to any person, an affidavit shall be filed verifying the amount due under the order and showing how that amount is arrived at.

In a case to which CCR Order 25 rule 11 (which deals with the enforcement of a High Court judgment in the county court) applies, the information required to be given in an affidavit under this paragraph , may be given in the affidavit filed pursuant to that rule.

(2) Except with the leave of the district judge, no writ of fieri facias or warrant of execution shall be issued to enforce payment of any sum due under an order for ancillary relief or an order made under the provisions of section 27 of the Act of 1973 or an order under Part 9 of Schedule 5 to the Act of 2004 where an application for a variation order is pending.

(3) Where a warrant of execution has been issued to enforce an order made in family proceedings pending in the principal registry which are treated as pending in a designated county court, the goods and chattels against which the warrant has been issued shall wherever they are situate, be treated for the purposes of section 103 of the County Courts Act 1984 as being out of the jurisdiction of the principal registry.

(4) The Attachment of Earnings Act 1971 and CCR Order 27 (which deals with attachment of earnings) shall apply to the enforcement of an order made in family proceedings in the principal registry which are treated as pending in a designated county court as if the order were an order made by such a court.

(5) Where —

(a) an application under CCR Order 25, rule 3 (which deals with the oral examination of a judgment debtor) relates to an order made by a divorce county court, the application shall be made to such divorce county court as in the opinion of the applicant is nearest to the place where the debtor resides or carries on business,

(b) an application under CCR Order 25, rule 3 (which deals with the oral examination of a judgment debtor) relates to an order made by a civil partnership proceedings county court, the application shall be made to such civil partnership proceedings county court as in the opinion of the applicant is nearest to the place where the debtor resides, or carries on business, and

(c) in either case, paragraph (2) of rule 3 shall not apply.

(6) In a case to which paragraph (5) relates there shall be filed the affidavit required by paragraph (1) of this rule and, except where the application is made to the court in which the order sought to be enforced was made, a copy of the order shall be exhibited to the affidavit.

Amendments—SI 2005/2922, r 1, 91(a).

7.2 Committal and injunction

(1) Subject to RSC Order 52, rule 6 (which, except in certain cases, requires an application for an order of committal to be heard in open court) an application for an order of committal in family proceedings pending in the High Court shall be made by summons.

(2) Where no judge is conveniently available to hear the application, then, without prejudice to CCR Order 29, rule 3(2) (which in certain circumstances gives jurisdiction to a district judge) an application for —

(a) the discharge of any person committed, or

(b) the discharge by consent of an injunction granted by a judge,

may be made to the district judge who may, if satisfied of the urgency of the matter and that it is expedient to do so, make any order on the application which a judge could have made.

(3) Where an order or warrant for the committal of any person to prison has been made or issued in family proceedings pending in the principal registry which are treated as pending in a designated county court or a county court, that person shall, wherever he may be, be treated for the purposes of section 122 of the County Courts Act 1984 as being out of the jurisdiction of the principal registry; but if the committal is for failure to comply with the terms of an injunction, the order or warrant may, if the court so directs, be executed by the tipstaff within any county court district.

(3A) Where an order or warrant for the arrest or committal of any person has been made or issued in proceedings under Part IV of the Family Law Act 1996 pending in the principal registry which are treated as pending in a county court, the order or warrant may, if the court so directs, be executed by the tipstaff within any county court district.

(4) For the purposes of section 118 of the County Courts Act 1984 in its application to the hearing of family proceedings at the Royal Courts of Justice or the principal registry, the tipstaff shall be deemed to be an officer of the court.

Amendments—SI 1997/1893, rr 5, 9, 17(1), (2); SI 2005/2922, r 92.

7.3 Transfer of county court order to High Court

(1) Any person who desires the transfer to the High Court of any order made by a designated county court in family proceedings except an order for periodical payments or for the recovery of arrears of periodical payments shall apply to the court ex parte by affidavit stating the amount which remains due under the order, and on the filing of the application the transfer shall have effect.

(2) Where an order is so transferred, it shall have the same force and effect and the same proceedings may be taken on it as if it were an order of the High Court.

Amendments—SI 2005/2922, r 92.

Chapter 2. Judgment summonses

7.4 General provisions

(1) In this chapter, unless the context otherwise requires —

'order' means an order made in family proceedings for the payment of money;
'judgment creditor' means a person entitled to enforce an order under section 5 of the Debtors Act 1869;
'debtor' means a person liable under an order;
'judgment summons' means a summons under the said section 5 requiring a debtor to attend court.

(2) An application for the issue of a judgment summons may be made —

(a) in the case of an order of the High Court—
  (i) where the order was made in a matrimonial cause, to the principal registry, a district registry or a divorce county court, whichever in the opinion of the judgment creditor is most convenient,
  (ii) where the order was made in a civil partnership cause, to the principal registry, a district registry or a civil partnership proceedings county court, whichever in the opinion of the judgment creditor is most convenient, and

(iii)   in any other case, to the principal registry, a district registry or a designated county court, whichever in the opinion of the judgment creditor is most convenient,

(b)   in the case of an order of a divorce county court, to whichever divorce county court is in the opinion of the judgment creditor most convenient, and

(c)   in the case of an order of a civil partnership proceedings county court, to whichever civil partnership proceedings county court is in the opinion of the judgment creditor most convenient,

having regard (in any case) to the place where the debtor resides or carries on business and irrespective of the court or registry in which the order was made.

(3) The application shall be made by filing a request in Form M16 together with the affidavit required by rule 7.1(1) and, except where the application is made to the registry or designated county court in which the order was made, a copy of the order shall be exhibited to the affidavit.

(3A) The judgment creditor must file with the request copies of all written evidence on which he intends to rely.

(4) A judgment summons shall not be issued without the leave of a judge if the debtor is in default under an order of commitment made on a previous judgment summons in respect of the same order.

(5) Every judgment summons shall be in Form M17 and shall be served on the debtor personally together with copies of the written evidence referred to in paragraph (3A) not less than 14 days before the hearing and at the time of service there shall be paid or tendered to the debtor a sum reasonably sufficient to cover his expenses in travelling to and from the court at which he is summoned to appear.

(6) CCR Order 28, rule 3 (which deals among other things with the issue of successive judgment summonses) shall apply to a judgment summons, whether issued in the High Court or a designated county court, but as if the said rule 3 did not apply CCR Order 7, rule 19(2).

(7) Successive judgment summonses may be issued notwithstanding that the judgment debtor has ceased to reside or carry on business at the address stated in Form M16 since the issue of the original judgment summons.

(7A) The following documents must be served personally on the debtor —

(a)   where the proceedings are in the High Court and the court has summoned the debtor to attend and he has failed to do so, the notice of the day and time fixed for the adjourned hearing;

(b)   where the proceedings are in the county court, an order made under section 110(1) of the County Courts Act 1984;

(c)   in either case, copies of the judgment summons, the affidavit required by rule 7.1(1) and all written evidence referred to in paragraph (3A).

(7B) No person may be committed on an application for a judgment summons unless —

(a)   where the proceedings are in the High Court, the court has summoned the debtor to attend, he has failed to do so, and he has also failed to attend the adjourned hearing;

(b)   where the proceedings are in the county court, an order is made under section 110(2) of the County Courts Act 1984; or

(c)   the judgment creditor proves that the debtor —

    (i)   has or has had since the date of the order the means to pay the sum in respect of which he has made default; and

    (ii)   has refused or neglected, or refuses or neglects, to pay that sum.

(7C) The debtor may not be compelled to give evidence.

(8) Where an applicant has obtained one or more orders in the same application but for the benefit of different persons —

(a)   he shall be entitled to issue a judgment summons in respect of those orders on behalf of any judgment creditor without (where the judgment creditor is a child) seeking leave to act as his next friend; and

(b)   only one judgment summons need be issued in respect of those orders.

(9) On the hearing of the judgment summons the judge may —

(a)   where the order is for lump sum provision or costs, or

(b)   where the order is for maintenance pending suit or outcome of proceedings ,or other periodical payments and it appears to him that the order would have been varied or suspended if the debtor had made an application for that purpose,

make a new order for payment of the amount due under the original order, together with the costs of the judgment summons, either at a specified time or by instalments.

(10) If the judge makes an order of committal, he may direct its execution to be suspended on terms that the debtor pays to the judgment creditor the amount due, together with the costs of the judgment summons, either at a specified time or by instalments, in addition to any sums accruing due under the original order.

(11) All payments under a new order or an order of committal shall be made to the judgment creditor unless the judge otherwise directs.

(12) Where an order of committal is suspended on such terms as are mentioned in paragraph (10) —

(a)   all payments thereafter made under the said order shall be deemed to be made, first, in or towards the discharge of any sums from time to time accruing due under the original order and, secondly, in or towards the discharge of a debt in respect of which the judgment summons was issued and the costs of the summons;

(b)   CCR Order 28, rule 7(4) and (5) (which deal with an application for a further suspension) shall apply to the said order, whether it was made in the High Court or a designated county court; and

(c)   the said order shall not be issued until the judgment creditor has filed an affidavit of default on the part of the debtor.

Amendments—SI 2003/184, r 11(1), (2), (3)(a), (b), (4); SI 2005/2922, r 94(a), 94(b).

7.5 Special provisions as to judgment summonses in the High Court

(1) (*revoked*)

(2) Witnesses may be summoned to prove the means of the debtor in the same manner as witnesses are summoned to give evidence on the hearing of a cause, and writs of subpoena may for that purpose be issued out of the registry in which the judgment summons is issued.

(3) Where the debtor appears at the hearing, the travelling expenses paid to him may, if the judge so directs, be allowed as expenses of a witness, but if the debtor appears at the hearing and no order of committal is made, the judge may allow to the debtor, by way of set-off or otherwise, his proper costs, including compensation for loss of time, as upon an attendance by a defendant at a trial in court.

(4) Where a new order or an order of committal is made, the proper officer of the registry in which the judgment summons was issued shall send notice of the order to the debtor and, if the original order was made in another registry, to the proper officer of that registry.

(5) An order of committal shall be directed to the tipstaff, for execution by him, or to the proper officer of the county court within the district of which the debtor is to be found, for execution by a deputy tipstaff.

(6), (7) (*revoked*)

Amendments—SI 2003/184, r 12.

7.6 Special provisions as to judgment summonses in designated county courts

(1) CCR Order 25, rules 3, 4 and 11 (which deal with the oral examination of debtors and the execution of High Court orders in county courts) and Order 28, rules 1, 2, 3(2), 5, 7(3), 9(2) and 10(3) (which deal with the issue of a judgment summons in a county court and the subsequent procedure) shall not apply to a judgment summons issued in a designated county court.

(2) CCR Order 28, rule 9(1) (which relates to a judgment summons heard in a county court on a judgment or order of the High Court) shall apply to such a summons as if for the words 'the High Court' there were substituted the words 'any other court' where they first appear and 'that other court' where they next appear.

(3) On any appeal to which paragraph (2) applies —

(a)   the appeal shall be limited to a review of the decision or order of the district judge unless the judge considers that in the circumstances of the case it would be in the interests of justice to hold a rehearing;

(b) oral evidence or evidence which was not before the district judge may be admitted if in all circumstances of the case it would be in the interests of justice to do so, irrespective of whether the appeal be by way of review or rehearing.

Amendments—SI 2003/184, r 13; SI 2005/2922, r 1(2).

. . .

Chapter 4. Enforcement of maintenance orders

7.16 Interpretation

In this chapter —

'the Act of 1920' means the Maintenance Orders (Facilities for Enforcement) Act 1920;
'the Act of 1950' means the Maintenance Orders Act 1950;
'the Act of 1958' means the Maintenance Orders Act 1958;
'the Act of 1965' means the Matrimonial Causes Act 1965;
'the Act of 1971' means the Attachment of Earnings Act 1971;
'the Act of 1972' means the Maintenance Orders (Reciprocal Enforcement) Act 1972;
'English maintenance order' means a maintenance order made in the High Court.

7.17 Registration etc of orders under Act of 1920

(1) The prescribed officer for the purposes of section 1(1) of the Act of 1920 shall be the senior district judge, and on receiving from the Secretary of State a copy of a maintenance order made by a court in any part of Her Majesty's dominions outside the United Kingdom to which the Act of 1920 extends he shall cause the order to be registered in the register kept for the purpose of that Act (in this rule referred to as 'the register').

The copy of the order received from the Secretary of State shall be filed in the principal registry.

(2) An application for the transmission of an English maintenance order under section 2 of the Act of 1920 shall be made to the district judge by lodging in the principal registry a certified copy of the order and an affidavit stating the applicant's reasons for believing that the person liable to make payments under the order is resident in some part of Her Majesty's dominions outside the United Kingdom to which the Act of 1920 extends, together with full particulars, so far as known to the applicant, of that person's address and occupation and any other information which may be required by the law of that part of Her Majesty's dominions for the purpose of the enforcement of the order.

(3) If it appears to the district judge mentioned in paragraph (2) that the person liable to make payments under the English maintenance order is resident in some part of Her Majesty's dominions outside the United Kingdom to which

the Act of 1920 extends, he shall send the certified copy of the order to the Secretary of State for transmission to the Governor of that part of Her Majesty's dominions.

Particulars of any English maintenance order sent to the Secretary of State under the said section 2 shall be entered in the register and the fact that this has been done shall be noted in the records of the court.

(4) Where an English maintenance order has been made in a cause or matter proceeding in a district registry, an application for the transmission of the order under the said section 2 may be made to the district judge of that registry and paragraphs (2) and (3) of this rule shall have effect as if for reference to the principal registry there were substituted references to the district registry.

The proper officer shall send to the principal registry for entry in the register particulars of any order sent by him to the Secretary of State.

(5) Any person who satisfies a district judge that he is entitled to or liable to make payments under an English maintenance order or a maintenance order made by a court in any part of Her Majesty's dominions outside the United Kingdom to which the Act of 1920 extends or a solicitor acting on behalf of any such person or, with the leave of a district judge, any other person may inspect the register and bespeak copies of any order which has been registered and of any document filed therewith.

Proceedings under Part II of Act of 1950

7.18 Interpretation of rules 7.18 to 7.21

In this rule and rules 7.19 to 7.21 —

'the clerk of the Court of Session' means the deputy principal clerk in charge of the petition department of the Court of Session;
'maintenance order' means a maintenance order to which section 16 of the Act of 1950 applies;
'Northern Irish order' means a maintenance order made by the Supreme Court of Northern Ireland;
'register' means the register kept for the purposes of the Act of 1950;
'the registrar in Northern Ireland' means the chief registrar of the Queen's Bench Division (Matrimonial) of the High Court of Justice in Northern Ireland;
'registration' means registration under Part II of the Act of 1950 and 'registered' shall be construed accordingly;
'Scottish order' means a maintenance order made by the Court of Session.

7.19 Registration etc of English order

(1) An application for the registration of an English maintenance order may be made by lodging with the proper officer a certified copy of the order, together with an affidavit by the applicant (and a copy thereof) stating —

(a) the address in the United Kingdom, and the occupation, of the person liable to make payments under the order;

(b) the date of service of the order on the person liable to make payments thereunder or, if the order has not been served, the reason why service has not been effected;

(c) the reason why it is convenient that the order should be enforceable in Scotland or Northern Ireland, as the case may be;

(d) the amount of any arrears due to the applicant under the order; and

(e) that the order is not already registered.

(2) If it appears to the district judge that the person liable to make payments under the order resides in Scotland or Northern Ireland and that it is convenient that the order should be enforceable there, the proper officer shall (subject to paragraph (6) below) send a certified copy of the order and the applicant's affidavit to the clerk of the Court of Session or to the registrar in Northern Ireland, as the case may be.

(3) On receipt of notice of the registration of an English maintenance order in the Court of Session or the Supreme Court of Northern Ireland, the proper officer shall —

(a) cause particulars of the notice to be entered in the register;

(b) note the fact of registration in the records of the court; and

(c) send particulars of the notice to the principal registry.

(4) Where an English order registered in the Court of Session or the Supreme Court of Northern Ireland is discharged or varied the proper officer of the court ordering the discharge or variation shall give notice thereof to the clerk of the Court of Session or to the registrar in Northern Ireland, as the case may be, by sending him a certified copy of the order discharging or varying the maintenance order.

(5) Where the registration of an English maintenance order registered in the Court of Session or the Supreme Court of Northern Ireland is cancelled under section 24(1) of the Act of 1950, notice of the cancellation shall be sent (as required by section 24(3)(a) of that Act) to the proper officer, and on receipt of such notice he shall cause particulars of it to be entered in Part I of the register.

(6) Where the order sought to be registered was made in a county court, this rule shall apply as though references to the Court of Session, the clerk of the Court of Session, the Supreme Court of Northern Ireland and the registrar of Northern Ireland were references to the sheriff court, the sheriff-clerk of the sheriff court, the court of summary jurisdiction and the clerk of the court of summary jurisdiction respectively.

7.20 Registration etc of Scottish and Northern Irish orders

(1) In relation to a Scottish or Northern Irish order the prescribed officer for the purposes of section 17(2) of the Act of 1950 shall be the proper officer of the principal registry.

(2) On receipt of a certified copy of a Scottish or Northern Irish order for registration, the proper officer shall —

(a) cause the order to be registered in Part II of the register and notify the clerk of the Court of Session or the registrar in Northern Ireland, as the case may be, that this has been done; and

(b) file the certified copy and any statutory declaration or affidavit as to the amount of any arrears due under the order.

(3) An application under section 21(2) of the Act of 1950 by a person liable to make payments under a Scottish order registered in the High Court to adduce before that court such evidence as is mentioned in that section shall be made by lodging a request for an appointment before a district judge of the principal registry; and notice of the date, time and place fixed for the hearing shall be sent by post to the applicant and to the person entitled to payments under the order.

(4) The prescribed officer to whom notice of the discharge or variation of a Scottish or Northern Irish order registered in the High Court is to be given under section 23(1)(a) of the Act of 1950 shall be the proper officer, and on receipt of the notice he shall cause particulars of it to be registered in Part II of the register.

(5) An application under section 24(1) of the Act of 1950 for the cancellation of the registration of a Scottish or Northern Irish order shall be made ex parte by affidavit to a district judge of the principal registry who, if he cancels the registration, shall note the cancellation in Part II of the register, whereupon the proper officer shall send notice of the cancellation to the clerk of the Court of Session or the registrar in Northern Ireland, as the case may be, and also to the clerk of any magistrates' court in which the order has been registered in accordance with section 2(5) of the Act of 1958.

(6) A person entitled to payments under a Scottish or Northern Irish order registered in the High Court who wishes to take proceedings for or with respect to the enforcement of the order in a district registry may apply by letter to the senior district judge of the principal registry who may, if satisfied that the order ought to be enforceable in the district registry, make an order accordingly on such terms, if any, as may be just.

Amendments—SI 1997/1893, r 18.

7.21 Inspection of register

Any person who satisfies a district judge of the principal registry that he is entitled to or liable to make payments under a maintenance order of a superior court or a solicitor acting on behalf of any such person or, with the leave of the district judge, any other person may inspect the register and bespeak copies of any such order which is registered in the High Court under Part II of the Act of 1950 and of any statutory declaration or affidavit filed therewith.

Registration etc of certain orders under the Act of 1958

7.22 Application and interpretation of rules 7.22 to 7.29

Section 21 of the Act of 1958 shall apply to the interpretation of this rule and rules 7.23 to 7.29 as it applies to the interpretation of that Act; and in those rules —

'cause book' includes cause card; and
'the register' means any register kept for the purposes of the Act of 1958.

7.23 Application for registration

(1) An application under section 2(1) of the Act of 1958 for the registration in a magistrates' court of a maintenance order shall be made by lodging with the proper officer —

(i)   a certified copy of the maintenance order, and
(ii)   two copies of the application in Form M33.

(2) The period required to be prescribed by rules of court for the purpose of section 2(2) of the Act of 1958 shall be 14 days.

(3) The proper officer shall cause the certified copy of an order required by the said section 2(2) to be sent to the designated officer for a magistrates' court to be endorsed with a note that the application for registration of the order has been granted and to be accompanied by a copy of the application lodged under paragraph (1).

(4) On receipt of notice that a maintenance order has been registered in a magistrates' court in accordance with section 2(5) of the Act of 1958, the proper officer shall enter particulars of the registration in the records of the court.

Amendments—SI 1992/2067, r 16; SI 2001/821, r 28. SI 2005/617.

7.24 Registration in a magistrates' court of an order registered in the High Court

On receipt of notice that a maintenance order registered in the High Court in accordance with section 17(4) of the Act of 1950 has been registered in a magistrates' court in accordance with section 2(5) of the Act of 1958, the proper officer shall cause particulars of the registration to be entered in Part II of the register.

7.25 Registration of magistrates' court order

On receipt of a certified copy of a magistrates' court order sent to him pursuant to section 2(4)(c) of the Act of 1958, the proper officer shall cause the order to be registered in the High Court by filing the copy and making an entry in the register or, where the copy order is received in a district registry, in the cause book and shall send notice to the justices' chief executive for the magistrates' court that the order has been duly registered.

Amendments—SI 2001/821, r 28.

7.26 Registration in the High Court of an order registered in a magistrates' court

(1) This rule applies where a sheriff court in Scotland or a magistrates' court in Northern Ireland has made an order for the registration in the High Court of an order previously registered in a magistrates' court in England and Wales in accordance with section 17(4) of the Act of 1950, and has sent a certified copy of the maintenance order to the proper officer of the High Court, pursuant to section 2(4)(c) of the Act of 1958.

(2) On receipt of the certified copy, the proper officer shall cause the order to be registered in the High Court by filing the copy and making an entry in the register, and shall send notice of the registration to the designated officer for the original court and also to the designated officer for the magistrates' court in which the order was registered in accordance with section 17(4) of the Act of 1950.

Amendments—SI 2001/821, r 28; SI 2005/617.

7.27 Variation or discharge of registered order

(1) Where the court makes an order varying or discharging an order registered in a magistrates' court under Part I of the Act of 1958, the proper officer shall send a certified copy of the first-mentioned order to the designated officer for the magistrates' court.

(2) Where a certified copy of an order varying an order registered in a magistrates' court under Part I of the Act of 1958 is received from the designated officer for the magistrates' court, the proper officer shall file the copy and enter particulars of the variation on the same documents or in the same records as particulars of registration are required by rule 7.23(4) to be entered.

(3) Where a certified copy of an order varying or discharging an order made by a magistrates' court and registered in the High Court under Part I of the Act of 1958 is received from the designated officer for the magistrates' court, the proper officer shall —

    (a)   file the copy,
    (b)   enter particulars of the variation or discharge in the register or, where the copy order is received in a district registry, in the cause book, and
    (c)   send notice of the variation or discharge to any proper officer of a county court —
        (i)   who has given notice to the proper officer of proceedings taken in that court for the enforcement of the registered order, or
        (ii) to whom any payment is to be made under an attachment of earnings order made by the High Court for the enforcement of the registered order.

Amendments—SI 2001/821, r 28; SI 2005/617.

7.28 Appeal from variation etc of order by magistrates' court

An appeal to the High Court under section 4(7) of the Act of 1958 shall be heard and determined by a Divisional Court of the Family Division, and rule 8.2 shall apply as it applies in relation to an appeal from a magistrates' court under the Domestic Proceedings and Magistrates' Courts Act 1978.

7.29 Cancellation of registration

(1) A notice under section 5 of the Act of 1958 by a person entitled to receive payments under an order registered in the High Court must be given to the proper officer.

(2) Where the High Court gives notice under the said section 5, the proper officer shall endorse the notice on the certified copy mentioned in rule 7.27(1).

(3) Where notice under the said section 5 is given in respect of an order registered in the High Court, the proper officer on being satisfied by an affidavit by the person entitled to receive payments under the order that no process for the enforcement of the order issued before the giving of the notice remains in force, shall —

(a) cancel the registration by entering particulars of the notice in the register or cause book, as the case may be, and

(b) send notice of the cancellation to the justices' chief executive for the court by which the order was made and, where applicable, to the designated officer for the magistrates' court in which the order was registered in accordance with section 17(4) of the Act of 1950 stating, if such be the case, that the cancellation is in consequence of a notice given under subsection (1) of the said section 5.

(4) On receipt of notice from the designated officer for a magistrates' court that the registration in that court under the Act of 1958 of an order made by the High Court or a county court has been cancelled, the proper officer shall enter particulars of the cancellation on the same documents or in the same records as particulars of registration are required by rule 7.23(4) to be entered.

(5) On receipt of notice from the designated officer for a magistrates' court that the registration in that court under the Act of 1958 of an order registered in the High Court in accordance with section 17(4) of the Act of 1950 has been cancelled, the proper officer shall note the cancellation in Part II of the register.

Amendments—SI 2001/821, r 28; SI 2005/617.

Proceedings under Act of 1972

7.30 Interpretation of rules 7.31 to 7.39

(1) Expressions used in rules 7.31 to 7.39 which are used in the Act of 1972 have the same meanings as in that Act.

(2) The references in the Act of 1972 to the prescribed officer shall be construed as references to the proper officer within the meaning of rule 1.2(1).

(3) The reference in section 21 of the Act of 1972 to the proper officer shall be the proper officer within the meaning of rule 1.2(1).

Amendments—SI 1996/816, r 5(1), (2).

7.31 Application for transmission of maintenance order to reciprocating country

An application for a maintenance order to be sent to a reciprocating country under section 2 of the Act of 1972 shall be made by lodging with the court —

- (a) an affidavit by the applicant stating —
  - (i) the applicant's reason for believing that the payer under the maintenance order is residing in that country, and
  - (ii) the amount of any arrears due to the applicant under the order, the date to which those arrears have been calculated and the date on which the next payment under the order falls due;
- (b) a certified copy of the maintenance order,
- (c) a statement giving such information as the applicant possesses as to the whereabouts of the payer,
- (d) a statement giving such information as the applicant possesses for facilitating the identification of the payer (including, if known to the applicant, the name and address of any employer of the payer, his occupation and the date and place of issue of any passport of the payer) and
- (e) if available to the applicant, a photograph of the payer.

7.32 Certification of evidence given on provisional order

Where the court makes a provisional order under section 5 of the Act of 1972 the document required by subsection (4) of that section to set out or summarise the evidence given in the proceedings shall be authenticated by a certificate signed by the district judge.

7.33 Confirmation of provisional order

(1) On receipt of a certified copy of a provisional order made in a reciprocating country, together with the document mentioned in section 5(5) of the Act of 1972, the proper officer shall fix a date, time and place for the court to consider whether or not the provisional order should be confirmed, and shall send to the payee under the maintenance order notice of the date, time and place so fixed together with a copy of the provisional order and that document.

(2) The proper officer shall send to the court which made the provisional order a certified copy of any order confirming or refusing to confirm that order.

7.34 Taking of evidence for court in reciprocating country

(1) The High Court shall be the prescribed court for the purposes of taking evidence pursuant to a request by a court in a reciprocating country under section 14 of the Act of 1972 where —

(a)   the request for evidence relates to a maintenance order made by a
       superior court in the United Kingdom, and
(b)   the witness resides in England and Wales.

(2) The evidence may be taken before a judge or officer of the High Court as
the court thinks fit, and the provisions of RSC Order 39 shall apply with the
necessary modifications as if the evidence were required to be taken pursuant
to an order made under rule 1 of that Order.

(3) The county court shall be the prescribed court for the purposes of taking
evidence pursuant to a request by a court in a reciprocating country pursuant
to section 14 of the Act of 1972 where the request for evidence relates to a
maintenance order made by a county court which has not been registered in a
magistrates' court under the Act of 1958.

(4) Paragraph (2) shall apply to the taking of such evidence as though
references therein to the High Court and RSC Order 39 were to the county
court and CCR Order 20, rule 13 respectively.

7.35 Notification of variation or revocation

Where the court makes an order (other than a provisional order) varying or
revoking a maintenance order a copy of which has been sent to a reciprocating
country in pursuance of section 2 of the Act of 1972, the proper officer shall
send a certified copy of the order to the court in the reciprocating country.

7.36 Transmission of documents

Any document required to be sent to a court in a reciprocating country under
section 5(4) or section 14(1) of the Act of 1972 or by rule 7.33(2) or 7.36 shall
be sent to the Lord Chancellor for transmission to that court unless the district
judge is satisfied that, in accordance with the law of that country, the document
may properly be sent by him direct to that court.

7.37 Application of rules 7.30 to 7.36 to Republic of Ireland

(1) In relation to the Republic of Ireland rules 7.30 to 7.36 shall have effect
subject to the provisions of this rule.

(1A) A reference to the Act of 1972 in this rule, and in any rule which has effect
in relation to the Republic of Ireland by virtue of this rule, shall be a reference
to the said Act as modified by Schedule 2 to the Reciprocal Enforcement of
Maintenance Orders (Republic of Ireland) Order 1993.

(2) The following paragraphs shall be added to rule 7.31 —

'(f)   a statement as to whether or not the payer appeared in the
        proceedings in which the maintenance order was made and, if he
        did not, the original or a copy certified by the applicant or his
        solicitor to be a true copy of a document which establishes that
        notice of the institution of the proceedings was served on the
        payer;

(g)   a document that establishes that notice of the order was sent to the payer, and

(h)   if the payer received legal aid in the proceedings in which the order was made, a copy certified by the applicant or his solicitor to be a true copy of the legal aid certificate.'

(3) For rule 7.32 there shall be substituted the following rule —

'7.32 Certification of evidence given on application for variation or revocation

(1) Where an application is made to the court for the variation or revocation of an order to which section 5 of the Act of 1972 applies, the certified copy of the application and the documents required by subsection (3) of that section to set out or summarise the evidence in support of the application shall be authenticated by a certificate signed by the district judge.'

(4) Rule 7.33 shall not apply.

(5) For rule 7.35 there shall be substituted the following rule —

'7.35 Notification of variation or revocation

Where the High Court makes an order varying or revoking a maintenance order to which section 5 of the Act of 1972 applies, the proper officer shall send a certified copy of the order and a statement as to the service on the payer of the documents mentioned in subsection (3) of that section to the court in the Republic of Ireland by which the maintenance order is being enforced.'

(6) Rule 7.36 shall not apply.

Amendments—SI 1996/816, r 6(1), (2), (3).

7.38 Application of rules 7.30 to 7.36 to the Hague Convention countries

(1) In relation to the Hague Convention countries, rules 7.30, 7.31, 7.34, 7.35 and 7.36 shall have effect subject to the provisions of this rule, but rules 7.32 and 7.33 shall not apply.

(1A) A reference to the Act of 1972 in this rule, and in any rule which has effect in relation to the Hague Convention countries by virtue of this rule, shall be a reference to the said Act as modified by Schedule 3 to the Reciprocal Enforcement of Maintenance Orders (Hague Convention Countries) Order 1993.

(2) A reference in rules 7.31 and 7.34 to a reciprocating country shall be construed as a reference to a Hague Convention country.

(3) The following words shall be inserted after paragraph (a)(ii) of rule 7.31 —

'and

(iii) whether the time for appealing against the order has expired and whether an appeal is pending;'

(4) The following paragraphs shall be inserted after paragraph (e) of rule 7.31 —

'(f) a statement as to whether or not the payer appeared in the proceedings in which the maintenance order was made, and, if he did not, the original or a copy certified by the applicant or his solicitor to be a true copy of a document which establishes that notice of the institution of proceedings, including notice of the substance of the claim, was served on the payer;

(g) a document that establishes that notice of the order was sent to the payer;

(h) a written statement as to whether or not the payee received legal aid in the proceedings in which the order was made, or in connection with the application under section 2 of the Act of 1972 and, if he did, a copy certified by the applicant or his solicitor to be a true copy of the legal aid certificate.'

(5) In relation to the Hague Convention countries the following rules shall apply in place of rules 7.35 and 7.36 —

'7.35 Notification of variation or revocation

(1) Where the court makes an order varying or revoking a maintenance order to which section 5 of the Act of 1972, as modified, applies, and the time for appealing has expired without an appeal having been entered, the proper officer shall send to the Lord Chancellor such documents as are required by subsection (8) of that section, as it applies to Hague Convention countries, including a certificate signed by the district judge that the order of variation or revocation is enforceable and that it is no longer subject to the ordinary forms of review.

(2) Where either party enters an appeal against the order of variation or revocation he shall, at the same time, inform the proper officer thereof by a notice in writing.

7.36 Transmission of documents

Any document required to be sent to a court in a Hague Convention country shall be sent to the Lord Chancellor for transmission to the court.'

Amendments—SI 1996/816, r 7(1), (2).

7.39 Application of rules 7.30 to 7.36 to a specified State of the United States of America

(1) In this rule unless the context otherwise requires —

'specified State' means a State of the United States of America specified in Schedule 1 to the Reciprocal Enforcement of Maintenance Orders (United States of America) Order 1995.

(2) In relation to a specified State, rules 7.30, 7.31, 7.34, 7.35 and 7.36 shall have effect subject to the provisions of this rule, but rules 7.32 and 7.33 shall not apply.

(3) A reference to the Act of 1972 in this rule, and in any rule which has effect in relation to a specified State by virtue of this rule, shall be a reference to the said Act as modified by Schedule 3 to the Reciprocal Enforcement of Maintenance Orders (United States of America) Order 1995.

(4) A reference in rules 7.31 and 7.34 to a reciprocating country shall be construed as a reference to a specified State.

(5) Paragraph (c) of rule 7.31 shall not apply to a specified State.

(6) The following paragraphs shall be inserted after paragraph (a)(ii) of rule 7.31 —

'(iii) the address for the payee;
(iv) such information as is known as to the whereabouts of the payer; and
(v) a description, so far as is known, of the nature and location of any assets of the payer available for execution.'

(7) A reference in paragraph (b) of rule 7.31 to a certified copy shall be construed as a reference to 3 certified copies.

(8) In relation to a specified State the following rules shall apply in place of rules 7.35 and 7.36 —

'7.35 Notification of variation of revocation

Where the court makes an order varying or revoking a maintenance order to which section 5 of the Act of 1972, as modified, applies, the proper officer shall send to the Secretary of State such documents as are required by subsection (7) of that section, as it applies to specified States.

7.36 Transmission of documents

Any document required to be sent to a court in a specified State shall be sent to the Secretary of State for transmission to the court.'

Amendments—Inserted by SI 1996/816, r 8.

Chapter 5

Registration and Enforcement under the Council Regulation

. . .

Amendments—Inserted by SI 2001/821, r 29.

APPENDIX 1
FORMS

. . .

FORM M16

Request to issue Judgment Summons

Click here to clear your fields

seal

Judgment Creditor's full name and address

Judgment Debtor's full name and address

In the	*[County Court]
	*[Principal Registry of the Family Division]

Case No.	*Always quote this*
Petitioner	
Solicitor's Ref.	
Respondent	
Solicitor's Ref.	
Co-Respondent	
Solicitor's Ref.	

* delete as appropriate

I apply for the issue of a judgment summons against the above named debtor in respect of an order made in this Court

(1) state nature of order

on the   day of   20   for (1)

[I intend to apply to the Court at the hearing of the proposed judgment summons for leave to enforce arrears which became due more than twelve months before the date of the proposed summons.]

I am aware that, if I do not prove to the satisfaction of the Court at the hearing that the debtor has, or has had since the date of the said order, the means to pay the sum in respect of which he has made default and that he has refused or neglected, or refuses or neglects, to pay it, I may have to pay the costs of the summons.

(2) delete where Judgment Summons is to issue in designated county court

(2) I certify that the said order has not been modified or discharged and that there is no order of commitment in this matter which remains unsatisfied.

(3) if writ or warrant has been issued, give details and state what return to it has been made

(3) I further certify that no [writ or] warrant of execution has been issued to enforce the said order.

Dated this   day of   20   .

Signed...

[Solicitor for the] Judgment Creditor

Amount due and unpaid in respect of the order and costs............. £

Costs of this summons.. £

Travelling expenses to be paid to debtor....................................... £

Total... £   0.00

The court office at

is open between 10 am and 4 pm Monday to Friday. Address all communications to the Court Manager and quote the above Case Number

D62 Request to issue Judgment Summons (12.05)   HMCS

FORM M17

SCHEDULE 1   Rule 18

Form M17
                                                                (Seal)

JUDGMENT SUMMONS

[Heading as in Form M16]

To the debtor

On   [19   ] [20   ], in the [   ],
[   ] ("the judgment creditor") obtained an order against you in the
following terms:

The judgment creditor says that you have not paid as ordered and has requested that this judgment
summons be issued against you.

If the judge is satisfied that—

the amount ordered to be paid has not been paid;
you have (or since the date of the order have had) the means to pay it; and
you are refusing or neglecting (or have refused or neglected) to pay it;

the judge may order your committal to prison.

[**AND TAKE NOTICE** that the judgment creditor intends to apply to the Court for leave to
enforce arrears which became due more than twelve months before the date of this judgment
summons.]

On   20   at   o'clock

at

**the judge will consider the evidence given by the judgment creditor and any evidence you may wish
to give.**

                                        Dated   20   .
_____

To the Debtor:

A copy of the written evidence filed by the judgment creditor is served with this judgment
summons.

If you fail to attend the hearing the judge may:—

• make an order in your absence; or
• order you to attend at a later hearing.

Amount claimed as due and unpaid in respect of the order and any costs   £
Court fee paid to issue this judgment summons   £
Amount (if any) paid to you for your travelling expenses to the court   £
                                                                         _____
                                        Total amount   £

If payment is made too late to prevent the judgment creditor's attendance on the day of the
hearing, you may be liable for further costs. If you pay the total amount above before the
hearing, an order committing you to prison will not be made.

[The judgment creditor's solicitor is

                                                                                ].

M17 Judgment Summons under the Debtors Act 1869 (09.02)

5

FORM M19

Rule 3.1

Form M19

ORIGINATING APPLICATION ON GROUND OF FAILURE
TO PROVIDE REASONABLE MAINTENANCE

In the   County Court
[Principle Registry]
No. of
Matter
(Seal)

[In the Matter of an Application under section 27 of the Matrimonial Causes Act 1973]

[In the Matter of an Application under Part 9 of Schedule 5 to the Civil Partnership Act 2004]

Between   Applicant
and   Respondent

I,   ,of ,   the spouse [civil partner]
of   (hereinafter called the 'respondent') say that the respondent has
failed to provide reasonable maintenance for myself [and has failed to provide, or to make a proper
contribution towards, maintenance for the child[ren] of our family, namely]
and I apply for an order for *[here set out the financial relief claimed]*

If you are applying for any periodical payments or secured periodical payments for **children**,
please say here whether you are applying for payment ☐ for a stepchild or step children ☐ in
addition to child support maintenance already paid under a Child Support Agency assessment ☐ to
meet expenses arising from a child's disability ☐ to meet expenses incurred by a child in being
educated or training for work ☐ when either • the child OR • the person with care of the child,
OR • the absent parent of the child is not habitually resident in the United Kingdom ☐ other
(please specify)

My address for service is *[Where the applicant sues by a solicitor, state the solicitor's name or
firm and address or, where the applicant sues in person, state her place of residence as given
above, or, if no place of residence in England or Wales is given, the address of a place in England
and Wales at or to which the documents for her may be delivered or sent].*

Dated

FORM M20

Rule 3.1(4) and 3.2(4)

Form M20

*NOTICE OF APPLICATION ON GROUND OF FAILURE TO PROVIDE REASONABLE
MAINTENANCE OR FOR ALTERATION OF MAINTENANCE DURING PARTIES LIFETIME*

(1) Delete as
appropriate

[IN THE   COUNTY COURT]

[IN THE PRINCIPAL REGISTRY OF THE FAMILY DIVISION][1]

No. of Matter: (SEAL)

[*In the Matter of an Application under section 27 of the Matrimonial Causes Act 1973*]
[*In the Matter of an Application under section 35 of the Matrimonial Causes Act 1973*]
[*In the Matter of an Application under Part 9 of Schedule 5 to the Civil Partnership Act 2004*]
[*In the Matter of an Application under paragraph 69 of Schedule 5 to the Civil Partnership Act 2004*]

Between   (Applicant)
and   (Respondent)
TAKE NOTICE that this application will be heard
at

(1) Delete if not
appropriate and
insert the date
of hearing

on [a date to be fixed[2]][   ]

and if you do not attend at that time and place, such order will be made as the Court thinks just.

This notice is accompanied by the following documents:

— a sealed copy of the application

— the affidavit in support [and verification]

— the Notice of Proceedings and Acknowledgement of Service.

Dated this   day of   20

FORM M21

Rule 3.2(1)   **Form M21**

ORIGINATING APPLICATION FOR ALTERATION OF MAINTENANCE
AGREEMENT DURING PARTIES' LIFETIME

In the   County Court
                                                          [Principle Registry.]
                                                          No. of
                                                          Matter
                                                                        (Seal)

[*In the Matter of an Application under section 35 of the Matrimonial Causes Act 1973*]

[*In the Matter of an Application under paragraph 69 of Schedule 5 to the Civil
Partnership Act 2004*]

Between   Applicant
And   Respondent

1. I,   the spouse [*or* civil partner] of
(hereinafter called 'the respondent'), apply for an order altering the maintenance agreement made
between me and the respondent on the day of   20   .

2. I reside at   and the respondent resides at
[*Add, unless both parties are resident in England or Wales.* We are both domiciled in England
and Wales [*or as the case may be*]].

3. On   [insert date],   I [was lawfully, married to the
respondent at] [formed a civil partnership with the respondent at]   .";
I [*or in the case of an application by the husband* The respondent] was then [*state full name and
status of wife before marriage*].

4. There is [are] [no [*or state number*] child[ren] of the family. [namely, [*state the full name
(including surname) of each child now, living and his date of birth or, if it be the case, that he is
over 18 and, in the case of each minor child over the age of 16, whether he is or, will be, or if an
order or provision were made would be, receiving instruction at an education establishment or
undergoing training for a trade, profession or vocation*] who is now residing at [*state the place*]
with [*stale the person*] [and [*state name of any. child who has died since the date of the
agreement*]
who died on   the day of   20   .] [The agreement also makes
financial arrangements for [*give similar particulars of any other child for whom the agreement
makes such arrangements*]].

5. There have been no previous proceedings in any court with reference to the agreement or to the
civil partnership [or to the child[ren] of the family.] [or to the other child[ren] for whom the
agreement makes financial arrangements] or between the applicant and the respondent with
reference to any property, of either or both of them [except *state the nature of the proceedings
and the date and effect of any order or decree*].

6. My means are as follows:-

7. I ask for the following alteration[s] to be made in the agreement:-

8. The facts on which I rely to justify the alteration[s] are:-

[*if there are or have been any proceedings in the Child Support Agency with reference to the maintenance of a child of the family please give details here.*]

My address for service is [*Where the applicant sues by a solicitor, state the solicitor's name or firm and address, or, where the applicant sues in person, state his or her place of residence as given in paragraph 2 or, if no place of residence in England or Wales is given, the address of a place in England or Wales at or to which documents for him or her mail be delivered or sent*].

Dated this   day of   20   .

FORM M22

Rule 3.3(1)							**Form M22**

ORIGINATING SUMMONS FOR ALTERATION OF MAINTENANCE AGREEMENT
AFTER DEATH OF ONE OF THE PARTIES

In the High Court of Justice
Family Division

[				District Registry]
[*In the Matter of an Application under section 36 of the Matrimonial Causes Act 1973*]
[*In the Matter of an Application under paragraph 73 of Schedule 5 to the Civil
Partnership Act 2004*]

Between						Applicant[s]
And						Respondent[s].

Let				of				attend before District Judge
in chambers at the Principle Registry, Somerset House, London, WC2R 1 LP, *[or as the case may
be]* on		day, the			day of			20	, at		o'clock,
on the hearing of an application by			that the agreement made on the
day of			20	, between [the applicant and]		who died on the
day of			20	, [and the respondent] should be altered as shown in the affidavit
accompanying this summons so as to make different *[or* contain] financial arrangements.

					Dated this		day of	20	.
This summons was taken out by
[Solicitor for] the above-named applicant[s].

To the Respondent.

TAKE NOTICE THAT:-

1.	A copy of the affidavit to be used in support of the application is delivered herewith.

2.	You must complete the accompanying acknowledgment of service and send it so as to
reach the Court within eight days after you receive this summons.

3.	[*If the respondent is a personal representative of the deceased*: You must also file an
affidavit in answer to the applicant's application containing full particulars of the value of the
deceased's estate for probabe, after providing for the discharge of the funeral, testamentary and
administration expenses, debts and liabilities, including the amount of the estate duty and interest
thereon, and the persons or classes of persons beneficially interested in the estate, with the names
and addresses of all living beneficiaries and stating whether any beneficiary is a minor or
incapable, by reason of mental disorder, of managing and administering his property and affairs.]
	[Or, *if the respondent is not a personal representative of the deceased*: You may also
file an affidavit in answer to the application.]

[*Add, in either case*: The affidavit must be filed by sending or delivering it, together with a copy for the applicant, so as to reach the Court within 14 days after the time allowed for sending the acknowledgment of service.]

4.   If you intend to instruct a solicitor to act for you, you should at once give him all the documents which have been served on you, so that he may take the necessary steps on your behalf.

APPENDIX 1A

FORM A

Notice of [intention to proceed with] an Application for Ancillary Relief

In the	
	*[County Court]
	*[Principal Registry of the Family Division]

Respondents (Solicitor(s))
name and address

Case No. *Always quote this*	
Applicant's Solicitor's reference	
Respondent's Solicitor's reference	

(*delete as appropriate*)

Postcode

Between   (petitioner)

and   (respondent)

Take Notice that

the Applicant intends; *to apply** to the Court for

*delete as
appropriate
*to proceed** with the application in the [petition][answer] for

*to apply to vary:**

☐ an order for maintenance pending suit or outcome of proceedings   ☐ a periodical payments order
☐ a secured provision order   ☐ a lump sum order
☐ a property adjustment order *(please provide address)*   ☐ a pension sharing order or a
                                                                          pension attachment order

If an application is made for any periodical payments or secured periodical payments for children:

• and there is a written agreement made before 5 April 1993 about maintenance for the benefit of children,
  tick this box ☐

• and there is a written agreement made on or after 5 April 1993 about maintenance for the benefit of children,
  tick this box ☐

• but there is no agreement, tick any of the boxes below to show if you are applying for payment:

  ☐ for a stepchild or stepchildren

  ☐ in addition to child support maintenance already paid under a Child Support Agency assessment

  ☐ to meet expenses arising from a child's disability

  ☐ to meet expenses incurred by a child in being educated or training for work

  ☐ when either the child **or** the person with care of the child **or** the absent parent of the child
      is not habitually resident in the United Kingdom

  ☐ Other *(please state)*

Signed: Dated:
          [Applicant/Solicitor for the Applicant]

The court office at

is open between 10 am and 4 pm (4.30pm at the Principal Registry of the Family Division) Monday to Friday. When corresponding with the court, please address forms or
letters to the Court Manager and quote the case number. If you do not do so, your correspondence may be returned.

Form A Notice of [Intention to proceed with] an Application for Ancillary Relief (12.05)   HMCS

FORM B

Notice of an application under Rule 2.45

In the	
	[County Court]
	*[Principal Registry of the Family Division]
Case No. *Always quote this*	
Applicant's Solicitor's reference	
Respondent's Solicitor's reference	

(*delete as appropriate)

Between (petitioner)

and (respondent)

Take Notice that

The Respondent intends to apply to the Court under [section 10(2) of the Matrimonial
Causes Act 1973 for the Court to consider the financial position of the Respondent after
the divorce*][section 48(2) of the Civil Partnership Act 2004 for the Court to consider the financial
position of the Respondent after the dissolution of the civil partnership*].

(*delete as appropriate)

Signed: Dated:

      [Respondent/Solicitor for the Respondent]

The court office at

is open between 10 am and 4 pm (4.30pm at the Principal Registry of the Family Division) Monday to Friday. When corresponding with the court, please address forms or
letters to the Court Manager and quote the case number. If you do not do so, your correspondence may be returned.

Form B Notice of an Application under Rule 2.45 (12.05)   HMCS

FORM C

Notice of a First Appointment

In the	
	[County Court] *[Principal Registry of the Family Division]*
Case No. *Always quote this*	
Applicant's Solicitor's reference	
Respondent's Solicitor's reference	

(*delete as appropriate)

Between   (petitioner)

and   (respondent)

Take Notice that

By [   ] you must file with the Court a statement which gives full details of your property and income. You must sign and swear the statement. At the same time each party must exchange a copy of the statement with the [legal representative of the] other party. You must use the standard form of statement (Form E) which you may obtain from the Court office.

By [   ] you must file with the Court and the [legal representative of the] other party:

- a concise statement of the apparent issues between yourself and the other party;
- a chronology;
- a questionnaire setting out the further information and documents you require from the other party, or a statement that no information or documents are required;
- a Notice in Form G.

The First Appointment will be heard by

(the District Judge in chambers) at

on   20

at   [a.m.][p.m.]

The probable length of the hearing is

> **You and your legal representative, if you have one, must attend the appointment. At the appointment you must provide the Court with a written estimate (in Form H) of any legal costs which you have incurred. Non-compliance may render you liable to costs penalties.**

Dated:

The court office at

is open between 10 am and 4 pm (4.30pm at the Principal Registry of the Family Division) Monday to Friday. When corresponding with the court, please address forms or letters to the Court Manager and quote the case number. If you do not do so, your correspondence may be returned.

Form C Notice of a First Appointment (12.05)   HMCS

FORM D

Notice of a Financial Dispute Resolution Appointment

In the	
	*[County Court] *[Principal Registry of the Family Division]
Case No. *Always quote this*	
Applicant's Solicitor's reference	
Respondent's Solicitor's reference	

*(*delete as appropriate)*

Between (petitioner)

and (respondent)

Take Notice that

By [   ] the Applicant must provide the Court with details of all offers, proposals and responses concerning the Application.

• An appointment for a Financial Dispute Resolution will take place at

on   20

at   [a.m.][p.m.]

The probable length of the hearing is

At the appointment

- You, and your legal representative, if you have one, must attend this appointment.
- The hearing will define, as far as possible, the issues in this matter and explore the possibility of settlement. If the matter proceeds to a full hearing, the date of the full hearing will be fixed.
- You must provide the Court with a written estimate (in Form H) of any legal costs .

Dated:

The court office at

is open between 10 am and 4 pm (4.30pm at the Principal Registry of the Family Division) Monday to Friday. When corresponding with the court, please address forms or letters to the Court Manager and quote the case number. If you do not do so, your correspondence may be returned.

Form D Notice of a Financial Dispute Resolution Appointment (12.05)   HMCS

FORM E

FINANCIAL STATEMENT OF

In the	*[High/County Court]*[Principal Registry of the Family Division]
Case No. *Always quote this*	
Petitioner's Solicitor's reference	
Respondent's Solicitor's reference	

*Husband/*Wife/*Civil partner

*(*delete as apprpriate)*

Between

	and	

Who is the *husband/*wife/*civil partner
*Petitioner/*Respondent in the
*divorce/*dissolution suit

Applicant in this matter

Who is the *husband/*wife/*civil partner
*Petitioner/*Respondent in the
*divorce/*dissolution suit

Respondent in this matter

Please fill in this form fully and accurately. Where any box is not applicable, write 'N/A'.

You have a duty to the court to give a full, frank and clear disclosure of all your financial and other relevant circumstances.

A failure to give full and accurate disclosure may result in any order the court makes being set aside.

If you are found to have been deliberately untruthful, criminal proceedings for perjury may be taken against you.

You must attach documents to the form where they are specifically sought and you may attach other documents where it is necessary to explain or clarify any of the information that you give.

Essential documents that must accompany this statement are detailed in the form.

If there is not enough room on the form for any particular piece of information, you may continue on an attached sheet of paper.

If you are in doubt about how to complete any part of this form you should seek legal advice.

This Statement must be sworn before a solicitor, a commissioner for oaths or an Officer of the Court or, if abroad, a notary or duly authorised official, before it is filed with the Court or sent to the other party (see last page).

This statement is filed by

Name and address of solicitor

1 General Information

1.1 Full name

1.2 Date of birth

Date	Month	Year

1.3 Date of the marriage/ civil partnership

Date	Month	Year

1.4 Occupation

1.5 Date of the separation

Date	Month	Year	
			Tick here if not applicable ☐

1.6 Date of the

Petition			Decree nisi/Decree of judicial separation Conditional order/ Separation order			Decree absolute/ Final order (if applicable)		
Date	Month	Year	Date	Month	Year	Date	Month	Year

1.7 If you have subsequently married or formed a civil partnership, or will do so, state the date

Date	Month	Year

1.8 Are you co-habiting?   Yes ☐ No ☐

1.9 Do you intend to co-habit within the next six months?   Yes ☐ No ☐

1.10 Details of any children of the family

Full names	Date of birth			With whom does the child live?
	Date	Month	Year	

1.11 Details of the state of health of yourself and the children if you think this should be taken into account

Yourself	Children

1.12 Details of the present and proposed future educational arrangements for the children.

Present arrangements	Future arrangements

1.13 Details of any child support maintenance calculation or any maintenance order or agreement made in respect of any children of the family. If no calculation, order or agreement has been made, give an estimate of the liability of the non-resident parent in respect of the children of the family under the Child Support Act 1991.

1.14 If this application is to vary an order, attach a copy of the order and give details of the part that is to be varied and the changes sought. You may need to continue on a separate sheet.

1.15 Details of any other court cases between you and your spouse/civil partner, whether in relation to money, property, children or anything else.

Case No	Court

1.16 Your present residence and the occupants of it and on what terms you occupy it (e.g. tenant, owner-occupier).

Address	Occupants	Terms of occupation

3

2 Financial Details *Part 1 Real Property and Personal Assets*

2.1 **Complete this section in respect of the family home (the last family home occupied by you and your spouse/civil partner) if it remains unsold.**

Documentation required for attachment to this section:

a) A copy of any valuation of the property obtained within the last six months. If you cannot provide this document, please give your own realistic estimate of the current market value

b) A recent mortgage statement confirming the sum outstanding on **each** mortgage

Property name and address	
Land Registry title number	
Mortgage company name(s) and address(es) and account number(s)	
Type of mortgage	
Details of who owns the property and the extent of your legal and beneficial interest in it (i.e. state if it is owned by you solely or jointly owned with your spouse/civil partner or with others)	
If you consider that the legal ownership as recorded at the Land Registry does not reflect the true position, state why	
Current market value of the property	
Balance outstanding on any mortgage(s)	
If a sale at this stage would result in penalties payable under the mortgage, state amount	
Estimate the costs of sale of the property	
Total equity in the property (i.e. market value less outstanding mortgage(s), penalties if any and the costs of sale)	

TOTAL value of your interest in the family home:
Total A £

2.2 Details of your interest in any other property, land or buildings. Complete one page for each property you have an interest in.

Documentation required for attachment to this section:

a)   A copy of any valuation of the property obtained within the last six months. If you cannot provide this document, please give your own realistic estimate of the current market value

b)   A recent mortgage statement confirming the sum outstanding on **each** mortgage

Property name and address	
Land Registry title number	
Mortgage company name(s) and address(es) and account number(s)	
Type of mortgage	
Details of who owns the property and the extent of your legal and beneficial interest in it (i.e. state if it is owned by you solely or jointly owned with your spouse/civil partner or with others)	
If you consider that the legal ownership as recorded at the Land Registry does not reflect the true position, state why	
Current market value of the property	
Balance outstanding on any mortgage(s)	
If a sale at this stage would result in penalties payable under the mortgage, state amount	
Estimate the costs of sale of the property	
Total equity in the property (i.e. market value less outstanding mortgage(s), penalties if any and the costs of sale)	
Total value of your interest in this property	

TOTAL value of your interest in ALL other property:
Total B £

2.3 **Details of all personal bank, building society and National Savings Accounts that you hold or have held at any time in the last twelve months and which are or were either in your own name or in which you have or have had any interest. This applies whether any such account is in credit or in debit. For joint accounts give your interest and the name of the other account holder. If the account is overdrawn, show a minus figure.**

Documentation required for attachment to this section:
For each account listed, all statements covering the last 12 months.

Name of bank or building society, including branch name	Type of account *(e.g. current)*	Account number	Name of other account holder *(if applicable)*	Balance at the date of this statement	Total current value of your interest
TOTAL value of your interest in ALL accounts: (C1)					£

2.4 **Details of all investments, including shares, PEPs, ISAs, TESSAs, National Savings Investments (other than already shown above), bonds, stocks, unit trusts, investment trusts, gilts and other quoted securities that you hold or have an interest in. (Do not include dividend income as this will be dealt with separately later on.)**

Documentation required for attachment to this section:
Latest statement or dividend counterfoil relating to each investment.

Name	Type of Investment	Size of Holding	Current value	Name of any other account holder *(if applicable)*	Total current value of your interest
TOTAL value of your interest in ALL holdings: (C2)					£

2.5 **Details of all life insurance policies including endowment policies that you hold or have an interest in. Include those that do not have a surrender value. Complete one page for each policy.**

Documentation required for attachment to this section:
A surrender valuation of each policy that has a surrender value.

Name of company			
Policy type			
Policy number			
If policy is assigned, state in whose favour and amount of charge			
Name of any other owner and the extent of your interest in the policy			
Maturity date *(if applicable)*	Date	Month	Year
Current surrender value *(if applicable)*			
If policy includes life insurance, the amount of the insurance and the name of the person whose life is insured			
Total current surrender value of your interest in this policy			

TOTAL value of your interest in ALL policies: (C3) £

2.6 **Details of all monies that are OWED TO YOU. Do not include sums owed in director's or partnership accounts which should be included at section 2.11.**

Brief description of money owed and by whom	Balance outstanding	Total current value of your interest

TOTAL value of your interest in ALL debts owed to you: (C4) £

7

2.7 Details of all cash sums held in excess of £500. You must state where it is held and the currency it is held in.

Where held	Amount	Currency	Total current value of your interest

TOTAL value of your interest in ALL cash sums: (C5)	£

2.8 Details of personal belongings individually worth more than £500.

INCLUDE:
- Cars (gross value)
- Collections, pictures and jewellery
- Furniture and house contents

Brief description of item	Total current value of your interest

TOTAL value of your interest in ALL personal belongings: (C6)	£
Add together all the figures in boxes C1 to C6 to give the TOTAL current value of your interest in personal assets: TOTAL C	£

2 Financial Details *Part 2 Capital: Liabilities and Capital Gains Tax*

2.9 Details of any liabilities you have.

EXCLUDE liabilities already shown such as:
- Mortgages
- Any overdrawn bank, building society or National Savings accounts

INCLUDE:
- Money owed on credit cards and store cards
- Bank loans
- Hire purchase agreements

List all credit and store cards held including those with a nil or positive balance. Where the liability is not solely your own, give the name(s) of the other account holder(s) and the amount of your share of the liability.

Liability	Name(s) of other account holder(s) *(if applicable)*	Total liability	Total current value of your interest in the liability
TOTAL value of your interest in ALL liabilities: (D1)			£

2.10 If any Capital Gains Tax would be payable on the disposal now of any of your real property or personal assets, give your estimate of the tax liability.

Asset	Total Capital Gains Tax liability
TOTAL value of ALL your potential Capital Gains Tax liabilities: (D2)	£
Add together D1 and D2 to give the TOTAL value of your liabilities: TOTAL D	£

9

2 Financial Details *Part 3 Capital: Business assets and directorships*

2.11 Details of all your business interests. Complete one page for each business you have an interest in.

Documentation required for attachment to this section:

a) Copies of the business accounts for the last two financial years

b) Any documentation, if available at this stage, upon which you have based your estimate of the current value of your interest in this business, for example a letter from an accountant or a formal valuation. It is not essential to obtain a formal valuation at this stage

Name of the business	
Briefly describe the nature of the business	
Are you *(Please delete all those that are not applicable)*	a) Sole trader b) Partner in a partnership with others c) Shareholder in a limited company
If you are a partner or a shareholder, state the extent of your interest in the business **(i.e. partnership share or the extent of your shareholding compared to the overall shares issued)**	
State when your next set of accounts will be available	
If any of the figures in the last accounts are not an accurate reflection of the current position, state why. **For example, if there has been a material change since the last accounts, or if the valuations of the assets are not a true reflection of their value (e.g. because property or other assets have not been re-valued in recent years or because they are shown at a book value)**	
Total amount of any sums owed to you by the business by way of a director's loan account, partnership capital or current accounts or the like. Identify where these appear in the business accounts	
Your estimate of the current value of your business interest. Explain briefly the basis upon which you have reached that figure	
Your estimate of any Capital Gains Tax that would be payable if you were to dispose of your business now	
Net value of your interest in this business after any Capital Gains Tax liability	

TOTAL value of ALL your interests in business assets: TOTAL E £

2.12 List any directorships you hold or have held in the last 12 months (other than those already disclosed in Section 2.11).

11

2 Financial Details *Part 4 Capital: Pensions*

2.13 Give details of all your pension rights. Complete a separate page for each pension.

EXCLUDE:
*   **Basic State Pension**

INCLUDE (complete a separate page for each one):
*   **Additional State Pension (SERPS and State Second Pension (S2P))**
*   **Free Standing Additional Voluntary Contribution Schemes (FSAVC) separate from the scheme of your employer**
*   **Membership of ALL pension plans or schemes**

Documentation required for attachment to this section:

a) A recent statement showing the cash equivalent transfer value (CETV) provided by the trustees or managers of each pension arrangement (or, in the case of the additional state pension, a valuation of these rights)

b) If any valuation is not available, give the estimated date when it will be available and attach a copy of your letter to the pension company or administrators from whom the information was sought and/or state the date on which an application for a valuation of a State Earnings Related Pension Scheme was submitted to the Department of Work and Pensions

Name and address of pension arrangement	
Your National Insurance Number	
Number of pension arrangement or reference number	
Type of scheme e.g. occupational or personal, final salary, money purchase, additional state pension or other (if other, please give details)	
Date the CETV was calculated	
Is the pension in payment or drawdown or deferment? *(Please answer Yes or No)*	
State the cash equivalent transfer value (CETV) quotation, or in the additional state pension, the valuation of those rights	
If the arrangement is an occupational pension arrangement that is paying reduced CETVs, please quote what the CETV would have been if not reduced. If this is not possible, please indicate if the CETV quoted is a reduced CETV	

TOTAL value of ALL your pension assets: TOTAL F £

2　Financial Details　*Part 5　Capital: Other assets*

2.14 Give details of any other assets not listed in Parts 1 to 4 above.

INCLUDE (the following list is not exhaustive):
- Any personal or business assets not yet disclosed
- Unrealisable assets
- Share option schemes, stating the estimated net sale proceeds of the shares if the options were capable of exercise now, and whether Capital Gains Tax or income tax would be payable
- Business expansion schemes
- Futures
- Commodities
- Trust interests (including interests under a discretionary trust), stating your estimate of the value of the interest and when it is likely to become realisable. If you say it will never be realisable, or has no value, give your reasons
- Any asset that is likely to be received in the foreseeable future
- Any asset held on your behalf by a third party
- Any asset not disclosed elsewhere on this form even if held outside England and Wales

You are reminded of your obligation to disclose all your financial assets and interests of ANY nature.

Type of asset	Value	Total NET value of your interest
TOTAL value of ALL your other assets: TOTAL G		£

2   Financial Details   *Part 6   Income: Earned income from employment*

2.15 Details of earned income from employment. Complete one page for each employment.

Documentation required for attachment to this section:

a)   P60 for the last financial year (you should have received this from your employer shortly after the last 5th April)

b)   Your last three payslips

c)   Your last Form P11D if you have been issued with one

Name and address of your employer	
Job title and brief details of the type of work you do	
Hours worked per week in this employment	
How long have you been with this employer?	
Explain the basis of your income i.e. state whether it is based on an annual salary or an hourly rate of pay and whether it includes commissions or bonuses	
Gross income for the last financial year as shown on your P60	
Net income for the last financial year i.e. gross income less income tax and national insurance	
Average net income for the last three months i.e. total income less income tax and national insurance divided by three	
Briefly explain any other entries on the attached payslips other than basic income, income tax and national insurance	
If the payslips attached for the last three months are not an accurate reflection of your normal income briefly explain why	
Details and value of any bonuses or other occasional payments that you receive from this employment not otherwise already shown, including the basis upon which they are paid	
Details and value of any benefits in kind, perks or other remuneration received from this employer in the last year (e.g. provision of a car, payment of travel, accommodation, meal expenses, etc.)	
Your estimate of your net income from this employment for the next 12 months. If this differs significantly from your current income explain why in box 4.1.2	

Estimated TOTAL of ALL net earned income from employment for the next 12 months: TOTAL H £

2   Financial Details   *Part 7 Income: Income from self-employment or partnership*

2.16 You will have already given details of your business and provided the last two years accounts at section 2.11. Complete this section giving details of your income from your business. Complete one page for each business.

Documentation required for attachment to this section:

a)   A copy of your last tax assessment or, if that is not available, a letter from your accountant confirming your tax liability

b)   If net income from the last financial year and estimated net income for the next 12 months is significantly different, a copy of management accounts for the period since your last account

Name of the business	
Date to which your last accounts were completed	
Your share of gross business profit from the last completed accounts	
Income tax and national insurance payable on your share of gross business profit above	
Net income for that year (using the two figures directly above, gross business profit less income tax and national insurance payable)	
Details and value of any benefits in kind, perks or other remuneration received from this business in the last year **e.g. provision of a car, payment of travel, accommodation, meal expenses, etc.**	
Amount of any regular monthly or other drawings that you take from this business	
If the estimated figure directly below is different from the net income as at the end date of the last completed accounts, briefly explain the reason(s)	
Your estimate of your net annual income for the next 12 months	

Estimated TOTAL of ALL net income from self-employment or partnership for the next 12 months: TOTAL I	£

15

2 Financial Details *Part 8 Income: Income from investments*
e.g. dividends, interest or rental income

2.17 Details of income received in the last financial year (the year ended last 5th April), and your estimate of your income for the current financial year. Indicate whether the income was paid gross or net of income tax. You are not required to calculate any tax payable that may arise.

Nature of income and the asset from which it derived	Paid gross or net	Income received in the last financial year	Estimated income for the next 12 months

Estimated TOTAL investment income for the next 12 months: TOTAL J	£

2 Financial Details   *Part 9 Income: Income from state benefits (including state pension and child benefit)*

2.18 Details of all state benefits that you are currently receiving.

Name of benefit	Amount paid	Frequency of payment	Estimated income for the next 12 months

Estimated TOTAL benefit income for the next 12 months: TOTAL K   £

2   Financial Details   *Part 10   Income: Any other income*

2.19 Details of any other income not disclosed above.

INCLUDE:
- Any source from which income has been received during the last 12 months (even if it has now ceased)
- Any source from which income is likely to be received during the next 12 months

You are reminded of your obligation to give full disclosure of your financial circumstances.

Nature of income	Paid gross or net	Income received in the last financial year	Estimated income for the next 12 months

Estimated TOTAL other income for the next 12 months: TOTAL L	£

2 Financial Details *Summaries*

2.20 Summary of your capital (Parts 1 to 5).

Description	Reference of the section on this statement	Value
Current value of your interest in the family home	A	
Current value of your interest in all other property	B	
Current value of your interest in personal assets	C	
Current value of your liabilities	D	
Current value of your interest in business assets	E	
Current value of your pension assets	F	
Current value of all your other assets	G	
TOTAL value of your assets (Totals A to G less D):		£

2.21 Summary of your estimated income for the next 12 months (Parts 6 to 10).

Description	Reference of the section on this statement	Value
Estimated net total of income from employment	H	
Estimated net total of income from self-employment or partnership	I	
Estimated net total of investment income	J	
Estimated state benefit receipts	K	
Estimated net total of all other income	L	
Estimated TOTAL income for the next 12 months (Totals H to L):		£

3 Financial Requirements *Part 1 Income needs*

3.1 Income needs for yourself and for any children living with you or provided for by you. ALL figures should be annual, monthly or weekly (state which). You *must not* use a combination of these periods. State your current income needs and, if these are likely to change in the near future, explain the anticipated change and give an estimate of the future cost.

The income needs below are:	Weekly	Monthly	Annual
(delete those not applicable)			

I anticipate my income needs are going to change because

3.1.1 Income needs for yourself.

INCLUDE:
- All income needs for yourself
- Income needs for any children living with you or provided for by you only if these form part of your total income needs (e.g. housing, fuel, car expenses, holidays, etc)

Item	Current cost	Estimated future cost
SUB-TOTAL your income needs:	£	

3.1.2 Income needs for children living with you or provided for by you.

INCLUDE:
- Only those income needs that are different to those of your household shown above

Item	Current cost	Estimated future cost
SUB-TOTAL children's income needs:	£	
TOTAL of ALL income needs:	£	

3 Financial Requirements *Part 2 Capital needs*

3.2 Set out below the reasonable future capital needs for yourself and for any children living with you or provided for by you.

3.2.1 Capital needs for yourself.

INCLUDE:
- All capital needs for yourself
- Capital needs for any children living with you or provided for by you only if these form part of your total capital needs (e.g. housing, car, etc.)

Item	Cost
SUB-TOTAL your capital needs:	£

3.2.2 Capital needs for children living with you or provided for by you.

INCLUDE:
- Only those capital needs that are different to those of your household shown above

Item	Cost
SUB-TOTAL your children's capital needs:	£
TOTAL of ALL capital needs:	£

4 Other Information

4.1 Details of any significant changes in your assets or income.

At both sections 4.1.1 and 4.1.2, INCLUDE:
- ALL assets held both within and outside England and Wales
- The disposal of any asset

4.1.1 Significant changes in assets or income during the LAST 12 months.

4.1.2 Significant changes in assets or income likely to occur during the NEXT 12 months.

4.2 Brief details of the standard of living enjoyed by you and your spouse/civil partner during the marriage/ civil partnership.

4.3 Are there any particular contributions to the family property and assets or outgoings, or to family life, or the welfare of the family that have been made by you, your partner or anyone else that you think should be taken into account? If there are any such items, briefly describe the contribution and state the amount, when it was made and by whom.

INCLUDE:
- Contributions already made
- Contributions that will be made in the foreseeable future

4.4 Bad behaviour or conduct by the other party will only be taken into account in very exceptional circumstances when deciding how assets should be shared after divorce/dissolution. If you feel it should be taken into account in your case, identify the nature of the behaviour or conduct below.

4.5 Give details of any other circumstances that you consider could significantly affect the extent of the financial provision to be made by or for you or any child of the family.

INCLUDE (the following list is not exhaustive):
- Earning capacity
- Disability
- Inheritance prospects
- Redundancy
- Retirement
- Any plans to marry, form a civil partnership or cohabit
- Any contingent liabilities

23

4.6 If you have subsequently married or formed a civil partnership (or intend to) or are living with another person (or intend to), give brief details, so far as they are known to you, of his or her income, assets and liabilities.

Annual Income		Assets and Liabilities	
Nature of income	Value (if known, state whether gross or net))	Item	Value (if known)
Total income: £		**Total assets/liabilities:** £	

5   Order Sought

5.1 If you are able at this stage, specify what kind of orders you are asking the court to make.
Even if you cannot be specific at this stage, if you are able to do so, indicate:

a) If the family home is still owned, whether you are asking for it to be transferred to yourself or
your spouse/civil partner or whether you are saying it should be sold

b) Whether you consider this is a case for continuing spousal maintenance/maintenance for your
civil partner or whether you see the case as being appropriate for a "clean break". *(A 'clean break'
means a settlement or order which provides amongst other things, that neither you nor your spouse/civil
partner will have any further claim against the income or capital of the other party. A 'clean break'
does not terminate the responsibility of a parent to a child.)*

c) Whether you are seeking a pension sharing or pension attachment order

d) If you are seeking a transfer or settlement of any property or assets, identify the property or
assets in question

5.2 If you are seeking a variation of an ante-nuptial or post-nuptial settlement or a relevant settlement
made during, or in anticipation of, a civil partnership, identify the settlement, by whom it was made,
its trustees and beneficiaries and state why you allege it is a settlement which the court can vary.

5.3 If you are seeking an avoidance of disposition order, or if you have already applied for such an order,
identify the property to which the disposition relates and the person or body in whose favour the
disposition is alleged to have been made.

25

Sworn confirmation of the information

I ☐ *(the above-named Applicant/Respondent)*

of ☐

MAKE OATH and confirm that the information given above is a full, frank, clear and accurate disclosure of my financial and other relevant circumstances.

Sworn by the above named

at ....)
....)
....)
....)
this   day of   20)   ....

Before me, ...

A solicitor, commissioner for oaths, an Officer of the Court appointed by the Judge to take affidavits, a notary or duly authorised official.

Address all communications to the Court Manager of the Court and quote the case number. If you do not quote this number, your correspondence may be returned.

SCHEDULE OF DOCUMENTS TO ACCOMPANY FORM E

The following list shows the documents you must attach to your Form E if applicable. You may attach other documents where it is necessary to explain or clarify any of the information that you give in the Form E.

Form E paragraph	Document	Attached	Not applicable	To follow
		Please tick		
1.14	**Application to vary an order:** if applicable, attach a copy of the relevant order.			
2.1	**Matrimonial home valuation:** a copy of any valuation relating to the matrimonial home that has been obtained in the last six months.			
2.1	**Matrimonial home mortgage(s):** a recent mortgage statement in respect of each mortgage on the matrimonial home confirming the amount outstanding.			
2.2	**Any other property:** a copy of any valuation relating to each other property disclosed that has been obtained in the last six months.			
2.2	**Any other property:** a recent mortgage statement in respect of each mortgage on each other property disclosed confirming the amount outstanding.			
2.3	**Personal bank, building society and National Savings accounts:** copies of statements for the last 12 months for each account that has been held in the last twelve months, either in your own name or in which you have or have had any interest.			
2.4	**Other investments:** the latest statement or dividend counterfoil relating to each investment as disclosed in paragraph 2.4.			
2.5	**Life insurance (including endowment) policies:** a surrender valuation for each policy that has a surrender value as disclosed under paragraph 2.5.			
2.11	**Business interests:** a copy of the business accounts for the last two financial years for each business interest disclosed.			
2.11	**Business interests:** any documentation that is available to confirm the estimate of the current value of the business, for example, a letter from an accountant or formal valuation if that has been obtained.			
2.13	**Pension rights:** a recent statement showing the cash equivalent transfer value (CETV) provided by the trustees or managers of each pension arrangement that you have disclosed (or, in the case of the additional state pension, a valuation of these rights). If not yet available, attach a copy of the letter sent to the pension company or administrators requesting the information.			
2.15	**Employment income:** your P60 for the last financial year in respect of each employment that you have.			
2.15	**Employment income:** your last three payslips in respect of each employment that you have.			
2.15	**Employment income:** your last form P11D if you have been issued with one.			
2.16	**Self-employment or partnership income:** a copy of your last tax assessment or if that is not available, a letter from your accountant confirming your tax liability.			
2.16	**Self-employment or partnership income:** if net income from the last financial year and the estimated income for the next twelve months is significantly different, a copy of the management accounts for the period since your last accounts.			
State relevant Form E paragraph	Description of other documents attached:			

Case no.

*Delete as
appropriate

In the

*[High/County Court]
*[Principal Registry of the Family Division]

In the marriage/Civil Partnership between

who is the husband/wife/civil partner

and

who is the husband/wife/civil partner

Financial Statement on behalf of

who is the husband/wife/civil partner
and the Petitioner/Respondent in the
divorce/dissolution suit

This statement is filed by

who are solicitors for the husband/wife/civil partner

Form E Financial Statement (12.05)   HMCS

FORM F

Notice of Allegation in Proceedings for Ancillary Relief

In the	
	[County Court] *[Principal Registry of the Family Division]
Case No. *Always quote this*	
Applicant's Solicitor's reference	
Respondent's Solicitor's reference	

(*delete as appropriate)

Between   (petitioner)

and   (respondent)

Take Notice that

The following statement has been filed in proceedings for ancillary relief:

Signed: Dated:

[Applicant / Respondent/Solicitor for the Applicant / Respondent]

If you wish to be heard on any matter affecting you in these proceedings you may intervene by applying to the Court for directions regarding:

- the filing and service of pleadings
- the conduct of further proceedings

You must apply for directions **within seven days** after you receive this Notice. The period of seven days includes the day you receive it.

The court office at

is open between 10 am and 4 pm (4.30pm at the Principal Registry of the Family Division) Monday to Friday. When corresponding with the court, please address forms or letters to the Court Manager and quote the case number. If you do not do so, your correspondence may be returned.

Form F Notice of allegation in proceedings for ancillary relief (12.05)   HMCS

FORM G

Notice of response to First Appointment

In the	
	[County Court] *[Principal Registry of the Family Division]
Case No. *Always quote this*	
Applicant's Solicitor's reference	
Respondent's Solicitor's reference	

(*delete as appropriate)

Between   (petitioner)

and   (respondent)

Take Notice that

At the First Appointment which will be heard on   20

at   [am][pm]

the [Applicant] [Respondent] [will][will not] be in a position to proceed on that occasion with a Financial Dispute Resolution appointment for the following reasons:-

Dated:

The court office at

is open between 10 am and 4 pm (4.30pm at the Principal Registry of the Family Division) Monday to Friday. When corresponding with the court, please address forms or letters to the Court Manager and quote the case number. If you do not do so, your correspondence may be returned.

Form G Notice of response to First Appointment (12.05)   HMCS

FORM H

Ancillary Relief
Costs Estimate of
*[Applicant]
*[Respondent]

In the	
	*[County Court] *[Principal Registry of the Family Division]
Case No. *Always quote this*	
Applicant's Solicitor's reference	
Respondent's Solicitor's reference	

(*delete as appropriate)

The marriage of   **and**

PART 1

	Prescribed rates for publicly funded services £	Indemnity Rate £
1. Ancillary relief solicitor's costs *(including VAT)* including costs of the current hearing, and any previous solicitor's costs.		
2. Disbursements *(include VAT, if appropriate, and any incurred by previous solicitors)*		
3. All Counsel's fees *(including VAT)*		
TOTAL	£0.00	£0.00

PART 2

4. Add any private client costs previously incurred *(In publicly funded cases only)*		
5. **GRAND TOTAL**	£0.00	£0.00

PART 3

6. State what has been paid towards the total at 5 above		
7. Amount of any contributions paid by the funded client towards their publicly funded services		

NB. If you are publicly funded and might be seeking an order for costs against the other party complete both rates.

Dated _____

The court office at

is open between 10 am and 4 pm (4.30pm at the Principal Registry of the Family Division) Monday to Friday. When corresponding with the court, please address forms or letters to the Court Manager and quote the case number. If you do not do so, your correspondence may be returned.

Form H Costs Estimate (12.00)   *Printed on behalf of The Court Service*

FORM H1

Statement of Costs (Ancillary Relief) of

_____

(name of party)

the   Applicant ☐
     Resondent ☐

Between

and

In the	
	[County Court] ***[Principal Registry of the Family Division]***
Case No. *Always quote this*	
Applicant's Solicitor's reference	
Respondent's Solicitor's reference	

*(*delete as appropriate)*

Statement of costs relating to ancillary relief application for hearing on: [   ]

Please Note: it is a requirement of the rules to provide full costs information to the court

(Do not include in this form costs incurred in respect of other aspects of the case, for example, the divorce or civil partnership proceedings, children matters, injunctions, etc.)

Description of fee earner:
(a) Name: Status: Hourly Rate Claimed: £
(b) Name: Status: Hourly Rate Claimed: £
(c) Name: Status: Hourly Rate Claimed: £
(d) Name: Status: Hourly Rate Claimed: £

SUMMARY OF COSTS STATEMENT

	Prescribed rates for publicly funded services £	Indemnity Rate £
TOTAL SECTION A (Box 7)	0.00	0.00
TOTAL SECTION B (Box 14)	0.00	0.00
TOTAL SECTION C (Box 21)	0.00	0.00
TOTAL SECTION D (Box 25)	0.00	0.00
TOTAL SECTION E (Box 26) (if completed)		
GRAND TOTAL (A +B +C + D + E)	0.00	0.00
State what has been paid towards the grand total above.		
Amount of any contributions paid by the funded client towards their publicly funded services.		

Signature of solicitor: _____   Dated: _____
(or party, if not represented)

Name of firm of solicitors: _____   Ref: _____

The court office at

is open between 10 am and 4 pm (4.30pm at the Principal Registry of the Family Division) Monday to Friday. When corresponding with the court, please address forms or letters to the Court Manager and quote the case number. If you do not do so, your correspondence may be returned.

SECTION A:

Costs incurred in the Ancillary Relief proceedings **prior** to issue of Form A

PART 1

	Prescribed rates for publicly funded services £	Indemnity Rate £
1. Ancillary Relief solicitors' costs (including VAT) incurred by any previous solicitors.		
2. Ancillary Relief solicitors' costs (including VAT) incurred by the current solicitors.		
3. Disbursements (including VAT, if appropriate) incurred by any previous solicitors.		
4. Disbursements (including VAT, if appropriate) incurred by current solicitors.		
5. All counsel's fees (including VAT).		
SUB-TOTAL	0.00	0.00

PART 2

6. Add any private client costs previously incurred (in publicly funded cases only)		
7. **TOTAL OF SECTION A**	0.00	0.00

SECTION B:

Costs incurred in the Ancillary Relief proceedings **after** issue of Form A up to and including FDR appointment (or, if none, the date of the last Form H)

PART 3

	Prescribed rates for publicly funded services £	Indemnity Rate £
8. Ancillary Relief solicitors' costs (including VAT) incurred by any previous solicitors.		
9. Ancillary Relief solicitors' costs (including VAT) incurred by the current solicitors.		
10. Disbursements (including VAT, if appropriate) incurred by any previous solicitors.		
11. Disbursements (including VAT, if appropriate) incurred by current solicitors.		
12. All counsel's fees (including VAT).		
SUB-TOTAL	0.00	0.00

PART 4

13. Add any private client costs previously incurred (in publicly funded cases only).		
14. **TOTAL OF SECTION B**	0.00	0.00

2

SECTION C:
Costs incurred in the Ancillary Relief proceedings **after** FDR appointment (or, if none, the date of the last Form H) up to the date of this form.

PART 5

	Prescribed rates for publicly funded services £	Indemnity Rate £
15. Ancillary Relief solicitors' costs (including VAT) incurred by any previous solicitors.		
16. Ancillary Relief solicitors' costs (including VAT) incurred by the current solicitors.		
17. Disbursements (including VAT, if appropriate) incurred by any previous solicitors.		
18. Disbursements (including VAT, if appropriate) incurred by current solicitors.		
19. All counsel's fees (including VAT). (Counsel's fees for final hearing should not be included here, but given in Section D.)		
SUB-TOTAL	0.00	0.00

PART 6

20. Add any private client costs previously incurred (in publicly funded cases only).		
21. **TOTAL OF SECTION C**	0.00	0.00

SECTION D:
Estimate of costs expected and incurred in the Ancillary Relief proceedings **after** the date of this form up to the end of the final hearing.

PART 7

	Prescribed rates for publicly funded services £	Indemnity Rate £
22. Ancillary Relief solicitors' costs (including VAT)		
23. Disbursements (including VAT, if appropriate)		
24. Counsel's fees (including VAT). (All counsel's fees expected to be incurred for final hearing should be included here.)		
25. **TOTAL OF SECTION D**	0.00	0.00

3

SECTION E:

Estimate of costs to be incurred in implementing proposed order for ancillary relief.

(Note: Include only those costs which it is known or anticipated will be incurred in giving effect to the order.
If the work to be carried out is only conveyancing, the prescribed rates for public funding services do not apply.)

PART 8

	Prescribed rates for publicly funded services £	Indemnity Rate £
26. **TOTAL OF SECTION E** **(Total estimated costs of implementing proposed order)**		

FORM I

Notice of Request for Periodical Payments Order at same rate as Order for Maintenance Pending Suit or Outcome of Proceedings	In the	
		***[County Court]** ***[Principal Registry of the Family Division]**
	Case No. *Always quote this*	
	Applicant's Solicitor's reference	
	Respondent's Solicitor's reference	

*(*delete as appropriate)*

Between   (petitioner)

and   (respondent)

Take Notice that

On   20   the Applicant obtained an Order for you to pay maintenance
pending [suit][outcome of proceedings]* at the rate of £   .

The Applicant having applied in his/her petition (answer) for a Periodical Payments Order for
himself/ herself has requested the Court to make such an Order at the same rate as above.

*(*delete as appropriate)*

What to do if you object to this Order being made.

**If you object to the making of such a Periodical Payments Order, you must notify the District Judge
and the Applicant/Respondent of your objections within 14 days of this notice being served on you. If
you do not do so, the District Judge may make an Order without notifying you further.**

The court office at

is open between 10 am and 4 pm (4.30pm at the Principal Registry of the Family Division) Monday to Friday. When corresponding with the court, please address forms or
letters to the Court Manager and quote the case number. If you do not do so, your correspondence may be returned.

Form I Notice of Request for Periodical Payments Order at same rate as Order for Maintenance Pending Suit or Outcome of Proceedings (12.05)   HMCS

FORM P

Pension Inquiry Form

Information needed when a Pension Sharing Order or Pension Attachment Order may be made

(Insert details of pension scheme here)
To:
of:
Reference Number:

A. To be completed by Pension Scheme member or policy holder:

1. Name of pension scheme member or policy holder:

Address:

Reference:

2. Solicitors details:

Address:

Reference:

Tel:

3. Address to which the form should be sent once completed if different from 2 above:

Signature ....

of Pension Scheme member or policy holder

(The scheme member's signature is necessary to authorise the release of the requested information, unless a court order requiring the information is attached to this form.)

B.   To be completed by the pension arrangement.

This section deals with information required to be provided under the Pensions on Divorce etc (Provision of Information) Regulations 2000 S.I.1048/2000, Regulations 2 and 3 and Rule 2.70(2) of the Family Proceedings Rules 1991 (as amended). If a request for a Cash Equivalent Transfer Value has been made, the pension arrangement has 3 months to provide the information or 6 weeks if notified that the information is needed in connection with matrimonial or civil partnership proceedings, or such shorter time as notified by the court. Otherwise, the information should be provided within one month or such shorter time as notified by the court. The valuation referred to in paragraph 1(a) below must have been made not more than 12 months before the date fixed for the first appointment.

If this information has already been prepared in a standard form please send this instead.

1.	(a) Please confirm that you have already provided a valuation of the member's pension rights to the scheme member or to the Court.	Yes ☐	No ☐
	(b) If the answer to (a) is No, details of the CETV quotation should be attached and the date on which it was calculated.		

2.   Provide a statement summarising the way in which the valuation referred to above has been or will be calculated.

3.   State the pension benefits included in the valuation referred to in B1 above.

4.	(a) Does the person responsible for the pension arrangement offer scheme membership to the person entitled to a pension credit?	Yes ☐	No ☐
	(b) If Yes, does this depend on Employer and/or trustee approval?	Yes ☐	No ☐

5.   If the answer to 4(a) is Yes, what benefits are available to the person with the pension credit?

6.   **Charging Policy**

•	Does the arrangement charge for providing information or implementing a pension sharing order?	Yes ☐	No ☐

If Yes, please:

• provide a list of charges

• indicate when these must be paid, and

• whether they can be paid directly from benefits held in the scheme or policy, or the pension credit.

C.   To be completed by the pension arrangement.

This information is required to be provided by the pension arrangement under the Pension on Divorce (Provision of Information) Regulations 2000 S.I. 1048, Regulation 4 within 21 days of being notified that a pension sharing order may be made. If such notification has not already been given, please treat this document as notification that such an order may be made. Alternatively the Court may specifiy a date by which this information should be provided.

If this information has already been prepared in a standard form please send this instead.

1.   The full name of the pension arrangement and address to which a pension sharing order should be sent.

2.   In the case of an occupational pension scheme only, is the scheme winding up?   Yes ☐   No ☐

If Yes:

  • when did the winding up commence, and

  • give the name and address of the trustees who are dealing with the winding up.

3.   In the case of an occupational pension scheme only, assuming that a calculation of the member's CETV was carried out on the day the pension scheme received notification that a pension sharing order may be made, would that CETV be reduced?   Yes ☐   No ☐

4.   As far as you are aware, are the member's rights under the pension scheme subject to any of the following:

  • a pension sharing order   Yes ☐   No ☐
  • a pension attachment order made under section   Yes ☐   No ☐
    23 of the Matrimonial Causes Act 1973 (England
    and Wales), section 12A(2) or (3) of the Family
    Law (Scotland) Act 1985 or under Article 25
    of the Matrimonial Causes (Northern Ireland)
    Order 1978

  • a pension attachment order made under Part 1   Yes ☐   No ☐
    of Schedule 5 to the Civil Partnership Act 2004
    (England and Wales), section 12A(2) or (3) of the
    Family Law (Scotland) Act 1985 or under Part 1
    of Schedule 15 to the Civil Partnership Act 2004
    (Northern Ireland)

  • a forfeiture order   Yes ☐   No ☐
  • a bankruptcy order   Yes ☐   No ☐
  • an award of sequestration on a member's estate   Yes ☐   No ☐
    or the making of the appointment on his estate of
    a judicial factor under section 41 of the Solicitors
    (Scotland) Act 1980.

5.   Do the member's rights include rights which are not shareable by virtue of regulation 2 of the Pension Sharing (Valuation) Regulations 2000?   Yes ☐   No ☐

If Yes, please provide details.

6.   Does the pension arrangement propose to levy additional charges specified in Regulation 6 of the Pensions on Divorce (Charging) Regulations 2000?   Yes ☐   No ☐

If Yes, please provide the scale of the additional charges likely to made.

7.	Is the scheme member a trustee of the pension scheme?	Yes ☐		No ☐

8.	If a pension sharing order is made, will the person responsible for the pension arrangement require information regarding the scheme member's state of health before implementing the pension sharing order?	Yes ☐		No ☐

9.	Does the person responsible for the pension sharing arrangement require any further information other than that contained in regulation 5 of the Pensions on Divorce etc. (Provision of Information Regulations) 2000, before implementing any Pension Sharing Order?	Yes ☐		No ☐

If Yes, specify what.

D.   To be completed by the pension arrangement.

The following information should be provided if the scheme member requests it or the Court orders it pursuant to its powers under the Pensions on Divorce etc (Provision of Information) Regulations 2000, S.I. 1048/2000. Please note that pension arrangements may make an additional charge for providing this information.

1. Disregarding any future service or premiums that might be paid and future inflation, what is the largest lump sum payment that the member would be entitled to take if s/he were to retire at a normal retirement age?

2. What is the earliest date on which the member has the right to take benefits, excluding retirement on grounds of ill health?

3.	Are spouse's or civil partner's benefits payable?	Yes ☐		No ☐

4. What lump sum would be payable on death at the date of completion of this form?

5. What proportion of the member's pension would be payable as of right to the spouse or civil partner of the member if the member were to die

   (a) before retirement, and

   (b) after retirement, disregarding any future service or premiums that might be paid and future inflation?

6.	Is the pension in payment, drawdown or deferment?	Yes ☐		No ☐

If Yes, which?

7. Please provide a copy of the scheme booklet.

Date: ....

FORM P1

| Pension Sharing Annex under [section 24B of the Matrimonial Causes Act 1973] [paragraph 15 of Schedule 5 to the Civil Partnership Act 2004] | In the *[County Court] *[Principal Registry of the Family Division] |

In the	*[County Court] *[Principal Registry of the Family Division]
Case No. *Always quote this*	
Transferor's Solicitor's reference	
Transferee's Solicitor's reference	

Between   **(Petitioner)**

and   **(Respondent)**

Take Notice that:

On _____ the court

- made a pension sharing order under Part IV of the Welfare Reform and Pensions Act 1999.

- [varied] [discharged] an order which included provision for pension sharing under Part IV of the Welfare Reform and Pensions Act 1999 and dated _____ .

This annex to the order provides the person responsible for the pension arrangement with the information required by virtue of rules of court:

_____

A.   Transferor's Details

(i)   The full name by which the Transferor is known:

(ii)   All names by which the Transferor has been known:

(iii)   The Transferor's date of birth:

(iv)   The Transferor's address:

(v)   The Transferor's National Insurance Number:

B.   Transferee's Details

(i)   The full name by which the Transferee is known:

(ii)   All names by which the Transferee has been known:

(iii)   The Transferee's date of birth:

(iv)   The Transferee's address:

(v)   The Transferee's National Insurance Number:

(vi)   If the Transferee is also a member of the pension scheme from which the credit is derived, or a beneficiary of the same scheme because of survivor's benefits, the membership number:

_____ Page 1 _____

Form P1 Pension Sharing Annex under section 24B of the Matrimonial Causes Act 1973
or under paragraph 15 of Schedule 5 to the Civil Partnership Act 2004   (12.05)

HMCS

C.   Details of the Transferor's Pension Arrangement

(i)   Name of the arrangement:

(ii)   Name and address of the person responsible for the pension arrangement:

(iii) Policy Reference Number:

(iv)   If appropriate, such other details to enable the pension arrangement to be identified:

(v)   The specified percentage of the member's CETV to be transferred: ____ . ____ %

D.   Pension Sharing Charges

It is directed that:

* The pension sharing charges be apportioned between the parties as follows:

or

* The pension sharing charges be paid in full by the Transferor.

(*Delete as appropriate)

E.

Have you filed Form M1 (Statement of Information for a Consent Order)?

If 'Yes' delete the text opposite.

Yes ☐   No ☐

The parties certify that:

(i)   they have received the information required by Regulation 4 of the Pensions on Divorce etc (Provisions of Information) Regulations 2000;

(ii)   that information is attached on Form P (Pension Inquiry Form); and

(iii) it appears from that information that there is power to make an order including provision under [section 24B of the Matrimonial Causes Act 1973] [paragraph 15 of Schedule 5 to the Civil Partnership Act 2004].

F.

In cases where the Transferee has a choice of an internal or external transfer, if the Transferee has indicated a preference, indicate what this is.

Internal Transfer ☐   External Transfer ☐

G.   In the case of external transfer only (recommended but optional information)

(i)   The name of the qualifying arrangement which has agreed to accept the pension credit:

(ii)   The address of the qualifying arrangement:

(iii) If known, the Transferee's membership or policy number in the qualifying arrangement and reference number of the new provider:

G. Continued

(iv) The name, or title, business address, phone and fax
numbers and email address of the person who may
be contacted in respect of the discharge of liability
for the pension credit on behalf of the Transferee:

(This may be an Independent Financial Advisor, for example, if
one is advising the Transferee or the new pension scheme itself.)

(v) Please attach a copy of the letter from the qualifying
arrangement indicating its willingness to accept the
pension credit.

Please complete boxes H to J where applicable

H.

Where the credit is derived from an occupational   Yes ☐   No ☐
scheme which is being wound up, has the Transferee
indicated whether he wishes to transfer his pension
credit rights to a qualifying arrangement?

I.

Where the pension arrangement has requested   Yes ☐   No ☐
details of the Transferor's health, has that
information been provided?

J.

Where the pension arrangement has requested   Yes ☐   No ☐
further information, has that information been
provided?

Note: Until the information requested in A, B, (and as far as applicable G, H, I and J) is provided the pension sharing order cannot be
implemented although it may be made. Even if all the information requested has been provided, further information may be required
before implementation can begin. If so, reasons why implementation cannot begin should be sent by the pension arrangement to the
Transferor and Transferee within 21 days of receipt of the pension sharing order and this annex.

THIS ORDER TAKES EFFECT FROM the date on which the Decree Absolute of Divorce or Nullity of marriage is granted,
or the Final Order of Dissolution or Nullity of civil partnership is made, or if later, either

    a.   21 days from the date of this order, unless an Appeal has been lodged, in which case

    b.   the effective date of the order determining that appeal.

To the person responsible for the pension arrangement:

(*Delete as appropriate)

*1. Take notice that you must discharge your liability within the period of 4 months beginning with the later of:

    • the day on which this order takes effect; or

    • the first day on which you are in receipt of –

    a.   the pension sharing order including this annex (and where appropriate any attachments);

    b.   in a matrimonial cause, a copy of the decree of divorce or nullity of marriage and a copy of the certificate that
the decree has been made absolute;

    c.   in a civil partnership cause, a copy of the final order of dissolution or order of nullity of civil partnership and a
copy of the certificate that the order has been made final;

    d.   the information specified in paragraphs A, B and C of this annex and, where applicable, paragraphs G to J of
this annex; and

    e.   payment of all outstanding charges requested by the pension scheme.

*2. The court directs that the implementation period for discharging your liability should be determined by regulations
made under section 34(4) or 41(2)(a) of the Welfare Reform and Pensions Act 1999, in that:

FORM P2

Pension Attachment Annex
under [section 25B or 25C of the
Matrimonial Causes Act 1973]
[paragraph 25 or 26 of Schedule 5
to the Civil Partnership Act 2004]

In the	
	*[County Court] *[Principal Registry of the Family Division]
Case No. *Always quote this*	
Applicant's Solicitor's reference	
Respondent's Solicitor's reference	

Between   **(Petitioner)**

and   **(Respondent)**

Take Notice that:

On _____ the court

• made an order including provision under [section [25B][25C]* of the Matrimonial Causes Act 1973]*
  [paragraph [25][26]* or Schedule 5 to the Civil Partnership Act 2004]*.

• [varied] [discharged] an order which included provision under [section [25B][25C]* of the Matrimonial Causes Act
  1973] [paragraph [25][26] of Schedule 5 to the Civil Partnership Act 2004]* and dated _____ .

(*Delete as appropriate)

This annex to the order provides the person responsible for the pension arrangement with the information required by virtue
of rules of court:

1. Name of the party with the pension rights:

2. Name of the other party:

3. The National Insurance Number of the party with
   pension rights:

4. Details of the Pension Arrangement:-
   (i) Name and address of the person responsible for
       the pension arrangement:
   (ii) Policy Reference Number:
   *(iii) if appropriate, such other details to enable the
        pension arrangement to be identified:*

5A. **(i) To be completed where a Periodical Payments
    Order is made under s.25B of the Matrimonial
    Causes Act 1973.**
    The specified percentage of any payment due to the
    party with the pension rights that is to be paid for the
    benefit of the other party: ____ . ____ %

    **(ii) To be completed where the court orders
    that the party with pension rights commutes a
    percentage of his pension to a tax free lump sum
    on retirement under s.25B of the Matrimonial
    Causes Act 1973.**

    (a) the specified percentage of the maximum lump
        sum available that is to be commuted: ____ . ____ %
    (b) the specified percentage of the commuted sum
        which is to be paid to the spouse or the former
        spouse of the party with pension rights: ____ . ____ %

Form P2 Pension Attachment Annex under section 25B or 25C of the Matrimonial Causes Act 1973
  or paragraph 25 or 26 of Schedule 5 to the Civil Partnership Act 2004   (12.05)   HMCS

(iii) To be completed where the court orders, under s.25C of the Matrimonial Causes Act 1973, that all or part of a lump sum payable to the party with pension rights in respect of his death be paid to the other party.

(a) the percentage of the lump sum to be paid by the person responsible for the pension arrangement to the other party: _____ . _____ %

(b) the percentage of the lump sum payable (in accordance with a nomination by the party with pension rights) to the other party: _____ . _____ %

(c) the percentage of the lump sum to be paid by the person responsible for the pension arrangement for the benefit of the other party: _____ . _____ %

5B. **(i) To be completed where a Periodical Payments Order is made under paragraph 25 of Schedule 5 to the Civil Partnership Act 2004.**

The specified percentage of any payment due to the civil partner with the pension rights that is to be paid for the benefit of the other civil partner: _____ . _____ %

(ii) To be completed where the court orders that the civil partner with pension rights commutes a percentage of his pension to a tax free lump sum on retirement under paragraph 25 of Schedule 5 to the Civil Partnership Act 2004.

(a) the specified percentage of the maximum lump sum available that is to be commuted: _____ . _____ %

(b) the specified percentage of the commuted sum which is to be paid to the civil partner or the former civil partner of the civil partner with pension rights: _____ . _____ %

(iii) To be completed where the court orders, under paragraph 26 of Schedule 5 to the Civil Partnership Act 2004, that all or part of a lump sum payable to the civil partner with pension rights in respect of his death be paid to the other civil partner.

(a) the percentage of the lump sum to be paid by the person responsible for the pension arrangement to the other civil partner: _____ . _____ %

(b) the percentage of the lump sum payable (in accordance with a nomination by the civil partner with pension rights) to the other civil partner: _____ . _____ %

(c) the percentage of the lump sum to be paid by the person responsible for the pension arrangement for the benefit of the other civil partner: _____ . _____ %

To the person responsible for the pension arrangement:
(* Delete if this information has already been provided to the person responsible for the pension arrangement)

1. *You are required to serve any notice under the
   Divorce etc. (Pensions) Regulations 2000 or the
   Dissolution etc. (Pensions) Regulations 2005 on the
   other party at the following address:

2. *You are required to make any payments due under
   the pension arrangement to the other party at the
   following address:

3. *If the address at 2. above is that of a bank, building
   society or the Department of National Savings the
   following details will enable you to make payment
   into the account of the other party (e.g. Account
   Name, Number, Bank/Building Society/etc. Sort code):

Note: Where the order to which this annex applies was made by consent the following section should also be completed.

The court also confirms:
(*Delete as appropriate)

- *That notice has been served on the person responsible for the pension arrangement and that no objection has been received.

- *That notice has been served on the person responsible for the pension arrangement and that the court has considered any objection received.

3. THE PENSIONS ON DIVORCE ETC (PROVISION OF INFORMATION) REGULATIONS 2000, SI 2000/1048

1 Citation, commencement and interpretation

(1) These Regulations may be cited as the Pensions on Divorce etc (Provision of Information) Regulations 2000 and shall come into force on 1 December 2000.

(2) In these Regulations —

'the 1993 Act' means the Pension Schemes Act 1993;
'the 1995 Act' means the Pensions Act 1995;
'the 1999 Act' means the Welfare Reform and Pensions Act 1999;
'the Board for Actuarial Standards' means the operating body of that name of the Financial Reporting Council;
'the Charging Regulations' means the Pensions on Divorce etc (Charging) Regulations 2000;
'the Implementation and Discharge of Liability Regulations' means the Pension Sharing (Implementation and Discharge of Liability) Regulations 2000;
'the Valuation Regulations' means the Pension Sharing (Valuation) Regulations 2000;
'active member' has the meaning given by section 124(1) of the 1995 Act;
'day' means any day other than —

   (a)   Christmas Day or Good Friday; or
   (b)   a bank holiday, that is to say, a day which is, or is to be observed as, a bank holiday or a holiday under Schedule 1 to the Banking and Financial Dealings Act 1971;

'deferred member' has the meaning given by section 124(1) of the 1995 Act;
'implementation period' has the meaning given by section 34(1) of the 1999 Act;
'member' means a person who has rights to future benefits, or has rights to benefits payable, under a pension arrangement;
'money purchase benefits' has the meaning given by section 181(1) of the 1993 Act;
'normal benefit age' has the meaning given by section 101B of the 1993 Act;
'notice of discharge of liability' means a notice issued to the member and his former spouse or former civil partner by the person responsible for a pension arrangement when that person has discharged his liability in respect of a pension credit in accordance with Schedule 5 to the 1999 Act;
'notice of implementation' means a notice issued by the person responsible for a pension arrangement to the member and his former spouse at the beginning of the implementation period notifying them of the day on which the implementation period for the pension credit begins;
'occupational pension scheme' has the meaning given by section 1 of the 1993 Act;

'the party with pension rights' and 'the other party' have the meanings given by section 25D(3) of the Matrimonial Causes Act 1997;

'pension arrangement' has the meaning given in section 46(1) of the 1999 Act;

'pension credit' means a credit under section 29(1)(b) of the 1999 Act;

'pension credit benefit' means the benefits payable under a pension arrangement or a qualifying arrangement to or in respect of a person by virtue of rights under the arrangement in question which are attributable (directly or indirectly) to a pension credit;

'pension credit rights' means rights to future benefits under a pension arrangement or a qualifying arrangement which are attributable (directly or indirectly) to a pension credit;

'pension sharing order or provision' means an order or provision which is mentioned in section 28(1) of the 1999 Act;

'pensionable service' has the meaning given by section 124(1) of the 1995 Act;

'person responsible for a pension arrangement' has the meaning given by section 46(2) of the 1999 Act;

'personal pension scheme' has the meaning given by section 1 of the 1993 Act;

'qualifying arrangement' has the meaning given by paragraph 6 of Schedule 5 to the 1999 Act;

'retirement annuity contract' means a contract or scheme which is to be treated as becoming a registered pension scheme under 153 (9) of the Finance Act 2004 in accordance with paragraph 1 (1) (f) of Schedule 36 to that Act;

'salary related occupational pension scheme' has the meaning given by regulation 1A of the Occupational Pension Schemes (Transfer Values) Regulations 1996;

'the Regulatory Authority' means the Occupational Pensions Regulatory Authority;

'transfer day' has the meaning given by section 29(8) of the 1999 Act;

'transferee' has the meaning given by section 29(8) of the 1999 Act;

'transferor' has the meaning given by section 29(8) of the 1999 Act;

'trustees or managers' has the meaning given by section 46(1) of the 1999 Act.

Amendments—Definition 'relevant date' revoked by SI 2000/2691, r 8(1), (2); amended by SI 2005/2877; SI 2006/744; SI 2007/60.

2 Basic information about pensions and divorce or dissolution of a civil partnership

(1) The requirements imposed on a person responsible for a pension arrangement for the purposes of section 23(1)(a) of the 1999 Act (supply of pension information in connection with divorce etc) are that he shall furnish —

(a)   on request from a member, the information referred to in paragraphs (2) and (3)(b) to (f);

(b) on request from the spouse or civil partner of a member, the information referred to in paragraph (3); or

(c) pursuant to an order of the court, the information referred to in paragraph (2), (3) or (4),

to the member, the spouse or civil partner of the member, or, as the case may be, to the court.

(2) The information in this paragraph is a valuation of pension rights or benefits accrued under that member's pension arrangement.

(3) The information in this paragraph is —

(a) a statement that on request from the member, or pursuant to an order of the court, a valuation of pension rights or benefits accrued under that member's pension arrangement, will be provided to the member, or, as the case may be, to the court;

(b) a statement summarising the way in which the valuation referred to in paragraph (2) and sub-paragraph (a) is calculated;

(c) the pension benefits which are included in a valuation referred to in paragraph (2) and sub-paragraph (a);

(d) whether the person responsible for the pension arrangement offers membership to a person entitled to a pension credit, and if so, the types of benefits available to pension credit members under that arrangement;

(e) whether the person responsible for the pension arrangements intends to discharge his liability for a pension credit other than by offering membership to a person entitled to a pension credit; and

(f) the schedule of charges which the person responsible for the pension arrangement will levy in accordance with regulation 2(2) of the Charging Regulations (general requirements as to charges).

(4) The information in this paragraph is any other information relevant to any power with respect to the matters specified in section 23(1)(a) of the 1999 Act and which is not specified in Schedule 1 or 2 to the Occupational Pension Schemes (Disclosure of Information) Regulations 1996 (basic information about the scheme and information to be made available to individuals), or in Schedule 1 or 2 to the Personal Pension Schemes (Disclosure of Information) Regulations 1987 (basic information about the scheme and information to be made available to individuals), in a case where either of those Regulations applies.

(5) Where the member's request for, or the court order for the provision of, information includes a request for, or an order for the provision of, a valuation under paragraph (2), the person responsible for the pension arrangement shall furnish all the information requested, or ordered, to the member —

(a) within 3 months beginning with the date the person responsible for the pension arrangement receives that request or order for the provision of the information;

(b) within 6 weeks beginning with the date the person responsible for the pension arrangement receives the request, or order, for the provision of the information, if the member has notified that person on the date of the request or order that the information is needed in connection with proceedings commenced under any of the provisions referred to in section 23(1)(a) of the 1999 Act; or

(c)   within such shorter period specified by the court in an order requiring the person responsible for the pension arrangement to provide a valuation in accordance with paragraph (2).

(6) Where —

(a)   the member's request for, or the court order for the provision of, information does not include a request or an order for a valuation under paragraph (2); or

(b)   the member's spouse or civil partner requests the information specified in paragraph (3),

the person responsible for the pension arrangement shall furnish that information to the member, his spouse, civil partner or the court, as the case may be, within one month beginning with the date that person responsible for the pension arrangement receives the request for, or the court order for the provision of, the information.

(7) At the same time as furnishing the information referred to in paragraph (1), the person responsible for a pension arrangement may furnish the information specified in regulation 4(2) (provision of information in response to a notification that a pension sharing order or provision may be made).

Amendments—SI 2005/2877.

3 Information about pensions and divorce and dissolution of a civil partnership: valuation of pension benefits

(1) Where an application for financial relief under any of the provisions referred to in section 23(a)(i), (ia), (iii) or (iv) of the 1999 Act (supply of pension information in connection with domestic and overseas divorce etc in England and Wales and corresponding Northern Ireland powers) has been made or is in contemplation, the valuation of benefits under a pension arrangement shall be calculated and verified for the purposes of regulation 2 of these Regulations in accordance with —

(a)   paragraph (3), if the person with pension rights is a deferred member of an occupational pension scheme;

(b)   paragraph (4), if the person with pension rights is an active member of an occupational pension scheme;

(c)   paragraphs (5) and (6), if —

(i)   the person with pension rights is a member of a personal pension scheme; or

(ii)   those pension rights are contained in a retirement annuity contract; or

(d)   paragraphs (7) to (9), if —

(i)   the pension of the person with pension rights is in payment;

(ii)   the rights of the person with pension rights are contained in an annuity contract other than a retirement annuity contract; or

(iii) the rights of the person with pension rights are contained in a deferred annuity contract other than a retirement annuity contract.

(2) Where an application for financial provision under any of the provisions referred to in section 23(1)(a)(ii) of the 1999 Act (corresponding Scottish powers) has been made, or is in contemplation, the valuation of benefits under a pension arrangement shall be calculated and verified for the purposes of regulation 2 of these Regulations in accordance with regulation 3 of the Divorce etc (Pensions) (Scotland) Regulations 2000 (valuation).

(3) Where the person with pension rights is a deferred member of an occupational pension scheme, the value of the benefits which he has under that scheme shall be taken to be —

(a)   in the case of an occupational pension scheme other than a salary related scheme, the cash equivalent to which he acquired a right under section 94(1)(a) if the 1993 Act (right to cash equivalent) on the termination of his pensionable service, calculated on the assumption that he has made an application under section 95 of that Act (ways of taking right to cash equivalent) on the date on which the request for the valuation was received; or

(b)   in the case of a salary related occupational pension scheme, the guaranteed cash equivalent to which he would have acquired a right under section 94(1)(aa) of the 1993 Act if he had made an application under section 95(1) of that Act, calculated on the assumption that he has made such an application on the date on which the request for the valuation was received.

(4) Where the person with pension rights is an active member of an occupational pension scheme, the valuation of the benefits which he has accrued under that scheme shall be calculated and verified —

(a)   on the assumption that the member had made a request for an estimate of the cash equivalent that would be available to him were his pensionable services to terminate on the date on which the request for the valuation was received; and

(b)   in accordance with regulation 11 of and Schedule 1 to the Occupational Pension Schemes (Transfer Values) Regulations 1996 (disclosure).

(5) Where the person with pension rights is a member of a personal pension scheme, or those rights are contained in a retirement annuity contract, the value of the benefits which he has under that scheme or contract shall be taken to be the cash equivalent to which he would have acquired a right under section 94(1)(b) of the 1993 Act, if he had made an application under section 95(1) of that Act on the date on which the request for the valuation was received.

(6) In relation to a personal pension scheme which is comprised in a retirement annuity contract made before 4 January 1988, paragraph (5) shall apply as if such a scheme were not excluded from the scope of Chapter IV of Part IV of the 1993 Act by section 93(1)(b) of that Act (scope of Chapter IV).

(7) Except in case to which, or to the extent to which, paragraph (9) applies, the cash equivalent of benefits in respect of a person referred to in paragraph (1)(d) shall be calculated and verified in such manner as may be approved in a particular case by —

(a)   a Fellow of the Institute of Actuaries;

(b)   a Fellow of the Faculty of Actuaries; or

(c)   a person with other actuarial qualifications who is approved by the Secretary of State, at the request of the person responsible for the pension arrangement in question, as being a proper person to act for the purposes of this regulation in connection with that arrangement.

(8) Except in a case to which paragraph (9) applies, cash equivalents are to be calculated and verified by adopting methods and making assumptions which —

(a)   if not determined by the person responsible for the pension arrangement in question, are notified to him by an actuary referred to in paragraph (7); and

(b)   are certified by the actuary to the person responsible for the pension arrangement in question as being consistent with 'Retirement Benefit Schemes – Transfer Values (GN11)' adopted or prepared, and from time to time revised, by the Board for Actuarial Standards and current on the date on which the request for the valuation is received.

(9) Where the cash equivalent, or any portion of it represents rights to money purchase benefits under the pension arrangement in question of the person with pension rights, and those rights do not fall, either wholly or in part, to be valued in a manner which involves making estimates of the value of benefits, then that cash equivalent, or that portion of it, shall be calculated and verified in such manner as may be approved in a particular case by the person responsible for the pension arrangement in question, and by adopting methods consistent with the requirements of Chapter IV of Part IV of the 1993 Act (protection for early leavers – transfer values).

(10) Where paragraph (3), (4) or (9) has effect by reference to provisions of Chapter IV of Part IV of the 1993 Act, section 93(1)(a)(i) of that Act (scope of Chapter IV) shall apply to those provisions as if the words 'at least one year' had been omitted from section 93(1)(a)(i).

Amendments—SI 2005/2877; SI 2007/60, reg 1.

4 Provision of information in response to a notification that a pension sharing order or provision may be made

(1) A person responsible for a pension arrangement shall furnish the information specified in paragraph (2) to the member or to the court, as the case may be —

(a)   within 21 days beginning with the date that the person responsible for the pension arrangement received the notification that a pension sharing order or provision may be made; or

(b)   if the court has specified a date which is outside the 21 days referred to in sub-paragraph (a), by that date.

(2) The information referred to in paragraph (1) is —

(a)   the full name of the pension arrangement and address to which any order or provision referred to in section 28(1) of the 1999 Act (activation of pension sharing) should be sent;

(b)   in the case of an occupational pension scheme, whether the scheme is winding up, and, if so —

   (i)   the date on which the winding up commenced; and

   (ii)   the name and address of the trustees who are dealing with the winding up;

(c)   in the case of an occupational pension scheme, whether a cash equivalent of the member's pension rights, if calculated on the date the notification referred to in paragraph (1)(a) was received by the trustees or managers of that scheme, would be reduced in accordance with the provisions of regulation 8(4), (4A), (6) or (12) of the Occupational Pension Schemes (Transfer Values) Regulations 1996 (further provisions as to reductions of cash equivalents);

(d)   whether the person responsible for the pension arrangement is aware that the member's rights under the pension arrangement are subject to any, and if so, to specify which, of the following —

   (i)   any order or provision specified in section 28(1) of the 1999 Act;

   (ii)   an order under section 23 of the Matrimonial Causes Act 1973 (financial provision orders in connection with divorce etc), so far as it includes provision made by virtue of section 25B or 25C of that Act (powers to include provisions about pensions);

   (iii) an order under section 12A(2) or (3) of the Family Law (Scotland) Act 1982 (powers in relation to pensions lump sums when making a capital sum order) which relates to benefits or future benefits to which the member is entitled under the pension arrangement;

   (iv)   an order under Article 25 of the Matrimonial Causes (Northern Ireland) Order 1978, so far as it includes provision made by virtue of Article 27B or 27C of that Order (Northern Ireland powers corresponding to those mentioned in paragraph (2)(d)(ii));

   (v)   a forfeiture order;

   (vi)   a bankruptcy order;

   (vii) an award of sequestration on a member's estate or the making of the appointment on his estate of a judicial factor under section 41 of the Solicitors (Scotland) Act 1980 (appointment of judicial factor);

(e)   whether the member's rights under the pension arrangement include rights specified in regulation 2 of the Valuation Regulations (rights under a pension arrangement which are not shareable);

(f)   if the person responsible for the pension arrangement has not at an earlier stage provided the following information, whether that person requires the charges specified in regulation 3 (charges recoverable in respect of the provision of basic information), 5 (charges in respect of pension sharing activity), or 6 (additional amounts recoverable in respect of pension sharing activity) of the Charging Regulations to be paid before the commencement of the implementation period, and if so, —

   (i)   whether that person requires those charges to be paid in full; or

   (ii)   the proportion of those charges which he requires to be paid;

(g)   whether the person responsible for the pension arrangement may levy additional charges specified in regulation 6 of the Charging Regulations, and if so, the scale of the additional charges which are likely to be made;

(h)   whether the member is a trustee of the pension arrangement;

(i)   whether the person responsible for the pension arrangement may request information about the member's state of health from the member if a pension sharing order or provision were to be made;

(j)   (*revoked*); and

(k)   whether the person responsible for the pension arrangement requires information additional to that specified in regulation 5 (information required by the person responsible for the pension arrangement before the implementation period may begin) in order to implement the pension sharing order or provision.

Amendments—Revoked by SI 2000/2691, r 8(1), (3); substituted by SI 2003/1727, r 3.

5 Information required by the person responsible for the pension arrangement before the implementation period may begin

The information prescribed for the purposes of section 34(1)(b) of the 1999 Act (information relating to the transferor and the transferee which the person responsible for the pension arrangement must receive) is —

(a)   in relation to the transferor —

   (i)   all names by which the transferor has been known;

   (ii)   date of birth;

   (iii)   address;

   (iv)   National Insurance number;

   (v)   the name of the pension arrangement to which the pension sharing order or provision relates; and

   (vi)   the transferor's membership or policy number in that pension arrangement;

(b)   in relation to the transferee —

   (i)   all names by which the transferee has been known;

   (ii)   date of birth;

   (iii)   address;

      (iv)   National Insurance number; and

      (v)   if the transferee is a member of the pension arrangement from which the pension credit is derived, his membership or policy number in that pension arrangement;

  (c)   where the transferee has given his consent in accordance with paragraph 1(3)(c), 3(3)(c) or 4(2)(c) of Schedule 5 to the 1999 Act (mode of discharge of liability for a pension credit) to the payment of the pension credit to the person responsible for a qualifying arrangement —

      (i)   the full name of that qualifying arrangement;

      (ii) its address;

      (iii) if known, the transferee's membership number or policy number in that arrangement; and

      (iv) the name or title, business address, business telephone number, and, where available, the business facsimile number and electronic mail address of a person who may be contacted in respect of the discharge of liability for the pension credit;

  (d)   where the rights from which the pension credit is derived are held in an occupational pension scheme which is being wound up, whether the transferee has given an indication whether he wishes to transfer his pension credit rights which may have been reduced in accordance with the provisions of regulation 16(1) of the Implementation and Discharge of Liability Regulations (adjustments to the amount of the pension credit – occupational pension schemes which are underfunded on the valuation day) to a qualifying arrangement; and

  (e)   any information requested by the person responsible for the pension arrangement in accordance with regulation 4(2)(i) or (k).

6 Provision of information after the death of the person entitled to the pension credit before liability in respect of the pension credit has been discharged

(1) Where the person entitled to the pension credit dies before the person responsible for the pension arrangement has discharged his liability in respect of the pension credit, the person responsible for the pension arrangement shall, within 21 days of the date of receipt of the notification of the death of the person entitled to the pension credit, notify in writing any person whom the person responsible for the pension arrangement considers should be notified of the matters specified in paragraph (2).

(2) The matters specified in this paragraph are —

  (a)   how the person responsible for the pension arrangement intends to discharge his liability in respect of the pension credit;

  (b)   whether the person responsible for the pension arrangement intends to recover charges from the person nominated to receive pension credit benefits, in accordance with regulations 2 to 9 of the Charging Regulations, and if so, a copy of the schedule of charges issued to the parties to pension sharing in accordance with regulation 2(2)(b) of the Charging Regulations (general requirements as to charges); and

(c)   a list of any further information which the person responsible for the pension arrangement requires in order to discharge his liability in respect of the pension credit.

Amendments—Substituted by SI 2000/2691, r 8(1), (4).

7 Provision of information after receiving a pension sharing order or provision

(1) A person responsible for a pension arrangement who is in receipt of a pension sharing order or provision relating to that arrangement shall provide in writing to the transferor and transferee, or, where regulation 6(1) applies, to the person other than the person entitled to the pension credit referred to in regulation 6 of the Implementation and Discharge of Liability Regulations (discharge of liability in respect of a pension credit following the death of the person entitled to the pension credit), as the case may be —

(a)   a notice in accordance with the provisions of regulation 7(1) of the Charging Regulations (charges in respect of pension sharing activity – postponement of implementation period);
(b)   a list of information relating to the transferor or the transferee, or, where regulation 6(1) applies, the person other than the person entitled to the pension credit referred to in regulation 6 of the Implementation and Discharge of Liability Regulations, as the case may be, which —
  (i)   has been requested in accordance with regulation 4(2)(i) and (k), or, where appropriate, 6(2)(c), or should have been provided in accordance with regulation 5;
  (ii)   the person responsible for the pension arrangement considers he needs in order to begin to implement the pension sharing order or provision; and
  (iii)   remains outstanding;
(c)   a notice of implementation; or
(d)   a statement by the person responsible for the pension arrangement explaining why he is unable to implement the pension sharing order or agreement.

(2) The information specified in paragraph (1) shall be furnished in accordance with that paragraph within 21 days beginning with —

(a)   in the case of sub-paragraph (a), (b) or (d) of that paragraph, the day on which the person responsible for the pension arrangement receives the pension sharing order or provision; or
(b)   in the case of sub-paragraph (c) of that paragraph, the later of the days specified in section 34(1)(a) and (b) of the 1999 Act (implementation period).

8 Provision of information after the implementation of a pension sharing order or provision

(1) The person responsible for the pension arrangement shall issue a notice of discharge of liability to the transferor and the transferee, or, as the case may be, the person entitled to the pension credit by virtue of regulation 6 of the

Implementation and Discharge of Liability Regulations no later than the end of the period of 21 days beginning with the day on which the discharge of liability in respect of the pension credit is completed.

(2) In the case of a transferor whose pension is not in payment, the notice of discharge of liability shall include the following details —

    (a)   the value of the transferor's accrued rights as determined by reference to the cash equivalent value of those rights calculated and verified in accordance with regulation 3 of the Valuation Regulations (calculation and verification of cash equivalents for the purposes of the creation of pension debits and credits);

    (b)   the value of the pension debit;

    (c)   any amount deducted from the value of the pension rights in accordance with regulation 9(2)(c) of the Charging Regulations (charges in respect of pension sharing activity – method of recovery);

    (d)   the value of the transferor's rights after the amounts referred to in sub-paragraphs (b) and (c) have been deducted; and

    (e)   the transfer day.

(3) In the case of a transferor whose pension is in payment, the notice of discharge of liability shall include the following details —

    (a)   the value of the transferor's benefits under the pension arrangement as determined by reference to the cash equivalent value of those rights calculated and verified in accordance with regulation 3 of the Valuation Regulations;

    (b)   the value of the pension debit;

    (c)   the amount of the pension which was in payment before liability in respect of the pension credit was discharged;

    (d)   the amount of pension which is payable following the deduction of the pension debit from the transferor's pension benefits;

    (e)   the transfer day;

    (f)   if the person responsible for the pension arrangement intends to recover charges, the amount of any unpaid charges —

        (i)   not prohibited by regulation 2 of the Charging Regulations (general requirements as to charges); and

        (ii)   specified in regulations 3 and 6 of those Regulations;

    (g)   how the person responsible for the pension arrangement will recover the charges referred to in sub-paragraph (f), including —

        (i)   whether the method of recovery specified in regulation 9(2)(d) of the Charging Regulations will be used;

        (ii)   the date when payment of those charges in whole or in part is required; and

        (iii)   the sum which will be payable by the transferor, or which will be deducted from his pension benefits, on that date.

(4) In the case of a transferee —

    (a)   whose pension is not in payment; and

(b)   who will become a member of the pension arrangement from which the pension credit rights were derived,

the notice of discharge of liability to the transferee shall include the following details —

(i)   the value of the pension credit;

(ii)   any amount deducted from the value of the pension credit in accordance with regulation 9(2)(b) of the Charging Regulations;

(iii)   the value of the pension credit after the amount referred to in sub-paragraph (b)(ii) has been deducted;

(iv)   the transfer day;

(v)   any periodical charges the person responsible for the pension arrangement intends to make, including how and when those charges will be recovered from the transferee; and

(vi)   information concerning membership of the pension arrangement which is relevant to the transferee as a pension credit member.

(5) In the case of a transferee who is transferring his pension credit rights out of the pension arrangement from which those rights were derived, the notice of discharge of liability to the transferee shall include the following details —

(a)   the value of the pension credit;

(b)   any amount deducted from the value of the pension credit in accordance with regulation 9(2)(b) of the Charging Regulations;

(c)   the value of the pension credit after the amount referred to in sub-paragraph (b) has been deducted;

(d)   the transfer day; and

(e)   details of the pension arrangement, including its name, address, reference number, telephone number, and, where available, the business facsimile number and electronic mail address, to which the pension credit has been transferred.

(6) In the case of a transferee, who has reached normal benefit age on the transfer day, and in respect of whose pension credit liability has been discharged in accordance with paragraph 1(2), 2(2), 3(2) or 4(4) of Schedule 5 to the 1999 Act (pension credits: mode of discharge – funded pension schemes, unfunded public service pension schemes, other unfunded pension schemes, or other pension arrangements), the notice or discharge of liability to the transferee shall include the following details —

(a)   the amount of pension credit benefit which is to be paid to the transferee;

(b)   the date when the pension credit benefit is to be paid to the transferee;

(c)   the transfer day;

(d)   if the person responsible for the pension arrangement intends to recover charges, the amount of any unpaid charges —

(i)   not prohibited by regulation 2 of the Charging Regulations; and

(ii)   specified in regulations 3 and 16 of those Regulations; and

(e)   how the person responsible for the pension arrangement will recover the charges referred to in sub-paragraph (d), including —

(i)   whether the method of recovery specified in regulation 9(2)(e) of the Charging Regulations will be used;

(ii)   the date when payment of those charges in whole or in part is required; and

(iii)   the sum which will be payable by the transferee, or which will be deducted from his pension credit benefits, on that date.

(7) In the case of a person entitled to the pension credit by virtue of regulation 7 of the Implementation and Discharge of Liability Regulations, the notice of discharge of liability shall include the following details —

(a)   the value of the pension credit rights as determined in accordance with regulation 10 of the Implementation and Discharge of Liability Regulations (calculation of the value of appropriate rights);

(b)   any amount deducted from the value of the pension credit in accordance with regulation 9(2)(b) of the Charging Regulations;

(c)   the value of the pension credit;

(d)   the transfer day; and

(e)   any periodical charges the person responsible for the pension arrangement intends to make, including how and when those charges will be recovered from the payments made to the person entitled to the pension credit by virtue of regulation 6 of the Implementation and Discharge of Liability Regulations.

9 Penalties

Where any trustee or manager of an occupational pension scheme fails, without reasonable excuse, to comply with any requirement imposed under regulation 6, 7 or 8, the Regulatory Authority may require that trustee or manager to pay within 28 days from the date of its imposition, a penalty which shall not exceed —

(a)   £200 in the case of an individual, and

(b)   £1,000 in any other case.

10 Provision of information after receipt of an earmarking order

(1) The person responsible for the pension arrangement shall, within 21 days beginning with the day that he receives —

(a)   an order under section 23 of the Matrimonial Causes Act 1973, so far as it includes provision made by virtue of section 25B or 25C of that Act (powers to include provision about pensions);

(b)   an order under section 12A(2) or (3) of the Family Law (Scotland) Act 1985; or

(c)   an order under Article 25 of the Matrimonial Causes (Northern Ireland) Order 1978, so far as it includes provision made by virtue of Article 27B or 27C of that Order (Northern Ireland powers corresponding to those mentioned in sub-paragraph (a)) issue to the party with pension rights and the other party a notice which includes the information specified in paragraphs (2) and (5), or (3), (4) and (5), as the case may be.

(2) Where an order referred to in paragraph (1)(a), (b) or (c) is made in respect of the pension rights or benefits of a party with pension rights whose pension is not in payment, the notice issued by the person responsible for a pension arrangement to the party with pension rights and the other party shall include a list of the circumstances in respect of any changes of which the party with pension rights or the other party must notify the person responsible for the pension arrangement.

(3) Where an order referred to in paragraph (1)(a) or (c) is made in respect of the pension rights or benefits of a party with pension rights whose pension is in payment, the notice issued by the person responsible for a pension arrangement to the party with pension rights and the other party shall include —

(a)   the value of the pension rights or benefits of the party with pension rights;
(b)   the amount of the pension of the party with pension rights after the order has been implemented;
(c)   the first date when a payment pursuant to the order is to be made; and
(d)   a list of the circumstances, in respect of any changes of which the party with pension rights or the other party must notify the person responsible for the pension arrangement.

(4) Where an order referred to in paragraph (1)(a) or (c) is made in respect of the pension rights of a party with pension rights whose pension is in payment, the notice issued by the person responsible for a pension arrangement to the party with pension rights shall, in addition to the items specified in paragraph (3), include —

(a)   the amount of the pension of the party with pension rights which is currently in payment; and
(b)   the amount of pension which will be payable to the party with pension rights after the order has been implemented.

(5) Where an order referred to in paragraph (1)(a), (b) or (c) is made the notice issued by the person responsible for a pension arrangement to the party with pension rights and the other party shall include —

(a)   the amount of any charges which remain unpaid by —
  (i)   the party with pension rights; or
  (ii)   the other party,
  in respect of the provision by the person responsible for the pension arrangement of information about pensions and divorce or dissolution of a civil partnership pursuant to regulation 3 of the Charging Regulations, and in respect of complying with an order referred to in paragraph (1)(a), (b) or (c); and
(b)   information as to the manner in which the person responsible for the pension arrangement will recover the charges referred to in sub-paragraph (a), including —

    (i)   the date when payment of those charges in whole or in part is required;

    (ii) the sum which will be payable by the party with pension rights or the other party, as the case may be; and

    (iii) whether the sum will be deducted from payments of pension to the party with pension rights, or, as the case may be, from payments to be made to the other party pursuant to an order referred to in paragraph (1)(a), (b) or (c).

Amendments—Inserted by SI 2005/2877.

4. PENSION SHARING (VALUATION) REGULATIONS 2000, SI 2000/1052

1 Citation, commencement and interpretation

(1) These Regulations may be cited as the Pension Sharing (Valuation) Regulations 2000 and shall come into force on 1 December 2000.

(2) In these Regulations —

'the 1993 Act' means the Pension Schemes Act 1993;

'the 1995 Act' means the Pensions Act 1995;

'the 1999 Act' means the Welfare Reform and Pensions Act 1999;

'the 2004 Act' means the Pensions Act 2004;

'the Board for Actuarial Standards' means the operating body of that name of the Financial Reporting Council;

'effective date' in paragraph (3) or (3A) of regulation 5 means the date as at which the assets and liabilities are valued;

'employer' has the meaning given by section 181(1) of the 1993 Act;

'occupational pension scheme' has the meaning given by section 1 of the 1993 Act;

'pension arrangement' has the meaning given by section 46(1) of the 1999 Act;

'relevant arrangement' has the meaning given by section 29(8) of the 1999 Act;

'scheme' means an occupational pension scheme;

'scheme actuary', in relation to a scheme to which section 47(1)(b) of the 1995 Act applies, means the actuary mentioned in section 47(1)(b) of that Act;

'transfer credits' has the meaning given by section 181(1) of the 1993 Act;

'transfer day' has the meaning given by section 29(8) of the 1999 Act;

'transferor' has the meaning given by section 29(8) of the 1999 Act;

'trustees or managers' has the meaning given by section 46(1) of the 1999 Act;

'valuation day' has the meaning given by section 29(7) of the 1999 Act.

Amendments—SI 2000/2691, r 10(1), (2); SI 2003/1727, r 4(1), (2); SI 2005/3377, r 20(1); SI 2006/744; SI 2007/60.

2 Rights under a pension arrangement which are not shareable

(1) Rights under a pension arrangement which are not shareable are —

    (a)   subject to paragraph (2), any rights accrued between 1961 and 1975 which relate to contracted-out equivalent pension benefit within the meaning of section 57 of the National Insurance Act 1965 (equivalent pension benefits, etc);

    (b)   any rights in respect of which a person is in receipt of —

        (i)   a pension;

        (ii)   an annuity;

        (iii)   payments under an interim arrangement within the meaning of section 28(1A) of the 1993 Act (ways of giving effect to protected rights); or

        (iv)   dependants' income withdrawal within the meaning of paragraph 21 of Schedule 28 to the Finance Act 2004 (dependants' income withdrawal.

        by virtue of being the widow, widower, surviving civil partner or other dependant of a deceased person with pension rights under a pension arrangement; and

    (c)   any rights which will result in the payment of a benefit which is to be provided solely by reason of the —

        (i)   disablement, or

        (ii)   death,

        due to an accident suffered by a person occurring during his pensionable service.

(2) Paragraph (1)(a) applies only when those rights are the only rights held by a person under a pension arrangement.

Amendments—SI 2005/2877; SI 2006/744.

3 Calculation and verification of cash equivalents for the purposes of the creation of pension debits and credits

For the purposes of section 29 of the 1999 Act (creation of pension debits and credits), cash equivalents may be calculated and verified —

    (a)   where the relevant arrangement is an occupational pension scheme in accordance with regulations 4 and 5; or

    (b)   in any other case, in accordance with regulations 6 and 7.

4 Occupational pension schemes: manner of calculation and verification of cash equivalents

(1) In a case to which, or to the extent to which, paragraph (2),(2C) or (5) does not apply, cash equivalents are to be calculated and verified in such manner as may be approved in a particular case by the scheme actuary or, in relation to a scheme to which section 47(1)(b) of the 1995 Act (professional advisers) does not apply, by —

    (a)   a Fellow of the Institute of Actuaries;

(b)   a Fellow of the Faculty of Actuaries; or

(c)   a person with other actuarial qualifications who is approved by the Secretary of State, at the request of the trustees or managers of the scheme in question, as being a proper person to act for the purposes of these Regulations in connection with that scheme.

and, subject to paragraph (2), in the following paragraphs of this regulation and in regulation 5 'actuary' means the scheme actuary or, in relation to a scheme to which section 47(1)(b) of the 1995 Act does not apply, the actuary referred to in sub-paragraph (a), (b) or (c) of this paragraph.

(2) Where the transferor in respect of whose rights a cash equivalent is to be calculated and verified, is a member of a scheme having particulars from time to time set out in regulations made under section 7 of the Superannuation Act 1972 (superannuation of persons employed in local government service, etc), that cash equivalent shall be calculated and verified in such manner as may be approved by the Government Actuary or by an actuary authorised by the Government Actuary to act on his behalf for that purpose and in such a case 'actuary' in this regulation and in regulation 5 means the Government Actuary or the actuary so authorised.

(2A) Where the person with pension rights is a deferred member of an occupational pension scheme on the transfer day, the value of the benefits which he has accrued under that scheme shall be taken to be —

(a)   in the case of an occupational pension scheme other than a salary related scheme, the cash equivalent to which he acquired a right under section 94(1)(a) of the 1993 Act (right to cash equivalent) on the termination of his pensionable service, calculated on the assumption that he has made an application under section 95(1) of that Act (ways of taking right to cash equivalent); or

(b)   in the case of a salary related occupational pension scheme, the guaranteed cash equivalent to which he would have acquired a right under section 94(1)(aa) of the 1993 Act if he had made an application under section 95(1) of that Act.

(2B) Where the person with pension rights is an active member of an occupational pension scheme on the transfer day, the value of the benefits which he has accrued under that scheme shall be calculated and verified —

(a)   on the assumption that the member had made a request for an estimate of the cash equivalent that would be available to him were his pensionable service to terminate on the transfer day; and

(b)   in accordance with regulation 11 of, and Schedule 1 to, the Occupational Pension Schemes (Transfer Values) Regulations 1996 (disclosure).

(2C) Where a transferor, in relation to whom a cash equivalent is to be calculated and verified, is a member of a scheme modified by —

(a)   the British Coal Staff Superannuation Scheme (Modification) Regulations 1994; or

(b)   the Mineworkers' Pension Scheme (Modification) Regulations 1994,

the cash equivalent of his bonus shall be calculated and verified by the actuary to reflect the fact that a reduced bonus, or no bonus, may become payable in accordance with the provisions governing the scheme in question.

(2D) For the purposes of paragraph (2C) 'bonus' means any —

(a)   augmentation of his benefits; or
(b)   new, additional or alternative benefits,

which the trustees of the scheme in question have applied to the transferor's benefits, or granted to him in accordance with the provisions governing that scheme, on the basis of findings as to that scheme's funding position.

(3) Except in a case to which paragraph (5) applies, cash equivalents are to be calculated and verified by adopting methods and making assumptions which —

(a)   if not determined by the trustees or managers of the scheme in question, are notified to them by the actuary; and
(b)   are certified by the actuary to the trustees or managers of the Scheme —
   (i)   as being consistent with 'Retirement Benefit Schemes – Transfer Values (GN11)' adopted or prepared, and from time to time revised, by the Board for Actuarial Standards and current on the valuation day; and
   (ii)   as being consistent with the methods adopted and assumptions made, at the time when the certificate is issued, in calculating the benefits to which entitlement arises under the rules of the scheme in question for a person who is acquiring transfer credits under those rules;
   (iii) *(revoked)*

(4) *(revoked)*

(5) Where a cash equivalent or any portion of a cash equivalent relates to money purchase benefits which do not fall to be valued in a manner which involves making estimates of the value of benefits, then that cash equivalent or that portion shall be calculated and verified in such manner as may be approved in particular cases by the trustees or managers of the scheme, and by adopting methods consistent with the requirements of Chapter IV of Part IV of the 1993 Act (protection for early leavers–transfers values).

Amendments—Inserted by SI 2000/2691, r 10(1), (3)(a), (b); revoked by SI 2005/3377; substituted by SI 2006/34, r 4(1), (2); substituted by SI 2007/60, r 2.

5 Occupational pension schemes: further provisions as to the calculation of cash equivalents and increases and reductions of cash equivalents

(1) Where it is the established custom for additional benefits to be awarded from the scheme at the discretion of the trustees or managers or the employer, the cash equivalent shall, unless the trustees or managers have given a direction

that cash equivalents shall not take account of such benefits, take account of any such additional benefits as will accrue to the transferor if the custom continues unaltered.

(2) The trustees or managers shall not make a direction such as is mentioned in paragraph (1) unless, within 3 months before making the direction, they have consulted the actuary and have obtained the actuary's written report on the implications for the state of funding of the scheme of making such a direction, including the actuary's advice as to whether or not in the actuary's opinion there would be any adverse implications for the funding of the scheme should the trustees or managers not make such a direction.

(3) In the case of a scheme to which Part 3 of the 2004 Act applies, the cash equivalent may be reduced by the trustees or managers if the GN11 insufficiency conditions are met.

(3A) The GN11 insufficiency conditions are that the actuary's last relevant GN11 report (see paragraph (3J)) shows that at the effective date of the report —

    (a)   the scheme had assets that were insufficient to pay the full amount of the cash equivalent in respect of all the members, and

    (b)   the assets were insufficient to pay in full any category of liabilities that is a category of liabilities for the benefits in respect of which the cash equivalent is being calculated.

(3B) If the GN11 insufficiency conditions are met, the trustees or managers may reduce any part of the cash equivalent that relates to such a category of liabilities as are mentioned in paragraph (3A)(b) by a percentage not exceeding the GN11 deficiency percentage.

(3C) The GN11 deficiency percentage for any such part of the cash equivalent is the percentage by which the actuary's last relevant GN11 report shows that the assets were insufficient to pay that category of liabilities.

(3D)–(3I) (*revoked*)

(3J) The references in this regulation to the actuary's last relevant GN11 report are to his last report before the valuation day in accordance with 'Retirement Benefit Schemes – Transfer Values (GN11)' adopted or prepared, and from time to time revised, by the Board for Actuarial Standards and current on the valuation day.

(3K)–(3L) (*revoked*)

(4) If, by virtue of Schedule 2 to the Occupational Pension Schemes (Scheme Funding) Regulations 2005, Part 3 of the 2004 Act applies to a section of a scheme as if that section were a separate scheme, paragraphs (3) and (3A) shall apply as if that section were a separate scheme, and as if the references therein to a scheme were accordingly references to that section.

(5) The reduction referred to in paragraph (3) shall not apply to a case where liability in respect of a pension credit is to be discharged in accordance with —

(a)   paragraph 1(2) of Schedule 5 to the 1999 Act (pension credits: mode of discharge – funded pension schemes); or

(b)   paragraph 1(3) of that Schedule, in a case where regulation 7(2) of the Pension Sharing (Implementation and Discharge of Liability) Regulations 2000 applies.

(6) Where a scheme has begun to be wound up, a cash equivalent may be reduced to the extent necessary for the scheme to comply with the winding up provisions as defined in section 73B(10) (a) of the 1995 Act and regulations made under those provisions.

(7) If, by virtue of regulations made under section 73B(4)(b)(i) of the 1995 Act by virtue of section 73B(5) of that Act, the winding up provisions (as so defined) apply to a section of a scheme as if that section were a separate scheme, paragraph (6) shall apply as if that section were a separate scheme and as if the references therein to a scheme were accordingly references to that section.

(8) Where all or any of the benefits to which a cash equivalent relates have been surrendered, commuted or forfeited before the date on which the trustees or managers discharge their liability in respect of the pension credit in accordance with the provisions of Schedule 5 to the 1999 Act, the cash equivalent of the benefits so surrendered, commuted or forfeited shall be reduced to nil.

(9) In a case where two or more of the paragraphs of this regulation fall to be applied to a calculation, they shall be applied in the order in which they occur in this regulation.

Amendments—Substituted by SI 2000/2691, r 10(1), (4); substituted by SI 2003/1727, r 4(1), (3); SI 2005/706; SI 2005/3377; SI 2007/60.

6 Other relevant arrangements: manner of calculation and verification of cash equivalents

(1) Except in a case to which paragraph (3) applies, cash equivalents are to be calculated and verified in such manner as may be approved in a particular case by —

(a)   a Fellow of the Institute of Actuaries;

(b)   a Fellow of the Faculty of Actuaries; or

(c)   a person with other actuarial qualifications who is approved by the Secretary of State, at the request of the person responsible for the relevant arrangement, as being a proper person to act for the purposes of this regulation and regulation 7 in connection with that arrangement,

and in paragraph (2) 'actuary' means any person such as is referred to in sub-paragraph (a), (b) or (c) of this paragraph.

(1A) Where the person with pension rights is a member of a personal pension scheme, or those rights are contained in a retirement annuity contract, the value of the benefits which he has accrued under that scheme or contract on the transfer day shall be taken to be the cash equivalent to which he would have acquired a right under section 94(1)(b) of the 1993 Act, if he had made an application under section 95(1) of that Act on the date on which the request for the valuation was received.

(1B) In relation to a personal pension scheme which is comprised in a retirement annuity contract made before 4th January 1988, paragraph (2) shall apply as if such a scheme were not excluded from the scope of Chapter IV of Part IV of the 1993 Act by section 93(1)(b) of that Act (scope of Chapter IV).

(2) Except in a case to which paragraph (3) applies, cash equivalents are to be calculated and verified by adopting methods and making assumptions which —

    (a)   if not determined by the person responsible for the relevant arrangement, are notified to them by an actuary; and

    (b)   are certified by an actuary to the person responsible for the relevant arrangement as being consistent with 'Retirement Benefit Schemes – Transfer Values (GN11)', adopted or prepared, and from time to time revised, by the Board for Actuarial Standards and current on the valuation day.

(3) Where a transferor's cash equivalent, or any portion of it —

    (a)   represents his rights to money purchase benefits under the relevant arrangement; and

    (b)   those rights do not fall, either wholly or in part, to be valued in a manner which involves making estimates of the value of benefits,

then that cash equivalent, or that portion of it, shall be calculated and verified in such manner as may be approved in a particular case by the person responsible for the relevant arrangement, and by adopting methods consistent with the requirements of Chapter IV of Part IV of the 1993 Act.

(4) This regulation and regulation 7 apply to a relevant arrangement other than an occupational pension scheme.

Amendments—Inserted by SI 2000/2691, r 10(1), (5)(a), (b); amended by SI 2007/60.

7 Other relevant arrangements: reduction of cash equivalents

Where all or any of the benefits to which a cash equivalent relates have been surrendered, commuted or forfeited before the date on which the person responsible for the relevant arrangement discharges his liability for the pension credit in accordance with the provisions of Schedule 5 to the 1999 Act, the cash equivalent of the benefits so surrendered, commuted or forfeited shall be reduced in proportion to the reduction in the total value of the benefits.

5. DIVORCE ETC (PENSIONS) REGULATIONS 2000, SI 2000/1123

1 Citation, commencement and transitional provisions

(1) These Regulations may be cited as the Divorce etc (Pensions) Regulations 2000 and shall come into force on 1 December 2000.

(2) These Regulations shall apply to any proceedings for divorce, judicial separation or nullity of marriage commenced on or after 1 December 2000, and any such proceedings commenced before that date shall be treated as if these Regulations had not come into force.

2 Interpretation

In these Regulations —

(a) a reference to a section by number alone means the section so numbered in the Matrimonial Causes Act 1973;

(b) 'the 1984 Act' means the Matrimonial and Family Proceedings Act 1984;

(c) expressions defined in sections 21A and 25D(3) have the meanings assigned by those sections;

(d) every reference to a rule by number alone means the rule so numbered in the Family Proceedings Rules 1991.

3 Valuation

(1) For the purposes of the court's functions in connection with the exercise of any of its powers under Part II of the Matrimonial Causes Act 1973, benefits under a pension arrangement shall be calculated and verified in the manner set out in regulation 3 of the Pensions on Divorce etc (Provision of Information) Regulations 2000, and —

(a) the benefits shall be valued as at a date to be specified by the court (being not earlier than one year before the date of the petition and not later than the date on which the court is exercising its power);

(b) in determining that value the court may have regard to information furnished by the person responsible for the pension arrangement pursuant to any of the provisions set out in paragraph (2); and

(c) in specifying a date under sub-paragraph (a) above the court may have regard to the date specified in any information furnished as mentioned in sub-paragraph (b) above.

(2) The relevant provisions for the purposes of paragraph (1)(b) above are —

(a) the Pensions on Divorce etc (Provision of Information) Regulations 2000;

(b)   regulation 5 of and Schedule 2 to the Occupational Pension Schemes (Disclosure of Information) Regulations 1996 and regulation 11 of and Schedule 1 to the Occupational Pension Schemes (Transfer Value) Regulations 1996;

(c)   section 93A or 94(1)(a) or (aa) of the Pension Schemes Act 1993;

(d)   section 94(1)(b) of the Pension Schemes Act 1993 or paragraph 2(a) (or, where applicable, 2(b)) of Schedule 2 to the Personal Pension Schemes (Disclosure of Information) Regulations 1987.

4 Pension attachment: notices

(1) This regulation applies in the circumstances set out in section 25D(1)(a) (transfers of pension rights).

(2) Where this regulation applies, the person responsible for the first arrangement shall give notice in accordance with the following paragraphs of this regulation to —

(a)   the person responsible for the new arrangement, and

(b)   the other party.

(3) The notice to the person responsible for the new arrangement shall include copies of the following documents —

(a)   every order made under section 23 imposing any requirement on the person responsible for the first arrangement in relation to the rights transferred;

(b)   any order varying such an order;

(c)   all information or particulars which the other party has been required to supply under any provision of rule 2.70 for the purpose of enabling the person responsible for the first arrangement:

    (i)   to provide information, documents or representations to the court to enable it to decide what if any requirement should be imposed on that person; or

    (ii)   to comply with any order imposing such a requirement;

(d)   any notice given by the other party to the person responsible for the first arrangement under regulation 6;

(e)   where the pension rights under the first arrangement were derived wholly or partly from rights held under a previous pension arrangement, any notice given to the person responsible for the previous arrangement under paragraph (2) of this regulation on the occasion of that acquisition of rights.

(4) The notice to the other party shall contain the following particulars —

(a)   the fact that the pension rights have been transferred;

(b)   the date on which the transfer takes effect;

(c)   the name and address of the person responsible for the new arrangement;

(d)   the fact that the order made under section 23 is to have effect as if it had been made in respect of the person responsible for the new arrangement.

(5) Both notices shall be given —

(a)   within the period provided by section 99 of the Pension Schemes Act 1993 for the person responsible for the first arrangement to carry out what the member requires; and

(b)   before the expiry of 21 days after the person responsible for the first arrangement has made all required payments to the person responsible for the new arrangement.

5 Pension attachment: reduction in benefits

(1) This regulation applies where —

(a)   an order under section 23 or under section 17 of the 1984 Act has been made by virtue of section 25B or 25C imposing any requirement on the person responsible for a pension arrangement;

(b)   an event has occurred which is likely to result in a significant reduction in the benefits payable under the arrangement, other than —

(i)   the transfer from the arrangement of all the rights of the party with pension rights in the circumstances set out in section 25D(1)(a), or

(ii)   a reduction in the value of assets held for the purposes of the arrangement by reason of a change in interest rates or other market conditions.

(2) Where this regulation applies, the person responsible for the arrangement shall, within 14 days of the occurrence of the event mentioned in paragraph (1)(b), give notice to the other party of —

(a)   that event;

(b)   the likely extent of the reduction in the benefits payable under the arrangement.

(3) Where the event mentioned in paragraph (1)(b) consists of a transfer of some but not all of the rights of the party with pension rights from the arrangement, the person responsible for the first arrangement shall, within 14 days of the transfer, give notice to the other party of the name and address of the person responsible for any pension arrangement under which the party with pension rights has acquired rights as a result of that event.

6 Pension attachment: change of circumstances

(1) This regulation applies where —

(a)   an order under section 23 or under section 17 of the 1984 Act has been made by virtue of section 25B or 25C imposing any requirement on the person responsible for a pension arrangement; and

(b)   any of the events set out in paragraph (2) has occurred.

(2) Those events are —

(a) any of the particulars supplied by the other party under rule 2.70 for the purpose mentioned in regulation 4(3)(c) has ceased to be accurate; or

(b) by reason of the remarriage of the other party or his having formed a subsequent civil partnership, or otherwise, the order has ceased to have effect.

(3) Where this regulation applies, the other party shall, within 14 days of the event, give notice of it to the person responsible for the pension arrangement.

(4) Where, because of the inaccuracy of the particulars supplied by the other party under rule 2.70 or because the other party has failed to give notice of their having ceased to be accurate, it is not reasonably practicable for the person responsible for the pension arrangement to make a payment to the other party as required by the order —

(a) it may instead make that payment to the party with pension rights, and

(b) it shall then be discharged of liability to the other party to the extent of that payment.

(5) Where an event set out in paragraph (2)(b) has occurred and, because the other party has failed to give notice in accordance with paragraph (3), the person responsible for the pension arrangement makes a payment to the other party as required by the order —

(a) its liability to the party with pension rights shall be discharged to the extent of that payment, and

(b) the other party shall, within 14 days of the payment being made, make a payment to the party with pension rights to the extent of that payment.

Amendments—inserted by SI 2005/2114.

7 Pension attachment: transfer of rights

(1) This regulation applies where —

(a) a transfer of rights has taken place in the circumstances set out in section 25D(1)(a);

(b) notice has been given in accordance with regulation 4(2)(a) and (b);

(c) any of the events set out in regulation 6(2) has occurred; and

(d) the other party has not, before receiving notice under regulation 4(2)(b), given notice of that event to the person responsible for the first arrangement under regulation 6(3).

(2) Where this regulation applies, the other party shall, within 14 days of the event, give notice of it to the person responsible for the new arrangement.

(3) Where, because of the inaccuracy of the particulars supplied by the other party under rule 2.70 for any purpose mentioned in regulation 4(3)(c) or because the other party has failed to give notice of their having ceased to be accurate, it is not reasonably practicable for the person responsible for the new arrangement to make a payment to the other party as required by the order:

(a)   it may instead make that payment to the party with pension rights, and

(b)   it shall then be discharged of liability to the other party to the extent of that payment.

(4) Subject to paragraph (5), where this regulation applies and the other party, within one year from the transfer, gives to the person responsible for the first arrangement notice of the event set out in regulation 6(2) in purported compliance with regulation 7(2), the person responsible for the first arrangement shall —

(a)   send that notice to the person responsible for the new arrangement, and

(b)   give the other party a second notice under regulation 4(2)(b);

and the other party shall be deemed to have given notice under regulation 7(2) to the person responsible for the new arrangement.

(5) Upon complying with paragraph (4) above, the person responsible for the first arrangement shall be discharged from any further obligation under regulation 4 or 7(4), whether in relation to the event in question or any further event set out in regulation 6(2) which may be notified to it by the other party.

8 Service

A notice under regulation 4, 5, 6 or 7 may be sent by fax or by ordinary first class post to the last known address of the intended recipient and shall be deemed to have been received on the seventh day after the day on which it was sent.

9 Pension sharing order not to take effect pending appeal

(1) No pension sharing order under section 24B or variation of a pension sharing order under section 31 shall take effect earlier than 7 days after the end of the period for filing notice of appeal against the order.

(2) The filing of a notice of appeal within the time allowed for doing so prevents the order taking effect before the appeal has been dealt with.

10 Revocation

The Divorce etc (Pensions) Regulations 1996 and the Divorce etc (Pensions) (Amendment) Regulations 1997 are revoked.

6. PRACTICE DIRECTION OF 27 JULY 2006 FAMILY PROCEEDINGS: COURT BUNDLES (UNIVERSAL PRACTICE TO BE APPLIED IN ALL COURTS OTHER THAN THE FAMILY PROCEEDINGS COURT)

Citations: [2006] 2 FLR 199

1 The President of the Family Division has issued this practice direction to achieve consistency across the country in all family courts (other than the Family Proceedings Court) in the preparation of court bundles and in respect of other related matters.

Application of the practice direction

2.1 Except as specified in para 2.4, and subject to specific directions given in any particular case, the following practice applies to:

(*a*) all hearings of whatever nature (including but not limited to hearings in family proceedings, Civil Procedure Rules 1998 Part 7 and Part 8 claims and appeals) before a judge of the Family Division of the High Court wherever the court may be sitting;

(*b*) all hearings in family proceedings in the Royal Courts of Justice (RCJ);

(*c*) all hearings in the Principal Registry of the Family Division (PRFD) at First Avenue House; and

(*d*) all hearings in family proceedings in all other courts except for Family Proceedings Courts.

2.2 'Hearings' includes all appearances before a judge or district judge, whether with or without notice to other parties and whether for directions or for substantive relief.

2.3 This practice direction applies whether a bundle is being lodged for the first time or is being re-lodged for a further hearing (see para 9.2).

2.4 This practice direction does not apply to:

(*a*) cases listed for one hour or less at a court referred to in para 2.1(*c*) or 2.1(*d*); or

(*b*) the hearing of any urgent application if and to the extent that it is impossible to comply with it.

2.5 The designated family judge responsible for any court referred to in para 2.1(*c*) or 2.1(*d*) may, after such consultation as is appropriate (but in the case of hearings in the PRFD at First Avenue House only with the agreement of the Senior District Judge), direct that in that court this practice direction shall apply to all family proceedings irrespective of the length of hearing.

Responsibility for the preparation of the bundle

3.1 A bundle for the use of the court at the hearing shall be provided by the party in the position of applicant at the hearing (or, if there are cross-applications, by the party whose application was first in time) or, if that person is a litigant in person, by the first listed respondent who is not a litigant in person.

3.2 The party preparing the bundle shall paginate it. If possible the contents of the bundle shall be agreed by all parties.

Contents of the bundle

4.1 The bundle shall contain copies of all documents relevant to the hearing, in chronological order from the front of the bundle, paginated and indexed, and divided into separate sections (each section being separately paginated) as follows:

(a)   preliminary documents (see para 4.2) and any other case management documents required by any other practice direction;

(b)   applications and orders;

(c)   statements and affidavits (which must be dated in the top right corner of the front page);

(d)   care plans (where appropriate);

(e)   experts' reports and other reports (including those of a guardian, children's guardian or litigation friend); and

(f)   other documents, divided into further sections as may be appropriate.

Copies of notes of contact visits should normally not be included in the bundle unless directed by a judge.

4.2 At the commencement of the bundle there shall be inserted the following documents (the preliminary documents):

(i)   an up to date summary of the background to the hearing confined to those matters which are relevant to the hearing and the management of the case and limited, if practicable, to one A4 page;

(ii)   a statement of the issue or issues to be determined (1) at that hearing and (2) at the final hearing;

(iii)   a position statement by each party including a summary of the order or directions sought by that party (1) at that hearing and (2) at the final hearing;

(iv)   an up to date chronology, if it is a final hearing or if the summary under (i) is insufficient;

(v)   skeleton arguments, if appropriate, with copies of all authorities relied on; and

(vi)   a list of essential reading for that hearing.

4.3 Each of the preliminary documents shall state on the front page immediately below the heading the date when it was prepared and the date of the hearing for which it was prepared.

4.4 The summary of the background, statement of issues, chronology, position statement and any skeleton arguments shall be cross-referenced to the relevant pages of the bundle.

4.5 The summary of the background, statement of issues, chronology and reading list shall in the case of a final hearing, and shall so far as practicable in the case of any other hearing, each consist of a single document in a form agreed by all parties. Where the parties disagree as to the content the fact of their disagreement and their differing contentions shall be set out at the appropriate places in the document.

4.6 Where the nature of the hearing is such that a complete bundle of all documents is unnecessary, the bundle (which need not be repaginated) may comprise only those documents necessary for the hearing, but

   (i)   the summary (para 4.2(i)) must commence with a statement that the bundle is limited or incomplete; and

   (ii)   the bundle shall if reasonably practicable be in a form agreed by all parties.

4.7 Where the bundle is re-lodged in accordance with para 9.2, before it is re-lodged:

   (*a*)   the bundle shall be updated as appropriate; and

   (*b*)   all superseded documents (and in particular all outdated summaries, statements of issues, chronologies, skeleton arguments and similar documents) shall be removed from the bundle.

Format of the bundle

5.1 The bundle shall be contained in one or more A4 size ring binders or lever arch files (each lever arch file being limited to 350 pages).

5.2 All ring binders and lever arch files shall have clearly marked on the front and the spine:

   (*a*)   the title and number of the case;

   (*b*)   the court where the case has been listed;

   (*c*)   the hearing date and time;

   (*d*)   if known, the name of the judge hearing the case; and

   (*e*)   where there is more than one ring binder or lever arch file, a distinguishing letter (A, B, C etc).

Timetable for preparing and lodging the bundle

6.1 The party preparing the bundle shall, whether or not the bundle has been agreed, provide a paginated index to all other parties not less than 4 working days before the hearing (in relation to a case management conference to which the provisions of the *Protocol for Judicial Case Management in Public Law Children Act Cases* [2003] 2 FLR 719 apply, not less than 5 working days before the case management conference).

6.2 Where counsel is to be instructed at any hearing, a paginated bundle shall (if not already in counsel's possession) be delivered to counsel by the person instructing that counsel not less than 3 working days before the hearing.

6.3 The bundle (with the exception of the preliminary documents if and insofar as they are not then available) shall be lodged with the court not less than 2 working days before the hearing, or at such other time as may be specified by the judge.

6.4 The preliminary documents shall be lodged with the court no later than 11 am on the day before the hearing and, where the hearing is before a judge of the High Court and the name of the judge is known, shall at the same time be sent by email to the judge's clerk.

Lodging the bundle

7.1 The bundle shall be lodged at the appropriate office. If the bundle is lodged in the wrong place the judge may:

(*a*)   treat the bundle as having not been lodged; and
(*b*)   take the steps referred to in para 12.

7.2 Unless the judge has given some other direction as to where the bundle in any particular case is to be lodged (for example a direction that the bundle is to be lodged with the judge's clerk) the bundle shall be lodged:

(*a*)   for hearings in the RCJ, in the office of the Clerk of the Rules, Room TM 9.09, Royal Courts of Justice, Strand, London WC2A 2LL (DX 44450 Strand);
(*b*)   for hearings in the PRFD at First Avenue House, at the List Office counter, 3rd floor, First Avenue House, 42/49 High Holborn, London, WC1V 6NP (DX 396 Chancery Lane); and
(*c*)   for hearings at any other court, at such place as may be designated by the designated family judge or other judge at that court and in default of any such designation at the court office of the court where the hearing is to take place.

7.3 Any bundle sent to the court by post, DX or courier shall be clearly addressed to the appropriate office and shall show the date and place of the hearing on the outside of any packaging as well as on the bundle itself.

Lodging the bundle – additional requirements for cases being heard at First Avenue House or at the RCJ

8.1 In the case of hearings at the RCJ or First Avenue House, parties shall:

(*a*)   if the bundle or preliminary documents are delivered personally, ensure that they obtain a receipt from the clerk accepting it or them; and
(*b*)   if the bundle or preliminary documents are sent by post or DX, ensure that they obtain proof of posting or despatch.

The receipt (or proof of posting or despatch, as the case may be) shall be brought to court on the day of the hearing and must be produced to the court if requested. If the receipt (or proof of posting or despatch) cannot be produced to the court the judge may: (i) treat the bundle as having not been lodged; and (ii) take the steps referred to in para 12.

8.2 For hearings at the RCJ:

(*a*) bundles or preliminary documents delivered after 11 am on the day before the hearing will not be accepted by the Clerk of the Rules and shall be delivered:

(i) in a case where the hearing is before a judge of the High Court, directly to the clerk of the judge hearing the case;

(ii) in a case where the hearing is before a Circuit Judge, Deputy High Court Judge or Recorder, directly to the messenger at the Judge's entrance to the Queen's Building (with telephone notification to the personal assistant to the Designated Family Judge, 020 7947 7155, that this has been done).

(*b*) upon learning before which judge a hearing is to take place, the clerk to counsel, or other advocate, representing the party in the position of applicant shall no later than 3 pm the day before the hearing:

(i) in a case where the hearing is before a judge of the High Court, telephone the clerk of the judge hearing the case;

(ii) in a case where the hearing is before a circuit judge, deputy high court judge or recorder, telephone the personal assistant to the designated family judge;

to ascertain whether the judge has received the bundle (including the preliminary documents) and, if not, shall organise prompt delivery by the applicant's solicitor.

Removing and re-lodging the bundle

9.1 Following completion of the hearing the party responsible for the bundle shall retrieve it from the court immediately or, if that is not practicable, shall collect it from the court within 5 working days. Bundles which are not collected in due time may be destroyed.

9.2 The bundle shall be re-lodged for the next and any further hearings in accordance with the provisions of this practice direction and in a form which complies with para 4.7.

Time estimates

10.1 In every case a time estimate (which shall be inserted at the front of the bundle) shall be prepared which shall so far as practicable be agreed by all parties and shall:

(a)   specify separately: (i) the time estimated to be required for judicial pre-reading; and (ii) the time required for hearing all evidence and submissions; and (iii) the time estimated to be required for preparing and delivering judgment; and

(b)   be prepared on the basis that before they give evidence all witnesses will have read all relevant filed statements and reports.

10.2   Once a case has been listed, any change in time estimates shall be notified immediately by telephone (and then immediately confirmed in writing):

(a)   in the case of hearings in the RCJ, to the Clerk of the Rules;

(b)   in the case of hearings in the PRFD at First Avenue House, to the List Officer at First Avenue House; and

(c)   in the case of hearings elsewhere, to the relevant listing officer.

Taking cases out of the list

11   As soon as it becomes known that a hearing will no longer be effective, whether as a result of the parties reaching agreement or for any other reason, the parties and their representatives shall immediately notify the court by telephone and by letter. The letter, which shall wherever possible be a joint letter sent on behalf of all parties with their signatures applied or appended, shall include:

(a)   a short background summary of the case;

(b)   the written consent of each party who consents and, where a party does not consent, details of the steps which have been taken to obtain that party's consent and, where known, an explanation of why that consent has not been given;

(c)   a draft of the order being sought; and

(d)   enough information to enable the court to decide (i) whether to take the case out of the list and (ii) whether to make the proposed order.

Penalties for failure to comply with the practice direction

12   Failure to comply with any part of this practice direction may result in the judge removing the case from the list or putting the case further back in the list and may also result in a "wasted costs" order in accordance with CPR, Part 48.7 or some other adverse costs order.

Commencement of the practice direction and application of other practice directions

13   This practice direction replaces *Practice Direction (Family Proceedings: Court Bundles) (10 March 2000)* [2000] 1 WLR 737, [2000] 1 FLR 536 and shall have effect from 2 October 2006.

14   Any reference in any other practice direction to *Practice Direction (Family Proceedings: Court Bundles) (10 March 2000)* shall be read as if substituted by a reference to this practice direction.

15 This practice direction should where appropriate be read in conjunction with *Practice Direction (Family Proceedings: Human Rights)* [2000] 1 WLR 1782, [2000] 2 FLR 429 and with *Practice Direction (Care Cases: Judicial Continuity and Judicial Case Management)* appended to the *Protocol for Judicial Case Management in Public Law Children Act Cases.* In particular, nothing in this practice direction is to be read as removing or altering any obligation to comply with the requirements of the *Public Law Protocol.*

This Practice Direction is issued:

(i)   in relation to family proceedings, by the President of the Family Division, as the nominee of the Lord Chief Justice, with the agreement of the Lord Chancellor; and

(ii) to the extent that it applies to proceedings to which s 5 of the Civil Procedure Act 1997 applies, by the Master of the Rolls as the nominee of the Lord Chief Justice, with the agreement of the Lord Chancellor.

The Right Honourable
Sir Mark Potter
President of the Family Division & Head of Family Justice

The Right Honourable
Sir Anthony Clarke
Master of the Rolls & Head of Civil Justice

7. PRESIDENT'S DIRECTION OF 25 MAY 2000 (ANCILLARY RELIEF PROCEDURE) AND PRE-APPLICATION PROTOCOL

[2000] 1 WLR 1480, [2000] 3 All ER 379, [2000] 1 FLR 997

1 Introduction

1.1 The Family Proceedings (Amendment No 2) Rules 1999 make important amendments to the Family Proceedings Rules 1991, as from 5 June 2000. The existing 'pilot scheme' rules in relation to ancillary relief which have applied since 1996 but only in specified courts will become, with significant revisions, of general application. In the same way as the pilot scheme, the new procedure is intended to reduce delay, facilitate settlements, limit costs incurred by parties and provide the court with greater and more effective control over the conduct of the proceedings.

2 Pre-Application Protocol

2.1 The 'Pre-application Protocol' annexed to this Direction outlines the steps parties should take to seek and provide information from and to each other prior to the commencement of any ancillary relief application. The court will expect the parties to comply with the terms of the protocol.

3 Financial Dispute Resolution (FDR) Appointment

3.1 A key element in the new procedure is the Financial Dispute Resolution (FDR) appointment. Rule 2.61E provides that the FDR appointment is to be treated as a meeting held for the purposes of discussion and negotiation. Such meetings which were previously described as meetings held for the purposes of conciliation have been developed as a means of reducing the tension which inevitably arises in matrimonial and family disputes and facilitating settlement of those disputes.

3.2 In order for the FDR appointment to be effective, parties must approach the occasion openly and without reserve. Non-disclosure of the content of such meetings is accordingly vital and is an essential prerequisite for fruitful discussion directed to the settlement of the dispute between the parties. The FDR appointment is an important part of the settlement process. As a consequence of *Re D* [1993] Fam 231, evidence of anything said or of any admission made in the course of an FDR appointment will not be admissible in evidence, except at the trial of a person for an offence committed at the appointment or in the very exceptional circumstances indicated in *Re D*.

3.3 Courts will therefore expect —

- parties to make offers and proposals;
- recipients of offers and proposals to give them proper consideration;
- that parties, whether separately or together, will not seek to exclude from consideration at the appointment any such offer or proposal.

3.4 In order to make the most effective use of the first appointment and the FDR appointment, the legal representatives attending those appointments will be expected to have full knowledge of the case.

4 Single Joint Expert

4.1 The introduction of expert evidence in proceedings is likely to increase costs substantially and consequently the court will use its powers to restrict the unnecessary use of experts. Accordingly, where expert evidence is sought to be relied upon, parties should if possible agree upon a single expert whom they can jointly instruct. Where parties are unable to agree upon the expert to be instructed, the court will consider using its powers under Part 35 of the Civil Procedure Rules 1998 to direct that evidence be given by one expert only. In such cases parties must be in a position at the first appointment or when the matter comes to be considered by the court to provide the court with a list of suitable experts or to make submissions as to the method by which the expert is to be selected.

5

This direction shall have effect as from 5 June 2000 and replaces the direction 'Ancillary Relief Procedure – Pilot Scheme' dated 16 June 1997.

6

Issued with the approval and concurrence of the Lord Chancellor.

DAME ELIZABETH BUTLER-SLOSS
President

PRE-APPLICATION PROTOCOL

1 Introduction

1.1.1 Lord Woolf in his final Access to Justice Report of July 1996 recommended the development of pre-application protocols:

> *'to build on and increase the benefits of early but well informed settlement which genuinely satisfy both parties to dispute'*

1.1.2 Subsequently, in April 2000 the Lord Chancellor's Ancillary Relief Advisory Committee agreed this pre-application protocol.

1.2 The aim of the pre-application protocol is to ensure that —

(a)   Pre-application disclosure and negotiation takes place in appropriate cases.

(b)   Where there is pre-application disclosure and negotiation, it is dealt with —
   i.   cost effectively;
   ii.   in line with the overriding objective of the Family Proceedings (Amendments) Rules 1999.

(c)   The parties are in a position to settle the case fairly and early without litigation.

1.3 The court will be able to treat the standard set in the pre-application protocol as the normal reasonable approach to pre-application conduct. If proceedings are issued, the court will decide whether there has been non-compliance with the protocol and, if so, whether non-compliance merits consequences.

2 Notes of Guidance

Scope of the Protocol

2.1 This protocol is intended to apply to all claims for ancillary relief as defined by FPR r 1(2). It is designed to cover all classes of case, ranging from a simple application for periodical payments to an application for a substantial lump sum and property adjustment order. The protocol is designed to facilitate the operation of what was called the pilot scheme and is from 5 June 2000 the standard procedure for ancillary relief application.

2.2 In considering the option of pre-application disclosure and negotiation, solicitors should bear in mind the advantage of having a court timetable and court managed process. There is sometimes an advantage in preparing disclosure before proceedings are commenced. However solicitors should bear in mind the objective of controlling costs and in particular the costs of discovery and that the option of pre-application disclosure and negotiation has risks of excessive and uncontrolled expenditure and delay. This option should only be encouraged where both parties agree to follow this route and disclosure is not likely to be an issue or has been adequately dealt with in mediation or otherwise.

2.3 Solicitors should consider at an early stage and keep under review whether it would be appropriate to suggest mediation to the clients as an alternative to solicitor negotiation or court-based litigation.

2.4 Making an application to the court should not be regarded as a hostile step or a last resort, rather as a way of starting the court timetable, controlling disclosure and endeavouring to avoid the costly final hearing and the preparation for it.

First Letter

2.5 The circumstances of parties to an application for ancillary relief are so various that it would be difficult to prepare a specimen first letter. The request for information will be different in every case. However, the tone of the initial letter is important and the guidelines in para 3.7 should be followed. Solicitors writing to an unrepresented party should always recommend that he seeks independent legal advice and enclose a second copy of the letter to be passed to any solicitor instructed. A reasonable time limit for a response may be 14 days.

Negotiation and Settlement

2.6 In the event of pre-application disclosure and negotiation, as envisaged in paragraph 2.2 an application should not be issued when a settlement is a reasonable prospect.

Disclosure 2.7 The protocol underlines the obligation of parties to make full and frank disclosure of all material facts, documents and other information relevant to the issues. Solicitors owe their clients a duty to tell them in clear terms of this duty and of the possible consequences of breach of the duty. This duty of disclosure is an ongoing obligation and includes the duty to disclose any material changes after initial disclosure has been given. Solicitors are referred to the Good Practice Guide for Disclosure produced by the Solicitors Family Law Association (obtainable from the Administrative Director, 366A Crofton Road, Orpington, Kent BR2 8NN).

3 The Protocol

General Principles

3.1 All parties must always bear in mind the overriding objective set out at FPR Rule 2.51B and try to ensure that all claims should be resolved and a just resolution achieved as speedily as possible without costs being unreasonably incurred. The needs of any children should be addressed and safeguarded. The procedures which it is appropriate to follow should be conducted with minimum distress to the parties and in a manner designed to promote as good a continuing relationship between the parties and any children affected as is possible in the circumstances.

3.2 The principle of proportionality must be borne in mind at all times. It is unacceptable for the costs of any case to outweigh the financial value of the subject matter of the dispute.

3.3 Parties should be informed that where a court exercises a discretion as to whether costs are payable by one party to another, this discretion extends to pre-application offers to settle and conduct of disclosure (Rule 44.3 Paragraph 1 of the Civil Procedure Rules).

Identifying the Issues

3.4 Parties must seek to clarify their claims and identify the issues between them as soon as possible. So that this can be achieved they must provide full, frank and clear disclosure of facts, information and documents which are material and sufficiently accurate to enable proper negotiations to take place to settle their differences. Openness in all dealings is essential.

Disclosure

3.5 If parties carry out voluntary disclosure before the issue of proceedings the parties should exchange schedules of assets, income, liabilities and other material facts, using Form E as a guide to the format of the disclosure. Documents should only be disclosed to the extent that they are required by Form E. Excessive or disproportionate costs should not be incurred.

Correspondence

3.6 Any first letter and subsequent correspondence must focus on the clarification of claims and identification of issues and their resolution. Protracted and unnecessary correspondence and 'trial by correspondence' must be avoided.

3.7 The impact of any correspondence upon the reader and in particular the parties must always be considered. Any correspondence which raises irrelevant issues or which might cause the other party to adopt an entrenched, polarised or hostile position is to be discouraged.

Experts

3.8 Expert valuation evidence is only necessary where the parties cannot agree or do not know the value of some significant asset. The cost of a valuation should be proportionate to the sums in dispute. Wherever possible, valuations of properties, shares etc should be obtained from a single valuer instructed by both parties. To that end, a party wishing to instruct an expert (the first party) should first give the other party a list of the names of one or more experts in the relevant speciality whom he considers are suitable to instruct. Within 14 days the other party may indicate an objection to one or more of the named experts and, if so, should supply the names of one or more experts whom he considers suitable.

3.9 Where the identity of the expert is agreed, the parties should agree the terms of a joint letter of instructions.

3.10 Where no agreement is reached as to the identity of the expert, each party should think carefully before instructing his own expert because of the costs implications. Disagreements about disclosure such as the use and identity of an expert may be better managed by the court within the context of an application for ancillary relief.

3.11 Whether a joint report is commissioned or the parties have chosen to instruct separate experts, it is important that the expert is prepared to answer reasonable questions raised by either party.

3.12 When experts' reports are commissioned pre-application, it should be made clear to the expert that they may in due course be reporting to the court and that they should therefore consider themselves bound by the guidance as to expert witnesses in Part 39 of the Civil Procedure Rules 1998.

3.13 Where the parties propose to instruct a joint expert, there is a duty on both parties to disclose whether they have already consulted that expert in respect of the assets in issue.

3.14 If the parties agree to instruct separate experts the parties should be encouraged to agree in advance that the reports will be disclosed.

Summary

3.15 The aim of all pre-application proceedings steps must be to assist the parties to resolve their differences speedily and fairly or at least narrow the issues and, should that not be possible, to assist the Court to do so.

8. PRESIDENT'S DIRECTION OF 16 MARCH 2001 (COMMITTAL APPLICATIONS AND PROCEEDINGS IN WHICH A COMMITTAL ORDER MAY BE MADE)

[2001] 1 FLR 949, [2001] Fam Law 730

(1) As from the date of this direction, the Civil Procedure Practice Direction supplemental to the Rules of the Supreme Court 1965 (SI 1965/1766), Ord 52 (Sch 1 to the Civil Procedure Rules 1998 (SI 1998/3132) and the County Court Rules 1981 (SI 1981/1687), Ord 29 (Sch 2 to the Civil Procedure Rules 1998) ('the CPR Direction'), shall apply to all applications in family proceedings for

an order of committal in the same manner and to the same extent as it applies to proceedings governed by the Civil Procedure Rules 1998 ('the CPR') but subject to —

(a)   the provisions of the Family Proceedings Rules 1991 (SI 1991/1247) ('the FPR') and the Rules applied by those Rules namely, the Rules of the Supreme Court 1965 ('RSC') and the County Court Rules 1981 ('CCR') in force immediately before 26 April 1999; and

(b)   the appropriate modifications consequent upon the limited application of the CPR to family proceedings.

(1.1) In particular, the following modification should apply —

(a)   Where the alleged contempt is in connection with existing proceedings (other than contempt in the face of the court) or with an order made or an undertaking given in existing proceedings, the committal application shall be made in those proceedings;

(b)   As required by the FPR, r 7.2, committal applications in the High Court are to be made by summons. In county court proceedings applications are to be made in the manner prescribed by CCR Ord 9. References in the CPR Direction to 'claim form' and 'application notice' are to be read accordingly;

(c)   In instances where the CPR Direction requires more information to be provided than is required to be provided under the RSC and the CCR, the court will expect the former to be observed;

(d)   Having regard to the periods specified in RSC Ord 52, r 3, Ord 32, r 3(2)(a) and CCR Ord 13, r 1(2), the time specified in para 4.2 of the CPR Direction shall not apply. Nevertheless, the court will ensure that adequate time is afforded to the respondent for the preparation of his defence;

(e)   Paragraph 9 of the CPR Direction is to be read with para 3 of each of the Directions issued on 17 December 1997, entitled 'Children Act 1989 – Exclusion requirement' and 'Family Law Act 1996 – Part IV'.

(2) In any family proceedings (not falling within (1) above), in which a committal order may be made, including proceedings for the enforcement of an existing order by way of judgment summons or other process, full effect will be given to the Human Rights Act 1998 and to the rights afforded under that Act. In particular, Art 6 of the European Convention for the Protection of Human Rights and Fundamental Freedoms 1950 (as set out in Sch 1 to the Human Rights Act 1998) is fully applicable to such proceedings. Those involved must ensure that in the conduct of the proceedings there is due observance of the Human Rights Act 1998 in the same manner as if the proceedings fell within the CPR Direction.

(3) As with all family proceedings, the CPR costs provisions apply to all committal proceedings.

(4) Issued with the approval and concurrence of the Lord Chancellor.

DAME ELIZABETH BUTLER-SLOSS
President

INDEX

References are to paragraph numbers.